Other Books By Bill Welch

The Tenth Man
*How A Major League Team
Can Gain A 2 To 3 Run Advantage
Every Game*

**The Baseball Analysis And Reporting System
National League Report**

The Baseball Analysis And Reporting System
American League Report
Ballpark Edition

By Bill Welch

With Jeff Moses

A Baseball Analysis And Reporting System Publication

A BARS System Book
Published by Baseball Analysis And Reporting System, Inc.
Box 50
Chillicothe, Missouri 64601
The BARS System is a registered trademark of
Baseball Analysis And Reporting System. Inc.
Manufactured in the United States of America
Library of Congress Catalogue Number Applied For

The Baseball Analysis And Reporting System
American League Report
Ballpark Edition

"A BARS book."
Includes index.
ISBN 0-929633-03-2

Contents

The New Age Of Baseball Statistics

When a Kirby Puckett or a Darryl Strawberry — or any of the great hitters active in baseball today — comes to the plate with runners in scoring position during the late innings of a close game, everyone in the ballpark knows he is capable of driving in the runners. The opposing pitcher knows it. The opposing fielders know it. And every fan watching the game knows it.

Everyone knows that certain hitters usually have good batting averages, get a lot of hits, and drive in a lot of runs. But when a hitter is at the plate, the opposing team needs specific information about how to get him out. The opposing team needs to know what strengths and weaknesses the hitter has, what types and locations of pitches he is most vulnerable to on specific ball-and-strike counts, and where fielders should be positioned to be most effective on every pitch. In other words, the team in the field needs specific, practical information that will help on the spot and at the moment.

The Baseball Analysis And Reporting System

Such statistics are exactly what the Baseball Analysis And Reporting System attempts to provide.

The Baseball Analysis and Reporting System (The BARS System) is a privately owned organization using a nationwide scouting system and a powerful computer to generate practical baseball statistics that can be used in actual game situations by any major league team.

The key word here is "practical." "Practical statistics" are defined as statistics that can be of use in actual play — during key moments in an actual game. The BARS System generates statistics that are meant to be used. In this book many of these statistics will be presented for the fans' enjoyment (and perhaps a deeper understanding of the game), but overall the statistics are designed for actual use.

The BARS System has scouted over 800 major league games during each of the last five seasons and has collected an enormous amount of data on every player in both leagues. This data is coordinated by a powerful computer to generate scouting and reporting charts that could revolutionize the game if used regularly by any team.

When put into play by major league teams, the BARS System can increase the effectiveness of pitchers and hitters, set up defensive strategy that is much more effective than the strategy now being used in the majors, and — when used in conjunction with other BARS strategies — prevent an average of two to three runs that each team is now allowing every game. Over the course of a 162-game schedule, this would make a tremendous difference in a team's final standing.

This book shows how this can be done, and gives detailed team-by-team BARS records for regular hitters in the American League.

The BARS System Super Summary Report

The BARS System calculates batting averages for nine locations in the strike zone for every player in the majors. Nine-location batting grids are calculated for four types of pitches: fastballs, curves, sliders and change-ups. In addition, batting grids are calculated for each of these four types of pitches in several different situations that can affect a hitter's performance: when he is ahead, behind, and even in the count, and when facing right- and left-handed pitchers. These batting charts are called Super Summary Reports in the BARS System, because they are a summary of several other BARS Reports.

The chart shown below illustrates how the BARS Super Summary batting grid is set up. The chart below is for a right-handed hitter. It shows the strike zone as the hitter would see it from the batter's box looking out at the pitcher. Inside and outside would be reversed for a left-handed hitter.

	Inside	Middle	Outside
High	High Inside	High Over The Middle	High Outside
Medium	Medium-High Inside	Medium Over The Middle	Medium-High Outside
Low	Low Inside	Low Over The Middle	Low Outside

The BARS System calculates a separate batting percentage in each of the nine locations. The sample chart on the next page shows how the batting average and other statistics are displayed.

(Please see the chart on the following page.)

1

BARS SYSTEM BATTING CHART
Sample Nine-Location Grid

	Inside	Middle	Outside
High	185/ 270 / 50	222/ 338 / 75	136/ 257 / 35
Medium	310/ 316 / 98	108/ 417 / 45	268/ 280 / 75
Low	140/ 221 / 31	191/ 309 / 59	155/ 181 / 28

Batting average for the specific location.

Total at-bats.

Total base hits resulting from pitches to the location.

The sample chart above shows how information is displayed. Notice that a separate batting percentage is shown in bold for each of the nine locations. For greater clarity, the decimal point is not included.

The number above and to the left of the slash is the total number of at-bats ended by pitches to that particular location. This includes all strike outs, fly-ball outs, ground-ball outs, base hits (singles, doubles, triples and home runs), hit balls resulting in fielders' errors or fielders' choices, and pop-outs into foul or fair territory. It does not include walks and sacrifices.

The number below and to the right of the slash is the number of base hits resulting from pitches to the location (singles, doubles, triples and home runs). Dividing the number below the slash by the number above the slash results in the batting average for the location.

This exactness gives a new dimension to baseball scouting and analysis. It's no longer adequate to speak in generalities, saying that a certain hitter has difficulties with inside fastballs, or problems with curves against right-handers. When pitchers can know with great precision what a hitter's strong and weak locations are, great accuracy can be achieved. In key moments of games, use of the BARS System can give managers and pitchers the practical information they need to plan the best strategy.

The BARS System Fielding Strategy

In each Super Summary Report there are areas of strength and weakness. By focussing on a hitter's weak batting locations, a pitcher will have a greater chance of getting the hitter out. But there is another aspect to getting a hitter out: positioning fielders properly.

For any pitcher, or the pitchers on a team as a whole, much of their success is based on the quality of the team's defense. Low ERAs can mean that the pitching is good, but often a pitcher who has a low ERA with one team will have a higher ERA when transferred to a team with a weaker defense.

It is often said that a pitcher can make hitters hit ground balls but can't make them hit the grounders to fielders. But is that really the case? Is there no way for fielders to know where to position themselves to be most effective? The BARS System has developed such a way.

The BARS System has determined that trends can be found in a hitter's performance when large numbers of instances are taken into consideration. Each hitter has his own characteristic trends. For instance, a player may hit a medium-high inside fastball a different distance and direction than he would hit a medium-high outside fastball. BARS research shows that many hitters also tend to hit the same type and location of pitch different distances and directions when ahead and behind in the count. Direction and distance of hit balls will vary with the type of pitch, location of pitch, when the batter faces right- and left-handed pitchers, and when he is ahead and behind in the count.

Generally, hitters tend to pull the ball more when they are ahead in the count than when they are behind. This is probably because when they are ahead they look for fastballs and time their swing accordingly. It's not unusual to see a batter hit medium-high outside fastballs, for example, completely differently when ahead and when behind in the count. This could be true for any of the pitch types and locations.

Since the distance and direction of each hit ball is recorded by the BARS scouts along with the type of each pitch and location of each pitch, it is not difficult for the BARS computer to calculate the best position for the fielders on a pitch-by-pitch basis.

For example, say that 310 instances have been recorded for a hitter in a certain location. This means that 310 at-bats for the hitter have ended with pitches to that particular location. Other than strikeouts, all instances would have resulted in the ball being hit. (Remember that walks and sacrifices are not included in the total.) Some of the hit balls would have been pop flies, some line drives and some ground balls. Some of these would have been base hits (singles, doubles, triples and home runs) and some would have been outs.

Based on this information, the BARS computer calculates the best possible fielding position for each of the fielders — for that type of pitch and location of pitch on that particular count. Thus if a hitter had 310 at-bats ended by pitches to a certain location, the BARS computer would calculate where each fielder should be positioned when the hitter is thrown pitches to that location.

How The Fielding Strategy Works

In the BARS System fielding strategy, the baseball field is divided into designated areas. Optimal fielding positions are calculated for the three outfielders, the shortstop and the second baseman. Each of the outfielders has nine suggested positions. The left fielder's positions are shown below. The center and right fielders have similar designated positions:

Deep and shifted toward the left field line
Deep in straightaway left field
Deep and shifted toward center field
Medium-deep and shifted toward the left field line
Medium-deep in straightaway left field
Medium-deep and shifted toward center field
Short and shifted toward the left field line
Short in straightaway left field
Short and shifted toward center field

The positions for the shortstop are:

Shifted toward third base
Normal position
Up middle (shifted toward second base)

The positions for the second baseman are:

Up middle (shifted toward second base)
Normal position
Shifted toward first base

Fielding strategy is not calculated for the first and third basemen. The first baseman is often forced to hold runners close to the base, and BARS strategy would not affect him as much as the other fielders. Although strategy is not presently calculated for the third baseman, BARS research has shown that the third baseman is out of position much more often than was originally thought. Because of this, the BARS System will soon begin calculating the third baseman's best position on a pitch-by-pitch basis.

There has long been a debate in baseball about whether in certain situations it is better to place the third baseman close to the bag so he can cut off potential extra-base hits down the line, or to place him in his normal position so he can field ground balls hit into the hole between third and short. When the BARS analysis is completed, this decision can be based on the comprehensive study of each hitter's past performance, rather than on theory or conjecture. The two designated fielding positions for the third baseman will be *Shifted toward the line* and *Normal position*.

The BARS System positions fielders for each of the nine locations in each batting grid. Taking the batting chart on the opposite page as an example, the .181 average in the low-outside location is the lowest. As will be seen throughout this book, the suggested positions for each fielder vary greatly with the pitching locations, the types of pitches, when the batter is ahead or behind in the count, and when he is facing a right- or left-handed pitcher. Assuming that the fielding strategy would require each fielder to be in the straightaway position, the BARS fielding information for the location would look like this:

LOW-OUTSIDE

BATTING AVERAGE .181
   Play
Left   Deep in straightaway left field
Center   Deep in straightaway center field
Right   Deep in straightaway right field
Short   Normal position
Second   Normal position

The next-lowest average is .221 in the low-inside location. The fielding strategy for that location would be similarly designated, depending on where the BARS strategy has found it best for each fielder to be positioned. Each of the nine locations would have designations for each of the fielders.

The chart on the following page shows how the field is divided for the purpose of positioning fielders.

The field chart is a graphic representation of a baseball field, divided into fielding positions.

Field Chart

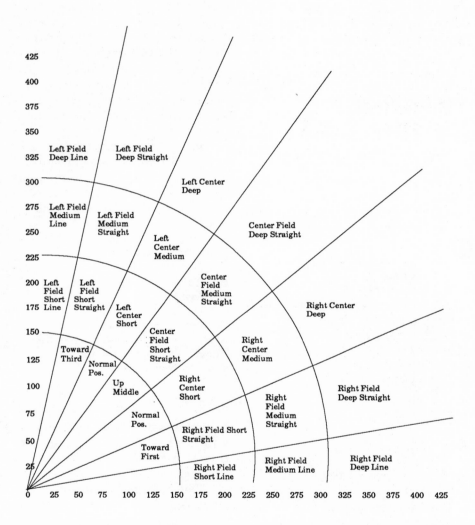

The BARS System records all balls hit to these field positions. Coordinating this information with the type and location of pitch (and with the ball-and-strike count when the pitch was made) allows the BARS computer to calculate the best possible position for each fielder when pitches are made to each location.

Such a high number of instances are recorded by the BARS System that when all the balls hit by a batter are recorded graphically on the Field Chart, the human eye can't differentiate one hit from another. Fortu-

nately, the computer can make sense out the information. Without use of a computer, the computations necessary to position fielders would be extremely complicated and time consuming.

The BARS System is unique in that it gathers an enormous amount of information — more than can be calculated by human beings — and analyzes it with a powerful computer to generate simple, easily understood charts that can be practically implemented by any major league team.

4

Diagrams Of The Fielding Strategy

The BARS Super Summary fielding strategy positions fielders for every pitch, based on the Field Chart shown on the opposite page. The positions for the shortstop and the second baseman are shown below. The positions for the outfielders are shown on the following page. These diagrams are for descriptive purposes only. The size of the players and their positions on the field are not meant to be exact.

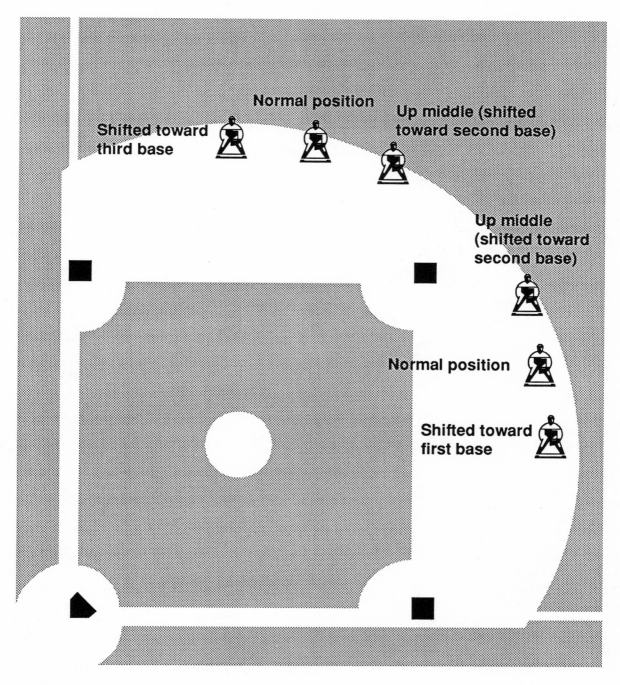

The Outfielders

The left fielder's nine designated fielding locations are shown in the diagram below. The center fielder and right fielder are positioned similarly in their respective fields but for the sake of clearness in the diagram they are not shown.

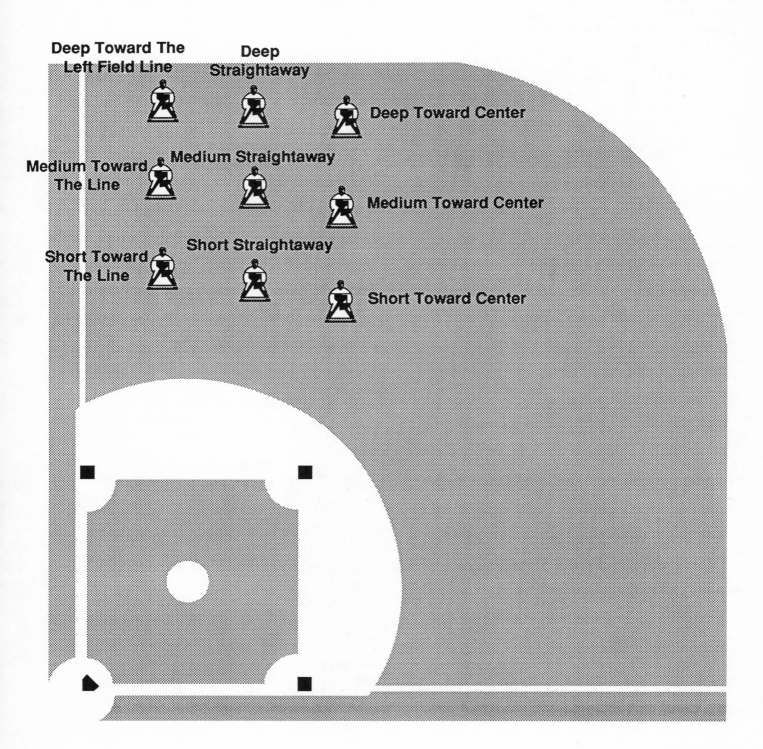

BARS Fielding Strategy Correct Over 90 Percent Of The Time

Sometimes during crucial moments in a game you'll see a coach come out of the dugout and wave to his fielders to take certain positions against a hitter. Maybe the coach will wave the outfielders more toward the right, or toward the left, or to come in, or to play deeper. These efforts are well-intended, but when the ensuing pattern of pitches to the hitter is, for example, a high-inside fastball followed by a low-outside curve, a low-inside slider and a low-outside fastball, the batter is being thrown pitches that he will tend to hit varying directions and distances. It's almost a waste of time for fielders to take set positions and hold them through all the pitches. They can be right only in the most general sense.

BARS analysis has shown that traditional fielding strategy is right about 75 percent of the time. This means that fielders are out of position about 25 percent of the time when balls are hit in their direction. When a "seeing eye" ground ball slips past an infielder or a line drive single falls just in front of a charging outfielder who was playing deep, that 25 percent factor is coming into effect.

The BARS System fielding strategy is accurate more than 90 percent of the time. This means that by following the BARS strategy, fielders would be in the right position nine times out of ten to field balls hit in their direction. The difference between 90 percent and 75 percent means that about two to three base hits that could have been prevented by using the BARS fielding strategy are being allowed by each team in every game.

This 15 percent differential — two to three hits per game — could make a tremendous difference in a team's final standing. It could turn any team into a highly organized defensive unit. If a team has strong defensive players, the team would become even better. If the team has weak defensive players, it would become more than adequate. Almost any fielder can field the ball when he is in the right position to start with.

I know that some teams have tried to make charts on where to put their fielders against certain hitters. These teams have kept records of the distance and direction hitters have hit against them. But these records are based only on how hitters have performed against that team, or against specific pitchers on that team. At best, this can give inconclusive information.

The BARS System consistently has gained 90 percent accuracy by breaking its batting and fielding strategy into specific charts for hitters against right- and left-handed pitchers, and for when ahead and behind in the count.

The previously-published BARS book, *The Tenth Man: How A Major League Team Can Gain A Two To Three Run Advantage Every Game*, goes into great detail about the BARS fielding strategy. *The Tenth Man* gives dozens of examples of games won and lost because of hits that could have been prevented by using the BARS fielding strategy.

The Number of Games Scouted

During the last six years, the BARS System has scouted about one-third of all major league games on a pitch-by-pitch basis. Many teams have had over half of their games scouted during the past few seasons. The Chicago Cubs had 137 games scouted in 1988, the Kansas City Royals had 118, the Baltimore Orioles 95, the Boston Red Sox 93, the New York Yankees 89, and the Atlanta Braves 88. Many teams had 50, 60 or 70 games scouted. During 1989 the BARS System scouted over 600 games, and during the upcoming season with more games being shown on TV we should approach a thousand games scouted. (Team-by-team scouting records for 1983-1987 are available in *The Tenth Man*.) This extensive scouting effort has resulted in a large amount of information that the BARS computer uses with great accuracy.

The BARS System records:

1. The exact location of every pitch in and around the strike zone.
2. The type of pitch: fastball, curve, slider, knuckleball, screwball, sinkerball, split-fingered fastball and change-up.
3. Exact details of the results of every hit: distance and direction of hit ball (fair or foul), fielder fielding the ball, accuracy of throws made, result of hit, runners advanced, runs scored, RBIs, errors, etc.
4. Called strikes and swing strikes, balls, fouls, bunts and bunt attempts, passed balls, balks, stolen bases, sacrifices, etc. — all events are recorded so that complete accuracy can be attained.

The computer is a powerful tool that has not yet come into its own in baseball. Many other sports utilize the computer's great potential, both in scouting and in game situations. Baseball today is such big business, on both the major and minor league levels, that it is only a matter of time until computers are used. The BARS System fielding strategy combined with other BARS strategies can give any team a two to three run advantage every game. Once a team implements the BARS System, it will have an edge for three or four years, until other teams have the chance to catch up.

The Best Way To Get A Batter Out

The BARS System calculates exact batting percentages by dividing the strike zone and the area immediately around the strike zone into nine locations. The BARS System batting report, which is called the Super Summary Report because it is a composite of several BARS System reports, calculates a separate nine-location batting-average grid for fastballs, curves and sliders. The BARS System can calculate batting averages for any type of pitch (change-ups, knuckleballs, sinkers and split-fingered fastballs, etc.), but this book shows only the charts for fastballs, curves and sliders because these are the three most common types of pitches. In the next year or so we will include a chart on split-fingered fastballs because this pitch is becoming more widely used today.

Overall, six separate Super Summary Reports are printed for each batter:

Against Right-Handed Pitchers

1. When ahead in the count
2. When behind in the count
3. Overall for all counts

Against Left-Handed Pitchers

4. When ahead in the count
5. When behind in the count
6. Overall for all counts

The breakdown into these different categories is important because, as will be seen, a batter may hit very differently not only against left- and right-handed pitchers and against different types of pitches, but when ahead and behind in the count.

The BARS System batting average may not correspond exactly with a player's official batting average, because the BARS batting charts are composites of a player's records over many seasons.

Batting Reports for Kirby Puckett

The BARS batting charts of Kirby Puckett, hard-hitting Minnesota Twins' slugger, will be used as examples.

Kirby Puckett Against Right-Handed Pitchers
Overall BARS Batting Average .294

Fastball Average .305

	Inside	Middle	Outside
High	16 / 187 / 3	24 / 291 / 7	13 / 230 / 3
Med	44 / 363 / 16	25 / 440 / 11	115 / 313 / 36
Low	18 / 166 / 3	32 / 312 / 10	31 / 258 / 8

Curve Average .280

	Inside	Middle	Outside
High	5 / 400 / 2	5 / 600 / 3	6 / 333 / 2
Med	6 / 333 / 2	8 / 625 / 5	34 / 352 / 12
Low	0 / 0 / 0	14 / 71 / 1	29 / 103 / 3

Slider Average .268

	Inside	Middle	Outside
High	1 / 0 / 0	2 / 500 / 1	4 / 0 / 0
Med	1 / 0 / 0	5 / 200 / 1	21 / 380 / 8
Low	2 / 0 / 0	16 / 250 / 4	30 / 266 / 8

Kirby Puckett Against Left-Handed Pitchers
Overall BARS Batting Average .300

Fastball Average .308

	Inside	Middle	Outside
High	8 / 750 / 3	9 / 222 / 2	10 / 200 / 2
Med	20 / 150 / 3	5 / 800 / 4	45 / 311 / 14
Low	9 / 333 / 3	13 / 307 / 4	14 / 214 / 3

Curve Average .333

	Inside	Middle	Outside
High	1 / 0 / 0	0 / 0 / 0	2 / 500 / 1
Med	5 / 400 / 2	1 / 0 / 0	9 / 333 / 3
Low	2 / 500 / 1	8 / 375 / 3	11 / 272 / 3

Slider Average .275

	Inside	Middle	Outside
High	2 / 500 / 1	3 / 666 / 2	0 / 0 / 0
Med	6 / 333 / 2	1 / 1000 / 1	3 / 0 / 0
Low	13 / 153 / 2	8 / 375 / 3	4 / 0 / 0

Puckett's Super Summary Report shows that he hits .294 overall against right-handed pitchers and .300 overall against left-handed pitchers. These overall averages include types of pitches not shown in the individual nine-location batting grids. For example, change-ups, knuckleballs, split-fingered fastballs and screwballs are included in the overall average but not shown as individual charts.

Puckett has areas of strength and areas of weakness in his charts, as do all hitters. Against right-handed pitchers he hits well against medium-high inside fastballs (.363), medium-over-the-middle fastballs (.440), medium-high outside fastballs (.313) and low-over-the-middle fastballs (.312). He also hits well in a few curve locations, most notably medium-high outside (.352).

But when facing right-handed pitchers he has weaknesses in the four fastball corners: low-inside fastballs (.166), high-inside fastballs (.187), high-outside fastballs (.230), and low-outside fastballs (.258). His most notable curve weakness against right-handers is in the low-outside location (.103).

When facing left-handed pitchers, Winfield has a higher overall fastball average than when facing right-handers (.300 against left-handers, .294 against right-handers). Note that when thrown medium-high inside fastballs by left-handers he hits only .150. And against low-outside fastballs he hits .214. He hits well against medium-high outside fastballs (.311) and low-over-the-middle fastballs (.307). He hits low curves and outside curves well against left-handers.

Puckett Ahead And Behind In The Count

Puckett's Super Summary batting report shows that he hits better against right-handed pitchers when ahead in the count (.348) than when behind in the count (.318). Notice in the charts below that Puckett has some very strong fastball locations when ahead in the count. He has much more difficulty with fastballs when he is behind in the count. When behind, he has a lot of trouble with medium-high outside fastballs (.235).

In the ongoing battle between pitcher and batter, the batter is considered to be ahead in the count when the count is 1-0 (one ball and no strikes), 3-0, 3-1, 2-0 and 2-1. The batter is considered behind when the count is 0-1, 0-2, 1-2 and 2-2. The other ball and strike counts — 0-0, 1-1 and 3-2 — are thought of as even counts.

Kirby Puckett   Right-Handed Hitter
Ahead In The Count Against Right-Handed Pitchers
BARS Average .348

Fastball Average .368

	Inside	Middle	Outside
High	10/200 / 2	15/400 / 6	2/500 / 1
Med	26/461 / 12	15/333 / 5	47/340 / 16
Low	8/375 / 3	20/250 / 5	9/666 / 6

Curve Average .342

	Inside	Middle	Outside
High	1/0 / 0	3/666 / 2	3/333 / 1
Med	2/500 / 1	3/666 / 2	12/500 / 6
Low	0/0 / 0	7/0 / 0	4/0 / 0

Kirby Puckett   Right-Handed Hitter
Behind In The Count Against Right-Handed Pitchers
BARS Average .318

Fastball Average .277

	Inside	Middle	Outside
High	3/333 / 1	4/250 / 1	3/333 / 1
Med	6/0 / 0	6/666 / 4	17/235 / 4
Low	5/0 / 0	7/571 / 4	3/0 / 0

Curve Average .518

	Inside	Middle	Outside
High	1/1000 / 1	1/1000 / 1	1/1000 / 1
Med	2/500 / 1	3/1000 / 3	8/625 / 5
Low	0/0 / 0	3/0 / 0	8/250 / 2

Examples Of The Fielding Strategy

The Super Summary shows fielding strategy for each of the nine locations for fastballs, curves and sliders. The chart below shows the fastball fielding strategy from Puckett's Super Summary against right-handed pitchers. Below the batting-percentage grid for fastballs are the best possible fielding positions for each of the nine pitch locations.

Fastball Average .305

	Inside	Middle	Outside
High	16/187 / 3	24/291 / 7	13/230 / 3
Med	44/363 /16	25/440 /11	115/313 /36
Low	18/166 / 3	32/312 /10	31/258 / 8

(Taken from Puckett's overall BARS Super Summary against right-handed pitchers.)

There are nine fielding categories, one for each of the nine locations in the strike zone. In each of these categories the best position for each fielder is shown. These positions are calculated by computer, based on the direction and distance of the many balls that Puckett has hit from each of the pitch locations during the past seasons.

1. LOW-INSIDE FASTBALLS

BATTING AVERAGE .166
Play
Left Deep in straightaway left field
Center Deep and shifted toward right field
Right Deep and shifted toward the right field line
Short Normal position
Second Normal position

2. HIGH-INSIDE FASTBALLS

BATTING AVERAGE .187
Play
Left *No instances recorded*
Center Medium-deep in straightaway center field
Right Deep and shifted toward the right field line
Short Up middle (shifted toward second base)
Second Shifted toward first base

3. HIGH-OUTSIDE FASTBALLS

BATTING AVERAGE .230
Play
Left *No instances recorded*
Center *No instances recorded*
Right Deep in straightaway right field
Short Shifted toward third base
Second Shifted toward first base

4. LOW-OUTSIDE FASTBALLS

BATTING AVERAGE .258
Play
Left Short in straightaway left field
Center Deep and shifted toward left field
Right Deep in straightaway right field
Short Up middle (shifted toward second base)
Second Normal position

5. HIGH-OVER-THE-MIDDLE FASTBALLS

BATTING AVERAGE .291
Play
Left Deep and shifted toward the left field line
Center Deep and shifted toward right field
Right Medium-deep in straightaway right field
Short Up middle (shifted toward second base)
Second *No instances recorded*

6. LOW-OVER-THE-MIDDLE FASTBALLS

BATTING AVERAGE .312
Play
Left Medium-deep in straightaway left field
Center Deep in straightaway center field
Right Deep in straightaway right field
Short Up middle (shifted toward second base)
Second Shifted toward first base

7. MEDIUM-HIGH OUTSIDE FASTBALLS

BATTING AVERAGE .313
Play
Left Deep in straightaway left field
Center Deep in straightaway center field
Right Medium-deep in straightaway right field
Short Up middle (shifted toward second base)
Second Shifted toward first base

8. MEDIUM-HIGH INSIDE FASTBALLS

BATTING AVERAGE .363
Play
Left Deep in straightaway left field
Center Medium-deep in straightaway center field
Right Medium-deep and shifted toward center field
Short Up middle (shifted toward second base)
Second Normal position

9. MEDIUM-OVER-THE-MIDDLE FASTBALLS

BATTING AVERAGE .440
Play
Left Deep and shifted toward the left field line
Center Medium-deep in straightaway center field
Right Deep in straightaway right field
Short Normal position
Second Shifted toward first base

The field diagrams on the opposite page illustrate the fielding strategy for each of Puckett's nine fastball locations against right-handed pitchers.

Fielding Strategy For Kirby Puckett Against Fastballs Thrown By Right-Handed Pitchers

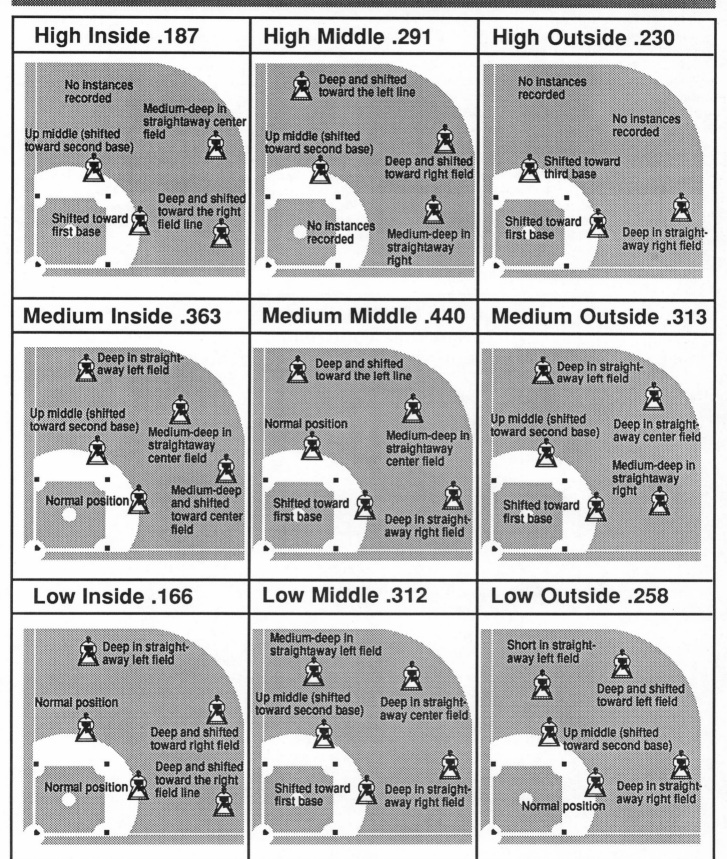

High Inside .187
No instances recorded

Up middle (shifted toward second base)

Medium-deep in straightaway center field

Shifted toward first base

Deep and shifted toward the right field line

High Middle .291
Deep and shifted toward the left line

Up middle (shifted toward second base)

Deep and shifted toward right field

No instances recorded

Medium-deep in straightaway right

High Outside .230
No instances recorded

No instances recorded

Shifted toward third base

Shifted toward first base

Deep in straightaway right field

Medium Inside .363
Deep in straightaway left field

Up middle (shifted toward second base)

Medium-deep in straightaway center field

Normal position

Medium-deep and shifted toward center field

Medium Middle .440
Deep and shifted toward the left line

Normal position

Medium-deep in straightaway center field

Shifted toward first base

Deep in straightaway right field

Medium Outside .313
Deep in straightaway left field

Up middle (shifted toward second base)

Deep in straightaway center field

Medium-deep in straightaway right

Shifted toward first base

Low Inside .166
Deep in straightaway left field

Normal position

Deep and shifted toward right field

Normal position

Deep and shifted toward the right field line

Low Middle .312
Medium-deep in straightaway left field

Up middle (shifted toward second base)

Deep in straightaway center field

Shifted toward first base

Deep in straightaway right field

Low Outside .258
Short in straightaway left field

Deep and shifted toward left field

Up middle (shifted toward second base)

Normal position

Deep in straightaway right field

11

An Overall Defensive Strategy

In general, the best way for a pitcher to get Puckett out with a fastball is to throw to the location in which he has the lowest average. In this case Puckett's lowest average against right-handers is .166, which is in the low-inside location. In addition to throwing to the weakest location, positioning the fielders according to the suggested fielding strategy will increase the chances of getting Puckett out. (This of course assumes that the pitch is not hit for a home run. The BARS System will soon include the number of home runs hit in each location of the batting grid.)

Since the fielding strategy is accurate 90 percent of the time, positioning fielders according to the suggested strategy for any particular pitch location will tend to lower the hitter's average in that location.

Puckett may hit .313 against medium-high outside fastballs, but if all fielders were properly positioned, his average in that location would decline. The same is true of all locations in Puckett's, and in any hitter's, Super Summary.

Thus, it is just as important — if not more important — to position fielders correctly for particular types and locations of pitches as it is to pitch to a hitter's weak locations. It does not matter whether a batter has been hitting .300 or even .400 in a particular location, if the fielders know where to position themselves.

As in any system that works with probability, the larger the number of instances a computer has to work with, the greater the accuracy will be. In the BARS System, the larger the number of instances recorded in any particular location, the greater the accuracy of the BARS fielding strategy for that location.

In some cases it may be better to pitch to a location with a very high average than to pitch to a location with a very low average — if the location with a high average has a large number of recorded instances.

BARS Fielding Strategy
Low-Inside Fastballs
Overall Against Right-Handed Pitchers

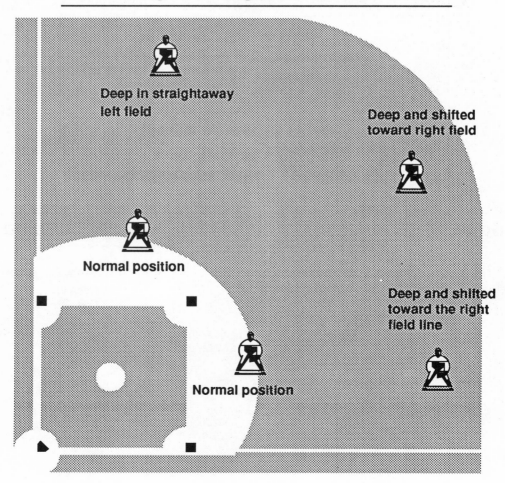

Deep in straightaway left field

Deep and shifted toward right field

Normal position

Deep and shifted toward the right field line

Normal position

Exactness Of The BARS System

The BARS System produces such accurate batting averages and fielding strategy that fielders are required to shift for pitches in adjacent locations of the strike zone. Pitchers may have difficulty targeting their pitches for the BARS System locations, but since fielders have to position themselves somewhere, they should be in coordination with the expected type and location of pitch.

The examples below from Puckett's charts show how critical even a few inches in the strike zone can be.

LOW-INSIDE FASTBALLS

BATTING AVERAGE .166
Play

Left	Deep in straightaway left field
Center	Deep and shifted toward right field
Right	Deep and shifted toward the right field line
Short	Normal position
Second	Normal position

Notice how differently the fielders would have to be positioned when a fastball is thrown to the low-over-the-middle location, which is immediately adjacent to the low-inside location. The diagram on the opposite page shows how each fielder would be required to shift.

LOW-OVER-THE-MIDDLE FASTBALLS

BATTING AVERAGE .312
Play

Left	Medium-deep in straightaway left field
Center	Deep in straightaway center field
Right	Deep in straightaway right field
Short	Up middle (shifted toward second base)
Second	Shifted toward first base

Each fielder would be required to shift in order to be correctly positioned on a low-over-the-middle fastball as compared to a low-inside fastball. If the fielders did not shift, they would be completely out of position for one of the pitches, and would likely have difficulty fielding a hit ball.

BARS Fielding Strategy
Low-Over-The-Middle Fastballs
(Compared To Low-Inside)
Overall Against Right-Handed Pitchers

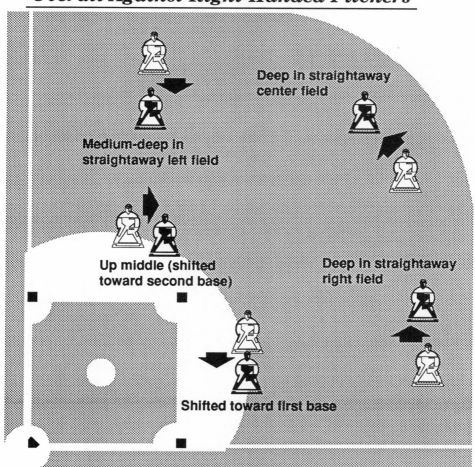

Deep in straightaway center field

Medium-deep in straightaway left field

Up middle (shifted toward second base)

Deep in straightaway right field

Shifted toward first base

How To Get Robin Yount Out, or The Anatomy Of A Hitter, BARS Style

In sports, as in life generally, the difference between a champion and an also-ran can be exceedingly small. In a horse race, the difference between the winning horse and a horse finishing out of the money is often measured in fractions of a second. Olympic running events and ski races are just as close. Hundredths of a second separate gold medalists from also-rans. It's not unusual for golf tournaments to be determined by a single stroke after 72 holes, and increasingly it seems that golf tournaments end in ties and have to be settled in playoffs. In major league baseball the difference between a .300 hitter and a .250 hitter is only 25 hits during the season — assuming a hitter has 500 official at-bats. That averages out to about one hit per week during the season.

That extra hit per week can be a fluke, a bloop hit that falls in for a single, or a ground ball that takes a lucky hop over a fielder's glove.

But for the most part the same players hit .300 or better year after year. They keep finding ways to get that extra bloop single or lucky bounce every week. Somehow they find a way to succeed. Over the years their hit totals increase consistently. But only the great hitters amass 2,500-3,000 hits or more during their career.

Robin Yount is among the great ones. He achieved the 2,500-hit level on July 2 of the '89 season, putting him on schedule for a Hall of Fame career. There are other great hitters in the game today, and this book gives all the details about their BARS statistics. But let's focus on Robin Yount in this chapter.

The Best Way To Get Robin Yount Out

When it comes to the best way to get a batter out, there are two things to consider:

(1) pitching to the batter's weaknesses
(2) positioning the fielders correctly on a pitch-by-pitch basis.

Of these, the more important is positioning the fielders correctly. It's true that when a batter's BARS charts show that he has very low batting percentages in certain locations, in general it may be better to pitch to those locations. But even if a batter is hitting .400 in a certain location, his average in that location will drop when the fielders are positioned correctly. Since the BARS fielding strategy is correct over 90 percent of the time, a player will hit no more than .100 in any location when the fielders follow the BARS strategy for that location.

The charts in this chapter show that the right-handed hitting Yount has a much higher overall BARS batting average against right-handed than against left-handed pitchers (.303 overall against right-handers, .257 overall against left-handers). This is fairly unusual because most right-handed hitters have a higher average against left-handed pitchers.

First let's look at his performance against right-handed pitchers. The BARS batting grids shown below give a complete look at Yount's career BARS statistics against fastballs, curves, and sliders vs. right-handers.

Robin Yount Against Right-Handed Pitchers
Overall BARS Batting Average .303

	Fastball Average .301			Curve Average .282			Slider Average .338		
	Inside	Middle	Outside	Inside	Middle	Outside	Inside	Middle	Outside
High	27/259 /7	25/360 /9	25/240 /6	0/0 /0	2/0 /0	3/666 /2	1/0 /0	3/0 /0	3/666 /2
Med	53/301 /16	26/461 /12	116/301 /35	12/166 /2	7/857 /6	28/142 /4	6/500 /3	7/428 /3	17/235 /4
Low	20/450 /9	41/195 /8	29/241 /7	3/333 /1	8/375 /3	15/266 /4	3/1000 /3	2/0 /0	17/294 /5

Yount hits well against all three types of pitches. Notice in the charts that Yount has very strong locations in each chart. He hits waist-high fastballs for solid averages — .301, .461 and .301, inside to outside. (His .301 against medium-high outside fastballs is somewhat low for a hitter of his ability.) He hits an excellent .360 against high-over-the-middle fastballs and a blazing .450 against low-inside fastballs.

He has weaknesses against fastballs high-inside (.259), low-outside (.241), high-outside (.240), and low-over-the-middle (.195).

Every hitter has strengths and weaknesses. The BARS batting grids pinpoint these with great accuracy. These statistics give pitchers an overall guide for facing a hitter, and they give a hitter information about his own strengths and weaknesses that he may not know. For instance, Yount probably knows that he has some trouble with low-outside and low-over-the-middle fastballs (.241 and .195, respectively). But he might not know this two-location sector is his major area of weakness. Yount can work to improve his performance against these pitches, or know to not swing at them until he has two strikes.

Notice in Yount's curve chart that he hits very poorly in the medium-high outside location (.142). His .266 against low-outside curves is somewhat better but is still not strong. He is also weak against medium-high outside sliders (.235), but is very strong against low-outside sliders (.294).

These charts show that many pitchers have been pitching Yount outside. In fact, the medium-high outside fastball location is almost always the most highly pitched location for a batter. Most pitches are fastballs and most pitchers try to keep fastballs away from hitters.

The BARS fielding strategy shows that Yount hits medium-high outside fastballs deep to the left-center, deep to straightaway center, and medium-deep to straightaway right.

(Please see diagram below)

BARS Fielding Strategy
Medium-High Outside Fastballs
Overall Against Right-Handed Pitchers

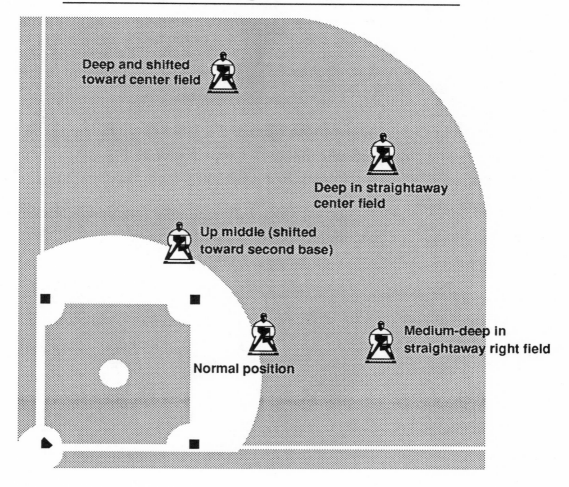

Deep and shifted toward center field

Deep in straightaway center field

Up middle (shifted toward second base)

Normal position

Medium-deep in straightaway right field

But Yount hits high-outside fastballs much differently than he hits medium-high outside fastballs. The following charts show that fielders may need to be positioned differently for pitches to each location in the BARS batting grids, even when the locations are adjacent in the strike zone.

MEDIUM-HIGH OUTSIDE FASTBALLS

BATTING AVERAGE .301

Play

Left	Deep and shifted toward center field
Center	Deep in straightaway center field
Right	Medium-deep in straightaway right field
Short	Up middle
Second	Normal position

HIGH-OUTSIDE FASTBALLS

BATTING AVERAGE .240

Play

Left	Medium-deep and shifted toward center field
Center	Deep and shifted toward right field
Right	Deep in straightaway right field
Short	Shifted toward third base
Second	Normal position

The field chart below compares the BARS fielding strategy necessary for these two pitches. The dark fielders represent the fielding positions for medium-high outside fastballs to Yount. The light fielders represent the positions for high-outside fastballs.

BARS Fielding Strategy
Medium-High Outside Fastballs (dark fielders)
Compared To High-Outside Fastballs (light fielders)
Overall Against Right-Handed Pitchers

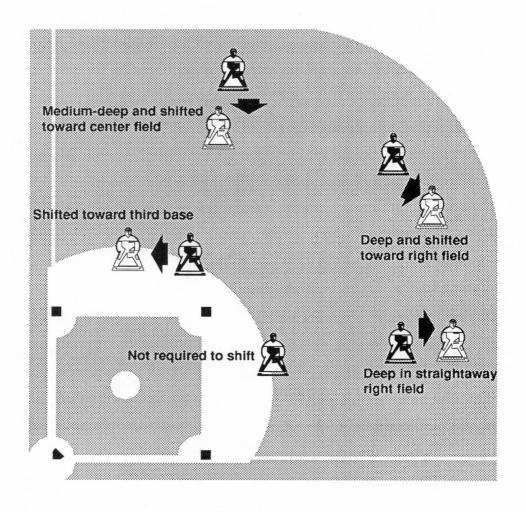

Medium-deep and shifted toward center field

Shifted toward third base

Deep and shifted toward right field

Not required to shift

Deep in straightaway right field

The field diagram below illustrates the changes necessary for low-outside fastballs (light fielders) compared to medium-high outside fastballs (dark fielder).

Notice in particular how great the adjustment is for the left fielder. In addition, the shortstop needs to shift from 'up middle' to 'shifted toward third base.'

LOW-OUTSIDE FASTBALLS

BATTING AVERAGE .241
Play

Left	Short in straightaway left field
Center	Deep and shifted toward right field
Right	Medium-deep in straightaway right field
Short	Shifted toward third base
Second	Shifted toward first base

BARS Fielding Strategy
Medium-High Outside Fastballs
Compared To Low-Outside Fastballs
Overall Against Right-Handed Pitchers

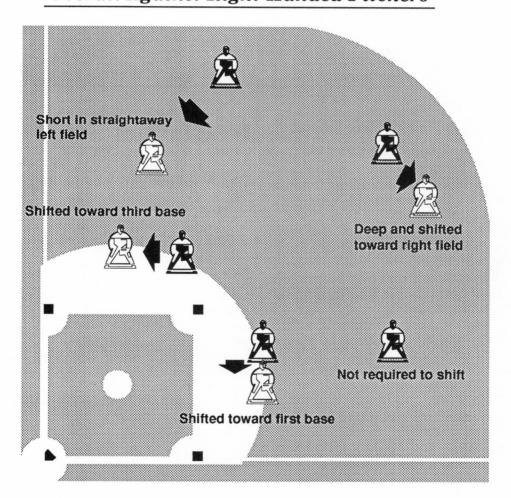

Short in straightaway left field

Shifted toward third base

Deep and shifted toward right field

Not required to shift

Shifted toward first base

Yount Ahead Against Right-Handed Pitchers

Fastball Average .351

	Inside	Middle	Outside
High	12 / 333 / 4	12 / 583 / 7	11 / 272 / 3
Med	25 / 360 / 9	12 / 583 / 7	54 / 277 / 15
Low	7 / 714 / 5	24 / 208 / 5	8 / 375 / 3

Curve Average .444

	Inside	Middle	Outside
High	0 / 0 / 0	1 / 0 / 0	1 / 1000 / 1
Med	3 / 333 / 1	3 / 1000 / 3	7 / 285 / 2
Low	2 / 500 / 1	1 / 0 / 0	0 / 0 / 0

Yount Behind Against Right-Handed Pitchers

Fastball Average .368

	Inside	Middle	Outside
High	5 / 0 / 0	4 / 500 / 2	5 / 200 / 1
Med	16 / 312 / 5	5 / 400 / 2	26 / 500 / 13
Low	3 / 0 / 0	4 / 250 / 1	8 / 500 / 4

Curve Average .185

	Inside	Middle	Outside
High	0 / 0 / 0	1 / 0 / 0	1 / 0 / 0
Med	3 / 0 / 0	2 / 500 / 1	13 / 153 / 2
Low	1 / 0 / 0	3 / 0 / 0	3 / 666 / 2

The charts above show how Yount hits fastballs and curves when he is ahead and behind in the count against right-handed pitchers.

He hits fastballs excellently both when ahead and behind, but he has trouble with curves when behind. Also notice that he hits differently in the same location when he is ahead and behind. For instance, he hits medium-high outside fastballs at a .500 clip when behind but only .277 when ahead.

Not only does Yount hit the same type and location of pitch for a different average when ahead and behind, he hits the ball different distances and directions. The following charts show how Yount hits medium-high outside fastballs when ahead and behind.

MEDIUM-HIGH OUTSIDE FASTBALLS (THROWN WHEN YOUNT IS BEHIND IN THE COUNT)

BATTING AVERAGE .500
Play
Left	Deep in straightaway left field
Center	Deep and shifted toward left field
Right	Medium-deep in straightaway right field
Short	Shifted toward third base
Second	Normal position

MEDIUM-HIGH OUTSIDE FASTBALLS (THROWN WHEN YOUNT IS AHEAD IN THE COUNT)

BATTING AVERAGE .277
Play
Left	Medium-deep and shifted toward the left field line
Center	Deep in straightaway center field
Right	Deep in straightaway right field
Short	Up middle (shifted toward second base)
Second	Normal position

Notice that every fielder except the second baseman needs to shift to be properly positioned for both pitches. This emphasizes the importance of adjusting fielders not only for all types and locations of pitches, but when the count changes.

Many times fielders assume one position then do not shift throughout all the pitches to a batter. Using the BARS System fielding strategy, fielders can adjust on a pitch-by-pitch basis. This will allow them to be in the proper position over 90 percent of the time.

The field diagram on the opposite page illustrates the shift in fielding strategy necessary for a medium-high outside fastball when Yount is ahead and behind in the count.

BARS Fielding Strategy
Medium-High Outside Fastballs
Light Fielders Represent Behind In The Count
Dark Fielders Represent Ahead In The Count

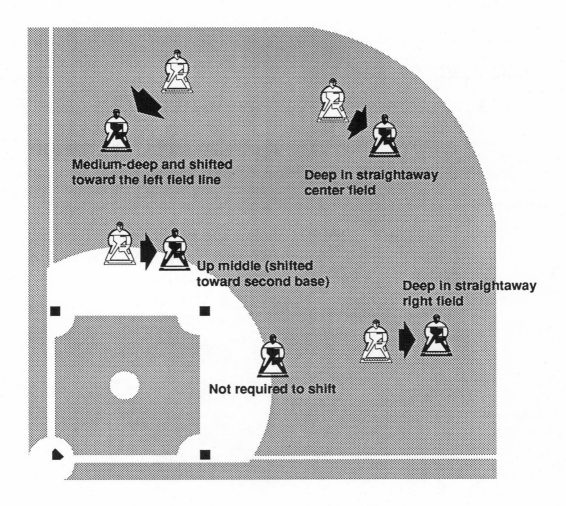

Medium-deep and shifted
toward the left field line

Deep in straightaway
center field

Up middle (shifted
toward second base)

Deep in straightaway
right field

Not required to shift

The preceding pages illustrate the BARS System findings that fielders need to assume specific fielding positons for each type and location of pitch and when the count on the batter changes. The discussion about each player included in this book will focus on various aspects of the player's BARS statistics. It is not possible to cover every aspect of a player's BARS information. This book highlights some of the most characteristic trends in each player's records.

Yount's BARS analysis continues on the following page with a look at his performance against left-handed pitchers.

Robin Yount Against Left-Handed Pitchers
Overall BARS Batting Average .257

	Fastball Average .246			Curve Average .216			Slider Average .352		
	Inside	Middle	Outside	Inside	Middle	Outside	Inside	Middle	Outside
High	3/ 0 /0	9/ 222 /2	8/ 125 /1	1/ 0 /0	0/ 0 /0	0/ 0 /0	2/ 500 /1	2/ 500 /1	5/ 400 /2
Med	17/ 294 /5	11/ 363 /4	57/ 245 /14	4/ 250 /1	2/ 1000 /2	16/ 125 /2	8/ 125 /1	4/ 750 /3	1/ 1000 /1
Low	14/ 71 /1	16/ 375 /6	23/ 260 /6	3/ 333 /1	3/ 333 /1	8/ 125 /1	4/ 250 /1	5/ 400 /2	3/ 0 /0

Yount has a considerably higher overall BARS batting average against right-handed pitchers than against left-handed pitchers (.303 overall against right-handers, .257 overall against left-handers).

Notice in the above fastball chart how much trouble Yount has with outside fastballs thrown by lefties (.125, .245, and .260, high to low). He also has trouble with all high fastballs and with low-inside fastballs.

He hits medium-high outside and medium-high inside fastballs much differently (see below).

BARS Fielding Strategy
Medium-High Fastballs Vs. Left-Handed Pitchers
Dark Fielders Represent Medium-High Outside
Light Fielders Represent Medium-High Inside

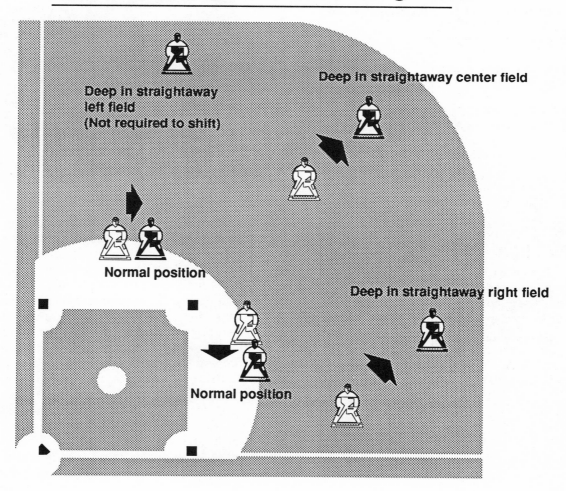

Deep in straightaway left field (Not required to shift)

Deep in straightaway center field

Normal position

Deep in straightaway right field

Normal position

MEDIUM-HIGH OUTSIDE FASTBALLS
(THROWN TO YOUNT BY
LEFT-HANDED PITCHERS)

BATTING AVERAGE .245
Play

Left	Deep in straightaway left field
Center	Deep in straightaway center field
Right	Deep in straightaway right field
Short	Normal position
Second	Normal position

MEDIUM-HIGH INSIDE FASTBALLS
(THROWN TO YOUNT BY
LEFT-HANDED PITCHERS)

BATTING AVERAGE .294
Play

Left	Deep in straightaway left field
Center	Short in straightaway center field
Right	Short and shifted toward the right field line
Short	Shifted toward third base
Second	Up middle (shifted toward second base)

Yount hits low-over-the-middle fastballs for a strong .375 average against left-handers. He pulls this pitch deep to the outfield. But notice that the second baseman is required to play shifted toward first base. The chart and field diagram below illustrate this.

LOW-OVER-THE-MIDDLE FASTBALLS
(THROWN TO YOUNT BY
LEFT-HANDED PITCHERS)

BATTING AVERAGE .375
Play

Left	Deep and shifted toward the left field line
Center	Deep and shifted toward left field
Right	Deep and shifted toward center field
Short	Normal position
Second	Shifted toward first base

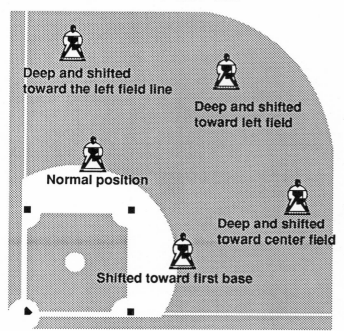

Yount has a lot of trouble with medium-high outside curves against left-handers (.125). He hits medium-high outside curves deep and straightaway to all fields. His low average indicates that most of his hit balls in this location are probably easy fly balls and ground outs (see chart and field diagram below).

MEDIUM-HIGH OUTSIDE CURVEBALLS
(THROWN TO YOUNT BY
LEFT-HANDED PITCHERS)

BATTING AVERAGE .125
Play

Left	Deep in straightaway left field
Center	Deep in straightaway center field
Right	Deep in straightaway right field
Short	Normal position
Second	*No instances recorded*

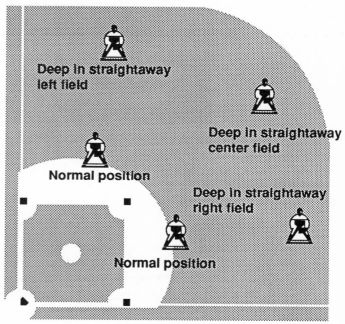

A Comprehensive BARS Analysis

This analysis of Robin Yount's BARS batting records is by no means comprehensive. The fielding strategies for a few key locations have been shown in this chapter but, for the greatest possible accuracy, fielders should position themselves on a pitch-by-pitch basis for Yount, as they should for any hitter. That would mean examining the fielding strategy for every type and location of pitch when ahead and behind in the count against both right- and left-handed pitchers.

The easiest way for a team to start using BARS fielding strategy would be to position fielders only for fastballs. Communication could be worked out between the fielders and the bench. Shifting only for fastballs would make the transition to BARS fielding strategy easier and, since most pitches are fastballs, most pitches would be covered.

A lot of people think that it would be too complicated for the fielders to shift before each pitch, but there are always at least twenty to thirty seconds between pitches. This is more than enough time to transfer information around the field.

If someone twenty years ago had suggested that professional football teams analyze opposing teams and shift on every play, based on computer read-outs of strengths, weaknesses and probable patterns of plays, he probably would have been told that it's too complicated and would take too much time.

Now every professional and major-college football team does just that. Before a game, a staff of coaches analyzes the opposing team, and their accuracy of analysis has a strong bearing on winning or losing. During a game, each team has scouts and analysts in the pressbox, calling game plans and changes in strategy to the coaches on the sidelines. This procedure is familiar to all football fans, and the complexity of the modern game has made it much more enjoyable for fans both at the stadium and on television.

The same will happen in baseball. The time will come when a strategic scouting system like the BARS System will be used by a team. When a team starts with the BARS System, it will have a three- or four-year advantage on the rest of the league, because it will take time for other teams to gather as much information as the BARS System has gathered. Once a team does start, others will follow. They will have to maintain the accelerating pace of fielding excellence that will result.

Fielding Strategy In Action

Few game-winning RBIs have had greater potential for lasting significance than Gary Carter's game-winning double in game one of the 1988 National League playoffs.

The event was dramatic enough to have been written by a Hollywood scriptwriter. The Mets came to bat in the top of the ninth trailing 2-0. Dodger pitcher Orel Hershiser, who had finished the regular season with a major-league record 59 scoreless innings, had handcuffed the Mets to that point. But when Gregg Jefferies singled to lead off the inning, moved to second on Keith Hernandez's ground out and scored on Darryl Strawberry's double to right center, the Dodgers lead was cut to 2-1 and Hershiser was taken out.

Right-handed reliever Jay Howell came in to face Kevin McReynolds. McReynolds drew a walk, but Howell then fanned Howard Johnson for the second out. That brought up Mets catcher Gary Carter.

With Strawberry on second and McReynolds on first, Howell threw Carter two straight low-outside curves. Carter reached for the next pitch, another curve low and away, and hit a soft line drive into shallow center field. Dodger centerfielder John Shelby, who had been playing very deep in center, made a mad dash and dived for the ball. He got it in his glove but it popped out as he hit the ground. Strawberry and McReynolds scored, giving the Mets a dramatic come-from-behind 3-2 victory.

The Much-Publicized Fielding Strategy

Only moments before Carter's hit, TV announcer Tim McCarver mentioned that he thought the Dodger outfielders were playing Carter extremely deep — too deep for the way Carter hit the ball as opposed to five years ago. The camera scanned the field, showing each of the outfielders playing straight-away and backed up nearly to the wall.

One pitch later, Carter's bloop hit made a prophet out of McCarver, and left millions of baseball fans with the impression that the Dodgers blew the game by playing Carter incorrectly. Next morning the papers called McCarver's observation one of the best in television history. Perhaps more than any other hit in recent years, this base hit brought national attention to the vital importance of fielding strategy.

Pitch-By-Pitch Fielding Strategy

The important fact to note is that the Dodger outfielders were not necessarily out of position simply because they were playing Carter deep. The BARS fielding strategy shows that it is often correct for the outfielders to play Carter deep — but only for specific types and locations of pitches. The Dodger fielding strategy broke down because the outfielders played Carter deep for all pitches to him, even though the pitches thrown to him did not call for them to be playing deep.

If some of the pitches to Carter had been medium-high outside fastballs, high-over-the-middle fastballs or even medium-high outside curves (among many other types and locations of pitches), it would have been correct for the outfielders to be positioned deep — *for those particular types and locations of pitches.* But by positioning themselves deep and staying deep for each of the three low-outside curves thrown to Carter, the Dodger outfielders found themselves out of position for Carter's hit.

The BARS System fielding strategy shows that for a low-outside curve thrown to Carter by a right-handed pitcher, the center fielder should play short in straight-away center field.

The BARS batting charts below show Carter's overall performance against right-handed pitchers. In particular, note his average against low-outside curves.

Gary Carter Against Right-Handed Pitchers
Overall BARS Batting Average .277

	Fastball Average .291			Curve Average .266			Slider Average .237		
	Inside	Middle	Outside	Inside	Middle	Outside	Inside	Middle	Outside
High	29/137 /4	41/292 /12	28/285 /8	5/200 /1	8/375 /3	6/166 /1	3/333 /1	7/571 /4	4/500 /2
Med	37/486 /18	17/235 /4	101/237 /24	4/500 /2	3/333 /1	43/302 /13	5/0 /0	5/400 /2	30/133 /4
Low	22/227 /5	51/392 /20	52/288 /15	0/0 /0	8/375 /3	28/142 /4	5/0 /0	12/333 /4	30/233 /7

If Shelby had been playing short in center, the ball would have been hit almost directly to him. Even if he had not wanted to play Carter short, Shelby could have played medium-deep (to guard against long hits), while realizing that the BARS fielding strategy indicates that Carter tends to hit low-outside curves short to straight-away center field.

The following diagram shows how Shelby would have been positioned had he followed the BARS fielding strategy.

BARS Fielding Strategy
Low-Outside Curveballs
Against Right-Handed Pitchers

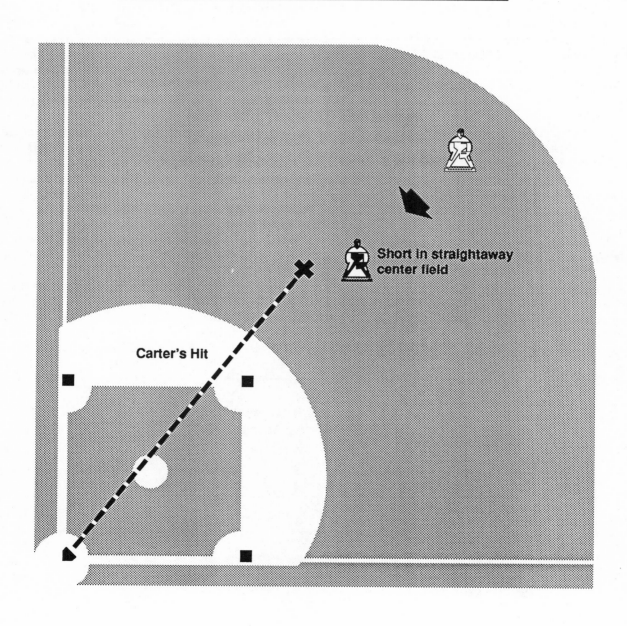

Short in straightaway center field

Carter's Hit

There was nothing wrong with the pitch itself. In fact, Carter's .142 against low-outside curves is his lowest curve average. But when the fielders are not positioned correctly, it really doesn't matter how good the pitch is, unless of course it results in a strikeout.

The opposite is also true: a pitcher can safely throw to the locations in which a hitter has a high average, if the fielders are correctly positioned for how the hitter tends to hit those pitches. Since the BARS System fielding strategy is correct over 90 percent of the time, a hitter will not have an average of over .100 in any location — if the fielders play him correctly for that location.

The BARS fielding chart shows where each of the fielders should have been playing for the low-outside curve thrown to Carter. These fielding positions are based on the computer analysis of Carter's past performance against this type of pitch.

LOW-OUTSIDE CURVEBALLS

BATTING AVERAGE .142

Play

Left	*No instances recorded*
Center	Short in straightaway center field
Right	Medium-deep and shifted toward center field
Short	Normal position
Second	Normal position

The ball was hit so softly that if the center fielder had been playing as suggested by the BARS System, he could have caught the ball. Even though the center fielder was playing very deep, he nearly made the catch. He had it in his glove but lost it in his fall. The following diagram shows Carter's hit and the fielding position of John Shelby, the Dodger's center fielder, in the actual game.

Dodger Center Fielder John Shelby's Position For Carter's Hit In Actual Game

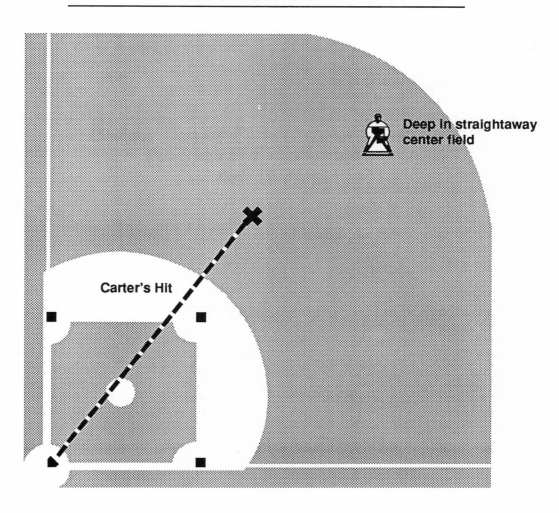

Deep in straightaway center field

Carter's Hit

Thus, if Shelby had been playing short (or even medium-deep) in straightaway center field on this particular pitch, he would have been correctly positioned to catch the ball. As it was, he couldn't reach the ball and two runners scored, giving the Mets a 3-2 ninth-inning victory.

Fielding Strategy Varies For Different Types And Locations Of Pitches

It is typical to hear managers, announcers and players comment that teams should position fielders a specific way when a certain hitter comes up. They say that fielders should play the hitter deep, or play him to pull the ball or to hit it to the opposite field. But the fact is that the same hitter will hit various types and locations of pitches differently, and if fielders do not adjust for each pitch, they run the risk of being out of position when the ball is hit.

Taking right-handed hitting Gary Carter as an example, when right-handed pitchers throw him a high-outside fastball, each of the outfielders should play deep.

HIGH-OUTSIDE FASTBALLS

BATTING AVERAGE .285
Play

Left	Deep and shifted toward the left field line
Center	Deep in straightaway center field
Right	Deep in straightaway right field
Short	Normal position
Second	Shifted toward first base

But when pitchers throw him a high-inside fastball, the center and right fielders need to play short. Only the left fielder should play deep for this particular type and location of pitch.

HIGH-INSIDE FASTBALLS

BATTING AVERAGE .137
Play

Left	Deep in straightaway left field
Center	Short in straightaway center field
Right	Short and shifted toward center field
Short	Shifted toward third base
Second	Normal position

When pitchers throw Carter a medium-high outside curve, the left and right fielders need to play deep and the center fielder needs to be medium-deep.

MEDIUM-HIGH OUTSIDE CURVEBALLS

BATTING AVERAGE .302
Play

Left	Deep in straightaway left field
Center	Medium-deep and shifted toward left field
Right	Deep and shifted toward the right field line
Short	Shifted toward third base
Second	Normal position

When pitchers throw Carter a low-outside slider, the left fielder needs to play short and the center and right fielders need to play medium-deep.

LOW-OUTSIDE SLIDERS

BATTING AVERAGE .233
Play

Left	Short and shifted toward the left field line
Center	Medium-deep in straightaway center field
Right	Medium-deep and shifted toward the right
Short	Up middle (shifted toward second base)
Second	Normal position

You may notice in each of these fielding strategies that the shortstop and second baseman are also required to shift for different types and locations of pitches. Notice too that the outfielders often are required to shift significantly to the left or to the right, in addition to adjusting by moving deep, medium-deep or short.

A Coordinated Defensive Unit

The bottom line is that fielders cannot take one position and hold that position through all the pitches to a hitter, unless all the pitches are going to the same location.

In game one of the NL playoffs, the Dodgers threw Carter three straight low-outside curves but they were not positioned correctly for how Carter tends to hit that pitch. It cost them the game.

This chapter is certainly not meant to single out the Dodger's fine organization for making a strategic error. The fact is that nearly every team does the same thing time and time again — in every game. BARS research has shown that if a team aligned itself on a pitch-by-pitch basis using the BARS fielding strategy, it would prevent an average of two to three base hits that it is now allowing in every game. Since teams allow an average of about nine hits per game, preventing two to three of those hits would make a tremendous improvement in a team's performance. Over the course of an entire season, the effect on a team's final standing would be dramatic.

A Game Of Yards

It's been said that baseball is a game of inches. A ball hit down the line can be fair or foul by a matter of inches — or even less. Throws to first base often beat runners by surprisingly small margins; even instant replays in slow motion leave viewers undecided about whether the runner was safe or out. An attempted pick-off, a pitch just missing the corner of the plate, a ball hitting a pebble and bouncing over an infielder's glove — time and again inches make the difference in a baseball game.

Outfielders and infielders are instructed from their earliest years in baseball that it is vital to get a jump on the ball when it's hit. Again, the rule is that even inches can make the difference, and we see that this is true. Almost every game has a base hit (or extra-base hit) that falls just out of a fielder's reach. These hits often make the difference in the game.

But positioning fielders according to the BARS strategy can make a difference of not mere inches — it can position fielders *yards* closer to where the ball will be hit. Getting a good jump on the ball is and always will be important, but when a player can be positioned yards closer to where he ultimately needs to be, the difference in fielding effectiveness will be immense.

For example, if the center fielder were playing deep in center field and the ball were lined to medium-deep or short center, he most likely would not be able to reach it in time to prevent the base hit. If, however, the BARS fielding strategy called for him to be playing medium-deep or short (see Example A below), by following the BARS strategy he would be a dozen or more yards closer to where he ultimately needs to be. Fast reaction time and a jump on the ball are certainly important, but when a fielder can be yards closer to where the ball is going to fall — and be there before the pitch is made — he is going to have a tremendously increased chance of making the play.

Another example, even more dramatic but no less likely, would be when a center fielder is playing deep and shifted toward left field. A ball hit short or medium-deep into *right center* would almost certainly fall in for a base hit, or slip through for an extra-base hit. But if the center fielder were positioned medium-deep or short and shifted toward right field, he would be 20 or 25 yards closer to where the ball will land. This is illustrated in Example B on the following page.

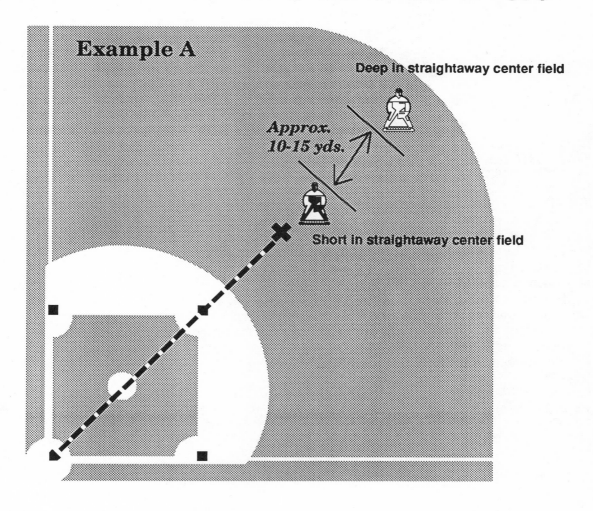

Example A

Deep in straightaway center field

Approx. 10-15 yds.

Short in straightaway center field

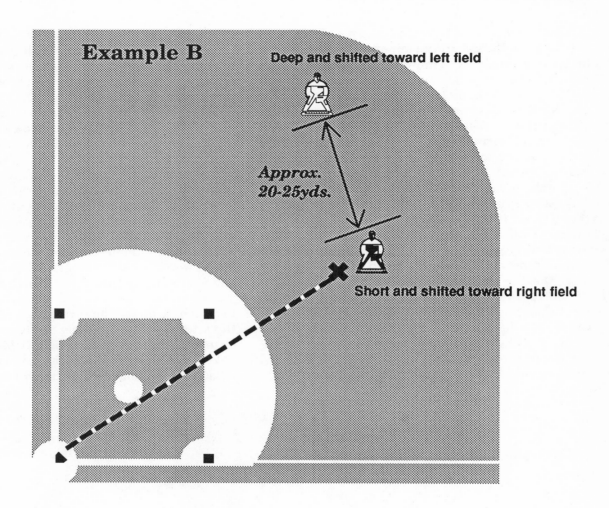

Example B

Deep and shifted toward left field

Approx. 20-25yds.

Short and shifted toward right field

Hard-Hit Balls

Some hit balls are easy to field. A pop-up to the infield often results in two or three infielders deciding among them who will take it. A lazy fly ball to the outfield is easy to catch no matter where the outfielder is playing. But hard-hit line drives require fielders to be in just the right positions. If they're not, the ball is past them in a second or less.

If a shortstop, for example, plays shifted toward second base and the ball is hit like a shot into the hole between short and third, the ball will be into left field before he even has time to take a step or two. (See Example C on opposite page.) If a right fielder plays deep and shifted toward center field when the ball is hit hard down the right-field line, the ball will go to the wall. (See Example D on opposite page.)

Example C

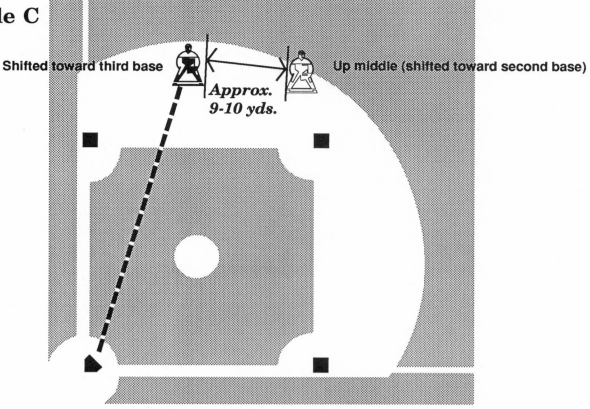

Shifted toward third base

Up middle (shifted toward second base)

Approx. 9-10 yds.

Example D

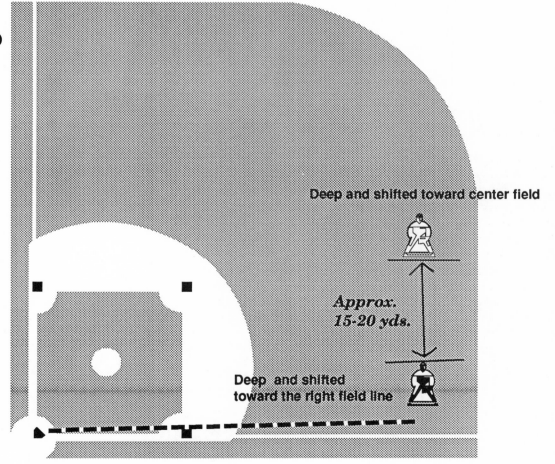

Deep and shifted toward center field

Approx. 15-20 yds.

Deep and shifted toward the right field line

Soft fly balls or easy grounders usually don't demand perfect fielding strategy. It's only when the ball is hit hard or to an unusual spot that accurate fielding strategy is essential. In these key moments, which often determine the course of a game, the action takes place so quickly that fielders are either in the right spot or not. There's little time after the pitch for adjusting or reacting.

Fielders need to be positioned correctly before the pitch is made. Positioning fielders in the best possible way for every pitch is exactly what the BARS System fielding strategy attempts to do. It's been found that by positioning fielders according to the type and location of pitch, and according to whether the hitter is ahead and behind in the count, the BARS fielding strategy is right over 90 percent of the time. Since traditional fielding strategy is right about 75 percent of the time, using the BARS strategy will prevent an average of two to three base hits that are now being allowed every game.

As a rule it's best to position fielders for every pitch according to the BARS fielding strategy. Key hits can happen at any time. They can change the complexion of a game in a matter of seconds. By placing fielders in the best possible positions *before the pitch is made*, the greatest number of hits can be prevented.

Hit 'Em Where They Are

William "Wee Willie" Keeler's famous phrase, "Hit 'em where they ain't," sums up the art of the singles and doubles hitter. Keeler practiced what he preached. Playing for Baltimore, he won the 1897 and 1898 National League batting titles with .432 and .379 averages. His .432 in 1897 is the second highest average ever recorded, trailing only Hugh Duffy's .438 for the Red Sox in 1894. After transferring to the New York Yankees, Keeler led the American League in singles for three straight seasons from 1904-1906.

"Hit 'em where they ain't" may have been the batter's motto for nearly a century, but now the BARS System offers teams a chance to make hitters "hit 'em where they are." The BARS System has found that every hitter has predictable hitting patterns. The fielding strategy is accurate over 90 percent of the time, and by positioning fielders according to the strategy for each pitch, the number of ground-ball base hits and extra-base hits into the gaps can be reduced significantly.

It has been shown that every team allows 2-3 base hits in each game that could be prevented by following the BARS fielding strategy. *The Tenth Man*, my first book, gives numerous examples from actual games of hits, runs, and even game-winning RBIs that could have been prevented by aligning fielders according to the BARS fielding strategy. It was found that nearly one-third of all game-winning RBIs resulted from hits that could have been prevented. Preventing 2-3 base hits every game — and the resulting runs — would make a tremendous difference in a team's final standing.

Let Singles Hitters Hit The Ball

Since the BARS fielding strategy is accurate over 90 percent of the time, positioning the fielders for a particular type and location of pitch (medium-high outside fastballs, low-outside curves, etc.) will lower any hitter's average in that location to about .100.

Since this is the case, it would make sense to simply align fielders appropriately for a particular type and location of pitch, throw the batter that pitch and let him hit it. As long as he doesn't hit the ball out of the park, he'll be out more than 90 percent of the time.

Even hitters like Wade Boggs or Tony Gwynn who punch and slash for high averages every year would be out more than 90 percent of the time if fielders were positioned properly for each pitch.

Pitchers Throw To Their Own Strengths, Not To Batter's Weaknesses

The BARS System has determined that pitchers throw more to their own strengths than to batters' weaknesses. This is evident from the batting charts. Looking through this book you'll see that batters often have their highest averages in locations in which they are thrown the most pitches. These are usually high-outside or high-inside fastballs. Pitchers either don't know or don't care what a hitter's strong and weak locations are.

When using the BARS fielding strategy, it would be easy to have pitchers aim at the medium-high inside location or at the medium-high outside location, letting the batter hit away. In fact, pitching to what usually are considered easy-to-hit locations could increase the accuracy of using the BARS System because normally there are more recorded instances in those locations. As with any system of probability, the more instances to calculate from, the more accurate the results will be. By pitching to locations with high numbers of instances, the BARS fielding strategy has the greatest chance to be correct.

It could be that the accuracy of the BARS fielding strategy is much higher than 90 percent for, say, medium-high outside fastballs — the location that almost always has the highest number of recorded instances for a hitter. Also included in the category of highly pitched locations would be the medium-high inside, medium-over-the-middle, low-over-the-middle, and high-over-the-middle locations. In this book the records for players show that most pitches go to these locations anyway, so having pitchers throw to them should not be difficult.

Starting The BARS System

One easy way to start using the BARS System would be to use the fielding strategy only for fastballs. Most pitches that are hit are fastballs anyway, so not much would be lost. Pitchers are usually more accurate with fastballs than with other types of pitches, so the chances are greatest that fastballs would find their way to the selected location and be hit by the batter.

It would not be necessary for pitchers to throw 90 m.p.h. fastballs. The most important thing when using the BARS System would to get the ball to the selected location. A team could save a pitcher's arm by letting him throw 85 m.p.h. fastballs — as long as he hit the right location. It wouldn't matter how well the hitter hit the ball — when the fielders are in the right place, they'll make the out.

There is ample time between pitches to transfer information around the field. There could come the time when teams use electronic communication to designate type and location of pitch, and to align fielders accordingly.

Most Teams Really Don't Have A Fielding Strategy

Most fielders take positions when a batter comes to the plate and maintain those positions through all the pitches to the batter.

This is clearly not effective because the pitcher delivers different types and locations of pitches. If five pitches are thrown before the batter hits the ball, and each pitch is to a different location, it would be only by chance that the fielders were in the best possible positions to field the hit ball. This is why so many base hits are allowed that could be prevented by the BARS System.

Using the BARS System will allow teams to coordinate their defense. When all fielders are aligned for a specific type and location of pitch, tremendous effectiveness can be gained.

Teams spend considerable amounts of money on players and player development, but nothing on finding out the strengths and weaknesses of hitters. And no time or resources are devoted to learning how to field hitters.

Professional football is now devoting tremendous resources to scouting the strengths and weaknesses of opponents. Extensive computer research is undertaken for every game, and the success of any particular game is greatly determined by the accuracy of the scouts and their computers.

Baseball offers an even better opportunity for effective computer analysis. In baseball the same thing happens again and again — a pitcher throws the ball to a stationary batter. The BARS System bases its statistics on extremely large numbers of instances. This results in a high degree of accuracy not only in determining areas of strength and weakness in a batter's charts, but in positioning fielders for specific pitches.

And in baseball the defense initiates each play (by pitching the ball). In football the defense has no control over the start of each play and never really knows what their opponent's offense will do. Overall, computers can be even more valuable in baseball than in football, though the potential has hardly been tapped by baseball scouts, players and managers.

Major league players have plenty of time on their hands (especially when on the road) to study the BARS System and be thoroughly prepared for every game. They could meet to organize their coordination of pitches and fielding positions, and be ready for every hitter.

New Excitement In The Game

We will see a lot of creativity in defense once teams start using the BARS System. While updating our records, we notice that some hitters never hit specific types and locations of pitches to certain fields. For instance, a certain hitter may never hit a medium-high inside fastball to right field. After 20 or 30 instances have been recorded in the medium-high inside fastball location without a ball hit to right, the percentages become significant that the hitter will not hit this pitch to right field.

This would allow the right fielder to be daring. He could break with the pitch toward center field to help cover that area. Or he could break toward the infield if it were found that the hitter tended to hit a lot of grounders to the right side.

You'll notice in this book that the BARS fielding positions occasionally require fielders to be spread out more than normal. For instance, the fielding strategy for a certain type and location of pitch to a batter might require the center fielder to be shifted toward left field and the right fielder to be shifted toward the right field line. This results in a large gap in right-center. While it's true that hitters tend to hit specific pitches the same way over and over, most major league hitters can adjust their swings enough to poke the ball into large empty areas. Fielders might want to break toward their suggested BARS positions with the pitch so the batter doesn't see the openings before the pitch is thrown.

There are numerous strategies that will be utilized when teams implement the BARS System. Once a team starts using the BARS fielding strategy, it will have a tremendous edge over teams that do not. The time is coming when every major league team will be forced to mold itself into a highly-coordinated defensive unit. The "hit 'em where they are" strategies that develop will be fascinating for fans and players alike.

The Overall Evaluation

Each player discussed in this book is given an Overall Evaluation. To make this easier to see and read, the Overall Evaluation is set up in chart form, with performance in each category designated as follows:

Excellent ⚾ ⚾ ⚾ ⚾
Good ⚾ ⚾ ⚾
Fair ⚾ ⚾
Poor ⚾

Since most players hit fastballs better than they hit curves and sliders, the excellent, good, fair and poor batting average criteria are slightly higher for fastballs than for curves and sliders.

Fastballs

Excellent	*.325 and above*
Good	*.300-.324*
Fair	*.275-.299*
Poor	*Below .275*

Curves and Sliders

Excellent	*.300 and above*
Good	*.275-.299*
Fair	*.250-.274*
Poor	*Below .250*

When looking through the BARS records it can be seen that the above designations are appropriate for most hitters. Many players hit over .300 against fastballs, while few hit over .300 against curves and sliders.

The BARS Overall Batting Averages

In addition to batting averages for fastballs, curves and sliders, the BARS System gives an overall average against right-handed pitchers and against left-handed pitchers. In some instances these overall averages may be higher or lower than the collective fastball, curve and slider averages would seem to indicate. This discrepancy can occur because the overall averages take into consideration types of pitches other than fastballs, curves and sliders. Among these other pitches are knuckleballs, sinkerballs, screwballs and change-ups. In particular, many pitchers have added split-fingered fastballs to their collection of pitches. Certain hitters may have a very high — or, in many cases — a very low average against split-fingered fastballs. This can cause the overall averages against right- or left-handed pitchers to be higher or lower than the fastball, curve and slider averages would suggest.

Realizing this, the BARS System will soon redesign its charts to account for the increasing number of split-fingered fastballs that are being thrown. Next year the BARS System will either replace the slider chart with a split-fingered fastball chart or simply add a split-fingered fastball chart to the analysis.

The BARS overall batting averages for a player against right- and left-handed pitchers may differ from his official averages against right- and left-handers because the BARS System scouts only about one-third of all major league games played. A player's BARS records and his official records are usually similar, but some variance is inevitable.

The Overall Evaluation shown for each player discussed in this book contains six overall categories:

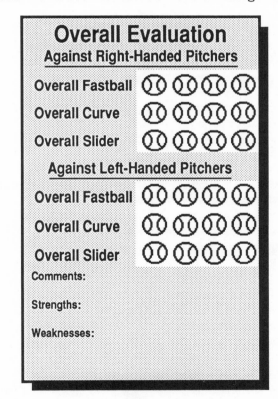

The number of baseballs shown for each category corresponds with the player's overall BARS average in that category. The Overall Evaluation includes a brief comment about each player's batting performance and a brief description of his most significant batting strengths and weaknesses.

The BARS System currently does not show home runs in the Super Summary. Starting next year it will. This will give a more complete indication of strength and weakness in each location of the batting grids.

Bradley, Phil
Hulett, Tim
Melvin, Bob
Moreland, Keith
Orsulak, Joe
Ripken, Bill
Ripken, Cal, Jr.
Sheets, Larry
Tettleton, Mickey
Traber, Jim

Baltimore Orioles
BARS System
Hitting Analysis

Phil Bradley Against Right-Handed Pitchers
Overall BARS Batting Average .282

Fastball Average .282

	Inside	Middle	Outside
High	19/157/3	16/375/6	13/153/2
Med	52/326/17	9/333/3	73/315/23
Low	23/173/4	50/280/14	28/285/8

Curve Average .312

	Inside	Middle	Outside
High	2/500/1	6/166/1	5/200/1
Med	9/333/3	4/750/3	23/304/7
Low	3/0/0	13/461/6	31/258/8

Slider Average .226

	Inside	Middle	Outside
High	2/0/0	0/0/0	1/0/0
Med	3/0/0	2/500/1	17/294/5
Low	5/0/0	8/250/2	15/266/4

Phil Bradley Against Left-Handed Pitchers
Overall BARS Batting Average .214

Fastball Average .215

	Inside	Middle	Outside
High	10/100/1	12/416/5	9/0/0
Med	21/142/3	4/250/1	39/282/11
Low	14/214/3	16/250/4	19/157/3

Curve Average .241

	Inside	Middle	Outside
High	0/0/0	1/0/0	1/0/0
Med	3/333/1	1/1000/1	4/500/2
Low	5/0/0	9/222/2	5/200/1

Slider Average .105

	Inside	Middle	Outside
High	4/250/1	0/0/0	0/0/0
Med	4/0/0	0/0/0	1/0/0
Low	9/111/1	0/0/0	1/0/0

Right-handed hitter Phil Bradley has a higher BARS average against right-handed pitchers (.282 overall vs. right-handers, .215 overall vs. left-handers). It's unusual for a right-handed hitter to have his average against right-handed pitchers be so much higher.

He hits waist-high fastballs very well against right-handers (.326, .333 and .315, inside to outside). He hits medium-high outside fastballs down both lines.

MEDIUM-HIGH OUTSIDE FASTBALLS

BATTING AVERAGE .315

Play

Left	Deep and shifted toward the left field line
Center	Medium-deep in straightaway center field
Right	Medium-deep and shifted toward the right line
Short	Up middle (shifted toward second base)
Second	Shifted toward first base

Bradley's .326 against medium-high inside fastballs is excellent. He hits this pitch down both lines also. Comparing the fielding strategies for Bradley's medium-high inside and medium-high outside fastballs locations shows how important it is for fielders to shift on a pitch-by-pitch basis.

MEDIUM-HIGH INSIDE FASTBALLS

BATTING AVERAGE .326

Play

Left	Deep and shifted toward the left field line
Center	Medium-deep and shifted toward right field
Right	Deep and shifted toward the right field line
Short	Up middle (shifted toward second base)
Second	Normal position

Bradley hits high-inside and high-outside fastballs poorly (.157 and .153, respectively), but his .375 against high-over-the-middle fastballs is excellent.

HIGH-OVER-THE-MIDDLE FASTBALLS

BATTING AVERAGE .375

Play

Left	Deep and shifted toward the left field line
Center	Deep in straightaway center field
Right	Medium-deep and shifted toward center field
Short	Shifted toward third base
Second	Shifted toward first base

Bradley Against Curves And Sliders

Bradley hits a strong .304 against medium-high outside curves thrown by right-handed pitchers.

MEDIUM-HIGH OUTSIDE CURVEBALLS

BATTING AVERAGE .304

Play

Left	Deep and shifted toward the left field line
Center	Deep in straightaway center field
Right	Deep in straightaway right field
Short	Normal position
Second	*No instances recorded*

His .258 against low-outside curves thrown by right-handers is fair.

LOW-OUTSIDE CURVEBALLS

BATTING AVERAGE .258

Play

Left	Medium-deep in straightaway left field
Center	Deep and shifted toward left field
Right	Deep in straightaway right field
Short	Up middle (shifted toward second base)
Second	Normal position

He hits low-over-the-middle curves for an excellent .461 average. He goes to his opposite field (right field) with this pitch. If fielders positioned themselves correctly, they could prevent most of his base hits from this location.

LOW-OVER-THE-MIDDLE CURVEBALLS

BATTING AVERAGE .461

Play

Left	*No instances recorded*
Center	*No instances recorded*
Right	Deep in straightaway right field
Short	Up middle (shifted toward second base)
Second	Shifted toward first base

Bradley hits .294 against medium-outside sliders thrown by right-handers. His .266 against low-outside sliders is adequate.

Bradley Against Left-Handed Pitchers

Bradley has a low .215 overall fastball average against left-handed pitchers. He's weak against low fastballs and inside fastballs thrown by left-handers, but he hits medium-high outside fastballs for a .282 average. He goes to right field with this pitch.

MEDIUM-HIGH OUTSIDE FASTBALLS (THROWN BY LEFT-HANDED PITCHERS)

BATTING AVERAGE .282

Play

Left	*No instances recorded*
Center	Deep and shifted toward right field
Right	Deep and shifted toward the right field line
Short	Normal position
Second	Normal position

He hits high-over-the-middle fastballs for an excellent .416 against lefties.

HIGH-OVER-THE-MIDDLE FASTBALLS (THROWN BY LEFT-HANDED PITCHERS)

BATTING AVERAGE .416

Play

Left	Deep and shifted toward the left field line
Center	Deep and shifted toward right field
Right	Medium-deep in straightaway right field
Short	Normal position
Second	Normal position

Ahead And Behind In The Count Vs. RH

Ahead

Fastball Average .380

	Inside	Middle	Outside
High	4/250 /1	7/571 /4	0/0 /0
Med	22/454 /10	5/200 /1	28/428 /12
Low	9/333 /3	26/230 /6	4/750 /3

Curve Average .363

	Inside	Middle	Outside
High	0/0 /0	0/0 /0	1/0 /0
Med	1/1000 /1	0/0 /0	2/500 /1
Low	0/0 /0	3/333 /1	4/250 /1

Behind

Fastball Average .274

	Inside	Middle	Outside
High	4/250 /1	6/333 /2	1/0 /0
Med	13/307 /4	1/0 /0	16/375 /6
Low	8/125 /1	6/333 /2	7/142 /1

Curve Average .388

	Inside	Middle	Outside
High	0/0 /0	1/0 /0	0/0 /0
Med	5/400 /2	2/500 /1	11/454 /5
Low	2/0 /0	6/500 /3	9/333 /3

Overall Evaluation

Against Right-Handed Pitchers

Overall Fastball	
Overall Curve	
Overall Slider	

Against Left-Handed Pitchers

Overall Fastball	
Overall Curve	
Overall Slider	

Comments: Strong against waist-high fastballs vs. RH. Strengths: Waist-high fastballs, high-middle fastballs, waist-high curves, low-middle curves, medium-outside sliders vs. RH; high-middle fastballs vs. LH. Weaknesses: High-inside, high-outside, low-inside fastballs vs. RH; all fastballs except high-middle and medium-outside vs. LH, low curves and low-inside sliders vs. LH.

Tim Hulett Against Right-Handed Pitchers
Overall BARS Batting Average .251

	Fastball Average .257			Curve Average .303			Slider Average .100		
	Inside	Middle	Outside	Inside	Middle	Outside	Inside	Middle	Outside
High	14/ 214 /3	15/ 133 /2	4/ 0 /0	1/ 0 /0	3/ 333 /1	2/ 0 /0	0/ 0 /0	0/ 0 /0	0/ 0 /0
Med	37/ 189 /7	13/ 461 /6	73/ 287 /21	5/ 200 /1	4/ 750 /3	24/ 250 /6	2/ 0 /0	1/ 0 /0	7/ 0 /0
Low	13/ 230 /3	32/ 343 /11	20/ 200 /4	1/ 1000 /1	2/ 500 /1	14/ 285 /4	1/ 0 /0	2/ 0 /0	17/ 176 /3

Tim Hulett Against Left-Handed Pitchers
Overall BARS Batting Average .262

	Fastball Average .280			Curve Average .230			Slider Average .277		
	Inside	Middle	Outside	Inside	Middle	Outside	Inside	Middle	Outside
High	5/ 200 /1	2/ 0 /0	6/ 166 /1	0/ 0 /0	1/ 0 /0	1/ 1000 /1	0/ 0 /0	1/ 0 /0	0/ 0 /0
Med	19/ 315 /6	6/ 500 /3	61/ 278 /17	3/ 333 /1	1/ 0 /0	10/ 400 /4	4/ 750 /3	1/ 0 /0	3/ 0 /0
Low	7/ 428 /3	14/ 285 /4	19/ 210 /4	6/ 0 /0	1/ 0 /0	3/ 0 /0	2/ 500 /1	3/ 0 /0	4/ 250 /1

Right-handed hitting Tim Hulett has trouble with fastballs against right-handed pitchers (.257 overall). His .280 overall against fastballs thrown by left-handed pitchers is fairly good. In contrast, he hits curves excellently against right-handers (.303 overall) but poorly against left-handers (.230) overall.

Starting with right-handers, Hulett hits .287 against medium-high outside fastballs. His Ahead and Behind charts on the opposite page show that he hits this pitch much better when behind in the count than when ahead (.333 when behind, .259 when ahead).

The following BARS charts show that the center and right fielders and the shortstop need to shift to be correctly positioned for medium-high outside fastballs against right-handers when Hulett is ahead and behind in the count.

MEDIUM-HIGH OUTSIDE FASTBALLS (WHEN BEHIND IN THE COUNT)

BATTING AVERAGE .333
Play
Left Deep and shifted toward the left field line
Center Deep in straightaway center field
Right Deep in straightaway right field
Short Up middle (shifted toward second base)
Second Shifted toward first base

MEDIUM-HIGH OUTSIDE FASTBALLS (WHEN AHEAD IN THE COUNT)

BATTING AVERAGE .259
Play
Left Deep and shifted toward the left field line
Center Medium-deep in straightaway center field
Right Medium-deep in straightaway right field
Short Normal position
Second Shifted toward first base

Hulett has trouble with low-outside and low-inside fastballs (.200 and .230, respectively). But he hits low-over-the-middle fastballs for an excellent .343 average.

LOW-OVER-THE-MIDDLE FASTBALLS

BATTING AVERAGE .343
Play
Left Deep and shifted toward center field
Center Deep in straightaway center field
Right Medium-deep and shifted toward the right line
Short Normal position
Second *No instances recorded*

Notice that he has a fine .461 average against medium-over-the-middle fastballs. He has a relatively-high number of recorded instances in this location (13). That means either that pitchers are not pitching him carefully enough or that he is patient and waiting for good pitches. Overall, right-handers would be best to keep fastballs inside or high to Hulett because these are his weak sectors.

Hulett Against Curves And Sliders

Hulett has trouble with medium-high outside curves thrown by right-handed pitchers (.250) but he hits low-outside curves fairly well (.285).

LOW-OUTSIDE CURVEBALLS

BATTING AVERAGE .285
Play

Left	*No instances recorded*
Center	Medium-deep in straightaway center field
Right	Medium-deep and shifted toward center field
Short	Up middle (shifted toward second base)
Second	*No instances recorded*

He has trouble with medium-outside and low-outside sliders against right-handers. (.000 on 0 for 7 and .176, respectively).

Hulett Against Left-Handed Pitchers

Hulett hits .278 against medium-high outside fastballs thrown by left-handed pitchers.

**MEDIUM-HIGH OUTSIDE FASTBALLS
(THROWN BY LEFT-HANDED PITCHERS)**

BATTING AVERAGE .278
Play

Left	Deep in straightaway left field
Center	Deep in straightaway center field
Right	Medium-deep and shifted toward the right line
Short	Normal position
Second	Normal position

He hits a solid .315 against medium-high inside fastballs.

**MEDIUM-HIGH INSIDE FASTBALLS
(THROWN BY LEFT-HANDED PITCHERS)**

BATTING AVERAGE .315
Play

Left	Deep in straightaway left field
Center	Medium-deep and shifted toward left field
Right	Medium-deep and shifted toward center field
Short	Normal position
Second	*No instances recorded*

Overall, he has trouble with outside fastballs thrown by left-handers (.166, .278 and .210, high to low). His .210 against low-outside fastballs is weak.

He hits .400 against medium-high outside curves thrown by lefties.

**MEDIUM-HIGH OUTSIDE CURVEBALLS
(THROWN BY LEFT-HANDED PITCHERS)**

BATTING AVERAGE .400
Play

Left	Medium-deep and shifted toward the left field line
Center	Medium-deep in straightaway center field
Right	Deep and shifted toward the right field line
Short	Up middle (shifted toward second base)
Second	Shifted toward first base

Ahead And Behind In The Count Vs. RH

Ahead

Fastball Average .290

	Inside	Middle	Outside
High	8 / 125 / 1	5 / 200 / 1	0 / 0 / 0
Med	14 / 214 / 3	6 / 666 / 4	27 / 259 / 7
Low	8 / 375 / 3	11 / 272 / 3	7 / 428 / 3

Curve Average .166

	Inside	Middle	Outside
High	0 / 0 / 0	0 / 0 / 0	0 / 0 / 0
Med	0 / 0 / 0	0 / 0 / 0	5 / 200 / 1
Low	0 / 0 / 0	1 / 0 / 0	0 / 0 / 0

Behind

Fastball Average .266

	Inside	Middle	Outside
High	3 / 333 / 1	4 / 0 / 0	1 / 0 / 0
Med	9 / 0 / 0	3 / 666 / 2	18 / 333 / 6
Low	0 / 0 / 0	6 / 500 / 3	1 / 0 / 0

Curve Average .375

	Inside	Middle	Outside
High	0 / 0 / 0	1 / 0 / 0	1 / 0 / 0
Med	1 / 0 / 0	1 / 1000 / 1	7 / 285 / 2
Low	0 / 0 / 0	1 / 1000 / 1	4 / 500 / 2

Overall Evaluation

Against Right-Handed Pitchers

Overall Fastball	⚾
Overall Curve	⚾ ⚾ ⚾ ⚾
Overall Slider	⚾

Against Left-Handed Pitchers

Overall Fastball	⚾ ⚾
Overall Curve	⚾
Overall Slider	⚾ ⚾ ⚾

Comments: Difficulty with inside fastballs and high fastballs vs. RH.
Strengths: Medium-middle and low-middle fastballs vs. RH; medium-inside, low-inside and medium-middle fastballs, medium-outside curves vs. LH.
Weaknesses: Inside fastballs, high fastballs, low-outside fastballs, low-outside sliders vs. RH; high fastballs, low-outside fastballs vs. LH.

Bob Melvin (Right Handed)   *Baltimore Orioles*

Bob Melvin Against Right-Handed Pitchers
Overall BARS Batting Average .152

Fastball Average .197

	Inside	Middle	Outside
High	12 / 83/1	10 / 300/3	7 / 142/1
Med	14 / 428/6	2 / 500/1	18 / 166/3
Low	7 / 142/1	10 / 100/1	11 / 90/1

Curve Average .032

	Inside	Middle	Outside
High	2 / 0/0	1 / 0/0	3 / 0/0
Med	2 / 500/1	1 / 0/0	9 / 0/0
Low	1 / 0/0	2 / 0/0	10 / 0/0

Slider Average .148

	Inside	Middle	Outside
High	0 / 0/0	2 / 0/0	2 / 500/1
Med	0 / 0/0	0 / 0/0	6 / 333/2
Low	2 / 0/0	4 / 0/0	11 / 90/1

Bob Melvin Against Left-Handed Pitchers
Overall BARS Batting Average .302

Fastball Average .515

	Inside	Middle	Outside
High	3 / 0/0	3 / 666/2	4 / 500/2
Med	3 / 666/2	2 / 500/1	8 / 625/5
Low	2 / 500/1	1 / 0/0	7 / 571/4

Curve Average .176

	Inside	Middle	Outside
High	0 / 0/0	0 / 0/0	0 / 0/0
Med	2 / 0/0	1 / 0/0	4 / 250/1
Low	4 / 250/1	4 / 250/1	2 / 0/0

Slider Average .142

	Inside	Middle	Outside
High	0 / 0/0	0 / 0/0	0 / 0/0
Med	0 / 0/0	0 / 0/0	1 / 0/0
Low	3 / 0/0	3 / 333/1	0 / 0/0

Right-handed hitter Bob Melvin has considerable trouble with outside fastballs thrown by right-handed pitchers. He also has trouble with low fastballs. But he hits medium-high inside fastballs for an excellent .428 average. The chart below and the field diagram on the opposite page show how fielders need to play for this pitch.

MEDIUM-HIGH INSIDE FASTBALLS

BATTING AVERAGE .428

Play

Left	Deep and shifted toward the left field line
Center	Deep and shifted toward left field
Right	Medium-deep and shifted toward the right line
Short	Shifted toward third base
Second	Normal position

He hits .300 against high-over-the-middle fastballs thrown by right-handers. He hits this pitch medium-deep down the left line and into the hole between third and short.

HIGH-OVER-THE-MIDDLE FASTBALLS

BATTING AVERAGE .300

Play

Left	Medium-deep and shifted toward the left field line
Center	Medium-deep in straightaway center field
Right	Deep in straightaway right field
Short	Shifted toward third base
Second	*No instances recorded*

Notice the difficulty Melvin has with medium-outside and low-outside curves against right-handers. He has almost as much trouble with low-outside sliders (.090) but he hits medium-high outside sliders well (.333).

Melvin has a much higher overall fastball average against left-handed pitchers. He hits all waist-high and all outside fastballs very well. His .625 against medium-high outside fastballs indicates strength, as does the .571 against low-outside fastballs.

MEDIUM-HIGH OUTSIDE FASTBALLS
(THROWN BY LEFT-HANDED PITCHERS)

BATTING AVERAGE .625

Play

Left	Medium-deep and shifted toward center field
Center	Medium-deep in straightaway center field
Right	Deep and shifted toward the right field line
Short	Up middle (shifted toward second base)
Second	*No instances recorded*

LOW-OUTSIDE FASTBALLS
(THROWN BY LEFT-HANDED PITCHERS)

BATTING AVERAGE .571

Play

Left	Medium-deep and shifted toward center field
Center	Medium-deep in straightaway center field
Right	Deep in straightaway right field
Short	Shifted toward third base
Second	*No instances recorded*

Medium-High Inside Fastballs
(Thrown By Right-Handed Pitchers)

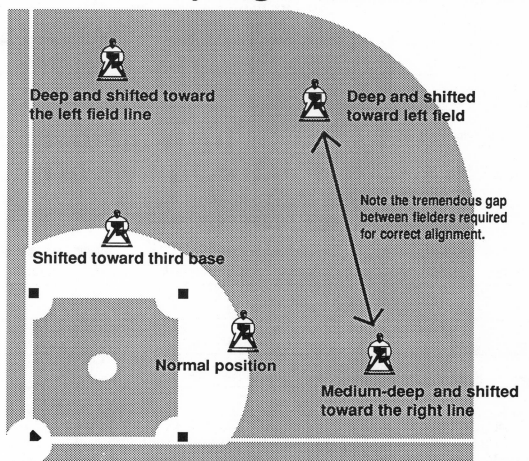

Deep and shifted toward the left field line

Deep and shifted toward left field

Note the tremendous gap between fielders required for correct alignment.

Shifted toward third base

Normal position

Medium-deep and shifted toward the right line

Ahead And Behind In The Count Vs. RH

Ahead

Fastball Average .153

	Inside	Middle	Outside
High	5/ 0 /0	3/ 333 /1	1/ 0 /0
Med	4/ 500 /2	1/ 1000 /1	6/ 0 /0
Low	1/ 0 /0	4/ 0 /0	1/ 0 /0

Curve Average .000

	Inside	Middle	Outside
High	0/ 0 /0	0/ 0 /0	1/ 0 /0
Med	1/ 0 /0	0/ 0 /0	1/ 0 /0
Low	0/ 0 /0	0/ 0 /0	2/ 0 /0

Behind

Fastball Average .291

	Inside	Middle	Outside
High	5/ 200 /1	4/ 500 /2	3/ 333 /1
Med	5/ 200 /1	0/ 0 /0	4/ 500 /2
Low	2/ 0 /0	0/ 0 /0	1/ 0 /0

Curve Average .100

	Inside	Middle	Outside
High	0/ 0 /0	1/ 0 /0	1/ 0 /0
Med	1/ 1000 /1	0/ 0 /0	3/ 0 /0
Low	1/ 0 /0	1/ 0 /0	2/ 0 /0

Overall Evaluation
Against Right-Handed Pitchers

Overall Fastball ⚾

Overall Curve ⚾

Overall Slider ⚾

Against Left-Handed Pitchers

Overall Fastball ⚾ ⚾ ⚾ ⚾

Overall Curve ⚾

Overall Slider   Not enough Information

Comments: Weak against outside fastballs, low fastballs, and curves in general vs. RH.
Strengths: Medium-inside and high-middle fastballs vs. RH; waist-high and outside fastballs vs. LH.
Weaknesses: High-inside, all outside and low fastballs, curves in general, low sliders vs. RH; low curves vs. LH.

Keith Moreland (Right Handed) *Baltimore Orioles*

Keith Moreland Against Right-Handed Pitchers
Overall BARS Batting Average .281

Fastball Average .296

	Inside	Middle	Outside
High	51/ 176 /9	121/ 297 /36	59/ 254 /15
Med	120/ 433 /52	40/ 300 /12	235/ 297 /70
Low	52/ 326 /17	217/ 327 /71	145/ 179 /26

Curve Average .262

	Inside	Middle	Outside
High	4/ 750 /3	12/ 416 /5	10/ 200 /2
Med	10/ 100 /1	10/ 300 /3	60/ 300 /18
Low	9/ 333 /3	38/ 394 /15	83/ 144 /12

Slider Average .213

	Inside	Middle	Outside
High	0/ 0 /0	7/ 142 /1	11/ 363 /4
Med	5/ 600 /3	2/ 500 /1	62/ 209 /13
Low	6/ 333 /2	13/ 153 /2	72/ 166 /12

Keith Moreland Against Left-Handed Pitchers
Overall BARS Batting Average .293

Fastball Average .321

	Inside	Middle	Outside
High	11/ 90 /1	13/ 538 /7	40/ 200 /8
Med	18/ 444 /8	7/ 285 /2	96/ 406 /39
Low	14/ 357 /5	65/ 261 /17	56/ 285 /16

Curve Average .252

	Inside	Middle	Outside
High	1/ 0 /0	4/ 500 /2	5/ 200 /1
Med	3/ 0 /0	2/ 500 /1	23/ 173 /4
Low	8/ 500 /4	23/ 304 /7	26/ 192 /5

Slider Average .433

	Inside	Middle	Outside
High	2/ 500 /1	0/ 0 /0	0/ 0 /0
Med	5/ 600 /3	2/ 1000 /2	1/ 0 /0
Low	6/ 333 /2	9/ 333 /3	5/ 400 /2

Right-handed hitter Keith Moreland has a fairly good .296 overall fastball average against right-handed pitchers and a good .321 overall fastball average against left-handed pitchers.

Against right-handers, he has some very strong locations. His .433 against medium-high inside fastballs is excellent. He hits this pitch well both when ahead and when behind in the count, though better when ahead. Notice the differences in fielding positions required in the diagram on the opposite page.

**MEDIUM-HIGH INSIDE FASTBALLS
(WHEN AHEAD IN THE COUNT)**

BATTING AVERAGE .490
Play
Left   Deep and shifted toward the left field line
Center Medium-deep in straightaway center field
Right   Medium-deep in straightaway right field
Short   Shifted toward third base
Second Normal position

**MEDIUM-HIGH INSIDE FASTBALLS
(WHEN BEHIND IN THE COUNT)**

BATTING AVERAGE .375
Play
Left   Deep and shifted toward the left field line
Center Deep in straightaway center field

Right   Deep in straightaway right field
Short   Up middle (shifted toward second base)
Second Normal position

Moreland hits medium-high outside curves (.300) and all over-the-middle curves excellently against right-handers. He has trouble, however, with low-outside curves (.144).

Moreland Against Left-Handed Pitchers

Moreland hits medium-high inside fastballs (.444) and medium-high outside fastballs (.406) excellently against left-handed pitchers.

**MEDIUM-HIGH OUTSIDE FASTBALLS
(THROWN BY LEFT-HANDED PITCHERS)**

BATTING AVERAGE .406
Play
Left   Deep in straightaway left field
Center Medium-deep in straightaway center field
Right   Medium-deep in straightaway right field
Short   Normal position
Second Shifted toward first base

He has trouble with outside curves against left-handers. He hits low-over-the-middle curves very well, however (.304).

Medium-High Inside Fastballs Vs. RH
Dark Fielders — Behind In The Count
Light Fielders — Ahead In The Count

Deep and shifted toward the left field line (Not required to shift)

Medium-deep in straightaway center field

Shifted toward third base

Normal position (Not required to shift)

Medium-deep in straightaway right field

Ahead And Behind In The Count Vs. RH

Ahead

	Fastball Average .358			**Curve Average .347**		
	Inside	Middle	Outside	Inside	Middle	Outside
High	16/ 125 /2	67/ 313 /21	21/ 285 /6	1/ 1000 /1	2/ 0 /0	1/ 0 /0
Med	55/ 490 /27	19/ 315 /6	111/ 342 /38	2/ 0 /0	4/ 250 /1	17/ 352 /6
Low	23/ 521 /12	115/ 382 /44	41/ 292 /12	4/ 500 /2	7/ 571 /4	8/ 250 /2

Behind

	Fastball Average .271			**Curve Average .337**		
	Inside	Middle	Outside	Inside	Middle	Outside
High	10/ 100 /1	23/ 304 /7	21/ 333 /7	1/ 1000 /1	4/ 500 /2	7/ 285 /2
Med	32/ 375 /12	9/ 222 /2	60/ 366 /22	5/ 200 /1	2/ 500 /1	22/ 409 /9
Low	12/ 250 /3	45/ 200 /9	35/ 114 /4	1/ 0 /0	11/ 545 /6	30/ 200 /6

Overall Evaluation
Against Right-Handed Pitchers

Overall Fastball ⚾⚾ ⚾⚾

Overall Curve ⚾⚾ ⚾⚾

Overall Slider ⚾⚾

Against Left-Handed Pitchers

Overall Fastball ⚾⚾ ⚾⚾ ⚾⚾

Overall Curve ⚾⚾ ⚾⚾

Overall Slider ⚾⚾ ⚾⚾ ⚾⚾ ⚾⚾ ⚾⚾

Comments: Strong vs. medium-inside fastballs.
Strengths: Medium-inside and low-middle fastballs, medium-outside and all over-the-middle curves vs. RH; medium-outside, medium-inside and high-middle fastballs, low-middle curves, low sliders vs. LH.
Weaknesses: Low-outside, high-outside and high-inside fastballs, low-outside curves and sliders, medium-outside sliders vs. RH; low-middle and high-outside fastballs, outside curves vs. LH.

Joe Orsulak (Left Handed)   *Baltimore Orioles*

Joe Orsulak Against Right-Handed Pitchers
Overall BARS Batting Average .282

Fastball Average .319

	Outside	Middle	Inside
High	8/ 250 /2	19/ 421 /8	9/ 444 /4
Med	44/ 250 /11	7/ 285 /2	25/ 360 /9
Low	10/ 0 /0	27/ 370 /10	20/ 400 /8

Curve Average .261

	Outside	Middle	Inside
High	2/ 0 /0	4/ 500 /2	1/ 0 /0
Med	10/ 200 /2	1/ 0 /0	8/ 500 /4
Low	1/ 0 /0	11/ 181 /2	4/ 250 /1

Slider Average .318

	Outside	Middle	Inside
High	0/ 0 /0	1/ 0 /0	2/ 500 /1
Med	1/ 0 /0	1/ 1000 /1	2/ 0 /0
Low	3/ 666 /2	7/ 142 /1	5/ 400 /2

Joe Orsulak Against Left-Handed Pitchers
Overall BARS Batting Average .177

Fastball Average .103

	Outside	Middle	Inside
High	0/ 0 /0	4/ 250 /1	5/ 0 /0
Med	8/ 0 /0	1/ 1000 /1	5/ 200 /1
Low	3/ 0 /0	1/ 0 /0	2/ 0 /0

Curve Average .333

	Outside	Middle	Inside
High	1/ 0 /0	0/ 0 /0	0/ 0 /0
Med	2/ 500 /1	0/ 0 /0	0/ 0 /0
Low	0/ 0 /0	0/ 0 /0	0/ 0 /0

Slider Average .428

	Outside	Middle	Inside
High	0/ 0 /0	0/ 0 /0	0/ 0 /0
Med	3/ 333 /1	0/ 0 /0	0/ 0 /0
Low	1/ 1000 /1	2/ 500 /1	1/ 0 /0

Left-handed hitting Joe Orsulak has a good .319 overall fastball average against right-handed pitchers. He hits curves for a .261 average against right-handers and hits sliders excellently (.318 on fewer instances).

Orsulak's fastball weaknesses are in the outside locations. Every other fastball location is solid. He hits medium-high outside fastballs deep to center and right while scattering grounders to the left and right sides of the infield.

MEDIUM-HIGH OUTSIDE FASTBALLS

BATTING AVERAGE .250
Play

Left	Medium-deep in straightaway left field
Center	Deep and shifted toward right field
Right	Deep in straightaway right field
Short	Shifted toward third base
Second	Shifted toward first base

Note in his Ahead and Behind charts on the opposite page that Orsulak hits medium-high outside fastballs better when ahead in the count. When ahead, he hits this pitch deep and straightaway to the outfield.

MEDIUM-HIGH OUTSIDE FASTBALLS (WHEN AHEAD IN THE COUNT)

BATTING AVERAGE .300
Play

Left	Deep in straightaway left field
Center	Deep in straightaway center field

Right	Deep in straightaway right field
Short	Shifted toward third base
Second	Shifted toward first base

Orsulak has very high averages in some of his other fastball locations. His .360 in the medium-high inside location is strong. He hits this pitch deep down both lines and to straightaway center. Note that he pulls medium-high inside fastballs to the right side of the infield.

MEDIUM-HIGH INSIDE FASTBALLS

BATTING AVERAGE .360
Play

Left	Deep and shifted toward the left field line
Center	Deep in straightaway center field
Right	Deep and shifted toward the right field line
Short	Up middle (shifted toward second base)
Second	Shifted toward first base

He hits high-over-the-middle fastballs very well.

HIGH-OVER-THE-MIDDLE FASTBALLS

BATTING AVERAGE .421
Play

Left	Deep and shifted toward the left field line
Center	Deep in straightaway center field
Right	Deep in straightaway right field
Short	Up middle (shifted toward second base)
Second	Normal position

His low-over-the-middle average is also excellent (.370). He hits this pitch completely differently than the other locations analyzed.

LOW-OVER-THE-MIDDLE FASTBALLS

BATTING AVERAGE .370
Play
Left   Medium-deep and shifted toward the left field line
Center   Medium-deep in straightaway center field
Right   Deep and shifted toward center field
Short   Up middle (shifted toward second base)
Second   Normal position

He hits low-inside fastballs medium-deep to left and center fields, deep to right.

LOW-INSIDE FASTBALLS

BATTING AVERAGE .400
Play
Left   Medium-deep and shifted toward center field
Center   Medium-deep in straightaway center field
Right   Deep in straightaway right field
Short   Normal position
Second   Normal position

It's clear from the variations in the BARS fielding strategy for Orsulak that fielders should adjust for every location of pitch.

Orsulak Against Curves

Orsulak hits low-over-the-middle curves very poorly (.181). He hits this pitch straightaway.

LOW-OVER-THE-MIDDLE CURVEBALLS

BATTING AVERAGE .181
Play
Left   Medium-deep in straightaway left field
Center   Deep in straightaway center field
Right   Deep in straightaway right field
Short   *No instances recorded*
Second   *No instances recorded*

In contrast, he hits medium-high outside curves mostly to the infield.

MEDIUM-HIGH OUTSIDE CURVEBALLS

BATTING AVERAGE .200
Play
Left   *No instances recorded*
Center   Deep in straightaway center field
Right   *No instances recorded*
Short   Normal position
Second   Shifted toward first base

He hits medium-high inside curves medium deep to all fields.

Orsulak Against Left-Handed Pitchers

Fewer instances have been recorded for Orsulak against left-handed pitchers. However, his 0-for-8 in the medium-high outside fastball location and his 0-for-3 in the low-outside fastball location indicate possible weaknesses.

Ahead And Behind In The Count Vs. RH

Ahead

	Fastball Average .355			Curve Average .222		
	Outside	Middle	Inside	Outside	Middle	Inside
High	2/ 0 /0	6/ 666 /4	3/ 666 /2	0/ 0 /0	0/ 0 /0	0/ 0 /0
Med	20/ 300 /6	4/ 500 /2	13/ 384 /5	4/ 250 /1	0/ 0 /0	3/ 333 /1
Low	5/ 0 /0	14/ 285 /4	9/ 444 /4	0/ 0 /0	2/ 0 /0	0/ 0 /0

Behind

	Fastball Average .282			Curve Average .307		
	Outside	Middle	Inside	Outside	Middle	Inside
High	2/ 0 /0	4/ 500 /2	4/ 0 /0	1/ 0 /0	3/ 666 /2	0/ 0 /0
Med	9/ 222 /2	2/ 0 /0	5/ 400 /2	3/ 333 /1	0/ 0 /0	1/ 0 /0
Low	2/ 0 /0	6/ 666 /4	5/ 200 /1	0/ 0 /0	4/ 250 /1	1/ 0 /0

Overall Evaluation

Against Right-Handed Pitchers

Overall Fastball   ⚾ ⚾⚾ ⚾
Overall Curve   ⚾ ⚾
Overall Slider   ⚾ ⚾⚾⚾ ⚾

Against Left-Handed Pitchers

Overall Fastball   ⚾
Overall Curve   Not enough information
Overall Slider   Not enough information

Comments: Hitting mostly against RH, Orsulak performs very well against fastballs.
Strengths: Fastballs against RH (except for outside fastballs).
Weaknesses: Outside fastballs vs. RH, low curves and outside curves vs. RH; outside fastballs vs. LH.

Bill Ripken Against Right-Handed Pitchers
Overall BARS Batting Average .238

Fastball Average .277

	Inside	Middle	Outside
High	7/ 571/4	10/ 100/1	10/ 600/6
Med	6/ 0/0	7/ 428/3	54/ 222/12
Low	7/ 428/3	10/ 300/3	15/ 200/3

Curve Average .125

	Inside	Middle	Outside
High	0/ 0/0	2/ 0/0	2/ 0/0
Med	2/ 0/0	1/ 0/0	8/ 250/2
Low	0/ 0/0	1/ 0/0	8/ 125/1

Slider Average .111

	Inside	Middle	Outside
High	1/ 0/0	0/ 0/0	0/ 0/0
Med	0/ 0/0	0/ 0/0	6/ 0/0
Low	1/ 1000/1	2/ 500/1	8/ 0/0

Bill Ripken Against Left-Handed Pitchers
Overall BARS Batting Average .286

Fastball Average .328

	Inside	Middle	Outside
High	3/ 666/2	6/ 0/0	7/ 428/3
Med	6/ 666/4	2/ 500/1	44/ 318/14
Low	1/ 0/0	1/ 0/0	6/ 166/1

Curve Average .285

	Inside	Middle	Outside
High	2/ 0/0	0/ 0/0	1/ 0/0
Med	0/ 0/0	0/ 0/0	3/ 333/1
Low	1/ 1000/1	0/ 0/0	0/ 0/0

Slider Average .066

	Inside	Middle	Outside
High	0/ 0/0	0/ 0/0	0/ 0/0
Med	2/ 0/0	0/ 0/0	5/ 0/0
Low	2/ 500/1	0/ 0/0	6/ 0/0

Bill Ripken, right-handed hitter, has very strong and very weak locations in his charts. He hits fastballs only adequately against right-handers (.277 overall) and excellently against left-handers (.328 overall) but he has trouble with curves against right-handers.

The most prominent aspect of Ripken's fastball chart against right-handers is his weak .222 in the highly pitched medium-high outside location. He hits this pitch very differently when ahead and behind in the count. Overall, he seems to hit with more authority when ahead.

MEDIUM-HIGH OUTSIDE FASTBALLS (WHEN BEHIND IN THE COUNT)

BATTING AVERAGE .181

Play

Left	Deep and shifted toward the left field line
Center	Short and shifted toward left field
Right	Medium-deep and shifted toward the right line
Short	Up middle (shifted toward second base)
Second	Normal position

MEDIUM-HIGH OUTSIDE FASTBALLS (WHEN AHEAD IN THE COUNT)

BATTING AVERAGE .318

Play

Left	Deep in straightaway left field
Center	Deep in straightaway center field
Right	Deep and shifted toward the right field line
Short	Normal position
Second	Normal position

He hits high-outside fastballs in such a way that fielders would have to adjust significantly to this pitch in comparison with a medium-high outside fastball.

HIGH-OUTSIDE FASTBALLS

BATTING AVERAGE .600

Play

Left	Deep in straightaway left field
Center	Deep and shifted toward left field
Right	Medium-deep in straightaway right field
Short	Up middle (shifted toward second base)
Second	Shifted toward first base

In contrast, he hits low-outside fastballs strongly to the opposite field (right field).

LOW-OUTSIDE FASTBALLS

BATTING AVERAGE .200

Play

Left	*No instances recorded*
Center	Deep and shifted toward right field
Right	Medium-deep and shifted toward the right line
Short	Up middle (shifted toward second base)
Second	Normal position

He spreads low-inside fastballs out to all fields.

LOW-INSIDE FASTBALLS

BATTING AVERAGE .428
Play

Left	Medium-deep and shifted toward the left field line
Center	Medium-deep and shifted toward right field
Right	Medium-deep in straightaway right field
Short	Shifted toward third base
Second	Shifted toward first base

Fielders need to be positioned in yet another alignment for high-over-the-middle fastballs.

HIGH-OVER-THE-MIDDLE FASTBALLS

BATTING AVERAGE .100
Play

Left	Medium-deep and shifted toward the left field line
Center	Deep in straightaway center field
Right	Medium-deep and shifted toward the right line
Short	Up middle (shifted toward second base)
Second	*No instances recorded*

It is apparent that fielders need to shift radically for many of Ripken's locations. If they didn't shift, they would be badly out of position for pitches to many of his locations. This could explain why Ripken's locations have either high or low averages. He seems to have nothing in between.

Ripken has weaknesses against both curves and sliders in the medium-high outside and low-outside locations.

Ripken Against Left-Handed Pitchers

Ripken is thrown predominantly outside fastballs by left-handed pitchers. Since he hits medium-high outside and high-outside fastballs very well (.318 and .428, respectively), perhaps left-handers should try more breaking pitches against him. Note especially that he has problems with low-outside and medium-high outside sliders.

He hits medium-high outside fastballs much better when he is ahead in the count (.200 when behind, .333 when ahead). The left fielder and the shortstop need to be positioned differently for this pitch when Ripken is ahead and behind.

MEDIUM-HIGH OUTSIDE FASTBALLS (WHEN BEHIND IN THE COUNT AGAINST LEFT-HANDED PITCHERS)

BATTING AVERAGE .200
Play

Left	Deep and shifted toward the left field line
Center	Deep in straightaway center field
Right	Medium-deep and shifted toward center field
Short	Normal position
Second	Normal position

MEDIUM-HIGH OUTSIDE FASTBALLS (WHEN AHEAD IN THE COUNT AGAINST LEFT-HANDED PITCHERS)

BATTING AVERAGE .333
Play

Left	Deep and shifted toward center field
Center	Deep in straightaway center field
Right	Medium-deep and shifted toward center field
Short	Up middle (shifted toward second base)
Second	*No instances recorded*

Ahead And Behind In The Count Vs. RH

Ahead

Fastball Average .306

	Inside	Middle	Outside
High	0/0	8/125	3/333
Med	2/0	4/500	22/318
Low	2/500	5/600	3/0

Curve Average .200

	Inside	Middle	Outside
High	0/0	0/0	0/0
Med	0/0	1/0	1/0
Low	0/0	1/0	2/500

Behind

Fastball Average .250

	Inside	Middle	Outside
High	4/500	2/0	4/500
Med	2/0	0/0	11/181
Low	0/0	2/0	3/333

Curve Average .500

	Inside	Middle	Outside
High	0/0	1/0	1/0
Med	0/0	0/0	2/1000
Low	0/0	0/0	0/0

Overall Evaluation

Against Right-Handed Pitchers

Overall Fastball	⚾⚾
Overall Curve	⚾
Overall Slider	⚾

Against Left-Handed Pitchers

Overall Fastball	⚾⚾⚾⚾
Overall Curve	Not enough information
Overall Slider	⚾

Comments: Fielders need to adjust on nearly every pitch for Ripken because he hits the ball so differently in many of his pitch locations.
Strengths: High-inside, low-inside, medium-middle, low-middle and high-outside fastballs vs. RH; waist-high fastballs, high-outside fastballs vs. LH.
Weaknesses: Medium-outside, low-outside and high-over-the-middle fastballs vs. RH, outside curves and outside sliders vs. RH, low-outside fastballs vs. LH.

Cal Ripken, Jr. (Right Handed) — *Baltimore Orioles*

Cal Ripken, Jr. Against Right-Handed Pitchers
Overall BARS Batting Average .283

Fastball Average .288

	Inside	Middle	Outside
High	51/215/11	38/342/13	22/272/6
Med	106/377/40	55/345/19	239/271/65
Low	37/378/14	69/347/24	58/51/3

Curve Average .236

	Inside	Middle	Outside
High	5/400/2	7/285/2	2/0/0
Med	10/400/4	9/444/4	39/153/6
Low	6/166/1	19/315/6	34/176/6

Slider Average .297

	Inside	Middle	Outside
High	2/500/1	8/375/3	4/250/1
Med	5/200/1	5/600/3	36/333/12
Low	2/0/0	13/384/5	46/217/10

Cal Ripken, Jr. Against Left-Handed Pitchers
Overall BARS Batting Average .333

Fastball Average .353

	Inside	Middle	Outside
High	11/454/5	21/428/9	18/388/7
Med	26/307/8	19/421/8	110/336/37
Low	25/400/10	49/387/19	18/111/2

Curve Average .279

	Inside	Middle	Outside
High	0/0/0	0/0/0	2/0/0
Med	3/333/1	6/833/5	10/100/1
Low	6/166/1	10/300/3	6/166/1

Slider Average .260

	Inside	Middle	Outside
High	4/250/1	1/0/0	0/0/0
Med	11/363/4	2/500/1	12/250/3
Low	9/333/3	9/111/1	2/0/0

Right-handed Cal Ripken, Jr., hits fastballs extremely well against left-handed pitchers (.353 overall). Against right-handed pitchers he hits fastballs fairly well (.288) but has trouble with curves (.236). He hits sliders only adequately against left-handers (.260 overall) but well against right-handers (.297).

Ripken has five very strong fastball locations against right-handed pitchers: medium-high inside (.377), low-inside (.378) and the three over-the-middle locations (.342, .345 and .347, high to low).

He hits medium-high inside fastballs in a very unusual way. He hits this pitch to short straightaway center and medium-deep into the right-center gap. If fielders positioned themselves properly for this pitch, they could prevent almost all of his line-drive base hits to this area of the field.

MEDIUM-HIGH INSIDE FASTBALLS

BATTING AVERAGE .377
Play

Left	Deep and shifted toward the left field line
Center	Short in straightaway center field
Right	Medium-deep and shifted toward center field
Short	Shifted toward third base
Second	Normal position

He hits medium-high outside fastballs much differently than he hits medium-high inside fastballs.

MEDIUM-HIGH OUTSIDE FASTBALLS

BATTING AVERAGE .271
Play

Left	Deep and shifted toward the left field line
Center	Deep in straightaway center field
Right	Medium-deep in straightaway right field
Short	Up middle (shifted toward second base)
Second	Normal position

Notice his weak .051 average against low-outside fastballs and .215 against high-inside fastballs. These two locations bring down his overall fastball average.

He has trouble with outside curves against right-handed pitchers. The sector consisting of the medium-high outside curve (.153) and low-outside curve (.176) locations gives pitchers an area of weakness on which to focus.

Ripken also has trouble with low-outside sliders (.217) but hits medium-high outside sliders very well (.333). The following charts show how differently he hits these two pitches. To be correctly positioned, every fielder would have to shift.

MEDIUM-HIGH OUTSIDE SLIDERS

BATTING AVERAGE .333
Play

Left	Deep in straightaway left field

48

Center	Deep and shifted toward left field
Right	Deep in straightaway right field
Short	Shifted toward third base
Second	Normal position

LOW-OUTSIDE SLIDERS

BATTING AVERAGE .217
Play

Left	Medium-deep and shifted toward the left field line
Center	Medium-deep in straightaway center field
Right	Medium-deep and shifted toward the right line
Short	Up middle (shifted toward second base)
Second	Normal position

Ripken Against Left-Handed Pitchers

Ripken's overall .353 fastball average against left-handers is top rate. He hits medium-high outside fastballs for a solid .336. His .387 average in the low-over-the-middle location is also outstanding. He hits pitches to this location much differently when ahead and when behind in the count.

LOW-OVER-THE-MIDDLE FASTBALLS
(THROWN BY LEFT-HANDED PITCHERS
WHEN RIPKEN IS BEHIND IN THE COUNT)

BATTING AVERAGE .181 (2 for 11)
Play

Left	Deep and shifted toward the left field line
Center	Deep and shifted toward left field
Right	Deep and shifted toward center field
Short	Up middle (shifted toward second base)
Second	*No instances recorded*

LOW-OVER-THE-MIDDLE FASTBALLS
(THROWN BY LEFT-HANDED PITCHERS
WHEN RIPKEN IS AHEAD IN THE COUNT)

BATTING AVERAGE .434 (10 for 23)
Play

Left	Deep in straightaway left field
Center	Deep in straightaway center field
Right	Short and shifted toward center field
Short	Normal position
Second	*No instances recorded*

Ripken also hits high-over-the-middle fastballs very well (.428). He hits this pitch deep down the line and into medium-deep right center.

Notice in the following fielding strategy that Ripken hits high-outside fastballs against lefties down both lines and deep into left center. Notice also that the shortstop needs to play shifted toward second base and the second baseman needs to play shifted toward first base. This required fielding strategy is considerably different from the strategy for many other locations and underscores the necessity of positioning fielders specifically for the type and location of every pitch.

HIGH-OUTSIDE FASTBALLS
(THROWN BY LEFT-HANDED PITCHERS)

BATTING AVERAGE .388
Play

Left	Deep and shifted toward the left field line
Center	Deep and shifted toward left field
Right	Medium-deep and shifted toward the right line
Short	Up middle (shifted toward second base)
Second	Shifted toward first base

Ahead And Behind In The Count Vs. RH

Ahead

	Fastball Average .369			Curve Average .250		
	Inside	Middle	Outside	Inside	Middle	Outside
High	20/350 /7	18/444 /8	7/428 /3	1/1000 /1	2/0 /0	0/0 /0
Med	41/365 /15	31/354 /11	98/346 /34	0/0 /0	3/333 /1	6/333 /2
Low	14/571 /8	33/424 /14	14/142 /2	0/0 /0	4/0 /0	0/0 /0

Behind

	Fastball Average .280			Curve Average .325		
	Inside	Middle	Outside	Inside	Middle	Outside
High	5/0 /0	10/200 /2	2/0 /0	1/0 /0	5/400 /2	0/0 /0
Med	27/370 /10	7/285 /2	49/326 /16	4/500 /2	1/0 /0	11/90 /1
Low	8/250 /2	19/315 /6	12/83 /1	3/333 /1	5/600 /3	10/400 /4

Overall Evaluation
Against Right-Handed Pitchers

Overall Fastball	⚾⚾
Overall Curve	⚾
Overall Slider	⚾⚾⚾

Against Left-Handed Pitchers

Overall Fastball	⚾⚾⚾⚾
Overall Curve	⚾⚾⚾
Overall Slider	⚾⚾

Comments: Weak vs. low-outside pitches.
Strengths: Medium- & low-inside fastballs, over-the-middle fastballs, medium-inside curves, low-middle & medium-outside sliders vs. RH; all fastball locations vs. LH except low-outside, over-the-middle curves, low-inside and medium-inside sliders vs. LH.
Weaknesses: Outside fastballs, high-inside fastballs, outside curves, low-outside sliders vs. RH; low-outside fastballs and low-middle sliders vs. LH.

49

Larry Sheets Against Right-Handed Pitchers
Overall BARS Batting Average .300

Fastball Average .309

	Outside	Middle	Inside
High	27/259 /7	23/478 /11	20/300 /6
Med	155/277 /43	27/629 /17	43/395 /17
Low	25/160 /4	40/175 /7	37/297 /11

Curve Average .228

	Outside	Middle	Inside
High	3/333 /1	3/333 /1	0/0 /0
Med	19/263 /5	4/250 /1	8/250 /2
Low	4/250 /1	19/157 /3	10/200 /2

Slider Average .342

	Outside	Middle	Inside
High	1/0 /0	2/1000 /2	1/0 /0
Med	3/333 /1	3/333 /1	11/363 /4
Low	1/0 /0	5/200 /1	11/363 /4

Larry Sheets Against Left-Handed Pitchers
Overall BARS Batting Average .268

Fastball Average .287

	Outside	Middle	Inside
High	5/200 /1	5/600 /3	5/200 /1
Med	35/228 /8	4/500 /2	21/333 /7
Low	6/0 /0	7/285 /2	6/500 /3

Curve Average .250

	Outside	Middle	Inside
High	0/0 /0	1/0 /0	4/250 /1
Med	7/142 /1	2/500 /1	2/1000 /2
Low	6/166 /1	6/333 /2	4/0 /0

Slider Average .166

	Outside	Middle	Inside
High	0/0 /0	1/0 /0	1/1000 /1
Med	2/0 /0	0/0 /0	2/500 /1
Low	5/0 /0	0/0 /0	1/0 /0

Left-handed hitter Larry Sheets hits fastballs well overall against right-handed pitchers (.309). He has trouble with curves (.228 overall vs. right-handers) but hits sliders very well (.342).

Sheets has some outstanding fastball locations against right-handers. The .629 in his medium-over-the-middle location is extremely high, and the .478 in his high-over-the-middle fastball location is also excellent. Almost as impressive is the .395 in his medium-high inside fastball location. He hits this pitch medium-deep down the left line, deep into left-center and deep to straightaway right field. Notice that the shortstop and the second baseman need to play the left-handed hitting Sheets to pull the ball when hitting grounders to the infield.

MEDIUM-HIGH INSIDE FASTBALLS

BATTING AVERAGE .395
Play

Left	Medium-deep and shifted toward the left line
Center	Deep and shifted toward left field
Right	Deep in straightaway right field
Short	Up middle (shifted toward second base)
Second	Shifted toward first base

He hits medium-high outside fastballs mostly into center field and toward the right side of the infield.

MEDIUM-HIGH OUTSIDE FASTBALLS

BATTING AVERAGE .277
Play

Left	Deep and shifted toward center field
Center	Deep in straightaway center field
Right	Deep and shifted toward center field
Short	Up middle (shifted toward second base)
Second	Shifted toward first base

Notice in the Ahead and Behind charts for Sheets that he hits high-over-the-middle fastballs very poorly when behind in the count (.142) but very strongly when ahead (.615). Fielders need to be aligned much differently for this pitch when he is ahead and behind. When behind, he hits the ball to medium-deep center and deep right-center. When ahead, he hits the ball deep down both lines.

HIGH-OVER-THE-MIDDLE FASTBALLS (WHEN AHEAD IN THE COUNT)

BATTING AVERAGE .615
Play

Left	Deep and shifted toward the left field line
Center	Deep and shifted toward right field
Right	Deep and shifted toward the right field line
Short	Shifted toward third base
Second	*No instances recorded*

Sheets' fastball weaknesses are apparent. He hits .160 against low-outside fastballs and .175 against low-over-the-middle fastballs. Of course his average would drop considerably in every fastball location if fielders aligned themselves according to the BARS fielding strategy.

Sheets Against Curves And Sliders

Sheets hits medium-high outside curves only adequately (.263). He has definite problems with low-over-the-middle curves (.157).

But he hits sliders excellently overall. He hits medium-high inside and low-inside sliders at a .363 clip. His BARS fielding strategy for medium-high inside sliders shows that center fielders need to play fairly short for this pitch.

MEDIUM-HIGH INSIDE SLIDERS

BATTING AVERAGE .363
Play
Left   *No instances recorded*
Center   Short in straightaway center field
Right   Deep in straightaway right field
Short   Up middle (shifted toward second base)
Second   Normal position

Sheets Against Left-Handed Pitchers

Sheets has trouble with outside fastballs thrown by left-handed pitchers. He hits only .228 (8 for 35) against medium-high outside fastballs.

MEDIUM-HIGH OUTSIDE FASTBALLS (THROWN BY LEFT-HANDED PITCHERS)

BATTING AVERAGE .228
Play
Left   Medium-deep and shifted toward center field
Center   Deep in straightaway center field
Right   Medium-deep in straightaway right field
Short   Up middle (shifted toward second base)
Second   Shifted toward first base

He hits better against medium-high inside fastballs (.333). He hits this pitch medium-deep into center and right. The shortstop and the second baseman need to be shifted uniquely for this pitch — the shortstop toward third and the second baseman toward first. Notice also that, for this pitch, there are no recorded instances of hit balls into left field.

MEDIUM-HIGH INSIDE FASTBALLS (THROWN BY LEFT-HANDED PITCHERS)

BATTING AVERAGE .333
Play
Left   *No instances recorded*
Center   Medium-deep in straightaway center field
Right   Medium-deep in straightaway right field
Short   Shifted toward third base
Second   Shifted toward first base

Sheets seems to have trouble with outside curves thrown by lefties. He hits .142 against medium-high outside curves and .166 against low-outside curves.

Ahead And Behind In The Count Vs. RH

Ahead

	Fastball Average .374			Curve Average .222		
	Outside	Middle	Inside	Outside	Middle	Inside
High	9/444 /4	13/615 /8	5/600 /3	1/0 /0	0/0 /0	0/0 /0
Med	67/268 /18	15/600 /9	24/541 /13	5/600 /3	1/0 /0	3/0 /0
Low	5/200 /1	29/206 /6	20/400 /8	0/0 /0	7/142 /1	1/0 /0

Behind

	Fastball Average .349			Curve Average .466		
	Outside	Middle	Inside	Outside	Middle	Inside
High	4/250 /1	7/142 /1	5/200 /1	0/0 /0	1/0 /0	0/0 /0
Med	38/394 /15	7/571 /4	8/500 /4	6/333 /2	2/500 /1	1/1000 /1
Low	6/333 /2	5/0 /0	3/333 /1	1/1000 /1	3/333 /1	1/1000 /1

Overall Evaluation

Against Right-Handed Pitchers

Overall Fastball ⚾⚾ ⚾⚾ ⚾⚾
Overall Curve ⚾⚾
Overall Slider ⚾⚾ ⚾⚾ ⚾⚾ ⚾⚾

Against Left-Handed Pitchers

Overall Fastball ⚾⚾ ⚾⚾
Overall Curve ⚾⚾ ⚾⚾
Overall Slider   Not enough information

Comments: A good fastball hitter vs. RH, Sheets has trouble with curves vs. RH.
Strengths: Medium-middle, high-middle and medium-inside fastballs vs. RH, medium-inside and low-inside sliders against RH; medium-inside fastballs vs. LH.
Weaknesses: Outside fastballs, low-middle fastballs, low curves vs. RH; outside fastballs and outside curves against LH.

Mickey Tettleton (Switch Hitter) — *Baltimore Orioles*

Mickey Tettleton Against Right-Handed Pitchers
Overall BARS Batting Average .228

Fastball Average .268

	Outside	Middle	Inside
High	7/ 0/0	12/ 83/1	4/ 500/2
Med	32/ 312/10	9/ 222/2	4/ 0/0
Low	10/ 300/3	12/ 500/6	7/ 285/2

Curve Average .047

	Outside	Middle	Inside
High	1/ 0/0	1/ 0/0	0/ 0/0
Med	5/ 200/1	2/ 0/0	0/ 0/0
Low	2/ 0/0	4/ 0/0	6/ 0/0

Slider Average .222

	Outside	Middle	Inside
High	0/ 0/0	2/ 500/1	0/ 0/0
Med	1/ 0/0	0/ 0/0	0/ 0/0
Low	0/ 0/0	4/ 250/1	2/ 0/0

Mickey Tettleton Against Left-Handed Pitchers
Overall BARS Batting Average .247

Fastball Average .245

	Inside	Middle	Outside
High	3/ 0/0	11/ 181/2	2/ 500/1
Med	2/ 0/0	2/ 0/0	20/ 400/8
Low	3/ 0/0	4/ 500/2	10/ 100/1

Curve Average .250

	Inside	Middle	Outside
High	0/ 0/0	2/ 0/0	0/ 0/0
Med	1/ 0/0	1/ 0/0	6/ 500/3
Low	6/ 0/0	2/ 500/1	2/ 500/1

Slider Average .250

	Inside	Middle	Outside
High	1/ 0/0	0/ 0/0	0/ 0/0
Med	4/ 0/0	0/ 0/0	3/ 333/1
Low	0/ 0/0	3/ 666/2	1/ 0/0

Switch-hitter Mickey Tettleton has weak overall fastball averages against both right- and left-handed pitchers. But he does have strong locations in his fastballs charts. Against right-handers, he hits a solid .312 against medium-high outside fastballs. He hits this pitch deep to straightaway center and right-center.

MEDIUM-HIGH OUTSIDE FASTBALLS

BATTING AVERAGE .312
Play

Left	*No instances recorded*
Center	Deep in straightaway center field
Right	Deep and shifted toward center field
Short	Up middle (shifted toward second base)
Second	Normal position

He has a very strong .500 in his low-over-the-middle fastball location. His field diagram on the opposite page illustrates how fielders need to play for this pitch.

LOW-OVER-THE-MIDDLE FASTBALLS

BATTING AVERAGE .500
Play

Left	Deep and shifted toward the left field line
Center	Medium-deep and shifted toward left field
Right	Deep and shifted toward the right field line

Short	Normal position
Second	Normal position

Tettleton is fairly strong against low-outside fastballs (.300). He hits this pitch straightaway to all fields.

He has a weak sector consisting of high-outside and high-over-the-middle fastballs. This is where right-handers should focus to get an edge. Notice also his troubles with low curves against right-handers.

Against left-handed pitchers, Tettleton has trouble with low-outside fastballs (.100), high-middle fastballs (.181) and all inside fastballs.

He hits a strong .400 against medium-high outside fastballs, however.

MEDIUM-HIGH OUTSIDE FASTBALLS (THROWN BY LEFT-HANDED PITCHERS)

BATTING AVERAGE .400
Play

Left	Deep in straightaway left field
Center	Deep in straightaway center field
Right	Deep and shifted toward center field
Short	Normal position
Second	Normal position

He hits outside curves well against lefties but seems to have trouble with low-inside curves.

Low-Over-The-Middle Fastballs
(Thrown By Right-Handed Pitchers)

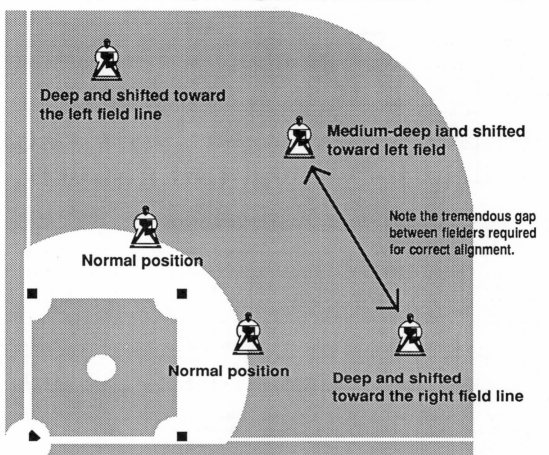

Deep and shifted toward the left field line

Medium-deep and shifted toward left field

Note the tremendous gap between fielders required for correct alignment.

Normal position

Normal position

Deep and shifted toward the right field line

Ahead And Behind In The Count Vs. RH

Ahead

Fastball Average .365

	Outside	Middle	Inside
High	2 / 0 / 0	6 / 0 / 0	1 / 1000 / 1
Med	10 / 300 / 3	5 / 200 / 1	1 / 0 / 0
Low	3 / 666 / 2	8 / 750 / 6	5 / 400 / 2

Curve Average .000

	Outside	Middle	Inside
	0 / 0 / 0	0 / 0 / 0	0 / 0 / 0
	1 / 0 / 0	0 / 0 / 0	0 / 0 / 0
	0 / 0 / 0	1 / 0 / 0	1 / 0 / 0

Behind

Fastball Average .333

	Outside	Middle	Inside
High	0 / 0 / 0	1 / 1000 / 1	1 / 0 / 0
Med	5 / 400 / 2	0 / 0 / 0	0 / 0 / 0
Low	3 / 333 / 1	1 / 0 / 0	1 / 0 / 0

Curve Average .200

	Outside	Middle	Inside
	0 / 0 / 0	0 / 0 / 0	0 / 0 / 0
	1 / 1000 / 1	1 / 0 / 0	0 / 0 / 0
	1 / 0 / 0	2 / 0 / 0	0 / 0 / 0

Overall Evaluation
Against Right-Handed Pitchers

Overall Fastball ⚾⚾

Overall Curve ⚾⚾

Overall Slider   Not enough information

Against Left-Handed Pitchers

Overall Fastball ⚾⚾

Overall Curve ⚾⚾ ⚾⚾

Overall Slider ⚾⚾ ⚾⚾

Comments: Has a strong fastball sector vs. RH consisting of the medium-outside, low-outside and low-middle locations.
Strengths: Medium-outside, low-outside and low-middle fastballs vs. RH; medium-outside and low-middle fastballs, medium-outside curves vs. LH.
Weaknesses: High-outside and high-middle fastballs, low curves vs. RH; low-outside, high-middle and inside fastballs, inside curves vs. LH.

Jim Traber (Left Handed)   *Baltimore Orioles*

Jim Traber Against Right-Handed Pitchers
Overall BARS Batting Average .282

Fastball Average .252

	Outside	Middle	Inside
High	12/ 166 /2	4/ 0 /0	7/ 285 /2
Med	42/ 309 /13	4/ 250 /1	11/ 363 /4
Low	4/ 0 /0	6/ 333 /2	9/ 111 /1

Curve Average .357

	Outside	Middle	Inside
High	0/ 0 /0	2/ 500 /1	0/ 0 /0
Med	2/ 500 /1	0/ 0 /0	2/ 500 /1
Low	2/ 0 /0	3/ 0 /0	3/ 666 /2

Slider Average .833

	Outside	Middle	Inside
High	1/ 0 /0	0/ 0 /0	0/ 0 /0
Med	2/ 1000 /2	0/ 0 /0	2/ 1000 /2
Low	0/ 0 /0	1/ 1000 /1	0/ 0 /0

Jim Traber Against Left-Handed Pitchers
Overall BARS Batting Average .338

Fastball Average .400

	Outside	Middle	Inside
High	1/ 1000 /1	3/ 666 /2	2/ 0 /0
Med	16/ 437 /7	4/ 250 /1	8/ 250 /2
Low	0/ 0 /0	4/ 500 /2	2/ 500 /1

Curve Average .230

	Outside	Middle	Inside
High	0/ 0 /0	0/ 0 /0	2/ 0 /0
Med	5/ 400 /2	0/ 0 /0	2/ 0 /0
Low	0/ 0 /0	3/ 333 /1	1/ 0 /0

Slider Average .333

	Outside	Middle	Inside
High	0/ 0 /0	2/ 500 /1	0/ 0 /0
Med	4/ 500 /2	0/ 0 /0	0/ 0 /0
Low	3/ 0 /0	0/ 0 /0	0/ 0 /0

Left-handed hitter Jim Traber has a higher overall BARS average against left-handed pitchers. This is unusual for a left-handed hitter.

He hits medium-high outside fastballs better against right-handed pitchers when ahead in the count (.380 when ahead, .300 when behind). The charts below and the field diagram on the opposite page show that all the outfielders need to shift to be correctly positioned for this pitch when Traber is ahead and behind.

MEDIUM-HIGH OUTSIDE FASTBALLS (WHEN AHEAD IN THE COUNT)

BATTING AVERAGE .380
Play

Left	Deep in straightaway left field
Center	Deep and shifted toward left field
Right	Deep and shifted toward center field
Short	Up middle (shifted toward second base)
Second	Normal position

MEDIUM-HIGH OUTSIDE FASTBALLS (WHEN BEHIND IN THE COUNT)

BATTING AVERAGE .300
Play

Left	Medium-deep in straightaway left field
Center	Medium-deep in straightaway center field
Right	Medium-deep in straightaway right field
Short	Up middle (shifted toward second base)
Second	Normal position

Traber hits a fine .363 against medium-high inside fastballs thrown by right-handers.

MEDIUM-HIGH INSIDE FASTBALLS

BATTING AVERAGE .363
Play

Left	Medium-deep and shifted toward the left field line
Center	Short and shifted toward right field
Right	Deep and shifted toward the right field line
Short	Up middle (shifted toward second base)
Second	Shifted toward first base

Against left-handed pitchers, Traber hits a solid .437 in his medium-high outside fastball location. He hits this pitch straightaway to the outfield. The shortstop, however, needs to play shifted toward second.

MEDIUM-HIGH OUTSIDE FASTBALLS (THROWN BY LEFT-HANDED PITCHERS)

BATTING AVERAGE .437
Play

Left	Deep in straightaway left field
Center	Medium-deep in straightaway center field
Right	Deep in straightaway right field
Short	Up middle (shifted toward second base)
Second	Normal position

Medium-High Outside Fastballs Vs. RH

Dark Fielders — Ahead In The Count
Light Fielders — Behind In The Count

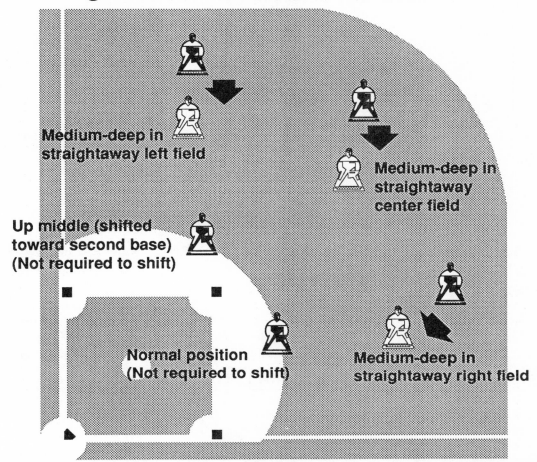

Medium-deep in straightaway left field

Medium-deep in straightaway center field

Up middle (shifted toward second base) (Not required to shift)

Normal position (Not required to shift)

Medium-deep in straightaway right field

Ahead And Behind In The Count Vs. RH

Ahead

	Fastball Average .333			Curve Average .400		
	Outside	Middle	Inside	Outside	Middle	Inside
High	6 / 333 2	1 / 0 0	5 / 400 2	0 / 0 0	2 / 500 1	0 / 0 0
Med	21 / 380 8	3 / 333 1	8 / 375 3	0 / 0 0	0 / 0 0	2 / 500 1
Low	1 / 0 0	4 / 250 1	5 / 200 1	0 / 0 0	1 / 0 0	0 / 0 0

Behind

	Fastball Average .176			Curve Average .000		
	Outside	Middle	Inside	Outside	Middle	Inside
High	0 / 0 0	2 / 0 0	0 / 0 0	0 / 0 0	0 / 0 0	0 / 0 0
Med	10 / 300 3	1 / 0 0	1 / 0 0	0 / 0 0	0 / 0 0	0 / 0 0
Low	1 / 0 0	0 / 0 0	2 / 0 0	0 / 0 0	0 / 0 0	0 / 0 0

Overall Evaluation
Against Right-Handed Pitchers

Overall Fastball ⚾

Overall Curve ⚾ ⚾ ⚾ ⚾

Overall Slider   Not enough information

Against Left-Handed Pitchers

Overall Fastball ⚾ ⚾ ⚾ ⚾

Overall Curve ⚾

Overall Slider   Not enough information

Comments: Hits better when ahead in the count vs. RH.
Strengths: Medium-outside and medium-inside fastballs vs. RH; medium-outside fastballs vs. LH.
Weaknesses: High-outside and low-inside fastballs vs. RH; medium-inside fastballs vs. LH.

Barrett, Marty
Boggs, Wade
Burks, Ellis
Evans, Dwight
Gedman, Rich
Greenwell, Mike
Heep, Danny
Pena, Tony
Reed, Jody
Rivera, Luis
Romine, Kevin

*Boston Red Sox
BARS System
Hitting Analysis*

Marty Barrett (Right Handed) *Boston Red Sox*

Marty Barrett Against Right-Handed Pitchers
Overall BARS Batting Average .260

Fastball Average .266

	Inside	Middle	Outside
High	49 / 306 / 15	64 / 343 / 22	25 / 160 / 4
Med	116 / 267 / 31	55 / 345 / 19	259 / 274 / 71
Low	41 / 170 / 7	72 / 250 / 18	31 / 96 / 3

Curve Average .256

	Inside	Middle	Outside
High	6 / 0 / 0	8 / 375 / 3	4 / 250 / 1
Med	14 / 428 / 6	6 / 166 / 1	34 / 323 / 11
Low	2 / 0 / 0	17 / 294 / 5	34 / 147 / 5

Slider Average .196

	Inside	Middle	Outside
High	1 / 0 / 0	2 / 0 / 0	2 / 0 / 0
Med	7 / 0 / 0	3 / 666 / 2	28 / 285 / 8
Low	1 / 1000 / 1	10 / 100 / 1	12 / 83 / 1

Marty Barrett Against Left-Handed Pitchers
Overall BARS Batting Average .291

Fastball Average .298

	Inside	Middle	Outside
High	9 / 333 / 3	13 / 384 / 5	18 / 333 / 6
Med	42 / 452 / 19	20 / 400 / 8	99 / 282 / 28
Low	20 / 200 / 4	44 / 159 / 7	20 / 250 / 5

Curve Average .239

	Inside	Middle	Outside
High	1 / 0 / 0	1 / 1000 / 1	3 / 333 / 1
Med	5 / 200 / 1	0 / 0 / 0	16 / 187 / 3
Low	2 / 0 / 0	10 / 200 / 2	8 / 375 / 3

Slider Average .304

	Inside	Middle	Outside
High	2 / 500 / 1	2 / 500 / 1	1 / 0 / 0
Med	9 / 222 / 2	5 / 400 / 2	4 / 250 / 1
Low	12 / 250 / 3	8 / 500 / 4	3 / 0 / 0

Right-handed Marty Barrett hits .266 overall against fastballs thrown by right-handed pitchers and a solid .298 against fastballs thrown by left-handed pitchers. His overall curve averages are .256 against right-handers, .239 against right-handers.

Barrett hits .274 against medium-high outside fastballs thrown by right-handers. He hits these pitches straightaway to the outfield and toward the right side of the infield. It's interesting that he tends to hit medium-high inside fastballs more down the right field line than he does medium-high outside fastballs.

MEDIUM-HIGH OUTSIDE FASTBALLS

BATTING AVERAGE .274
Play

Left	Deep in straightaway left field
Center	Deep in straightaway center field
Right	Medium-deep in straightaway right field
Short	Up middle (shifted toward second base)
Second	Shifted toward first base

MEDIUM-HIGH INSIDE FASTBALLS

BATTING AVERAGE .267
Play

Left	Medium-deep in straightaway left field
Center	Medium-deep in straightaway center field
Right	Medium-deep and shifted toward the right line
Short	Up middle (shifted toward second base)
Second	Shifted toward first base

Barrett has weaknesses against low-outside fastballs (.096), low-inside fastballs (.170) and high-outside fastballs (.160). He hits high-over-the-middle fastballs excellently (.343).

HIGH-OVER-THE-MIDDLE FASTBALLS

BATTING AVERAGE .343
Play

Left	Deep and shifted toward center field
Center	Deep in straightaway center field
Right	Medium-deep in straightaway right field
Short	Normal position
Second	Normal position

Barrett's overall fastball average is much higher when he is ahead than when he is behind in the count (.240 when behind, .302 when ahead). His high-over-the-middle fielding strategy indicates that he pulls the ball more when ahead.

HIGH-OVER-THE-MIDDLE FASTBALLS
(WHEN BEHIND IN THE COUNT)

BATTING AVERAGE .285
Play

Left	Medium-deep and shifted toward the left field line
Center	Deep and shifted toward left field
Right	Medium-deep and shifted toward the right line
Short	Up middle (shifted toward second base)
Second	Shifted toward first base

HIGH-OVER-THE-MIDDLE FASTBALLS
(WHEN AHEAD IN THE COUNT)

BATTING AVERAGE .375
Play

Left	Deep and shifted toward the left field line
Center	Deep in straightaway center field
Right	Medium-deep and shifted toward center field
Short	Normal position
Second	Normal position

Barrett Against Curves And Sliders

Barrett has trouble with low curves against right-handed pitchers but he hits medium-high outside and medium-high inside curves excellently (.323 and .428 respectively).

He hits medium-high outside curves down both lines.

MEDIUM-HIGH OUTSIDE CURVEBALLS

BATTING AVERAGE .323
Play

Left	Deep and shifted toward the left field line
Center	Deep in straightaway center field
Right	Medium-deep and shifted toward the right line
Short	Up middle (shifted toward second base)
Second	Normal position

He hits medium-high outside sliders fairly well against right-handers (.285) but has trouble with low sliders.

Barrett Against Left-Handed Pitchers

Barrett has some very strong fastball averages against left-handers. His .452 in the medium-high inside location is excellent, as is his .282 in the medium-high outside fastball location. If fielders would play him medium-deep for this pitch against left-handed pitchers, they would catch most of his line drives that now fall for hits.

MEDIUM-HIGH OUTSIDE FASTBALLS
(THROWN BY LEFT-HANDED PITCHERS)

BATTING AVERAGE .282
Play

Left	Medium-deep in straightaway left field
Center	Medium-deep in straightaway center field
Right	Medium-deep in straightaway right field
Short	Up middle (shifted toward second base)
Second	Normal position

He pulls medium-high inside fastballs medium-deep down the left line against left-handers.

MEDIUM-HIGH INSIDE FASTBALLS
(THROWN BY LEFT-HANDED PITCHERS)

BATTING AVERAGE .452
Play

Left	Medium-deep and shifted toward the left line
Center	Medium-deep in straightaway center field
Right	Deep and shifted toward center field
Short	Up middle (shifted toward second base)
Second	Normal position

Ahead And Behind In The Count Vs. RH

Ahead

Fastball Average .302

	Inside	Middle	Outside
High	20 / 500 /10	32 / 375 /12	6 / 333 /2
Med	46 / 239 /11	27 / 370 /10	120 / 275 /33
Low	17 / 176 /3	27 / 333 /9	6 / 166 /1

Curve Average .384

	Inside	Middle	Outside
High	0 / 0 /0	2 / 0 /0	0 / 0 /0
Med	2 / 1000 /2	1 / 0 /0	4 / 250 /1
Low	0 / 0 /0	2 / 500 /1	2 / 500 /1

Behind

Fastball Average .240

	Inside	Middle	Outside
High	13 / 230 /3	14 / 285 /4	6 / 0 /0
Med	31 / 322 /10	9 / 333 /3	52 / 288 /15
Low	8 / 0 /0	16 / 62 /1	9 / 222 /2

Curve Average .285

	Inside	Middle	Outside
High	5 / 0 /0	3 / 333 /1	3 / 333 /1
Med	5 / 400 /2	2 / 500 /1	16 / 375 /6
Low	1 / 0 /0	6 / 333 /2	15 / 200 /3

Overall Evaluation
Against Right-Handed Pitchers

Overall Fastball	⚾
Overall Curve	⚾ ⚾
Overall Slider	⚾

Against Left-Handed Pitchers

Overall Fastball	⚾ ⚾
Overall Curve	⚾
Overall Slider	⚾ ⚾ ⚾ ⚾

Comments: Has trouble with low fastballs vs. RH. Strengths: High-middle, medium-middle and high-inside fastballs, medium-inside and medium-outside curves vs. RH; all high and waist-high fastballs, low-outside curves, low-middle sliders vs. LH. Weaknesses: Low fastballs, medium-inside and high-outside fastballs, low-outside curves and low sliders vs. RH; low fastballs, low-middle and medium-outside curves vs. LH.

Wade Boggs (Left Handed)   *Boston Red Sox*

Wade Boggs Against Right-Handed Pitchers
Overall BARS Batting Average .379

Fastball Average .365

	Outside	Middle	Inside
High	54/ 277 /15	48/ 375 /18	35/ 485 /17
Med	311/ 350 /109	71/ 436 /31	122/ 409 /50
Low	34/ 264 /9	65/ 369 /24	59/ 322 /19

Curve Average .493

	Outside	Middle	Inside
High	4/ 1000 /4	11/ 272 /3	7/ 428 /3
Med	29/ 655 /19	11/ 545 /6	28/ 642 /18
Low	6/ 166 /1	20/ 450 /9	32/ 312 /10

Slider Average .300

	Outside	Middle	Inside
High	1/ 1000 /1	3/ 333 /1	4/ 250 /1
Med	8/ 250 /2	3/ 1000 /3	24/ 250 /6
Low	8/ 250 /2	15/ 266 /4	14/ 285 /4

Wade Boggs Against Left-Handed Pitchers
Overall BARS Batting Average .322

Fastball Average .362

	Outside	Middle	Inside
High	7/ 428 /3	23/ 304 /7	20/ 200 /4
Med	124/ 362 /45	26/ 384 /10	66/ 409 /27
Low	14/ 285 /4	44/ 386 /17	26/ 384 /10

Curve Average .177

	Outside	Middle	Inside
High	2/ 1000 /2	8/ 250 /2	1/ 1000 /1
Med	17/ 58 /1	6/ 166 /1	16/ 187 /3
Low	12/ 0 /0	12/ 333 /4	5/ 0 /0

Slider Average .260

	Outside	Middle	Inside
High	2/ 0 /0	2/ 1000 /2	0/ 0 /0
Med	13/ 153 /2	2/ 500 /1	6/ 166 /1
Low	9/ 222 /2	12/ 250 /3	4/ 500 /2

Left-handed hitter Wade Boggs hits fastballs excellently against both right- and left-handed pitchers (.365 vs. right-handers, .362 vs. left-handers). His .362 and his overall .322 against lefties are extremely high for a left-handed hitter. His .493 curve average against right-handers is also extremely high.

Note the .409 in his highly pitched medium-high inside fastball location, the .485 in his high-inside location, and the .375 in his high-over-the-middle location.

These are brilliant enough, but looking to his curve chart against right-handers, one wonders why pitchers even bother throwing him curves. The .655 in his medium-high outside curve location, the .642 medium-high inside and the .450 low-over-the-middle serve as warnings to right-handers.

It's interesting that right-handers throw Boggs so few low-outside curves in comparison with the number of curves they throw to other locations. Since this is his only apparent weakness, they should focus on this location.

Looking at Boggs' Ahead and Behind charts on the opposite page, it can be seen that he hits medium-high outside fastballs for a higher average when ahead in the count. Notice how the fielders need to shift for this pitch when Boggs is ahead and behind.

**MEDIUM-HIGH OUTSIDE FASTBALLS
(WHEN AHEAD IN THE COUNT)**

BATTING AVERAGE .391
Play

Left	Deep and shifted toward the left field line
Center	Medium-deep in straightaway center field
Right	Medium-deep in straightaway right field
Short	Up middle (shifted toward second base)
Second	Shifted toward first base

**MEDIUM-HIGH OUTSIDE FASTBALLS
(WHEN BEHIND IN THE COUNT)**

BATTING AVERAGE .349
Play

Left	Deep and shifted toward the left field line
Center	Deep in straightaway center field
Right	Deep and shifted toward the right field line
Short	Up middle (shifted toward second base)
Second	Normal position

Boggs' .409 medium-high inside fastball average is extraordinary, especially considering the high number of recorded instances in the location (122).

MEDIUM-HIGH INSIDE FASTBALLS

BATTING AVERAGE .409
Play

Left	Medium-deep in straightaway left field
Center	Medium-deep in straightaway center field
Right	Deep and shifted toward center field

Short   Up middle (shifted toward second base)
Second   Shifted toward first base

His .369 against low-over-the-middle fastballs is solid.

LOW-OVER-THE-MIDDLE FASTBALLS

BATTING AVERAGE .369
Play
Left   Deep in straightaway left field
Center   Medium-deep in straightaway center field
Right   Deep and shifted toward center field
Short   Up middle (shifted toward second base)
Second Shifted toward first base

Boggs Against Curves And Sliders

Although his average is high in both locations, Boggs hits medium-high inside curves much differently than he hits medium-high outside curves.

MEDIUM-HIGH INSIDE CURVES

BATTING AVERAGE .642
Play
Left   Deep in straightaway left field
Center   Medium-deep in straightaway center field
Right   Deep and shifted toward the right field line
Short   Up middle (shifted toward second base)
Second Shifted toward first base

MEDIUM-HIGH OUTSIDE CURVEBALLS

BATTING AVERAGE .655
Play
Left   Medium-deep and shifted toward the left field line

Center   Medium-deep in straightaway center field
Right   Deep and shifted toward center field
Short   Up middle (shifted toward second base)
Second Shifted toward first base

Medium-high inside curves (along with high-inside curves) are one of the few pitches Boggs pulls down the right line.

Boggs Against Left-Handed Pitchers

Boggs hits fastballs very strongly against left-handed pitchers but has difficulty with many curve locations. He hits .409 in his medium-high inside fastball location.

MEDIUM-HIGH INSIDE FASTBALLS (THROWN BY LEFT-HANDED PITCHERS)

BATTING AVERAGE .409
Play
Left   Deep and shifted toward the left field line
Center   Medium-deep in straightaway center field
Right   Medium-deep and shifted toward center field
Short   Up middle (shifted toward second base)
Second Shifted toward first base

His .386 low-middle fastball average, .384 low-inside fastball average and .362 medium-high outside fastball average are also excellent. There is not enough room to describe all of Boggs' strong locations.

Boggs has difficulty with many curve locations against left-handers. He has trouble with low-outside (.000 on 0 for 12) and medium-high outside curves (.058). He also has trouble with outside sliders. These are locations for left-handers to attack.

Ahead And Behind In The Count Vs. RH

Ahead

Fastball Average .398

	Outside	Middle	Inside
High	12/ 500 /6	15/ 533 /8	8/ 500 /4
Med	115/ 391 /45	28/ 285 /8	49/ 367 /18
Low	5/ 200 /1	19/ 473 /9	25/ 440 /11

Curve Average .645

	Outside	Middle	Inside
High	0/ 0 /0	0/ 0 /0	2/ 500 /1
Med	12/ 750 /9	3/ 333 /1	8/ 750 /6
Low	0/ 0 /0	3/ 333 /1	3/ 666 /2

Behind

Fastball Average .376

	Outside	Middle	Inside
High	18/ 388 /7	11/ 363 /4	13/ 615 /8
Med	83/ 349 /29	11/ 363 /4	29/ 482 /14
Low	13/ 384 /5	14/ 285 /4	15/ 200 /3

Curve Average .462

	Outside	Middle	Inside
High	4/ 1000 /4	8/ 375 /3	3/ 333 /1
Med	7/ 571 /4	6/ 666 /4	12/ 500 /6
Low	3/ 0 /0	11/ 636 /7	13/ 153 /2

Overall Evaluation

Against Right-Handed Pitchers

Overall Fastball	⚾ ⚾ ⚾ ⚾
Overall Curve	⚾ ⚾ ⚾ ⚾
Overall Slider	⚾ ⚾ ⚾ ⚾

Against Left-Handed Pitchers

Overall Fastball	⚾ ⚾ ⚾ ⚾
Overall Curve	⚾
Overall Slider	⚾ ⚾

Comments: Weakest fastball location low-outside vs. RH. Trouble with curves vs. LH.
Strengths: Pick a location.
Weaknesses: Low-outside fastballs vs. RH; high-inside fastballs, low-outside, medium-outside and medium-inside curves, outside sliders vs. LH.

Ellis Burks (Right Handed)   *Boston Red Sox*

Ellis Burks Against Right-Handed Pitchers
Overall BARS Batting Average .280

Fastball Average .273

	Inside	Middle	Outside
High	19/ 210 /4	16/ 375 /6	21/ 142 /3
Med	21/ 285 /6	9/ 444 /4	159/ 264 /42
Low	5/ 200 /1	27/ 407 /11	23/ 217 /5

Curve Average .337

	Inside	Middle	Outside
High	0/ 0 /0	1/ 1000 /1	3/ 0 /0
Med	6/ 500 /3	4/ 750 /3	39/ 384 /15
Low	1/ 0 /0	1/ 0 /0	19/ 157 /3

Slider Average .234

	Inside	Middle	Outside
High	0/ 0 /0	1/ 0 /0	4/ 0 /0
Med	7/ 428 /3	3/ 666 /2	15/ 266 /4
Low	2/ 500 /1	5/ 0 /0	10/ 100 /1

Ellis Burks Against Left-Handed Pitchers
Overall BARS Batting Average .338

Fastball Average .349

	Inside	Middle	Outside
High	2/ 500 /1	3/ 333 /1	8/ 500 /4
Med	12/ 166 /2	6/ 166 /1	54/ 481 /26
Low	4/ 0 /0	5/ 0 /0	9/ 111 /1

Curve Average .076

	Inside	Middle	Outside
High	0/ 0 /0	0/ 0 /0	1/ 1000 /1
Med	0/ 0 /0	0/ 0 /0	3/ 0 /0
Low	2/ 0 /0	1/ 0 /0	6/ 0 /0

Slider Average .500

	Inside	Middle	Outside
High	1/ 1000 /1	1/ 1000 /1	0/ 0 /0
Med	1/ 1000 /1	1/ 0 /0	2/ 1000 /2
Low	3/ 0 /0	3/ 333 /1	2/ 500 /1

Right-handed Ellis Burks hits fastballs much better overall against left-handed pitchers (.349 against left-handers, .273 against right-handers) but has an excellent curve average against right-handers (.337).

Looking at Burks' fastball chart against right-handed pitchers, notice that a high percentage of the fastballs thrown to him are in the medium-high outside location. He gets so many pitches in this location that he could just sit back and wait for them.

He hits medium-high outside fastballs deep to all fields.

MEDIUM-HIGH OUTSIDE FASTBALLS

BATTING AVERAGE .264
Play

Left	Deep and shifted toward the left field line
Center	Deep in straightaway center field
Right	Deep in straightaway right field
Short	Normal position
Second	Shifted toward first base

He hits low-over-the-middle fastballs medium-deep down the left line for an excellent .407 average. If fielders aligned themselves as suggested by the BARS fielding strategy for this pitch they could prevent most of his base hits resulting from this location.

LOW-OVER-THE-MIDDLE FASTBALLS

BATTING AVERAGE .407
Play

Left	Medium-deep and shifted toward the left field line
Center	Medium-deep in straightaway center field
Right	Deep and shifted toward center field
Short	Normal position
Second	Normal position

Burks hits medium-high outside fastballs for a higher average when he is behind in the count, as the charts on the opposite page show. It's interesting to note that the BARS fielding strategy for this pitch shows that he hits the ball deeper when ahead in the count. Fielders apparently are positioned correctly for this and are getting him out. When behind, he hits the ball to short right field. It seems that fielders aren't positioned correctly for this, and his hits are dropping in.

MEDIUM-HIGH OUTSIDE FASTBALLS
(WHEN BEHIND IN THE COUNT)

BATTING AVERAGE .321
Play

Left	*No instances recorded*
Center	Deep in straightaway center field
Right	Short in straightaway right field
Short	Up middle (shifted toward second base)
Second	Normal position

MEDIUM-HIGH OUTSIDE FASTBALLS (WHEN AHEAD IN THE COUNT)

BATTING AVERAGE .205
Play
Left	Deep and shifted toward the left field line
Center	Deep and shifted toward left field
Right	Deep in straightaway right field
Short	Normal position
Second	Normal position

Burks Against Curves And Sliders

Burks hits excellently against medium-high outside curves thrown by right-handers (.384). He hits this pitch deep down the left line and deep into right-center.

MEDIUM-HIGH OUTSIDE CURVEBALLS

BATTING AVERAGE .384
Play
Left	Deep and shifted toward the left field line
Center	Deep in straightaway center field
Right	Deep and shifted toward center field
Short	Up middle (shifted toward second base)
Second	*No instances recorded*

In contrast, he hits low-outside curves very poorly. The only recorded hit ball to the outfield was deep down the left line. He has trouble with low-outside sliders thrown by right-handers.

Burks Against Left-Handed Pitchers

Left-handed pitchers throw Burks as high a percentage of medium-high outside fastballs as right-handers do. He hits them at a .481 clip.

MEDIUM-HIGH OUTSIDE FASTBALLS (THROWN BY LEFT-HANDED PITCHERS)

BATTING AVERAGE .481
Play
Left	Deep in straightaway left field
Center	Deep and shifted toward left field
Right	Deep and shifted toward center field
Short	Up middle (shifted toward second base)
Second	Normal position

He has trouble with low fastballs thrown by left-handers. The .111 in his low-outside fastball location indicates a weakness.

LOW-OUTSIDE FASTBALLS (THROWN BY LEFT-HANDED PITCHERS)

BATTING AVERAGE .111
Play
Left	Deep in straightaway left field
Center	Medium-deep in straightaway center field
Right	Short in straightaway right field
Short	Normal position
Second	Normal position

Few instances have been recorded for Burks' curve and slider charts against left-handers. He seems to have problems with outside curves, going 0-for-3 and 0-for-6 in the medium-high outside and low-outside locations, respectively.

Ahead And Behind In The Count Vs. RH

Ahead

Fastball Average .288

	Inside	Middle	Outside
High	4/500 /2	9/444 /4	3/0 /0
Med	9/222 /2	9/444 /4	68/205 /14
Low	1/1000 /1	7/571 /4	8/375 /3

Curve Average .538

	Inside	Middle	Outside
High	0/0 /0	0/0 /0	1/0 /0
Med	2/500 /1	1/1000 /1	7/714 /5
Low	0/0 /0	0/0 /0	2/0 /0

Behind

Fastball Average .285

	Inside	Middle	Outside
High	7/142 /1	3/333 /1	8/250 /2
Med	3/333 /1	0/0 /0	28/321 /9
Low	1/0 /0	4/500 /2	2/0 /0

Curve Average .344

	Inside	Middle	Outside
High	0/0 /0	1/1000 /1	1/0 /0
Med	2/1000 /2	1/1000 /1	16/312 /5
Low	0/0 /0	1/0 /0	7/142 /1

Overall Evaluation

Against Right-Handed Pitchers

Overall Fastball	⚾
Overall Curve	⚾ ⚾ ⚾ ⚾
Overall Slider	⚾

Against Left-Handed Pitchers

Overall Fastball	⚾ ⚾ ⚾ ⚾
Overall Curve	⚾
Overall Slider	⚾ ⚾ ⚾ ⚾

Comments: Excellent medium-outside fastball hitter vs. LH.
Strengths: Over-the-middle fastballs, waist-high curves vs. RH; medium-outside fastballs vs. LH.
Weaknesses: Outside fastballs, high-inside fastballs, low-outside curves, low-outside sliders vs. RH; medium-inside and low fastballs vs. LH.

Dwight Evans (Right Handed)   *Boston Red Sox*

Dwight Evans Against Right-Handed Pitchers
Overall BARS Batting Average .304

	Fastball Average .320			Curve Average .261			Slider Average .271		
	Inside	Middle	Outside	Inside	Middle	Outside	Inside	Middle	Outside
High	32 / 125 / 4	37 / 324 / 12	36 / 250 / 9	2 / 500 / 1	6 / 500 / 3	8 / 125 / 1	1 / 0 / 0	4 / 250 / 1	5 / 400 / 2
Med	91 / 351 / 32	56 / 410 / 23	264 / 329 / 87	11 / 272 / 3	13 / 538 / 7	66 / 303 / 20	2 / 500 / 1	5 / 800 / 4	35 / 171 / 6
Low	28 / 250 / 7	79 / 405 / 32	51 / 196 / 10	5 / 200 / 1	20 / 200 / 4	41 / 121 / 5	3 / 333 / 1	14 / 428 / 6	38 / 210 / 8

Dwight Evans Against Left-Handed Pitchers
Overall BARS Batting Average .312

	Fastball Average .314			Curve Average .343			Slider Average .255		
	Inside	Middle	Outside	Inside	Middle	Outside	Inside	Middle	Outside
High	13 / 153 / 2	16 / 375 / 6	19 / 263 / 5	1 / 1000 / 1	1 / 0 / 0	1 / 0 / 0	1 / 0 / 0	1 / 0 / 0	1 / 0 / 0
Med	26 / 269 / 7	18 / 333 / 6	108 / 351 / 38	10 / 300 / 3	5 / 1000 / 5	14 / 214 / 3	8 / 250 / 2	3 / 666 / 2	10 / 300 / 3
Low	11 / 272 / 3	33 / 393 / 13	20 / 150 / 3	7 / 142 / 1	16 / 375 / 6	12 / 333 / 4	9 / 444 / 4	7 / 142 / 1	7 / 0 / 0

Right-handed Dwight Evans is a good fastball hitter (.320 vs. right-handers, .314 vs. left-handers). He hits curves fairly well against right-handers (.261) and excellently against left-handers (.343).

Against right-handers, Evans hits all waist-high fastballs well (.351, .410 and .329, inside to outside). He hits low-over-the-middle fastballs very strongly (.405) but has trouble with low-outside (.196) and high-inside (.125) fastballs.

He hits medium-high outside fastballs straightaway to the outfield and to the right side of the infield.

MEDIUM-HIGH OUTSIDE FASTBALLS

BATTING AVERAGE .329
Play
Left   Deep in straightaway left field
Center   Deep in straightaway center field
Right   Medium-deep in straightaway right field
Short   Up middle (shifted toward second base)
Second   Shifted toward first base

He hits medium-high inside fastballs much differently than medium-high outside fastballs.

MEDIUM-HIGH INSIDE FASTBALLS

BATTING AVERAGE .351
Play
Left   Deep in straightaway left field
Center   Deep and shifted toward left field

Right   Medium-deep in straightaway right field
Short   Normal position
Second   Normal position

He hits low-over-the-middle fastballs extremely well. He hits this pitch straightaway to all fields.

LOW-OVER-THE-MIDDLE FASTBALLS

BATTING AVERAGE .405
Play
Left   Deep in straightaway left field
Center   Medium-deep in straightaway center field
Right   Medium-deep in straightaway right field
Short   Up middle (shifted toward second base)
Second   Normal position

A pitcher would not want to throw Evans, or any hitter, a medium-over-the-middle fastball. But Evans hits this pitch for such a high average it's interesting to see how fielders need to play.

MEDIUM-OVER-THE-MIDDLE FASTBALLS

BATTING AVERAGE .410
Play
Left   Deep and shifted toward the left field line
Center   Deep and shifted toward right field
Right   Deep in straightaway right field
Short   Up middle (shifted toward second base)
Second   Normal position

Evans Against Curves And Sliders

Evans hits medium-high outside curves excellently (.303). He hits this pitch deep to left and into the left-center field gap.

MEDIUM-HIGH OUTSIDE CURVEBALLS

BATTING AVERAGE .303

Play

Left	Deep in straightaway left field
Center	Deep and shifted toward left field
Right	Medium-deep in straightaway right field
Short	Up middle (shifted toward second base)
Second	Normal position

Evans has trouble with low-outside and low-over-the-middle curves (.121 and .200 respectively). It's interesting that Evans does not have one recorded instance of hitting a low-outside or a low-over-the-middle curve to right field. This means he gets around on these pitches.

LOW-OUTSIDE CURVEBALLS

BATTING AVERAGE .121

Play

Left	Deep in straightaway left field
Center	Short in straightaway center field
Right	*No instances recorded*
Short	Normal position
Second	Shifted toward first base

Evans has trouble with both medium-high outside and low-outside sliders. He pulls low-over-the-middle sliders deep to left and center, much as he does low-over-the-middle and low-outside curves.

Evans Against Left-Handed Pitchers

Evans hits very well against left-handed pitchers. His .314 overall fastball average is built upon an excellent .351 average in his medium-high outside fastball location. He hits this pitch deep to the outfield and to the right side of the infield.

MEDIUM-HIGH OUTSIDE FASTBALLS (THROWN BY LEFT-HANDED PITCHERS)

BATTING AVERAGE .351

Play

Left	Deep and shifted toward center field
Center	Deep in straightaway center field
Right	Deep and shifted toward center field
Short	Up middle (shifted toward second base)
Second	Shifted toward first base

He hits all over-the-middle fastballs excellently against left-handers. His .393 against low-over-the-middle fastballs is exceptional.

LOW-OVER-THE-MIDDLE FASTBALLS (THROWN BY LEFT-HANDED PITCHERS)

BATTING AVERAGE .393

Play

Left	Deep and shifted toward center field
Center	Medium-deep in straightaway center field
Right	Medium-deep in straightaway right field
Short	Up middle (shifted toward second base)
Second	Normal position

Ahead And Behind In The Count Vs. RH

Ahead

Fastball Average .377   Curve Average .413

	Inside	Middle	Outside	Inside	Middle	Outside
High	8/125 /1	19/368 /7	17/411 /7	0/0 /0	1/0 /0	0/0 /0
Med	38/289 /11	28/428 /12	112/428 /48	4/250 /1	3/1000 /3	10/300 /3
Low	13/230 /3	46/434 /20	16/187 /3	0/0 /0	7/428 /3	4/500 /2

Behind

Fastball Average .379   Curve Average .450

	Inside	Middle	Outside	Inside	Middle	Outside
High	4/500 /2	5/400 /2	5/0 /0	0/0 /0	4/500 /2	3/333 /1
Med	13/461 /6	9/333 /3	60/383 /23	4/500 /2	5/600 /3	22/545 /12
Low	5/200 /1	14/500 /7	9/333 /3	1/0 /0	4/250 /1	8/250 /2

Overall Evaluation

Against Right-Handed Pitchers

Overall Fastball ⚾ ⚾ ⚾

Overall Curve ⚾ ⚾

Overall Slider ⚾ ⚾

Against Left-Handed Pitchers

Overall Fastball ⚾ ⚾ ⚾

Overall Curve ⚾ ⚾ ⚾ ⚾

Overall Slider ⚾ ⚾

Comments: Weak vs. all low-outside pitches vs. RH. Strengths: Waist-high and over-the-middle fastballs, medium-outside and medium-middle curves, low-middle sliders vs. RH; over-the-middle and medium-outside fastballs, low-outside and low-middle curves vs. LH. Weaknesses: Fastball corners, low curves, low-outside and medium-outside sliders vs. RH; four fastball corners, medium-outside curves vs. LH.

Rich Gedman (Left Handed)   *Boston Red Sox*

Rich Gedman Against Right-Handed Pitchers
Overall BARS Batting Average .265

<table>
<tr><td colspan="4">Fastball Average .290</td><td colspan="3">Curve Average .154</td><td colspan="3">Slider Average .232</td></tr>
<tr><td></td><td>Outside</td><td>Middle</td><td>Inside</td><td>Outside</td><td>Middle</td><td>Inside</td><td>Outside</td><td>Middle</td><td>Inside</td></tr>
<tr><td>High</td><td>38/131 /5</td><td>26/461 /12</td><td>11/272 /3</td><td>1/0 /0</td><td>4/0 /0</td><td>5/200 /1</td><td>1/1000 /1</td><td>2/0 /0</td><td>1/0 /0</td></tr>
<tr><td>Med</td><td>175/331 /58</td><td>38/289 /11</td><td>64/281 /18</td><td>22/136 /3</td><td>2/500 /1</td><td>12/250 /3</td><td>9/444 /4</td><td>2/0 /0</td><td>4/500 /2</td></tr>
<tr><td>Low</td><td>31/161 /5</td><td>76/355 /27</td><td>34/117 /4</td><td>11/181 /2</td><td>15/200 /3</td><td>25/80 /2</td><td>1/0 /0</td><td>6/0 /0</td><td>17/176 /3</td></tr>
</table>

Rich Gedman Against Left-Handed Pitchers
Overall BARS Batting Average .259

<table>
<tr><td colspan="4">Fastball Average .272</td><td colspan="3">Curve Average .285</td><td colspan="3">Slider Average .178</td></tr>
<tr><td></td><td>Outside</td><td>Middle</td><td>Inside</td><td>Outside</td><td>Middle</td><td>Inside</td><td>Outside</td><td>Middle</td><td>Inside</td></tr>
<tr><td>High</td><td>4/500 /2</td><td>11/272 /3</td><td>12/0 /0</td><td>2/0 /0</td><td>5/600 /3</td><td>3/666 /2</td><td>2/0 /0</td><td>2/0 /0</td><td>1/1000 /1</td></tr>
<tr><td>Med</td><td>40/250 /10</td><td>12/500 /6</td><td>26/192 /5</td><td>18/333 /6</td><td>3/333 /1</td><td>5/200 /1</td><td>7/142 /1</td><td>1/1000 /1</td><td>4/0 /0</td></tr>
<tr><td>Low</td><td>6/166 /1</td><td>18/388 /7</td><td>7/428 /3</td><td>14/142 /2</td><td>10/300 /3</td><td>3/0 /0</td><td>6/166 /1</td><td>2/0 /0</td><td>3/333 /1</td></tr>
</table>

Left-handed hitting Rich Gedman hits fastballs pretty well against right-handed pitchers (.290 overall) but he has considerable trouble with curves (.154 overall) and sliders (.232 overall).

He hits a strong .331 against medium-high outside fastballs thrown by right-handers. In contrast, he hits only .131 against high-outside fastballs and .161 against low-outside fastballs. If pitchers are going to throw him an outside fastball, they should keep it high or low.

He goes with medium-high outside fastballs, hitting them deep down the line to left (his opposite field). He does, however, pull them to the right side of the infield when he hits grounders.

MEDIUM-HIGH OUTSIDE FASTBALLS

BATTING AVERAGE .331
Play
Left	Deep and shifted toward the left field line
Center	Deep in straightaway center field
Right	Deep in straightaway right field
Short	Up middle (shifted toward second base)
Second	Shifted toward first base

He hits a sparkling .461 against high-over-the-middle fastballs. He hits this pitch to left center and right center.

HIGH-OVER-THE-MIDDLE FASTBALLS

BATTING AVERAGE .461
Play
Left	Deep and shifted toward center field
Center	Deep and shifted toward right field
Right	Deep in straightaway right field
Short	Up middle (shifted toward second base)
Second	Normal position

Gedman also hits low-over-the-middle fastballs excellently (.355). He hits low-inside fastballs very poorly (.117). It seems that, location to location, Gedman either hits spectacularly or poorly.

Pitchers throw Gedman a lot of low fastballs. He tends to hit low-over-the-middle fastballs extremely well when ahead in the count, sending the ball deep to left and center fields.

LOW-OVER-THE-MIDDLE FASTBALLS
(WHEN AHEAD IN THE COUNT)

BATTING AVERAGE .414
Play
Left	Deep and shifted toward the left field line
Center	Deep and shifted toward left field
Right	Medium-deep in straightaway right field
Short	Up middle (shifted toward second base)
Second	Shifted toward first base

LOW-OVER-THE-MIDDLE FASTBALLS
(WHEN BEHIND IN THE COUNT)

BATTING AVERAGE .294
Play

Left   Deep in straightaway left field
Center   Medium-deep in straightaway center field
Right   Medium-deep in straightaway right field
Short   Up middle (shifted toward second base)
Second   Shifted toward first base

It may be noticed that Gedman has a strong tendency to pull the ball to the infield (shortstop up middle and first baseman shifted toward first base). This is the case in many of his fastball locations against right- and left-handed pitchers.

Gedman Against Curves And Sliders

Gedman does not have a strong curve location against right-handers. He hits .500 against medium-over-the-middle, but there are only two instances to go by in that location. He has definite trouble with all low and outside curves against right-handers. His .250 against medium-high inside curves is barely adequate.

He has similar trouble with low sliders. His .176 against low-inside sliders thrown by right-handers is a weakness. But he hits .444 against medium-high outside sliders.

MEDIUM-HIGH OUTSIDE SLIDERS

BATTING AVERAGE .444
Play

Left   Deep and shifted toward the left field line
Center   Deep and shifted toward right field

Right   *No instances recorded*
Short   Up middle (shifted toward second base)
Second   Normal position

Gedman Against Left-Handed Pitchers

Gedman's .272 overall fastball average against left-handers is decent enough, but he has some very weak locations in his fastball chart.

The .250 in his medium-high outside location and the .192 in his medium-high inside location are detriments. In contrast he hits a solid .388 in his low-over-the-middle location and a .428, on fewer instances, in his low-inside location.

He hits low-over-the-middle fastballs thrown by left-handers deep down the line and into the short right-center gap. Fielders could not be expected to position themselves correctly for this pitch to Gedman without use of the BARS System fielding strategy.

**LOW-OVER-THE-MIDDLE FASTBALLS
(THROWN BY LEFT-HANDED PITCHERS)**

BATTING AVERAGE .388
Play

Left   Deep and shifted toward the left field line
Center   Medium-deep in straightaway center field
Right   Short and shifted toward center field
Short   Up middle (shifted toward second base)
Second   Normal position

Gedman hits medium-high outside curves well against lefties (.333) but he has trouble with low-outside curves (.142). He has trouble with outside sliders.

Ahead And Behind In The Count Vs. RH

Ahead

	Fastball Average .336			Curve Average .233		
	Outside	Middle	Inside	Outside	Middle	Inside
High	11/272 /3	10/500 /5	3/333 /1	0/0 /0	3/0 /0	3/0 /0
Med	84/357 /30	18/388 /7	27/296 /8	8/375 /3	2/500 /1	4/0 /0
Low	9/0 /0	41/414 /17	11/90 /1	0/0 /0	7/285 /2	3/333 /1

Behind

	Fastball Average .361			Curve Average .227		
	Outside	Middle	Inside	Outside	Middle	Inside
High	5/200 /1	8/750 /6	3/333 /1	0/0 /0	0/0 /0	0/0 /0
Med	38/394 /15	8/250 /2	15/266 /4	8/0 /0	0/0 /0	3/666 /2
Low	6/333 /2	17/294 /5	5/400 /2	4/500 /2	4/0 /0	3/333 /1

Overall Evaluation

Against Right-Handed Pitchers

Overall Fastball ⚾⚾ ⚾⚾
Overall Curve ⚾⚾
Overall Slider ⚾⚾

Against Left-Handed Pitchers

Overall Fastball ⚾⚾
Overall Curve ⚾⚾ ⚾⚾ ⚾⚾
Overall Slider ⚾⚾

Comments: A fairly good fastball hitter against RH.
Strengths: Medium-outside, low-middle and high-middle fastballs, medium-outside sliders vs. RH; low-middle and medium-middle fastballs, medium-outside and over-the-middle curves vs. LH.
Weaknesses: The four fastball corners, low and outside curves, low sliders vs. RH; medium-outside, high-middle, high-inside and medium-inside fastballs, low-outside curves and outside sliders vs. LH.

Mike Greenwell (Left Handed)   *Boston Red Sox*

Mike Greenwell Against Right-Handed Pitchers
Overall BARS Batting Average .362

	Fastball Average .345			Curve Average .406			Slider Average .421		
	Outside	Middle	Inside	Outside	Middle	Inside	Outside	Middle	Inside
High	16/250/4	18/444/8	20/300/6	2/500/1	3/666/2	4/750/3	1/1000/1	1/0/0	5/400/2
Med	137/350/48	15/466/7	47/361/17	22/318/7	3/666/2	8/625/5	9/111/1	0/0/0	9/666/6
Low	5/200/1	25/280/7	12/333/4	4/250/1	5/400/2	8/125/1	1/0/0	2/500/1	10/500/5

Mike Greenwell Against Left-Handed Pitchers
Overall BARS Batting Average .327

	Fastball Average .348			Curve Average .318			Slider Average .187		
	Outside	Middle	Inside	Outside	Middle	Inside	Outside	Middle	Inside
High	7/0/0	6/333/2	9/333/3	0/0/0	2/500/1	1/0/0	1/0/0	0/0/0	1/0/0
Med	52/326/17	4/750/3	19/421/8	3/333/1	1/1000/1	2/0/0	7/142/1	0/0/0	2/0/0
Low	4/500/2	6/500/3	5/200/1	7/142/1	4/750/3	2/0/0	3/333/1	2/500/1	0/0/0

Left-handed hitter Mike Greenwell is a top-rate fastball hitter against both right- and left-handed pitchers. His .327 overall average against left-handers is one of the best for a left-handed hitter, especially since he has such good power.

Looking first at Greenwell's fastball chart against right-handers, notice his strength against all waist-high fastballs (.350, .466 and .361, outside to inside).

He hits medium-high outside fastballs much differently than he hits medium-high inside fastballs. He goes down both lines with medium-high inside while hitting more straightaway with medium-high outside.

MEDIUM-HIGH INSIDE FASTBALLS

BATTING AVERAGE .361
Play
Left	Medium-deep and shifted toward the left field line
Center	Deep and shifted toward right field
Right	Deep and shifted toward the right field line
Short	Shifted toward third base
Second	Shifted toward first base

MEDIUM-HIGH OUTSIDE FASTBALLS

BATTING AVERAGE .350
Play
Left	Deep and shifted toward center field
Center	Deep in straightaway center field
Right	Medium-deep in straightaway right field

Short   Up middle (shifted toward second base)
Second   Shifted toward first base

Notice how few low-outside fastballs right-handers throw to Greenwell in comparison to other locations. Pitchers should try throwing him more low and away, especially since he hits most other locations so well.

Greenwell hits high-inside fastballs in such a way that the fielders would be extremely fortunate to position themselves correctly without use of the BARS fielding strategy.

HIGH-INSIDE FASTBALLS

BATTING AVERAGE .300
Play
Left	Short and shifted toward the left field line
Center	Medium-deep in straightaway center field
Right	Deep in straightaway right field
Short	Up middle (shifted toward second base)
Second	Shifted toward first base

Greenwell hits high-over-the-middle fastballs deep into the left-center gap.

HIGH-OVER-THE-MIDDLE FASTBALLS

BATTING AVERAGE .444
Play
Left	Deep and shifted toward center field

Center	Deep in straightaway center field
Right	Deep in straightaway right field
Short	*No instances recorded*
Second	Normal position

Greenwell hits medium-high outside fastballs much differently when ahead and when behind in the count. Every fielder except the shortstop is required to shift for this pitch when Greenwell is ahead and behind.

MEDIUM-HIGH OUTSIDE FASTBALLS (WHEN BEHIND IN THE COUNT)

BATTING AVERAGE .400
Play

Left	Medium-deep and shifted toward center field
Center	Deep and shifted toward right field
Right	Medium-deep and shifted toward the right line
Short	Up middle (shifted toward second base)
Second	Shifted toward first base

MEDIUM-HIGH OUTSIDE FASTBALLS (WHEN AHEAD IN THE COUNT)

BATTING AVERAGE .373
Play

Left	Deep and shifted toward center field
Center	Deep in straightaway center field
Right	Medium-deep in straightaway right field
Short	Up middle (shifted toward second base)
Second	Normal position

Greenwell has quite a bit less recorded information for curves and sliders than he does for fastballs, but it can be seen that he hits both excellently against right-handed pitchers. He hits a solid .318 in his medium-high outside curve location against right-handers.

MEDIUM-HIGH OUTSIDE CURVEBALLS

BATTING AVERAGE .318
Play

Left	Deep in straightaway left field
Center	Deep in straightaway center field
Right	Deep in straightaway right field
Short	Shifted toward third base
Second	Shifted toward first base

Greenwell Against Left-Handed Pitchers

Against left-handed pitchers, Greenwell hits fastballs excellently overall (.348). He has a solid .326 average in his medium-high outside fastball location, hitting straightaway to left and center fields and deep down the right field line.

MEDIUM-HIGH OUTSIDE FASTBALLS (THROWN BY LEFT-HANDED PITCHERS)

BATTING AVERAGE .326
Play

Left	Deep in straightaway left field
Center	Medium-deep in straightaway center field
Right	Deep and shifted toward the right field line
Short	Up middle (shifted toward second base)
Second	Shifted toward first base

One thing can be said about the second baseman's required position for Greenwell: play normal or shifted toward first base for fastballs thrown by both right- and left-handed pitchers. Not one instance is recorded in which the second baseman should play up middle.

Ahead And Behind In The Count Vs. RH

Ahead

Fastball Average .378

	Outside	Middle	Inside
High	5 / 200 /1	11 / 454 /5	9 / 333 /3
Med	75 / 373 /28	11 / 454 /5	23 / 391 /9
Low	0 / 0 /0	9 / 222 /2	5 / 600 /3

Curve Average .500

	Outside	Middle	Inside
High	1 / 1000 /1	2 / 1000 /2	2 / 500 /1
Med	8 / 375 /3	2 / 500 /1	5 / 600 /3
Low	0 / 0 /0	2 / 500 /1	2 / 0 /0

Behind

Fastball Average .360

	Outside	Middle	Inside
High	4 / 750 /3	1 / 0 /0	6 / 166 /1
Med	25 / 400 /10	1 / 1000 /1	8 / 250 /2
Low	0 / 0 /0	4 / 250 /1	1 / 0 /0

Curve Average .285

	Outside	Middle	Inside
High	1 / 0 /0	1 / 0 /0	1 / 1000 /1
Med	3 / 0 /0	0 / 0 /0	1 / 0 /0
Low	3 / 333 /1	1 / 1000 /1	3 / 333 /1

Overall Evaluation

Against Right-Handed Pitchers

Overall Fastball	⚾⚾ ⚾⚾ ⚾⚾ ⚾⚾
Overall Curve	⚾⚾ ⚾⚾ ⚾⚾ ⚾⚾
Overall Slider	⚾⚾ ⚾⚾ ⚾⚾ ⚾⚾

Against Left-Handed Pitchers

Overall Fastball	⚾⚾ ⚾⚾ ⚾⚾ ⚾⚾
Overall Curve	⚾⚾ ⚾⚾ ⚾⚾ ⚾⚾
Overall Slider	⚾⚾

Comments: RH and LH should avoid throwing Greenwell waist-high or over-the-middle fastballs. Strengths: Waist-high and over-the-middle fastballs, low-inside fastballs, waist-high and over-the-middle curves, inside sliders vs. RH; waist-high and over-the-middle fastballs vs. LH. Weaknesses: High-outside fastballs, low-inside curves and medium-outside sliders vs. RH; low-outside curves and medium-outside sliders vs. LH.

Danny Heep (Left Handed) — *Boston Red Sox*

Danny Heep Against Right-Handed Pitchers
Overall BARS Batting Average .306

Fastball Average .304

	Outside	Middle	Inside
High	22/ 136 /3	20/ 150 /3	9/ 111 /1
Med	65/ 307 /20	21/ 380 /8	45/ 333 /15
Low	14/ 428 /6	49/ 387 /19	31/ 290 /9

Curve Average .258

	Outside	Middle	Inside
High	3/ 333 /1	1/ 0 /0	2/ 0 /0
Med	9/ 333 /3	5/ 400 /2	7/ 428 /3
Low	9/ 222 /2	15/ 200 /3	7/ 142 /1

Slider Average .333

	Outside	Middle	Inside
High	0/ 0 /0	1/ 0 /0	2/ 0 /0
Med	6/ 500 /3	2/ 500 /1	8/ 250 /2
Low	0/ 0 /0	8/ 500 /4	9/ 222 /2

Danny Heep Against Left-Handed Pitchers
Overall BARS Batting Average .214

Fastball Average .166

	Outside	Middle	Inside
High	2/ 500 /1	2/ 0 /0	1/ 0 /0
Med	6/ 166 /1	1/ 0 /0	4/ 250 /1
Low	3/ 0 /0	8/ 125 /1	3/ 333 /1

Curve Average .333

	Outside	Middle	Inside
High	0/ 0 /0	0/ 0 /0	0/ 0 /0
Med	2/ 500 /1	0/ 0 /0	0/ 0 /0
Low	2/ 0 /0	2/ 500 /1	0/ 0 /0

Slider Average .333

	Outside	Middle	Inside
High	0/ 0 /0	0/ 0 /0	0/ 0 /0
Med	0/ 0 /0	0/ 0 /0	0/ 0 /0
Low	4/ 250 /1	2/ 500 /1	0/ 0 /0

Left-handed hitter Danny Heep has a consistent .304 overall fastball average against right-handed pitchers. His only weaknesses are in his high locations (.136, .150, and .111, outside to inside). He probably doesn't realize he's such a poor high-fastball hitter. If he could hold off on these pitches until he has two strikes, he might be able to improve his effectiveness significantly.

He tends to hit high fastballs deep to the outfield, but his low averages in these locations indicate that he is not hitting the ball hard and most of his hit balls are easy pop flies.

He hits waist-high fastballs very well against right-handers. His .307 against medium-high outside fastballs is solid.

MEDIUM-HIGH OUTSIDE FASTBALLS

BATTING AVERAGE .307

Play
Left	Deep and shifted toward center field
Center	Medium-deep in straightaway center field
Right	Medium-deep and shifted toward center field
Short	Up middle (shifted toward second base)
Second	Normal position

He hits .333 against medium-high inside fastballs.

MEDIUM-HIGH INSIDE FASTBALLS

BATTING AVERAGE .333

Play
Left	Deep in straightaway left field
Center	Medium-deep in straightaway center field
Right	Deep in straightaway right field
Short	Shifted toward third base
Second	Shifted toward first base

His .387 against low-over-the-middle fastballs is very strong. By following the fielding strategy for this pitch shown in the chart below fielders could prevent most of his base hits from this location.

LOW-OVER-THE-MIDDLE FASTBALLS

BATTING AVERAGE .387

Play
Left	Medium-deep in straightaway left field
Center	Medium-deep in straightaway center field
Right	Medium-deep and shifted toward the right line
Short	Up middle (shifted toward second base)
Second	Shifted toward first base

Heep hits .428 against low-outside fastballs, showing that not all hitters have trouble with this pitch.

LOW-OUTSIDE FASTBALLS

BATTING AVERAGE .428

Play
Left	Deep in straightaway left field

Center	Deep and shifted toward left field
Right	Deep and shifted toward center field
Short	Normal position
Second	*No instances recorded*

He hits medium-over-the-middle fastballs at a .380 clip, sending the ball deep to the outfield.

MEDIUM-OVER-THE-MIDDLE FASTBALLS

BATTING AVERAGE .380
Play

Left	Deep and shifted toward the left field line
Center	Deep in straightaway center field
Right	Deep in straightaway right field
Short	Normal position
Second	Normal position

His .290 against low-inside fastballs is pretty good. He hits this pitch deep down the left line (his opposite field) but to the right side of the infield.

LOW-INSIDE FASTBALLS

BATTING AVERAGE .290
Play

Left	Deep and shifted toward the left field line
Center	Deep and shifted toward right field
Right	Deep in straightaway right field
Short	Up middle (shifted toward second base)
Second	Shifted toward first base

Heep Against Curves And Sliders

Heep has trouble with low curves against right-handed pitchers (.222, .200, and .142, outside to inside).

But he hits all waist-high curves excellently. He hits .333 against medium-high outside curves and .428 against medium-high inside curves.

MEDIUM-HIGH INSIDE CURVEBALLS

BATTING AVERAGE .428
Play

Left	Deep in straightaway left field
Center	Deep in straightaway center field
Right	Deep and shifted toward the right field line
Short	Normal position
Second	Shifted toward first base

He has some trouble with inside sliders against right-handers. But his .500 against medium-high outside and low-over-the-middle sliders is strong.

LOW-OVER-THE-MIDDLE SLIDERS

BATTING AVERAGE .500
Play

Left	*No instances recorded*
Center	Deep in straightaway center field
Right	Deep and shifted toward the right field line
Short	Up middle (shifted toward second base)
Second	Normal position

The BARS System has recorded few instances for Heep when facing left-handed pitchers. For this reason we won't go into his performance against lefties. It's apparent that he has some trouble with low-over-the-middle fastballs (.125) and medium-high outside fastballs (.166). It will be interesting to see if he can become as effective against left-handers as he is against right-handers.

Ahead And Behind In The Count Vs. RH

Ahead

Fastball Average .331

	Outside	Middle	Inside
High	15/133 /2	8/125 /1	4/0 /0
Med	36/333 /12	15/333 /5	23/478 /11
Low	5/600 /3	34/411 /14	17/235 /4

Curve Average .100

	Outside	Middle	Inside
High	0/0 /0	0/0 /0	0/0 /0
Med	1/0 /0	0/0 /0	2/0 /0
Low	2/0 /0	4/0 /0	1/1000 /1

Behind

Fastball Average .352

	Outside	Middle	Inside
High	2/500 /1	4/250 /1	1/0 /0
Med	6/500 /3	2/500 /1	8/250 /2
Low	2/500 /1	6/166 /1	3/666 /2

Curve Average .409

	Outside	Middle	Inside
High	2/500 /1	0/0 /0	1/0 /0
Med	3/333 /1	2/500 /1	4/750 /3
Low	4/500 /2	4/250 /1	2/0 /0

Overall Evaluation

Against Right-Handed Pitchers

Overall Fastball	⚾⚾⚾
Overall Curve	⚾⚾
Overall Slider	⚾⚾⚾⚾

Against Left-Handed Pitchers

Overall Fastball	⚾
Overall Curve	Not enough information
Overall Slider	Not enough information

Comments: Weak vs. high fastballs vs. RH, strong vs. waist-high and low fastballs vs. RH.
Strengths: Waist-high and low fastballs, waist-high curves, medium-outside and low-middle sliders vs. RH.
Weaknesses: High fastballs, low curves, inside sliders vs. RH; low fastballs vs. LH.

Tony Pena (Right Handed)   *Boston Red Sox*

Tony Pena Against Right-Handed Pitchers
Overall BARS Batting Average .287

	Fastball Average .311			Curve Average .238			Slider Average .250		
	Inside	Middle	Outside	Inside	Middle	Outside	Inside	Middle	Outside
High	33/212 /7	44/409 /18	22/318 /7	5/0 /0	11/363 /4	5/200 /1	0/0 /0	3/666 /2	5/0 /0
Med	47/170 /8	14/428 /6	51/490 /25	4/250 /1	3/666 /2	32/250 /8	0/0 /0	3/0 /0	25/320 /8
Low	20/150 /3	60/266 /16	43/325 /14	4/250 /1	7/428 /3	38/157 /6	2/0 /0	8/375 /3	34/205 /7

Tony Pena Against Left-Handed Pitchers
Overall BARS Batting Average .378

	Fastball Average .362			Curve Average .400			Slider Average .411		
	Inside	Middle	Outside	Inside	Middle	Outside	Inside	Middle	Outside
High	5/200 /1	7/0 /0	8/375 /3	1/0 /0	1/0 /0	1/0 /0	1/0 /0	0/0 /0	0/0 /0
Med	8/500 /4	5/600 /3	25/360 /9	2/500 /1	2/500 /1	5/600 /3	0/0 /0	1/0 /0	3/666 /2
Low	7/142 /1	24/541 /13	24/291 /7	2/0 /0	10/600 /6	11/272 /3	3/0 /0	4/1000 /4	5/200 /1

Right-handed hitting Tony Pena has a good .311 overall fastball average against right-handed pitchers. He hits a very strong .490 against medium-high outside fastballs.

MEDIUM-HIGH OUTSIDE FASTBALLS

BATTING AVERAGE .490
Play
Left Deep in straightaway left field
Center Medium-deep in straightaway center field
Right Medium-deep in straightaway right field
Short Up middle (shifted toward second base)
Second Normal position

His .409 against high-over-the-middle fastballs is also impressive. He hits this pitch into a corridor in left-center field. By aligning themselves according to the following unusual fielding strategy, fielders could get to most of Pena's hits that are now falling in.

HIGH-OVER-THE-MIDDLE FASTBALLS

BATTING AVERAGE .409
Play
Left Medium-deep and shifted toward center field
Center Deep and shifted toward left field
Right Deep in straightaway right field
Short Up middle (shifted toward second base)
Second Shifted toward first base

Pena is weak against inside fastballs and low-over-the-middle fastballs thrown by right-handers. He is also weak against outside curves (.200, .250 and .157). He has trouble with low-outside sliders (.205) but hits medium-high outside sliders excellently (.320).

Pena hits a vibrant .362 against fastballs thrown by left-handed pitchers. He hits medium-outside fastballs (.360) deep to all fields.

MEDIUM-HIGH OUTSIDE FASTBALLS
(THROWN BY LEFT-HANDED PITCHERS)

BATTING AVERAGE .360
Play
Left Deep in straightaway left field
Center Deep and shifted toward left field
Right Deep and shifted toward center field
Short Up middle (shifted toward second base
Second Normal position

He hits low-over-the-middle fastballs deep into the right-center gap for a very high .541 average.

LOW-OVER-THE-MIDDLE FASTBALLS
(THROWN BY LEFT-HANDED PITCHERS)

BATTING AVERAGE .541
Play
Left Deep in straightaway left field
Center Medium-deep in straightaway center field
Right Deep and shifted toward center field
Short Up middle (shifted toward second base)
Second *No instances recorded*

High-Over-The-Middle Fastballs
(Thrown By Right-Handed Pitchers)

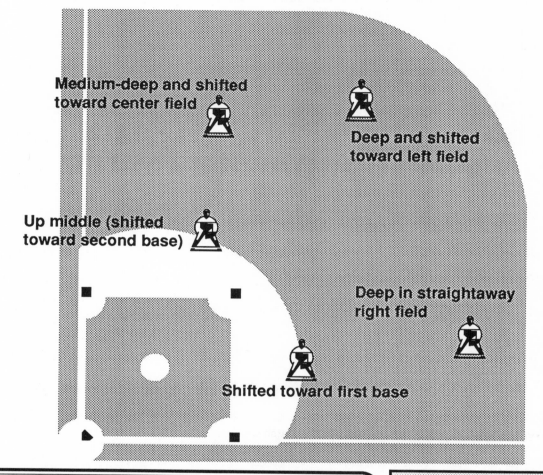

Medium-deep and shifted toward center field

Deep and shifted toward left field

Up middle (shifted toward second base)

Deep in straightaway right field

Shifted toward first base

Ahead And Behind In The Count Vs. RH

Ahead

Fastball Average .321

	Inside	Middle	Outside
High	11/363 /4	22/363 /8	11/181 /2
Med	29/137 /4	8/375 /3	27/629 /17
Low	7/142 /1	35/228 /8	15/400 /6

Curve Average .250

	Inside	Middle	Outside
High	2/0 /0	6/333 /2	0/0 /0
Med	3/0 /0	0/0 /0	10/200 /2
Low	3/333 /1	2/500 /1	6/333 /2

Behind

Fastball Average .411

	Inside	Middle	Outside
High	12/166 /2	11/727 /8	6/500 /3
Med	7/285 /2	3/666 /2	8/375 /3
Low	5/400 /2	7/428 /3	9/333 /3

Curve Average .281

	Inside	Middle	Outside
High	1/0 /0	1/0 /0	3/0 /0
Med	1/1000 /1	0/0 /0	12/333 /4
Low	0/0 /0	2/500 /1	12/250 /3

Overall Evaluation
Against Right-Handed Pitchers

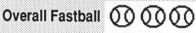

Overall Fastball ⚾⚾ ⚾⚾⚾

Overall Curve ⚾⚾

Overall Slider ⚾⚾ ⚾⚾

Against Left-Handed Pitchers

Overall Fastball ⚾⚾ ⚾⚾ ⚾⚾ ⚾⚾

Overall Curve ⚾⚾ ⚾⚾ ⚾⚾ ⚾⚾

Overall Slider ⚾⚾ ⚾⚾ ⚾⚾ ⚾⚾

Comments: Weak against inside fastballs vs. RH. Strong hitter vs. LH (especially outside fastballs). Strengths: High-middle, medium-middle, medium-outside and low-outside fastballs, over-the-middle curves, medium-outside sliders vs. RH; waist-high, outside and low-middle fastballs, low-middle curves vs. LH. Weaknesses: Inside fastballs, low-middle fastballs, outside and inside curves, low-outside sliders vs. RH.

Jody Reed (Right Handed)   *Boston Red Sox*

Jody Reed Against Right-Handed Pitchers
Overall BARS Batting Average .286

Fastball Average .310

	Inside	Middle	Outside
High	10/ 200 /2	18/ 444 /8	10/ 500 /5
Med	18/ 333 /6	13/ 461 /6	94/ 276 /26
Low	5/ 0 /0	14/ 357 /5	11/ 181 /2

Curve Average .280

	Inside	Middle	Outside
High	1/ 0 /0	2/ 500 /1	2/ 500 /1
Med	1/ 1000 /1	0/ 0 /0	10/ 200 /2
Low	1/ 0 /0	2/ 500 /1	6/ 166 /1

Slider Average .200

	Inside	Middle	Outside
High	0/ 0 /0	2/ 0 /0	3/ 666 /2
Med	0/ 0 /0	0/ 0 /0	5/ 0 /0
Low	0/ 0 /0	0/ 0 /0	0/ 0 /0

Jody Reed Against Left-Handed Pitchers
Overall BARS Batting Average .250

Fastball Average .213

	Inside	Middle	Outside
High	7/ 428 /3	2/ 0 /0	7/ 142 /1
Med	3/ 333 /1	2/ 0 /0	28/ 214 /6
Low	3/ 0 /0	6/ 333 /2	3/ 0 /0

Curve Average .333

	Inside	Middle	Outside
High	0/ 0 /0	0/ 0 /0	0/ 0 /0
Med	0/ 0 /0	0/ 0 /0	4/ 500 /2
Low	1/ 0 /0	0/ 0 /0	1/ 0 /0

Slider Average .600

	Inside	Middle	Outside
High	0/ 0 /0	0/ 0 /0	0/ 0 /0
Med	2/ 1000 /2	0/ 0 /0	2/ 500 /1
Low	0/ 0 /0	0/ 0 /0	1/ 0 /0

Jody Reed has a solid .310 overall fastball average against right-handed pitchers but only a .213 overall fastball average against left-handed pitchers. This is somewhat unusual for a right-handed hitter.

He has some very strong fastball averages against right-handers. He hits waist-high and over-the-middle fastballs well, although his .276 against medium-high outside fastballs is only adequate.

MEDIUM-HIGH OUTSIDE FASTBALLS

BATTING AVERAGE .276
Play
Left   Deep in straightaway left field
Center   Deep and shifted toward left field
Right   Medium-deep in straightaway right field
Short   Up middle (shifted toward second base)
Second   Shifted toward first base

His .333 against medium-high inside fastballs is excellent.

MEDIUM-HIGH INSIDE FASTBALLS

BATTING AVERAGE .333
Play
Left   Medium-deep in straightaway left field
Center   Deep in straightaway center field
Right   *No instances recorded*
Short   Shifted toward third base

Second   *No instances recorded*

He hits .444 against high-over-the-middle fastballs against right-handers.

HIGH-OVER-THE-MIDDLE FASTBALLS

BATTING AVERAGE .444
Play
Left   Deep in straightaway left field
Center   Deep and shifted toward left field
Right   Medium-deep in straightaway right field
Short   Normal position
Second   Normal position

He pulls low-over-the-middle fastballs (.357) when hitting to the outfield.

LOW-OVER-THE-MIDDLE FASTBALLS

BATTING AVERAGE .357
Play
Left   Deep and shifted toward the left field line
Center   Deep and shifted toward left field
Right   *No instances recorded*
Short   Normal position
Second   Normal position

Reed's .461 against medium-over-the-middle fastballs is a warning to pitchers.

MEDIUM-OVER-THE-MIDDLE FASTBALLS

BATTING AVERAGE .461
Play

Left	Medium-deep in straightaway left field
Center	Deep and shifted toward left field
Right	*No instances recorded*
Short	Shifted toward third base
Second	Normal position

He hits a strong .500 against high-outside fastballs. Note that he goes to the right side of the infield with this pitch. It is one of the few he hits that way.

HIGH-OUTSIDE FASTBALLS

BATTING AVERAGE .500
Play

Left	Deep in straightaway left field
Center	Deep and shifted toward left field
Right	Medium-deep in straightaway right field
Short	Up middle (shifted toward second base)
Second	Shifted toward first base

Against right-handers, Reed has trouble with medium-high outside curves (.200) and low-outside curves (.166). He pulls medium-high outside curves, but his low average indicates that most of his hit balls from this location are easy outs.

MEDIUM-HIGH OUTSIDE CURVEBALLS

BATTING AVERAGE .200
Play

Left	Deep and shifted toward the left field line
Center	Deep and shifted toward left field
Right	*No instances recorded*

Short	Normal position
Second	*No instances recorded*

Reed Against Left-Handed Pitchers

Against left-handed pitchers, Reed has trouble with medium-high outside fastballs. His .214 in this highly pitched location brings down his average against left-handers.

MEDIUM-HIGH OUTSIDE FASTBALLS (THROWN BY LEFT-HANDED PITCHERS)

BATTING AVERAGE .214
Play

Left	Medium-deep in straightaway left field
Center	Deep in straightaway center field
Right	Medium-deep in straightaway right field
Short	Normal position
Second	Normal position

He hits a strong .428 against high-inside fastballs, sending the ball straightaway to the outfield and to the right side of the infield.

He hits low-over-the-middle fastballs medium-deep to the outfield.

LOW-OVER-THE-MIDDLE FASTBALLS

BATTING AVERAGE .333
Play

Left	Medium-deep in straightaway left field
Center	Medium-deep in straightaway center field
Right	Medium-deep and shifted toward center field
Short	Normal position
Second	*No instances recorded*

Ahead And Behind In The Count Vs. RH

Ahead

Fastball Average .360

	Inside	Middle	Outside
High	8/250 /2	9/444 /4	4/500 /2
Med	8/500 /4	8/625 /5	35/285 /10
Low	1/0 /0	8/375 /3	5/200 /1

Curve Average .500

	Inside	Middle	Outside
High	0/0 /0	0/0 /0	0/0 /0
Med	1/1000 /1	0/0 /0	0/0 /0
Low	1/0 /0	0/0 /0	0/0 /0

Behind

Fastball Average .258

	Inside	Middle	Outside
High	1/0 /0	6/333 /2	0/0 /0
Med	2/0 /0	1/0 /0	18/277 /5
Low	0/0 /0	2/500 /1	1/0 /0

Curve Average .230

	Inside	Middle	Outside
High	0/0 /0	1/0 /0	1/0 /0
Med	0/0 /0	0/0 /0	6/333 /2
Low	0/0 /0	1/1000 /1	4/0 /0

Overall Evaluation

Against Right-Handed Pitchers

Overall Fastball	
Overall Curve	
Overall Slider	Not enough information

Against Left-Handed Pitchers

Overall Fastball	
Overall Curve	Not enough information
Overall Slider	Not enough information

Comments: Very strong against over-the-middle fastballs vs. RH.

Strengths: Over-the-middle fastballs, high-outside fastballs vs. RH; high-inside and low-middle fastballs vs. LH.

Weaknesses: High-inside and low-outside fastballs, medium-outside and low-outside curves vs. RH; outside fastballs vs. LH.

Luis Rivera (Right Handed)   *Boston Red Sox*

Luis Rivera Against Right-Handed Pitchers
Overall BARS Batting Average .233

Fastball Average .228

	Inside	Middle	Outside
High	9/ 222 /2	4/ 250 /1	8/ 125 /1
Med	10/ 400 /4	3/ 333 /1	42/ 238 /10
Low	8/ 125 /1	6/ 333 /2	15/ 133 /2

Curve Average .235

	Inside	Middle	Outside
High	1/ 1000 /1	1/ 1000 /1	2/ 0 /0
Med	5/ 200 /1	2/ 500 /1	3/ 333 /1
Low	3/ 333 /1	2/ 500 /1	15/ 66 /1

Slider Average .250

	Inside	Middle	Outside
High	0/ 0 /0	1/ 0 /0	3/ 0 /0
Med	1/ 0 /0	3/ 333 /1	11/ 454 /5
Low	0/ 0 /0	1/ 0 /0	4/ 0 /0

Luis Rivera Against Left-Handed Pitchers
Overall BARS Batting Average .215

Fastball Average .220

	Inside	Middle	Outside
High	5/ 0 /0	5/ 0 /0	4/ 500 /2
Med	4/ 500 /2	3/ 333 /1	22/ 272 /6
Low	5/ 0 /0	10/ 200 /2	1/ 0 /0

Curve Average .125

	Inside	Middle	Outside
High	1/ 1000 /1	0/ 0 /0	1/ 0 /0
Med	1/ 0 /0	0/ 0 /0	8/ 0 /0
Low	2/ 0 /0	1/ 0 /0	2/ 500 /1

Slider Average .500

	Inside	Middle	Outside
High	0/ 0 /0	0/ 0 /0	0/ 0 /0
Med	1/ 1000 /1	0/ 0 /0	1/ 0 /0
Low	0/ 0 /0	1/ 1000 /1	1/ 0 /0

Right-handed hitter Luis Rivera has low BARS fastball averages against both right- and left-handed pitchers (.228 overall fastball against right-handers, .220 against left-handers). His low .238 medium-high outside fastball average against right-handers brings down his overall average. The chart below and the field diagram on the opposite page show how fielders need to play for this pitch.

MEDIUM-HIGH OUTSIDE FASTBALLS

BATTING AVERAGE .238
Play

Left Deep and shifted toward the left field line
Center Medium-deep in straightaway center field
Right Deep in straightaway right field
Short Normal position
Second Normal position

He has trouble with high fastballs and low-inside fastballs against right-handers. But he hits medium-high inside fastballs for a strong .400.

MEDIUM-HIGH INSIDE FASTBALLS

BATTING AVERAGE .400
Play

Left Deep and shifted toward the left field line
Center Medium-deep in straightaway center field
Right Short in straightaway right field
Short Up middle (shifted toward second base)

Second Normal position

Rivera has trouble with low-outside curves against right-handers (.066). He hits medium-high outside sliders excellently (.454).

MEDIUM-HIGH OUTSIDE SLIDERS

BATTING AVERAGE .454
Play

Left Deep in straightaway left field
Center Medium-deep and shifted toward right field
Right Medium-deep in straightaway right field
Short Shifted toward third base
Second *No instances recorded*

When facing left-handed pitchers Rivera is weak against low-over-the-middle fastballs (.200) and medium-outside curves (.000 on 0 for 8). But he hits .272 against medium-high outside fastballs.

MEDIUM-HIGH OUTSIDE FASTBALLS
(THROWN BY LEFT-HANDED PITCHERS)

BATTING AVERAGE .272
Play

Left Deep in straightaway left field
Center Deep in straightaway center field
Right Deep and shifted toward center field
Short Normal position
Second Normal position

Medium-High Outside Fastballs
(Thrown By Right-Handed Pitchers)

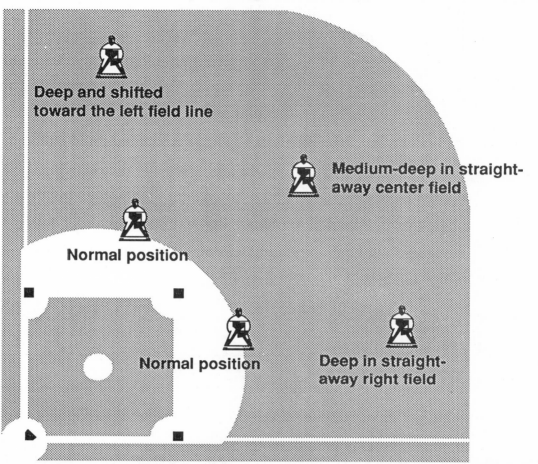

Deep and shifted toward the left field line

Medium-deep in straight-away center field

Normal position

Normal position

Deep in straight-away right field

Ahead And Behind In The Count Vs. RH

Ahead

Fastball Average .187

	Inside	Middle	Outside
High	250 — 4/1	500 — 2/1	250 — 4/1
Med	333 — 3/1	0 — 2/0	166 — 18/3
Low	166 — 6/1	250 — 4/1	0 — 5/0

Curve Average .600

	Inside	Middle	Outside
High	0 — 0/0	1000 — 1/1	0 — 0/0
Med	0 — 1/0	0 — 0/0	500 — 2/1
Low	0 — 0/0	0 — 0/0	1000 — 1/1

Behind

Fastball Average .312

	Inside	Middle	Outside
High	0 — 0/0	0 — 1/0	0 — 0/0
Med	333 — 3/1	1000 — 1/1	250 — 8/2
Low	0 — 1/0	0 — 1/0	1000 — 1/1

Curve Average .111

	Inside	Middle	Outside
High	0 — 0/0	0 — 0/0	0 — 1/0
Med	333 — 3/1	0 — 0/0	0 — 0/0
Low	0 — 1/0	0 — 0/0	0 — 4/0

Overall Evaluation

Against Right-Handed Pitchers

Overall Fastball ⚾⚾

Overall Curve ⚾⚾

Overall Slider ⚾⚾ ⚾⚾

Against Left-Handed Pitchers

Overall Fastball ⚾⚾

Overall Curve ⚾⚾

Overall Slider Not enough information

Comments: Weak against high and outside fastballs vs. RH.

Strengths: Medium-inside and low-middle fastballs, medium-outside sliders vs. RH; waist-high fastballs vs. LH.

Weaknesses: High and outside fastballs, low-inside fastballs, low-outside curves vs. RH; low-middle and low-inside fastballs, medium-outside curves vs. LH.

Kevin Romine (Right Handed) — *Boston Red Sox*

Kevin Romine Against Right-Handed Pitchers
Overall BARS Batting Average .242

Fastball Average .295

	Inside	Middle	Outside
High	1/ 0/0	2/ 0/0	0/ 0/0
Med	7/ 428/3	1/ 1000/1	25/ 280/7
Low	3/ 333/1	2/ 0/0	3/ 333/1

Curve Average .000

	Inside	Middle	Outside
High	0/ 0/0	0/ 0/0	0/ 0/0
Med	1/ 0/0	0/ 0/0	4/ 0/0
Low	0/ 0/0	0/ 0/0	3/ 0/0

Slider Average .100

	Inside	Middle	Outside
High	1/ 0/0	1/ 0/0	0/ 0/0
Med	0/ 0/0	1/ 1000/1	3/ 0/0
Low	1/ 0/0	0/ 0/0	3/ 0/0

Kevin Romine Against Left-Handed Pitchers
Overall BARS Batting Average .403

Fastball Average .461

	Inside	Middle	Outside
High	1/ 0/0	1/ 0/0	6/ 166/1
Med	2/ 0/0	1/ 1000/1	18/ 555/10
Low	2/ 0/0	4/ 750/3	4/ 750/3

Curve Average .363

	Inside	Middle	Outside
High	0/ 0/0	0/ 0/0	1/ 0/0
Med	0/ 0/0	1/ 1000/1	3/ 333/1
Low	2/ 0/0	2/ 500/1	2/ 500/1

Slider Average .200

	Inside	Middle	Outside
High	1/ 1000/1	0/ 0/0	0/ 0/0
Med	0/ 0/0	0/ 0/0	2/ 0/0
Low	0/ 0/0	2/ 0/0	0/ 0/0

Right-handed hitting Kevin Romine has solid fastball averages against right-handed and left-handed pitchers (.295 overall fastball against right-handers, .461 against left-handers).

Starting with right-handers, he hits .280 against medium-high outside fastballs.

MEDIUM-HIGH OUTSIDE FASTBALLS

BATTING AVERAGE .280

Play	
Left	*No instances recorded*
Center	Medium-deep in straightaway center field
Right	Deep in straightaway right field
Short	Up middle (shifted toward second base)
Second	Normal position

He hits .428 (with fewer recorded instances) against medium-high inside fastballs thrown by right-handers.

MEDIUM-HIGH INSIDE FASTBALLS

BATTING AVERAGE .428

Play	
Left	*No instances recorded*
Center	Deep and shifted toward left field
Right	Medium-deep and shifted toward the right line
Short	Shifted toward third base
Second	Normal position

Romine does not yet have a recorded base hit in his outside curve or slider locations against right-handers.

Romine Against Left-Handed Pitchers

Romine hits an extremely solid .555 against medium-high outside fastballs thrown by left-handed pitchers. He hits this pitch medium-deep to all fields. If fielders played him as suggested in the chart below and the field diagram on the opposite page they could prevent most of his base hits from this location.

MEDIUM-HIGH OUTSIDE FASTBALLS
(THROWN BY LEFT-HANDED PITCHERS)

BATTING AVERAGE .555

Play	
Left	Medium-deep in straightaway left field
Center	Medium-deep in straightaway center field
Right	Medium-deep in straightaway right field
Short	Normal position
Second	Shifted toward first base

Romine has fewer recorded instances in his low fastball locations against left-handers, but it is evident that he hits low-over-the-middle and low-outside fastballs well (.750 on 3 for 4 in each location).

Medium-High Outside Fastballs
(Thrown By Left-Handed Pitchers)

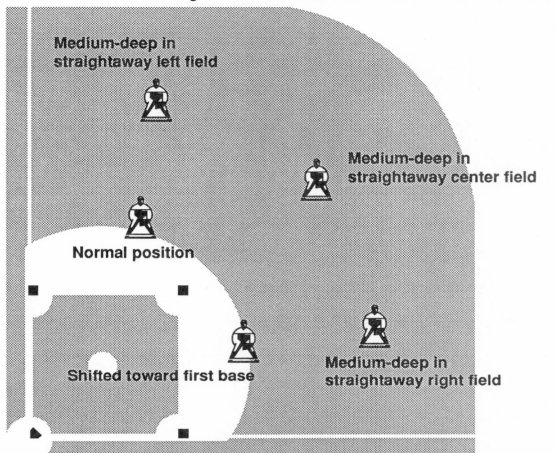

Medium-deep in straightaway left field

Medium-deep in straightaway center field

Normal position

Shifted toward first base

Medium-deep in straightaway right field

Ahead And Behind In The Count Vs. RH

Ahead

Fastball Average .285

	Inside	Middle	Outside
High	1/0 /0	2/0 /0	0/0 /0
Med	4/500 /2	1/1000 /1	11/272 /3
Low	2/0 /0	0/0 /0	0/0 /0

Curve Average .000

	Inside	Middle	Outside
High	0/0 /0	0/0 /0	0/0 /0
Med	0/0 /0	0/0 /0	1/0 /0
Low	0/0 /0	0/0 /0	0/0 /0

Behind

Fastball Average .500

	Inside	Middle	Outside
High	0/0 /0	0/0 /0	0/0 /0
Med	1/1000 /1	0/0 /0	4/250 /1
Low	1/1000 /1	0/0 /0	0/0 /0

Curve Average .000

	Inside	Middle	Outside
High	0/0 /0	0/0 /0	0/0 /0
Med	0/0 /0	0/0 /0	0/0 /0
Low	0/0 /0	0/0 /0	0/0 /0

Overall Evaluation
Against Right-Handed Pitchers

Overall Fastball

Overall Curve — Not enough information

Overall Slider — Not enough information

Against Left-Handed Pitchers

Overall Fastball

Overall Curve

Overall Slider — Not enough information

Comments: Excellent medium-outside fastball hitter vs. LH.

Strength: Medium-inside and medium-outside fastballs vs. RH; medium-outside, low-middle and low-outside fastballs vs. LH.

Weaknesses: Outside curves and sliders vs. RH.

Cleveland Indians

Aguayo, Luis
Allanson, Andy
Brookens, Tom
Browne, Jerry
Hernandez, Keith
Jacoby, Brook
James, Chris
James, Dion
Komminsk, Brad
Maldonado, Candy
Skinner, Joel
Snyder, Cory
Webster, Mitch

Cleveland Indians
BARS System
Hitting Analysis

Luis Aguayo (Right Handed) — *Cleveland Indians*

Luis Aguayo Against Right-Handed Pitchers
Overall BARS Batting Average .201

Fastball Average .223

	Inside	Middle	Outside
High	9/ 444 /4	9/ 222 /2	4/ 0 /0
Med	13/ 307 /4	4/ 0 /0	28/ 321 /9
Low	6/ 166 /1	9/ 111 /1	12/ 0 /0

Curve Average .111

	Inside	Middle	Outside
High	1/ 0 /0	1/ 0 /0	0/ 0 /0
Med	1/ 0 /0	1/ 0 /0	5/ 0 /0
Low	1/ 0 /0	2/ 500 /1	6/ 166 /1

Slider Average .176

	Inside	Middle	Outside
High	0/ 0 /0	3/ 333 /1	0/ 0 /0
Med	0/ 0 /0	0/ 0 /0	5/ 200 /1
Low	1/ 0 /0	1/ 1000 /1	7/ 0 /0

Luis Aguayo Against Left-Handed Pitchers
Overall BARS Batting Average .225

Fastball Average .280

	Inside	Middle	Outside
High	5/ 0 /0	4/ 750 /3	2/ 500 /1
Med	2/ 500 /1	1/ 0 /0	17/ 235 /4
Low	4/ 0 /0	12/ 416 /5	3/ 0 /0

Curve Average .000

	Inside	Middle	Outside
High	0/ 0 /0	0/ 0 /0	0/ 0 /0
Med	1/ 0 /0	2/ 0 /0	1/ 0 /0
Low	1/ 0 /0	0/ 0 /0	1/ 0 /0

Slider Average .000

	Inside	Middle	Outside
High	0/ 0 /0	0/ 0 /0	0/ 0 /0
Med	0/ 0 /0	1/ 0 /0	1/ 0 /0
Low	3/ 0 /0	0/ 0 /0	1/ 0 /0

Right-handed hitter Luis Aguayo has a low overall fastball average against right-handed pitchers (.223) but an adequate .280 overall fastball average against left-handed pitchers.

Against right-handers he hits well against waist-high fastballs and high-inside fastballs but he has a terrible time with all low fastballs (.166, .111, and .000 on 0 for 12, inside to outside). These locations bring his average down significantly. If right-handers pitch Aguayo fastballs low, they'll have an edge.

Aguayo hits medium-high outside fastballs for a solid .321 average against right-handers. He hits this pitch deep down the left line, medium-deep to straightaway center and short to straightaway right.

MEDIUM-HIGH OUTSIDE FASTBALLS

BATTING AVERAGE .321
Play

Left	Deep and shifted toward the left field line
Center	Medium-deep in straightaway center field
Right	Short in straightaway right field
Short	Normal position
Second	Normal position

He hits medium-high inside fastballs for a .307 average against right-handers.

MEDIUM-HIGH INSIDE FASTBALLS

BATTING AVERAGE .307
Play

Left	Deep in straightaway left field
Center	*No instances recorded*
Right	Short in straightaway right field
Short	Shifted toward third base
Second	Shifted toward first base

He hits high-inside fastballs for an excellent .444 average. Notice that he hits this pitch medium-deep to all fields (and probably sharply, judging by his high average). By playing him as suggested by the BARS fielding strategy for this pitch, fielders could prevent most of his hits from this location.

HIGH-INSIDE FASTBALLS

BATTING AVERAGE .444
Play

Left	Medium-deep and shifted toward center field
Center	Medium-deep in straightaway center field
Right	Medium-deep and shifted toward the right line
Short	Shifted toward third base
Second	Normal position

Checking out a few of Aguayo's other locations, he hits .222 against high-over-the-middle fastballs.

HIGH-OVER-THE-MIDDLE FASTBALLS

BATTING AVERAGE .222
Play

Left	Medium-deep in straightaway left field
Center	Medium-deep in straightaway center field
Right	Deep and shifted toward the right field line
Short	*No instances recorded*
Second	Shifted toward first base

He has trouble getting the ball out of the infield when thrown low-outside fastballs.

LOW-OUTSIDE FASTBALLS

BATTING AVERAGE .000
Play

Left	*No instances recorded*
Center	Deep in straightaway center field
Right	*No instances recorded*
Short	Normal position
Second	Normal position

Aguayo has trouble with outside curves and sliders. His low-outside location is especially weak in each of these pitching charts (.166 low-outside curves, .000 on 0 for 7 low-outside sliders).

Aguayo Against Left-Handed Pitchers

Aguayo's fastball chart against left-handed pitchers is unusual in that he has a fairly good .280 overall fastball average but a very low .235 average in his highly pitched medium-high outside fastball location. This location usually is predominant in determining the overall average.

Aguayo's low-over-the-middle location (.416) bolsters his fastball average.

LOW-OVER-THE-MIDDLE FASTBALLS (THROWN BY LEFT-HANDED PITCHERS)

BATTING AVERAGE .416
Play

Left	*No instances recorded*
Center	Short in straightaway center field
Right	Deep in straightaway right field
Short	Normal position
Second	*No instances recorded*

He hits medium-high outside fastballs straightaway to all fields against left-handers. His low average in this location probably means that his hit balls are going for easy outs.

MEDIUM-HIGH OUTSIDE FASTBALLS (THROWN BY LEFT-HANDED PITCHERS)

BATTING AVERAGE .235
Play

Left	Medium-deep in straightaway left field
Center	Medium-deep in straightaway center field
Right	Deep in straightaway right field
Short	Shifted toward third base
Second	*No instances recorded*

Ahead And Behind In The Count Vs. RH

Ahead

Fastball Average .250

	Inside	Middle	Outside
High	500 4/2	250 4/1	0 2/0
Med	250 4/1	0 2/0	333 12/4
Low	1000 1/1	0 3/0	0 4/0

Curve Average .000

	Inside	Middle	Outside
High	0 0/0	0 0/0	0 0/0
Med	0 1/0	0 0/0	0 0/0
Low	0 0/0	0 0/0	0 0/0

Behind

Fastball Average .176

	Inside	Middle	Outside
High	0 0/0	1 0/0	0 0/0
Med	1 0/0	0 0/0	375 8/3
Low	2 0/0	3 0/0	2 0/0

Curve Average .000

	Inside	Middle	Outside
High	0 0/0	0 0/0	0 0/0
Med	0 0/0	1 0/0	1 0/0
Low	0 0/0	0 0/0	1 0/0

Overall Evaluation

Against Right-Handed Pitchers

Overall Fastball	⚾⚾
Overall Curve	⚾⚾
Overall Slider	⚾⚾

Against Left-Handed Pitchers

Overall Fastball	⚾⚾ ⚾⚾
Overall Curve	Not enough information
Overall Slider	Not enough information

Comments: Weak against low fastballs vs. RH.
Strengths: Medium-inside, medium-outside and high-inside fastballs vs. RH; low-middle fastballs vs. LH.
Weaknesses: Low fastballs, high-middle fastballs, outside curves and outside sliders vs. RH; medium-outside fastballs vs. LH.

Andy Allanson (Right Handed)   *Cleveland Indians*

Andy Allanson Against Right-Handed Pitchers
Overall BARS Batting Average .200

Fastball Average .205

	Inside	Middle	Outside
High	16/375/6	8/125/1	3/333/1
Med	12/166/2	8/500/4	40/150/6
Low	5/200/1	12/83/1	8/125/1

Curve Average .227

	Inside	Middle	Outside
High	3/666/2	2/500/1	1/0/0
Med	0/0/0	1/1000/1	6/166/1
Low	1/0/0	1/0/0	7/0/0

Slider Average .142

	Inside	Middle	Outside
High	0/0/0	1/0/0	0/0/0
Med	0/0/0	1/0/0	4/0/0
Low	0/0/0	4/250/1	11/181/2

Andy Allanson Against Left-Handed Pitchers
Overall BARS Batting Average .261

Fastball Average .272

	Inside	Middle	Outside
High	2/1000/2	3/333/1	2/500/1
Med	3/333/1	2/0/0	9/222/2
Low	3/333/1	5/200/1	4/0/0

Curve Average .250

	Inside	Middle	Outside
High	0/0/0	0/0/0	0/0/0
Med	0/0/0	0/0/0	2/500/1
Low	0/0/0	1/0/0	0/0/0

Slider Average .200

	Inside	Middle	Outside
High	0/0/0	0/0/0	0/0/0
Med	0/0/0	0/0/0	1/1000/1
Low	0/0/0	1/0/0	3/0/0

Right-handed hitter Andy Allanson has a lot of trouble with fastballs and curves against right-handed pitchers (.205 and .227, respectively). He is strong against high-inside fastballs (.375). He hits this pitch medium-deep to all fields. Even though his average is high in this location, if fielders played him as suggested by the BARS fielding strategy (see the chart below and the field diagram on the opposite page), they could prevent most of his base hits from this location.

HIGH-INSIDE FASTBALLS

BATTING AVERAGE .375

Play

Left	Medium-deep in straightaway left field
Center	Medium-deep in straightaway center field
Right	Medium-deep in straightaway right field
Short	Normal position
Second	Normal position

Note the weak .150 average in his medium-high-outside fastball location. He hits this ball straightaway to all fields. His low average in this location indicates that most of his hit balls are probably easy flies or grounders.

MEDIUM-HIGH OUTSIDE FASTBALLS

BATTING AVERAGE .150

Play

Left	Medium-deep in straightaway left field
Center	Deep in straightaway center field
Right	Deep in straightaway right field
Short	Normal position
Second	Shifted toward first base

He hits only .166 against medium-high inside fastballs. His .083 against low-over-the-middle fastballs is indicative of his weakness against all low fastballs. He pulls this pitch deep to all fields but his low average means fielders are having little trouble getting to the ball for the out.

LOW-OVER-THE-MIDDLE FASTBALLS

BATTING AVERAGE .083

Play

Left	Deep and shifted toward the left field line
Center	Deep and shifted toward left field
Right	Deep and shifted toward center field
Short	Normal position
Second	Normal position

Allanson has trouble with low-outside curves and low-outside sliders (.000 and .181, respectively). He hits both these pitches to his opposite field, but he's obviously not hitting them hard enough to cause problems.

Allanson hits .272 overall against fastballs thrown by left-handed pitchers. His strength is spread across his locations, but he hits only .222 in his medium-high outside fastball location.

High-Inside Fastballs
(Thrown By Right-Handed Pitchers)

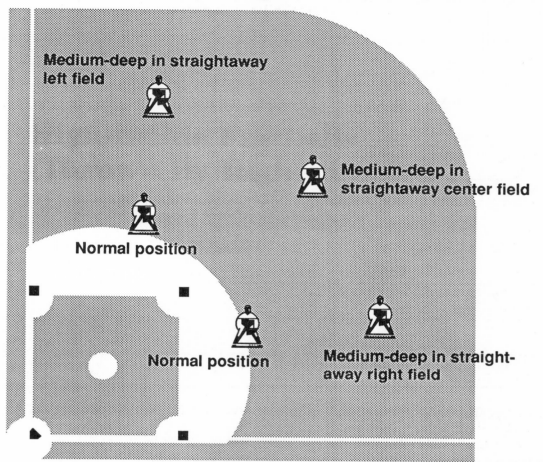

Ahead And Behind In The Count Vs. RH

Ahead

	Fastball Average .290			Curve Average .200		
	Inside	Middle	Outside	Inside	Middle	Outside
High	12/416 /5	4/250 /1	1/1000 /1	0/0 /0	1/1000 /1	0/0 /0
Med	8/250 /2	3/333 /1	19/263 /5	0/0 /0	0/0 /0	3/0 /0
Low	0/0 /0	6/0 /0	2/500 /1	0/0 /0	0/0 /0	1/0 /0

Behind

	Fastball Average .095			Curve Average .200		
	Inside	Middle	Outside	Inside	Middle	Outside
High	1/1000 /1	1/0 /0	1/0 /0	2/500 /1	1/0 /0	1/0 /0
Med	3/0 /0	2/500 /1	7/0 /0	0/0 /0	0/0 /0	2/500 /1
Low	2/0 /0	2/0 /0	2/0 /0	0/0 /0	1/0 /0	3/0 /0

Overall Evaluation

Against Right-Handed Pitchers

Overall Fastball

Overall Curve ⚾

Overall Slider ⚾

Against Left-Handed Pitchers

Overall Fastball ⚾

Overall Curve — Not enough information

Overall Slider — Not enough information

Comments: RH should avoid throwing Allanson high-inside fastballs.

Strengths: High-inside and medium-middle fastballs vs. RH.

Weaknesses: Low fastballs, medium-inside, medium-outside and high-middle fastballs, low and outside curves and sliders vs. RH; medium-outside fastballs vs. LH.

Tom Brookens (Right Handed) — *Cleveland Indians*

Tom Brookens Against Right-Handed Pitchers
Overall BARS Batting Average .246

Fastball Average .229

	Inside	Middle	Outside
High	13/ 230/3	32/ 187/6	17/ 58/1
Med	31/ 258/8	20/ 400/8	77/ 272/21
Low	16/ 312/5	28/ 178/5	27/ 111/3

Curve Average .289

	Inside	Middle	Outside
High	5/ 0/0	8/ 250/2	3/ 0/0
Med	7/ 714/5	8/ 500/4	22/ 136/3
Low	5/ 600/3	12/ 416/5	13/ 153/2

Slider Average .256

	Inside	Middle	Outside
High	0/ 0/0	3/ 0/0	4/ 750/3
Med	4/ 500/2	3/ 666/2	18/ 166/3
Low	1/ 0/0	14/ 357/5	27/ 148/4

Tom Brookens Against Left-Handed Pitchers
Overall BARS Batting Average .335

Fastball Average .346

	Inside	Middle	Outside
High	7/ 0/0	13/ 615/8	20/ 350/7
Med	17/ 294/5	14/ 428/6	62/ 338/21
Low	15/ 266/4	30/ 400/12	21/ 285/6

Curve Average .319

	Inside	Middle	Outside
High	1/ 0/0	1/ 0/0	2/ 500/1
Med	1/ 0/0	3/ 0/0	9/ 333/3
Low	13/ 307/4	10/ 400/4	7/ 428/3

Slider Average .272

	Inside	Middle	Outside
High	0/ 0/0	0/ 0/0	1/ 0/0
Med	4/ 500/2	0/ 0/0	2/ 500/1
Low	7/ 142/1	5/ 200/1	3/ 333/1

Right-handed hitting Tom Brookens has a low overall fastball average against right-handed pitchers (.229). He hits curves fairly well against right-handers (.289) but has trouble with sliders (.256).

Against left-handed pitchers, he hits fastballs and curves excellently (.346 fastballs, .319 curves). His slider average against left-handers (.272) is adequate.

Starting with his performance against right-handed pitchers, note his weaknesses against high fastballs (.230, .187 and .058 from inside to outside). He also has trouble with low-outside (.111) and low-over-the-middle fastballs (.178).

He hits medium-high outside fastballs at .272. He hits this pitch deep to all fields.

MEDIUM-HIGH OUTSIDE FASTBALLS

BATTING AVERAGE .272
Play

Left	Deep and shifted toward center field
Center	Deep in straightaway center field
Right	Deep in straightaway right field
Short	Up middle (shifted toward second base)
Second	Shifted toward first base

He pulls the ball down the left line when thrown medium-high inside fastballs (.258).

MEDIUM-HIGH INSIDE FASTBALLS

BATTING AVERAGE .258
Play

Left	Deep and shifted toward the left field line
Center	Medium-deep in straightaway center field
Right	Medium-deep in straightaway right field
Short	Normal position
Second	Normal position

He pulls low-inside fastballs to the outfield. But note that the second baseman must play shifted toward first base.

LOW-INSIDE FASTBALLS

BATTING AVERAGE .312
Play

Left	Deep and shifted toward the left field line
Center	Deep and shifted toward left field
Right	Deep and shifted toward center field
Short	Normal position
Second	Shifted toward first base

Brookens Against Curves And Sliders

Brookens has trouble with medium-high outside and low-outside curves and sliders against right-handed pitchers. But he hits low-over-the-middle curves and sliders excellently.

LOW-OVER-THE-MIDDLE CURVEBALLS

BATTING AVERAGE .416
Play

Left	Deep in straightaway left field
Center	Short in straightaway center field
Right	Deep in straightaway right field
Short	Shifted toward third base
Second	*No instances recorded*

LOW-OVER-THE-MIDDLE SLIDERS

BATTING AVERAGE .357
Play

Left	Medium-deep and shifted toward the left field line
Center	Medium-deep in straightaway center field
Right	Deep and shifted toward the right field line
Short	Shifted toward third base
Second	Normal position

Brookens Against Left-Handed Pitchers

Brookens hits fastballs extremely well overall against left-handers. Notice his strength in all outside and over-the-middle locations. He hits medium-high outside fastballs much better against left-handers when ahead in the count.

MEDIUM-HIGH OUTSIDE FASTBALLS (THROWN BY LEFT-HANDED PITCHERS WHEN BROOKENS IS AHEAD IN THE COUNT)

BATTING AVERAGE .416
Play

Left	Deep in straightaway left field
Center	Medium-deep and shifted toward left field

Right	Medium-deep and shifted toward the right line
Short	Normal position
Second	Shifted toward first base

MEDIUM-HIGH OUTSIDE FASTBALLS (THROWN BY LEFT-HANDED PITCHERS WHEN BROOKENS IS BEHIND IN THE COUNT)

BATTING AVERAGE .166
Play

Left	Deep and shifted toward the left field line
Center	Deep in straightaway center field
Right	Medium-deep in straightaway right field
Short	Normal position
Second	Normal position

His .400 in the low-over-the-middle location against left-handers is top rate. If fielders aligned themselves as suggested by the BARS fielding strategy for this location, they would undoubtedly be able to prevent most of his line-drive hits and extra-base hits.

LOW-OVER-THE-MIDDLE FASTBALLS (THROWN BY LEFT-HANDED PITCHERS)

BATTING AVERAGE .400
Play

Left	Medium-deep and shifted toward the left field line
Center	Medium-deep in straightaway center field
Right	Short and shifted toward the right field line
Short	Normal position
Second	*No instances recorded*

Brookens hits low curves excellently against left-handers (.307, .400 and .428 from inside to outside).

Ahead And Behind In The Count Vs. RH

Ahead

Fastball Average .263

	Inside	Middle	Outside
High	4/500 /2	11/363 /4	3/0 /0
Med	15/266 /4	10/500 /5	41/243 /10
Low	7/285 /2	12/166 /2	11/90 /1

Curve Average .333

	Inside	Middle	Outside
High	2/0 /0	1/0 /0	0/0 /0
Med	1/1000 /1	3/666 /2	4/0 /0
Low	1/1000 /1	0/0 /0	0/0 /0

Behind

Fastball Average .266

	Inside	Middle	Outside
High	3/333 /1	5/200 /1	4/250 /1
Med	7/142 /1	4/500 /2	11/363 /4
Low	2/500 /1	3/0 /0	6/166 /1

Curve Average .307

	Inside	Middle	Outside
High	0/0 /0	3/333 /1	2/0 /0
Med	2/500 /1	4/250 /1	7/142 /1
Low	1/1000 /1	5/400 /2	2/500 /1

Overall Evaluation

Against Right-Handed Pitchers

Overall Fastball	⚾⚾
Overall Curve	⚾⚾ ⚾⚾ ⚾⚾
Overall Slider	⚾⚾ ⚾⚾

Against Left-Handed Pitchers

Overall Fastball	⚾⚾ ⚾⚾ ⚾⚾ ⚾⚾
Overall Curve	⚾⚾ ⚾⚾ ⚾⚾ ⚾⚾
Overall Slider	⚾⚾ ⚾⚾

Comments: Weak against high fastballs vs. RH.
Strengths: Medium-middle and low-inside fastballs, low-middle medium-middle and medium-inside curves, low-middle sliders vs. RH; all fastballs except high-inside and low-inside, low curves, medium-outside curves vs. LH.
Weaknesses: All high and all outside fastballs, low-middle and medium-inside fastballs, outside curves, low-outside and medium-outside sliders vs. RH.

Jerry Browne (Switch Hitter)　　　*Cleveland Indians*

Jerry Browne Against Right-Handed Pitchers
Overall BARS Batting Average .280

	Fastball Average .289			Curve Average .235			Slider Average .266		
	Outside	Middle	Inside	Outside	Middle	Inside	Outside	Middle	Inside
High	16/187 /3	9/222 /2	10/200 /2	3/333 /1	0/0 /0	0/0 /0	0/0 /0	0/0 /0	2/0 /0
Med	62/322 /20	8/375 /3	19/263 /5	9/0 /0	2/500 /1	4/500 /2	2/0 /0	0/0 /0	3/0 /0
Low	17/176 /3	14/500 /7	14/285 /4	3/0 /0	8/125 /1	5/600 /3	0/0 /0	3/666 /2	5/400 /2

Jerry Browne Against Left-Handed Pitchers
Overall BARS Batting Average .371

	Fastball Average .333			Curve Average .500			Slider Average .500		
	Inside	Middle	Outside	Inside	Middle	Outside	Inside	Middle	Outside
High	4/0 /0	4/0 /0	4/500 /2	0/0 /0	2/1000 /2	0/0 /0	0/0 /0	1/1000 /1	0/0 /0
Med	4/250 /1	1/1000 /1	37/378 /14	0/0 /0	1/0 /0	2/0 /0	2/0 /0	0/0 /0	1/1000 /1
Low	3/0 /0	3/666 /2	0/0 /0	1/0 /0	3/666 /2	1/1000 /1	1/1000 /1	3/333 /1	0/0 /0

Switch-hitting Jerry Browne hits fastballs fairly well against right-handed pitchers (.289 overall) and excellently against left-handed pitchers (.333 overall). He has problems with curves against right-handers (.235 overall).

Starting with right-handers, notice the solid strength in his medium-high outside fastball location (.322). His Ahead and Behind charts show that he hits this pitch considerably better when ahead in the count (.352 when ahead, .222 when behind). The following charts show how fielders need to play for this pitch as the count changes.

MEDIUM-HIGH OUTSIDE FASTBALLS (WHEN AHEAD IN THE COUNT)

BATTING AVERAGE .352
Play
Left   Deep and shifted toward the left field line
Center   Medium-deep in straightaway center field
Right   *No instances recorded*
Short   Shifted toward third base
Second   Shifted toward first base

MEDIUM-HIGH OUTSIDE FASTBALLS (WHEN BEHIND IN THE COUNT)

BATTING AVERAGE .222

Play
Left   Deep and shifted toward the left field line
Center   Deep in straightaway center field
Right   Medium-deep and shifted toward center field
Short   Up middle (shifted toward second base)
Second   Normal position

He has trouble with high-outside and low-outside fastballs (.187 and .176). In fact he has trouble with all high fastballs thrown by right-handers (.187, .222, and .200, outside to inside).

He hits high-outside fastballs deep to left down the line and deep into the left-center alley. Most of these hits balls are probably easy outs, as indicated by his low average in this location.

HIGH-OUTSIDE FASTBALLS

BATTING AVERAGE .187
Play
Left   Deep and shifted toward the left field line
Center   Deep and shifted toward left field
Right   *No instances recorded*
Short   Normal position
Second   Normal position

His .263 against medium-high inside fastballs is not quite adequate. He hits this pitch deep to left and center and medium-deep down the right line. Note that the infielders need to play toward the right side.

MEDIUM-HIGH INSIDE FASTBALLS

BATTING AVERAGE .263
Play

Left	Deep in straightaway left field
Center	Deep and shifted toward right field
Right	Medium-deep and shifted toward the right line
Short	Up middle (shifted toward second base)
Second	Shifted toward first base

He hits a solid .500 against low-over-the-middle fastballs. He hits this pitch down the left line, but note that the infielders need to play shifted toward the right side.

LOW-OVER-THE-MIDDLE FASTBALLS

BATTING AVERAGE .500
Play

Left	Medium-deep and shifted toward the left field line
Center	Deep in straightaway center field
Right	*No instances recorded*
Short	Up middle (shifted toward second base)
Second	Shifted toward first base

His .285 against low-inside fastballs is fair.

LOW-INSIDE FASTBALLS

BATTING AVERAGE .285
Play

Left	Medium-deep and shifted toward center field
Center	Deep in straightaway center field
Right	Medium-deep and shifted toward center field
Short	Up middle (shifted toward second base)
Second	*No instances recorded*

Browne has an L-shaped weak sector against curves thrown by right-handers: medium-high outside (.000)/low-outside (.000)/low-over-the-middle (.125).

Browne Against Left-Handed Pitchers

Against left-handed pitchers he hits medium-high outside fastballs extremely well (.378) This bolsters his entire average against left-handers because so many pitches are thrown to him in this location.

MEDIUM-HIGH OUTSIDE FASTBALLS (THROWN BY LEFT-HANDED PITCHERS)

BATTING AVERAGE .378
Play

Left	Medium-deep in straightaway left field
Center	Medium-deep in straightaway center field
Right	Deep in straightaway right field
Short	Up middle (shifted toward second base)
Second	Normal position

Ahead And Behind In The Count Vs. RH

Ahead

Fastball Average .333   Curve Average .142

	Outside	Middle	Inside	Outside	Middle	Inside
High	3/ 333 /1	4/ 500 /2	4/ 0 /0	0/ 0 /0	0/ 0 /0	0/ 0 /0
Med	17/ 352 /6	4/ 250 /1	12/ 250 /3	3/ 0 /0	0/ 0 /0	0/ 0 /0
Low	3/ 666 /2	4/ 500 /2	3/ 333 /1	1/ 0 /0	2/ 0 /0	1/ 1000 /1

Behind

Fastball Average .317   Curve Average .600

	Outside	Middle	Inside	Outside	Middle	Inside
High	5/ 400 /2	2/ 0 /0	1/ 1000 /1	0/ 0 /0	0/ 0 /0	0/ 0 /0
Med	18/ 222 /4	2/ 500 /1	4/ 250 /1	1/ 0 /0	0/ 0 /0	1/ 1000 /1
Low	1/ 0 /0	5/ 800 /4	3/ 0 /0	0/ 0 /0	2/ 500 /1	1/ 1000 /1

Overall Evaluation
Against Right-Handed Pitchers

Overall Fastball	
Overall Curve	
Overall Slider	

Against Left-Handed Pitchers

Overall Fastball	🎾🎾🎾🎾
Overall Curve	Not enough information
Overall Slider	Not enough information

Comments: Weak against high fastballs vs. RH.
Strengths: Medium-outside, medium-middle and low-middle fastballs, inside curves vs. RH; medium-outside fastballs vs. LH.
Weaknesses: High fastballs, low-outside fastballs, medium-outside and low-middle curves vs. RH; inside fastballs vs. LH.

Keith Hernandez Against Right-Handed Pitchers
Overall BARS Batting Average .307

Fastball Average .332

	Outside	Middle	Inside
High	31/ 290 /9	55/ 345 /19	32/ 343 /11
Med	88/ 329 /29	33/ 272 /9	70/ 371 /26
Low	34/ 205 /7	87/ 379 /33	60/ 333 /20

Curve Average .261

	Outside	Middle	Inside
High	3/ 333 /1	15/ 200 /3	5/ 400 /2
Med	12/ 333 /4	4/ 0 /0	3/ 666 /2
Low	15/ 133 /2	15/ 400 /6	16/ 187 /3

Slider Average .163

	Outside	Middle	Inside
High	1/ 0 /0	5/ 0 /0	2/ 0 /0
Med	4/ 500 /2	3/ 0 /0	11/ 181 /2
Low	7/ 0 /0	7/ 428 /3	21/ 142 /3

Keith Hernandez Against Left-Handed Pitchers
Overall BARS Batting Average .285

Fastball Average .305

	Outside	Middle	Inside
High	6/ 0 /0	30/ 266 /8	19/ 315 /6
Med	27/ 296 /8	8/ 625 /5	61/ 377 /23
Low	11/ 272 /3	32/ 406 /13	42/ 142 /6

Curve Average .257

	Outside	Middle	Inside
High	1/ 1000 /1	4/ 250 /1	4/ 0 /0
Med	11/ 272 /3	3/ 666 /2	8/ 250 /2
Low	18/ 222 /4	15/ 200 /3	2/ 500 /1

Slider Average .210

	Outside	Middle	Inside
High	1/ 1000 /1	2/ 0 /0	0/ 0 /0
Med	5/ 200 /1	2/ 0 /0	2/ 500 /1
Low	16/ 187 /3	7/ 142 /1	3/ 333 /1

Left-handed hitting Keith Hernandez has an excellent BARS fastball average against right-handed pitchers (.332 overall). Against right-handers, he has only one weak fastball location (low outside, .205), although his medium-over-the-middle fastball average of .272 is only barely adequate.

He hits medium-high outside fastballs for a strong .329 average. He hits this pitch straightaway to the outfield while pulling it to the right side of the infield.

MEDIUM-HIGH OUTSIDE FASTBALLS

BATTING AVERAGE .329
Play

Left	Deep in straightaway left field
Center	Deep in straightaway center field
Right	Medium-deep in straightaway right field
Short	Up middle (shifted toward second base)
Second	Shifted toward first base

Hernandez hits medium-high inside fastballs for a sparkling .371 average, but his Ahead and Behind charts on the opposite page show that he hits medium-high inside fastballs very poorly when behind in the count (.100) and extremely well when ahead in the count (.575). He pulls this pitch sharply when ahead. The following charts show how vital it can be for fielders to adjust when the count on a batter changes.

MEDIUM-HIGH INSIDE FASTBALLS (WHEN AHEAD IN THE COUNT)

BATTING AVERAGE .575
Play

Left	Deep and shifted toward center field
Center	Deep in straightaway center field
Right	Deep and shifted toward the right field line
Short	Up middle (shifted toward second base)
Second	Shifted toward first base

MEDIUM-HIGH INSIDE FASTBALLS (WHEN BEHIND IN THE COUNT)

BATTING AVERAGE .100
Play

Left	Medium-deep in straightaway left field
Center	Deep and shifted toward left field
Right	Medium-deep in straightaway right field
Short	Normal position
Second	Normal position

Hernandez Against Curves And Sliders

Hernandez hits low-outside curves poorly against right-handers (.133), but he hits medium-high outside (.333) and low-over-the-middle curves (.400) very well.

He goes to his opposite field (left field) with low-over-the-middle curves. Note, however, that the shortstop needs to play shifted toward second base.

LOW-OVER-THE-MIDDLE CURVEBALLS

BATTING AVERAGE .400
Play
Left   Deep and shifted toward the left field line
Center Deep and shifted toward left field
Right   Deep and shifted toward center field
Short   Up middle (shifted toward second base)
Second Normal position

He has a lot of trouble with inside sliders thrown by right-handers. His .181 against medium-high inside sliders and .142 against low-inside sliders give a target for right-handers.

Hernandez Against Left-Handed Pitchers

Hernandez's BARS charts show that left-handed pitchers throw him more inside than outside fastballs. This is good strategy if pitchers keep the ball low (.142 against low-inside fastballs vs. left-handers); but it could be a mistake if they let the ball get up to the medium-high inside (.377) or high-inside (.315) fastball locations.

Hernandez hits medium-high inside fastballs in such a unique way against left-handers that fielders need to pay careful attention to the following BARS fielding strategy for this pitch.

MEDIUM-HIGH INSIDE FASTBALLS (THROWN BY LEFT-HANDED PITCHERS)

BATTING AVERAGE .377
Play
Left   Medium-deep and shifted toward center field
Center Short in straightaway center field
Right   Deep and shifted toward the right field line
Short   Up middle (shifted toward second base)
Second Shifted toward first base

His .406 against low-over-the-middle fastballs thrown by left-handers is also excellent.

LOW-OVER-THE-MIDDLE FASTBALLS (THROWN BY LEFT-HANDED PITCHERS)

BATTING AVERAGE .406
Play
Left   Deep and shifted toward the left field line
Center Deep and shifted toward right field
Right   Deep in straightaway right field
Short   Up middle (shifted toward second base)
Second Shifted toward first base

He has trouble with low-outside and low-over-the-middle curves against left-handers (.222 and .200 respectively). He also has trouble with sliders in these two locations against left-handers (.187 and .142 respectively).

Ahead And Behind In The Count Vs. RH

Ahead

	Fastball Average .396			Curve Average .454		
	Outside	Middle	Inside	Outside	Middle	Inside
High	10/200 /2	29/448 /13	12/583 /7	0/0 /0	6/500 /3	0/0 /0
Med	39/410 /16	18/277 /5	33/575 /19	0/0 /0	0/0 /0	0/0 /0
Low	12/250 /3	57/368 /21	32/312 /10	1/1000 /1	3/333 /1	1/0 /0

Behind

	Fastball Average .296			Curve Average .360		
	Outside	Middle	Inside	Outside	Middle	Inside
High	4/750 /3	6/166 /1	12/250 /3	0/0 /0	4/0 /0	2/500 /1
Med	21/380 /8	6/166 /1	10/100 /1	4/500 /2	2/0 /0	2/1000 /2
Low	4/500 /2	9/222 /2	9/333 /3	5/200 /1	4/500 /2	2/500 /1

Overall Evaluation
Against Right-Handed Pitchers

Overall Fastball ⚾⚾ ⚾⚾ ⚾⚾
Overall Curve   ⚾ ⚾
Overall Slider   ⚾

Against Left-Handed Pitchers

Overall Fastball ⚾ ⚾ ⚾
Overall Curve   ⚾ ⚾
Overall Slider   ⚾

Comments: Hits significantly better when ahead in the count against RH.
Strengths: All fastballs vs. RH (except low-outside), medium-outside and low-middle curves, low-middle sliders vs. RH; high-inside, medium-inside, medium-middle and low-middle fastballs vs. LH.
Weaknesses: Low-outside fastballs, low-outside, low-inside and high-middle curves, inside sliders vs. RH; low-inside fastballs, outside sliders vs. LH.

91

Brook Jacoby (Right Handed)   *Cleveland Indians*

Brook Jacoby Against Right-Handed Pitchers
Overall BARS Batting Average .329

Fastball Average .342	Inside	Middle	Outside
High	23/304 /7	26/115 /3	14/214 /3
Med	52/288 /15	28/464 /13	89/337 /30
Low	19/210 /4	46/478 /22	36/194 /7

Curve Average .262	Inside	Middle	Outside
High	0/0 /0	3/333 /1	2/0 /0
Med	3/0 /0	3/333 /1	31/387 /12
Low	5/400 /2	9/444 /4	24/41 /1

Slider Average .345	Inside	Middle	Outside
High	0/0 /0	5/600 /3	3/0 /0
Med	2/500 /1	7/857 /6	16/312 /5
Low	2/0 /0	7/285 /2	13/153 /2

Brook Jacoby Against Left-Handed Pitchers
Overall BARS Batting Average .294

Fastball Average .270	Inside	Middle	Outside
High	7/571 /4	11/454 /5	7/285 /2
Med	13/76 /1	12/166 /2	46/217 /10
Low	7/285 /2	13/384 /5	17/294 /5

Curve Average .409	Inside	Middle	Outside
High	0/0 /0	0/0 /0	0/0 /0
Med	3/333 /1	1/1000 /1	4/500 /2
Low	3/333 /1	7/428 /3	4/250 /1

Slider Average .333	Inside	Middle	Outside
High	0/0 /0	0/0 /0	0/0 /0
Med	2/0 /0	0/0 /0	2/500 /1
Low	4/250 /1	4/500 /2	3/333 /1

Right-handed hitting Brook Jacoby has a higher overall average against right-handed than against left-handed pitchers (.329 vs. 294). His overall fastball average is 72 points higher against right-handers.

Against right-handers, Jacoby has an excellent .337 average in his medium-high outside fastball location. He hits this pitch deep and straightaway to all fields.

MEDIUM-HIGH OUTSIDE FASTBALLS

BATTING AVERAGE .337
Play
Left — Deep in straightaway left field
Center — Deep in straightaway center field
Right — Deep in straightaway right field
Short — Normal position
Second — Normal position

He hits low-over-the-middle fastballs at a .478 clip against right-handers. He hits this pitch medium-deep to all fields. By playing him medium-deep, fielders could take away most of his base hits from this location.

LOW-OVER-THE-MIDDLE FASTBALLS

BATTING AVERAGE .478
Play
Left — Medium-deep in straightaway left field
Center — Medium-deep in straightaway center field

Right — Medium-deep in straightaway right field
Short — Normal position
Second — Normal position

He has trouble with low-outside fastballs (.194). He hits this pitch to right field.

LOW-OUTSIDE FASTBALLS

BATTING AVERAGE .194
Play
Left — *No instances recorded*
Center — Deep and shifted toward right field
Right — Deep and shifted toward the right field line
Short — Normal position
Second — Normal position

One of Jacoby's weakest fastball sectors consists of his high-over-the-middle/high-outside locations. By focussing on this area pitchers could gain an advantage.

HIGH-OVER-THE-MIDDLE FASTBALLS

BATTING AVERAGE .115
Play
Left — Deep and shifted toward the left field line
Center — Deep in straightaway center field
Right — Medium-deep in straightaway right field
Short — Normal position
Second — Normal position

92

HIGH-OUTSIDE FASTBALLS

BATTING AVERAGE .214

Play

Left	Deep and shifted toward center field
Center	Deep and shifted toward right field
Right	Deep in straightaway right field
Short	*No instances recorded*
Second	*No instances recorded*

He hits high-inside fastballs medium-deep down both lines for a good .304 average. There are exceptions, but more often than not Jacoby has a higher average for the locations in which he tends to hit the ball medium-deep. This indicates he hits the ball hard in these locations and fielders need to be positioned correctly or the ball will fall in for base hits.

HIGH-INSIDE FASTBALLS

BATTING AVERAGE .304

Play

Left	Medium-deep and shifted toward the left field line
Center	Deep and shifted toward center field
Right	Medium-deep and shifted toward the right line
Short	Shifted toward third base
Second	*No instances recorded*

Jacoby Against Curves And Sliders

Jacoby hits medium-high outside curves and sliders well, while hitting low-outside curves and sliders poorly. He hits a strong .387 against medium-high outside curves against right-handed pitchers. Notice that he hits this pitch medium-deep to center and right.

MEDIUM-HIGH OUTSIDE CURVEBALLS

BATTING AVERAGE .387

Play

Left	Deep in straightaway left field
Center	Medium-deep and shifted toward right field
Right	Medium-deep in straightaway right field
Short	Normal position
Second	*No instances recorded*

Jacoby Against Left-Handed Pitchers

Jacoby has a .294 overall average against left-handers. He hits fastballs at .270 overall, with a weak .217 average in his medium-high outside fastball location. In the fielding strategy shown below for this pitch, notice that he hits it deep to the outfield and down both lines.

MEDIUM-HIGH OUTSIDE FASTBALLS (THROWN BY LEFT-HANDED PITCHERS)

BATTING AVERAGE .217

Play

Left	Deep and shifted toward the left field line
Center	Deep in straightaway center field
Right	Deep and shifted toward the right field line
Short	Shifted toward third base
Second	Shifted toward first base

He hits low-over-the-middle fastballs well against left-handers, as he does against right-handers. He hits this pitch medium-deep to left and center for a .384 average. His .454 against high-over-the-middle fastballs is also excellent.

Ahead And Behind In The Count Vs. RH

Ahead

	Fastball Average .419			Curve Average .500		
	Inside	Middle	Outside	Inside	Middle	Outside
High	10/700 /7	12/166 /2	8/375 /3	0/0 /0	0/0 /0	0/0 /0
Med	26/384 /10	20/400 /8	44/431 /19	1/0 /0	1/0 /0	13/615 /8
Low	7/285 /2	25/520 /13	10/400 /4	1/0 /0	3/666 /2	3/333 /1

Behind

	Fastball Average .325			Curve Average .500		
	Inside	Middle	Outside	Inside	Middle	Outside
High	3/0 /0	4/250 /1	0/0 /0	0/0 /0	1/0 /0	1/0 /0
Med	9/444 /4	1/1000 /1	9/222 /2	1/0 /0	0/0 /0	3/1000 /3
Low	4/0 /0	7/571 /4	3/333 /1	0/0 /0	2/500 /1	0/0 /0

Overall Evaluation

Against Right-Handed Pitchers

Overall Fastball	⚾⚾⚾
Overall Curve	⚾⚾
Overall Slider	⚾⚾⚾⚾

Against Left-Handed Pitchers

Overall Fastball	⚾
Overall Curve	⚾⚾⚾⚾
Overall Slider	⚾⚾⚾⚾

Comments: Fielders need to play Jacoby medium-deep when indicated by the BARS fielding strategy. **Strengths:** Waist-high, low-middle and high-inside fastballs, medium-outside curves and medum-outside sliders vs. RH; high fastballs, low-middle fastballs, low-middle curves vs. LH. **Weaknesses:** Low-inside, low-outside, high-outside and high-middle fastballs, low-outside curves and sliders vs. RH; waist-high fastballs vs. LH.

Chris James Against Right-Handed Pitchers
Overall BARS Batting Average .285

Fastball Average .293

	Inside	Middle	Outside
High	12/333 /4	3/333 /1	14/357 /5
Med	11/272 /3	0/0 /0	17/294 /5
Low	8/125 /1	14/357 /5	13/230 /3

Curve Average .219

	Inside	Middle	Outside
High	2/500 /1	0/0 /0	4/250 /1
Med	2/0 /0	1/0 /0	13/307 /4
Low	2/500 /1	1/0 /0	16/125 /2

Slider Average .360

	Inside	Middle	Outside
High	0/0 /0	1/0 /0	1/0 /0
Med	2/0 /0	0/0 /0	7/714 /5
Low	0/0 /0	2/0 /0	12/333 /4

Chris James Against Left-Handed Pitchers
Overall BARS Batting Average .322

Fastball Average .333

	Inside	Middle	Outside
High	7/428 /3	5/400 /2	7/285 /2
Med	10/400 /4	0/0 /0	14/357 /5
Low	6/666 /4	4/0 /0	10/100 /1

Curve Average .285

	Inside	Middle	Outside
High	1/1000 /1	1/0 /0	0/0 /0
Med	3/666 /2	0/0 /0	2/500 /1
Low	3/0 /0	2/0 /0	2/0 /0

Slider Average .300

	Inside	Middle	Outside
High	1/0 /0	0/0 /0	0/0 /0
Med	3/333 /1	0/0 /0	1/0 /0
Low	2/500 /1	2/500 /1	1/0 /0

Right-handed hitter Chris James has a strong .293 overall fastball average against right-handed pitchers and an excellent .333 overall fastball average against left-handed pitchers.

Starting with his performance against right-handers, notice his strength against high fastballs (.333, .333 and .357, inside to outside). He hits high-outside fastballs straightaway to the outfield.

HIGH-OUTSIDE FASTBALLS

BATTING AVERAGE .357
Play
Left   Deep in straightaway left field
Center   Medium-deep in straightaway center field
Right   Medium-deep in straightaway right field
Short   Shifted toward third base
Second   *No instances recorded*

He hits high-inside fastballs much more to his opposite field (right field).

HIGH-INSIDE FASTBALLS

BATTING AVERAGE .333
Play
Left   *No instances recorded*
Center   Deep and shifted toward right field
Right   Deep and shifted toward the right field line
Short   Up middle (shifted toward second base)

Second   Normal position

He hits excellently against low-over-the-middle fastballs thrown by right-handers (.357). He pulls this pitch to left.

LOW-OVER-THE-MIDDLE FASTBALLS

BATTING AVERAGE .357
Play
Left   Medium-deep and shifted toward the left field line
Center   Medium-deep and shifted toward left field
Right   *No instances recorded*
Short   Shifted toward third base
Second   Normal position

He hits .294 against medium-high outside fastballs, hitting straightaway to all fields.

MEDIUM-HIGH OUTSIDE FASTBALLS

BATTING AVERAGE .294
Play
Left   Deep in straightaway left field
Center   Deep in straightaway center field
Right   Medium-deep in straightaway right field
Short   Normal position
Second   Normal position

James has a strong .307 average in his medium-high outside curve location against right-handers.

MEDIUM-HIGH OUTSIDE CURVEBALLS

BATTING AVERAGE .307
Play

Left	Medium-deep and shifted toward the left field line
Center	Deep and shifted toward left field
Right	Deep in straightaway right field
Short	Up middle (shifted toward second base)
Second	*No instances recorded*

In contrast, he has trouble with low-outside curves (.125).

He hits well against both medium-high outside and low-outside sliders (.714 and .333). He scatters medium-high outside sliders to all fields.

MEDIUM-HIGH OUTSIDE SLIDERS

BATTING AVERAGE .714
Play

Left	Medium-deep and shifted toward the left field line
Center	Deep and shifted toward left field
Right	Medium-deep and shifted toward the right line
Short	Up middle (shifted toward second base)
Second	*No instances recorded*

He hits low-outside sliders medium-deep and straightaway to the outfield.

LOW-OUTSIDE SLIDERS

BATTING AVERAGE .333
Play

Left	Medium-deep in straightaway left field
Center	Medium-deep in straightaway center field
Right	Medium-deep in straightaway right field
Short	Normal position

Second   *No instances recorded*

James Against Left-Handed Pitchers

James hits excellently against both medium-high outside fastballs (.357) and medium-high inside fastballs (.400) against left-handed pitchers. He hits medium-high outside fastballs deep down the left line.

MEDIUM-HIGH OUTSIDE FASTBALLS (THROWN BY LEFT-HANDED PITCHERS)

BATTING AVERAGE .357
Play

Left	Deep and shifted toward the left field line
Center	Deep in straightaway center field
Right	Medium-deep in straightaway right field
Short	Normal position
Second	*No instances recorded*

He pulls medium-high inside fastballs to the outfield but hits them to the right side of the infield.

MEDIUM-HIGH INSIDE FASTBALLS (THROWN BY LEFT-HANDED PITCHERS)

BATTING AVERAGE .400
Play

Left	Deep and shifted toward the left field line
Center	Deep and shifted toward left field
Right	Deep and shifted toward center field
Short	Up middle (shifted toward second base)
Second	Shifted toward first base

He has a lot of trouble with low-outside fastballs thrown by left-handers (.100).

Ahead And Behind In The Count Vs. RH

Ahead

	Fastball Average .333			Curve Average .181		
	Inside	Middle	Outside	Inside	Middle	Outside
High	500/4/2	0/0/0	375/8/3	0/1/0	0/0/0	0/1/0
Med	0/3/0	0/0/0	333/3/1	0/0/0	0/0/0	200/5/1
Low	333/3/1	375/8/3	250/4/1	500/2/1	0/0/0	0/2/0

Behind

	Fastball Average .400			Curve Average .230		
	Inside	Middle	Outside	Inside	Middle	Outside
High	500/4/2	1000/1/1	1000/1/1	1000/1/1	0/0/0	0/2/0
Med	333/3/1	0/0/0	250/4/1	0/0/0	0/0/0	0/3/0
Low	0/2/0	333/3/1	500/2/1	0/0/0	0/1/0	333/6/2

Overall Evaluation
Against Right-Handed Pitchers

Overall Fastball	⚾ ⚾
Overall Curve	⚾
Overall Slider	⚾ ⚾ ⚾ ⚾ ⚾

Against Left-Handed Pitchers

Overall Fastball	⚾ ⚾ ⚾ ⚾
Overall Curve	⚾ ⚾ ⚾
Overall Slider	Not enough information

Comments: Excellent vs. high fastballs vs. RH.
Strengths: High fastballs, low-middle fastballs, medium-outside curves and medium-outside sliders, low-outside sliders vs. RH; inside fastballs, medium-outside fastballs vs. LH.
Weaknesses: Medium-inside, low-inside and low-outside fastballs, low-outside curves vs. RH; low-outside fastballs vs. LH.

Dion James (Left Handed)   *Cleveland Indians*

Dion James Against Right-Handed Pitchers
Overall BARS Batting Average .307

Fastball Average .307

	Outside	Middle	Inside
High	30/ 233/7	31/ 322/10	25/ 160/4
Med	98/ 326/32	27/ 555/15	49/ 408/20
Low	40/ 75/3	63/ 365/23	34/ 235/8

Curve Average .268

	Outside	Middle	Inside
High	3/ 666/2	4/ 0/0	0/ 0/0
Med	11/ 454/5	1/ 1000/1	5/ 200/1
Low	7/ 142/1	2/ 0/0	8/ 125/1

Slider Average .400

	Outside	Middle	Inside
High	1/ 0/0	1/ 1000/1	1/ 1000/1
Med	1/ 0/0	1/ 1000/1	5/ 600/3
Low	4/ 250/1	4/ 250/1	2/ 0/0

Dion James Against Left-Handed Pitchers
Overall BARS Batting Average .320

Fastball Average .376

	Outside	Middle	Inside
High	3/ 666/2	5/ 600/3	5/ 0/0
Med	16/ 312/5	5/ 600/3	22/ 363/8
Low	8/ 125/1	10/ 600/6	3/ 333/1

Curve Average .238

	Outside	Middle	Inside
High	3/ 0/0	0/ 0/0	0/ 0/0
Med	4/ 250/1	1/ 0/0	4/ 250/1
Low	4/ 500/2	2/ 500/1	3/ 0/0

Slider Average .000

	Outside	Middle	Inside
High	0/ 0/0	1/ 0/0	1/ 0/0
Med	3/ 0/0	0/ 0/0	0/ 0/0
Low	3/ 0/0	0/ 0/0	0/ 0/0

Left-handed hitter Dion James hits a solid .307 overall against fastballs thrown by right-handed pitchers and a sparkling .376 overall against fastballs thrown by left-handed pitchers. It's unusual for a left-handed hitter to hit fastballs this well against left-handed pitchers.

Starting against right-handers, his .408 against medium-high inside fastballs is outstanding.

MEDIUM-HIGH INSIDE FASTBALLS

BATTING AVERAGE .408
Play
Left   Medium-deep and shifted toward the left field line
Center   Medium-deep in straightaway center field
Right   Deep in straightaway right field
Short   Up middle (shifted toward second base)
Second   Normal position

His .326 against medium-high outside fastballs thrown by right-handers is excellent. He hits this pitch deep down both lines. The chart below and the field diagram on the opposite page show how fielders need to play for fastballs to this location.

MEDIUM-HIGH OUTSIDE FASTBALLS

BATTING AVERAGE .326
Play

Left   Deep and shifted toward the left field line
Center   Deep in straightaway center field
Right   Deep and shifted toward the right field line
Short   Up middle (shifted toward second base)
Second   Shifted toward first base

James has weaknesses in the four fastball corners. He also has trouble with low curves against right-handers.

James Against Left-Handed Pitchers

James hits all waist-high and all over-the-middle fastballs well against left-handed pitchers. His .363 against medium-high inside fastballs is excellent.

MEDIUM-HIGH INSIDE FASTBALLS (THROWN BY LEFT-HANDED PITCHERS)

BATTING AVERAGE .363
Play
Left   Medium-deep in straightaway left field
Center   Deep and shifted toward left field
Right   Deep and shifted toward the right field line
Short   Normal position
Second   Shifted toward first base

He hits .312 against medium-high outside fastballs thrown by left-handers.

Medium-High Outside Fastballs
(Thrown By Right-Handed Pitchers)

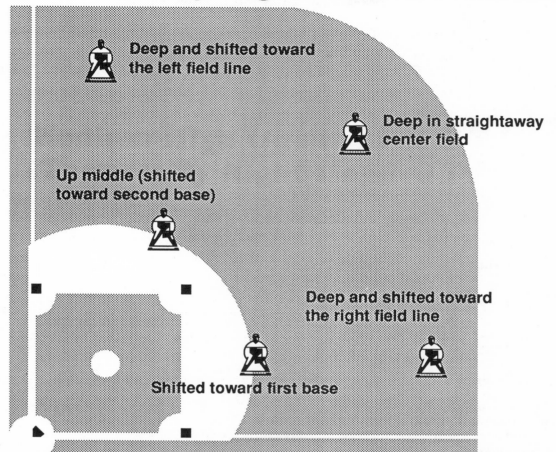

Deep and shifted toward the left field line

Deep in straightaway center field

Up middle (shifted toward second base)

Deep and shifted toward the right field line

Shifted toward first base

Ahead And Behind In The Count Vs. RH

Ahead

Fastball Average .364

	Outside	Middle	Inside
High	15/266 /4	16/312 /5	11/181 /2
Med	51/411 /21	13/615 /8	30/500 /15
Low	17/58 /1	37/378 /14	13/307 /4

Curve Average .400

	Outside	Middle	Inside
High	0/0 /0	0/0 /0	0/0 /0
Med	1/1000 /1	0/0 /0	3/333 /1
Low	1/0 /0	0/0 /0	0/0 /0

Behind

Fastball Average .300

	Outside	Middle	Inside
High	4/250 /1	4/750 /3	6/166 /1
Med	22/272 /6	6/500 /3	7/285 /2
Low	7/285 /2	10/200 /2	4/250 /1

Curve Average .333

	Outside	Middle	Inside
High	1/0 /0	3/0 /0	0/0 /0
Med	4/750 /3	1/1000 /1	1/0 /0
Low	4/250 /1	0/0 /0	1/0 /0

Overall Evaluation
Against Right-Handed Pitchers

Overall Fastball ⚾⚾⚾

Overall Curve ⚾⚾

Overall Slider ⚾⚾⚾⚾

Against Left-Handed Pitchers

Overall Fastball ⚾⚾⚾⚾

Overall Curve ⚾

Overall Slider   Not enough information

Comments: Strong vs. waist-high and over-the-middle fastballs vs. both RH and LH.

Strengths: Waist-high and over-the-middle fastballs, medium-outside curves vs. RH; waist-high and over-the-middle fastballs vs. LH.

Weaknesses: The four fastball corners, low curves vs. RH; low-outside fastballs vs. LH.

Brad Komminsk (Right Handed)　　*Cleveland Indians*

Brad Komminsk Against Right-Handed Pitchers
Overall BARS Batting Average .191

Fastball Average .248

	Inside	Middle	Outside
High	6 / 0/0	14 / 142/2	7 / 142/1
Med	16 / 375/6	17 / 352/6	24 / 208/5
Low	5 / 200/1	27 / 296/8	13 / 230/3

Curve Average .125

	Inside	Middle	Outside
High	0 / 0/0	4 / 0/0	0 / 0/0
Med	4 / 0/0	1 / 0/0	13 / 153/2
Low	0 / 0/0	5 / 0/0	13 / 230/3

Slider Average .100

	Inside	Middle	Outside
High	0 / 0/0	2 / 500/1	2 / 0/0
Med	1 / 0/0	3 / 0/0	1 / 0/0
Low	1 / 0/0	6 / 166/1	14 / 71/1

Brad Komminsk Against Left-Handed Pitchers
Overall BARS Batting Average .188

Fastball Average .220

	Inside	Middle	Outside
High	8 / 500/4	9 / 0/0	4 / 250/1
Med	14 / 214/3	10 / 200/2	28 / 214/6
Low	3 / 333/1	33 / 181/6	18 / 277/5

Curve Average .096

	Inside	Middle	Outside
High	2 / 500/1	0 / 0/0	0 / 0/0
Med	4 / 0/0	1 / 0/0	3 / 666/2
Low	7 / 0/0	6 / 0/0	8 / 0/0

Slider Average .142

	Inside	Middle	Outside
High	0 / 0/0	0 / 0/0	0 / 0/0
Med	2 / 500/1	3 / 666/2	1 / 0/0
Low	6 / 0/0	7 / 0/0	2 / 0/0

Right-handed hitter Brad Komminsk has trouble with all outside fastballs and high fastballs against right-handed pitchers. He does, however, hit very well against medium-high inside, medium-over-the-middle, and low-over-the-middle fastballs.

He hits medium-high inside fastballs for a strong .375 average.

MEDIUM-HIGH INSIDE FASTBALLS

BATTING AVERAGE .375

Play

Left	Deep and shifted toward the left field line
Center	Medium-deep in straightaway center field
Right	Deep in straightaway right field
Short	Normal position
Second	*No instances recorded*

He gets quite a few medium-over-the-middle fastballs against right-handers. This means either he is a patient hitter, waiting for his pitch to come in over the plate, or pitchers aren't pitching him carefully enough.

MEDIUM-OVER-THE-MIDDLE FASTBALLS

BATTING AVERAGE .352

Play

Left	Medium-deep in straightaway left field
Center	Deep in straightaway center field
Right	Medium-deep in straightaway right field
Short	Shifted toward third base
Second	Shifted toward first base

He is thrown a lot of low-over-the-middle fastballs.

LOW-OVER-THE-MIDDLE FASTBALLS

BATTING AVERAGE .296

Play

Left	Deep and shifted toward the left field line
Center	Medium-deep in straightaway center field
Right	Deep in straightaway right field
Short	Normal position
Second	Normal position

Against right-handed pitchers, Komminsk has trouble with medium-high outside curves (.153) and low-outside curves (.230). He hits medium-outside curves deep down the left line, but he seems to have trouble getting his bat on the ball against low-outside curves.

MEDIUM-HIGH OUTSIDE CURVEBALLS

BATTING AVERAGE .153

Play

Left	Deep and shifted toward the left field line
Center	Deep in straightaway center field
Right	Medium-deep and shifted toward center field
Short	Normal position
Second	*No instances recorded*

LOW-OUTSIDE CURVEBALLS

BATTING AVERAGE .230

Left	Short and shifted toward the left field line
Center	*No instances recorded*
Right	Medium-deep and shifted toward the right line
Short	*No instances recorded*
Second	*No instances recorded*

Against right-handers, he has a lot of problem with low-outside and low-over-the-middle sliders (.071 and .166)

Komminsk Against Left-Handed Pitchers

Against left-handed pitchers Komminsk has difficulties in almost all his fastball locations. He hits a barely adequate .277 against low-outside fastballs thrown by left-handers.

LOW-OUTSIDE FASTBALLS
(THROWN BY LEFT-HANDED PITCHERS)

BATTING AVERAGE .277

Play

Left	Medium-deep and shifted toward the left field line
Center	Deep and shifted toward left field
Right	Deep in straightaway right field
Short	Shifted toward third base
Second	Normal position

He hits a solid enough .500 against high-inside fastballs thrown by left-handers.

HIGH-INSIDE FASTBALLS
(THROWN BY LEFT-HANDED PITCHERS)

BATTING AVERAGE .500

Play

Left	Medium-deep and shifted toward the left field line

Center	Medium-deep in straightaway center field
Right	Medium-deep and shifted toward center field
Short	Up middle (shifted toward second base)
Second	*No instances recorded*

His .181 against low-over-the-middle fastballs is a detriment.

LOW-OVER-THE-MIDDLE FASTBALLS
(THROWN BY LEFT-HANDED PITCHERS)

BATTING AVERAGE .181

Play

Left	Deep in straightaway left field
Center	Deep in straightaway center field
Right	Deep and shifted toward center field
Short	Normal position
Second	Normal position

He hits .214 against medium-high outside fastballs thrown by lefties. His low average indicates that most of his hit balls from pitches to this location are probably easy outs.

MEDIUM-HIGH OUTSIDE FASTBALLS
(THROWN BY LEFT-HANDED PITCHERS)

BATTING AVERAGE .214

Play

Left	Medium-deep and shifted toward center field
Center	Medium-deep and shifted toward right field
Right	Deep in straightaway right field
Short	Normal position
Second	Shifted toward first base

Komminsk has trouble with low curves and low sliders against left-handers. The BARS System has yet to record a base hit for him in these locations.

Ahead And Behind In The Count Vs. RH

Ahead

Fastball Average .290

	Inside	Middle	Outside
High	1/ 0/0	5/ 200/1	2/ 0/0
Med	7/ 571/4	12/ 333/4	14/ 214/3
Low	0/ 0/0	12/ 250/3	2/ 500/1

Curve Average .142

	Inside	Middle	Outside
High	0/ 0/0	0/ 0/0	0/ 0/0
Med	1/ 0/0	0/ 0/0	4/ 250/1
Low	0/ 0/0	2/ 0/0	0/ 0/0

Behind

Fastball Average .333

	Inside	Middle	Outside
High	1/ 0/0	4/ 250/1	1/ 0/0
Med	4/ 250/1	2/ 500/1	0/ 0/0
Low	1/ 1000/1	1/ 0/0	4/ 500/2

Curve Average .250

	Inside	Middle	Outside
High	0/ 0/0	1/ 0/0	0/ 0/0
Med	0/ 0/0	0/ 0/0	1/ 0/0
Low	0/ 0/0	0/ 0/0	2/ 500/1

Overall Evaluation
Against Right-Handed Pitchers

Overall Fastball	⚾⚾
Overall Curve	⚾⚾
Overall Slider	⚾⚾

Against Left-Handed Pitchers

Overall Fastball	⚾⚾
Overall Curve	⚾⚾
Overall Slider	⚾⚾

Comments: Has a strong fastball sector medium-inside/medium-middle vs. RH.
Strengths: Medium-middle and medium-inside fastballs vs. RH; high-inside fastballs vs. LH.
Weaknesses: Fastballs except as above vs. RH, outside curves and outside sliders vs. RH; all fastballs except low-inside, high-inside and low-outside vs. LH, low curves and low sliders vs. LH.

Candy Maldonado (RightHanded) *Cleveland Indians*

Candy Maldonado Against Right-Handed Pitchers
Overall BARS Batting Average .256

Fastball Average .282

	Inside	Middle	Outside
High	17/ 352/6	18/ 333/6	12/ 250/3
Med	21/ 190/4	6/ 500/3	37/ 324/12
Low	18/ 55/1	22/ 272/6	26/ 346/9

Curve Average .178

	Inside	Middle	Outside
High	1/ 0/0	2/ 500/1	2/ 0/0
Med	2/ 0/0	1/ 0/0	6/ 333/2
Low	0/ 0/0	3/ 0/0	11/ 181/2

Slider Average .200

	Inside	Middle	Outside
High	1/ 0/0	1/ 0/0	2/ 500/1
Med	3/ 333/1	0/ 0/0	16/ 187/3
Low	2/ 0/0	6/ 333/2	19/ 157/3

Candy Maldonado Against Left-Handed Pitchers
Overall BARS Batting Average .301

Fastball Average .312

	Inside	Middle	Outside
High	9/ 0/0	14/ 428/6	9/ 222/2
Med	10/ 300/3	4/ 0/0	33/ 454/15
Low	7/ 285/2	14/ 357/5	28/ 250/7

Curve Average .285

	Inside	Middle	Outside
High	0/ 0/0	1/ 1000/1	1/ 1000/1
Med	4/ 500/2	0/ 0/0	6/ 333/2
Low	3/ 333/1	8/ 125/1	5/ 0/0

Slider Average .266

	Inside	Middle	Outside
High	0/ 0/0	1/ 0/0	2/ 0/0
Med	4/ 500/2	2/ 0/0	7/ 428/3
Low	4/ 250/1	6/ 166/1	4/ 250/1

Right-handed hitter Candy Maldonado hits fastballs fairly well against right-handed pitchers (.282 overall) and very well against left-handed pitchers (.312 overall).

Starting with right-handers, Maldonado hits .324 against medium-high outside fastballs.

MEDIUM-HIGH OUTSIDE FASTBALLS

BATTING AVERAGE .324
Play

Left	Medium-deep and shifted toward the left field line
Center	Deep and shifted toward right field
Right	Deep and shifted toward the right field line
Short	Up middle (shifted toward second base)
Second	Normal position

When right-handers throw low or medium-high, they should keep the ball inside against Maldonado. He hits a strong .346 against low-outside fastballs.

LOW-OUTSIDE FASTBALLS

BATTING AVERAGE .346
Play

Left	Deep in straightaway left field
Center	Deep and shifted toward left field
Right	Deep and shifted toward center field
Short	Normal position
Second	Normal position

Maldonado receives quite a few low-outside curves and sliders. He has trouble with these pitches.

Against left-handed pitchers Maldonado hits medium-high outside fastballs for an exceptional .454 average. See the field diagram on the opposite page.

MEDIUM-HIGH OUTSIDE FASTBALLS
(THROWN BY LEFT-HANDED PITCHERS)

BATTING AVERAGE .454
Play

Left	Medium-deep and shifted toward the left field line
Center	Medium-deep in straightaway center field
Right	Deep in straightaway right field
Short	Normal position
Second	Normal position

His .357 against low-over-the-middle fastballs thrown by left-handers is also very strong.

LOW-OVER-THE-MIDDLE FASTBALLS
(THROWN BY LEFT-HANDED PITCHERS)

BATTING AVERAGE .357
Play

Left	Deep and shifted toward the left field line
Center	Medium-deep and shifted toward left field
Right	Medium-deep in straightaway right field
Short	Normal position
Second	Normal position

His high-over-the-middle and medium-high inside fastball locations (.428 and .300 respectively) show overall strength against left-handers.

Medium-High Outside Fastballs
(Thrown By Left-Handed Pitchers)

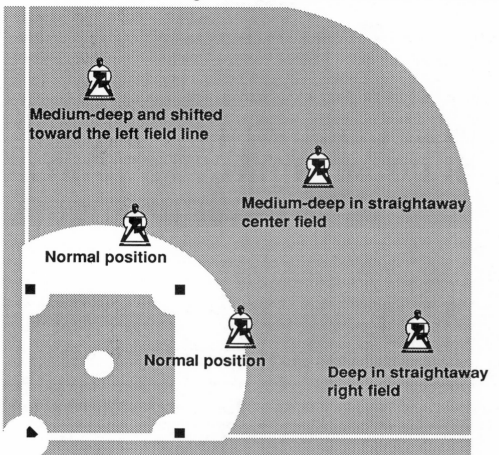

Medium-deep and shifted toward the left field line

Medium-deep in straightaway center field

Normal position

Normal position

Deep in straightaway right field

Ahead And Behind In The Count Vs. RH

Ahead

Fastball Average .367

	Inside	Middle	Outside
High	5/400 /2	10/300 /3	6/166 /1
Med	12/250 /3	2/500 /1	16/500 /8
Low	5/200 /1	12/333 /4	11/545 /6

Curve Average .500

	Inside	Middle	Outside
High	0/0 /0	1/1000 /1	1/0 /0
Med	0/0 /0	0/0 /0	2/1000 /2
Low	0/0 /0	0/0 /0	2/0 /0

Behind

Fastball Average .361

	Inside	Middle	Outside
High	4/500 /2	5/600 /3	2/1000 /2
Med	1/0 /0	2/500 /1	6/166 /1
Low	6/0 /0	5/400 /2	5/400 /2

Curve Average .100

	Inside	Middle	Outside
High	0/0 /0	1/0 /0	1/0 /0
Med	1/0 /0	1/0 /0	3/0 /0
Low	0/0 /0	0/0 /0	3/333 /1

Overall Evaluation
Against Right-Handed Pitchers

Overall Fastball
Overall Curve
Overall Slider

Against Left-Handed Pitchers

Overall Fastball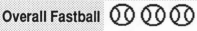
Overall Curve
Overall Slider

Comments: Strong against medium-outside fastballs.
Strengths: High-inside, high-middle, medium-outside, low-outside fastballs vs. RH; high-middle, low-middle and medium-outside fastballs, medium-outside sliders vs. LH.
Weaknesses: medium-inside, low-inside, low-middle and high-outside fastballs, low-outside curves, medium-outside and low-outside sliders vs. RH; low-outside fastballs and curves vs. LH.

Joel Skinner Against Right-Handed Pitchers
Overall BARS Batting Average .207

Fastball Average .230

	Inside	Middle	Outside
High	13 / 76 / 1	6 / 333 / 2	7 / 0 / 0
Med	14 / 285 / 4	16 / 312 / 5	65 / 276 / 18
Low	13 / 76 / 1	19 / 315 / 6	12 / 83 / 1

Curve Average .113

	Inside	Middle	Outside
High	1 / 0 / 0	3 / 333 / 1	1 / 0 / 0
Med	2 / 0 / 0	3 / 0 / 0	12 / 250 / 3
Low	4 / 0 / 0	6 / 166 / 1	12 / 0 / 0

Slider Average .215

	Inside	Middle	Outside
High	1 / 0 / 0	2 / 0 / 0	4 / 0 / 0
Med	3 / 666 / 2	5 / 400 / 2	15 / 333 / 5
Low	3 / 0 / 0	2 / 500 / 1	16 / 62 / 1

Joel Skinner Against Left-Handed Pitchers
Overall BARS Batting Average .215

Fastball Average .278

	Inside	Middle	Outside
High	1 / 0 / 0	6 / 166 / 1	3 / 0 / 0
Med	3 / 1000 / 3	1 / 1000 / 1	41 / 268 / 11
Low	2 / 0 / 0	12 / 250 / 3	10 / 300 / 3

Curve Average .038

	Inside	Middle	Outside
High	2 / 0 / 0	0 / 0 / 0	1 / 1000 / 1
Med	2 / 0 / 0	4 / 0 / 0	1 / 0 / 0
Low	5 / 0 / 0	3 / 0 / 0	8 / 0 / 0

Slider Average .181

	Inside	Middle	Outside
High	1 / 0 / 0	2 / 0 / 0	0 / 0 / 0
Med	2 / 0 / 0	0 / 0 / 0	3 / 666 / 2
Low	1 / 0 / 0	1 / 0 / 0	1 / 0 / 0

Right-handed hitter Joel Skinner has trouble with fastballs against right-handed pitchers (.230 overall). His .278 overall fastball average against left-handed pitchers is better, but still only adequate. He has trouble with curves and sliders against both right- and left-handers.

Against right-handers he hits .276 against medium-high outside fastballs.

MEDIUM-HIGH OUTSIDE FASTBALLS

BATTING AVERAGE .276
Play
Left   Deep and shifted toward center field
Center   Deep in straightaway center field
Right   Medium-deep in straightaway right field
Short   Normal position
Second   Normal position

He hits .285 against medium-high inside fastballs.

MEDIUM-HIGH INSIDE FASTBALLS

BATTING AVERAGE .285
Play
Left   Deep in straightaway left field
Center   Deep and shifted toward right field
Right   Medium-deep in straightaway right field
Short   Up middle (shifted toward second base)
Second   Shifted toward first base

He hits all over-the-middle fastballs solidly (.333,

.312, and .315, high to low). He hits low-over-the-middle fastballs deep to all fields.

LOW-OVER-THE-MIDDLE FASTBALLS

BATTING AVERAGE .315
Play
Left   Deep in straightaway left field
Center   Deep in straightaway center field
Right   Deep and shifted toward the right field line
Short   Normal position
Second   Normal position

He gets a lot of medium-over-the-middle fastballs against right-handers (16 instances). He's either patient and waits for good pitches or pitchers don't pitch him carefully enough.

MEDIUM-OVER-THE-MIDDLE FASTBALLS

BATTING AVERAGE .312
Play
Left   Deep and shifted toward the left field line
Center   Deep and shifted toward left field
Right   Deep in straightaway right field
Short   Shifted toward third base
Second   *No instances recorded*

Skinner has trouble in his four corner fastball locations. If right-handers can keep fastballs in these weak locations, they'll have a real advantage.

He also has trouble against outside curves thrown

by right-handers. His .000 on 0 for 12 against low-outside curves is extremely weak. His .250 against medium-high outside curves is fair.

MEDIUM-HIGH OUTSIDE CURVES

BATTING AVERAGE .250
Play

Left	Deep and shifted toward center field
Center	Medium-deep and shifted toward right field
Right	Medium-deep and shifted toward the right line
Short	Up middle (shifted toward second base)
Second	Normal position

He also has trouble with low-outside sliders against right-handers (.062 on 1 for 16). But he hits medium-high outside sliders excellently (.333).

MEDIUM-HIGH OUTSIDE SLIDERS

BATTING AVERAGE .333
Play

Left	Deep in straightaway left field
Center	Medium-deep and shifted toward left field
Right	Medium-deep and shifted toward center field
Short	Shifted toward third base
Second	Normal position

Skinner Against Left-Handed Pitchers

Against left-handed pitchers, Skinner hits .278 overall against fastballs. He has trouble with medium-high outside fastballs (.268). His Ahead and Behind charts are not shown for left-handers, but it's interesting that he hits this pitch significantly better when ahead in the count (.350 on 7 for 20 when ahead, .000 on 0 for 8 when behind).

MEDIUM-HIGH OUTSIDE FASTBALLS
(WHEN AHEAD IN THE COUNT
AGAINST LEFT-HANDED PITCHERS)

BATTING AVERAGE .350
Play

Left	*No instances recorded*
Center	Medium-deep in straightaway center field
Right	Deep in straightaway right field
Short	Normal position
Second	Shifted toward first base

MEDIUM-HIGH OUTSIDE FASTBALLS
(WHEN BEHIND IN THE COUNT
AGAINST LEFT-HANDED PITCHERS)

BATTING AVERAGE .000
Play

Left	Deep and shifted toward center field
Center	Deep and shifted toward right field
Right	Short in straightaway right field
Short	Normal position
Second	*No instances recorded*

He hits .300 overall against low-outside fastballs.

LOW-OUTSIDE FASTBALLS
(THROWN BY LEFT-HANDED PITCHERS)

BATTING AVERAGE .300
Play

Left	Deep and shifted toward center field
Center	Medium-deep in straightaway center field
Right	*No instances recorded*
Short	Up middle (shifted toward second base)
Second	*No instances recorded*

He has trouble with low curves thrown by lefties. He has yet to have a recorded base hit in these locations.

Ahead And Behind In The Count Vs. RH

Ahead

Fastball Average .229

	Inside	Middle	Outside
High	4/ 250 /1	3/ 333 /1	0/ 0 /0
Med	7/ 285 /2	11/ 181 /2	31/ 225 /7
Low	6/ 0 /0	8/ 375 /3	4/ 250 /1

Curve Average .000

	Inside	Middle	Outside
High	0/ 0 /0	1/ 0 /0	0/ 0 /0
Med	0/ 0 /0	2/ 0 /0	3/ 0 /0
Low	0/ 0 /0	1/ 0 /0	1/ 0 /0

Behind

Fastball Average .470

	Inside	Middle	Outside
High	0/ 0 /0	0/ 0 /0	2/ 0 /0
Med	3/ 666 /2	0/ 0 /0	9/ 555 /5
Low	0/ 0 /0	2/ 500 /1	1/ 0 /0

Curve Average .153

	Inside	Middle	Outside
High	1/ 0 /0	2/ 500 /1	1/ 0 /0
Med	1/ 0 /0	1/ 0 /0	3/ 0 /0
Low	1/ 0 /0	1/ 1000 /1	2/ 0 /0

Overall Evaluation
Against Right-Handed Pitchers

Overall Fastball	
Overall Curve	
Overall Slider	

Against Left-Handed Pitchers

Overall Fastball	
Overall Curve	
Overall Slider	Not enough information

Comments: Weak on the four fastball corners vs. RH. **Strengths:** Over-the-middle fastballs, medium-outside sliders vs. RH; low-outside fastballs vs. LH. **Weaknesses:** High-inside and low-inside fastballs, outside fastballs, low curves and low-outside sliders vs. RH; medium-outside and low-middle fastballs, low curves vs. LH.

Cory Snyder (Right Handed)   *Cleveland Indians*

Cory Snyder Against Right-Handed Pitchers
Overall BARS Batting Average .267

Fastball Average .231

	Inside	Middle	Outside
High	16/125/2	17/352/6	15/400/6
Med	20/100/2	4/0/0	70/200/14
Low	5/400/2	13/384/5	17/235/4

Curve Average .363

	Inside	Middle	Outside
High	2/500/1	2/500/1	5/400/2
Med	4/500/2	1/1000/1	13/538/7
Low	1/0/0	1/0/0	15/133/2

Slider Average .250

	Inside	Middle	Outside
High	0/0/0	4/500/2	3/333/1
Med	4/250/1	0/0/0	12/333/4
Low	2/0/0	3/333/1	12/83/1

Cory Snyder Against Left-Handed Pitchers
Overall BARS Batting Average .278

Fastball Average .287

	Inside	Middle	Outside
High	4/250/1	5/0/0	8/250/2
Med	7/285/2	3/666/2	23/347/8
Low	2/500/1	5/200/1	9/222/2

Curve Average .222

	Inside	Middle	Outside
High	0/0/0	0/0/0	2/500/1
Med	0/0/0	1/1000/1	1/0/0
Low	0/0/0	0/0/0	5/0/0

Slider Average .166

	Inside	Middle	Outside
High	0/0/0	1/0/0	0/0/0
Med	1/0/0	0/0/0	1/0/0
Low	0/0/0	3/333/1	0/0/0

Cory Snyder, right-handed hitter, has higher overall curve and slider averages agaìnst right-handed pitchers. But he hits fastablls better against left-handed pitchers (.287 overall fastball against left-handers, .231 overall fastball against right-handers). .

Starting first with his performance against right-handers, he has a low .200 average in his medium-high outside fastball location. Since this location has a high number of instances, Snyder's average here goes a long way to determining his overall average.

Snyder hits medium-high outside fastballs deep down the left line and straightaway to the other fields.

MEDIUM-HIGH OUTSIDE FASTBALLS

BATTING AVERAGE .200

Play

Left	Deep and shifted toward the left field line
Center	Deep in straightaway center field
Right	Deep in straightaway right field
Short	Normal position
Second	Normal position

Snyder hits .100 against medium-high inside fastballs. This is also weak for a highly pitched location.

MEDIUM-HIGH INSIDE FASTBALLS

BATTING AVERAGE .100

Play

Left	Deep and shifted toward center field
Center	Medium-deep and shifted toward left field
Right	Medium-deep in straightaway right field
Short	Shifted toward third base
Second	Shifted toward first base

Snyder hits high-over-the-middle and high-outside fastballs very well (.352 and .400, respectively).

HIGH-OVER-THE-MIDDLE FASTBALLS

BATTING AVERAGE .352

Play

Left	Deep in straightaway left field
Center	Medium-deep in straightaway center field
Right	Deep and shifted toward center field
Short	Shifted toward third base
Second	*No instances recorded*

HIGH-OUTSIDE FASTBALLS

BATTING AVERAGE .400

Play

Left	Deep in straightaway left field
Center	Deep and shifted toward right field
Right	Deep in straightaway right field
Short	*No instances recorded*
Second	*No instances recorded*

Snyder hits .384 against low-over-the-middle fastballs. He hits this pitch straightaway to all fields.

Snyder Against Curves And Sliders

Snyder hits extremely well against medium-high outside curves and sliders thrown by right-handers (.538 curves, .333 sliders). But he hits very poorly against low-outside curves and sliders (.133 curves, .083 sliders).

MEDIUM-HIGH OUTSIDE CURVEBALLS

BATTING AVERAGE .538

Play

Left	Deep in straightaway left field
Center	Deep and shifted toward left field
Right	Deep and shifted toward center field
Short	*No instances recorded*
Second	*No instances recorded*

MEDIUM-HIGH OUTSIDE SLIDERS

BATTING AVERAGE .333

Play

Left	*No instances recorded*
Center	Medium-deep in straightaway center field
Right	Deep in straightaway right field
Short	Up middle (shifted toward second base)
Second	Shifted toward first base

Snyder hits low-outside curves deep down the left line. Notice in the fielding strategy for this pitch that he has not had a recorded hit ball to the right fielder or to the second baseman.

LOW-OUTSIDE CURVEBALLS

BATTING AVERAGE .133

Play

Left	Deep and shifted toward the left field line
Center	Medium-deep in straightaway center field
Right	*No instances recorded*
Short	Normal position
Second	*No instances recorded*

Snyder seems to have trouble getting wood on the ball when thrown a low-outside slider; he has few recorded hit balls for the location.

LOW-OUTSIDE SLIDERS

BATTING AVERAGE .083

Play

Left	*No instances recorded*
Center	*No instances recorded*
Right	*No instances recorded*
Short	Shifted toward third base
Second	*No instances recorded*

Snyder Against Left-Handed Pitchers

Snyder hits medium-high outside fastballs excellently against left-handed pitchers. He hits this pitch deep to all fields.

MEDIUM-HIGH OUTSIDE FASTBALLS
(THROWN BY LEFT-HANDED PITCHERS)

BATTING AVERAGE .315

Play

Left	Deep in straightaway left field
Center	Deep in straightaway center field
Right	Deep and shifted toward center field
Short	Normal position
Second	*No instances recorded*

Ahead And Behind In The Count Vs. RH

Ahead

Fastball Average .353	Inside	Middle	Outside	Curve Average .666	Inside	Middle	Outside
High	6/333 /2	7/571 /4	2/0 /0		0/0 /0	0/0 /0	1/1000 /1
Med	8/250 /2	2/0 /0	28/285 /8		2/500 /1	1/1000 /1	6/666 /4
Low	2/500 /1	7/428 /3	3/1000 /3		0/0 /0	0/0 /0	2/500 /1

Behind

Fastball Average .378	Inside	Middle	Outside	Curve Average .384	Inside	Middle	Outside
High	0/0 /0	2/500 /1	7/857 /6		0/0 /0	1/0 /0	2/500 /1
Med	2/0 /0	1/0 /0	17/235 /4		1/1000 /1	0/0 /0	4/500 /2
Low	1/1000 /1	5/400 /2	2/0 /0		0/0 /0	0/0 /0	5/200 /1

Overall Evaluation

Against Right-Handed Pitchers

Overall Fastball	⚾
Overall Curve	⚾ ⚾ ⚾ ⚾
Overall Slider	⚾ ⚾

Against Left-Handed Pitchers

Overall Fastball	⚾ ⚾
Overall Curve	Not enough information
Overall Slider	Not enough information

Comments: Snyder hits fastballs better vs. LH, curves better vs. RH.

Strengths: High-middle, low-middle and high-outside fastballs, medium-outside curves and medium-outside sliders vs. RH; waist-high fastballs vs. LH.

Weaknesses: Waist-high fastballs, low-outside and high-inside fastballs, low-outside curves and sliders vs. RH; low-outside and all high fastballs vs. LH.

Mitch Webster (Switch Hitter) — *Cleveland Indians*

Mitch Webster Against Right-Handed Pitchers
Overall BARS Batting Average .267

Fastball Average .276

	Outside	Middle	Inside
High	24/ 208 /5	36/ 361 /13	19/ 263 /5
Med	72/ 263 /19	10/ 200 /2	49/ 244 /12
Low	45/ 155 /7	66/ 333 /22	44/ 363 /16

Curve Average .184

	Outside	Middle	Inside
High	1/ 0 /0	2/ 1000 /2	1/ 0 /0
Med	8/ 125 /1	4/ 500 /2	11/ 90 /1
Low	11/ 90 /1	12/ 250 /3	15/ 133 /2

Slider Average .333

	Outside	Middle	Inside
High	0/ 0 /0	1/ 1000 /1	1/ 0 /0
Med	4/ 250 /1	0/ 0 /0	7/ 571 /4
Low	3/ 333 /1	4/ 250 /1	7/ 142 /1

Mitch Webster Against Left-Handed Pitchers
Overall BARS Batting Average .340

Fastball Average .339

	Inside	Middle	Outside
High	16/ 437 /7	11/ 545 /6	12/ 250 /3
Med	18/ 166 /3	3/ 666 /2	32/ 468 /15
Low	8/ 375 /3	29/ 344 /10	24/ 125 /3

Curve Average .302

	Inside	Middle	Outside
High	0/ 0 /0	2/ 500 /1	1/ 1000 /1
Med	4/ 500 /2	2/ 1000 /2	11/ 272 /3
Low	8/ 0 /0	7/ 428 /3	8/ 125 /1

Slider Average .500

	Inside	Middle	Outside
High	1/ 0 /0	0/ 0 /0	0/ 0 /0
Med	1/ 1000 /1	0/ 0 /0	2/ 500 /1
Low	3/ 333 /1	3/ 666 /2	0/ 0 /0

Switch-hitting Mitch Webster hits .263 against medium-high outside fastballs thrown by right-handed pitchers. Batting left-handed, he hits this pitch down the left line and straightaway to the other fields. The shortstop needs to play shifted toward second base.

MEDIUM-HIGH OUTSIDE FASTBALLS

BATTING AVERAGE .263
Play

Left	Medium-deep and shifted toward the left field line
Center	Medium-deep and shifted toward left field
Right	Deep in straightaway right field
Short	Up middle (shifted toward second base)
Second	Normal position

He is weak against low-outside fastballs (.155) but he hits low-over-the-middle (.333) and low-inside fastballs (.363) excellently.

LOW-OVER-THE-MIDDLE FASTBALLS

BATTING AVERAGE .333
Play

Left	Medium-deep and shifted toward the left line
Center	Medium-deep in straightaway center field
Right	Deep in straightaway right field
Short	Normal position
Second	Shifted toward first base

LOW-INSIDE FASTBALLS

BATTING AVERAGE .363
Play

Left	Medium-deep and shifted toward the left field line
Center	Deep in straightaway center field
Right	Deep in straightaway right field
Short	*No instances recorded*
Second	Shifted toward first base

Webster has trouble with curves against right-handers. He really has no strong curve locations. By mixing in more curves, right-handers could get an advantage.

Webster has some excellent fastball locations against left-handed pitchers. His .468 against medium-high outside fastballs is exceptional. Batting right-handed, he pulls this pitch down the left line.

MEDIUM-HIGH OUTSIDE FASTBALLS
(THROWN BY LEFT-HANDED PITCHERS)

BATTING AVERAGE .468
Play

Left	Medium-deep and shifted toward the left field line
Center	Medium-deep in straightaway center field
Right	Medium-deep in straightaway right field
Short	Up middle (shifted toward second base)
Second	Normal position

Medium-High Outside Fastballs
(Thrown By Right-Handed Pitchers)

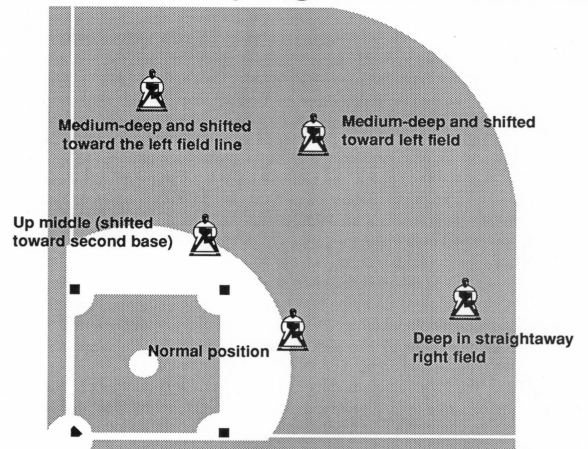

Medium-deep and shifted toward the left field line

Medium-deep and shifted toward left field

Up middle (shifted toward second base)

Normal position

Deep in straightaway right field

Ahead And Behind In The Count Vs. RH

Ahead

Fastball Average .339

	Outside	Middle	Inside
High	8/ 375 / 3	15/ 333 / 5	11/ 181 / 2
Med	31/ 322 / 10	3/ 333 / 1	24/ 291 / 7
Low	16/ 125 / 2	34/ 441 / 15	23/ 478 / 11

Curve Average .166

	Outside	Middle	Inside
High	0/ 0 / 0	0/ 0 / 0	1/ 0 / 0
Med	1/ 0 / 0	1/ 0 / 0	5/ 0 / 0
Low	2/ 0 / 0	4/ 250 / 1	4/ 500 / 2

Behind

Fastball Average .288

	Outside	Middle	Inside
High	2/ 500 / 1	8/ 375 / 3	4/ 250 / 1
Med	11/ 363 / 4	3/ 0 / 0	10/ 200 / 2
Low	6/ 333 / 2	8/ 375 / 3	7/ 142 / 1

Curve Average .500

	Outside	Middle	Inside
High	1/ 0 / 0	2/ 1000 / 2	0/ 0 / 0
Med	2/ 0 / 0	1/ 1000 / 1	3/ 333 / 1
Low	1/ 0 / 0	2/ 1000 / 2	0/ 0 / 0

Overall Evaluation
Against Right-Handed Pitchers

Overall Fastball

Overall Curve

Overall Slider

Against Left-Handed Pitchers

Overall Fastball

Overall Curve

Overall Slider 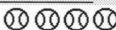 Not enough information

Comments: Very strong overall vs. LH.
Strengths: High-middle, low-middle and low-inside fastballs vs. RH; high-inside and low-inside fastballs, all over-the-middle fastballs, medium-high outside fastballs vs. LH.
Weaknesses: Outside fastballs, high-inside and medium-high inside fastballs, curves in general vs. RH; medium-inside, high-outside and low-outside fastballs, low-outside and low-inside curves vs. LH.

Bergman, Dave
Heath, Mike
Jones, Tracy
Nokes, Matt
Lemon, Chet
Moseby, Lloyd
Phillips, Tony
Schu, Rick
Trammell, Alan
Ward, Gary
Whitaker, Lou
Williams, Ken

Detroit Tigers
BARS System
Hitting Analysis

Dave Bergman (Left Handed)　　　　*Detroit Tigers*

Dave Bergman Against Right-Handed Pitchers
Overall BARS Batting Average .227

	Fastball Average .223			Curve Average .183			Slider Average .323		
	Outside	Middle	Inside	Outside	Middle	Inside	Outside	Middle	Inside
High	11/ 272 /3	19/ 263 /5	9/ 222 /2	0/ 0 /0	0/ 0 /0	1/ 0 /0	0/ 0 /0	1/ 0 /0	1/ 0 /0
Med	70/ 200 /14	17/ 176 /3	31/ 354 /11	14/ 142 /2	3/ 0 /0	4/ 250 /1	5/ 400 /2	0/ 0 /0	5/ 400 /2
Low	15/ 266 /4	38/ 105 /4	23/ 260 /6	4/ 500 /2	15/ 266 /4	8/ 0 /0	2/ 0 /0	5/ 400 /2	15/ 333 /5

Dave Bergman Against Left-Handed Pitchers
Overall BARS Batting Average .333

	Fastball Average .333			Curve Average .500			Slider Average .000		
	Outside	Middle	Inside	Outside	Middle	Inside	Outside	Middle	Inside
High	0/ 0 /0	1/ 1000 /1	6/ 166 /1	0/ 0 /0	0/ 0 /0	0/ 0 /0	0/ 0 /0	0/ 0 /0	0/ 0 /0
Med	9/ 222 /2	1/ 1000 /1	4/ 500 /2	1/ 1000 /1	0/ 0 /0	0/ 0 /0	0/ 0 /0	0/ 0 /0	0/ 0 /0
Low	0/ 0 /0	3/ 333 /1	3/ 333 /1	1/ 0 /0	0/ 0 /0	0/ 0 /0	0/ 0 /0	0/ 0 /0	1/ 0 /0

There is a shortage of BARS System information for left-handed hitting Dave Bergman against left-handed pitchers so only his performance against right-handers will be discussed here.

He hits a weak .223 overall against fastballs thrown by right-handers. His only strong location is medium-high inside (.354). He drives this pitch deep down the left line and into short left center.

MEDIUM-HIGH INSIDE FASTBALLS

BATTING AVERAGE .354
Play
Left	Deep and shifted toward the left field line
Center	Short and shifted toward left field
Right	Deep in straightaway right field
Short	Up middle (shifted toward second base)
Second	Shifted toward first base

He hits .260 against low-inside fastballs. But notice how much differently fielders need to play for low-inside fastballs compared to medium-high inside fastballs. Every fielder is required to shift, even though these two pitching locations are adjacent to each other in the strike zone.

LOW-INSIDE FASTBALLS

BATTING AVERAGE .260

Play
Left	Deep and shifted toward center field
Center	Medium-deep in straightaway center field
Right	Deep and shifted toward the right field line
Short	Normal position
Second	Normal position

He hits only .200 against medium-high outside fastballs thrown by right-handers. He hits this pitch deep to left center and right center. This shows a tendency to hit more to the opposite field, but notice that the shortstop and second baseman need to play him to pull the ball.

MEDIUM-HIGH OUTSIDE FASTBALLS

BATTING AVERAGE .200
Play
Left	Medium-deep in straightaway left field
Center	Deep and shifted toward left field
Right	Deep and shifted toward center field
Short	Up middle (shifted toward second base)
Second	Shifted toward first base

Notice Bergman's low average in his low-over-the-middle fastball location (.105). He hits this ball short to left down the line, to deep left center, to deep right center and to the right side of the infield. His low average indicates that most of his hit balls from this location are probably easy outs.

LOW-OVER-THE-MIDDLE FASTBALLS

BATTING AVERAGE .105
Play
Left	Short and shifted toward the left field line
Center	Deep and shifted toward left field
Right	Deep and shifted toward center field
Short	Up middle (shifted toward second base)
Second	Shifted toward first base

Bergman also has a relatively low average in the low-outside location. He hits this pitch down the left line.

LOW-OUTSIDE FASTBALLS

BATTING AVERAGE .266
Play
Left	Medium-deep and shifted toward the left field line
Center	Short and shifted toward left field
Right	*No instances recorded*
Short	Up middle (shifted toward second base)
Second	Normal position

He hits high-over-the-middle fastballs deep to all fields for a .263 average.

HIGH-OVER-THE-MIDDLE FASTBALLS

BATTING AVERAGE .263
Play
Left	Deep in straightaway left field
Center	Deep and shifted toward right field
Right	Deep in straightaway right field

Short	Up middle (shifted toward second base)
Second	Normal position

Bergman Against Curves And Sliders

Bergman hits a weak .142 against medium-high outside curves. He hits .266 against low-over-the-middle curves.

LOW-OVER-THE-MIDDLE CURVEBALLS

BATTING AVERAGE .266
Play
Left	Short in straightaway left field
Center	Medium-deep in straightaway center field
Right	Deep in straightaway right field
Short	Shifted toward third base
Second	Shifted toward first base

He hits low-inside sliders very well (.333). He pulls this pitch to the infield and the outfield with no recorded instances of hit balls to left and center fields.

LOW-INSIDE SLIDERS

BATTING AVERAGE .333
Play
Left	*No instances recorded*
Center	*No instances recorded*
Right	Deep in straightaway right field
Short	Up middle (shifted toward second base)
Second	Shifted toward first base

Against left-handed pitchers his .222 medium-high outside fastball average indicates a weakness.

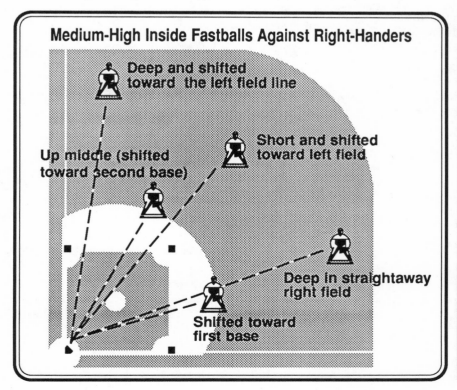

Medium-High Inside Fastballs Against Right-Handers

Deep and shifted toward the left field line

Short and shifted toward left field

Up middle (shifted toward second base)

Deep in straightaway right field

Shifted toward first base

Overall Evaluation
Against Right-Handed Pitchers

Overall Fastball ⚾⚾

Overall Curve ⚾⚾

Overall Slider ⚾⚾⚾⚾⚾

Against Left-Handed Pitchers

Overall Fastball ⚾⚾⚾⚾⚾

Overall Curve — Not enough information

Overall Slider — Not enough information

Comments: Only truly strong fastball location vs. RH is medium-inside.
Strengths: Medium-inside fastballs, low-inside sliders vs. RH.
Weaknesses: Medium-outside, high-inside, low-inside and all over-the-middle fastballs, medium-outside and low-inside curves vs. RH; medium-outside fastballs vs. LH.

Mike Heath (Right Handed)   *Detroit Tigers*

Mike Heath Against Right-Handed Pitchers
Overall BARS Batting Average .220

Fastball Average .226

	Inside	Middle	Outside
High	6/ 166 /1	13/ 307 /4	9/ 111 /1
Med	22/ 227 /5	14/ 357 /5	56/ 232 /13
Low	10/ 400 /4	30/ 266 /8	34/ 88 /3

Curve Average .200

	Inside	Middle	Outside
High	0/ 0 /0	2/ 500 /1	0/ 0 /0
Med	7/ 142 /1	4/ 500 /2	24/ 250 /6
Low	0/ 0 /0	8/ 250 /2	20/ 50 /1

Slider Average .219

	Inside	Middle	Outside
High	0/ 0 /0	1/ 0 /0	2/ 0 /0
Med	2/ 500 /1	1/ 1000 /1	15/ 66 /1
Low	3/ 0 /0	4/ 500 /2	13/ 307 /4

Mike Heath Against Left-Handed Pitchers
Overall BARS Batting Average .272

Fastball Average .285

	Inside	Middle	Outside
High	6/ 0 /0	15/ 333 /5	17/ 176 /3
Med	18/ 222 /4	5/ 600 /3	69/ 347 /24
Low	14/ 357 /5	23/ 347 /8	29/ 137 /4

Curve Average .268

	Inside	Middle	Outside
High	1/ 1000 /1	2/ 1000 /2	2/ 500 /1
Med	7/ 428 /3	2/ 500 /1	6/ 0 /0
Low	3/ 0 /0	9/ 111 /1	9/ 222 /2

Slider Average .066

	Inside	Middle	Outside
High	0/ 0 /0	2/ 0 /0	0/ 0 /0
Med	5/ 200 /1	0/ 0 /0	2/ 0 /0
Low	4/ 0 /0	2/ 0 /0	0/ 0 /0

Right-handed hitter Mike Heath has trouble with right-handed pitchers. He has some strong locations in his charts, but they are offset by weak locations. Against left-handed pitchers he has higher overall averages.

Starting with his charts against right-handers, note his troubles with outside fastballs (.111, .232, and .088, high to low). These locations, along with his .266 against low-over-the-middle fastballs, give right-handers a large reversed L-shaped sector to attack.

He hits low-outside fastballs to right field and to the right side of the infield. His low average indicates that he's not hitting this pitch hard.

LOW-OUTSIDE FASTBALLS

BATTING AVERAGE .088

Play
Left   No instances recorded
Center   No instances recorded
Right   Medium-deep in straightaway right field
Short   Up middle (shifted toward second base)
Second   Shifted toward first base

He hits medium-high outside fastballs deep down the right field line.

MEDIUM-HIGH OUTSIDE FASTBALLS

BATTING AVERAGE .232

Play
Left   Deep and shifted toward center field
Center   Medium-deep in straightaway center field
Right   Deep and shifted toward the right field line
Short   Normal position
Second   Normal position

His .266 against low-over-the-middle fastballs is barely adequate.

LOW-OVER-THE-MIDDLE FASTBALLS

BATTING AVERAGE .266

Play
Left   Medium-deep and shifted toward center field
Center   Medium-deep in straightaway center field
Right   Deep and shifted toward center field
Short   Normal position
Second   Shifted toward first base

He hits low-inside fastballs (.400), medium-over-the-middle fastballs (.357) and high-over-the-middle fastballs (.307) strongly.

Heath has trouble with medium-high inside curves (.142) and with low-outside curves (.050). His .250 against medium-high outside curves is fairly good, however.

In contrast he hits a very weak .066 against medium-high outside sliders and a very strong .307 against low-outside sliders. He hits this pitch short to left field and medium-deep to center and right fields.

LOW-OUTSIDE SLIDERS

BATTING AVERAGE .307
Play
Left   Short in straightaway left field
Center Medium-deep in straightaway center field
Right   Medium-deep and shifted toward center field
Short   Shifted toward third base
Second *No instances recorded*

Heath Against Left-Handed Pitchers

Heath hits fastballs pretty well overall against left-handed pitches (.285 overall). He hits medium-high outside and low-over-the-middle fastballs very strongly (.347 in each location).

MEDIUM-HIGH OUTSIDE FASTBALLS
(THROWN BY LEFT-HANDED PITCHERS)

BATTING AVERAGE .347
Play
Left   Deep and shifted toward center field
Center Medium-deep in straightaway center field
Right   Deep and shifted toward the right field line
Short   Normal position
Second Shifted toward first base

LOW-OVER-THE-MIDDLE FASTBALLS
(THROWN BY LEFT-HANDED PITCHERS)

BATTING AVERAGE .347
Play
Left   Deep in straightaway left field
Center Deep and shifted toward left field
Right   Medium-deep in straightaway right field

Short   Normal position
Second Normal position

He also hits high-over-the-middle and low-inside fastballs excellently.

HIGH-OVER-THE-MIDDLE FASTBALLS
(THROWN BY LEFT-HANDED PITCHERS)

BATTING AVERAGE .333
Play
Left   Deep and shifted toward center field
Center Deep in straightaway center field
Right   Deep and shifted toward center field
Short   Up middle (shifted toward second base)
Second *No instances recorded*

LOW-INSIDE FASTBALLS
(THROWN BY LEFT-HANDED PITCHERS)

BATTING AVERAGE .357
Play
Left   Deep and shifted toward the left field line
Center Medium-deep in straightaway center field
Right   Deep and shifted toward the right field line
Short   Shifted toward third base
Second *No instances recorded*

The fielding strategies for Heath's various fastball locations against left-handers show how necessary it is for fielders to assume positions on a pitch-by-pitch basis. His average is high in many of his fastball locations. This probably means that he hits the ball hard in these locations. If fielders don't adjust, they won't be able to get to the ball.

Ahead And Behind In The Count Vs. RH

Ahead

Fastball Average .270

	Inside	Middle	Outside
High	2/0	8/375/3	1/0
Med	10/200/2	8/375/3	30/266/8
Low	4/0	14/285/4	8/375/3

Curve Average .454

	Inside	Middle	Outside
High	0/0	1/1000/1	0/0
Med	1/0	0/0	5/400/2
Low	0/0	2/1000/2	2/0

Behind

Fastball Average .266

	Inside	Middle	Outside
High	1/0	1/1000/1	3/333/1
Med	4/250/1	3/333/1	7/285/2
Low	2/500/1	6/166/1	3/0

Curve Average .190

	Inside	Middle	Outside
High	0/0	0/0	0/0
Med	3/333/1	3/333/1	7/142/1
Low	0/0	2/0	6/166/1

Overall Evaluation
Against Right-Handed Pitchers

Overall Fastball ⚾⚾
Overall Curve ⚾⚾
Overall Slider ⚾⚾

Against Left-Handed Pitchers

Overall Fastball ⚾⚾ ⚾⚾
Overall Curve ⚾⚾ ⚾⚾
Overall Slider ⚾⚾

Comments: Weak against outside fastballs vs. RH.
Strengths: High-middle, medium-middle and low-inside fastballs, low-outside sliders vs. RH; over-the-middle, low-inside & medium-outside fastballs vs. LH.
Weaknesses: Outside fastballs, low-middle and medium-inside fastballs, medium-inside and low-outside curves, medium-outside sliders vs. RH; low-outside and high-outside fastballs, medium-inside fastballs, low curves vs. LH.

Tracy Jones (Right Handed)　　　　*Detroit Tigers*

Tracy Jones Against Right-Handed Pitchers
Overall BARS Batting Average .308

Fastball Average .355

	Inside	Middle	Outside
High	4/ 0/0	12/ 500/6	3/ 0/0
Med	9/ 444/4	0/ 0/0	20/ 400/8
Low	3/ 333/1	7/ 285/2	1/ 0/0

Curve Average .166

	Inside	Middle	Outside
High	1/ 0/0	1/ 0/0	2/ 0/0
Med	1/ 0/0	0/ 0/0	7/ 285/2
Low	0/ 0/0	1/ 0/0	5/ 200/1

Slider Average .294

	Inside	Middle	Outside
High	1/ 0/0	1/ 1000/1	1/ 0/0
Med	0/ 0/0	0/ 0/0	3/ 333/1
Low	0/ 0/0	2/ 500/1	9/ 222/2

Tracy Jones Against Left-Handed Pitchers
Overall BARS Batting Average .352

Fastball Average .382

	Inside	Middle	Outside
High	7/ 285/2	5/ 400/2	6/ 500/3
Med	4/ 750/3	3/ 666/2	21/ 380/8
Low	4/ 250/1	8/ 375/3	10/ 200/2

Curve Average .230

	Inside	Middle	Outside
High	2/ 1000/2	0/ 0/0	3/ 333/1
Med	1/ 0/0	0/ 0/0	2/ 0/0
Low	1/ 0/0	3/ 0/0	1/ 0/0

Slider Average .333

	Inside	Middle	Outside
High	0/ 0/0	0/ 0/0	0/ 0/0
Med	2/ 500/1	0/ 0/0	1/ 0/0
Low	0/ 0/0	1/ 1000/1	2/ 0/0

Right-handed hitter Tracy Jones has four very good fastball locations against right-handed pitchers: medium-high outside (.400), high-over-the-middle (.500), low-over-the-middle (.285), and medium-high inside (.444). Right-handers keep throwing him pitches in these locations, showing that they don't know (or care) what his strengths and weaknesses are. By looking at his BARS batting charts, pitchers can know exactly where to pitch him.

The chart below and the field diagram on the opposite page show where fielders need to play when a right-handed pitcher throws Jones a medium-high outside fastball.

MEDIUM-HIGH OUTSIDE FASTBALLS

BATTING AVERAGE .400
Play
Left	Medium-deep in straightaway left field
Center	Deep and shifted toward left field
Right	Deep and shifted toward center field
Short	Normal position
Second	Normal position

He hits .444 against medium-high inside fastballs thrown by right-handers and .500 against high-over-the-middle fastballs.

MEDIUM-HIGH INSIDE FASTBALLS

BATTING AVERAGE .444
Play

Left	*No instances recorded*
Center	Medium-deep in straightaway center field
Right	Medium-deep and shifted toward the right line
Short	Normal position
Second	*No instances recorded*

HIGH-OVER-THE-MIDDLE FASTBALLS

BATTING AVERAGE .500
Play
Left	Medium-deep in straightaway left field
Center	Medium-deep in straightaway center field
Right	Deep in straightaway right field
Short	Normal position
Second	Normal position

Against left-handed pitchers Jones hits over-the-middle, high and waist-high fastballs excellently. His fastball weaknesses are low-inside and low-outside.

He hits a solid .380 against medium-high outside fastballs thrown by left-handers.

MEDIUM-HIGH OUTSIDE FASTBALLS
(THROWN BY LEFT-HANDED PITCHERS)

BATTING AVERAGE .380
Play
Left	Deep in straightaway left field
Center	Deep and shifted toward left field
Right	Medium-deep in straightaway right field
Short	Shifted toward third base
Second	Shifted toward first base

Medium-High Outside Fastballs (Thrown By Right-Handed Pitchers)

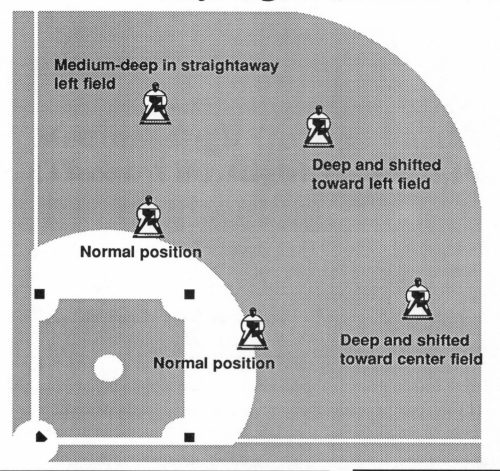

Medium-deep in straightaway left field

Deep and shifted toward left field

Normal position

Normal position

Deep and shifted toward center field

Ahead And Behind In The Count Vs. RH

Ahead

Fastball Average .400

	Inside	Middle	Outside
High	2 / 0 /0	8 / 500 /4	2 / 0 /0
Med	3 / 0 /0	0 / 0 /0	8 / 625 /5
Low	2 / 500 /1	4 / 500 /2	1 / 0 /0

Curve Average .000

	Inside	Middle	Outside
High	0 / 0 /0	0 / 0 /0	0 / 0 /0
Med	0 / 0 /0	0 / 0 /0	0 / 0 /0
Low	0 / 0 /0	0 / 0 /0	0 / 0 /0

Behind

Fastball Average .333

	Inside	Middle	Outside
High	0 / 0 /0	1 / 1000 /1	0 / 0 /0
Med	1 / 0 /0	0 / 0 /0	3 / 333 /1
Low	0 / 0 /0	1 / 0 /0	0 / 0 /0

Curve Average .250

	Inside	Middle	Outside
High	0 / 0 /0	0 / 0 /0	0 / 0 /0
Med	1 / 0 /0	0 / 0 /0	3 / 333 /1
Low	0 / 0 /0	0 / 0 /0	0 / 0 /0

Overall Evaluation

Against Right-Handed Pitchers

Overall Fastball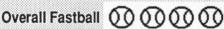

Overall Curve

Overall Slider

Against Left-Handed Pitchers

Overall Fastball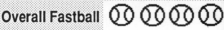

Overall Curve

Overall Slider Not enough information

Comments: Very strong against medium-outside fastballs vs. RH and LH.

Strengths: Medium-outside, high-middle, medium-inside and low-middle fastballs, medium-outside curves vs. RH; all fastballs except low-inside and low-outside vs. LH.

Weaknesses: Low-outside curves and low-outside sliders vs. RH; low-inside and low-outside fastballs vs. LH.

Matt Nokes (Left Handed)　　　　*Detroit Tigers*

Matt Nokes Against Right-Handed Pitchers
Overall BARS Batting Average .322

	Fastball Average .314			Curve Average .360			Slider Average .352		
	Outside	Middle	Inside	Outside	Middle	Inside	Outside	Middle	Inside
High	21/ 333 /7	9/ 333 /3	10/ 500 /5	1/ 1000 /1	1/ 1000 /1	1/ 1000/ 1	0/ 0 /0	2/ 0 /0	1/ 1000 /1
Med	79/ 265 /21	4/ 0 /0	16/ 500 /8	6/ 500 /3	0/ 0 /0	3/ 333 /1	2/ 500 /1	0/ 0 /0	2/ 500 /1
Low	14/ 214 /3	30/ 300 /9	14/ 428 /6	4/ 250 /1	4/ 250 /1	5/ 0 /0	0/ 0 /0	3/ 0 /0	7/ 428 /3

Matt Nokes Against Left-Handed Pitchers
Overall BARS Batting Average .185

	Fastball Average .161			Curve Average .210			Slider Average .250		
	Outside	Middle	Inside	Outside	Middle	Inside	Outside	Middle	Inside
High	3/ 333 /1	0/ 0 /0	3/ 0 /0	2/ 500 /1	1/ 0 /0	0/ 0 /0	0/ 0 /0	0/ 0 /0	0/ 0 /0
Med	10/ 100 /1	2/ 1000 /2	5/ 200 /1	4/ 500 /2	1/ 0 /0	1/ 0 /0	2/ 500 /1	0/ 0 /0	0/ 0 /0
Low	2/ 0 /0	2/ 0 /0	4/ 0 /0	5/ 0 /0	3/ 333 /1	2/ 0 /0	1/ 0 /0	1/ 0 /0	0/ 0 /0

Left-handed hitter Matt Nokes hits fastballs very well overall against right-handed pitchers (.314 overall). Against left-handed pitchers his fastball average is poor (.161 overall).

Nokes hits medium-high outside fastballs against right-handed pitchers much better when he is ahead in the count (.342 when ahead, .230 when behind).

MEDIUM-HIGH OUTSIDE FASTBALLS
(WHEN AHEAD IN THE COUNT)

BATTING AVERAGE .342
Play
Left　　　Medium-deep in straightaway left field
Center　Deep in straightaway center field
Right　　Deep and shifted toward center field
Short　　Normal position
Second　Shifted toward first base

MEDIUM-HIGH OUTSIDE FASTBALLS
(WHEN BEHIND IN THE COUNT)

BATTING AVERAGE .230
Play
Left　　　Medium-deep and shifted toward the left line
Center　Deep and shifted toward left field
Right　　Deep in straightaway right field
Short　　Up middle (shifted toward second base)
Second　Normal position

He hits high-outside fastballs (.333) straightaway to left and center fields and to deep right toward center.

HIGH-OUTSIDE FASTBALLS

BATTING AVERAGE .333
Play
Left　　　Deep in straightaway left field
Center　Medium-deep in straightaway center field
Right　　Deep and shifted toward center field
Short　　*No instances recorded*
Second　Shifted toward first base

Turning now to his extremely strong inside fastball locations (.500, .500 and .428, from high to low), notice in the fielding strategies below that the second baseman should be positioned toward first base for fastballs to all three locations but the outfielders need to shift for each pitch.

HIGH-INSIDE FASTBALLS

BATTING AVERAGE .500
Play
Left　　　Deep in straightaway left field
Center　Medium-deep in straightaway center field
Right　　Medium-deep in straightaway right field
Short　　Normal position
Second　Shifted toward first base

MEDIUM-HIGH INSIDE FASTBALLS

BATTING AVERAGE .500
Play

Left   *No instances recorded*
Center   Medium-deep in straightaway center field
Right   Medium-deep in straightaway right field
Short   *No instances recorded*
Second   Shifted toward first base

LOW-INSIDE FASTBALLS

BATTING AVERAGE .428
Play

Left   Deep in straightaway left field
Center   Medium-deep and shifted toward right field
Right   Deep in straightaway right field
Short   *No instances recorded*
Second   Shifted toward first base

Nokes hits a fine .300 against low-over-the-middle fastballs.

LOW-OVER-THE-MIDDLE FASTBALLS

BATTING AVERAGE .300
Play

Left   Medium-deep and shifted toward center field
Center   Deep in straightaway center field
Right   Deep and shifted toward center field
Short   *No instances recorded*
Second   Normal position

Pitchers throw Nokes very few medium-over-the-middle fastballs. This means that they are pitching him carefully, keeping the ball away from the heart of the plate. The relatively high number of instances in his medium-high outside fastball location (79) indicates that pitchers throw him more outside than inside fastballs, which is what they should be doing because he hits medium-high inside fastballs so strongly.

He hits low-outside fastballs for a .214 average. The low-outside/medium-high-outside sector is a good area for pitchers to attack.

LOW-OUTSIDE FASTBALLS

BATTING AVERAGE .214
Play

Left   Deep in straightaway left field
Center   Deep in straightaway center field
Right   Medium-deep in straightaway right field
Short   Up middle (shifted toward second base)
Second   *No instances recorded*

Nokes Against Left-Handed Pitchers

Nokes is weak generally against left-handed pitchers, although his BARS averages are based on fewer recorded instances.

He hits only .100 against medium-high outside fastballs thrown by left-handers. He hits this pitch down both lines.

MEDIUM-HIGH OUTSIDE FASTBALLS (THROWN BY LEFT-HANDED PITCHERS)

BATTING AVERAGE .100
Play

Left   Medium-deep and shifted toward the left field line
Center   Deep in straightaway center field
Right   Deep and shifted toward the right field line
Short   Normal position
Second   Shifted toward first base

Ahead And Behind In The Count Vs. RH

Ahead

Fastball Average .364

	Outside	Middle	Inside
High	8/375/3	6/333/2	3/333/1
Med	38/342/13	2/0/0	13/538/7
Low	5/400/2	15/266/4	6/500/3

Curve Average .750

	Outside	Middle	Inside
High	0/0/0	1/1000/1	0/0/0
Med	3/666/2	0/0/0	0/0/0
Low	0/0/0	0/0/0	0/0/0

Behind

Fastball Average .281

	Outside	Middle	Inside
High	3/333/1	3/333/1	2/500/1
Med	13/230/3	0/0/0	2/0/0
Low	2/0/0	5/400/2	2/500/1

Curve Average .444

	Outside	Middle	Inside
High	1/1000/1	0/0/0	1/1000/1
Med	2/500/1	0/0/0	1/0/0
Low	2/500/1	0/0/0	2/0/0

Overall Evaluation

Against Right-Handed Pitchers

Overall Fastball ⚾⚾⚾
Overall Curve ⚾⚾⚾⚾
Overall Slider ⚾⚾⚾⚾

Against Left-Handed Pitchers

Overall Fastball ⚾
Overall Curve ⚾
Overall Slider   Not enough information

Comments: Nokes hits high fastballs and inside fastballs extremely well against RH.
Strengths: High fastballs, inside fastballs, low-middle fastballs, medium-outside curves, low-inside sliders vs. RH.
Weaknesses: Low-outside and medium-outside fastballs, low curves vs. RH; medium-outside fastballs, inside fastballs vs. LH.

Chet Lemon Against Right-Handed Pitchers
Overall BARS Batting Average .259

Fastball Average .250			Curve Average .326			Slider Average .233		
Inside	Middle	Outside	Inside	Middle	Outside	Inside	Middle	Outside
High								
29/ 241/7	33/ 212/7	16/ 125/2	2/ 0/0	7/ 571/4	2/ 0/0	0/ 0/0	3/ 666/2	2/ 0/0
Med								
70/ 214/15	24/ 333/8	136/ 286/39	11/ 454/5	6/ 500/3	21/ 428/9	4/ 750/3	7/ 142/1	28/ 321/9
Low								
30/ 166/5	65/ 292/19	33/ 212/7	2/ 0/0	14/ 285/4	30/ 200/6	5/ 0/0	12/ 250/3	29/ 103/3

Chet Lemon Against Left-Handed Pitchers
Overall BARS Batting Average .290

Fastball Average .295			Curve Average .219			Slider Average .360		
Inside	Middle	Outside	Inside	Middle	Outside	Inside	Middle	Outside
High								
10/ 100/1	18/ 333/6	16/ 312/5	3/ 0/0	0/ 0/0	0/ 0/0	2/ 0/0	5/ 400/2	0/ 0/0
Med								
23/ 217/5	15/ 400/6	74/ 310/23	2/ 500/1	3/ 333/1	10/ 400/4	1/ 1000/1	2/ 500/1	1/ 0/0
Low								
12/ 250/3	32/ 406/13	23/ 173/4	5/ 400/2	12/ 83/1	6/ 0/0	5/ 0/0	5/ 600/3	4/ 500/2

Right-handed batter Chet Lemon hits fastballs better against left-handed than against right-handed pitchers (.295 overall vs. left-handers, .250 overall vs. right-handers). He hits curves much better, however, against right-handers (.326 overall against right-handers, .219 against left-handers).

He hits .286 against medium-high outside fastballs thrown by right-handed pitchers. He hits this pitch deep to the outfield and to the right side of the infield.

MEDIUM-HIGH OUTSIDE FASTBALLS

BATTING AVERAGE .286
Play
Left — Deep and shifted toward center field
Center — Deep in straightaway center field
Right — Deep and shifted toward the right field line
Short — Up middle (shifted toward second base)
Second — Shifted toward first base

He hits low-over-the-middle fastballs better when ahead than when behind in the count (.333 when ahead, .266 when behind). He tends to pull this pitch more when ahead.

LOW-OVER-THE-MIDDLE FASTBALLS
(WHEN AHEAD IN THE COUNT)

BATTING AVERAGE .333
Play
Left — Medium-deep and shifted toward the left field line
Center — Medium-deep in straightaway center field
Right — Deep and shifted toward center field
Short — Shifted toward third base
Second — Normal position

LOW-OVER-THE-MIDDLE FASTBALLS
(WHEN BEHIND IN THE COUNT)

BATTING AVERAGE .266
Play
Left — Deep in straightaway left field
Center — Deep in straightaway center field
Right — Deep and shifted toward center field
Short — Shifted toward third base
Second — Normal position

Lemon hits very well against both medium-high inside and medium-high outside curves. He hits these two pitches very differently, however. He tends to pull the inside curve much more than he does the outside curve.

MEDIUM-HIGH INSIDE CURVEBALLS

BATTING AVERAGE .454
Play
Left — Short in straightaway left field
Center — Medium-deep and shifted toward left field
Right — *No instances recorded*
Short — Shifted toward third base
Second — *No instances recorded*

MEDIUM-HIGH OUTSIDE CURVEBALLS

BATTING AVERAGE .428
Play
Left   Deep and shifted toward the left field line
Center   Deep in straightaway center field
Right   Medium-deep and shifted toward the right line
Short   Shifted toward third base
Second   Shifted toward first base

Lemon has trouble with low sliders (.000, .250 and .103, inside to outside). He hits an excellent .321 against medium-high outside sliders against right-handers.

Lemon Against Left-Handed Pitchers

Lemon hits a fine .310 against medium-high outside fastballs thrown by left-handed pitchers.

MEDIUM-HIGH OUTSIDE FASTBALLS
(THROWN BY LEFT-HANDED PITCHERS)

BATTING AVERAGE .310
Play
Left   Deep in straightaway left field
Center   Deep and shifted toward left field
Right   Deep in straightaway right field
Short   Normal position
Second   Normal position

His .406 against low-over-the-middle fastballs thrown by lefties is excellent. He pulls this pitch deep down the left line and into right field toward center.

LOW-OVER-THE-MIDDLE FASTBALLS
(THROWN BY LEFT-HANDED PITCHERS)

BATTING AVERAGE .406
Play
Left   Deep and shifted toward the left field line
Center   Deep in straightaway center field
Right   Deep and shifted toward center field
Short   Normal position
Second   Normal position

The BARS fielding strategy shows that each of the outfielders needs to be positioned differently for a high-over-the-middle fastball compared with a high-outside fastball when Lemon faces a left-handed pitcher.

HIGH-OVER-THE-MIDDLE FASTBALLS
(THROWN BY LEFT-HANDED PITCHERS)

BATTING AVERAGE .333
Play
Left   Deep in straightaway left field
Center   Deep and shifted toward left field
Right   Deep and shifted toward center field
Short   Up middle (shifted toward second base)
Second   *No instances recorded*

HIGH-OUTSIDE FASTBALLS
(THROWN BY LEFT-HANDED PITCHERS)

BATTING AVERAGE .312
Play
Left   Deep and shifted toward the left field line
Center   Deep and shifted toward right field
Right   Deep in straightaway right field
Short   Shifted toward third base
Second   *No instances recorded*

Ahead And Behind In The Count Vs. RH

Ahead

Fastball Average .274

	Inside	Middle	Outside
High	13/307 /4	13/153 /2	5/200 /1
Med	33/151 /5	12/416 /5	49/326 /16
Low	12/250 /3	27/333 /9	7/285 /2

Curve Average .379

	Inside	Middle	Outside
High	0/0 /0	3/666 /2	2/0 /0
Med	3/333 /1	5/400 /2	5/600 /3
Low	2/0 /0	3/0 /0	6/500 /3

Behind

Fastball Average .260

	Inside	Middle	Outside
High	3/333 /1	12/166 /2	1/0 /0
Med	14/214 /3	3/333 /1	37/324 /12
Low	3/0 /0	15/266 /4	8/250 /2

Curve Average .464

	Inside	Middle	Outside
High	1/0 /0	2/1000 /2	0/0 /0
Med	2/500 /1	1/1000 /1	7/571 /4
Low	0/0 /0	6/333 /2	9/333 /3

Overall Evaluation
Against Right-Handed Pitchers

Overall Fastball ⚾⚾
Overall Curve ⚾⚾⚾⚾⚾
Overall Slider ⚾⚾

Against Left-Handed Pitchers

Overall Fastball ⚾⚾⚾⚾
Overall Curve ⚾⚾
Overall Slider ⚾⚾⚾⚾⚾

Comments: Trouble vs. inside & high fastballs vs. RH.
Strengths: Medium-middle fastballs, waist-high curves, medium-outside sliders vs. RH; over-the-middle fastballs, medium-outside and high-outside fastballs, waist-high curves vs. LH.
Weaknesses: Inside fastballs, high fastballs, low-outside fastballs, low-outside curves, low sliders vs. RH; inside fastballs, low-outside fastballs, low-middle and low-outside curves vs. LH.

Lloyd Moseby (Left Handed)   *Detroit Tigers*

Lloyd Moseby Against Right-Handed Pitchers
Overall BARS Batting Average .295

Fastball Average .305

	Outside	Middle	Inside
High	23/ 173 /4	21/ 190 /4	9/ 111 /1
Med	116/ 327 /38	31/ 483 /15	42/ 285 /12
Low	24/ 250 /6	39/ 384 /15	19/ 210 /4

Curve Average .258

	Outside	Middle	Inside
High	3/ 666 /2	5/ 0 /0	2/ 0 /0
Med	27/ 333 /9	11/ 272 /3	12/ 500 /6
Low	3/ 0 /0	15/ 133 /2	11/ 90 /1

Slider Average .300

	Outside	Middle	Inside
High	2/ 500 /1	2/ 1000 /2	2/ 1000 /2
Med	2/ 500 /1	4/ 250 /1	10/ 200 /2
Low	3/ 0 /0	6/ 166 /1	9/ 222 /2

Lloyd Moseby Against Left-Handed Pitchers
Overall BARS Batting Average .220

Fastball Average .205

	Outside	Middle	Inside
High	7/ 285 /2	10/ 100 /1	13/ 153 /2
Med	57/ 210 /12	19/ 105 /2	24/ 166 /4
Low	5/ 200 /1	30/ 266 /8	20/ 300 /6

Curve Average .229

	Outside	Middle	Inside
High	2/ 0 /0	1/ 0 /0	0/ 0 /0
Med	14/ 214 /3	4/ 500 /2	7/ 285 /2
Low	7/ 285 /2	9/ 111 /1	4/ 250 /1

Slider Average .264

	Outside	Middle	Inside
High	1/ 0 /0	2/ 500 /1	1/ 0 /0
Med	14/ 285 /4	3/ 333 /1	5/ 600 /3
Low	16/ 125 /2	8/ 250 /2	3/ 333 /1

Left-handed hitting Lloyd Moseby hits fastballs well against right-handed pitchers (.305) but has trouble with fastballs against left-handed pitchers (.205).

Against right-handers, he hits .327 in his medium-high outside fastball location. He hits this pitch deep into the left-center alley and to the right side of the infield.

MEDIUM-HIGH OUTSIDE FASTBALLS

BATTING AVERAGE .327
Play
Left   Deep in straightaway left field
Center   Deep and shifted toward left field
Right   Medium-deep in straightaway right field
Short   Up middle (shifted toward second base)
Second   Shifted toward first base

He hits medium-high inside fastballs for a .285 average. He hits this pitch deep into the right-center gap.

MEDIUM-HIGH INSIDE FASTBALLS

BATTING AVERAGE .285
Play
Left   Medium-deep in straightaway left field
Center   Deep in straightaway center field
Right   Deep and shifted toward center field

Short   Up middle (shifted toward second base)
Second   Normal position

He has an excellent .384 average in his low-over-the-middle fastball location. He hits this pitch deep down the left line (his opposite field) and into the right-center gap. If fielders played him as suggested by the BARS fielding strategy shown below, they could prevent most of his base hits resulting from pitches to this location.

LOW-OVER-THE-MIDDLE FASTBALLS

BATTING AVERAGE .384
Play
Left   Deep and shifted toward the left field line
Center   Deep in straightaway center field
Right   Deep and shifted toward center field
Short   Normal position
Second   Normal position

Moseby has trouble with high fastballs against right-handers. He hits .173 against high-outside fastballs. Most of his hit balls in this location are probably easy fly balls or ground balls that fielders could get to no matter where they play.

HIGH-OUTSIDE FASTBALLS

BATTING AVERAGE .173
  Play
Left   Deep in straightaway left field
Center   Deep in straightaway center field
Right   Deep and shifted toward center field
Short   Up middle (shifted toward second base)
Second   Normal position

By keeping fastballs high or inside, right-handers could gain an advantage on Moseby.

Moseby Against Curves And Sliders

Moseby has trouble with low curves and low sliders against right-handed pitchers. But he hits waist-high curves very well. His .333 average against medium-high outside curves is excellent.

MEDIUM-HIGH OUTSIDE CURVEBALLS

BATTING AVERAGE .333
  Play
Left   Deep in straightaway left field
Center   Medium-deep in straightaway center field
Right   Deep and shifted toward center field
Short   Up middle (shifted toward second base)
Second   Shifted toward first base

He pulls medium-high inside curves down the right line for a strong .500 average

MEDIUM-HIGH INSIDE CURVEBALLS

BATTING AVERAGE .500
  Play
Left   *No instances recorded*
Center   Medium-deep in straightaway center field

Right   Medium-deep and shifted toward the right line
Short   Normal position
Second   Shifted toward first base

Moseby Against Left-Handed Pitchers

Moseby hits only .210 against medium-high outside fastballs thrown by left-handers. Most of his hit balls in this location are probably easy outs.

MEDIUM-HIGH OUTSIDE FASTBALLS

BATTING AVERAGE .210
  Play
Left   Deep in straightaway left field
Center   Medium-deep in straightaway center field
Right   Deep in straightaway right field
Short   Normal position
Second   Normal position

His highest fastball average against left-handers is in the low-inside location (.300). He hits this pitch down both lines when he hits to the outfield but to the right side of the infield when he hits ground balls.

LOW-INSIDE FASTBALLS

BATTING AVERAGE .300
  Play
Left   Medium-deep and shifted toward the left field line
Center   Deep and shifted toward left field
Right   Deep and shifted toward the right field line
Short   Up middle (shifted toward second base)
Second   Shifted toward first base

Moseby has trouble with curves against left-handers (.229 overall). He hits sliders fairly well (.264 overall).

Ahead And Behind In The Count Vs. RH

Ahead

Fastball Average .347

	Outside	Middle	Inside
High	6/ 333 /2	5/ 200 /1	1/ 1000/1
Med	38/ 342 /13	15/ 533 /8	16/ 312 /5
Low	10/ 200 /2	22/ 363 /8	8/ 250 /2

Curve Average .352

	Outside	Middle	Inside
High	0/ 0 /0	1/ 0 /0	0/ 0 /0
Med	7/ 428 /3	3/ 333 /1	2/ 0 /0
Low	0/ 0 /0	2/ 500 /1	2/ 500 /1

Behind

Fastball Average .353

	Outside	Middle	Inside
High	3/ 0 /0	7/ 285 /2	0/ 0 /0
Med	29/ 379 /11	6/ 500 /3	8/ 375 /3
Low	3/ 333 /1	4/ 750 /3	5/ 0 /0

Curve Average .307

	Outside	Middle	Inside
High	2/ 1000/2	0/ 0 /0	1/ 0 /0
Med	10/ 300 /3	2/ 500 /1	3/ 666 /2
Low	0/ 0 /0	5/ 0 /0	3/ 0 /0

Overall Evaluation
Against Right-Handed Pitchers

Overall Fastball ⚾ ⚾ ⚾

Overall Curve ⚾ ⚾

Overall Slider ⚾ ⚾ ⚾ ⚾

Against Left-Handed Pitchers

Overall Fastball ⚾

Overall Curve ⚾

Overall Slider ⚾ ⚾

Comments: Trouble with all high fastballs vs. RH.
Strengths: Medium-outside, medium-middle and low-middle fastballs vs. RH, waist-high curves vs. RH; low-inside fastballs vs. LH.
Weaknesses: High fastballs, low-outside and low-inside fastballs vs. RH, low curves and low sliders, medium-inside sliders vs. RH; all fastballs except low-inside, medium-outside and low-middle curves vs. LH, low-outside sliders vs. LH.

Tony Phillips (Switch Hitter) — Detroit Tigers

Tony Phillips Against Right-Handed Pitchers
Overall BARS Batting Average .239

Fastball Average .250

	Outside	Middle	Inside
High	10 / 200 / 2	35 / 200 / 7	9 / 111 / 1
Med	65 / 338 / 22	19 / 421 / 8	35 / 228 / 8
Low	15 / 266 / 4	43 / 162 / 7	20 / 200 / 4

Curve Average .184

	Outside	Middle	Inside
High	0 / 0 / 0	0 / 0 / 0	3 / 333 / 1
Med	7 / 285 / 2	3 / 333 / 1	4 / 250 / 1
Low	3 / 333 / 1	11 / 0 / 0	7 / 142 / 1

Slider Average .208

	Outside	Middle	Inside
High	0 / 0 / 0	4 / 250 / 1	0 / 0 / 0
Med	1 / 1000 / 1	2 / 0 / 0	7 / 428 / 3
Low	1 / 0 / 0	2 / 0 / 0	7 / 0 / 0

Tony Phillips Against Left-Handed Pitchers
Overall BARS Batting Average .285

Fastball Average .281

	Inside	Middle	Outside
High	0 / 0 / 0	7 / 285 / 2	8 / 0 / 0
Med	14 / 357 / 5	10 / 400 / 4	39 / 307 / 12
Low	5 / 200 / 1	13 / 230 / 3	7 / 285 / 2

Curve Average .285

	Inside	Middle	Outside
High	0 / 0 / 0	0 / 0 / 0	2 / 500 / 1
Med	1 / 0 / 0	2 / 0 / 0	5 / 400 / 2
Low	2 / 0 / 0	6 / 333 / 2	3 / 333 / 1

Slider Average .333

	Inside	Middle	Outside
High	0 / 0 / 0	0 / 0 / 0	0 / 0 / 0
Med	7 / 428 / 3	0 / 0 / 0	2 / 500 / 1
Low	8 / 375 / 3	6 / 166 / 1	1 / 0 / 0

Switch-hitter Tony Phillips has a low .250 overall fastball average against right-handed pitchers, but he hits fastballs at .281 overall against left-handed pitchers.

Against right-handers he has trouble with all high fastballs, inside fastballs, and low fastballs. Right-handers need to keep fastballs away from his medium-high outside/medium-over-the-middle sector. He hits medium-high outside fastballs for a solid .338 average deep down both lines and into the deep left-center alley.

MEDIUM-HIGH OUTSIDE FASTBALLS

BATTING AVERAGE .338

Play

Left	Deep and shifted toward the left field line
Center	Deep and shifted toward left field
Right	Deep and shifted toward the right field line
Short	Up middle (shifted toward second base)
Second	Normal position

He is thrown a relatively-high number of medium-over-the-middle fastballs (19 recorded instances). Pitchers need to make sure they don't give him this pitch because he hits .421 in this location.

MEDIUM-OVER-THE-MIDDLE FASTBALLS

BATTING AVERAGE .421

Play

Left	Deep in straightaway left field
Center	Deep in straightaway center field
Right	Deep in straightaway right field
Short	Normal position
Second	Shifted toward first base

He has trouble with medium-high inside fastballs (.228). He also hits this pitch deep to all fields, but his low average probably means that most of his hit balls in this location are not hit hard and are easy outs.

MEDIUM-HIGH INSIDE FASTBALLS

BATTING AVERAGE .228

Play

Left	Deep and shifted toward the left field line
Center	Deep in straightaway center field
Right	Deep in straightaway right field
Short	Up middle (shifted toward second base)
Second	Normal position

Phillips Against Curves And Sliders

Phillips hits well enough against medium-high outside curves (.285) but he has trouble with low-over-the-middle curves (.000 on 0 for 11), low-inside curves (.142) and low-inside sliders (.000 on 0 for 7). His BARS fielding strategy shows hardly any recorded hit balls in these locations. He seems to have trouble getting his bat on the ball for these pitches.

LOW-OVER-THE-MIDDLE CURVEBALLS

BATTING AVERAGE .000 (0 for 11)
> *Play*

Left   Short in straightaway left field
Center Deep in straightaway center field
Right   *No instances recorded*
Short   *No instances recorded*
Second *No instances recorded*

LOW-INSIDE SLIDERS

BATTING AVERAGE .000 (0 for 7)
> *Play*

Left   Medium-deep in straightaway left field
Center Deep in straightaway center field
Right   *No instances recorded*
Short   *No instances recorded*
Second *No instances recorded*

Phillips Against Left-Handed Pitchers

Against left-handed pitchers, Phillips hits a solid .307 against medium-high outside fastballs.

MEDIUM-HIGH OUTSIDE FASTBALLS (THROWN BY LEFT-HANDED PITCHERS)

BATTING AVERAGE .307
> *Play*

Left   Deep in straightaway left field
Center Deep in straightaway center field
Right   Medium-deep in straightaway right field
Short   Normal position
Second Shifted toward first base

He hits an excellent .357 against medium-high inside fastballs thrown by left-handers. He tends to hit this pitch up the middle of the field.

MEDIUM-HIGH INSIDE FASTBALLS (THROWN BY LEFT-HANDED PITCHERS)

BATTING AVERAGE .357
> *Play*

Left   Deep and shifted toward center field
Center Deep in straightaway center field
Right   Deep and shifted toward the right field line
Short   Up middle (shifted toward second base)
Second *No instances recorded*

He has trouble with low-over-the-middle fastballs (.230) and high-outside fastballs (.000 on 0 for 8) against lefties. He has a strong .400 average in his medium-over-the-middle location.

Phillips hits curves well overall against lefties (.285), but he really comes alive against inside sliders. His .428 against medium-inside sliders is excellent. By aligning themselves according to the following BARS fielding strategy for this pitch, fielders could catch most of his line drives that are now falling in for base hits.

MEDIUM-HIGH INSIDE SLIDERS (THROWN BY LEFT-HANDED PITCHERS)

BATTING AVERAGE .428
> *Play*

Left   Medium-deep in straightaway left field
Center Medium-deep in straightaway center field
Right   Short in straightaway right field
Short   Normal position
Second *No instances recorded*

Ahead And Behind In The Count Vs. RH

Ahead

Fastball Average .284

	Outside	Middle	Inside
High	4/250 /1	12/166 /2	6/0 /0
Med	29/413 /12	16/437 /7	13/384 /5
Low	4/500 /2	19/105 /2	13/153 /2

Curve Average .000

	Outside	Middle	Inside
High	0/0 /0	0/0 /0	0/0 /0
Med	0/0 /0	0/0 /0	0/0 /0
Low	0/0 /0	1/0 /0	0/0 /0

Behind

Fastball Average .282

	Outside	Middle	Inside
High	3/0 /0	7/285 /2	0/0 /0
Med	14/357 /5	1/0 /0	5/200 /1
Low	2/500 /1	6/333 /2	1/0 /0

Curve Average .428

	Outside	Middle	Inside
High	0/0 /0	0/0 /0	3/333 /1
Med	3/666 /2	2/500 /1	1/0 /0
Low	2/500 /1	2/0 /0	1/1000 /1

Overall Evaluation

Against Right-Handed Pitchers

Overall Fastball ⚾⚾
Overall Curve ⚾⚾
Overall Slider ⚾⚾

Against Left-Handed Pitchers

Overall Fastball ⚾⚾
Overall Curve ⚾⚾⚾
Overall Slider ⚾⚾⚾⚾⚾

Comments: Has a strong fastball sector medium-outside/medium-middle vs. RH.
Strengths: As above, medium-inside sliders vs. RH; waist-high fastballs, medium-inside and low-inside sliders vs. LH.
Weaknesses: High fastballs, low fastballs, medium-inside fastballs, low-middle and low-inside curves, low sliders vs. RH; low-middle, low-inside and high-outside fastballs, low-middle sliders vs. LH.

Rick Schu Against Right-Handed Pitchers
Overall BARS Batting Average .240

Fastball Average .272

	Inside	Middle	Outside
High	10/ 100 /1	14/ 214 /3	10/ 300 /3
Med	9/ 222 /2	14/ 357 /5	40/ 300 /12
Low	5/ 200 /1	14/ 285 /4	5/ 400 /2

Curve Average .171

	Inside	Middle	Outside
High	0/ 0 /0	0/ 0 /0	1/ 0 /0
Med	4/ 0 /0	3/ 333 /1	10/ 300 /3
Low	4/ 0 /0	2/ 0 /0	11/ 181 /2

Slider Average .157

	Inside	Middle	Outside
High	1/ 0 /0	1/ 0 /0	2/ 0 /0
Med	0/ 0 /0	0/ 0 /0	3/ 0 /0
Low	0/ 0 /0	4/ 500 /2	8/ 125 /1

Rick Schu Against Left-Handed Pitchers
Overall BARS Batting Average .241

Fastball Average .252

	Inside	Middle	Outside
High	7/ 285 /2	8/ 125 /1	10/ 400 /4
Med	10/ 200 /2	3/ 333 /1	30/ 200 /6
Low	3/ 333 /1	9/ 333 /3	11/ 272 /3

Curve Average .153

	Inside	Middle	Outside
High	1/ 1000 /1	0/ 0 /0	1/ 0 /0
Med	2/ 0 /0	0/ 0 /0	3/ 0 /0
Low	1/ 0 /0	3/ 0 /0	2/ 500 /1

Slider Average .250

	Inside	Middle	Outside
High	0/ 0 /0	0/ 0 /0	1/ 0 /0
Med	2/ 1000 /2	1/ 1000 /1	2/ 0 /0
Low	2/ 0 /0	1/ 0 /0	3/ 0 /0

Right-handed hitting Rick Schu has some trouble with fastballs (.272 overall vs. right-handed pitchers, .252 overall vs. left-handed pitchers).

Schu hits .300 against medium-high outside fastballs thrown by right-handers. His other strong fastball locations against right-handers are medium-over-the-middle (.357), low-over-the-middle (.285) and high-outside (.300). His weak locations are high-over-the-middle (.214), medium-high inside (.222) and high-inside (.100).

Schu hits medium-high outside fastballs thrown by right-handers deep to straightaway left field, into the deep right-center gap, and deep down the right field line.

MEDIUM-HIGH OUTSIDE FASTBALLS

BATTING AVERAGE .300
Play

Left	Deep in straightaway left field
Center	Deep and shifted toward right field
Right	Deep and shifted toward the right field line
Short	Up middle (shifted toward second base)
Second	Normal position

He hits high-outside fastballs deep to all fields.

HIGH-OUTSIDE FASTBALLS

BATTING AVERAGE .300
Play

Left	Deep and shifted toward the left field line
Center	Deep in straightaway center field
Right	Deep in straightaway right field
Short	*No instances recorded*
Second	Shifted toward first base

He hits low-over-the-middle fastballs into right-center. Fielders could prevent most of Schu's line-drive base hits if they positioned themselves correctly for this pitch.

LOW-OVER-THE-MIDDLE FASTBALLS

BATTING AVERAGE .285
Play

Left	*No instances recorded*
Center	Medium-deep in straightaway center field
Right	Deep and shifted toward center field
Short	Normal position
Second	Normal position

Schu's .357 medium-over-the-middle fastball average is very strong. A pitcher would not want to throw him this pitch, but it's interesting to see how he hits it.

MEDIUM-OVER-THE-MIDDLE FASTBALLS

BATTING AVERAGE .357

	Play
Left	Medium-deep and shifted toward the left line
Center	Deep in straightaway center field
Right	Medium-deep in straightaway right field
Short	Normal position
Second	Normal position

Schu Against Curves And Sliders

Schu has trouble with low-outside curves and low-outside sliders thrown by right-handed pitchers (.181 and .125 respectively).

He hits medium-high outside curves excellently (.300), sending the ball deep to left, short to center and medium-deep to right.

MEDIUM-HIGH OUTSIDE CURVEBALLS

BATTING AVERAGE .300

	Play
Left	Deep in straightaway left field
Center	Short in straightaway center field
Right	Medium-deep in straightaway right field
Short	Shifted toward third base
Second	*No instances recorded*

Schu Against Left-Handed Pitchers

Schu hits medium-high outside fastballs poorly against left-handers (.200).

MEDIUM-HIGH OUTSIDE FASTBALLS
(THROWN BY LEFT-HANDED PITCHERS)

BATTING AVERAGE .200

	Play
Left	Deep in straightaway left field
Center	Medium-deep in straightaway center field
Right	Medium-deep in straightaway right field
Short	Up middle (shifted toward second base)
Second	Shifted toward first base

It's interesting to see how Schu hits low-outside fastballs in comparison to medium-high outside fastballs. All fielders except the right fielder would have to shift to be correctly positioned for pitches to these locations.

LOW-OUTSIDE FASTBALLS
(THROWN BY LEFT-HANDED PITCHERS)

BATTING AVERAGE .272

	Play
Left	Deep and shifted toward the left field line
Center	Deep and shifted toward left field
Right	Medium-deep in straightaway right field
Short	Normal position
Second	Normal position

In contrast, he hits low-over-the-middle fastballs to deep right center and deep down the right line.

LOW-OVER-THE-MIDDLE FASTBALLS
(THROWN BY LEFT-HANDED PITCHERS)

BATTING AVERAGE .333

	Play
Left	Deep in straightaway left field
Center	Deep and shifted toward right field
Right	Deep and shifted toward the right field line
Short	Shifted toward third base
Second	Shifted toward first base

Ahead And Behind In The Count Vs. RH

Ahead

Fastball Average .272

	Inside	Middle	Outside
High	5/200 /1	6/166 /1	1/0 /0
Med	3/333 /1	6/500 /3	21/238 /5
Low	1/0 /0	9/333 /3	3/333 /1

Curve Average .166

	Inside	Middle	Outside
High	0/0 /0	0/0 /0	0/0 /0
Med	0/0 /0	1/1000 /1	3/0 /0
Low	0/0 /0	1/0 /0	1/0 /0

Behind

Fastball Average .466

	Inside	Middle	Outside
High	0/0 /0	0/0 /0	3/666 /2
Med	3/333 /1	3/666 /2	2/500 /1
Low	2/0 /0	1/0 /0	1/1000 /1

Curve Average .500

	Inside	Middle	Outside
High	0/0 /0	0/0 /0	1/0 /0
Med	0/0 /0	1/0 /0	1/1000 /1
Low	0/0 /0	0/0 /0	1/1000 /1

Overall Evaluation

Against Right-Handed Pitchers

Overall Fastball	⚾⚾
Overall Curve	⚾⚾
Overall Slider	⚾⚾

Against Left-Handed Pitchers

Overall Fastball	⚾⚾
Overall Curve	⚾⚾
Overall Slider	⚾⚾ ⚾⚾

Comments: Weak against inside fastballs vs. RH.
Strengths: Medium-outside, high-outside, medium-middle and low-middle fastballs, medium-outside curves vs. RH; high-outside and low-middle fastballs vs. LH.
Weaknesses: Inside fastballs, high-middle fastballs, low-outside curves and low-outside sliders vs. RH; medium-inside, medium-outside and high-middle fastballs vs. LH.

Alan Trammell (Right Handed) — *Detroit Tigers*

Alan Trammell Against Right-Handed Pitchers
Overall BARS Batting Average .285

Fastball Average .318

	Inside	Middle	Outside
High	34/ 294 /10	45/ 222 /10	20/ 250 /5
Med	77/ 428 /33	49/ 489 /24	158/ 316 /50
Low	27/ 148 /4	83/ 301 /25	38/ 210 /8

Curve Average .187

	Inside	Middle	Outside
High	1/ 0 /0	6/ 166 /1	1/ 1000 /1
Med	11/ 272 /3	7/ 0 /0	28/ 214 /6
Low	2/ 500 /1	9/ 222 /2	31/ 129 /4

Slider Average .186

	Inside	Middle	Outside
High	1/ 0 /0	5/ 200 /1	2/ 0 /0
Med	5/ 200 /1	5/ 200 /1	22/ 227 /5
Low	1/ 0 /0	8/ 375 /3	26/ 115 /3

Alan Trammell Against Left-Handed Pitchers
Overall BARS Batting Average .355

Fastball Average .374

	Inside	Middle	Outside
High	8/ 125 /1	17/ 352 /6	25/ 160 /4
Med	35/ 571 /20	20/ 550 /11	82/ 280 /23
Low	11/ 363 /4	30/ 433 /13	34/ 470 /16

Curve Average .296

	Inside	Middle	Outside
High	0/ 0 /0	3/ 333 /1	3/ 333 /1
Med	4/ 250 /1	3/ 333 /1	16/ 437 /7
Low	7/ 0 /0	10/ 300 /3	8/ 250 /2

Slider Average .305

	Inside	Middle	Outside
High	1/ 0 /0	1/ 1000 /1	1/ 1000 /1
Med	6/ 333 /2	3/ 333 /1	5/ 200 /1
Low	8/ 0 /0	7/ 571 /4	4/ 250 /1

Right-handed hitting Alan Trammell hits fastballs very well against right-handed pitchers (.318) and excellently against left-handers (.374).

Trammell has some very strong locations in his fastball chart against right-handed pitchers. In particular, notice his high averages in the three medium-high locations (.428, .489 and .316 from inside to outside).

Notice in his Ahead and Behind charts on the opposite page that Trammell hits medium-high outside fastballs much better when he is ahead in the count than when he is behind (.369 when ahead, .216 when behind). He pulls this pitch deep down the left line when he is ahead.

MEDIUM-HIGH OUTSIDE FASTBALLS (WHEN AHEAD IN THE COUNT)

BATTING AVERAGE .369

Play

Left	Deep and shifted toward the left field line
Center	Medium-deep in straightaway center field
Right	Medium-deep in straightaway right field
Short	Up middle (shifted toward second base)
Second	Normal position

MEDIUM-HIGH OUTSIDE FASTBALLS (WHEN BEHIND IN THE COUNT)

BATTING AVERAGE .216

Play

Left	Medium-deep in straightaway left field
Center	Medium-deep in straightaway center field
Right	Deep in straightaway right field
Short	Normal position
Second	Shifted toward first base

Trammell hits .428 against medium-high inside fastballs thrown by right-handers. He also hits this pitch considerably better when ahead (.500 when ahead, .250 when behind).

MEDIUM-HIGH INSIDE FASTBALLS (OVERALL FOR ALL COUNTS)

BATTING AVERAGE .428

Play

Left	Deep and shifted toward the left field line
Center	Medium-deep in straightaway center field
Right	Medium-deep and shifted toward center field
Short	Normal position
Second	Normal position

Trammell hits .301 against low-over-the-middle fastballs but only .210 against low-outside fastballs. Notice in the following BARS fielding strategies that each outfielder must shift to be in the best position for these two pitches.

LOW-OVER-THE-MIDDLE FASTBALLS

BATTING AVERAGE .301
Play

Left	Medium-deep in straightaway left field
Center	Deep and shifted toward left field
Right	Deep and shifted toward center field
Short	Up middle (shifted toward second base)
Second	Shifted toward first base

LOW-OUTSIDE FASTBALLS

BATTING AVERAGE .210
Play

Left	Medium-deep and shifted toward the left field line
Center	Medium-deep in straightaway center field
Right	Medium-deep and shifted toward center field
Short	Up middle (shifted toward second base)
Second	Shifted toward first base

Trammell has great difficulty with curves and sliders against right-handed pitchers. He has low averages in the medium-high outside and low-outside locations for both types of pitch. By keeping curves and sliders in this down and away sector, right-handers could gain quite an edge on Trammell.

Trammell Against Left-Handed Pitchers

Trammell hits fastballs excellently overall against left-handers. His only weak locations are high-inside and high-outside (.125 and .160). He hits an exceptional .470 against low-outside fastballs against lefties.

LOW-OUTSIDE FASTBALLS
(THROWN BY LEFT-HANDED PITCHERS)

BATTING AVERAGE .470
Play

Left	Deep and shifted toward center field
Center	Medium-deep and shifted toward right field
Right	Medium-deep in straightaway right field
Short	Normal position
Second	*No instances recorded*

He hits a blazing .571 against medium-high inside fastballs thrown by lefties. He pulls this pitch strongly to deep left down the line and to left center.

MEDIUM-HIGH INSIDE FASTBALLS

BATTING AVERAGE .571
Play

Left	Deep and shifted toward the left field line
Center	Deep and shifted toward left field
Right	Medium-deep in straightaway right field
Short	Shifted toward third base
Second	Normal position

Trammell hits curves and sliders very strongly against left-handed pitchers. His .437 medium-high outside curve average is excellent.

MEDIUM-HIGH OUTSIDE CURVEBALLS
(THROWN BY LEFT-HANDED PITCHERS)

BATTING AVERAGE .437
Play

Left	Deep in straightaway left field
Center	Deep and shifted toward left field
Right	Deep and shifted toward the right field line
Short	Up middle (shifted toward second base)
Second	Shifted toward first base

Ahead And Behind In The Count Vs. RH

Ahead

Fastball Average .344

	Inside	Middle	Outside
High	16/ 312 /5	24/ 291 /7	7/ 285 /2
Med	32/ 500 /16	24/ 458 /11	65/ 369 /24
Low	15/ 133 /2	45/ 266 /12	10/ 300 /3

Curve Average .454

	Inside	Middle	Outside
High	1/ 0 /0	0/ 0 /0	0/ 0 /0
Med	3/ 333 /1	0/ 0 /0	6/ 500 /3
Low	0/ 0 /0	1/ 1000 /1	0/ 0 /0

Behind

Fastball Average .281

	Inside	Middle	Outside
High	5/ 600 /3	9/ 111 /1	4/ 250 /1
Med	16/ 250 /4	11/ 454 /5	37/ 216 /8
Low	5/ 200 /1	14/ 500 /7	9/ 111 /1

Curve Average .280

	Inside	Middle	Outside
High	0/ 0 /0	2/ 0 /0	1/ 1000 /1
Med	5/ 200 /1	3/ 0 /0	6/ 333 /2
Low	1/ 1000 /1	0/ 0 /0	7/ 285 /2

Overall Evaluation

Against Right-Handed Pitchers

Overall Fastball ⚾⚾ ⚾⚾⚾

Overall Curve ⚾

Overall Slider ⚾

Against Left-Handed Pitchers

Overall Fastball ⚾⚾ ⚾⚾⚾ ⚾⚾

Overall Curve ⚾ ⚾⚾⚾ ⚾⚾

Overall Slider ⚾⚾ ⚾⚾⚾ ⚾⚾

Comments: A strong fastball hitter, Trammell has trouble with curves and sliders vs. RH.
Strengths: Waist-high and low-middle fastballs vs. RH; all fastballs except high-outside and high-inside, medium-outside and low-middle curves vs. LH.
Weaknesses: Low-inside, low-outside, high-outside and high-middle fastballs, curves and sliders in general vs. RH; high-outside and high-inside fastballs, low-inside curves and low-inside sliders vs. LH.

Gary Ward Against Right-Handed Pitchers
Overall BARS Batting Average .258

	Fastball Average .283			Curve Average .222			Slider Average .187		
	Inside	Middle	Outside	Inside	Middle	Outside	Inside	Middle	Outside
High	17/58 /1	39/102 /4	21/333 /7	1/0 /0	6/0 /0	3/333 /1	0/0 /0	5/400 /2	5/200 /1
Med	74/364 /27	50/520 /26	130/276 /36	7/428 /3	14/714 /10	45/222 /10	8/250 /2	3/333 /1	24/166 /4
Low	41/195 /8	64/250 /16	47/255 /12	9/0 /0	18/111 /2	41/146 /6	5/0 /0	8/250 /2	38/157 /6

Gary Ward Against Left-Handed Pitchers
Overall BARS Batting Average .360

	Fastball Average .383			Curve Average .295			Slider Average .306		
	Inside	Middle	Outside	Inside	Middle	Outside	Inside	Middle	Outside
High	6/166 /1	13/384 /5	17/352 /6	1/0 /0	1/1000 /1	1/1000 /1	1/0 /0	2/500 /1	2/0 /0
Med	30/366 /11	20/500 /10	90/400 /36	4/250 /1	4/500 /2	14/285 /4	7/142 /1	3/666 /2	8/375 /3
Low	19/578 /11	29/413 /12	21/95 /2	8/250 /2	4/250 /1	7/142 /1	12/333 /4	7/571 /4	7/0 /0

Right-handed hitter Gary Ward hits significantly better against left-handed pitchers. Against right-handers he hits .283 against fastballs, .222 against curves and .187 against sliders. Against left-handers, however, he hits a sparkling .383 against fastballs, .295 against curves and .306 against sliders.

Looking at Ward's fastball chart against right-handers, notice his strength against medium-over-the-middle fastballs (.520) and medium-high inside fastballs (.364). It is vital for pitchers to avoid throwing to this sector. They would be much better off throwing to his high-inside (.058)/high-over-the-middle (.102) sector, or to any of his low locations.

A pitcher would not want to throw Ward a medium-over-the-middle fastball, but he hits this pitch for such a strong average it's interesting to see how he hits pitches thrown to this location. He tends to hit into the left-center and right-center gaps. The second baseman needs to shift toward first base.

MEDIUM-OVER-THE-MIDDLE FASTBALLS

BATTING AVERAGE .520
Play

Left	Deep and shifted toward center field
Center	Medium-deep in straightaway center field
Right	Deep and shifted toward center field
Short	Normal position
Second	Shifted toward first base

Now look at his medium-over-the-middle curveball average. There aren't as many recorded instances to go on, but his .714 average in this location is exceptional. The BARS fielding strategy shows that he tends to hit these pitches almost exactly the same way that he hits medium-over-the-middle fastballs.

MEDIUM-OVER-THE-MIDDLE CURVEBALLS

BATTING AVERAGE .714
Play

Left	Deep and shifted toward center field
Center	Deep in straightaway center field
Right	Deep and shifted toward center field
Short	Shifted toward third base
Second	*No instances recorded*

It seems likely that most outfielders play Ward deep and to pull the ball to left field. His higher averages are in the locations in which he hits the ball either into the alleys or medium-deep.

The charts below show that he hits medium-high outside fastballs deep down the line to left for a fair .276 average. But he hits medium-high inside fastballs medium-deep to left and center fields for an excellent .364 average.

MEDIUM-HIGH OUTSIDE FASTBALLS

BATTING AVERAGE .276
Play
Left   Deep and shifted toward the left field line
Center   Medium-deep in straightaway center field
Right   Deep in straightaway right field
Short   Up middle (shifted toward second base)
Second   Normal position

MEDIUM-HIGH INSIDE FASTBALLS

BATTING AVERAGE .364
Play
Left   Medium-deep in straightaway left field
Center   Medium-deep in straightaway center field
Right   Deep in straightaway right field
Short   Normal position
Second   Normal position

Ward has considerable trouble with low curves and medium-high outside curves thrown by right-handers. This gives pitchers quite a sector to attack, and his overall .222 curve average indicates that they are taking advantage of it. The same is true with his weak medium-high outside and low-outside slider locations. His overall slider average of .187 is low.

Ward Against Left-Handed Pitchers

Ward hits very well overall against left-handers. His .383 against fastballs is one of the highest fastball averages recorded by the BARS System. Notice the many strong locations in his fastball chart. The .400 in his medium-high outside fastball location is top rate, as is the .413 in his low-over-the-middle fastball location.

MEDIUM-HIGH OUTSIDE FASTBALLS (THROWN BY LEFT-HANDED PITCHERS)

BATTING AVERAGE .400
Play
Left   Medium-deep and shifted toward center field
Center   Medium-deep in straightaway center field
Right   Deep in straightaway right field
Short   Up middle (shifted toward second base)
Second   Shifted toward first base

LOW-OVER-THE-MIDDLE FASTBALLS (THROWN BY LEFT-HANDED PITCHERS)

BATTING AVERAGE .413
Play
Left   Deep and shifted toward the left field line
Center   Deep in straightaway center field
Right   Medium-deep and shifted toward the right line
Short   Normal position
Second   *No instances recorded*

His .366 against medium-high inside fastballs is also excellent. His only significant fastball weakness against left-handers is low-outside (.095).

He has some trouble with low curves and inside curves against lefties, but his medium-high outside location is solid (.285). He hits excellently overall against sliders thrown by left-handers. His strong slider locations make up for his weak locations overall, but pitchers can become aware of his weaknesses by examining Ward's BARS charts.

Ahead And Behind In The Count Vs. RH

Ahead

	Fastball Average .330			Curve Average .292		
	Inside	Middle	Outside	Inside	Middle	Outside
High	3/0 /0	15/266 /4	10/600 /6	0/0 /0	1/0 /0	1/0 /0
Med	37/459 /17	27/518 /14	63/301 /19	3/666 /2	6/833 /5	17/176 /3
Low	18/277 /5	41/195 /8	22/227 /5	1/0 /0	7/285 /2	5/0 /0

Behind

	Fastball Average .342			Curve Average .341		
	Inside	Middle	Outside	Inside	Middle	Outside
High	2/500 /1	7/0 /0	3/0 /0	1/0 /0	2/0 /0	1/1000 /1
Med	10/400 /4	6/666 /4	22/454 /10	2/500 /1	6/666 /4	14/357 /5
Low	7/285 /2	10/100 /1	6/500 /3	3/0 /0	4/0 /0	8/375 /3

Overall Evaluation

Against Right-Handed Pitchers

Overall Fastball

Overall Curve

Overall Slider

Against Left-Handed Pitchers

Overall Fastball

Overall Curve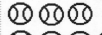

Overall Slider

Comments: Ward is much more effective vs. LH.
Strengths: Medium-inside, medium-middle and high-outside fastballs, medium-inside and medium-middle curves vs. RH; over-the-middle and waist-high fastballs, low-inside and high-outside fastballs vs. LH.
Weaknesses: Low fastballs, high-middle and high-inside fastballs, low curves, medium-outside curves, inside and outside sliders vs. RH; low-outside fastballs, low-outside curves and sliders vs. LH.

Lou Whitaker (Left Handed)   *Detroit Tigers*

Lou Whitaker Against Right-Handed Pitchers
Overall BARS Batting Average .313

	Fastball Average .312			Curve Average .340			Slider Average .262		
	Outside	Middle	Inside	Outside	Middle	Inside	Outside	Middle	Inside
High	43/232/10	43/232/10	20/300/6	8/375/3	11/363/4	3/0/0	2/0/0	3/333/1	1/0/0
Med	179/279/50	57/438/25	48/375/18	39/435/17	11/272/3	12/416/5	11/363/4	1/1000/1	7/285/2
Low	48/166/8	72/430/31	37/351/13	11/90/1	29/344/10	20/300/6	7/285/2	7/285/2	22/181/4

Lou Whitaker Against Left-Handed Pitchers
Overall BARS Batting Average .215

	Fastball Average .213			Curve Average .211			Slider Average .232		
	Outside	Middle	Inside	Outside	Middle	Inside	Outside	Middle	Inside
High	9/0/0	27/148/4	17/294/5	3/1000/3	8/125/1	6/333/2	0/0/0	3/333/1	0/0/0
Med	61/131/8	12/333/4	39/256/10	26/153/4	7/571/4	7/571/4	13/307/4	5/600/3	4/250/1
Low	12/416/5	32/218/7	16/312/5	17/0/0	10/0/0	6/166/1	7/0/0	7/0/0	4/250/1

Left-handed hitting Lou Whitaker's fastball average is 99 points higher against right-handed than against left-handed pitchers. (.312 overall vs. right-handers, .213 overall vs. left-handers). He also hits curves extremely well against right-handed pitchers (.340 overall).

Looking at Whitaker's fastball chart against right-handers, notice how well he hits medium-over-the-middle fastballs (.438), low-over-the-middle fastballs (.430) and all inside fastballs (.300, .375 and .351 from high to low).

He hits fairly well in the highly pitched medium-high outside fastball location. His Ahead and Behind charts on the opposite page show that he hits this pitch better when ahead in the count.

**MEDIUM-HIGH OUTSIDE FASTBALLS
(WHEN AHEAD IN THE COUNT)**

BATTING AVERAGE .304
Play
Left   Medium-deep and shifted toward the left field line
Center   Deep in straightaway center field
Right   Deep in straightaway right field
Short   Up middle (shifted toward second base)
Second   Shifted toward first base

**MEDIUM-HIGH OUTSIDE FASTBALLS
(WHEN BEHIND IN THE COUNT)**

BATTING AVERAGE .209
Play
Left   Deep in straightaway left field
Center   Deep and shifted toward left field
Right   Deep and shifted toward center field
Short   Up middle (shifted toward second base)
Second   Normal position

He hits low-over-the-middle fastballs down the line to left, medium-deep to straightaway center and to right center. Notice that the infielders need to play him to pull the ball.

LOW-OVER-THE-MIDDLE FASTBALLS

BATTING AVERAGE .430
Play
Left   Deep and shifted toward the left field line
Center   Medium-deep in straightaway center field
Right   Medium-deep and shifted toward center field
Short   Up middle (shifted toward second base)
Second   Shifted toward first base

He hits medium-over-the-middle fastballs deep and straightaway to the outfield. But he pulls the ball when he hits grounders to the infield. His .438 average in this location should serve as a warning to pitchers.

He hits medium-high inside and low-inside fast-balls for very high averages (.375 and .351). But notice in the BARS fielding strategy below that every fielder needs to be positioned differently for maximum effectiveness against pitches to these two locations.

MEDIUM-HIGH INSIDE FASTBALLS

BATTING AVERAGE .375
Play

Left	Deep and shifted toward the left field line
Center	Medium-deep in straightaway center field
Right	Deep and shifted toward the right field line
Short	Shifted toward third base
Second	Normal position

LOW-INSIDE FASTBALLS

BATTING AVERAGE .351
Play

Left	Deep in straightaway left field
Center	Deep in straightaway center field
Right	Medium-deep and shifted toward the right line
Short	Normal position
Second	Shifted toward first base

Whitaker Against Curves And Sliders

Whitaker hits curves extremely well against right-handers. His only weak location is low-outside (.090). His .435 against medium-high outside curves is exceptional. When behind in the count, he hits .583 in this location. He is obviously waiting for outside curves when behind.

MEDIUM-HIGH OUTSIDE CURVEBALLS (WHEN BEHIND IN THE COUNT)

BATTING AVERAGE .583
Play

Left	Deep and shifted toward the left field line
Center	Deep and shifted toward right field
Right	Medium-deep and shifted toward the right line
Short	Up middle (shifted toward second base)
Second	Normal position

Whitaker Against Left-Handed Pitchers

Whitaker has trouble with many fastball locations against left-handed pitchers. He hits medium-high outside fastballs very poorly (.131). And he has trouble with high-over-the-middle fastballs (.148). His .256 against medium-high inside fastballs is barely adequate.

MEDIUM-HIGH INSIDE FASTBALLS (THROWN BY LEFT-HANDED PITCHERS)

BATTING AVERAGE .256
Play

Left	Medium-deep and shifted toward the left line
Center	Deep in straightaway center field
Right	Deep and shifted toward center field
Short	Up middle (shifted toward second base)
Second	Shifted toward first base

He has many weak curve locations against left-handers. He has weaknesses in the three low curve locations and hits only .153 against medium-high outside curves. He also has trouble against low sliders.

Ahead And Behind In The Count Vs. RH

Ahead

	Fastball Average .357			Curve Average .400		
	Outside	Middle	Inside	Outside	Middle	Inside
High	17/235 /4	21/285 /6	8/500 /4	0/0 /0	5/400 /2	0/0 /0
Med	82/304 /25	23/521 /12	28/357 /10	8/250 /2	1/1000 /1	7/571 /4
Low	18/111 /2	48/479 /23	21/428 /9	2/0 /0	8/375 /3	4/500 /2

Behind

	Fastball Average .257			Curve Average .476		
	Outside	Middle	Inside	Outside	Middle	Inside
High	12/250 /3	12/333 /4	2/0 /0	2/500 /1	5/400 /2	1/0 /0
Med	43/209 /9	8/250 /2	5/200 /1	12/583 /7	2/500 /1	1/1000 /1
Low	4/250 /1	11/454 /5	4/250 /1	1/1000 /1	10/400 /4	8/375 /3

Overall Evaluation

Against Right-Handed Pitchers

Overall Fastball	⚾⚾ ⚾⚾⚾
Overall Curve	⚾⚾ ⚾⚾⚾ ⚾⚾
Overall Slider	⚾⚾ ⚾⚾

Against Left-Handed Pitchers

Overall Fastball	⚾⚾
Overall Curve	⚾⚾
Overall Slider	⚾⚾

Comments: Hits well against inside fastballs vs. RH. Strengths: Low-middle, medium-middle and all inside fastballs, all curves except low-outside, medium-outside sliders vs. RH; low-outside and medium-middle fastballs, medium-outside sliders vs. LH. Weaknesses: Low-outside, high-outside and high-middle fastballs, low-outside curves, low-inside sliders vs. RH; medium-outside and high-middle fastballs, low curves and sliders, medium-outside curves vs. LH.

Ken Williams (Right Handed)   *Detroit Tigers*

Ken Williams Against Right-Handed Pitchers
Overall BARS Batting Average .270

Fastball Average .290

	Inside	Middle	Outside
High	3 / 0 /0	4 / 0 /0	9 / 222 /2
Med	12 / 83 /1	2 / 0 /0	37 / 378 /14
Low	5 / 400 /2	10 / 500 /5	11 / 272 /3

Curve Average .205

	Inside	Middle	Outside
High	2 / 0 /0	3 / 0 /0	4 / 500 /2
Med	1 / 0 /0	1 / 1000 /1	12 / 250 /3
Low	2 / 500 /1	1 / 0 /0	8 / 0 /0

Slider Average .294

	Inside	Middle	Outside
High	0 / 0 /0	1 / 0 /0	1 / 0 /0
Med	2 / 500 /1	1 / 1000 /1	6 / 500 /3
Low	3 / 0 /0	0 / 0 /0	3 / 0 /0

Ken Williams Against Left-Handed Pitchers
Overall BARS Batting Average .307

Fastball Average .300

	Inside	Middle	Outside
High	1 / 0 /0	1 / 0 /0	6 / 0 /0
Med	6 / 333 /2	2 / 1000 /2	29 / 344 /10
Low	4 / 250 /1	4 / 500 /2	7 / 142 /1

Curve Average .222

	Inside	Middle	Outside
High	0 / 0 /0	0 / 0 /0	0 / 0 /0
Med	3 / 333 /1	0 / 0 /0	2 / 500 /1
Low	1 / 0 /0	1 / 0 /0	2 / 0 /0

Slider Average .363

	Inside	Middle	Outside
High	0 / 0 /0	0 / 0 /0	1 / 1000 /1
Med	1 / 0 /0	0 / 0 /0	4 / 250 /1
Low	1 / 1000 /1	2 / 500 /1	2 / 0 /0

Right-handed hitter Ken Williams hits medium-high outside fastballs excellently against both right- and left-handed pitchers (.378 vs. right-handers, .344 against left-handers). Nonetheless, pitchers keep feeding him this pitch. This shows pitchers don't look at all at hitter's strengths and weaknesses. By examining the BARS batting records, pitchers can know very exactly where to pitch a hitter.

The chart below and the diagram on the opposite page show how fielders need to play for medium-high outside fastballs thrown by right-handers.

MEDIUM-HIGH OUTSIDE FASTBALLS

BATTING AVERAGE .378
Play
Left   Deep and shifted toward the left field line
Center   Medium-deep in straightaway center field
Right   Medium-deep in straightaway right field
Short   Normal position
Second   Normal position

He's weak against medium-high inside fastballs against right-handers (.083). His .500 against low-over-the-middle fastballs is excellent.

LOW-OVER-THE-MIDDLE FASTBALLS

BATTING AVERAGE .500
Play
Left   Deep and shifted toward the left field line

Center   Deep in straightaway center field
Right   *No instances recorded*
Short   Normal position
Second   Shifted toward first base

He has trouble with low-outside curves (.000) but hits medium-high outside curves fairly well (.250).

MEDIUM-HIGH OUTSIDE CURVEBALLS

BATTING AVERAGE .250
Play
Left   Medium-deep in straightaway left field
Center   Deep and shifted toward right field
Right   *No instances recorded*
Short   Normal position
Second   Normal position

Against left-handed pitchers, Williams hits medium-high outside fastballs deep into left field toward center and deep down the right line.

**MEDIUM-HIGH OUTSIDE FASTBALLS
(THROWN BY LEFT-HANDED PITCHERS)**

BATTING AVERAGE .344
Play
Left   Deep and shifted toward center field
Center   Deep in straightaway center field
Right   Deep and shifted toward the right field line
Short   Up middle (shifted toward second base)
Second   Normal position

Medium-High Outside Fastballs
(Thrown By Right-Handed Pitchers)

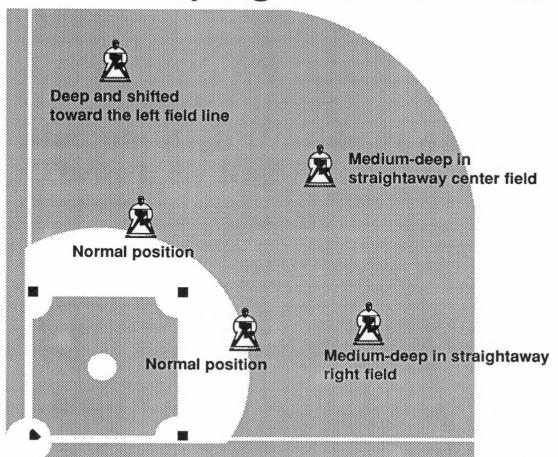

Deep and shifted toward the left field line

Medium-deep in straightaway center field

Normal position

Medium-deep in straightaway right field

Normal position

Ahead And Behind In The Count Vs. RH

Ahead

Fastball Average .382

	Inside	Middle	Outside
High	0 / 0 /0	0 / 0 /0	1 / 1000 /1
Med	2 / 0 /0	1 / 0 /0	17 / 352 /6
Low	4 / 500 /2	6 / 500 /3	3 / 333 /1

Curve Average .363

	Inside	Middle	Outside
High	0 / 0 /0	0 / 0 /0	1 / 0 /0
Med	1 / 0 /0	1 / 1000 /1	5 / 400 /2
Low	1 / 1000 /1	1 / 0 /0	1 / 0 /0

Behind

Fastball Average .272

	Inside	Middle	Outside
High	0 / 0 /0	0 / 0 /0	1 / 1000 /1
Med	5 / 200 /1	0 / 0 /0	3 / 333 /1
Low	0 / 0 /0	0 / 0 /0	2 / 0 /0

Curve Average .125

	Inside	Middle	Outside
High	1 / 0 /0	2 / 0 /0	1 / 1000 /1
Med	0 / 0 /0	0 / 0 /0	2 / 0 /0
Low	0 / 0 /0	0 / 0 /0	2 / 0 /0

Overall Evaluation
Against Right-Handed Pitchers

Overall Fastball

Overall Curve ⚾

Overall Slider ⚾⚾⚾

Against Left-Handed Pitchers

Overall Fastball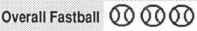

Overall Curve   Not enough information

Overall Slider   Not enough information

Comments: Strong against medium-outside fastballs vs. RH and LH.
Strengths: Medium-outside and low-middle fastballs, medium-outside sliders vs. RH; medium-outside fastballs vs. LH.
Weaknesses: High fastballs, medium-inside fastballs, low-outside curves vs. RH; low-outside fastballs vs. LH.

Braggs, Glenn
Brock, Greg
Deer, Rob
Felder, Mike
Francona, Terry
Gantner, Jim
Molitor, Paul
Parker, Dave
Surhoff, B.J.
Yount, Robin

Milwaukee Brewers
BARS System
Hitting Analysis

Glenn Braggs Against Right-Handed Pitchers
Overall BARS Batting Average .244

Fastball Average .241	Inside	Middle	Outside
High	8 / 125 / 1	5 / 600 / 3	8 / 250 / 2
Med	19 / 315 / 6	4 / 250 / 1	47 / 255 / 12
Low	7 / 142 / 1	13 / 307 / 4	13 / 0 / 0

Curve Average .333	Inside	Middle	Outside
High	2 / 500 / 1	0 / 0 / 0	2 / 1000 / 2
Med	0 / 0 / 0	2 / 1000 / 2	12 / 166 / 2
Low	1 / 0 / 0	3 / 0 / 0	8 / 375 / 3

Slider Average .166	Inside	Middle	Outside
High	0 / 0 / 0	0 / 0 / 0	2 / 0 / 0
Med	2 / 500 / 1	2 / 0 / 0	11 / 90 / 1
Low	0 / 0 / 0	1 / 1000 / 1	12 / 166 / 2

Glenn Braggs Against Left-Handed Pitchers
Overall BARS Batting Average .215

Fastball Average .211	Inside	Middle	Outside
High	3 / 0 / 0	2 / 0 / 0	3 / 0 / 0
Med	10 / 100 / 1	2 / 500 / 1	33 / 333 / 11
Low	4 / 250 / 1	7 / 142 / 1	7 / 0 / 0

Curve Average .250	Inside	Middle	Outside
High	0 / 0 / 0	0 / 0 / 0	0 / 0 / 0
Med	1 / 1000 / 1	0 / 0 / 0	3 / 0 / 0
Low	1 / 0 / 0	2 / 500 / 1	1 / 0 / 0

Slider Average .214	Inside	Middle	Outside
High	0 / 0 / 0	1 / 0 / 0	2 / 0 / 0
Med	3 / 333 / 1	0 / 0 / 0	3 / 0 / 0
Low	2 / 500 / 1	2 / 500 / 1	1 / 0 / 0

Right-handed hitting Glenn Braggs has trouble with outside fastballs against right-handed pitchers (.250, .255, and .000 on 0 for 13, high to low). He has trouble with low-outside fastballs against left-handed pitchers (.000 on 0 for 7) but he hits medium-high outside fastballs excellently against lefties (.333).

Notice in Braggs' Ahead and Behind charts against right-handers on the opposite page that he hits medium-high outside fastballs much better when behind in the count. When behind, he goes sharply to his opposite field (to right field and to the right side of the infield). It's unusual for a batter to hit so much better in this location when behind in the count.

MEDIUM-HIGH OUTSIDE FASTBALLS (WHEN BEHIND IN THE COUNT)

BATTING AVERAGE .428
Play
Left   Medium-deep and shifted toward center field
Center Deep and shifted toward right field
Right   Deep and shifted toward the right field line
Short   Up middle (shifted toward second base)
Second Shifted toward first base

MEDIUM-HIGH OUTSIDE FASTBALLS (WHEN AHEAD IN THE COUNT)

BATTING AVERAGE .187
Play
Left   Deep in straightaway left field

Center Medium-deep in straightaway center field
Right   Deep in straightaway right field
Short   Normal position
Second Normal position

It may be interesting to some readers to see how the above two fielding strategy charts combine to make the overall fielding chart. Remember that the overall chart also contains pitches thrown when the count was even.

MEDIUM-HIGH OUTSIDE FASTBALLS (OVERALL FOR ALL COUNTS)

BATTING AVERAGE .255
Play
Left   Deep in straightaway left field
Center Medium-deep and shifted toward left field
Right   Deep and shifted toward center field
Short   Normal position
Second Shifted toward first base

Braggs hits well against medium-high inside fastballs thrown by right-handed pitchers.

MEDIUM-HIGH INSIDE FASTBALLS

BATTING AVERAGE .315
Play
Left   Deep and shifted toward the left field line
Center Medium-deep in straightaway center field
Right   Deep in straightaway right field
Short   Up middle (shifted toward second base)
Second Normal position

His 0-for-13 in the low-outside fastball location indicates a weakness.

LOW-OUTSIDE FASTBALLS

BATTING AVERAGE .000 (0 for 13)

Play
Left *No instances recorded*
Center Medium-deep and shifted toward right field
Right Medium-deep in straightaway right field
Short Normal position
Second Normal position

Braggs Against Curves And Sliders

Braggs has a fine .333 overall curve average against right-handers. But he hits only .166 against medium-high outside curves.

MEDIUM-HIGH OUTSIDE CURVEBALLS

BATTING AVERAGE .166

Play
Left *No instances recorded*
Center Deep in straightaway center field
Right Deep and shifted toward center field
Short Shifted toward third base
Second Normal position

Braggs hits a fine .375 against low-outside curves against right-handers.

He has obvious troubles with outside sliders (1 for 11 in medium-high outside and 2 for 12 in low-outside).

LOW-OUTSIDE SLIDERS

BATTING AVERAGE .166

Play
Left Medium-deep and shifted toward center field
Center Deep in straightaway center field
Right Deep and shifted toward the right field line
Short Normal position
Second *No instances recorded*

Braggs Against Left-Handed Pitchers

Braggs hits medium-high outside fastballs excellently against left-handed pitchers (.333). As against right-handers, he hits this pitch much better when behind in the count.

MEDIUM-HIGH OUTSIDE FASTBALLS (THROWN BY LEFT-HANDED PITCHERS WHEN BRAGGS IS BEHIND IN THE COUNT)

BATTING AVERAGE .375

Play
Left Deep and shifted toward center field
Center Medium-deep in straightaway center field
Right Deep in straightaway right field
Short Up middle (shifted toward second base)
Second Normal position

MEDIUM-HIGH OUTSIDE FASTBALLS (THROWN BY LEFT-HANDED PITCHERS WHEN BRAGGS IS AHEAD IN THE COUNT)

BATTING AVERAGE .266

Play
Left Deep in straightaway left field
Center Deep in straightaway center field
Right Deep and shifted toward center field
Short Up middle (shifted toward second base)
Second Shifted toward first base

Ahead And Behind In The Count Vs. RH

Ahead

	Fastball Average .191			Curve Average .375		
	Inside	Middle	Outside	Inside	Middle	Outside
High	3/ 0 /0	3/ 666 /2	3/ 333 /1	0/ 0 /0	0/ 0 /0	2/ 1000 /2
Med	6/ 333 /2	1/ 0 /0	16/ 187 /3	0/ 0 /0	0/ 0 /0	3/ 0 /0
Low	4/ 0 /0	5/ 200 /1	6/ 0 /0	0/ 0 /0	1/ 0 /0	2/ 500 /1

Behind

	Fastball Average .370			Curve Average .428		
	Inside	Middle	Outside	Inside	Middle	Outside
High	0/ 0 /0	1/ 1000 /1	2/ 500 /1	2/ 500 /1	0/ 0 /0	0/ 0 /0
Med	4/ 250 /1	0/ 0 /0	14/ 428 /6	0/ 0 /0	0/ 0 /0	4/ 250 /1
Low	1/ 0 /0	3/ 333 /1	2/ 0 /0	0/ 0 /0	0/ 0 /0	1/ 1000 /1

Overall Evaluation
Against Right-Handed Pitchers

Overall Fastball ⚾⚾
Overall Curve ⚾⚾ ⚾⚾ ⚾⚾
Overall Slider ⚾⚾

Against Left-Handed Pitchers

Overall Fastball ⚾⚾
Overall Curve Not enough information
Overall Slider ⚾⚾

Comments: Has trouble with outside fastballs vs. RH; hits medium-outside fastballs excellently vs. LH.
Strengths: Medium-inside and low-middle fastballs, low-outside curves vs. RH; medium-outside fastballs vs. LH.
Weaknesses: Outside fastballs, medium-outside curves, medium-outside sliders and low-outside sliders vs. RH; low fastballs, medium-inside fastballs vs. LH.

Greg Brock (Left Handed) — *Milwaukee Brewers*

Greg Brock Against Right-Handed Pitchers
Overall BARS Batting Average .284

Fastball Average .291

	Outside	Middle	Inside
High	26 / 230 / 6	30 / 300 / 9	26 / 230 / 6
Med	86 / 348 / 30	14 / 285 / 4	54 / 277 / 15
Low	27 / 259 / 7	49 / 244 / 12	21 / 380 / 8

Curve Average .184

	Outside	Middle	Inside
High	3 / 0 / 0	1 / 0 / 0	2 / 0 / 0
Med	10 / 100 / 1	2 / 0 / 0	7 / 142 / 1
Low	8 / 250 / 2	18 / 333 / 6	14 / 142 / 2

Slider Average .394

	Outside	Middle	Inside
High	1 / 0 / 0	3 / 666 / 2	1 / 0 / 0
Med	6 / 833 / 5	2 / 0 / 0	2 / 0 / 0
Low	5 / 200 / 1	7 / 285 / 2	11 / 454 / 5

Greg Brock Against Left-Handed Pitchers
Overall BARS Batting Average .223

Fastball Average .206

	Outside	Middle	Inside
High	7 / 285 / 2	8 / 250 / 2	10 / 200 / 2
Med	24 / 291 / 7	4 / 0 / 0	11 / 0 / 0
Low	7 / 285 / 2	14 / 214 / 3	12 / 166 / 2

Curve Average .285

	Outside	Middle	Inside
High	2 / 1000 / 2	0 / 0 / 0	1 / 0 / 0
Med	10 / 200 / 2	1 / 0 / 0	1 / 1000 / 1
Low	7 / 142 / 1	6 / 333 / 2	0 / 0 / 0

Slider Average .214

	Outside	Middle	Inside
High	2 / 500 / 1	0 / 0 / 0	0 / 0 / 0
Med	2 / 500 / 1	0 / 0 / 0	2 / 0 / 0
Low	7 / 142 / 1	1 / 0 / 0	0 / 0 / 0

Left-handed hitting Greg Brock has a much higher overall fastball average against right-handed pitchers (.291 vs. right-handers, .206 vs. left-handers). He has trouble with curves but hits sliders very well against right-handers (.184 curves, .394 sliders).

Brock hits medium-high outside fastballs extremely well against right-handed pitchers. His .348 average in this location is excellent. He hits this pitch to his opposite field (slightly toward left). But note that the shortstop needs to be shifted toward second base.

MEDIUM-HIGH OUTSIDE FASTBALLS

BATTING AVERAGE .348
Play

Left	Deep and shifted toward the left field line
Center	Deep and shifted toward left field
Right	Deep in straightaway right field
Short	Up middle (shifted toward second base)
Second	Normal position

In contrast, he pulls medium-high inside fastballs thrown by right-handers. With the exception of the right fielder, every fielder needs to shift for a medium-high inside fastball compared to a medium-high outside fastball.

MEDIUM-HIGH INSIDE FASTBALLS

BATTING AVERAGE .277
Play

Left	Medium-deep and shifted toward center field
Center	Deep and shifted toward right field
Right	Deep in straightaway right field
Short	Normal position
Second	Shifted toward first base

Brock hits high-over-the-middle fastballs deep to the outfield.

LOW-OVER-THE-MIDDLE FASTBALLS

BATTING AVERAGE .300
Play

Left	Deep in straightaway left field
Center	Deep and shifted toward right field
Right	Deep in straightaway right field
Short	Shifted toward third base
Second	Shifted toward first base

Brock Ahead And Behind In The Count

It was noted above that Brock hits medium-high inside fastballs differently from the way he hits medium-high outside fastballs. But he also hits medium-high inside fastballs differently when ahead and when behind in the count. The following BARS fielding strategy charts show that he pulls this pitch more and hits it with greater authority when ahead in the count.

MEDIUM-HIGH INSIDE FASTBALLS (WHEN BEHIND IN THE COUNT)

BATTING AVERAGE .285
Play
Left	Medium-deep in straightaway left field
Center	Medium-deep in straightaway center field
Right	Short in straightaway right field
Short	Normal position
Second	Shifted toward first base

MEDIUM-HIGH INSIDE FASTBALLS (WHEN AHEAD IN THE COUNT)

BATTING AVERAGE .428
Play
Left	Medium-deep and shifted toward center field
Center	Deep and shifted toward right field
Right	Deep in straightaway right field
Short	Up middle (shifted toward second base)
Second	Shifted toward first base

Brock hits .380 against low-inside fastballs. This is the highest location in his overall fastball chart against right-handed pitchers.

LOW-INSIDE FASTBALLS

BATTING AVERAGE .380
Play
Left	Deep in straightaway left field
Center	Deep in straightaway center field
Right	Deep in straightaway right field
Short	Up middle (shifted toward second base)
Second	Normal position

Brock hits very poorly against curves thrown by right-handers. His .142 against both medium-high inside and low-inside curves indicates an area of weakness pitchers can attack. He hits low-over-the-middle curves very well, however (.333).

LOW-OVER-THE-MIDDLE CURVEBALLS

BATTING AVERAGE .333
Play
Left	Medium-deep in straightaway left field
Center	Deep and shifted toward right field
Right	Deep in straightaway right field
Short	*No instances recorded*
Second	Shifted toward first base

He hits low-inside sliders very well (.454). He hits this pitch deep down both lines and to the right side of the infield.

Brock Against Left-Handed Pitchers

Brock hits poorly overall against fastballs thrown by left-handers (.206). He does hit outside fastballs well overall, however. He hits medium-high outside fastballs straightaway to the outfield.

MEDIUM-HIGH OUTSIDE FASTBALLS (THROWN BY LEFT-HANDED PITCHERS)

BATTING AVERAGE .291
Play
Left	Deep in straightaway left field
Center	Deep in straightaway center field
Right	Deep in straightaway right field
Short	Up middle (shifted toward second base)
Second	Normal position

Ahead And Behind In The Count Vs. RH

Ahead

	Fastball Average .335			Curve Average .200		
	Outside	Middle	Inside	Outside	Middle	Inside
High	10/100 /1	15/400 /6	6/0 /0	1/0 /0	0/0 /0	1/0 /0
Med	48/333 /16	6/500 /3	21/428 /9	0/0 /0	2/0 /0	3/0 /0
Low	12/250 /3	24/375 /9	10/400 /4	1/1000 /1	1/1000 /1	1/0 /0

Behind

	Fastball Average .448			Curve Average .142		
	Outside	Middle	Inside	Outside	Middle	Inside
High	3/333 /1	4/500 /2	8/500 /4	1/0 /0	0/0 /0	0/0 /0
Med	14/571 /8	1/0 /0	7/285 /2	3/0 /0	0/0 /0	3/333 /1
Low	6/666 /4	2/0 /0	4/250 /1	3/0 /0	3/0 /0	1/1000 /1

Overall Evaluation

Against Right-Handed Pitchers

Overall Fastball	⚾⚾ ⚾⚾
Overall Curve	⚾⚾
Overall Slider	⚾⚾ ⚾⚾⚾ ⚾⚾

Against Left-Handed Pitchers

Overall Fastball	⚾⚾
Overall Curve	⚾⚾ ⚾⚾⚾
Overall Slider	⚾⚾

Comments: Weak vs. curves, strong vs. sliders vs. RH; hits fastballs much better vs. RH.

Strengths: Medium-outside, high-middle and low-inside fastballs, low-middle curves, medium-outside and low-inside sliders vs. RH.

Weaknesses: Low-outside, low-middle, high-outside and high-inside fastballs, outside and inside curves vs. RH; inside and middle fastballs, low-outside and medium-outside curves, low-outside sliders vs. LH.

Rob Deer (Right Handed) — *Milwaukee Brewers*

Rob Deer Against Right-Handed Pitchers
Overall BARS Batting Average .187

Fastball Average .215

	Inside	Middle	Outside
High	14/ 142 /2	11/ 363 /4	18/ 111 /2
Med	20/ 100 /2	4/ 500 /2	81/ 271 /22
Low	5/ 0 /0	13/ 384 /5	20/ 50 /1

Curve Average .137

	Inside	Middle	Outside
High	1/ 0 /0	3/ 0 /0	0/ 0 /0
Med	8/ 500 /4	2/ 500 /1	14/ 142 /2
Low	3/ 0 /0	5/ 0 /0	15/ 0 /0

Slider Average .146

	Inside	Middle	Outside
High	2/ 0 /0	0/ 0 /0	1/ 1000 /1
Med	2/ 500 /1	2/ 0 /0	13/ 307 /4
Low	1/ 0 /0	3/ 0 /0	17/ 0 /0

Rob Deer Against Left-Handed Pitchers
Overall BARS Batting Average .255

Fastball Average .337

	Inside	Middle	Outside
High	1/ 0 /0	5/ 400 /2	10/ 100 /1
Med	2/ 0 /0	0/ 0 /0	39/ 410 /16
Low	4/ 0 /0	11/ 545 /6	11/ 272 /3

Curve Average .181

	Inside	Middle	Outside
High	0/ 0 /0	1/ 1000 /1	2/ 0 /0
Med	0/ 0 /0	1/ 0 /0	8/ 250 /2
Low	3/ 0 /0	3/ 333 /1	4/ 0 /0

Slider Average .111

	Inside	Middle	Outside
High	1/ 0 /0	1/ 0 /0	2/ 0 /0
Med	3/ 333 /1	1/ 0 /0	2/ 0 /0
Low	4/ 0 /0	3/ 333 /1	1/ 0 /0

Right-handed hitting Rob Deer has tremendous difficulties against right-handed pitchers. He hits .215 overall against fastballs thrown by right-handers. He hits .271 in his medium-high outside fastball location. This is his most highly pitched location, and it brings up his overall average.

He hits medium-high outside fastballs very well against left-handed pitchers (.410). In addition, his .545 low-over-the-middle fastball average and .400 high-over-the-middle fastball average bring up his overall average against left-handers.

Looking first at Deer's performance against right-handed pitchers, notice that he hits medium-high outside fastballs better when he is ahead in the count than when he is behind (.480 ahead, .250 behind).

MEDIUM-HIGH OUTSIDE FASTBALLS (WHEN AHEAD IN THE COUNT)

BATTING AVERAGE .480

Play
Left — Deep and shifted toward the left field line
Center — Medium-deep in straightaway center field
Right — Medium-deep and shifted toward center field
Short — Shifted toward third base
Second — Shifted toward first base

His low average when behind indicates that most of his hit balls are easy fly balls or grounders.

MEDIUM-HIGH OUTSIDE FASTBALLS (WHEN BEHIND IN THE COUNT)

BATTING AVERAGE .250

Play
Left — Deep and shifted toward the left field line
Center — Deep and shifted toward left field
Right — *No instances recorded*
Short — Normal position
Second — *No instances recorded*

He hits low-over-the-middle fastballs deep to the outfield. In this location he does not have a recorded instance of a hit ball to the infield.

LOW-OVER-THE-MIDDLE FASTBALLS

BATTING AVERAGE .384

Play
Left — Deep and shifted toward center field
Center — Deep in straightaway center field
Right — Deep and shifted toward center field
Short — *No instances recorded*
Second — *No instances recorded*

He has such a low average in his low-outside fastball location that it's interesting to see how he hits this pitch. Most of his hit balls in this location are probably easy flies and grounders.

LOW-OUTSIDE FASTBALLS

BATTING AVERAGE .050
Play
Left	Medium-deep in straightaway left field
Center	Medium-deep and shifted toward right field
Right	Medium-deep and shifted toward the right line
Short	Shifted toward third base
Second	Normal position

Deer has problems in his medium-high outside and low-outside curve locations. He does not have a recorded base hit in his low-outside curve and slider locations.

LOW-OUTSIDE CURVEBALLS

BATTING AVERAGE .000 (0 for 15)
Play
Left	*No instances recorded*
Center	Deep and shifted toward left field
Right	*No instances recorded*
Short	Shifted toward third base
Second	*No instances recorded*

LOW-OUTSIDE SLIDERS

BATTING AVERAGE .000 (0 for 17)
Play
Left	*No instances recorded*
Center	*No instances recorded*
Right	*No instances recorded*

Short	Normal position
Second	*No instances recorded*

Deer Against Left-Handed Pitchers

Deer's .410 medium-high outside fastball average is excellent. He hits this pitch deep to all fields.

MEDIUM-HIGH OUTSIDE FASTBALLS (THROWN BY LEFT-HANDED PITCHERS)

BATTING AVERAGE .410
Play
Left	Deep and shifted toward the left field line
Center	Medium-deep in straightaway center field
Right	Deep in straightaway right field
Short	Normal position
Second	Shifted toward first base

Deer pulls low-over-the-middle fastballs thrown by lefties. He undoubtedly hits this pitch very hard, as indicated by his high average. Sharply hit balls are harder to reach than slowly hit balls, resulting in a higher average. Even so, fielders could prevent most of Deer's base hits resulting from this location by following the suggested BARS fielding strategy.

LOW-OVER-THE-MIDDLE FASTBALLS (THROWN BY LEFT-HANDED PITCHERS)

BATTING AVERAGE .545
Play
Left	Deep and shifted toward the left field line
Center	Deep and shifted toward left field
Right	*No instances recorded*
Short	Normal position
Second	*No instances recorded*

Ahead And Behind In The Count Vs. RH

Ahead

Fastball Average .377

	Inside	Middle	Outside
High	3/ 333/1	2/ 1000/2	5/ 0/0
Med	6/ 0/0	3/ 666/2	25/ 480/12
Low	0/ 0/0	6/ 333/2	3/ 333/1

Curve Average .300

	Inside	Middle	Outside
High	0/ 0/0	1/ 0/0	0/ 0/0
Med	1/ 1000/1	2/ 500/1	4/ 250/1
Low	0/ 0/0	0/ 0/0	2/ 0/0

Behind

Fastball Average .275

	Inside	Middle	Outside
High	2/ 0/0	0/ 0/0	3/ 666/2
Med	4/ 250/1	0/ 0/0	16/ 250/4
Low	0/ 0/0	3/ 333/1	1/ 0/0

Curve Average .000

	Inside	Middle	Outside
High	0/ 0/0	2/ 0/0	0/ 0/0
Med	1/ 0/0	0/ 0/0	3/ 0/0
Low	0/ 0/0	0/ 0/0	1/ 0/0

Overall Evaluation
Against Right-Handed Pitchers

Overall Fastball	⚾⚾
Overall Curve	⚾⚾
Overall Slider	⚾⚾

Against Left-Handed Pitchers

Overall Fastball	⚾⚾ ⚾⚾ ⚾⚾ ⚾⚾
Overall Curve	⚾⚾
Overall Slider	⚾⚾

Comments: Trouble with all outside and all inside fastballs vs. RH — especially weak against all low-outside pitches vs. RH.
Strengths: All middle fastballs, medium-inside curves, medium-outside sliders vs. RH; medium-outside and low-middle fastballs vs. LH.
Weaknesses: All inside and outside fastballs, all low and all outside curves and sliders vs. RH; high-outside and low-outside fastballs vs. LH.

Mike Felder Against Right-Handed Pitchers
Overall BARS Batting Average .247

Fastball Average .269

	Outside	Middle	Inside
High	5/ 0/0	9/ 111/1	6/ 166/1
Med	37/ 351/13	3/ 666/2	13/ 384/5
Low	3/ 0/0	6/ 166/1	7/ 142/1

Curve Average .100

	Outside	Middle	Inside
High	0/ 0/0	0/ 0/0	1/ 0/0
Med	0/ 0/0	2/ 500/1	3/ 0/0
Low	3/ 0/0	0/ 0/0	1/ 0/0

Slider Average .200

	Outside	Middle	Inside
High	0/ 0/0	0/ 0/0	0/ 0/0
Med	2/ 500/1	0/ 0/0	2/ 0/0
Low	0/ 0/0	1/ 0/0	0/ 0/0

Mike Felder Against Left-Handed Pitchers
Overall BARS Batting Average .209

Fastball Average .204

	Inside	Middle	Outside
High	2/ 0/0	0/ 0/0	5/ 200/1
Med	3/ 333/1	0/ 0/0	23/ 173/4
Low	0/ 0/0	4/ 0/0	7/ 428/3

Curve Average .285

	Inside	Middle	Outside
High	0/ 0/0	0/ 0/0	0/ 0/0
Med	0/ 0/0	0/ 0/0	4/ 250/1
Low	0/ 0/0	0/ 0/0	3/ 333/1

Slider Average .000

	Inside	Middle	Outside
High	0/ 0/0	0/ 0/0	0/ 0/0
Med	2/ 0/0	1/ 0/0	0/ 0/0
Low	0/ 0/0	1/ 0/0	0/ 0/0

Switch-hitter Mike Felder has trouble with high fastballs and low fastballs against right-handed pitchers, but he hits waist-high fastballs excellently (.351, .666, and .384, outside to inside).

He hits medium-high outside fastballs better when behind in the count. Notice that the right fielder and the shortstop need to shift to be correctly positioned for this pitch when Felder goes ahead or behind.

MEDIUM-HIGH OUTSIDE FASTBALLS (WHEN BEHIND IN THE COUNT)

BATTING AVERAGE .416
Play
Left	Medium-deep in straightaway left field
Center	Deep in straightaway center field
Right	Deep and shifted toward center field
Short	Normal position
Second	Normal position

MEDIUM-HIGH OUTSIDE FASTBALLS (WHEN AHEAD IN THE COUNT)

BATTING AVERAGE .294
Play
Left	Medium-deep in straightaway left field
Center	Deep in straightaway center field
Right	Medium-deep and shifted toward center field
Short	Up middle (shifted toward second base)
Second	Normal position

He hits an excellent .384 against medium-high inside fastballs against right-handers. The field diagram on the opposite page shows how fielders need to align themselves for this pitch.

MEDIUM-HIGH INSIDE FASTBALLS

BATTING AVERAGE .384
Play
Left	Medium-deep in straightaway left field
Center	Short in straightaway center field
Right	Medium-deep in straightaway right field
Short	Normal position
Second	Shifted toward first base

Batting right handed against left-handed pitchers, Felder has a lot of trouble with medium-high outside fastballs (.173). His low average in this location indicates that most of his hit balls from here are probably easy pop flies and grounders.

MEDIUM-HIGH OUTSIDE FASTBALLS (THROWN BY LEFT-HANDED PITCHERS)

BATTING AVERAGE .173
Play
Left	Deep and shifted toward center field
Center	Medium-deep in straightaway center field
Right	Deep in straightaway right field
Short	Up middle (shifted toward second base)
Second	Normal position

Medium-High Inside Fastballs
(Thrown By Right-Handed Pitchers)

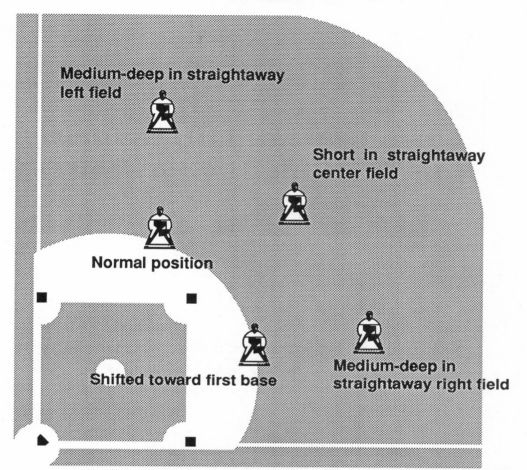

Medium-deep in straightaway left field

Short in straightaway center field

Normal position

Shifted toward first base

Medium-deep in straightaway right field

Ahead And Behind In The Count Vs. RH

Ahead

Fastball Average .256				Curve Average .000		
	Outside	Middle	Inside	Outside	Middle	Inside
High	0/ 0 /0	2/ 0 /0	5/ 0 /0	0/ 0 /0	0/ 0 /0	0/ 0 /0
Med	17/ 294 /5	2/ 1000 /2	5/ 400 /2	0/ 0 /0	0/ 0 /0	0/ 0 /0
Low	1/ 0 /0	4/ 0 /0	3/ 333 /1	0/ 0 /0	0/ 0 /0	1/ 0 /0

Behind

Fastball Average .322				Curve Average .000		
	Outside	Middle	Inside	Outside	Middle	Inside
High	4/ 0 /0	5/ 0 /0	1/ 1000 /1	0/ 0 /0	0/ 0 /0	0/ 0 /0
Med	12/ 416 /5	1/ 0 /0	5/ 600 /3	0/ 0 /0	1/ 0 /0	2/ 0 /0
Low	0/ 0 /0	2/ 500 /1	1/ 0 /0	1/ 0 /0	0/ 0 /0	0/ 0 /0

Overall Evaluation
Against Right-Handed Pitchers

Overall Fastball ⊙⊙

Overall Curve — Not enough information

Overall Slider — Not enough information

Against Left-Handed Pitchers

Overall Fastball ⊙⊙

Overall Curve — Not enough information

Overall Slider — Not enough information

Comments: Has trouble with high fastballs and low fastballs vs. RH.

Strengths: Waist-high fastballs vs. RH; low-outside fastballs vs. LH.

Weaknesses: High fastballs and low fastballs vs. RH.

Terry Francona Against Right-Handed Pitchers
Overall BARS Batting Average .265

Fastball Average .271

	Outside	Middle	Inside
High	19/ 210 /4	23/ 217 /5	18/ 166 /3
Med	51/ 235 /12	11/ 545 /6	38/ 315 /12
Low	14/ 214 /3	38/ 236 /9	20/ 450 /9

Curve Average .210

	Outside	Middle	Inside
High	3/ 333 /1	3/ 333 /1	0/ 0 /0
Med	6/ 0 /0	5/ 200 /1	4/ 500 /2
Low	5/ 400 /2	9/ 111 /1	3/ 0 /0

Slider Average .307

	Outside	Middle	Inside
High	0/ 0 /0	2/ 1000 /2	1/ 1000 /1
Med	1/ 0 /0	0/ 0 /0	4/ 250 /1
Low	0/ 0 /0	1/ 0 /0	4/ 0 /0

Terry Francona Against Left-Handed Pitchers
Overall BARS Batting Average .136

Fastball Average .166

	Outside	Middle	Inside
High	1/ 0 /0	2/ 500 /1	2/ 0 /0
Med	2/ 0 /0	1/ 1000 /1	2/ 0 /0
Low	1/ 0 /0	0/ 0 /0	1/ 0 /0

Curve Average .000

	Outside	Middle	Inside
High	1/ 0 /0	1/ 0 /0	0/ 0 /0
Med	0/ 0 /0	0/ 0 /0	0/ 0 /0
Low	3/ 0 /0	2/ 0 /0	0/ 0 /0

Slider Average .333

	Outside	Middle	Inside
High	0/ 0 /0	1/ 1000 /1	0/ 0 /0
Med	1/ 0 /0	0/ 0 /0	0/ 0 /0
Low	1/ 0 /0	0/ 0 /0	0/ 0 /0

Left-handed hitter Terry Francona has trouble with high fastballs and outside fastballs against right-handed pitchers. These locations offer the best sectors for right-handers to attack. He hits well against medium-high inside and low-inside fastballs, however (.315 and .450).

Notice in Francona's Ahead and Behind charts on the opposite page that he hits medium-high inside fastballs considerably better when ahead in the count (.350 when ahead, .181 when behind).

MEDIUM-HIGH INSIDE FASTBALLS (WHEN AHEAD IN THE COUNT)

BATTING AVERAGE .350
Play

Left	Medium-deep in straightaway left field
Center	Deep in straightaway center field
Right	Deep in straightaway right field
Short	Normal position
Second	Normal position

MEDIUM-HIGH INSIDE FASTBALLS (WHEN BEHIND IN THE COUNT)

BATTING AVERAGE .181
Play

Left	Short in straightaway left field
Center	Medium-deep and shifted toward left field
Right	*No instances recorded*
Short	Normal position
Second	Shifted toward first base

He hits low-inside fastballs for a strong .450 average. The field diagram on the opposite page shows how fielders need to play him for this pitch.

LOW-INSIDE FASTBALLS

BATTING AVERAGE .450
Play

Left	Deep in straightaway left field
Center	Deep and shifted toward left field
Right	Medium-deep in straightaway right field
Short	Shifted toward third base
Second	Shifted toward first base

He hits an exceptionally strong .545 against medium-over-the-middle fastballs. The .235 in his highly pitched medium-high outside fastball location brings down his overall average.

MEDIUM-HIGH OUTSIDE FASTBALLS

BATTING AVERAGE .235
Play

Left	Deep and shifted toward the left field line
Center	Deep and shifted toward left field
Right	Deep in straightaway right field
Short	Up middle (shifted toward second base)
Second	Normal position

Francona has trouble with low-over-the-middle curves against right-handers (.111 on 1 for 9).

Low-Inside Fastballs
(Thrown By Right-Handed Pitchers)

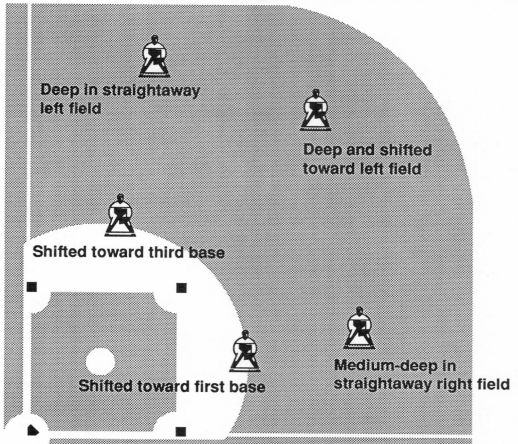

Deep in straightaway left field

Deep and shifted toward left field

Shifted toward third base

Shifted toward first base

Medium-deep in straightaway right field

Ahead And Behind In The Count Vs. RH

Ahead

Fastball Average .274

	Outside	Middle	Inside
High	6/ 0/0	8/ 0/0	6/ 166/1
Med	29/ 137/4	4/ 500/2	20/ 350/7
Low	3/ 1000/3	27/ 333/9	10/ 500/5

Curve Average .000

	Outside	Middle	Inside
	1/ 0/0	1/ 0/0	0/ 0/0
	1/ 0/0	1/ 0/0	2/ 0/0
	1/ 0/0	0/ 0/0	0/ 0/0

Behind

Fastball Average .250

	Outside	Middle	Inside
High	2/ 500/1	6/ 333/2	3/ 0/0
Med	8/ 375/3	5/ 600/3	11/ 181/2
Low	6/ 0/0	6/ 0/0	5/ 400/2

Curve Average .230

	Outside	Middle	Inside
	1/ 1000/1	2/ 500/1	0/ 0/0
	2/ 0/0	1/ 0/0	0/ 0/0
	0/ 0/0	6/ 166/1	1/ 0/0

Overall Evaluation
Against Right-Handed Pitchers

Overall Fastball

Overall Curve ⚾⚾

Overall Slider ⚾⚾ ⚾⚾ ⚾⚾ ⚾⚾

Against Left-Handed Pitchers

Overall Fastball — Not enough information

Overall Curve — Not enough information

Overall Slider — Not enough information

Comments: Weak against all high fastballs and outside fastballs vs. RH.
Strengths: Medium-middle, medium-inside and low-inside fastballs vs. RH.
Weaknesses: High fastballs, outside fastballs, low-middle fastballs, low-middle curves vs. RH.

Jim Gantner (Left Handed)

Milwaukee Brewers

Jim Gantner Against Right-Handed Pitchers
Overall BARS Batting Average .260

Fastball Average .277

	Outside	Middle	Inside
High	26/230 /6	39/282 /11	7/428 /3
Med	112/241 /27	48/312 /15	51/313 /16
Low	22/136 /3	42/452 /19	24/125 /3

Curve Average .185

	Outside	Middle	Inside
High	1/0 /0	5/200 /1	4/0 /0
Med	16/62 /1	6/333 /2	7/285 /2
Low	3/333 /1	16/312 /5	12/83 /1

Slider Average .291

	Outside	Middle	Inside
High	0/0 /0	1/0 /0	2/500 /1
Med	5/200 /1	0/0 /0	6/333 /2
Low	4/250 /1	5/400 /2	1/0 /0

Jim Gantner Against Left-Handed Pitchers
Overall BARS Batting Average .300

Fastball Average .333

	Outside	Middle	Inside
High	5/600 /3	18/111 /2	8/375 /3
Med	39/307 /12	12/416 /5	22/318 /7
Low	7/428 /3	22/454 /10	8/250 /2

Curve Average .272

	Outside	Middle	Inside
High	2/500 /1	3/333 /1	0/0 /0
Med	12/83 /1	1/1000 /1	8/750 /6
Low	9/0 /0	7/142 /1	2/500 /1

Slider Average .178

	Outside	Middle	Inside
High	0/0 /0	2/0 /0	0/0 /0
Med	1/0 /0	1/0 /0	6/166 /1
Low	11/90 /1	6/333 /2	1/1000 /1

Left-handed hitter Jim Gantner has an overall fastball average of .277 against right-handed pitchers. Fastballs against left-handed pitchers are a different story. His .333 overall fastball average against lefties is excellent. It's somewhat unusual for a left-handed hitter to hit fastballs so much better against left-handed pitchers.

Starting first with Gantner's performance against right-handers, note his contrasting strong and weak locations. His .452 in low-middle, .312 in medium-over-the-middle and .313 in medium-high inside are all very solid. But these are offset by his weaknesses in the three outside locations (.230, .241 and .136, high to low) and the low-inside location (.125).

The left-handed Gantner goes down the left line with medium-high outside fastballs. But the infielders need to be shifted for a pull.

MEDIUM-HIGH OUTSIDE FASTBALLS

BATTING AVERAGE .241
Play

Left	Deep and shifted toward the left field line
Center	Deep in straightaway center field
Right	Medium-deep in straightaway right field
Short	Up middle (shifted toward second base)
Second	Shifted toward first base

His Ahead and Behind charts show that Gantner hits medium-high outside fastballs much better when ahead in the count (.301 when ahead, .153 when behind). Fielders must adjust for this pitch depending on the count.

MEDIUM-HIGH OUTSIDE FASTBALLS
(WHEN AHEAD IN THE COUNT)

BATTING AVERAGE .301
Play

Left	Deep and shifted toward the left field line
Center	Deep in straightaway center field
Right	Deep and shifted toward center field
Short	Up middle (shifted toward second base)
Second	Shifted toward first base

MEDIUM-HIGH OUTSIDE FASTBALLS
(WHEN BEHIND IN THE COUNT)

BATTING AVERAGE .153
Play

Left	Deep and shifted toward the left field line
Center	Medium-deep in straightaway center field
Right	*No instances recorded*
Short	Up middle (shifted toward second base)
Second	Normal position

Gantner hits low-over-the-middle fastballs exceptionally well (.452).

LOW-OVER-THE-MIDDLE FASTBALLS

BATTING AVERAGE .452
Play

Left	Deep in straightaway left field
Center	Medium-deep in straightaway center field
Right	Deep in straightaway right field
Short	Up middle (shifted toward second base)
Second	Normal position

Gantner has some very weak curve locations. His .312 in the low-over-the-middle curve location is excellent, however.

LOW-OVER-THE-MIDDLE CURVEBALLS

BATTING AVERAGE .312
Play

Left	Deep in straightaway left field
Center	Medium-deep in straightaway center field
Right	*No instances recorded*
Short	Normal position
Second	Normal position

Gantner Against Left-Handed Pitchers

Against left-handers, Gantner hits fastballs excellently (.333 overall). Every fielder except the second baseman is required to shift for a medium-high inside as compared with a medium-high outside fastball.

MEDIUM-HIGH INSIDE FASTBALLS (THROWN BY LEFT-HANDED PITCHERS)

BATTING AVERAGE .318
Play

Left	Medium-deep and shifted toward the left field line
Center	Deep and shifted toward left field
Right	Medium-deep in straightaway right field
Short	Normal position
Second	Normal position

MEDIUM-HIGH OUTSIDE FASTBALLS (THROWN BY LEFT-HANDED PITCHERS)

BATTING AVERAGE .307
Play

Left	Medium-deep in straightaway left field
Center	Medium-deep in straightaway center field
Right	Deep and shifted toward center field
Short	Up middle (shifted toward second base)
Second	Normal position

As against right-handers, Gantner hits extremely well against low-over-the-middle fastballs thrown by left-handers (452 vs. right-handers, .454 vs. lefties.

LOW-OVER-THE-MIDDLE FASTBALLS (THROWN BY LEFT-HANDED PITCHERS)

BATTING AVERAGE .454
Play

Left	Deep in straightaway left field
Center	Deep in straightaway center field
Right	Medium-deep and shifted toward center field
Short	Up middle (shifted toward second base)
Second	Shifted toward first base

Gantner has weaknesses against low-outside curves and sliders thrown by left-handers (0-for-9 curves, 1-for-11 sliders). He also hits poorly against medium-high outside curves (.083 on 1-for-12).

Ahead And Behind In The Count Vs. RH

Ahead

	Fastball Average .318			Curve Average .318		
	Outside	Middle	Inside	Outside	Middle	Inside
High	16/187 /3	20/250 /5	3/333 /1	0/0 /0	1/0 /0	1/0 /0
Med	63/301 /19	31/290 /9	30/333 /10	7/142 /1	2/500 /1	4/250 /1
Low	6/333 /2	23/565 /13	9/222 /2	0/0 /0	5/600 /3	2/500 /1

Behind

	Fastball Average .207			Curve Average .160		
	Outside	Middle	Inside	Outside	Middle	Inside
High	3/0 /0	11/363 /4	1/1000 /1	1/0 /0	0/0 /0	3/0 /0
Med	13/153 /2	4/0 /0	6/166 /1	2/0 /0	3/0 /0	1/1000 /1
Low	3/0 /0	9/333 /3	3/0 /0	3/333 /1	10/200 /2	2/0 /0

Overall Evaluation

Against Right-Handed Pitchers

Overall Fastball	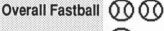
Overall Curve	
Overall Slider	

Against Left-Handed Pitchers

Overall Fastball	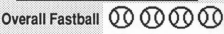
Overall Curve	
Overall Slider	

Comments: Hits fastballs excellently against LH.
Strengths: Low-middle, medium-middle and medium-inside fastballs, low-middle curves vs. RH; all fastballs vs. LH except high-middle and low-inside, medium-inside curves vs. LH.
Weaknesses: Low-inside and all outside fastballs, medium-outside and low-inside curves vs. RH; high-middle and low-inside fastballs, medium-outside and low-outside curves, low-outside sliders vs. LH.

Paul Molitor (Right Handed)   *Milwaukee Brewers*

Paul Molitor Against Right-Handed Pitchers
Overall BARS Batting Average .324

Fastball Average .333

	Inside	Middle	Outside
High	16/ 437/7	20/ 200/4	7/ 428/3
Med	51/ 313/16	12/ 416/5	114/ 342/39
Low	26/ 346/9	31/ 419/13	26/ 192/5

Curve Average .302

	Inside	Middle	Outside
High	3/ 333/1	10/ 300/3	1/ 0/0
Med	4/ 500/2	7/ 428/3	20/ 250/5
Low	2/ 0/0	11/ 545/6	28/ 214/6

Slider Average .290

	Inside	Middle	Outside
High	2/ 0/0	3/ 666/2	2/ 500/1
Med	7/ 428/3	5/ 400/2	19/ 157/3
Low	1/ 0/0	4/ 500/2	12/ 250/3

Paul Molitor Against Left-Handed Pitchers
Overall BARS Batting Average .289

Fastball Average .275

	Inside	Middle	Outside
High	5/ 600/3	9/ 444/4	6/ 333/2
Med	19/ 315/6	5/ 400/2	49/ 265/13
Low	5/ 0/0	11/ 272/3	18/ 111/2

Curve Average .285

	Inside	Middle	Outside
High	0/ 0/0	0/ 0/0	2/ 0/0
Med	2/ 0/0	1/ 1000/1	5/ 200/1
Low	3/ 0/0	2/ 1000/2	6/ 333/2

Slider Average .300

	Inside	Middle	Outside
High	1/ 0/0	0/ 0/0	1/ 1000/1
Med	4/ 250/1	1/ 1000/1	7/ 142/1
Low	7/ 142/1	7/ 428/3	2/ 500/1

Paul Molitor, a right-handed hitter, has an excellent overall fastball average against right-handed pitchers (.333). He has two distinctly weak fastball locations (.192 low-outside and .200 high-over-the-middle), but every other fastball location is solid.

He has an excellent .342 overall average in his medium-high outside location. He hits this pitch for a higher average when he is ahead in the count.

MEDIUM-HIGH OUTSIDE FASTBALLS (WHEN AHEAD IN THE COUNT)

BATTING AVERAGE .344
Play
Left	Deep in straightaway left field
Center	Medium-deep in straightaway center field
Right	Deep in straightaway right field
Short	Up middle (shifted toward second base)
Second	Normal position

MEDIUM-HIGH OUTSIDE FASTBALLS (WHEN BEHIND IN THE COUNT)

BATTING AVERAGE .307
Play
Left	Medium-deep in straightaway left field
Center	Medium-deep and shifted toward left field
Right	Medium-deep in straightaway right field
Short	Normal position
Second	Normal position

He hits medium-high inside fastballs mostly toward center field.

MEDIUM-HIGH INSIDE FASTBALLS

BATTING AVERAGE .313
Play
Left	Deep and shifted toward center field
Center	Deep in straightaway center field
Right	Medium-deep and shifted toward center field
Short	Normal position
Second	Normal position

He tends to hit low-over-the-middle fastballs to the opposite field (right field) for a high .419 average.

LOW-OVER-THE-MIDDLE FASTBALLS

BATTING AVERAGE .419
Play
Left	Medium-deep in straightaway left field
Center	Deep and shifted toward right field
Right	Deep and shifted toward the right field line
Short	Normal position
Second	Shifted toward first base

He goes deep down both lines with low-inside fastballs.

LOW-INSIDE FASTBALLS

BATTING AVERAGE .346
Play
Left	Deep and shifted toward the left field line
Center	Medium-deep and shifted toward left field
Right	Deep and shifted toward the right field line

Short Shifted toward third base
Second *No instances recorded*

He hits high-inside fastballs at a .437 clip.

HIGH-INSIDE FASTBALLS

BATTING AVERAGE .437
Play
Left Medium-deep and shifted toward the left field line
Center Short in straightaway center field
Right Medium-deep in straightaway right field
Short Normal position
Second Normal position

Molitor's lowest fastball average is in his low-outside location.

LOW-OUTSIDE FASTBALLS

BATTING AVERAGE .192
Play
Left Medium-deep in straightaway left field
Center Medium-deep and shifted toward right field
Right Deep in straightaway right field
Short Shifted toward third base
Second Normal position

Molitor hits curves excellently overall against right-handed pitchers (.302). But his .250 in the medium-high outside curve location and .214 in the low-outside location offer a sector of weakness for pitchers to attack. The same is true in his two most highly pitched slider locations: medium-high outside (.157) and low-outside (.250). He hits all over-the-middle curves very strongly: .300 high-middle, .428 medium-over-the-middle, and .545 low-over-the-middle.

Molitor Against Left-Handed Pitchers

Molitor has trouble with low-outside and medium-high outside fastballs thrown by left-handed pitchers. He hits medium-high outside fastballs deep down both lines.

MEDIUM-HIGH OUTSIDE FASTBALLS (THROWN BY LEFT-HANDED PITCHERS)

BATTING AVERAGE .265
Play
Left Deep and shifted toward the left field line
Center Deep in straightaway center field
Right Deep and shifted toward the right field line
Short Normal position
Second Shifted toward first base

He pulls medium-high inside fastballs thrown by left-handers. Note, however, that the infielders must play in their normal straightaway positions for this pitch.

MEDIUM-HIGH INSIDE FASTBALLS (THROWN BY LEFT-HANDED PITCHERS)

BATTING AVERAGE .315
Play
Left Deep and shifted toward the left field line
Center Deep and shifted toward left field
Right Deep and shifted toward center field
Short Normal position
Second Normal position

Left-handed pitchers throw Molitor few curves and sliders. By focusing on outside fastballs and by mixing in more breaking pitches, pitchers could gain an edge.

Ahead And Behind In The Count Vs. RH

Ahead

	Fastball Average .369			Curve Average .428		
	Inside	Middle	Outside	Inside	Middle	Outside
High	7/714 /5	7/142 /1	2/1000 /2	0/0 /0	7/428 /3	0/0 /0
Med	27/333 /9	6/500 /3	58/344 /20	3/333 /1	2/500 /1	8/375 /3
Low	9/444 /4	18/444 /8	12/166 /2	0/0 /0	5/600 /3	3/333 /1

Behind

	Fastball Average .369			Curve Average .272		
	Inside	Middle	Outside	Inside	Middle	Outside
High	8/250 /2	4/500 /2	3/0 /0	2/0 /0	1/0 /0	0/0 /0
Med	14/357 /5	4/500 /2	13/307 /4	0/0 /0	2/500 /1	5/400 /2
Low	8/500 /4	5/600 /3	6/333 /2	1/0 /0	3/333 /1	8/250 /2

Overall Evaluation

Against Right-Handed Pitchers

Overall Fastball ⚾⚾⚾⚾
Overall Curve ⚾⚾⚾⚾
Overall Slider ⚾⚾⚾

Against Left-Handed Pitchers

Overall Fastball ⚾⚾
Overall Curve ⚾⚾⚾
Overall Slider ⚾⚾⚾⚾

Comments: Molitor's a quality fastball hitter vs. RH; he has more trouble with fastballs vs. LH.
Strengths: All fastballs vs. RH except low-outside and high-middle, all over-the-middle curves and sliders vs. RH; medium-inside and all high fastballs vs. LH.
Weaknesses: Low-outside and high-middle fastballs, low-outside and medium-outside curves and sliders vs. RH; low-outside and medium-outside fastballs, low-inside and medium-inside sliders vs. LH.

Dave Parker Against Right-Handed Pitchers
Overall BARS Batting Average .329

Fastball Average .341

	Outside	Middle	Inside
High	34/ 352 /12	38/ 282 /11	29/ 241 /7
Med	85/ 376 /32	23/ 391 /9	59/ 338 /20
Low	17/ 411 /7	59/ 338 /20	45/ 333 /15

Curve Average .315

	Outside	Middle	Inside
High	3/ 0 /0	8/ 625 /5	1/ 0 /0
Med	13/ 153 /2	5/ 400 /2	10/ 500 /5
Low	9/ 111 /1	10/ 500 /5	14/ 214 /3

Slider Average .258

	Outside	Middle	Inside
High	2/ 0 /0	3/ 666 /2	3/ 333 /1
Med	8/ 125 /1	3/ 333 /1	6/ 666 /4
Low	5/ 200 /1	10/ 300 /3	18/ 111 /2

Dave Parker Against Left-Handed Pitchers
Overall BARS Batting Average .285

Fastball Average .347

	Outside	Middle	Inside
High	6/ 166 /1	9/ 333 /3	18/ 277 /5
Med	16/ 312 /5	12/ 416 /5	26/ 307 /8
Low	8/ 250 /2	14/ 500 /7	12/ 500 /6

Curve Average .147

	Outside	Middle	Inside
High	5/ 200 /1	5/ 0 /0	0/ 0 /0
Med	14/ 71 /1	3/ 666 /2	6/ 333 /2
Low	18/ 55 /1	10/ 200 /2	0/ 0 /0

Slider Average .320

	Outside	Middle	Inside
High	1/ 0 /0	2/ 0 /0	0/ 0 /0
Med	5/ 400 /2	3/ 333 /1	1/ 0 /0
Low	7/ 142 /1	6/ 666 /4	0/ 0 /0

Dave Parker, left-handed hitter, has excellent overall averages against fastballs (.341 vs. right-handed pitchers, .347 vs. left-handed pitchers). He hits curves well against right-handers (.315 overall) but very poorly against left-handers (.147).

Parker has only one weak fastball location against right-handers: high-inside (.241). He hits medium-high outside fastballs extremely well (.376). He hits this pitch straightaway to the outfield.

MEDIUM-HIGH OUTSIDE FASTBALLS

BATTING AVERAGE .376
Play

Left	Deep in straightaway left field
Center	Medium-deep in straightaway center field
Right	Deep in straightaway right field
Short	Up middle (shifted toward second base)
Second	Shifted toward first base

He goes down the left line (the opposite field for Parker) with medium-high inside fastballs.

MEDIUM-HIGH INSIDE FASTBALLS

BATTING AVERAGE .338
Play

Left	Medium-deep and shifted toward the left field line
Center	Medium-deep in straightaway center field
Right	Deep in straightaway right field
Short	Shifted toward third base
Second	Normal position

He also goes down the left line with low-inside fastballs.

LOW-INSIDE FASTBALLS

BATTING AVERAGE .333
Play

Left	Medium-deep and shifted toward the left field line
Center	Deep in straightaway center field
Right	Deep in straightaway right field
Short	Shifted toward third base
Second	Normal position

All in all, it seems that Parker's weakest fastball area is the high-over-the-middle/high-inside sector. He hits these pitches in such a way that fielders need to shift toward Parker's opposite field (left field). His low average against high-inside fastballs indicates that he hits mostly easy fly balls from this location.

HIGH-OVER-THE-MIDDLE FASTBALLS

BATTING AVERAGE .282
Play

Left	Deep and shifted toward the left field line
Center	Deep in straightaway center field
Right	Deep and shifted toward center field
Short	Normal position
Second	Normal position

Parker Against Curves And Sliders

Parker's overall curve average of .315 against right-handers is good, but he has some key weak locations. Notice his low averages against outside curves and against low-inside curves.

He's strong against all over-the-middle curves and against medium-high inside curves. He pulls low-over-the middle curves.

LOW-OVER-THE-MIDDLE CURVEBALLS

BATTING AVERAGE .500
Play
Left	*No instances recorded*
Center	Medium-deep in straightaway center field
Right	Deep and shifted toward the right field line
Short	Shifted toward third base
Second	Normal position

He scatters low-inside curves, even hitting down the line to left.

LOW-INSIDE CURVEBALLS

BATTING AVERAGE .214
Play
Left	Medium-deep and shifted toward the left field line
Center	*No instances recorded*
Right	Deep and shifted toward the right field line
Short	Normal position
Second	Shifted toward first base

Parker also has trouble with outside sliders. He hits low-over-the-middle sliders well, but hits only .111 against low-inside sliders.

Parker Against Left-Handed Pitchers

Parker hits for a very strong overall average against fastballs thrown by left-handers (.347). He hits medium-high inside fastballs up the center.

MEDIUM-HIGH INSIDE FASTBALLS (THROWN BY LEFT-HANDED PITCHERS)

BATTING AVERAGE .307
Play
Left	Deep and shifted toward center field
Center	Deep in straightaway center field
Right	Medium-deep and shifted toward center field
Short	Up middle (shifted toward second base)
Second	Shifted toward first base

He goes down the left line with low-over-the-middle fastballs thrown by left-handers.

LOW-OVER-THE-MIDDLE FASTBALLS (THROWN BY LEFT-HANDED PITCHERS)

BATTING AVERAGE .500
Play
Left	Medium-deep and shifted toward the left field line
Center	Deep and shifted toward left field
Right	Deep in straightaway right field
Short	Up middle (shifted toward second base)
Second	Normal position

Notice Parker's extreme weakness against outside curves and low curves thrown by left-handers. These curve locations are the greatest weakness of Parker's BARS charts.

Ahead And Behind In The Count Vs. RH

Ahead

Fastball Average .369

	Outside	Middle	Inside
High	10/ 500 /5	18/ 333 /6	9/ 333 /3
Med	46/ 413 /19	12/ 333 /4	26/ 384 /10
Low	7/ 428 /3	37/ 270 /10	30/ 400 /12

Curve Average .687

	Outside	Middle	Inside
High	0/ 0 /0	2/ 500 /1	0/ 0 /0
Med	3/ 666 /2	1/ 0 /0	5/ 800 /4
Low	0/ 0 /0	3/ 666 /2	2/ 1000 /2

Behind

Fastball Average .313

	Outside	Middle	Inside
High	8/ 500 /4	10/ 200 /2	10/ 200 /2
Med	12/ 333 /4	2/ 500 /1	8/ 125 /1
Low	3/ 666 /2	10/ 500 /5	4/ 0 /0

Curve Average .230

	Outside	Middle	Inside
High	2/ 0 /0	0/ 0 /0	0/ 0 /0
Med	4/ 0 /0	0/ 0 /0	1/ 1000 /1
Low	2/ 0 /0	2/ 500 /1	2/ 500 /1

Overall Evaluation
Against Right-Handed Pitchers

Overall Fastball	⚾⚾⚾⚾⚾
Overall Curve	⚾⚾⚾⚾⚾
Overall Slider	⚾⚾

Against Left-Handed Pitchers

Overall Fastball	⚾⚾⚾⚾
Overall Curve	⚾
Overall Slider	⚾⚾⚾⚾⚾

Comments: An excellent fastball hitter, Parker has trouble with curves against left-handers.
Strengths: All fastball locations vs. RH (except high-middle and high-inside), over-the-middle and medium-inside curves vs. RH, waist-high and over-the-middle fastballs vs. LH, low-inside fastballs vs. LH.
Weaknesses: High-middle and high-inside fastballs vs. RH, all outside curves & low-inside curves vs. RH, low-inside sliders vs. RH, all outside & low curves vs. LH.

B. J. Surhoff Against Right-Handed Pitchers
Overall BARS Batting Average .277

Fastball Average .280

	Outside	Middle	Inside
High	17/176/3	8/375/3	6/166/1
Med	63/301/19	3/666/2	16/312/5
Low	12/250/3	14/214/3	18/277/5

Curve Average .315

	Outside	Middle	Inside
High	1/0/0	2/500/1	2/0/0
Med	4/250/1	3/666/2	1/1000/1
Low	0/0/0	4/250/1	2/0/0

Slider Average .227

	Outside	Middle	Inside
High	0/0/0	1/1000/1	0/0/0
Med	7/142/1	1/1000/1	6/166/1
Low	3/0/0	1/1000/1	3/0/0

B. J. Surhoff Against Left-Handed Pitchers
Overall BARS Batting Average .240

Fastball Average .277

	Outside	Middle	Inside
High	2/0/0	3/333/1	7/285/2
Med	10/200/2	1/1000/1	5/400/2
Low	2/0/0	2/500/1	4/250/1

Curve Average .181

	Outside	Middle	Inside
High	3/0/0	1/0/0	0/0/0
Med	4/250/1	1/1000/1	0/0/0
Low	1/0/0	1/0/0	0/0/0

Slider Average .000

	Outside	Middle	Inside
High	0/0/0	1/0/0	0/0/0
Med	1/0/0	0/0/0	0/0/0
Low	1/0/0	0/0/0	0/0/0

B. J. Surhoff, left-handed hitter, has a .280 overall fastball average against right-handed pitchers. This is mainly built upon his solid .301 average in the medium-high outside location.

He hits medium-high outside fastballs thrown by right-handers deep to all fields. The center and right fielders need to be shifted toward Surhoff's opposite field (left field), but the shortstop and second baseman need to play for a pull. Only the left fielder plays straightaway.

MEDIUM-HIGH OUTSIDE FASTBALLS

BATTING AVERAGE .301
Play

Left	Deep in straightaway left field
Center	Deep and shifted toward left field
Right	Deep and shifted toward center field
Short	Up middle (shifted toward second base)
Second	Shifted toward first base

In contrast, Surhoff hits high-outside fastballs almost exclusively to the opposite field (toward left field). The shortstop and second baseman need to be in their normal positions, however.

HIGH-OUTSIDE FASTBALLS

BATTING AVERAGE .176
Play

Left	Deep and shifted toward the left field line
Center	Medium-deep and shifted toward left field
Right	*No instances recorded*
Short	Normal position
Second	Normal position

Surhoff also hits low-outside fastballs down the left line, but the center fielder needs to be straightaway.

LOW-OUTSIDE FASTBALLS

BATTING AVERAGE .250
Play

Left	Deep and shifted toward the left field line
Center	Medium-deep in straightaway center field
Right	Medium-deep and shifted toward center field
Short	Up middle (shifted toward second base)
Second	Normal position

Surhoff hits low-inside fastballs for a .277 average.

LOW-INSIDE FASTBALLS

BATTING AVERAGE .277
Play

Left	Medium-deep in straightaway left field
Center	Medium-deep and shifted toward left field
Right	Deep and shifted toward center field
Short	Normal position
Second	Shifted toward first base

He hits low-over-the-middle fastballs for a .214 average. His low average indicates that most of his hit balls in this location are probably easy pop-ups and ground outs.

LOW-OVER-THE-MIDDLE FASTBALLS

BATTING AVERAGE .214
Play

Left	Short in straightaway left field
Center	Medium-deep in straightaway center field
Right	Deep in straightaway right field
Short	Up middle (shifted toward second base)
Second	Shifted toward first base

His medium-high inside fastball average is very solid (.312). The BARS fielding strategy shows that he pulls this pitch.

MEDIUM-HIGH INSIDE FASTBALLS

BATTING AVERAGE .312

Play

Left	Medium-deep and shifted toward center field
Center	Deep and shifted toward right field
Right	Medium-deep and shifted toward the right line
Short	Normal position
Second	Shifted toward first base

Surhoff Against Left-Handed Pitchers

Less overall BARS information is available for Surhoff's performance against left-handed pitchers. He seems to have a weakness against outside fastballs thrown by left-handers. His average of .200 (2 for 10) in the medium-high outside location gives pitchers a weak spot on which to focus.

MEDIUM-HIGH OUTSIDE FASTBALLS (THROWN BY LEFT-HANDED PITCHERS)

BATTING AVERAGE .200
Play

Left	*No instances recorded*
Center	Deep in straightaway center field
Right	Deep in straightaway right field
Short	Normal position
Second	Normal position

Ahead And Behind In The Count Vs. RH

Ahead

Fastball Average .285

	Outside	Middle	Inside
High	9 / 111 / 1	4 / 250 / 1	1 / 0 / 0
Med	39 / 333 / 13	3 / 666 / 2	10 / 300 / 3
Low	7 / 142 / 1	9 / 111 / 1	9 / 444 / 4

Curve Average .000

	Outside	Middle	Inside
High	0 / 0 / 0	0 / 0 / 0	1 / 0 / 0
Med	0 / 0 / 0	0 / 0 / 0	0 / 0 / 0
Low	0 / 0 / 0	0 / 0 / 0	0 / 0 / 0

Behind

Fastball Average .533

	Outside	Middle	Inside
High	2 / 500 / 1	0 / 0 / 0	2 / 0 / 0
Med	6 / 500 / 3	0 / 0 / 0	2 / 500 / 1
Low	1 / 1000 / 1	1 / 1000 / 1	1 / 1000 / 1

Curve Average .444

	Outside	Middle	Inside
High	1 / 0 / 0	1 / 1000 / 1	0 / 0 / 0
Med	3 / 333 / 1	1 / 1000 / 1	1 / 1000 / 1
Low	0 / 0 / 0	2 / 0 / 0	0 / 0 / 0

Overall Evaluation

Against Right-Handed Pitchers

Overall Fastball	⚾ ⚾
Overall Curve	⚾ ⚾ ⚾ ⚾
Overall Slider	⚾

Against Left-Handed Pitchers

Overall Fastball	⚾ ⚾
Overall Curve	Not enough information
Overall Slider	Not enough information

Comments: Surhoff hits waist-high fastballs very well vs. RH.

Strength: Waist-high fastballs, high-middle fastballs vs. RH.

Weaknesses: High-outside, low-outside and low-middle fastballs vs. RH; outside fastballs vs. LH.

Robin Yount Against Right-Handed Pitchers
Overall BARS Batting Average .303

Fastball Average .300

	Inside	Middle	Outside
High	32/ 250 /8	25/ 360 /9	27/ 222 /6
Med	56/ 303 /17	26/ 461 /12	126/ 317 /40
Low	20/ 450 /9	44/ 181 /8	33/ 242 /8

Curve Average .289

	Inside	Middle	Outside
High	0/ 0 /0	2/ 0 /0	3/ 666 /2
Med	12/ 166 /2	7/ 857 /6	31/ 161 /5
Low	3/ 333 /1	8/ 375 /3	17/ 294 /5

Slider Average .344

	Inside	Middle	Outside
High	1/ 0 /0	3/ 0 /0	3/ 666 /2
Med	6/ 500 /3	7/ 428 /3	18/ 277 /5
Low	3/ 1000 /3	2/ 0 /0	18/ 277 /5

Robin Yount Against Left-Handed Pitchers
Overall BARS Batting Average .267

Fastball Average .257

	Inside	Middle	Outside
High	3/ 0 /0	10/ 300 /3	10/ 100 /1
Med	18/ 333 /6	11/ 363 /4	60/ 250 /15
Low	14/ 71 /1	17/ 411 /7	24/ 250 /6

Curve Average .216

	Inside	Middle	Outside
High	1/ 0 /0	0/ 0 /0	0/ 0 /0
Med	4/ 250 /1	2/ 1000 /2	16/ 125 /2
Low	3/ 333 /1	3/ 333 /1	8/ 125 /1

Slider Average .371

	Inside	Middle	Outside
High	2/ 500 /1	2/ 500 /1	5/ 400 /2
Med	9/ 222 /2	4/ 750 /3	1/ 1000 /1
Low	4/ 250 /1	5/ 400 /2	3/ 0 /0

Robin Yount, right-handed hitter, has an even .300 fastball average against right-handed pitchers. His averages are different here from the opening chapters of this book because the BARS System continually updates its records and these are the latest available for Yount at the time of publication.

Yount hits medium-high outside fastballs for a fine .317 average against right-handed pitchers.

MEDIUM-HIGH OUTSIDE FASTBALLS

BATTING AVERAGE .317

Play

Left	Medium-deep in straightaway left field
Center	Deep and shifted toward left field
Right	Medium-deep in straightaway right field
Short	Up middle (shifted toward second base)
Second	Normal position

He hits medium-high inside fastballs (.303) mostly toward center field.

MEDIUM-HIGH INSIDE FASTBALLS

BATTING AVERAGE .303

Play

Left	Deep and shifted toward center field
Center	Deep in straightaway center field
Right	Deep and shifted toward center field
Short	Normal position
Second	Shifted toward first base

Yount hits high-over-the-middle fastballs extremely well (.360). He pulls this pitch.

HIGH-OVER-THE-MIDDLE FASTBALLS

BATTING AVERAGE .360

Play

Left	Deep and shifted toward the left field line
Center	Medium-deep and shifted toward left field
Right	Medium-deep in straightaway right field
Short	Normal position
Second	*No instances recorded*

Yount's low averages in the low-over-the-middle fastball location and low-outside fastball location give a target for pitchers. He hits low-over-the-middle fastballs straightaway, probably mostly for easy outs.

LOW-OVER-THE-MIDDLE FASTBALLS

BATTING AVERAGE .181

Play

Left	Deep in straightaway left field
Center	Deep in straightaway center field
Right	Medium-deep in straightaway right field
Short	Normal position
Second	Shifted toward first base

He goes to medium-deep left center and deep right-center with high-outside fastballs. But notice that the shortstop needs to play for Yount to pull the ball.

HIGH-OUTSIDE FASTBALLS

BATTING AVERAGE .222
Play
Left	Medium-deep and shifted toward center field
Center	Deep and shifted toward right field
Right	Deep in straightaway right field
Short	Shifted toward third base
Second	Normal position

Yount Against Curves And Sliders

Yount has weaknesses in his medium-high inside (.166) and medium-high outside (.161) curve locations. But he hits low-outside curves well (.294).

LOW-OUTSIDE CURVEBALLS

BATTING AVERAGE .294
Play
Left	Deep in straightaway left field
Center	Medium-deep in straightaway center field
Right	*No instances recorded*
Short	Up middle (shifted toward second base)
Second	*No instances recorded*

He goes more to right (his opposite field) with low-outside sliders (.277).

LOW-OUTSIDE SLIDERS

BATTING AVERAGE .277
Play
Left	*No instances recorded*
Center	Medium-deep in straightaway center field
Right	Deep in straightaway right field
Short	Up middle (shifted toward second base)
Second	Normal position

Yount Against Left-Handed Pitchers

Yount has trouble with outside fastballs against left-handed pitchers. He hits medium-high outside fastballs straightaway and deep to all fields.

MEDIUM-HIGH OUTSIDE FASTBALLS (THROWN BY LEFT-HANDED PITCHERS)

BATTING AVERAGE .250
Play
Left	Deep in straightaway left field
Center	Deep in straightaway center field
Right	Deep in straightaway right field
Short	Normal position
Second	Normal position

He hits low-over-the-middle fastballs for an excellent .411 average against left-handers.

LOW-OVER-THE-MIDDLE FASTBALLS (THROWN BY LEFT-HANDED PITCHERS)

BATTING AVERAGE .411
Play
Left	Deep and shifted toward center field
Center	Deep and shifted toward right field
Right	Deep in straightaway right field
Short	Normal position
Second	Shifted toward first base

His .333 against medium-high inside fastballs, .363 against medium-over-the-middle fastballs and .300 against high-over-the-middle fastballs are all very solid.

He has trouble with outside curves against lefties. His .125 averages in his medium-high outside and low-outside curve locations offer targets for left-handers.

Ahead And Behind In The Count Vs. RH

Ahead

Fastball Average .359

	Inside	Middle	Outside
High	14/ 357/5	12/ 583/7	12/ 250/3
Med	26/ 346/9	12/ 583/7	59/ 322/19
Low	7/ 714/5	26/ 192/5	10/ 400/4

Curve Average .473

	Inside	Middle	Outside
High	0/ 0/0	1/ 0/0	1/ 1000/1
Med	3/ 333/1	3/ 1000/3	8/ 375/3
Low	2/ 500/1	1/ 0/0	0/ 0/0

Behind

Fastball Average .362

	Inside	Middle	Outside
High	5/ 0/0	4/ 500/2	5/ 200/1
Med	17/ 352/6	5/ 400/2	27/ 481/13
Low	3/ 0/0	5/ 200/1	9/ 444/4

Curve Average .214

	Inside	Middle	Outside
High	0/ 0/0	1/ 0/0	1/ 0/0
Med	3/ 0/0	2/ 500/1	13/ 153/2
Low	1/ 0/0	3/ 0/0	4/ 750/3

Overall Evaluation

Against Right-Handed Pitchers

Overall Fastball	●●●
Overall Curve	●●●
Overall Slider	●●●●

Against Left-Handed Pitchers

Overall Fastball	●
Overall Curve	●
Overall Slider	●●●●

Comments: Hits fastballs and curves better vs. RH.
Strengths: Waist-high fastballs, low-inside and high-middle fastballs, low curves, medium-middle curves and sliders vs. RH; over-the-middle and medium-inside fastballs vs. LH.
Weaknesses: Fastballs except as above, medium-inside and medium-outside curves vs. RH; outside fastballs, low-inside fastballs, outside curves vs. LH.

Balboni, Steve
Barfield, Jesse
Cerone, Rick
Espinoza, Alvaro
Garcia, Damaso
Hall, Mel
Kelly, Roberto
Mattingly, Don
Polonia, Luis
Sax, Steve
Tolleson, Wayne
Winfield, Dave

New York Yankees
BARS System
Hitting Analysis

Steve Balboni Against Right-Handed Pitchers
Overall BARS Batting Average .231

Fastball Average .241

	Inside	Middle	Outside
High	29/ 34 /1	47/ 276 /13	31/ 129 /4
Med	88/ 215 /19	59/ 423 /25	123/ 211 /26
Low	26/ 76 /2	93/ 333 /31	51/ 215 /11

Curve Average .195

	Inside	Middle	Outside
High	5/ 200 /1	15/ 533 /8	3/ 0 /0
Med	19/ 368 /7	24/ 458 /11	45/ 155 /7
Low	10/ 100 /1	28/ 107 /3	45/ 0 /0

Slider Average .240

	Inside	Middle	Outside
High	3/ 0 /0	13/ 461 /6	6/ 333 /2
Med	16/ 250 /4	16/ 500 /8	31/ 322 /10
Low	2/ 0 /0	18/ 277 /5	53/ 56 /3

Steve Balboni Against Left-Handed Pitchers
Overall BARS Batting Average .264

Fastball Average .270

	Inside	Middle	Outside
High	14/ 0 /0	21/ 190 /4	15/ 66 /1
Med	24/ 250 /6	27/ 481 /13	76/ 315 /24
Low	13/ 384 /5	42/ 333 /14	19/ 52 /1

Curve Average .294

	Inside	Middle	Outside
High	1/ 0 /0	9/ 333 /3	4/ 500 /2
Med	10/ 300 /3	10/ 300 /3	16/ 312 /5
Low	8/ 125 /1	13/ 384 /5	7/ 142 /1

Slider Average .157

	Inside	Middle	Outside
High	1/ 0 /0	3/ 0 /0	1/ 0 /0
Med	3/ 333 /1	4/ 500 /2	6/ 500 /3
Low	6/ 0 /0	8/ 0 /0	6/ 0 /0

Right-handed hitting Steve Balboni has higher overall fastball and curve averages against left-handed pitchers. He has some very strong locations in his charts, but these are offset by some very weak locations.

Against right-handers, Balboni hits .211 against medium-high outside fastballs. His Ahead and Behind charts on the opposite page show that he hits this pitch much better when ahead in the count (.340 when ahead, .153 when behind). He pulls this pitch to all fields when behind, but hits it more straightaway when ahead.

MEDIUM-HIGH OUTSIDE FASTBALLS (WHEN AHEAD IN THE COUNT)

BATTING AVERAGE .340
Play
Left — Deep and shifted toward center field
Center — Deep in straightaway center field
Right — Deep in straightaway right field
Short — Up middle (shifted toward second base)
Second — Normal position

MEDIUM-HIGH OUTSIDE FASTBALLS (WHEN BEHIND IN THE COUNT)

BATTING AVERAGE .153
Play
Left — Deep and shifted toward the left field line

Center — Deep and shifted toward left field
Right — Deep and shifted toward center field
Short — Normal position
Second — Shifted toward first base

Notice how well he hits low-over-the-middle fastballs against right-handers (.333). He also hits this pitch better when ahead, but his fielding strategy does not change as dramatically when he is ahead and behind as it does in his medium-high outside location. The fielding strategy below is for all counts.

LOW-OVER-THE-MIDDLE FASTBALLS

BATTING AVERAGE .333
Play
Left — Deep and shifted toward the left field line
Center — Deep in straightaway center field
Right — Deep in straightaway right field
Short — Shifted toward third base
Second — Shifted toward first base

Balboni is weak in the four fastball corners against right-handers. If right-handers avoid throwing fastballs high-over-the-middle, medium-over-the-middle or low-over-the-middle, they should have little trouble pitching to him.

Balboni Against Curves And Sliders

Balboni is weak against all outside and all low curves against right-handed pitchers.

His extremely low averages against low-outside curves and low-outside sliders deserve special note. His 0-for-45 against low-outside curves thrown by right-handers is, to my knowledge, the weakest single location in the BARS records. But this is contrasted by his fine averages against medium-high inside, medium-over-the-middle and high-over-the-middle curves. By keeping curves away from this reverse L-shaped sector, right-handers should gain an edge.

He pulls medium-high inside curves sharply.

MEDIUM-HIGH INSIDE CURVEBALLS

BATTING AVERAGE .368

Play

Left	Deep and shifted toward the left field line
Center	Deep and shifted toward left field
Right	*No instances recorded*
Short	Shifted toward third base
Second	*No instances recorded*

He also pulls high-over-the-middle curves. Notice that there are no recorded instances of Balboni hitting this pitch to right field or to the right side of the infield.

HIGH-OVER-THE-MIDDLE CURVEBALLS

BATTING AVERAGE .533

Play

Left	Deep and shifted toward the left field line
Center	Medium-deep and shifted toward left field

Right	*No instances recorded*
Short	Normal position
Second	*No instances recorded*

He also hits medium-over-the-middle, high-over-the-middle and medium-high outside sliders very well.

Balboni Against Left-Handed Pitchers

Balboni has a solid .315 average against medium-high outside fastballs thrown by left-handers. He hits this pitch deep to the outfield, mostly toward center field.

MEDIUM-HIGH OUTSIDE FASTBALLS (THROWN BY LEFT-HANDED PITCHERS)

BATTING AVERAGE .315

Play

Left	Deep and shifted toward center field
Center	Deep in straightaway center field
Right	Deep and shifted toward center field
Short	Up middle (shifted toward second base)
Second	Normal position

He has extreme trouble with high fastballs and with low-outside fastballs thrown by left-handers, but hits low-inside (.384), low-over-the-middle (.333) and medium-over-the-middle fastballs (.481) very well.

Balboni hits curves well against lefties, with great strength down-the-middle and waist-high. He has trouble with all low sliders, although he hits waist-high sliders excellently.

Ahead And Behind In The Count Vs. RH

Ahead

Fastball Average .346

	Inside	Middle	Outside
High	5/0	14/571 /8	6/500 /3
Med	35/257 /9	29/413 /12	50/340 /17
Low	8/125 /1	40/400 /16	21/285 /6

Curve Average .244

	Inside	Middle	Outside
High	2/0	6/500 /3	2/0
Med	4/250 /1	6/500 /3	13/153 /2
Low	2/500 /1	7/142 /1	3/0

Behind

Fastball Average .215

	Inside	Middle	Outside
High	7/142 /1	3/333 /1	6/0
Med	18/222 /4	12/500 /6	26/153 /4
Low	3/0	15/200 /3	3/333 /1

Curve Average .413

	Inside	Middle	Outside
High	2/0	5/600 /3	1/0
Med	8/625 /5	9/666 /6	8/375 /3
Low	3/0	7/285 /2	3/0

Overall Evaluation

Against Right-Handed Pitchers

Overall Fastball	⚾⚾
Overall Curve	⚾⚾
Overall Slider	⚾⚾

Against Left-Handed Pitchers

Overall Fastball	⚾⚾ ⚾⚾
Overall Curve	⚾⚾ ⚾⚾ ⚾⚾
Overall Slider	⚾⚾

Comments: Has trouble with all low-outside pitches. **Strengths:** Low-middle and medium-middle fastballs, medium-inside and medium-middle curves, high-middle, medium-middle and medium-outside sliders vs. RH; low-inside, low-middle and medium-middle fastballs, all waist-high and all middle curves vs. LH. **Weaknesses:** High, outside, and inside fastballs, outside and low curves, low-outside sliders vs. RH; high fastballs, low-outside curves, low sliders vs. LH.

Jesse Barfield (Right Handed)　　　*New York Yankees*

Jesse Barfield Against Right-Handed Pitchers
Overall BARS Batting Average .287

Fastball Average .326

	Inside	Middle	Outside
High	13/ 76 /1	25/ 440 /11	24/ 250 /6
Med	45/ 288 /13	33/ 575 /19	123/ 333 /41
Low	14/ 428 /6	39/ 358 /14	39/ 128 /5

Curve Average .211

	Inside	Middle	Outside
High	2/ 0 /0	7/ 571 /4	4/ 0 /0
Med	8/ 375 /3	9/ 333 /3	31/ 193 /6
Low	4/ 250 /1	14/ 285 /4	25/ 40 /1

Slider Average .200

	Inside	Middle	Outside
High	0/ 0 /0	3/ 666 /2	3/ 666 /2
Med	6/ 166 /1	3/ 0 /0	17/ 235 /4
Low	2/ 0 /0	6/ 166 /1	30/ 133 /4

Jesse Barfield Against Left-Handed Pitchers
Overall BARS Batting Average .290

Fastball Average .353

	Inside	Middle	Outside
High	5/ 400 /2	6/ 166 /1	17/ 294 /5
Med	14/ 214 /3	7/ 857 /6	70/ 385 /27
Low	7/ 142 /1	23/ 391 /9	18/ 277 /5

Curve Average .127

	Inside	Middle	Outside
High	0/ 0 /0	1/ 0 /0	1/ 0 /0
Med	1/ 0 /0	4/ 0 /0	10/ 300 /3
Low	8/ 125 /1	15/ 133 /2	7/ 0 /0

Slider Average .216

	Inside	Middle	Outside
High	1/ 0 /0	1/ 1000 /1	1/ 0 /0
Med	7/ 0 /0	0/ 0 /0	7/ 285 /2
Low	9/ 0 /0	4/ 750 /3	7/ 285 /2

Right-handed hitting Jesse Barfield has excellent fastball averages against both right- and left-handed pitchers, but his curve and slider averages are poor.

Starting with his fastball charts against right-handers, notice his excellent .333 average in the highly pitched medium-high outside location. He hits this pitch deep into the left-center gap, deep and straight-away to center and deep down the right line.

MEDIUM-HIGH OUTSIDE FASTBALLS

BATTING AVERAGE .333
Play
Left　Deep and shifted toward center field
Center　Deep in straightaway center field
Right　Deep and shifted toward the right field line
Short　Normal position
Second　Shifted toward first base

Barfield hits medium-high inside fastballs for a .288 average.

MEDIUM-HIGH INSIDE FASTBALLS

BATTING AVERAGE .288
Play
Left　Deep and shifted toward the left field line
Center　Deep in straightaway center field
Right　Medium-deep in straightaway right field

Short　Normal position
Second　Normal position

His only weak fastball locations are high-inside (.076) and low-outside (.128).

He is extremely strong against all over-the-middle fastballs (.440, .575, and .358, high to low).

HIGH-OVER-THE-MIDDLE FASTBALLS

BATTING AVERAGE .440
Play
Left　Deep in straightaway left field
Center　Deep in straightaway center field
Right　Deep and shifted toward center field
Short　Normal position
Second　*No instances recorded*

LOW-OVER-THE-MIDDLE FASTBALLS

BATTING AVERAGE .358
Play
Left　Deep and shifted toward center field
Center　Deep in straightaway center field
Right　Deep and shifted toward center field
Short　Normal position
Second　Normal position

Barfield Against Curves And Sliders

Barfield had trouble with curves and sliders against right-handers, especially in the outside locations. By keeping breaking balls low and away, right-handed pitchers can gain an advantage.

He hits medium-high outside curves deep to all fields.

MEDIUM-HIGH OUTSIDE CURVEBALLS

BATTING AVERAGE .193

Play	
Left	Deep in straightaway left field
Center	Deep and shifted toward right field
Right	Deep in straightaway right field
Short	Normal position
Second	Normal position

He has trouble getting his bat on the ball against low-outside curves.

LOW-OUTSIDE CURVEBALLS

BATTING AVERAGE .040

Play	
Left	Medium-deep in straightaway left field
Center	*No instances recorded*
Right	*No instances recorded*
Short	Up middle (shifted toward second base)
Second	*No instances recorded*

Barfield Against Left-Handed Pitchers

Barfield hits fastballs extremely well against left-handed pitchers (.353 overall). He hits medium-high outside fastballs at a .385 clip.

MEDIUM-HIGH OUTSIDE FASTBALLS (THROWN BY LEFT-HANDED PITCHERS)

BATTING AVERAGE .385

Play	
Left	Deep and shifted toward center field
Center	Deep in straightaway center field
Right	Deep in straightaway right field
Short	Up middle (shifted toward second base)
Second	Shifted toward first base

He hits .391 against low-over-the-middle fastballs thrown by left-handers.

LOW-OVER-THE-MIDDLE FASTBALLS (THROWN BY LEFT-HANDED PITCHERS)

BATTING AVERAGE .391

Play	
Left	Medium-deep and shifted toward center field
Center	Deep in straightaway center field
Right	Deep and shifted toward center field
Short	Normal position
Second	Normal position

He has some trouble with low-outside fastballs against left-handers (.277).

He has difficulty with low curves and inside sliders against left-handers, but he hits a solid .300 against medium-high inside curves.

Ahead And Behind In The Count Vs. RH

Ahead

Fastball Average .393

	Inside	Middle	Outside
High	4/250 /1	8/750 /6	8/500 /4
Med	20/350 /7	13/538 /7	40/325 /13
Low	6/666 /4	15/400 /6	13/153 /2

Curve Average .470

	Inside	Middle	Outside
High	0/0 /0	2/1000 /2	0/0 /0
Med	2/500 /1	2/500 /1	9/222 /2
Low	0/0 /0	2/1000 /2	0/0 /0

Behind

Fastball Average .414

	Inside	Middle	Outside
High	3/0 /0	4/500 /2	3/0 /0
Med	9/222 /2	7/714 /5	30/466 /14
Low	3/666 /2	8/500 /4	3/0 /0

Curve Average .294

	Inside	Middle	Outside
High	1/0 /0	5/400 /2	2/0 /0
Med	4/500 /2	3/333 /1	8/375 /3
Low	1/1000 /1	7/142 /1	3/0 /0

Overall Evaluation

Against Right-Handed Pitchers

Overall Fastball	⚾⚾⚾⚾
Overall Curve	⚾⚾
Overall Slider	⚾⚾

Against Left-Handed Pitchers

Overall Fastball	⚾⚾⚾⚾
Overall Curve	⚾⚾
Overall Slider	⚾⚾

Comments: Trouble with outside curves vs. RH. Strengths: Waist-high fastballs, over-the-middle fastballs and low-inside fastballs, medium-middle curves vs. RH; medium-outside and low-middle fastballs, medium-outside curves vs. LH. Weaknesses: High-inside and low-outside fastballs, outside curves, medium-outside and low-outside sliders vs. RH; medium-inside and low-inside fastballs, low curves and inside sliders vs. LH.

Rick Cerone (Right Handed) — *New York Yankees*

Rick Cerone Against Right-Handed Pitchers
Overall BARS Batting Average .251

Fastball Average .240

	Inside	Middle	Outside
High	19/ 210 /4	16/ 437 /7	12/ 416 /5
Med	38/ 236 /9	13/ 153 /2	97/ 216 /21
Low	7/ 142 /1	25/ 320 /8	22/ 136 /3

Curve Average .235

	Inside	Middle	Outside
High	0/ 0 /0	3/ 666 /2	4/ 0 /0
Med	6/ 0 /0	2/ 1000 /2	20/ 300 /6
Low	4/ 0 /0	7/ 428 /3	22/ 136 /3

Slider Average .320

	Inside	Middle	Outside
High	1/ 0 /0	4/ 250 /1	2/ 500 /1
Med	4/ 500 /2	5/ 600 /3	11/ 181 /2
Low	1/ 0 /0	6/ 166 /1	19/ 368 /7

Rick Cerone Against Left-Handed Pitchers
Overall BARS Batting Average .218

Fastball Average .207

	Inside	Middle	Outside
High	6/ 0 /0	10/ 200 /2	12/ 83 /1
Med	21/ 238 /5	10/ 500 /5	67/ 238 /16
Low	6/ 333 /2	26/ 192 /5	25/ 80 /2

Curve Average .184

	Inside	Middle	Outside
High	0/ 0 /0	1/ 1000 /1	1/ 0 /0
Med	2/ 500 /1	1/ 1000 /1	9/ 111 /1
Low	4/ 250 /1	9/ 222 /2	11/ 0 /0

Slider Average .363

	Inside	Middle	Outside
High	0/ 0 /0	3/ 666 /2	1/ 0 /0
Med	2/ 500 /1	1/ 1000 /1	5/ 600 /3
Low	5/ 0 /0	3/ 0 /0	2/ 500 /1

Cerone's .240 overall fastball average against right-handed pitchers is very low, but it is an improvement from his .212 at the end of last year. His strongest locations are high-over-the-middle (.437) and high-outside (.416), but his weaknesses in the highly pitched medium-high outside (.216) and medium-high inside (.236) locations bring his overall average down.

It's interesting to see how differently Cerone hits high-over-the-middle and high-outside fastballs. Even though these are adjoining locations, fielders would have to shift significantly to be positioned properly against pitches to both locations.

HIGH-OVER-THE-MIDDLE FASTBALLS

BATTING AVERAGE .437
Play

Left	Deep and shifted toward the left field line
Center	Deep and shifted toward left field
Right	Medium-deep and shifted toward the right line
Short	Up middle (shifted toward second base)
Second	Normal position

HIGH-OUTSIDE FASTBALLS

BATTING AVERAGE .416
Play

Left	Medium-deep in straightaway left field
Center	Deep in straightaway center field
Right	Deep and shifted toward the right field line
Short	Normal position
Second	Shifted toward first base

The diagram on the opposite page illustrates the necessary change in fielding strategy for these two pitch locations.

Cerone Against Left-Handed Pitchers

Against left-handers, Cerone has many weak fastball and curve locations. His .238 against medium-high outside fastballs is poor. His weaknesses against low and high fastballs present many good targets for left-handers.

MEDIUM-HIGH OUTSIDE FASTBALLS (THROWN BY LEFT-HANDED PITCHERS)

BATTING AVERAGE .238
Play

Left	Deep in straightaway left field
Center	Deep in straightaway center field
Right	Medium-deep in straightaway right field
Short	Normal position
Second	Normal position

Dark Fielders — High-Over-The-Middle Fastballs Vs. RH
Light Fielders — High-Outside Fastballs Vs. RH

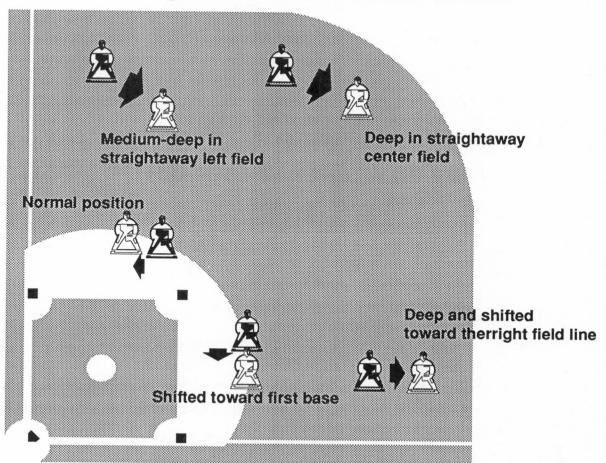

Medium-deep in straightaway left field

Deep in straightaway center field

Normal position

Deep and shifted toward therright field line

Shifted toward first base

Ahead And Behind In The Count Vs. RH

Ahead

Fastball Average .277

	Inside	Middle	Outside
High	11/90 /1	9/444 /4	6/500 /3
Med	27/296 /8	4/0 /0	42/285 /12
Low	2/0 /0	13/384 /5	12/166 /2

Curve Average .461

	Inside	Middle	Outside
High	0/0 /0	0/0 /0	0/0 /0
Med	2/0 /0	1/1000 /1	4/500 /2
Low	1/0 /0	4/750 /3	1/0 /0

Behind

Fastball Average .191

	Inside	Middle	Outside
High	5/600 /3	3/333 /1	3/333 /1
Med	4/250 /1	1/0 /0	21/95 /2
Low	2/0 /0	5/0 /0	3/333 /1

Curve Average .350

	Inside	Middle	Outside
High	0/0 /0	1/1000 /1	0/0 /0
Med	2/0 /0	0/0 /0	5/600 /3
Low	0/0 /0	1/0 /0	11/272 /3

Overall Evaluation
Against Right-Handed Pitchers

Overall Fastball ◯◯

Overall Curve ◯◯

Overall Slider ◯◯ ◯◯◯◯◯

Against Left-Handed Pitchers

Overall Fastball ◯◯

Overall Curve ◯◯

Overall Slider ◯◯ ◯◯◯◯

Comments: Weak against inside fastballs vs. RH.
Strengths: High-outside, high-middle and low-middle
fastballs, medium-outside and low-middle curves, low-
outside sliders vs. RH; medium-middle fastballs vs. LH.
Weaknesses: Fastballs except as above, inside and
low-outside curves, medium-outside sliders vs. RH;
high fastballs, outside fastballs, low-middle and
medium-inside fastballs, outside and low curves
vs. LH.

Alvaro Espinoza Against Right-Handed Pitchers
Overall BARS Batting Average .243

Fastball Average .282

	Inside	Middle	Outside
High	4 / 250 /1	5 / 400 /2	4 / 0 /0
Med	7 / 0 /0	3 / 666 /2	45 / 288 /13
Low	3 / 333 /1	7 / 571 /4	7 / 142 /1

Curve Average .200

	Inside	Middle	Outside
High	0 / 0 /0	2 / 0 /0	1 / 0 /0
Med	1 / 1000 /1	0 / 0 /0	2 / 500 /1
Low	0 / 0 /0	2 / 500 /1	7 / 0 /0

Slider Average .066

	Inside	Middle	Outside
High	0 / 0 /0	0 / 0 /0	0 / 0 /0
Med	0 / 0 /0	0 / 0 /0	8 / 0 /0
Low	0 / 0 /0	2 / 500 /1	5 / 0 /0

Alvaro Espinoza Against Left-Handed Pitchers
Overall BARS Batting Average .250

Fastball Average .250

	Inside	Middle	Outside
High	0 / 0 /0	0 / 0 /0	4 / 0 /0
Med	2 / 500 /1	0 / 0 /0	14 / 142 /2
Low	1 / 1000 /1	6 / 500 /3	1 / 0 /0

Curve Average .333

	Inside	Middle	Outside
High	0 / 0 /0	0 / 0 /0	0 / 0 /0
Med	2 / 0 /0	0 / 0 /0	1 / 1000 /1
Low	0 / 0 /0	0 / 0 /0	0 / 0 /0

Slider Average .000

	Inside	Middle	Outside
High	0 / 0 /0	0 / 0 /0	0 / 0 /0
Med	0 / 0 /0	0 / 0 /0	0 / 0 /0
Low	0 / 0 /0	1 / 0 /0	0 / 0 /0

Right-handed hitter Alvaro Espinoza hits .282 overall against fastballs thrown by right-handed pitchers. His .288 medium-high outside fastball average, though not outstanding, buoys up his fastball average. He gets so many pitches in this location he could just wait for them and really tee off.

He hits this pitch straightaway to left and center fields and deep into the right-center gap. The chart below and the field diagram on the opposite page illustrate how fielders should play for this pitch to him.

MEDIUM-HIGH OUTSIDE FASTBALLS

BATTING AVERAGE .288
Play
Left	Deep in straightaway left field
Center	Medium-deep in straightaway center field
Right	Deep and shifted toward center field
Short	Up middle (shifted toward second base)
Second	Normal position

He hits .571 against low-over-the-middle fastballs thrown by right-handers. The seven instances in this location are not a lot to go on, but there is no question he tends to hit this pitch well. He hits this pitch strongly to his opposite field (right field), but notice that the shortstop needs to be shifted toward third base.

LOW-OVER-THE-MIDDLE FASTBALLS

BATTING AVERAGE .571
Play
Left	*No instances recorded*
Center	Medium-deep and shifted toward right field
Right	Medium-deep and shifted toward the right line
Short	Shifted toward third base
Second	Shifted toward first base

Espinoza Against Left-Handed Pitchers

Against left-handed pitchers, Espinoza has trouble with medium-high outside fastballs (.142). He hits this pitch deep to all fields, but his low average indicates that he is not hitting the ball hard and it is easy for fielders to get him out.

MEDIUM-HIGH OUTSIDE FASTBALLS
(THROWN BY LEFT-HANDED PITCHERS)

BATTING AVERAGE .142
Play
Left	Deep and shifted toward center field
Center	Deep and shifted toward right field
Right	Deep in straightaway right field
Short	Normal position
Second	Normal position

Medium-High Outside Fastballs
(Thrown By Right-Handed Pitchers)

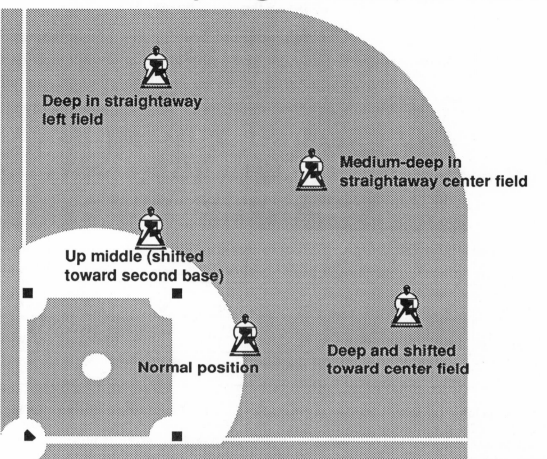

Deep in straightaway left field

Medium-deep in straightaway center field

Up middle (shifted toward second base)

Normal position

Deep and shifted toward center field

Ahead And Behind In The Count Vs. RH

Ahead

Fastball Average .351

	Inside	Middle	Outside
High	3/ 333 /1	3/ 666 /2	3/ 0 /0
Med	6/ 0 /0	1/ 1000 /1	27/ 370 /10
Low	1/ 1000 /1	5/ 600 /3	5/ 200 /1

Curve Average .000

	Inside	Middle	Outside
High	0/ 0 /0	1/ 0 /0	1/ 0 /0
Med	0/ 0 /0	0/ 0 /0	0/ 0 /0
Low	0/ 0 /0	0/ 0 /0	0/ 0 /0

Behind

Fastball Average .300

	Inside	Middle	Outside
High	0/ 0 /0	0/ 0 /0	1/ 0 /0
Med	1/ 0 /0	0/ 0 /0	5/ 400 /2
Low	1/ 0 /0	2/ 500 /1	0/ 0 /0

Curve Average .000

	Inside	Middle	Outside
High	0/ 0 /0	1/ 0 /0	0/ 0 /0
Med	0/ 0 /0	0/ 0 /0	1/ 0 /0
Low	0/ 0 /0	1/ 0 /0	0/ 0 /0

Overall Evaluation
Against Right-Handed Pitchers

Overall Fastball	⚾⚾ ⚾⚾
Overall Curve	⚾⚾
Overall Slider	⚾⚾

Against Left-Handed Pitchers

Overall Fastball	⚾⚾
Overall Curve	Not enough information
Overall Slider	Not enough information

Comments: Weak against low-outside pitches vs. RH.
Strengths: Low-middle and medium-outside fastballs vs. RH.
Weaknesses: Low-outside fastballs and curves, outside sliders vs. RH; medium-outside fastballs vs. LH.

Damaso Garcia Against Right-Handed Pitchers
Overall BARS Batting Average .250

Fastball Average .259

	Inside	Middle	Outside
High	12 / 250 / 3	20 / 300 / 6	10 / 300 / 3
Med	29 / 275 / 8	17 / 529 / 9	58 / 172 / 10
Low	8 / 250 / 2	42 / 261 / 11	24 / 208 / 5

Curve Average .255

	Inside	Middle	Outside
High	3 / 0 / 0	9 / 222 / 2	1 / 1000 / 1
Med	2 / 0 / 0	5 / 600 / 3	33 / 212 / 7
Low	0 / 0 / 0	16 / 250 / 4	29 / 275 / 8

Slider Average .172

	Inside	Middle	Outside
High	0 / 0 / 0	2 / 0 / 0	1 / 1000 / 1
Med	1 / 0 / 0	1 / 0 / 0	10 / 200 / 2
Low	0 / 0 / 0	3 / 333 / 1	11 / 90 / 1

Damaso Garcia Against Left-Handed Pitchers
Overall BARS Batting Average .247

Fastball Average .198

	Inside	Middle	Outside
High	3 / 333 / 1	8 / 375 / 3	10 / 100 / 1
Med	19 / 263 / 5	14 / 357 / 5	33 / 181 / 6
Low	7 / 142 / 1	21 / 95 / 2	21 / 142 / 3

Curve Average .414

	Inside	Middle	Outside
High	1 / 0 / 0	0 / 0 / 0	2 / 0 / 0
Med	1 / 0 / 0	3 / 666 / 2	12 / 416 / 5
Low	5 / 600 / 3	9 / 555 / 5	8 / 250 / 2

Slider Average .240

	Inside	Middle	Outside
High	2 / 0 / 0	1 / 0 / 0	0 / 0 / 0
Med	6 / 166 / 1	0 / 0 / 0	4 / 500 / 2
Low	7 / 142 / 1	4 / 500 / 2	1 / 0 / 0

Right-handed hitter Damaso Garcia has weak BARS fastball averages against both right-handed and left-handed pitchers (.259 against right-handers, .198 against left-handers). He hits curves for an adequate .255 average against right-handers and for an excellent .414 against left-handers.

He is weak against all low fastballs thrown by right-handers (.250, .261, and .208, inside to outside). He also has trouble with high-inside fastballs (.250) and medium-high outside fastballs (.172). Many hitters are strong in their medium-high outside fastball locations. Garcia's average here brings down his overall average significantly. He hits medium-high outside fastballs deep to all fields.

MEDIUM-HIGH OUTSIDE FASTBALLS

BATTING AVERAGE .172
Play
Left   Deep and shifted toward center field
Center   Deep in straightaway center field
Right   Deep in straightaway right field
Short   Up middle (shifted toward second base)
Second   Normal position

He hits high-over-the-middle fastballs (.300) and high-outside fastballs (.300) solidly. This is a sector right-handers should avoid.

It's interesting that every fielder except the right fielder needs to shift to be correctly positioned for these two pitches. Notice the left fielder in particular. He would have to shift the maximum possible distance for any fielder — deep toward center for high-over-the-middle fastballs to short toward the left line for high-outside fastballs.

HIGH-OVER-THE-MIDDLE FASTBALLS

BATTING AVERAGE .300
Play
Left   Deep and shifted toward center field
Center   Deep and shifted toward right field
Right   Medium-deep in straightaway right field
Short   Up middle (shifted toward second base)
Second   Shifted toward first base

HIGH-OUTSIDE FASTBALLS

BATTING AVERAGE .300
Play
Left   Short and shifted toward the left field line
Center   Deep and shifted toward right field
Right   Deep and shifted toward the right field line
Short   Normal position
Second   Normal position

Garcia has quite a few medium-over-the-middle fastball instances (17). This indicates that either he is a fairly patient hitter or pitchers are not pitching him carefully enough. His .529 average in this location is very high.

MEDIUM-OVER-THE-MIDDLE FASTBALLS

BATTING AVERAGE .529
Play

Left	Deep in straightaway left field
Center	Medium-deep in straightaway center field
Right	Medium-deep in straightaway right field
Short	Up middle (shifted toward second base)
Second	Normal position

Garcia his low-outside curves for a good .275 average against right-handers.

LOW-OUTSIDE CURVEBALLS

BATTING AVERAGE .275
Play

Left	Medium-deep and shifted toward center field
Center	Medium-deep in straightaway center field
Right	Deep in straightaway right field
Short	Normal position
Second	*No instances recorded*

In contrast, he has trouble with low-outside sliders (.090).

Garcia Against Left-Handed Pitchers

Garcia has trouble with all outside fastballs against left-handed pitchers (.100, .181, and .142, high to low). He also has trouble with all low fastballs. He hits medium-over-the-middle fastballs and high-over-the-middle fastballs excellently, (.357 and .375).

MEDIUM-OVER-THE-MIDDLE FASTBALLS (THROWN BY LEFT-HANDED PITCHERS)

BATTING AVERAGE .357
Play

Left	Deep and shifted toward center field
Center	Deep in straightaway center field
Right	Deep in straightaway right field
Short	Normal position
Second	Normal position

HIGH-OVER-THE-MIDDLE FASTBALLS (THROWN BY LEFT-HANDED PITCHERS)

BATTING AVERAGE .375
Play

Left	Deep in straightaway left field
Center	Medium-deep in straightaway center field
Right	Deep and shifted toward center field
Short	Up middle (shifted toward second base)
Second	Normal position

He hits most curve locations well. He hits low-over-the-middle curves (.555) and medium-high outside curves (.416) for exceptional averages. He pulls medium-high outside curves.

MEDIUM-HIGH OUTSIDE CURVEBALLS (THROWN BY LEFT-HANDED PITCHERS)

BATTING AVERAGE .416
Play

Left	Deep and shifted toward the left field line
Center	Deep and shifted toward left field
Right	*No instances recorded*
Short	Shifted toward third base
Second	Normal position

Ahead And Behind In The Count Vs. RH

Ahead

	Fastball Average .213			Curve Average .314		
	Inside	Middle	Outside	Inside	Middle	Outside
High	7/ 0/0	10/ 500/5	3/ 333/1	2/ 0/0	3/ 666/2	1/ 1000/1
Med	18/ 222/4	10/ 400/4	36/ 138/5	0/ 0/0	2/ 500/1	15/ 200/3
Low	6/ 333/2	26/ 153/4	15/ 200/3	0/ 0/0	5/ 200/1	7/ 428/3

Behind

	Fastball Average .300			Curve Average .360		
	Inside	Middle	Outside	Inside	Middle	Outside
High	0/ 0/0	7/ 0/0	4/ 250/1	0/ 0/0	1/ 0/0	0/ 0/0
Med	4/ 250/1	2/ 500/1	7/ 571/4	1/ 0/0	1/ 0/0	10/ 300/3
Low	0/ 0/0	5/ 400/2	1/ 0/0	0/ 0/0	3/ 666/2	9/ 444/4

Overall Evaluation

Against Right-Handed Pitchers

Overall Fastball	⚾
Overall Curve	⚾ ⚾
Overall Slider	⚾

Against Left-Handed Pitchers

Overall Fastball	⚾
Overall Curve	⚾ ⚾ ⚾ ⚾
Overall Slider	⚾

Comments: Weak vs. med-outside fastballs vs. RH. **Strengths:** Medium-middle, high-middle and high-outside fastballs vs. RH; medium-middle and high-middle fastballs, low-middle and medium-outside curves vs. LH. **Weaknesses:** Inside and low fastballs, medium-outside fastballs, medium-outside curves and sliders, low-outside sliders vs. RH; low and outside fastballs, medium-inside fastballs, inside sliders vs. LH.

Mel Hall Against Right-Handed Pitchers
Overall BARS Batting Average .297

Fastball Average .304

	Outside	Middle	Inside
High	33 / 363 /12	16 / 250 /4	13 / 76 /1
Med	100 / 260 /26	21 / 285 /6	31 / 451 /14
Low	23 / 260 /6	40 / 400 /16	22 / 272 /6

Curve Average .285

	Outside	Middle	Inside
High	2 / 0 /0	2 / 0 /0	2 / 500 /1
Med	22 / 409 /9	3 / 333 /1	4 / 250 /1
Low	6 / 166 /1	5 / 400 /2	10 / 100 /1

Slider Average .250

	Outside	Middle	Inside
High	1 / 1000 /1	3 / 333 /1	0 / 0 /0
Med	1 / 1000 /1	4 / 0 /0	3 / 333 /1
Low	4 / 250 /1	5 / 200 /1	15 / 200 /3

Mel Hall Against Left-Handed Pitchers
Overall BARS Batting Average .200

Fastball Average .250

	Outside	Middle	Inside
High	1 / 1000 /1	0 / 0 /0	1 / 0 /0
Med	13 / 153 /2	0 / 0 /0	4 / 250 /1
Low	1 / 0 /0	3 / 333 /1	1 / 1000 /1

Curve Average .142

	Outside	Middle	Inside
High	0 / 0 /0	0 / 0 /0	0 / 0 /0
Med	3 / 333 /1	0 / 0 /0	0 / 0 /0
Low	4 / 0 /0	0 / 0 /0	0 / 0 /0

Slider Average .000

	Outside	Middle	Inside
High	0 / 0 /0	1 / 0 /0	0 / 0 /0
Med	1 / 0 /0	0 / 0 /0	0 / 0 /0
Low	2 / 0 /0	0 / 0 /0	0 / 0 /0

Left-handed hitting Mel Hall hits .297 overall against right-handed pitchers and .200 overall against left-handed pitchers. He hits fastballs at .304 against right-handers and .250 against left-handers.

Hall hits medium-high outside fastballs for a fairly low .260 average, but he hits medium-high inside fastballs for an excellent .451 average. Compare the fielding strategy for medium-high outside fastballs with the strategy for medium-high inside fastballs and you'll see how necessary it can be for fielders to adjust on every pitch. Each of the outfielders would need to shift to be properly positioned.

MEDIUM-HIGH OUTSIDE FASTBALLS

BATTING AVERAGE .260
Play
Left   Deep and shifted toward center field
Center   Deep in straightaway center field
Right   Deep and shifted toward center field
Short   Up middle (shifted toward second base)
Second   Shifted toward first base

MEDIUM-HIGH INSIDE FASTBALLS

BATTING AVERAGE .458
Play
Left   Deep in straightaway left field
Center   Deep and shifted toward right field
Right   Medium-deep in straightaway right field

Short   Up middle (shifted toward second base)
Second   Shifted toward first base

He goes down the left line with high-outside fastballs (.363).

HIGH-OUTSIDE FASTBALLS

BATTING AVERAGE .363
Play
Left   Medium-deep and shifted toward the left line
Center   Medium-deep in straightaway center field
Right   Deep in straightaway right field
Short   Shifted toward third base
Second   Normal position

He hits low-outside fastballs medium-deep to left and center.

LOW-OUTSIDE FASTBALLS

BATTING AVERAGE .260
Play
Left   Medium-deep and shifted toward the left line
Center   Medium-deep and shifted toward left field
Right   *No instances recorded*
Short   Up middle (shifted toward second base)
Second   Normal position

He hits low-over-the-middle fastballs for a very high .400 average.

LOW-OVER-THE-MIDDLE FASTBALLS

BATTING AVERAGE .400
Play

Left	Deep and shifted toward center field
Center	Deep in straightaway center field
Right	Deep and shifted toward center field
Short	Up middle (shifted toward second base)
Second	Shifted toward first base

He has trouble with high-inside and high-over-the-middle fastballs (.076 and .250). This sector is a good target for right-handed pitchers to attack.

HIGH-OVER-THE-MIDDLE FASTBALLS

BATTING AVERAGE .250
Play

Left	Medium-deep and shifted toward the left line
Center	Deep and shifted toward left field
Right	Deep in straightaway right field
Short	Normal position
Second	Normal position

He hits low-inside fastballs deep to all fields for a .272 average.

LOW-INSIDE FASTBALLS

BATTING AVERAGE .272
Play

Left	Deep in straightaway left field
Center	Deep and shifted toward left field
Right	Deep in straightaway right field
Short	Up middle (shifted toward second base)
Second	Normal position

Hall hits medium-high outside curves extremely well against right-handed pitchers (.409).

MEDIUM-HIGH OUTSIDE CURVEBALLS

BATTING AVERAGE .409
Play

Left	Deep and shifted toward the left field line
Center	Medium-deep in straightaway center field
Right	Medium-deep in straightaway right field
Short	Normal position
Second	Shifted toward first base

He has a weak .100 average against low-inside curves. His .200 against low-inside sliders is also weak.

LOW-INSIDE CURVEBALLS

BATTING AVERAGE .100
Play

Left	*No instances recorded*
Center	*No instances recorded*
Right	Medium-deep and shifted toward the right line
Short	*No instances recorded*
Second	*No instances recorded*

LOW-INSIDE SLIDERS

BATTING AVERAGE .200
Play

Left	Medium-deep in straightaway left field
Center	Medium-deep and shifted toward right field
Right	Medium-deep and shifted toward the right line
Short	*No instances recorded*
Second	Shifted toward first base

Hall has fewer recorded instances against left-handed pitchers. His .153 against medium-high outside fastballs indicates a weakness.

Ahead And Behind In The Count Vs. RH

Ahead

Fastball Average .346

	Outside	Middle	Inside
High	14/428/6	9/222/2	7/0/0
Med	51/294/15	10/400/4	14/500/7
Low	14/214/3	17/588/10	14/357/5

Curve Average .421

	Outside	Middle	Inside
High	1/0/0	0/0/0	0/0/0
Med	10/600/6	1/0/0	2/500/1
Low	1/0/0	3/333/1	1/0/0

Behind

Fastball Average .365

	Outside	Middle	Inside
High	10/400/4	3/333/1	4/250/1
Med	27/333/9	1/0/0	6/833/5
Low	4/500/2	6/166/1	2/0/0

Curve Average .266

	Outside	Middle	Inside
High	0/0/0	1/0/0	2/500/1
Med	7/285/2	0/0/0	1/0/0
Low	1/0/0	0/0/0	3/333/1

Overall Evaluation
Against Right-Handed Pitchers

Overall Fastball	⚾⚾ ⚾⚾ ⚾⚾
Overall Curve	⚾⚾ ⚾⚾ ⚾⚾
Overall Slider	⚾⚾ ⚾⚾

Against Left-Handed Pitchers

Overall Fastball	⚾⚾
Overall Curve	Not enough information
Overall Slider	Not enough information

Comments: Has some strong fastball locations vs. RH.
Strengths: High-outside fastballs, medium-inside fastballs, low-middle fastballs, medium-outside curves vs. RH.
Weaknesses: High-inside fastballs, high-middle fastballs, low-outside and medium-outside fastballs, low-inside curves and low-inside sliders vs. RH; medium-outside fastballs vs. LH.

Roberto Kelly (Right Handed) — *New York Yankees*

Roberto Kelly Against Right-Handed Pitchers
Overall BARS Batting Average .216

Fastball Average .231

	Inside	Middle	Outside
High	1/ 0/0	4/ 250/1	2/ 0/0
Med	13/ 461/6	0/ 0/0	28/ 142/4
Low	8/ 125/1	5/ 400/2	8/ 250/2

Curve Average .166

	Inside	Middle	Outside
High	0/ 0/0	3/ 333/1	0/ 0/0
Med	0/ 0/0	0/ 0/0	5/ 200/1
Low	0/ 0/0	3/ 0/0	1/ 0/0

Slider Average .187

	Inside	Middle	Outside
High	0/ 0/0	2/ 0/0	0/ 0/0
Med	0/ 0/0	0/ 0/0	6/ 166/1
Low	1/ 0/0	3/ 666/2	4/ 0/0

Roberto Kelly Against Left-Handed Pitchers
Overall BARS Batting Average .264

Fastball Average .235

	Inside	Middle	Outside
High	0/ 0/0	0/ 0/0	3/ 0/0
Med	7/ 142/1	0/ 0/0	19/ 315/6
Low	1/ 0/0	1/ 0/0	3/ 333/1

Curve Average .545

	Inside	Middle	Outside
High	0/ 0/0	1/ 1000/1	1/ 0/0
Med	0/ 0/0	0/ 0/0	3/ 1000/3
Low	2/ 500/1	1/ 0/0	3/ 333/1

Slider Average .000

	Inside	Middle	Outside
High	1/ 0/0	0/ 0/0	0/ 0/0
Med	0/ 0/0	0/ 0/0	3/ 0/0
Low	2/ 0/0	1/ 0/0	1/ 0/0

Right-handed hitting Roberto Kelly has low fastball averages against both right- and left-handed pitchers (.231 against right-handers, .235 against left-handers).

He hits only .142 against medium-high outside fastballs thrown by right-handers. He hits this pitch deep into the right-center gap and medium-deep into straightaway right field.

MEDIUM-HIGH OUTSIDE FASTBALLS

BATTING AVERAGE .142
Play
- **Left** — *No instances recorded*
- **Center** — Deep and shifted toward right field
- **Right** — Medium-deep in straightaway right field
- **Short** — Up middle (shifted toward second base)
- **Second** — Normal position

He hits medium-high inside fastballs thrown by right-handers for a very strong .461 average.

MEDIUM-HIGH INSIDE FASTBALLS

BATTING AVERAGE .461
Play
- **Left** — Medium-deep in straightaway left field
- **Center** — Medium-deep in straightaway center field
- **Right** — Medium-deep in straightaway right field

- **Short** — Normal position
- **Second** — *No instances recorded*

Kelly Against Left-Handed Pitchers

Kelly hits a solid .315 against medium-high outside fastballs thrown by left-handed pitchers. The chart below and the field diagram on the opposite page show how fielders should play for this pitch.

MEDIUM-HIGH OUTSIDE FASTBALLS
(THROWN BY LEFT-HANDED PITCHERS)

BATTING AVERAGE .315
Play
- **Left** — Medium-deep and shifted toward the left field line
- **Center** — Deep and shifted toward left field
- **Right** — Deep in straightaway right field
- **Short** — Normal position
- **Second** — Normal position

He hits .142 against medium-high inside fastballs. There are fewer instances to go on in this location, but it is evident that left-handers would be better off throwing fastballs inside to Kelly.

Notice his difficulty with medium-high outside curves and medium-high outside sliders against left-handers. These are good targets for attack.

Medium-High Outside Fastballs
(Thrown By Left-Handed Pitchers)

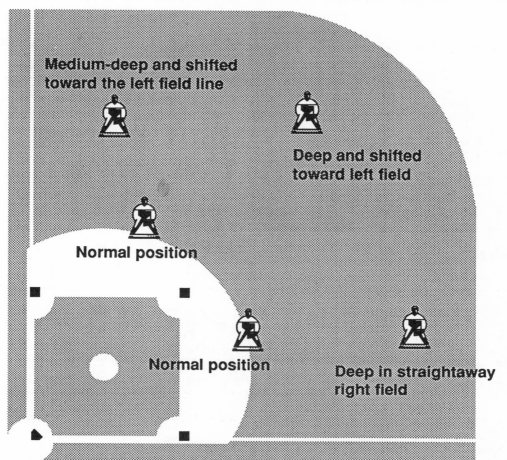

Medium-deep and shifted toward the left field line

Deep and shifted toward left field

Normal position

Normal position

Deep in straightaway right field

Ahead And Behind In The Count Vs. RH

Ahead

Fastball Average .291

	Inside	Middle	Outside
High	0/0	0/0	0/0
Med	5/600/3	0/0	13/153/2
Low	1/0/0	3/0/0	2/1000/2

Curve Average .000

	Inside	Middle	Outside
High	0/0	0/0	0/0
Med	0/0	0/0	1/0/0
Low	0/0	1/0/0	0/0

Behind

Fastball Average .200

	Inside	Middle	Outside
High	0/0	2/500/1	0/0
Med	5/400/2	0/0	6/0/0
Low	4/250/1	0/0	3/0/0

Curve Average .285

	Inside	Middle	Outside
High	0/0	3/333/1	0/0
Med	0/0	0/0	1/1000/1
Low	0/0	2/0/0	1/0/0

Overall Evaluation

Against Right-Handed Pitchers

Overall Fastball ⚾⚾
Overall Curve ⚾
Overall Slider ⚾⚾

Against Left-Handed Pitchers

Overall Fastball ⚾
Overall Curve — Not enough information
Overall Slider — Not enough information

Comments: Very strong against medium-inside fastballs vs. RH.
Strengths: Medium-inside fastballs vs. RH; medium-outside fastballs vs. LH.
Weaknesses: Outside fastballs, low-inside fastballs, outside curves and outside sliders vs. RH; medium-inside fastballs vs. LH.

Don Mattingly Against Right-Handed Pitchers
Overall BARS Batting Average .351

Fastball Average .374

	Outside	Middle	Inside
High	86/348/30	62/370/23	29/620/18
Med	256/316/81	47/425/20	64/421/27
Low	62/387/24	105/380/40	48/437/21

Curve Average .268

	Outside	Middle	Inside
High	5/800/4	8/125/1	6/166/1
Med	31/225/7	3/333/1	8/375/3
Low	12/333/4	20/300/6	15/133/2

Slider Average .228

	Outside	Middle	Inside
High	1/1000/1	3/333/1	2/500/1
Med	11/90/1	3/333/1	11/272/3
Low	13/307/4	12/333/4	14/0/0

Don Mattingly Against Left-Handed Pitchers
Overall BARS Batting Average .317

Fastball Average .350

	Outside	Middle	Inside
High	15/66/1	40/375/15	24/458/11
Med	108/379/41	38/421/16	44/318/14
Low	23/173/4	39/384/15	23/304/7

Curve Average .276

	Outside	Middle	Inside
High	5/200/1	5/200/1	9/222/2
Med	27/259/7	8/500/4	12/416/5
Low	20/250/5	16/187/3	3/333/1

Slider Average .228

	Outside	Middle	Inside
High	6/0/0	8/125/1	1/0/0
Med	27/296/8	1/0/0	5/400/2
Low	21/190/4	14/285/4	0/0/0

Left-handed Don Mattingly hits fastballs excellently against both right- and left-handed pitchers (.374 and .350, respectively). But he has trouble with curves and sliders.

Looking first at his charts against right-handed pitchers, notice that Mattingly does not have a weak fastball location. The .316 in his medium-high outside location is his lowest average. He hits extremely well against low-outside fastballs (.387) and low-over-the-middle fastballs (.380). His .620 average against high-inside fastballs is stunning.

Mattingly goes with the pitch and hits fastballs differently from location to location. If fielders play him in one position through all pitches to him, they'll find themselves chasing balls into the gaps and down the lines. It's very important for fielders to adjust on every pitch, as the following charts show.

MEDIUM-HIGH OUTSIDE FASTBALLS

BATTING AVERAGE .316
Play

Left	Deep in straightaway left field
Center	Deep in straightaway center field
Right	Deep in straightaway right field
Short	Up middle (shifted toward second base)
Second	Normal position

His .380 against low-over-the-middle fastballs is exceptional.

LOW-OVER-THE-MIDDLE FASTBALLS

BATTING AVERAGE .380
Play

Left	Deep in straightaway left field
Center	Medium-deep in straightaway center field
Right	Deep in straightaway right field
Short	Up middle (shifted toward second base)
Second	Normal position

Mattingly pulls high-inside fastballs deep down the right line and deep into the right-center gap.

HIGH-INSIDE FASTBALLS

BATTING AVERAGE .620
Play

Left	Medium-deep in straightaway left field
Center	Deep and shifted toward right field
Right	Deep and shifted toward the right field line
Short	Normal position
Second	Shifted toward first base

His .387 is one of the highest BARS averages recorded for low-outside fastballs, especially considering the high number of recorded instances in this location (62). He goes to his opposite field (left field) with this pitch.

LOW-OUTSIDE FASTBALLS

BATTING AVERAGE .387
Play
Left	Deep and shifted toward the left field line
Center	Deep and shifted toward left field
Right	Deep and shifted toward center field
Short	Up middle (shifted toward second base)
Second	Normal position

Mattingly Against Curves And Sliders

Mattingly has trouble with curves and sliders thrown by right-handed pitchers. In particular, notice his difficulty with low-inside curves and sliders (.133 curves, 0-for-14 sliders). He also has trouble in the medium-high outside location against both types of pitches (.225 vs. curves, .090 vs. sliders).

Mattingly hits medium-high outside curves straightaway to the outfield.

MEDIUM-HIGH OUTSIDE CURVEBALLS

BATTING AVERAGE .225
Play
Left	Deep and shifted toward center field
Center	Deep in straightaway center field
Right	Medium-deep in straightaway right field
Short	Up middle (shifted toward second base)
Second	Normal position

In contrast, he has a tendency to pull low-over-the-middle curves.

Mattingly Against Left-Handed Pitchers

Mattingly's .350 overall fastball average against left-handed pitchers in not as high as his overall .367 against right-handers, but it is still excellent. Notice he has two weak fastball locations against left-handers: high-outside (.066) and low-outside (.173). He hits high-inside fastballs very well against left-handers (.458), as he does against right-handers.

HIGH-INSIDE FASTBALLS
(THROWN BY LEFT-HANDED PITCHERS)

BATTING AVERAGE .458
Play
Left	Medium-deep and shifted toward the left line
Center	Medium-deep in straightaway center field
Right	Medium-deep in straightaway right field
Short	Up middle (shifted toward second base)
Second	Shifted toward first base

His .379 against medium-high outside fastballs thrown by left-handers is outstanding.

MEDIUM-HIGH OUTSIDE FASTBALLS
(THROWN BY LEFT-HANDED PITCHERS)

BATTING AVERAGE .379
Play
Left	Medium-deep in straightaway left field
Center	Deep in straightaway center field
Right	Medium-deep in straightaway right field
Short	Up middle (shifted toward second base)
Second	Normal position

Ahead And Behind In The Count Vs. RH

Ahead

Fastball Average .408

	Outside	Middle	Inside
High	27/370/10	21/428/9	12/583/7
Med	131/328/43	31/451/14	27/555/15
Low	32/406/13	60/433/26	21/523/11

Curve Average .454

	Outside	Middle	Inside
High	1/1000/1	2/0/0	2/0/0
Med	5/800/4	0/0/0	2/1000/2
Low	2/0/0	4/250/1	4/500/2

Behind

Fastball Average .355

	Outside	Middle	Inside
High	26/307/8	17/294/5	8/500/4
Med	55/363/20	7/428/3	14/285/4
Low	12/416/5	19/315/6	5/600/3

Curve Average .277

	Outside	Middle	Inside
High	4/750/3	3/333/1	0/0/0
Med	12/166/2	0/0/0	0/0/0
Low	5/200/1	10/300/3	2/0/0

Overall Evaluation
Against Right-Handed Pitchers

Overall Fastball	⚾ ⚾ ⚾ ⚾
Overall Curve	⚾ ⚾
Overall Slider	⚾

Against Left-Handed Pitchers

Overall Fastball	⚾ ⚾ ⚾ ⚾
Overall Curve	⚾ ⚾ ⚾
Overall Slider	⚾

Comments: Mattingly is a top-quality fastball hitter. **Strengths:** All fastballs, medium-inside and low-middle curves, middle sliders and low-outside sliders vs. RH; waist-high and middle fastballs, high-inside fastballs, medium-inside curves, medium-outside sliders vs. LH. **Weaknesses:** Medium-outside & low-inside sliders vs. RH; medium-outside and low-inside sliders vs. LH; low-outside and high-outside fastballs, outside curves, low-middle curves, low-outside sliders vs. LH.

Luis Polonia (Left Handed)　　　*New York Yankees*

Luis Polonia Against Right-Handed Pitchers
Overall BARS Batting Average .342

Fastball Average .354

	Outside	Middle	Inside
High	16 / 187 / 3	8 / 500 / 4	8 / 500 / 4
Med	56 / 392 / 22	3 / 333 / 1	15 / 466 / 7
Low	10 / 200 / 2	12 / 166 / 2	16 / 375 / 6

Curve Average .272

	Outside	Middle	Inside
High	2 / 500 / 1	1 / 0 / 0	1 / 1000 / 1
Med	4 / 0 / 0	3 / 666 / 2	1 / 1000 / 1
Low	6 / 166 / 1	1 / 0 / 0	3 / 0 / 0

Slider Average .333

	Outside	Middle	Inside
High	2 / 0 / 0	0 / 0 / 0	4 / 250 / 1
Med	2 / 500 / 1	0 / 0 / 0	3 / 0 / 0
Low	1 / 0 / 0	2 / 1000 / 2	7 / 428 / 3

Luis Polonia Against Left-Handed Pitchers
Overall BARS Batting Average .222

Fastball Average .200

	Outside	Middle	Inside
High	2 / 0 / 0	4 / 0 / 0	4 / 750 / 3
Med	11 / 90 / 1	3 / 333 / 1	3 / 333 / 1
Low	1 / 0 / 0	1 / 0 / 0	1 / 0 / 0

Curve Average .375

	Outside	Middle	Inside
High	0 / 0 / 0	1 / 1000 / 1	1 / 0 / 0
Med	4 / 500 / 2	1 / 0 / 0	0 / 0 / 0
Low	1 / 0 / 0	0 / 0 / 0	0 / 0 / 0

Slider Average .142

	Outside	Middle	Inside
High	0 / 0 / 0	0 / 0 / 0	0 / 0 / 0
Med	2 / 500 / 1	0 / 0 / 0	0 / 0 / 0
Low	3 / 0 / 0	1 / 0 / 0	1 / 0 / 0

Left-handed hitter Luis Polonia has an exceptionally good .354 fastball average against right-handed pitchers. Notice the .392 against medium-high outside fastballs. The Ahead and Behind charts on the opposite page show that he hits this pitch better when behind in the count (.454 when behind, .375 when ahead). When ahead, he pulls the ball more. Probably fielders are playing him more to pull — thus his lower average when ahead. By aligning themselves as suggested below and in the field diagram on the opposite page, fielders could prevent most of Polonia's hits in this location.

MEDIUM-HIGH OUTSIDE FASTBALLS (WHEN BEHIND IN THE COUNT)

BATTING AVERAGE .454
Play
Left　　Medium-deep and shifted toward the left field line
Center　Medium-deep and shifted toward left field
Right　Medium-deep in straightaway right field
Short　Normal position
Second　Normal position

MEDIUM-HIGH OUTSIDE FASTBALLS (WHEN AHEAD IN THE COUNT)

BATTING AVERAGE .375
Play

Left　　Deep in straightaway left field
Center　Deep in straightaway center field
Right　Deep in straightaway right field
Short　Up middle (shifted toward second base)
Second　Shifted toward first base

He hits an outstanding .466 against medium-high inside fastballs thrown by right-handers. He hits this pitch into a corridor in center field.

MEDIUM-HIGH INSIDE FASTBALLS

BATTING AVERAGE .466
Play
Left　　Medium-deep and shifted toward center field
Center　Deep in straightaway center field
Right　Medium-deep and shifted toward center field
Short　Up middle (shifted toward second base)
Second　Normal position

His .375 against low-inside fastballs is also excellent. He hits this pitch medium-deep down both lines and to the right side of the infield.

His fastball weaknesses are low- and high-outside and low-over-the-middle.

Polonia has fewer recorded instances against left-handed pitchers. It seems that he's weak against medium-outside fastballs thrown by lefties.

Medium-High Outside Fastballs Vs. RH

Dark Fielders — Behind In The Count
Light Fielders — Ahead In The Count

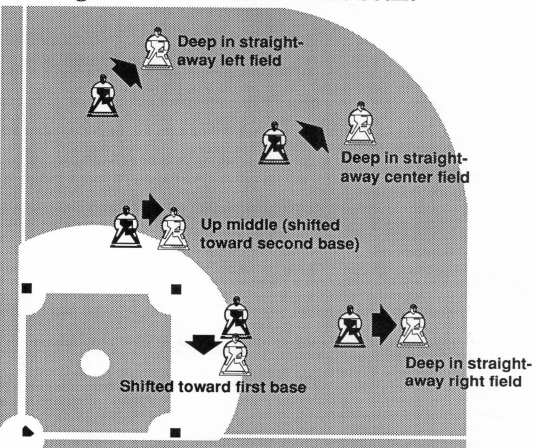

Deep in straight-away left field

Deep in straight-away center field

Up middle (shifted toward second base)

Shifted toward first base

Deep in straight-away right field

Ahead And Behind In The Count Vs. RH

Ahead

Fastball Average .423

	Outside	Middle	Inside
High	3/ 333 /1	1/ 0 /0	3/ 666 /2
Med	24/ 375 /9	2/ 0 /0	5/ 800 /4
Low	2/ 500 /1	6/ 333 /2	6/ 500 /3

Curve Average .000

	Outside	Middle	Inside
High	0/ 0 /0	0/ 0 /0	0/ 0 /0
Med	0/ 0 /0	0/ 0 /0	0/ 0 /0
Low	1/ 0 /0	1/ 0 /0	0/ 0 /0

Behind

Fastball Average .375

	Outside	Middle	Inside
High	6/ 333 /2	2/ 500 /1	3/ 333 /1
Med	11/ 454 /5	1/ 1000 /1	5/ 400 /2
Low	2/ 0 /0	2/ 0 /0	0/ 0 /0

Curve Average .250

	Outside	Middle	Inside
High	1/ 0 /0	0/ 0 /0	0/ 0 /0
Med	2/ 0 /0	1/ 1000 /1	0/ 0 /0
Low	3/ 333 /1	0/ 0 /0	1/ 0 /0

Overall Evaluation

Against Right-Handed Pitchers

Overall Fastball	⚾⚾ ⚾⚾ ⚾⚾ ⚾⚾
Overall Curve	⚾⚾ ⚾⚾
Overall Slider	⚾⚾ ⚾⚾ ⚾⚾ ⚾⚾

Against Left-Handed Pitchers

Overall Fastball	⚾⚾
Overall Curve	Not enough information
Overall Slider	Not enough information

Comments: Strong against waist-high fastballs vs. RH.
Strengths: Waist-high fastballs, high-middle fastballs, low-inside fastballs, low-inside sliders vs. RH.
Weaknesses: High-outside, low-outside and low-middle fastballs vs. RH; medium-outside fastballs vs. LH.

Steve Sax (Right Handed) — *New York Yankees*

Steve Sax Against Right-Handed Pitchers
Overall BARS Batting Average .319

Fastball Average .349

	Inside	Middle	Outside
High	49/285/14	69/376/26	25/360/9
Med	73/369/27	32/375/12	125/320/40
Low	39/307/12	90/422/38	48/291/14

Curve Average .225

	Inside	Middle	Outside
High	5/400/2	9/111/1	8/0/0
Med	12/166/2	10/300/3	31/387/12
Low	4/0/0	21/190/4	33/181/6

Slider Average .279

	Inside	Middle	Outside
High	0/0/0	4/750/3	5/200/1
Med	5/400/2	10/300/3	16/562/9
Low	1/0/0	10/300/3	42/119/5

Steve Sax Against Left-Handed Pitchers
Overall BARS Batting Average .352

Fastball Average .329

	Inside	Middle	Outside
High	6/166/1	18/333/6	19/210/4
Med	19/578/11	4/750/3	58/413/24
Low	13/230/3	25/280/7	23/86/2

Curve Average .538

	Inside	Middle	Outside
High	3/333/1	3/666/2	2/0/0
Med	0/0/0	2/1000/2	10/600/6
Low	5/400/2	7/714/5	7/428/3

Slider Average .153

	Inside	Middle	Outside
High	1/0/0	1/0/0	0/0/0
Med	6/166/1	2/500/1	3/0/0
Low	5/200/1	6/0/0	2/500/1

Right-handed hitter Steve Sax has a .319 BARS average against right-handed pitchers. This is primarily built on his excellent .349 overall fastball average.

Notice how strongly Sax hits all waist-high and over-the-middle fastballs against right-handers. His .422 average against low-over-the-middle fastballs is top-rate. If fielders positioned themselves correctly, they could prevent most of his base hits from this location.

LOW-OVER-THE-MIDDLE FASTBALLS

BATTING AVERAGE .422
Play

Left	Medium-deep in straightaway left field
Center	Deep in straightaway center field
Right	Medium-deep in straightaway right field
Short	Up middle (shifted toward second base)
Second	Normal position

Ahead and Behind charts on the opposite page show that he hits medium-high outside fastballs better when ahead in the count (.358 when ahead, .277 when behind). The charts below and the field diagram on the opposite page show how fielders need to play for this pitch as the count changes.

MEDIUM-HIGH OUTSIDE FASTBALLS
(WHEN AHEAD IN THE COUNT)

BATTING AVERAGE .358
Play

Left	Deep and shifted toward center field
Center	Deep in straightaway center field
Right	Deep and shifted toward the right field line
Short	Up middle (shifted toward second base)
Second	Shifted toward first base

MEDIUM-HIGH OUTSIDE FASTBALLS
(WHEN BEHIND IN THE COUNT)

BATTING AVERAGE .277
Play

Left	Deep in straightaway left field
Center	Deep in straightaway center field
Right	Deep in straightaway right field
Short	Up middle (shifted toward second base)
Second	Normal position

Sax Against Left-Handed Pitchers

Against left-handed pitchers, Sax hits very strongly against medium-high outside fastballs (.413) and medium-high inside fastballs (.578). He has a weakness in the four fastballs corners: low-outside .086, high-outside .210, high-inside .166, and low-inside .230.

Notice his strength against low curves and medium-high outside curves. His averages in these locations show great effectiveness against curves thrown by left-handers.

Medium-High Outside Fastballs Vs. RH

Dark Fielders — Behind In The Count
Light Fielders — Ahead In The Count

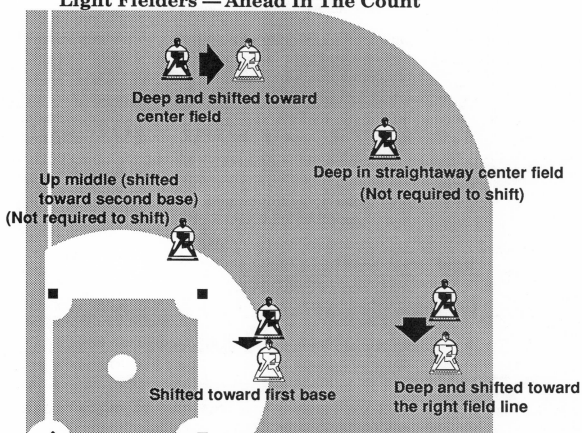

Deep and shifted toward center field

Deep in straightaway center field (Not required to shift)

Up middle (shifted toward second base) (Not required to shift)

Shifted toward first base

Deep and shifted toward the right field line

Ahead And Behind In The Count Vs. RH

Ahead

Fastball Average .405				Curve Average .333		
	Inside	Middle	Outside		Inside	Middle	Outside
High	18/277/5	39/461/18	7/571/4		0/0/0	3/333/1	1/0/0
Med	35/428/15	21/380/8	53/358/19		1/0/0	3/333/1	7/428/3
Low	19/421/8	44/454/20	18/333/6		0/0/0	5/400/2	4/250/1

Behind

Fastball Average .279				Curve Average .254		
	Inside	Middle	Outside		Inside	Middle	Outside
High	11/363/4	15/266/4	6/333/2		4/500/2	4/0/0	4/0/0
Med	13/307/4	2/0/0	36/277/10		3/333/1	4/250/1	15/400/6
Low	10/0/0	12/250/3	6/666/4		3/0/0	8/250/2	10/200/2

Overall Evaluation

Against Right-Handed Pitchers

Overall Fastball	⚾⚾⚾⚾
Overall Curve	⚾
Overall Slider	⚾⚾

Against Left-Handed Pitchers

Overall Fastball	⚾⚾⚾⚾
Overall Curve	⚾⚾⚾
Overall Slider	⚾

Comments: No fastball weakness vs. RH; very weak vs. low-outside fastballs vs. LH.

Strengths: Fastballs in general, medium-outside and medium-middle curves, waist-high and all middle sliders vs. RH; waist-high and high-middle fastballs, low curves and medium-outside curves vs. LH.

Weaknesses: All low curves, high-middle and high-outside curves, low-outside sliders vs. RH; low-outside fastballs and high-outside fastballs vs. LH.

Wayne Tolleson (Switch Hitter) — *New York Yankees*

Wayne Tolleson Against Right-Handed Pitchers
Overall BARS Batting Average .265

Fastball Average .279

	Outside	Middle	Inside
High	26 / 230 / 6	44 / 363 / 16	20 / 150 / 3
Med	115 / 313 / 36	39 / 358 / 14	61 / 196 / 12
Low	29 / 275 / 8	55 / 290 / 16	33 / 212 / 7

Curve Average .050

	Outside	Middle	Inside
High	1 / 0 / 0	2 / 0 / 0	0 / 0 / 0
Med	16 / 62 / 1	4 / 250 / 1	9 / 0 / 0
Low	3 / 0 / 0	12 / 83 / 1	13 / 0 / 0

Slider Average .400

	Outside	Middle	Inside
High	3 / 333 / 1	3 / 333 / 1	6 / 333 / 2
Med	5 / 400 / 2	3 / 1000 / 3	8 / 375 / 3
Low	3 / 666 / 2	8 / 375 / 3	11 / 272 / 3

Wayne Tolleson Against Left-Handed Pitchers
Overall BARS Batting Average .253

Fastball Average .245

	Inside	Middle	Outside
High	2 / 0 / 0	7 / 142 / 1	7 / 0 / 0
Med	17 / 176 / 3	23 / 391 / 9	56 / 250 / 14
Low	14 / 428 / 6	24 / 291 / 7	25 / 120 / 3

Curve Average .266

	Inside	Middle	Outside
High	0 / 0 / 0	1 / 0 / 0	2 / 0 / 0
Med	5 / 200 / 1	2 / 500 / 1	7 / 571 / 4
Low	3 / 666 / 2	2 / 0 / 0	8 / 0 / 0

Slider Average .281

	Inside	Middle	Outside
High	2 / 0 / 0	0 / 0 / 0	0 / 0 / 0
Med	8 / 375 / 3	0 / 0 / 0	3 / 0 / 0
Low	11 / 272 / 3	7 / 428 / 3	1 / 0 / 0

Switch-hitting Wayne Tolleson hits about the same overall against right- and left-handed pitchers (.265 against right-handers, .253 against left-handers). Batting left-handed against right-handers, Tolleson hits fastballs and sliders well (.279 and .400 respectively), but has tremendous difficulty with curves (.050).

Looking first at fastballs thrown by right-handers, notice that Tolleson hits medium-high outside fastballs at a .313 clip. He hits these pitches medium-deep to all fields.

MEDIUM-HIGH OUTSIDE FASTBALLS

BATTING AVERAGE .313
Play
Left Medium-deep and shifted toward the left field line
Center Medium-deep in straightaway center field
Right Medium-deep in straightaway right field
Short Up middle (shifted toward second base)
Second Shifted toward first base

One of the main points of interest in Tolleson's charts is his trouble with inside fastballs (.150, .196, and .212, high to low). He hits medium-high inside fastballs much differently than he hits medium-high outside fastballs.

MEDIUM-HIGH INSIDE FASTBALLS

BATTING AVERAGE .196
Play
Left Medium-deep and shifted toward center field
Center Deep and shifted toward left field
Right Medium-deep and shifted toward the right line
Short Up middle (shifted toward second base)
Second Normal position

Tolleson hits high-over-the-middle fastballs (.363) down the left line and to left center. If left fielders and center fielders adjusted properly when high fastballs are thrown to Tolleson, they would be able to prevent most of his base hits from this location.

HIGH-OVER-THE-MIDDLE FASTBALLS

BATTING AVERAGE .363
Play
Left Medium-deep and shifted toward the left field line
Center Deep and shifted toward left field
Right Medium-deep in straightaway right field
Short Up middle (shifted toward second base)
Second Normal position

Tolleson Against Curves And Sliders

Tolleson's curve chart against right-handed pitchers does not have a single strong location. He is weak against inside, outside, and low curves. He does not have a recorded low-inside curve hit to the outfield, but he does have hit balls to the right side of the infield.

LOW-INSIDE CURVEBALLS

BATTING AVERAGE .000 (0 for 13)

Play	
Left	No instances recorded
Center	No instances recorded
Right	No instances recorded
Short	No instances recorded
Second	Shifted toward first base

Tolleson hits sliders much better overall than he hits curves. He hits low-inside sliders medium-deep down the left line and to straightaway center.

LOW-INSIDE SLIDERS

BATTING AVERAGE .272

Play	
Left	Medium-deep and shifted toward the left field line
Center	Medium-deep in straightaway center field
Right	Deep and shifted toward center field
Short	Normal position
Second	No instances recorded

Tolleson Against Left-Handed Pitchers

Batting right-handed against left-handed pitchers, Tolleson has difficulty with fastballs overall. It's interesting that he hits .428 against low-inside fastballs thrown by lefties, but only .176 against medium-high inside fastballs. The BARS fielding strategies for these two locations show that every fielder except the second baseman needs to shift to be properly positioned for pitches to these two locations.

LOW-INSIDE FASTBALLS
(THROWN BY LEFT-HANDED PITCHERS)

BATTING AVERAGE .428

Play	
Left	Medium-deep in straightaway left field
Center	Medium-deep in straightaway center field
Right	Deep in straightaway right field
Short	Normal position
Second	Normal position

MEDIUM-HIGH INSIDE FASTBALLS
(THROWN BY LEFT-HANDED PITCHERS)

BATTING AVERAGE .176

Play	
Left	Deep and shifted toward the left field line
Center	Deep in straightaway center field
Right	Medium-deep in straightaway right field
Short	Up middle (shifted toward second base)
Second	Normal position

Ahead And Behind In The Count Vs. RH

Ahead

Fastball Average .298

	Outside	Middle	Inside
High	13 / 307 /4	25 / 400 /10	8 / 0 /0
Med	48 / 375 /18	20 / 300 /6	33 / 242 /8
Low	10 / 400 /4	27 / 222 /6	17 / 235 /4

Curve Average .111

	Outside	Middle	Inside
High	0 / 0 /0	1 / 0 /0	0 / 0 /0
Med	3 / 333 /1	1 / 0 /0	2 / 0 /0
Low	0 / 0 /0	1 / 0 /0	1 / 0 /0

Behind

Fastball Average .363

	Outside	Middle	Inside
High	3 / 666 /2	7 / 142 /1	2 / 500 /1
Med	19 / 315 /6	9 / 333 /3	6 / 333 /2
Low	4 / 500 /2	10 / 600 /6	6 / 166 /1

Curve Average .000

	Outside	Middle	Inside
High	1 / 0 /0	1 / 0 /0	0 / 0 /0
Med	5 / 0 /0	2 / 0 /0	5 / 0 /0
Low	1 / 0 /0	7 / 0 /0	2 / 0 /0

Overall Evaluation

Against Right-Handed Pitchers

Overall Fastball	⚾⚾
Overall Curve	⚾
Overall Slider	⚾⚾⚾⚾

Against Left-Handed Pitchers

Overall Fastball	⚾
Overall Curve	⚾⚾
Overall Slider	⚾⚾⚾

Comments: Weak against inside fastballs vs. RH. Strengths: Over-the-middle fastballs, medium-outside fastballs, waist-high and over-the-middle sliders vs. RH; low-inside and medium-middle fastballs, medium-outside curves, medium-inside sliders vs. LH. Weaknesses: Inside fastballs, high-outside fastballs and all curves vs. RH; high fastballs, outside fastballs, medium-inside fastballs, low-outside curves vs. LH.

Dave Winfield (Right Handed) — *New York Yankees*

Dave Winfield Against Right-Handed Pitchers
Overall BARS Batting Average .282

Fastball Average .300			Curve Average .283			Slider Average .220		
Inside	Middle	Outside	Inside	Middle	Outside	Inside	Middle	Outside
High 32/218/7	47/446/21	27/259/7	4/500/2	16/562/9	7/428/3	3/333/1	17/352/6	2/500/1
Med 60/333/20	39/307/12	176/318/56	13/384/5	11/454/5	43/255/11	5/600/3	8/500/4	52/173/9
Low 27/74/2	62/322/20	70/242/17	2/500/1	18/222/4	45/111/5	6/0/0	15/133/2	51/176/9

Dave Winfield Against Left-Handed Pitchers
Overall BARS Batting Average .301

Fastball Average .323			Curve Average .238			Slider Average .275		
Inside	Middle	Outside	Inside	Middle	Outside	Inside	Middle	Outside
High 12/250/3	17/411/7	34/352/12	1/0/0	5/400/2	6/333/2	2/0/0	2/500/1	1/0/0
Med 32/343/11	19/473/9	91/318/29	8/250/2	3/1000/3	27/296/8	11/181/2	0/0/0	9/333/3
Low 20/300/6	34/352/12	38/184/7	17/58/1	11/90/1	10/200/2	7/285/2	4/500/2	4/250/1

Winfield hits a little better against left-handed pitchers (.301 overall against left-handers, .282 overall against right-handers).

He hits fastballs very well against both right- and left-handers (.300 against right-handers, .323 against left-handers). His curve average is much higher against right-handers (.283 against right, .238 against left). First, against right-handers:

Winfield is solid against all waist-high fastballs (.333, .307 and .318, inside to outside). But he has difficulty with low-inside fastballs (.074), high-inside fastballs (.218) and low-outside fastballs (.242).

Winfield pulls medium-high outside fastballs deep down the left line. The shortstop, however, has to play him shifted toward second base.

MEDIUM-HIGH OUTSIDE FASTBALLS

BATTING AVERAGE .318
Play

Left	Deep and shifted toward the left field line
Center	Deep in straightaway center field
Right	Deep and shifted toward center field
Short	Up middle (shifted toward second base)
Second	Normal position

He hits medium-high inside fastball deep down the left line also.

MEDIUM-HIGH INSIDE FASTBALLS

BATTING AVERAGE .333
Play

Left	Deep and shifted toward the left field line
Center	Deep in straightaway center field
Right	Medium-deep in straightaway right field
Short	Shifted toward third base
Second	*No instances recorded*

He hits a spectacular .446 against high-over-the-middle fastballs. He also pulls this pitch down the left line.

HIGH-OVER-THE-MIDDLE FASTBALLS

BATTING AVERAGE .446
Play

Left	Deep and shifted toward the left field line
Center	Deep in straightaway center field
Right	Deep and shifted toward center field
Short	Shifted toward third base
Second	Normal position

He hits low-over-the-middle fastballs differently when ahead and behind in the count.

LOW-OVER-THE-MIDDLE FASTBALLS
(WHEN BEHIND IN THE COUNT)

BATTING AVERAGE .266
Play

Left	Medium-deep and shifted toward the left field line

Center	Deep and shifted toward left field	**Left**	Deep in straightaway left field
Right	Short and shifted toward center field	**Center**	Deep and shifted toward left field
Short	Normal position	**Right**	*No instances recorded*
Second	Shifted toward first base	**Short**	Shifted toward third base
		Second	Normal position

LOW-OVER-THE-MIDDLE FASTBALLS (WHEN AHEAD IN THE COUNT)

BATTING AVERAGE .310
Play

Left	Medium-deep in straightaway left field
Center	Medium-deep in straightaway center field
Right	Deep in straightaway right field
Short	Up middle (shifted toward second base)
Second	*No instances recorded*

Every fielder would have to shift for a low-over-the-middle fastball when Winfield is ahead in the count as opposed to when he is behind in the count.

Winfield Against Curves and Sliders

Against right-handers, Winfield hits curves well overall (.283) but has trouble with sliders (.220). His .111 against low-outside curves is very weak. Many people might think that Winfield would hit low-outside curves mostly to right field, but the BARS System has not recorded even one instance of this, although a relatively high number of low-outside curves have been recorded (45).

LOW-OUTSIDE CURVEBALLS

BATTING AVERAGE .111
Play

Winfield Against Left-Handed Pitchers

Winfield's strong overall fastball average of .323 against left-handed pitchers has only one truly weak location, the .184 in his low-outside location.

Each outfielder would have to shift to be correctly positioned for a low-outside fastball as opposed to a low-over-the-middle fastball.

LOW-OUTSIDE FASTBALLS (THROWN BY LEFT-HANDED PITCHERS)

BATTING AVERAGE .184
Play

Left	Deep in straightaway left field
Center	Deep and shifted toward left field
Right	Deep and shifted toward center field
Short	Up middle (shifted toward second base)
Second	Normal position

LOW-OVER-THE-MIDDLE FASTBALLS (THROWN BY LEFT-HANDED PITCHERS)

BATTING AVERAGE .352
Play

Left	Deep and shifted toward the left field line
Center	Deep in straightaway center field
Right	Short in straightaway right field
Short	Up middle (shifted toward second base)
Second	Normal position

Ahead And Behind In The Count Vs. RH

Ahead

Fastball Average .331

	Inside	Middle	Outside
High	11/90 /1	19/526 /10	10/200 /2
Med	28/321 /9	17/235 /4	72/347 /25
Low	7/285 /2	29/310 /9	24/416 /10

Curve Average .428

	Inside	Middle	Outside
High	1/1000/ 1	5/400 /2	0/0 /0
Med	2/500 /1	4/1000/ 4	11/272 /3
Low	0/0 /0	4/250 /1	8/375 /3

Behind

Fastball Average .333

	Inside	Middle	Outside
High	4/500 /2	9/222 /2	6/333 /2
Med	11/363 /4	6/666 /4	38/342 /13
Low	6/0 /0	15/266 /4	7/428 /3

Curve Average .348

	Inside	Middle	Outside
High	1/0 /0	3/1000 /3	4/500 /2
Med	5/600 /3	2/0 /0	14/357 /5
Low	0/0 /0	4/0 /0	10/200 /2

Overall Evaluation

Against Right-Handed Pitchers

Overall Fastball	⚾ ⚾ ⚾
Overall Curve	⚾ ⚾ ⚾
Overall Slider	⚾

Against Left-Handed Pitchers

Overall Fastball	⚾ ⚾ ⚾
Overall Curve	⚾
Overall Slider	⚾ ⚾ ⚾

Comments: Winfield is a good fastball hitter. Strengths: Waist-high and over-the-middle fastballs, high-middle, medium-inside and medium-middle curves, high-middle and medium-middle sliders vs. RH; over-the-middle and waist-high fastballs, high-outside fastballs, medium-outside curves vs. LH. Weaknesses: Fastball corners, low curves and sliders, medium-outside sliders vs. RH; low-outside and high-inside fastballs, low curves vs. LH.

Bell, George
Fernandez, Tony
Gruber, Kelly
Lee, Manny
Liriano, Nelson
McGriff, Fred
Mulliniks, Rance
Wilson, Mookie

Toronto Blue Jays
BARS System
Hitting Analysis

George Bell (Right Handed)   *Toronto Blue Jays*

George Bell Against Right-Handed Pitchers
Overall BARS Batting Average .317

Fastball Average .326			Curve Average .254			Slider Average .333		
Inside	Middle	Outside	Inside	Middle	Outside	Inside	Middle	Outside
High 22/181 /4	23/260 /6	19/315 /6	4/0 /0	4/250 /1	2/0 /0	2/500 /1	3/333 /1	3/333 /1
Med 38/263 /10	25/480 /12	117/358 /42	3/333 /1	14/357 /5	30/333 /10	4/500 /2	4/500 /2	17/235 /4
Low 15/266 /4	47/319 /15	37/351 /13	4/500 /2	10/300 /3	31/129 /4	2/0 /0	11/454 /5	23/304 /7

George Bell Against Left-Handed Pitchers
Overall BARS Batting Average .345

Fastball Average .342			Curve Average .365			Slider Average .333		
Inside	Middle	Outside	Inside	Middle	Outside	Inside	Middle	Outside
High 7/0 /0	13/230 /3	13/461 /6	1/0 /0	0/0 /0	2/0 /0	2/1000 /2	0/0 /0	1/1000 /1
Med 20/300 /6	14/500 /7	59/372 /22	3/333 /1	5/600 /3	10/400 /4	6/333 /2	0/0 /0	4/250 /1
Low 10/300 /3	22/409 /9	17/235 /4	4/500 /2	9/444 /4	7/142 /1	7/142 /1	7/428 /3	3/0 /0

Right-handed hitter George Bell hits fastballs very strongly against both right- and left-handed pitchers. He has a little trouble with curves against right-handers but hits them well against left-handers.

Starting against right-handers, notice how strong Bell is against all outside fastballs. His Ahead and Behind charts on the opposite page show that he hits medium-high fastballs better when ahead than when behind in the count (.403 when ahead, .333 when behind). He hits this pitch straightaway to the outfield when behind. When ahead, he pulls it deep down the left line.

MEDIUM-HIGH OUTSIDE FASTBALLS (WHEN AHEAD IN THE COUNT)

BATTING AVERAGE .403
Play
Left   Deep and shifted toward the left field line
Center   Deep in straightaway center field
Right   Deep in straightaway right field
Short   Shifted toward third base
Second   Shifted toward first base

MEDIUM-HIGH OUTSIDE FASTBALLS (WHEN BEHIND IN THE COUNT)

BATTING AVERAGE .333
Play
Left   Deep and straightaway in left field
Center   Deep and straightaway in center field
Right   Deep and straightaway in right field
Short   Normal position
Second   Shifted toward first base

His .351 average against low-outside fastballs is also excellent.

LOW-OUTSIDE FASTBALLS

BATTING AVERAGE .351
Play
Left   Deep and shifted toward the left field line
Center   Medium-deep in straightaway center field
Right   Deep and shifted toward the right field line
Short   Shifted toward third base
Second   Normal position

Notice in his charts that right-handers throw him more outside than inside fastballs. Pitchers are probably afraid that he will hit inside pitches out of the park. His BARS fielding strategy charts show that he hits both inside and outside fastballs deep so pitchers might as well throw him inside since his averages are lower against inside than outside fastballs.

Fielders are probably aligned more correctly for the way he hits inside fastballs. That's why his averages are lower in these locations.

Bell Against Curves And Sliders

Bell hits curves very well against right-handers — with the exception of the low-outside location (.129). He hits medium-high outside curves excellently (.333).

MEDIUM-HIGH OUTSIDE CURVEBALLS

BATTING AVERAGE .333

Play

Left	Deep in straightaway left field
Center	Deep in straightaway center field
Right	Medium-deep in straightaway right field
Short	Normal position
Second	Shifted toward first base

In contrast, he hits medium-high outside sliders poorly and low-outside sliders excellently.

LOW-OUTSIDE SLIDERS

BATTING AVERAGE .304

Play

Left	Medium-deep in straightaway left field
Center	Deep in straightaway center field
Right	Medium-deep in straightaway right field
Short	Shifted toward third base
Second	*No instances recorded*

Bell Against Left-Handed Pitchers

Bell hits medium-high outside fastballs for a very high average against left-handed pitchers (.372).

MEDIUM-HIGH OUTSIDE FASTBALLS (THROWN BY LEFT-HANDED PITCHERS)

BATTING AVERAGE .372

Play

Left	Deep in straightaway left field
Center	Deep in straightaway center field
Right	Deep in straightaway right field
Short	Normal position
Second	Normal position

He also hits low-over-the-middle fastballs for a high average (.409).

LOW-OVER-THE-MIDDLE FASTBALLS (THROWN BY LEFT-HANDED PITCHERS)

BATTING AVERAGE .409

Play

Left	Deep in straightaway left field
Center	Deep in straightaway center field
Right	Deep and shifted toward center field
Short	Normal position
Second	Normal position

He scatters high-outside fastballs (.461).

HIGH-OUTSIDE FASTBALLS (THROWN BY LEFT-HANDED PITCHERS)

BATTING AVERAGE .461

Play

Left	Deep and shifted toward the left field line
Center	Deep in straightaway center field
Right	Deep and shifted toward the right field line
Short	Normal position
Second	Shifted toward first base

Ahead And Behind In The Count Vs. RH

Ahead

Fastball Average .355

	Inside	Middle	Outside
High	12/83 /1	10/300 /3	5/400 /2
Med	16/250 /4	12/500 /6	52/403 /21
Low	7/428 /3	22/318 /7	16/437 /7

Curve Average .466

	Inside	Middle	Outside
High	0/0 /0	2/0 /0	0/0 /0
Med	0/0 /0	9/555 /5	9/444 /4
Low	4/500 /2	3/666 /2	3/333 /1

Behind

Fastball Average .375

	Inside	Middle	Outside
High	4/250 /1	2/1000 /2	6/333 /2
Med	11/272 /3	6/666 /4	24/333 /8
Low	1/0 /0	13/307 /4	5/600 /3

Curve Average .258

	Inside	Middle	Outside
High	1/0 /0	0/0 /0	0/0 /0
Med	2/500 /1	2/0 /0	11/454 /5
Low	0/0 /0	4/250 /1	11/90 /1

Overall Evaluation

Against Right-Handed Pitchers

Overall Fastball	⚾⚾⚾⚾
Overall Curve	⚾⚾
Overall Slider	⚾⚾⚾⚾

Against Left-Handed Pitchers

Overall Fastball	⚾⚾⚾⚾
Overall Curve	⚾⚾⚾⚾
Overall Slider	⚾⚾⚾⚾

Comments: Weak vs. inside fastballs vs. RH. **Strengths:** Fastballs vs. RH except as above, medium-outside, low-middle, medium-middle curves, low-middle and low-outside sliders vs. RH; all waist-high fastballs and curves vs. LH, low-middle and high-outside fastballs, low-middle curves & sliders vs. LH. **Weaknesses:** Inside fastballs, low-outside curves and medium-outside sliders vs. RH; high-middle and low-outside fastballs, low-outside curves vs. LH.

Tony Fernandez (Switch Hitter)   *Toronto Blue Jays*

Tony Fernandez Against Right-Handed Pitchers
Overall BARS Batting Average .275

Fastball Average .315

	Outside	Middle	Inside
High	15/200 /3	38/368 /14	15/266 /4
Med	118/338 /40	32/437 /14	59/203 /12
Low	14/214 /3	46/347 /16	37/324 /12

Curve Average .209

	Outside	Middle	Inside
High	0/0 /0	2/0 /0	1/0 /0
Med	10/300 /3	2/500 /1	4/0 /0
Low	8/0 /0	7/571 /4	9/111 /1

Slider Average .233

	Outside	Middle	Inside
High	0/0 /0	1/0 /0	3/0 /0
Med	2/0 /0	2/500 /1	7/571 /4
Low	1/0 /0	4/250 /1	10/100 /1

Tony Fernandez Against Left-Handed Pitchers
Overall BARS Batting Average .255

Fastball Average .255

	Inside	Middle	Outside
High	4/0 /0	11/90 /1	6/166 /1
Med	23/347 /8	12/500 /6	63/301 /19
Low	9/222 /2	28/214 /6	16/62 /1

Curve Average .333

	Inside	Middle	Outside
High	0/0 /0	2/1000 /2	0/0 /0
Med	0/0 /0	6/166 /1	10/300 /3
Low	3/333 /1	8/250 /2	4/500 /2

Slider Average .194

	Inside	Middle	Outside
High	2/0 /0	0/0 /0	0/0 /0
Med	6/0 /0	0/0 /0	2/0 /0
Low	12/83 /1	11/454 /5	3/333 /1

Switch-hitting Tony Fernandez hits fastballs better when batting left-handed against right-handed pitchers (.315 vs. right-handers, .255 vs. left-handers). He hits curves better when facing left-handers.

Starting with right-handers, note Fernandez's strength against fastballs thrown over the middle (.368, .437 and .347, high to low). Pitchers should keep fastballs away from the heart of the plate.

They should not, however, throw medium-high outside fastballs (.338). Fernandez hits this pitch medium-deep down the left line (his opposite field). By positioning themselves as suggested by the BARS fielding strategy, fielders could prevent most of the base hits resulting from pitches to this location.

MEDIUM-HIGH OUTSIDE FASTBALLS

BATTING AVERAGE .338
Play
Left   Medium-deep and shifted toward the left field line
Center   Medium-deep in straightaway center field
Right   Deep and shifted toward center field
Short   Up middle (shifted toward second base)
Second   Normal position

If pitchers throw low to Fernandez, they should keep the ball outside. He hits low-inside fastballs very well (.324) and low-over-the-middle fastballs excel-

lently (.347). The following fielding strategy shows that he hits low-over-the-middle fastballs medium-deep and straightaway to all fields. By playing medium-deep for this pitch, fielders could catch most of his line-drive base hits from this location. Notice that the infielders need to play him to pull when he hits grounders.

LOW-OVER-THE-MIDDLE FASTBALLS

BATTING AVERAGE .347
Play
Left   Medium-deep in straightaway left field
Center   Medium-deep in straightaway center field
Right   Medium-deep in straightaway right field
Short   Up middle (shifted toward second base)
Second   Shifted toward first base

He hits high-over-the-middle fastballs for a very strong average (.368).

HIGH-OVER-THE-MIDDLE FASTBALLS

BATTING AVERAGE .368
Play
Left   Medium-deep in straightaway left field
Center   Deep in straightaway center field
Right   Deep and shifted toward center field
Short   Up middle (shifted toward second base)
Second   Shifted toward first base

Fernandez has a weak sector in his fastball chart against right-handers in the high-inside/medium-high inside locations. In a pinch, pitchers could focus on this sector.

Fernandez Against Curves And Sliders

Fernandez is weak against low-inside curves and low-inside sliders against right-handed pitchers. He also has trouble with low-outside curves, although he hits medium-high outside curves excellently (.300).

MEDIUM-HIGH OUTSIDE CURVEBALLS

BATTING AVERAGE .300

Play

Left	Deep and shifted toward the left field line
Center	Deep in straightaway center field
Right	Medium-deep and shifted toward center field
Short	Shifted toward third base
Second	Normal position

Fernandez Against Left-Handed Pitchers

Fernandez has a lot of trouble with all low and high fastballs against left-handed pitchers. By keeping fastballs high or low to him, pitchers could gain an advantage.

He hits all waist-high fastballs well against left-handers. His .301 against medium-high outside fastballs is not spectacular, but more than adequate.

MEDIUM-HIGH OUTSIDE FASTBALLS (THROWN BY LEFT-HANDED PITCHERS)

BATTING AVERAGE .301

Play

Left	Deep and shifted toward center field
Center	Medium-deep in straightaway center field
Right	Medium-deep and shifted toward the right line
Short	Normal position
Second	Shifted toward first base

His .347 against medium-high inside fastballs is excellent. Notice in the fielding strategy that the right fielder needs to play short and straightaway for this pitch. If he did not want to play short against Fernandez, he could play medium-deep, anticipating that he might have to come in for a short hit.

MEDIUM-HIGH INSIDE FASTBALLS (THROWN BY LEFT-HANDED PITCHERS)

BATTING AVERAGE .347

Play

Left	Deep in straightaway left field
Center	Deep and shifted toward left field
Right	Short in straightaway right field
Short	Up middle (shifted toward second base)
Second	Normal position

Ahead And Behind In The Count Vs. RH

Ahead

Fastball Average .338

	Outside	Middle	Inside
High	5 / 200 / 1	19 / 315 / 6	10 / 300 / 3
Med	64 / 343 / 22	20 / 450 / 9	29 / 241 / 7
Low	7 / 428 / 3	29 / 413 / 12	18 / 277 / 5

Curve Average .363

	Outside	Middle	Inside
High	0 / 0 / 0	0 / 0 / 0	0 / 0 / 0
Med	4 / 250 / 1	1 / 1000 / 1	2 / 0 / 0
Low	0 / 0 / 0	2 / 500 / 1	2 / 500 / 1

Behind

Fastball Average .315

	Outside	Middle	Inside
High	3 / 0 / 0	10 / 400 / 4	1 / 1000 / 1
Med	24 / 375 / 9	5 / 400 / 2	10 / 0 / 0
Low	3 / 0 / 0	8 / 250 / 2	9 / 555 / 5

Curve Average .181

	Outside	Middle	Inside
High	0 / 0 / 0	2 / 0 / 0	1 / 0 / 0
Med	3 / 333 / 1	1 / 0 / 0	1 / 0 / 0
Low	0 / 0 / 0	2 / 500 / 1	1 / 0 / 0

Overall Evaluation

Against Right-Handed Pitchers

Overall Fastball	⚾⚾ ⚾⚾⚾
Overall Curve	⚾⚾
Overall Slider	⚾⚾

Against Left-Handed Pitchers

Overall Fastball	⚾⚾
Overall Curve	⚾⚾ ⚾⚾⚾ ⚾⚾
Overall Slider	⚾⚾

Comments: Strong vs. fastballs over the middle vs.RH.
Strengths: Fastballs as above, medium-outside and low-inside fastballs, medium-outside curves and medium-inside sliders vs. RH; waist-high fastballs, medium-outside curves and low-middle sliders vs. LH.
Weaknesses: Low-outside, high-outside, high-inside & medium-inside fastballs, low-outside and low-inside curves, low sliders vs. RH; all high and all low fastballs, all inside sliders vs. LH.

Kelly Gruber (Right Handed)   *Toronto Blue Jays*

Kelly Gruber Against Right-Handed Pitchers
Overall BARS Batting Average .305

Fastball Average .250

	Inside	Middle	Outside
High	6 / 166 / 1	2 / 500 / 1	12 / 166 / 2
Med	7 / 142 / 1	2 / 1000 / 2	41 / 268 / 11
Low	2 / 500 / 1	10 / 300 / 3	10 / 100 / 1

Curve Average .434

	Inside	Middle	Outside
High	0 / 0 / 0	2 / 500 / 1	2 / 1000 / 2
Med	2 / 0 / 0	1 / 1000 / 1	7 / 428 / 3
Low	0 / 0 / 0	2 / 1000 / 2	7 / 142 / 1

Slider Average .437

	Inside	Middle	Outside
High	0 / 0 / 0	2 / 500 / 1	0 / 0 / 0
Med	2 / 500 / 1	1 / 1000 / 1	4 / 250 / 1
Low	0 / 0 / 0	2 / 500 / 1	5 / 400 / 2

Kelly Gruber Against Left-Handed Pitchers
Overall BARS Batting Average .305

Fastball Average .309

	Inside	Middle	Outside
High	1 / 0 / 0	4 / 750 / 3	5 / 0 / 0
Med	5 / 600 / 3	3 / 666 / 2	34 / 323 / 11
Low	4 / 0 / 0	8 / 250 / 2	7 / 142 / 1

Curve Average .250

	Inside	Middle	Outside
High	0 / 0 / 0	1 / 0 / 0	0 / 0 / 0
Med	0 / 0 / 0	0 / 0 / 0	3 / 666 / 2
Low	5 / 0 / 0	1 / 1000 / 1	2 / 0 / 0

Slider Average .333

	Inside	Middle	Outside
High	2 / 0 / 0	1 / 0 / 0	0 / 0 / 0
Med	0 / 0 / 0	0 / 0 / 0	2 / 500 / 1
Low	2 / 500 / 1	2 / 1000 / 2	3 / 0 / 0

Right-handed hitter Kelly Gruber hits .250 overall against fastballs vs. right-handed pitchers, .309 overall vs. left-handed pitchers. His high average against curves and sliders thrown by right-handers shows that he is looking for breaking balls.

Starting against right-handers, he hits medium-high outside fastballs medium-deep to left and center and deep into the right-center gap. The fielding diagram on the opposite page shows how fielders should play Gruber for this pitch.

MEDIUM-HIGH OUTSIDE FASTBALLS

BATTING AVERAGE .268
Play

Left	Medium-deep in straightaway left field
Center	Deep in straightaway center field
Right	Deep and shifted toward center field
Short	Normal position
Second	Normal position

He has trouble with low-outside fastballs thrown by right-handers (.100).

LOW-OUTSIDE FASTBALLS

BATTING AVERAGE .100
Play

Left	*No instances recorded*
Center	*No instances recorded*
Right	Medium-deep in straightaway right field
Short	Shifted toward third base
Second	*No instances recorded*

Gruber has trouble with low-outside curves thrown by right-handers (.142). His hit balls from this location are probably mostly easy flies and grounders.

Gruber Against Left-Handed Pitchers

Against left-handed pitchers, Gruber hits medium-high outside fastballs deep to all fields for a fine .323 average.

MEDIUM-HIGH OUTSIDE FASTBALLS (THROWN BY LEFT-HANDED PITCHERS)

BATTING AVERAGE .323
Play

Left	Deep in straightaway left field
Center	Deep in straightaway center field
Right	Deep and shifted toward center field
Short	Normal position
Second	Normal position

He hits low-outside fastballs poorly against left-handers. If pitchers are going to throw him outside, they should keep the ball low.

Medium-High Outside Fastballs
(Thrown By Right-Handed Pitchers)

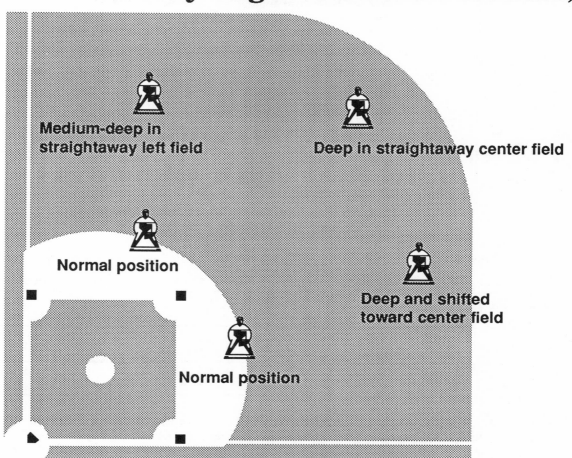

Medium-deep in straightaway left field

Deep in straightaway center field

Normal position

Deep and shifted toward center field

Normal position

Ahead And Behind In The Count Vs. RH

Ahead

	Fastball Average .229			Curve Average .250		
	Inside	Middle	Outside	Inside	Middle	Outside
High	5/200/1	2/500/1	5/400/2	0/0/0	0/0/0	0/0/0
Med	2/0/0	0/0/0	23/217/5	0/0/0	0/0/0	2/500/1
Low	1/0/0	6/166/1	4/250/1	0/0/0	0/0/0	2/0/0

Behind

	Fastball Average .375			Curve Average .625		
	Inside	Middle	Outside	Inside	Middle	Outside
High	0/0/0	0/0/0	2/0/0	0/0/0	2/500/1	2/1000/2
Med	2/0/0	2/1000/2	7/428/3	1/0/0	0/0/0	1/0/0
Low	0/0/0	2/500/1	1/0/0	0/0/0	1/1000/1	1/1000/1

Overall Evaluation
Against Right-Handed Pitchers

Overall Fastball ⚾

Overall Curve ⚾ ⚾ ⚾ ⚾

Overall Slider ⚾ ⚾ ⚾ ⚾

Against Left-Handed Pitchers

Overall Fastball ⚾ ⚾ ⚾

Overall Curve ⚾ ⚾

Overall Slider ⚾ ⚾ ⚾ ⚾

Comments: Has trouble with outside fastballs vs. RH, low fastballs vs. LH.

Strengths: Low-middle fastballs and medium-outside curves vs. RH; medium-outside, medium-inside, and high-middle fastballs vs. LH.

Weaknesses: Outside fastballs, medium-inside and high-inside fastballs, low-outside curves vs. RH; low fastballs vs. LH.

Manny Lee Against Right-Handed Pitchers
Overall BARS Batting Average .213

Fastball Average .237

	Outside	Middle	Inside
High	3 / 0/0	7 / 285/2	5 / 0/0
Med	16 / 312/5	1 / 0/0	8 / 250/2
Low	2 / 500/1	10 / 300/3	7 / 142/1

Curve Average .000

	Outside	Middle	Inside
High	0 / 0/0	1 / 0/0	1 / 0/0
Med	0 / 0/0	1 / 0/0	0 / 0/0
Low	1 / 0/0	4 / 0/0	2 / 0/0

Slider Average .300

	Outside	Middle	Inside
High	1 / 0/0	1 / 1000/1	0 / 0/0
Med	1 / 0/0	0 / 0/0	1 / 1000/1
Low	2 / 0/0	2 / 0/0	2 / 500/1

Manny Lee Against Left-Handed Pitchers
Overall BARS Batting Average .365

Fastball Average .380

	Inside	Middle	Outside
High	1 / 1000/1	2 / 0/0	3 / 333/1
Med	1 / 0/0	0 / 0/0	7 / 714/5
Low	4 / 0/0	3 / 333/1	0 / 0/0

Curve Average .500

	Inside	Middle	Outside
High	1 / 1000/1	0 / 0/0	1 / 0/0
Med	0 / 0/0	0 / 0/0	2 / 1000/2
Low	2 / 500/1	2 / 0/0	0 / 0/0

Slider Average .300

	Inside	Middle	Outside
High	0 / 0/0	0 / 0/0	0 / 0/0
Med	1 / 0/0	0 / 0/0	1 / 0/0
Low	3 / 0/0	4 / 750/3	1 / 0/0

Switch-hitting Manny Lee hits .312 against medium-high outside fastballs thrown by right-handed pitchers. Batting left-handed against right-handers, he hits this pitch to his opposite field (left field). But note that the shortstop needs to play shifted toward second base.

MEDIUM-HIGH OUTSIDE FASTBALLS

BATTING AVERAGE .312
Play

Left	Deep in straightaway left field
Center	Deep and shifted toward left field
Right	*No instances recorded*
Short	Up middle (shifted toward second base)
Second	*No instances recorded*

He hits a solid .300 against low-over-the-middle fastballs thrown by right-handers. Again there are no recorded instances of hit balls to right field. He hits this pitch medium-deep to straightaway left and center.

LOW-OVER-THE-MIDDLE FASTBALLS

BATTING AVERAGE .300
Play

Left	Medium-deep in straightaway left field
Center	Medium-deep in straightaway center field
Right	*No instances recorded*
Short	Up middle (shifted toward second base)
Second	Normal position

He has trouble with inside fastballs against right-handers (.000 on 0 for 5, .250 and .142, high to low). He hits a respectable .285 against high-over-the-middle fastballs.

HIGH-OVER-THE-MIDDLE FASTBALLS

BATTING AVERAGE .285
Play

Left	Deep in straightaway left field
Center	Deep and shifted toward right field
Right	Deep in straightaway right field
Short	*No instances recorded*
Second	Normal position

There are fewer recorded instances against left-handed pitchers, but Lee's .714 average on 5 for 7 in his medium-high outside fastball location indicates that he can hit this pitch well. The chart below and the field diagram on the opposite page shows how fielders need to play him for this pitch.

MEDIUM-HIGH OUTSIDE FASTBALLS
(THROWN BY LEFT-HANDED PITCHERS)

BATTING AVERAGE .714
Play

Left	Short and shifted toward center field
Center	Deep and shifted toward right field
Right	Deep and shifted toward the right field line
Short	Up middle (shifted toward second base)
Second	Shifted toward first base

Medium-High Outside Fastballs (Thrown By Left-Handed Pitchers)

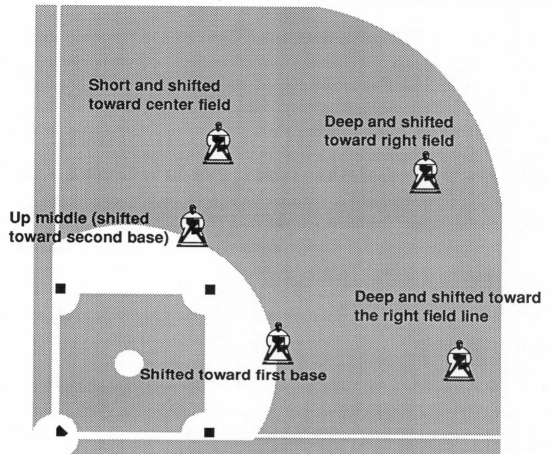

Short and shifted toward center field

Deep and shifted toward right field

Up middle (shifted toward second base)

Deep and shifted toward the right field line

Shifted toward first base

Ahead And Behind In The Count Vs. RH

Ahead

Fastball Average .291

	Outside	Middle	Inside
High	1/0 0/0	2/500 1	1/0 0/0
Med	5/400 2	1/0 0/0	4/250 1
Low	0/0 0/0	6/500 3	4/0 0/0

Curve Average .000

	Outside	Middle	Inside
High	0/0 0/0	0/0 0/0	0/0 0/0
Med	0/0 0/0	0/0 0/0	0/0 0/0
Low	0/0 0/0	0/0 0/0	0/0 0/0

Behind

Fastball Average .142

	Outside	Middle	Inside
High	0/0 0/0	2/0 0/0	2/0 0/0
Med	7/142 1	0/0 0/0	0/0 0/0
Low	1/1000 1	2/0 0/0	0/0 0/0

Curve Average .000

	Outside	Middle	Inside
High	0/0 0/0	1/0 0/0	0/0 0/0
Med	0/0 0/0	0/0 0/0	0/0 0/0
Low	0/0 0/0	3/0 0/0	0/0 0/0

Overall Evaluation

Against Right-Handed Pitchers

Overall Fastball

Overall Curve — Not enough information

Overall Slider — Not enough information

Against Left-Handed Pitchers

Overall Fastball

Overall Curve — Not enough information

Overall Slider — Not enough information

Comments: Strong medium-outside fastball hitter vs. both RH and LH.
Strengths: Medium-outside and low-middle fastballs vs. RH; medium-outside fastballs vs. LH.
Weaknesses: Inside fastballs vs. RH.

Nelson Liriano (Switch Hitter) — *Toronto Blue Jays*

Nelson Liriano Against Right-Handed Pitchers
Overall BARS Batting Average .354

Fastball Average .400

	Outside	Middle	Inside
High	3/ 0 /0	7/ 428 /3	5/ 400 /2
Med	24/ 500 /12	2/ 0 /0	.12/ 416 /5
Low	4/ 500 /2	3/ 333 /1	5/ 200 /1

Curve Average .333

	Outside	Middle	Inside
High	0/ 0 /0	0/ 0 /0	0/ 0 /0
Med	1/ 1000 /1	0/ 0 /0	0/ 0 /0
Low	1/ 0 /0	1/ 0 /0	0/ 0 /0

Slider Average .000

	Outside	Middle	Inside
High	0/ 0 /0	0/ 0 /0	1/ 0 /0
Med	0/ 0 /0	0/ 0 /0	0/ 0 /0
Low	0/ 0 /0	0/ 0 /0	1/ 0 /0

Nelson Liriano Against Left-Handed Pitchers
Overall BARS Batting Average .233

Fastball Average .272

	Inside	Middle	Outside
High	1/ 0 /0	1/ 1000 /1	1/ 0 /0
Med	1/ 0 /0	1/ 1000 /1	13/ 153 /2
Low	0/ 0 /0	3/ 666 /2	1/ 0 /0

Curve Average .000

	Inside	Middle	Outside
High	0/ 0 /0	0/ 0 /0	0/ 0 /0
Med	0/ 0 /0	0/ 0 /0	2/ 0 /0
Low	0/ 0 /0	1/ 0 /0	1/ 0 /0

Slider Average .250

	Inside	Middle	Outside
High	0/ 0 /0	0/ 0 /0	0/ 0 /0
Med	0/ 0 /0	0/ 0 /0	3/ 333 /1
Low	1/ 0 /0	0/ 0 /0	0/ 0 /0

Switch-hitting Nelson Liriano has a very high .500 average in his medium-high outside fastball location. The chart below and the field diagram on the opposite page show how fielders need to play for this pitch.

MEDIUM-HIGH OUTSIDE FASTBALLS

BATTING AVERAGE .500
Play
Left	Medium-deep in straightaway left field
Center	Deep and shifted toward right field
Right	Medium-deep in straightaway right field
Short	Up middle (shifted toward second base)
Second	Normal position

He hits .416 against medium-high inside fastballs, sending the ball medium-deep to all fields.

MEDIUM-HIGH INSIDE FASTBALLS

BATTING AVERAGE .416
Play
Left	Medium-deep in straightaway left field
Center	Medium-deep and shifted toward right field
Right	Medium-deep in straightaway right field
Short	*No instances recorded*
Second	Normal position

On fewer instances, he hits .428 against high-over-the-middle fastballs thrown by right-handers. He hits this pitch medium-deep down the left line, deep down the right line, and medium-deep to straight center field.

HIGH-OVER-THE-MIDDLE FASTBALLS

BATTING AVERAGE .428
Play
Left	Medium-deep and shifted toward the left field line
Center	Medium-deep in straightaway center field
Right	Deep and shifted toward the right field line
Short	Normal position
Second	Shifted toward first base

The BARS System has fewer recorded instances for Liriano against left-handed pitchers. He clearly has trouble with medium-high outside fastballs thrown by lefties (.153). He hits this pitch deep to all fields, but it is evident from his low average that most of his hit balls are easy flies or grounders.

MEDIUM-HIGH OUTSIDE FASTBALLS
(THROWN BY LEFT-HANDED PITCHERS)

BATTING AVERAGE .153
Play
Left	Deep in straightaway left field
Center	Deep in straightaway center field
Right	Deep in straightaway right field
Short	Normal position
Second	Normal position

Medium-High Outside Fastballs
(Thrown By Right-Handed Pitchers)

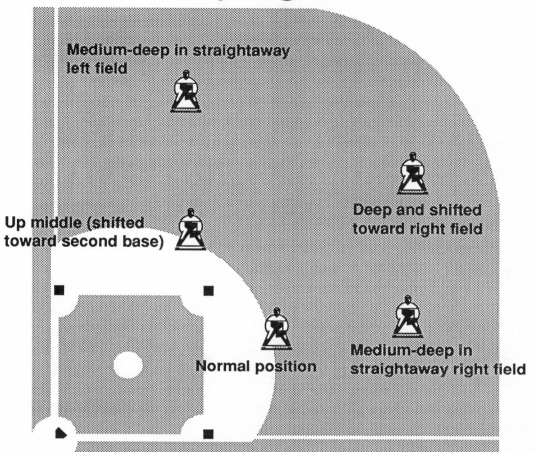

Medium-deep in straightaway left field

Up middle (shifted toward second base)

Deep and shifted toward right field

Normal position

Medium-deep in straightaway right field

Ahead And Behind In The Count Vs. RH

Ahead

Fastball Average .406

	Outside	Middle	Inside
High	1/ 0 /0	5/ 600 /3	3/ 666 /2
Med	13/ 461 /6	2/ 0 /0	6/ 333 /2
Low	0/ 0 /0	1/ 0 /0	1/ 0 /0

Curve Average .000

	Outside	Middle	Inside
High	0/ 0 /0	0/ 0 /0	0/ 0 /0
Med	0/ 0 /0	0/ 0 /0	0/ 0 /0
Low	0/ 0 /0	0/ 0 /0	0/ 0 /0

Behind

Fastball Average .461

	Outside	Middle	Inside
High	1/ 0 /0	2/ 0 /0	0/ 0 /0
Med	4/ 750 /3	0/ 0 /0	3/ 666 /2
Low	0/ 0 /0	1/ 1000 /1	2/ 0 /0

Curve Average .500

	Outside	Middle	Inside
High	0/ 0 /0	0/ 0 /0	0/ 0 /0
Med	1/ 1000 /1	0/ 0 /0	0/ 0 /0
Low	0/ 0 /0	1/ 0 /0	0/ 0 /0

Overall Evaluation
Against Right-Handed Pitchers

Overall Fastball ⚾⚾ ⚾⚾⚾ ⚾

Overall Curve Not enough information

Overall Slider Not enough information

Against Left-Handed Pitchers

Overall Fastball ⚾⚾

Overall Curve Not enough information

Overall Slider Not enough information

Comments: Very strong vs. medium-outside and medium-inside fastballs vs. RH.
Strengths: Medium-outside, low-outside, high-middle and medium-inside fastballs vs. RH.
Weaknesses: Low-inside fastballs vs. RH; medium-outside fastballs vs. LH.

Fred McGriff (Left Handed)   *Toronto Blue Jays*

Fred McGriff Against Right-Handed Pitchers
Overall BARS Batting Average .289

Fastball Average .342

	Outside	Middle	Inside
High	13/ 230/3	7/ 285/2	5/ 0/0
Med	38/ 394/15	6/ 500/3	9/ 333/3
Low	8/ 375/3	10/ 500/5	9/ 222/2

Curve Average .100

	Outside	Middle	Inside
High	0/ 0/0	1/ 0/0	1/ 0/0
Med	4/ 250/1	0/ 0/0	2/ 0/0
Low	2/ 0/0	0/ 0/0	0/ 0/0

Slider Average .272

	Outside	Middle	Inside
High	0/ 0/0	2/ 500/1	0/ 0/0
Med	2/ 0/0	1/ 1000/1	3/ 333/1
Low	0/ 0/0	1/ 0/0	2/ 0/0

Fred McGriff Against Left-Handed Pitchers
Overall BARS Batting Average .258

Fastball Average .263

	Outside	Middle	Inside
High	4/ 0/0	1/ 0/0	2/ 0/0
Med	4/ 250/1	3/ 333/1	5/ 600/3
Low	0/ 0/0	0/ 0/0	0/ 0/0

Curve Average .285

	Outside	Middle	Inside
High	0/ 0/0	0/ 0/0	0/ 0/0
Med	1/ 1000/1	0/ 0/0	0/ 0/0
Low	3/ 333/1	3/ 0/0	0/ 0/0

Slider Average .200

	Outside	Middle	Inside
High	1/ 0/0	0/ 0/0	0/ 0/0
Med	1/ 1000/1	0/ 0/0	0/ 0/0
Low	1/ 0/0	2/ 0/0	0/ 0/0

Left-handed hitter Fred McGriff has some strong fastball locations against right-handed pitchers. Notice the strong sector consisting of the low-over-the-middle, low-outside, medium-high outside, and medium-over-the-middle fastball locations. Right-handers would do better by avoiding these locations.

His .500 against low-over-the-middle fastballs is excellent. He pulls this pitch down the right line and to the right side of the infield. The diagram on the opposite page shows how fielders need to be positioned when McGriff is thrown this pitch.

LOW-OVER-THE-MIDDLE FASTBALLS

BATTING AVERAGE .500
Play
Left   Deep in straightaway left field
Center   Deep in straightaway center field
Right   Deep and shifted toward the right field line
Short   Up middle (shifted toward second base)
Second   Shifted toward first base

He hits medium-high outside fastballs for an excellent .394 average. He hits this pitch straightaway to the outfield and to the right side of the infield.

MEDIUM-HIGH OUTSIDE FASTBALLS

BATTING AVERAGE .394
Play
Left   Medium-deep in straightaway left field

Center   Deep in straightaway center field
Right   Deep in straightaway right field
Short   Up middle (shifted toward second base)
Second   Shifted toward first base

He goes down both lines with medium-high inside fastballs thrown by right-handers.

HIGH-OUTSIDE FASTBALLS

BATTING AVERAGE .333
Play
Left   Medium-deep and shifted toward the left field line
Center   Medium-deep and shifted toward right field
Right   Deep and shifted toward the right field line
Short   *No instances recorded*
Second   Shifted toward first base

His .375 against low-outside fastballs is excellent. He also hits this pitch down the left line (his opposite field).

LOW-OUTSIDE FASTBALLS

BATTING AVERAGE .375
Play
Left   Deep and shifted toward the left field line
Center   *No instances recorded*
Right   *No instances recorded*
Short   Normal position
Second   Shifted toward first base

Low-Over-The-Middle Fastballs
(Thrown By Right-Handed Pitchers)

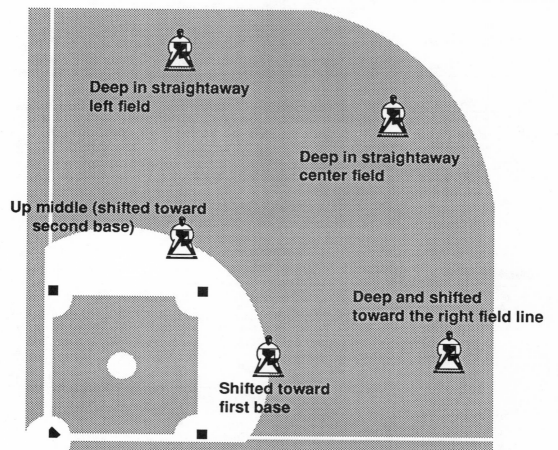

Deep in straightaway
left field

Deep in straightaway
center field

Up middle (shifted toward
second base)

Deep and shifted
toward the right field line

Shifted toward
first base

Ahead And Behind In The Count Vs. RH

Ahead

	Fastball Average .450			Curve Average .000		
	Outside	Middle	Inside	Outside	Middle	Inside
High	4/250 /1	2/500 /1	1/0 /0	0/0 /0	0/0 /0	0/0 /0
Med	12/583 /7	3/1000 /3	3/333 /1	0/0 /0	0/0 /0	0/0 /0
Low	3/333 /1	7/285 /2	5/400 /2	0/0 /0	0/0 /0	0/0 /0

Behind

	Fastball Average .466			Curve Average .000		
	Outside	Middle	Inside	Outside	Middle	Inside
High	3/666 /2	1/0 /0	0/0 /0	0/0 /0	0/0 /0	1/0 /0
Med	4/250 /1	1/0 /0	2/500 /1	0/0 /0	0/0 /0	0/0 /0
Low	3/666 /2	1/1000 /1	0/0 /0	0/0 /0	0/0 /0	0/0 /0

Overall Evaluation

Against Right-Handed Pitchers

Overall Fastball

Overall Curve — Not enough information

Overall Slider

Against Left-Handed Pitchers

Overall Fastball ⚾

Overall Curve — Not enough information

Overall Slider — Not enough information

Comments: Has a strong fastball sector low-middle/
low-outside/medium-outside/medium-middle vs. RH.
Strengths: As above vs. RH; medium-inside fastballs
vs. LH.
Weaknesses: High-outside and low-inside fastballs
vs. RH.

Rance Mulliniks (Left Handed)   *Toronto Blue Jays*

Rance Mulliniks Against Right-Handed Pitchers
Overall BARS Batting Average .279

Fastball Average .308

	Outside	Middle	Inside
High	19/368 /7	29/206 /6	18/222 /4
Med	101/287 /29	20/700 /14	35/257 /9
Low	22/227 /5	34/382 /13	20/250 /5

Curve Average .140

	Outside	Middle	Inside
High	3/333 /1	4/0 /0	2/0 /0
Med	14/142 /2	3/333 /1	4/250 /1
Low	10/200 /2	14/142 /2	10/0 /0

Slider Average .416

	Outside	Middle	Inside
High	1/1000 /1	0/0 /0	0/0 /0
Med	4/250 /1	0/0 /0	3/1000 /3
Low	0/0 /0	7/714 /5	9/0 /0

Rance Mulliniks Against Left-Handed Pitchers
Overall BARS Batting Average .219

Fastball Average .258

	Outside	Middle	Inside
High	0/0 /0	5/600 /3	4/0 /0
Med	7/428 /3	1/0 /0	9/111 /1
Low	1/0 /0	2/500 /1	2/0 /0

Curve Average .200

	Outside	Middle	Inside
High	0/0 /0	0/0 /0	0/0 /0
Med	2/500 /1	1/0 /0	2/0 /0
Low	0/0 /0	0/0 /0	0/0 /0

Slider Average .000

	Outside	Middle	Inside
High	1/0 /0	1/0 /0	0/0 /0
Med	0/0 /0	0/0 /0	0/0 /0
Low	1/0 /0	0/0 /0	1/0 /0

The BARS System has much more information for left-handed hitting Rance Mulliniks against right-handed pitchers. His charts against left-handers are included only for general interest.

Against right-handers, Mulliniks has a .308 average against fastballs. He has distinct bands of strength and weakness in his fastballs chart. By paying attention to these, pitchers could gain an advantage on him.

Note his weakness against inside fastballs and high-over-the-middle fastballs. These locations offer targets for pitchers to attack, and since there are four locations adjacent to each other, pitchers have a greater margin for error.

Mulliniks is also weak in his low-outside fastball location, but it is bounded by stronger locations (low-over-the-middle, medium-over-the-middle, and medium-high outside). These adjacent strong locations give pitchers less margin for error.

Mulliniks hits .287 against medium-high outside fastballs. He goes to the opposite field with this pitch.

MEDIUM-HIGH OUTSIDE FASTBALLS

BATTING AVERAGE .287
Play

Left	Deep and shifted toward the left field line
Center	Deep in straightaway center field
Right	Medium-deep and shifted toward center field
Short	Up middle (shifted toward second base)
Second	Normal position

He hits low-over-the-middle fastballs for an excellent .382 average. He goes deep down the left line with this pitch also.

LOW-OVER-THE-MIDDLE FASTBALLS

BATTING AVERAGE .382
Play

Left	Deep and shifted toward the left field line
Center	Deep in straightaway center field
Right	Deep and shifted toward center field
Short	Up middle (shifted toward second base)
Second	Normal position

He goes deep down both lines with medium-high inside fastballs, but his low average indicates that most of his hit balls in this location are easy pop flies or grounders.

MEDIUM-HIGH INSIDE FASTBALLS

BATTING AVERAGE .257
Play

Left	Deep and shifted toward the left field line
Center	Medium-deep in straightaway center field
Right	Deep and shifted toward the right field line

| Short | Normal position |
| Second | Normal position |

Mulliniks' problems with high fastballs are shown in his high-over-the-middle location (.206).

HIGH-OVER-THE-MIDDLE FASTBALLS

BATTING AVERAGE .206
Play

Left	Deep and shifted toward the left field line
Center	Deep in straightaway center field
Right	Deep in straightaway right field
Short	*No instances recorded*
Second	Normal position

He hits high-outside fastballs for an excellent .368 average.

HIGH-OUTSIDE FASTBALLS

BATTING AVERAGE .368
Play

Left	Deep and shifted toward the left field line
Center	Medium-deep in straightaway center field
Right	Medium-deep and shifted toward the right line
Short	Up middle (shifted toward second base)
Second	Normal position

Mulliniks has trouble with low curves and medium-high outside curves. He has trouble getting low-outside curves out of the infield.

He has a lot of trouble with low-inside sliders (.000 on 0 for 9). He hits low-over-the-middle sliders very well, however (.714).

Mulliniks When Ahead And Behind In The Count

Mulliniks hits medium-high outside fastballs better when ahead in the count (.306 when ahead, .200 when behind). The following fielding strategy charts show how fielders need to play for this pitch when Mulliniks is ahead and behind. Notice that every fielder is required to shift.

MEDIUM-HIGH OUTSIDE FASTBALLS (WHEN AHEAD IN THE COUNT)

BATTING AVERAGE .306
Play

Left	Deep and shifted toward the left field line
Center	Medium-deep in straightaway center field
Right	Medium-deep and shifted toward center field
Short	Up middle (shifted toward second base)
Second	Shifted toward first base

MEDIUM-HIGH OUTSIDE FASTBALLS (WHEN BEHIND IN THE COUNT)

BATTING AVERAGE .200
Play

Left	Medium-deep in straightaway left field
Center	Medium-deep and shifted toward left field
Right	*No instances recorded*
Short	Normal position
Second	Normal position

Ahead And Behind In The Count Vs. RH

Ahead

Fastball Average .385 — Curve Average .181

	Outside	Middle	Inside		Outside	Middle	Inside
High	7/ 571 /4	13/ 153 /2	9/ 444 /4		1/ 0 /0	0/ 0 /0	0/ 0 /0
Med	49/ 306 /15	13/ 769 /10	17/ 294 /5		3/ 333 /1	1/ 1000 /1	0/ 0 /0
Low	5/ 600 /3	16/ 375 /6	6/ 500 /3		0/ 0 /0	2/ 0 /0	4/ 0 /0

Behind

Fastball Average .285 — Curve Average .142

	Outside	Middle	Inside		Outside	Middle	Inside
High	2/ 500 /1	6/ 166 /1	4/ 0 /0		0/ 0 /0	2/ 0 /0	1/ 0 /0
Med	15/ 200 /3	1/ 1000 /1	7/ 428 /3		4/ 250 /1	0/ 0 /0	3/ 333 /1
Low	1/ 0 /0	11/ 454 /5	2/ 0 /0		3/ 333 /1	6/ 0 /0	2/ 0 /0

Overall Evaluation

Against Right-Handed Pitchers

Overall Fastball	⚾ ⚾ ⚾
Overall Curve	⚾
Overall Slider	⚾ ⚾ ⚾ ⚾

Against Left-Handed Pitchers

Overall Fastball	⚾
Overall Curve	Not enough information
Overall Slider	Not enough information

Comments: Has trouble with inside fastballs vs. RH.
Strengths: High-outside, medium-middle and low-middle fastballs vs. RH, low-middle sliders vs. RH.
Weaknesses: Inside fastballs, high-middle and low-outside fastballs vs. RH, low curves and medium-outside curves, low-inside sliders vs. RH; inside fastballs vs. LH.

Mookie Wilson Against Right-Handed Pitchers
Overall BARS Batting Average .271

Fastball Average .296

	Outside	Middle	Inside
High	22/ 90 /2	24/ 375 /9	16/ 375 /6
Med	47/ 361 /17	21/ 238 /5	49/ 285 /14
Low	18/ 111 /2	57/ 368 /21	39/ 282 /11

Curve Average .226

	Outside	Middle	Inside
High	6/ 333 /2	3/ 333 /1	1/ 0 /0
Med	15/ 333 /5	4/ 500 /2	12/ 333 /4
Low	10/ 100 /1	19/ 105 /2	14/ 142 /2

Slider Average .390

	Outside	Middle	Inside
High	0/ 0 /0	3/ 0 /0	2/ 500 /1
Med	3/ 666 /2	6/ 333 /2	12/ 500 /6
Low	0/ 0 /0	4/ 500 /2	11/ 272 /3

Mookie Wilson Against Left-Handed Pitchers
Overall BARS Batting Average .267

Fastball Average .264

	Inside	Middle	Outside
High	14/ 285 /4	14/ 285 /4	15/ 200 /3
Med	9/ 111 /1	13/ 153 /2	48/ 291 /14
Low	17/ 235 /4	24/ 375 /9	35/ 257 /9

Curve Average .268

	Inside	Middle	Outside
High	0/ 0 /0	1/ 0 /0	0/ 0 /0
Med	4/ 0 /0	0/ 0 /0	9/ 444 /4
Low	3/ 333 /1	13/ 307 /4	11/ 181 /2

Slider Average .354

	Inside	Middle	Outside
High	3/ 666 /2	2/ 0 /0	1/ 0 /0
Med	4/ 250 /1	0/ 0 /0	3/ 333 /1
Low	8/ 250 /2	6/ 333 /2	4/ 750 /3

Switch-hitter Mookie Wilson hits .296 against fastballs when batting left-handed against right-handed pitchers but only .264 right-handed against left-handed pitchers.

Against right-handers he hits very poorly against low-outside and high-outside fastballs (.111 and .090 respectively). But he hits medium-high outside fastballs excellently (.361). The chart below and the field diagram opposite show how fielders need to play.

MEDIUM-HIGH OUTSIDE FASTBALLS

BATTING AVERAGE .361

Play

Left	Deep and shifted toward the left field line
Center	Medium-deep in straightaway center field
Right	Medium-deep and shifted toward center field
Short	Up middle (shifted toward second base)
Second	Normal position

He hits high-over-the-middle and high-inside fastballs extremely well (.375 in both locations). Pitchers would do well to steer away from this sector.

His .368 against low-over-the-middle fastballs is very strong. Notice that this location has the highest number of recorded fastballs. Pitchers are trying to throw Wilson low fastballs, but he is hitting them well. If they throw him low, they should make sure it is outside.

LOW-OVER-THE-MIDDLE FASTBALLS

BATTING AVERAGE .368

Play

Left	Medium-deep in straightaway left field
Center	Medium-deep in straightaway center field
Right	Deep in straightaway right field
Short	Up middle (shifted toward second base)
Second	Normal position

Wilson has problems with low curves (.100, .105 and .142, outside to inside). He hits all other curve locations excellently.

Wilson Against Left-Handed Pitchers

Wilson also hits low-over-the-middle fastballs well against left-handed pitchers (.375).

LOW-OVER-THE-MIDDLE FASTBALLS
(THROWN BY LEFT-HANDED PITCHERS)

BATTING AVERAGE .375

Play

Left	Medium-deep and shifted toward the left field line
Center	Deep in straightaway center field
Right	Deep and shifted toward center field
Short	Up middle (shifted toward second base)
Second	Normal position

Medium-High Outside Fastballs
(Thrown By Right-Handed Pitchers)

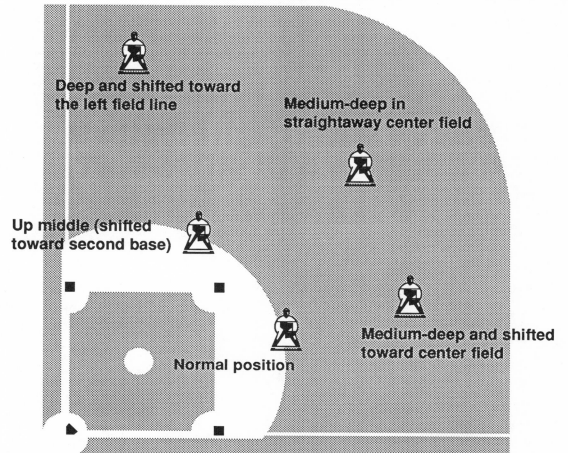

Deep and shifted toward the left field line

Medium-deep in straightaway center field

Up middle (shifted toward second base)

Normal position

Medium-deep and shifted toward center field

Ahead And Behind In The Count Vs. RH

Ahead

	Fastball Average .343			Curve Average .409		
	Outside	Middle	Inside	Outside	Middle	Inside
High	8/ 250 /2	13/ 384 /5	7/ 571 /4	2/ 500 /1	0/ 0 /0	0/ 0 /0
Med	22/ 454 /10	15/ 266 /4	21/ 380 /8	4/ 750 /3	3/ 666 /2	7/ 285 /2
Low	8/ 125 /1	23/ 391 /9	17/ 176 /3	4/ 0 /0	1/ 0 /0	1/ 1000 /1

Behind

	Fastball Average .313			Curve Average .208		
	Outside	Middle	Inside	Outside	Middle	Inside
High	0/ 0 /0	2/ 500 /1	6/ 166 /1	1/ 1000 /1	2/ 500 /1	0/ 0 /0
Med	8/ 250 /2	3/ 333 /1	14/ 357 /5	5/ 0 /0	1/ 0 /0	2/ 500 /1
Low	4/ 250 /1	6/ 333 /2	8/ 375 /3	2/ 0 /0	10/ 200 /2	1/ 0 /0

Overall Evaluation
Against Right-Handed Pitchers

Overall Fastball

Overall Curve

Overall Slider

Against Left-Handed Pitchers

Overall Fastball

Overall Curve

Overall Slider

Comments: Weak against low curves vs. RH.
Strengths: Medium-outside, low-middle, high-middle and high-inside fastballs vs. RH, medium-outside and medium-inside curves vs. RH, medium-inside sliders vs. RH; low-middle fastballs, low-middle and medium-outside curves vs. LH.
Weaknesses:High-outside and low-outside fastballs and low curves vs. RH; high-outside, low-outside, low-inside fastballs vs.LH, low-outside curves vs. LH.

Armas, Tony
Davis, Chili
Downing, Brian
Hoffman, Glenn
Howell, Jack
Joyner, Wally
Parrish, Lance
Ray, Johhny
Schroeder, Bill
Schofield, Dick
Washington, Claudell
White, Devon

California Angels
BARS System
Hitting Analysis

Tony Armas Against Right-Handed Pitchers
Overall BARS Batting Average .235

Fastball Average .262

	Inside	Middle	Outside
High	20/ 200 /4	33/ 242 /8	20/ 150 /3
Med	44/ 318 /14	23/ 347 /8	103/ 252 /26
Low	24/ 0 /0	41/ 365 /15	23/ 391 /9

Curve Average .183

	Inside	Middle	Outside
High	1/ 0 /0	6/ 333 /2	3/ 0 /0
Med	12/ 83 /1	1/ 1000 /1	37/ 216 /8
Low	3/ 0 /0	15/ 333 /5	31/ 96 /3

Slider Average .172

	Inside	Middle	Outside
High	1/ 0 /0	0/ 0 /0	2/ 500 /1
Med	5/ 200 /1	1/ 1000 /1	16/ 250 /4
Low	3/ 0 /0	9/ 111 /1	21/ 95 /2

Tony Armas Against Left-Handed Pitchers
Overall BARS Batting Average .329

Fastball Average .333

	Inside	Middle	Outside
High	5/ 0 /0	6/ 333 /2	13/ 230 /3
Med	22/ 272 /6	13/ 615 /8	47/ 297 /14
Low	9/ 222 /2	29/ 551 /16	15/ 133 /2

Curve Average .292

	Inside	Middle	Outside
High	0/ 0 /0	2/ 500 /1	0/ 0 /0
Med	2/ 1000 /2	6/ 0 /0	13/ 384 /5
Low	1/ 0 /0	9/ 222 /2	8/ 250 /2

Slider Average .352

	Inside	Middle	Outside
High	2/ 500 /1	7/ 714 /5	1/ 1000 /1
Med	4/ 250 /1	2/ 1000 /2	3/ 0 /0
Low	6/ 333 /2	6/ 0 /0	3/ 0 /0

Right-handed hitting Tony Armas has a much higher overall BARS average against left-handed pitchers (.220 overall vs. right-handers, .304 overall vs. left-handers).

Armas has trouble overall with medium-high outside fastballs against right-handed pitchers (.254). His Ahead and Behind charts show, however, that he murders this pitch when behind in the count (.571 when behind, .250 when ahead). This is unusual because most hitters look for fastballs more when they are ahead in the count.

MEDIUM-HIGH OUTSIDE FASTBALLS (WHEN BEHIND IN THE COUNT)

BATTING AVERAGE .571
Play
Left   Deep and shifted toward the left field line
Center   Deep and shifted toward left field
Right   Deep and shifted toward center field
Short   Up middle (shifted toward second base)
Second   Normal position

MEDIUM-HIGH OUTSIDE FASTBALLS (WHEN AHEAD IN THE COUNT)

BATTING AVERAGE .250
Play
Left   Deep in straightaway left field
Center   Deep in straightaway center field

Right   Medium-deep in straightaway right field
Short   Up middle (shifted toward second base)
Second   Normal position

In contrast, he hits medium-high inside fastballs better when ahead in the count (.692 when ahead, .142 when behind). These instances show that fielders need to adjust not only for the type and location of pitch, but for the count on the batter.

MEDIUM-HIGH INSIDE FASTBALLS (WHEN AHEAD IN THE COUNT)

BATTING AVERAGE .692
Play
Left   Deep in straightaway left field
Center   Deep and shifted toward left field
Right   Short and shifted toward center field
Short   Shifted toward third base
Second   Normal position

MEDIUM-HIGH INSIDE FASTBALLS (WHEN BEHIND IN THE COUNT)

BATTING AVERAGE .142
Play
Left   Short and shifted toward center field
Center   Medium-deep in straightaway center field
Right   *No instances recorded*
Short   Up middle (shifted toward second base)
Second   Shifted toward first base

Notice Armas' trouble with high fastballs. And his low-fastball locations are a study in contrasts. He hits .365 and .391 against low-over-the-middle and low-outside fastballs respectively, but is 0-for-24 against low-inside fastballs.

His trouble with low-inside fastballs could be that he cannot get his bat on this pitch or that he tends to swing at the ball when it is out of the strike zone low-inside. His BARS information shows that he should hold off on all low-inside pitches (fastballs, curves, and sliders) until he has to swing at them.

Against right-handers he has trouble with inside and outside curves and sliders. His low averages in these areas offer large targets for right-handers.

Armas Against Left-Handed Pitchers

Armas hits fastballs excellently overall against left-handed pitchers (.333). He hits .297 against medium-outside fastballs thrown by left-handers.

MEDIUM-HIGH OUTSIDE FASTBALLS
(THROWN BY LEFT-HANDED PITCHERS)

BATTING AVERAGE .297
Play

Left	Medium-deep in straightaway left field
Center	Deep and shifted toward left field
Right	Deep and shifted toward center field
Short	Up middle (shifted toward second base)
Second	Normal position

He hits medium-high inside fastballs for a .272 average against left-handers. The following fielding strategy shows that the outfielders and the shortstop need to shift to be properly positioned against both inside and outside medium-high fastballs thrown by left-handers.

MEDIUM-HIGH INSIDE FASTBALLS
(THROWN BY LEFT-HANDED PITCHERS)

BATTING AVERAGE .272
Play

Left	Deep in straightaway left field
Center	Deep and shifted toward right field
Right	Deep in straightaway right field
Short	Normal position
Second	Normal position

Armas hits a sterling .551 against low-over-the-middle fastballs thrown by left-handers.

LOW-OVER-THE-MIDDLE FASTBALLS
(THROWN BY LEFT-HANDED PITCHERS)

BATTING AVERAGE .551
Play

Left	Deep and shifted toward the left field line
Center	Deep in straightaway center field
Right	Deep and shifted toward center field
Short	Normal position
Second	Normal position

No pitcher would want to throw a medium-over-the-middle fastball to Armas (.615), but it's interesting to see how he hits this pitch against left-handers. He pulls it deep down the left line, deep to left-center, deep to straightaway right field, and to the shortstop in the hole between short and third. There are no recorded instances of Armas hitting this pitch to the second baseman.

Ahead And Behind In The Count Vs. RH

Ahead

Fastball Average .357

	Inside	Middle	Outside
High	4/250 /1	4/0 /0	6/333 /2
Med	13/692 /9	13/384 /5	40/250 /10
Low	5/0 /0	18/500 /9	9/444 /4

Curve Average .235

	Inside	Middle	Outside
High	0/0 /0	1/1000 /1	1/0 /0
Med	3/0 /0	0/0 /0	7/285 /2
Low	0/0 /0	2/500 /1	3/0 /0

Behind

Fastball Average .385

	Inside	Middle	Outside
High	4/500 /2	4/750 /3	6/0 /0
Med	7/142 /1	2/500 /1	21/571 /12
Low	4/0 /0	6/333 /2	3/333 /1

Curve Average .240

	Inside	Middle	Outside
High	1/0 /0	0/0 /0	0/0 /0
Med	3/0 /0	1/1000 /1	13/230 /3
Low	1/0 /0	3/333 /1	3/333 /1

Overall Evaluation

Against Right-Handed Pitchers

Overall Fastball ◯◯
Overall Curve ◯◯
Overall Slider ◯◯

Against Left-Handed Pitchers

Overall Fastball ◯◯ ◯◯ ◯◯ ◯◯
Overall Curve ◯◯ ◯◯ ◯◯
Overall Slider ◯◯ ◯◯ ◯◯ ◯◯

Comments: Has trouble with high fastballs vs. RH.
Strengths: Low-outside, low-middle, medium-middle and medium-inside fastballs, low-middle curves vs. RH; all over-the-middle fastballs, medium-outside curves vs. LH.
Weaknesses: High fastballs, low-inside and medium-outside fastballs, inside and outside curves and sliders vs. RH; inside fastballs, high-outside and low-outside fastballs, low curves vs. LH.

Chili Davis (Switch Hitter) — *California Angels*

Chili Davis Against Right-Handed Pitchers
Overall BARS Batting Average .264

Fastball Average .270

	Outside	Middle	Inside
High	18/ 111 /2	31/ 290 /9	20/ 100 /2
Med	57/ 228 /13	17/ 411 /7	52/ 365 /19
Low	26/ 153 /4	78/ 333 /26	52/ 250 /13

Curve Average .232

	Outside	Middle	Inside
High	0/ 0 /0	5/ 200 /1	3/ 333 /1
Med	11/ 181 /2	6/ 166 /1	11/ 272 /3
Low	9/ 222 /2	17/ 352 /6	11/ 90 /1

Slider Average .257

	Outside	Middle	Inside
High	1/ 0 /0	1/ 0 /0	2/ 0 /0
Med	3/ 0 /0	2/ 500 /1	12/ 250 /3
Low	1/ 0 /0	5/ 600 /3	8/ 250 /2

Chili Davis Against Left-Handed Pitchers
Overall BARS Batting Average .223

Fastball Average .219

	Inside	Middle	Outside
High	4/ 0 /0	8/ 500 /4	5/ 200 /1
Med	7/ 0 /0	4/ 250 /1	28/ 214 /6
Low	7/ 142 /1	23/ 304 /7	19/ 157 /3

Curve Average .130

	Inside	Middle	Outside
High	0/ 0 /0	0/ 0 /0	1/ 0 /0
Med	3/ 333 /1	1/ 0 /0	5/ 0 /0
Low	4/ 0 /0	5/ 200 /1	4/ 250 /1

Slider Average .360

	Inside	Middle	Outside
High	2/ 0 /0	0/ 0 /0	1/ 1000 /1
Med	2/ 500 /1	2/ 0 /0	1/ 1000 /1
Low	7/ 142 /1	6/ 500 /3	4/ 500 /2

Switch-hitting Chili Davis has a higher BARS average batting left-handed against right-handed pitchers. He has trouble with outside fastballs and curves against both right- and left-handed pitchers.

Davis' fastball chart against right-handers is unusual in that he has more recorded *inside* fastballs than *outside* fastballs. Pitchers are trying to throw him inside, but this could be a mistake because his .365 average against medium-high inside fastballs is one of his higher averages. He is looking for inside fastballs.

MEDIUM-HIGH INSIDE FASTBALLS

BATTING AVERAGE .365
Play

Left	Deep in straightaway left field
Center	Deep and shifted toward right field
Right	Deep and shifted toward the right field line
Short	Normal position
Second	Normal position

Pitchers also try to throw Davis low, as indicated by the higher number of instances in his low locations. This seems to be a mistake: he hits each low fastball location better than the corresponding high fastball location. By positioning themselves correctly for low-over-the-middle fastballs, fielders could prevent most of Davis' hits resulting from pitches to this location.

LOW-OVER-THE-MIDDLE FASTBALLS

BATTING AVERAGE .333
Play

Left	Deep in straightaway left field
Center	Medium-deep in straightaway center field
Right	Deep and shifted toward center field
Short	Up middle (shifted toward second base)
Second	Normal position

He has a lot of trouble with outside fastballs thrown by right-handers. His highest average is .228 in his medium-high outside location. He hits this pitch deep down both lines, probably for easy pop-flies.

MEDIUM-HIGH OUTSIDE FASTBALLS

BATTING AVERAGE .228
Play

Left	Deep and shifted toward the left field line
Center	Deep and shifted toward left field
Right	Deep and shifted toward the right field line
Short	Normal position
Second	Shifted toward first base

Davis hits .250 in his low-inside fastball location. Fielders could prevent even more base hits resulting from pitches to this location if they positioned themselves according to BARS strategy.

LOW-INSIDE FASTBALLS

BATTING AVERAGE .250

Play

Left	Deep and shifted toward the left field line
Center	Deep in straightaway center field
Right	Deep in straightaway right field
Short	Normal position
Second	Normal position

He has trouble with outside curves, but he hits low-over-the-middle curves very well (.352).

LOW-OVER-THE-MIDDLE CURVEBALLS

BATTING AVERAGE .352

Play

Left	Deep and shifted toward the left field line
Center	Deep in straightaway center field
Right	Deep and shifted toward center field
Short	Up middle (shifted toward second base)
Second	Normal position

He hits medium-high inside sliders for a .250 average, scattering the ball down both lines.

MEDIUM-HIGH INSIDE SLIDERS

BATTING AVERAGE .250

Play

Left	Deep and shifted toward the left field line
Center	*No instances recorded*
Right	Deep and shifted toward the right field line
Short	Normal position
Second	Shifted toward first base

Davis Against Left-Handed Pitchers

Davis has fewer recorded BARS instances against left-handed pitchers, but it is evident that he has more trouble overall with fastballs against left-handers than against right-handers.

His .304 against low-over-the-middle fastballs thrown by left-handers is good, but his .214 against medium-high outside fastballs is poor.

LOW-OVER-THE-MIDDLE FASTBALLS (THROWN BY LEFT-HANDED PITCHERS)

BATTING AVERAGE .304

Play

Left	Medium-deep and shifted toward center field
Center	Medium-deep in straightaway center field
Right	Deep in straightaway right field
Short	Normal position
Second	*No instances recorded*

MEDIUM-HIGH OUTSIDE FASTBALLS (THROWN BY LEFT-HANDED PITCHERS)

BATTING AVERAGE .214

Play

Left	Deep in straightaway left field
Center	Medium-deep and shifted toward right field
Right	Medium-deep in straightaway right field
Short	Up middle (shifted toward second base)
Second	Normal position

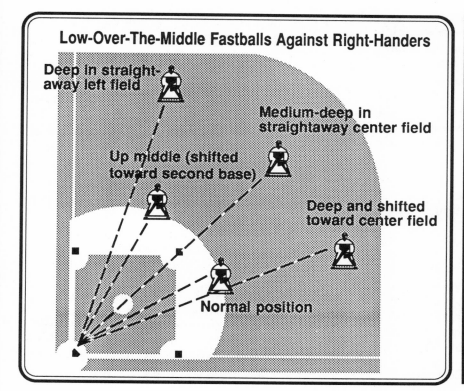

Low-Over-The-Middle Fastballs Against Right-Handers

Deep in straightaway left field

Medium-deep in straightaway center field

Up middle (shifted toward second base)

Deep and shifted toward center field

Normal position

Overall Evaluation
Against Right-Handed Pitchers

Overall Fastball	⚾
Overall Curve	⚾
Overall Slider	⚾ ⚾

Against Left-Handed Pitchers

Overall Fastball	⚾
Overall Curve	⚾
Overall Slider	⚾ ⚾ ⚾ ⚾

Comments: Weak against outside fastballs and curves vs. LH and RH.

Strengths: Low-middle, medium-middle and medium-inside fastballs, low-middle curves vs. RH; high-middle and low-middle fastballs vs. LH.

Weaknesses: Outside fastballs, high-inside and low-inside fastballs, outside curves, low-inside curves vs. RH; outside and inside fastballs, low curves, outside curves, low-inside sliders vs. LH.

Brian Downing (Right Handed)　　*California Angels*

Brian Downing Against Right-Handed Pitchers
Overall BARS Batting Average .280

Fastball Average .311

	Inside	Middle	Outside
High	21/142 /3	19/421 /8	15/200 /3
Med	41/268 /11	17/470 /8	76/302 /23
Low	20/500 /10	40/275 /11	43/325 /14

Curve Average .202

	Inside	Middle	Outside
High	4/250 /1	7/0 /0	1/0 /0
Med	9/222 /2	9/222 /2	28/321 /9
Low	2/0 /0	9/222 /2	25/120 /3

Slider Average .256

	Inside	Middle	Outside
High	1/0 /0	2/500 /1	5/200 /1
Med	3/333 /1	3/333 /1	23/391 /9
Low	5/200 /1	4/0 /0	28/178 /5

Brian Downing Against Left-Handed Pitchers
Overall BARS Batting Average .294

Fastball Average .290

	Inside	Middle	Outside
High	7/285 /2	12/333 /4	12/416 /5
Med	21/333 /7	12/416 /5	51/235 /12
Low	9/111 /1	37/297 /11	11/272 /3

Curve Average .411

	Inside	Middle	Outside
High	0/0 /0	1/1000 /1	2/0 /0
Med	1/0 /0	0/0 /0	3/333 /1
Low	0/0 /0	4/750 /3	6/333 /2

Slider Average .250

	Inside	Middle	Outside
High	1/0 /0	1/1000 /1	2/500 /1
Med	5/200 /1	2/500 /1	3/666 /2
Low	10/0 /0	6/333 /2	2/0 /0

Right-handed hitter Brian Downing hits fastballs consistently (.311 against right-handers, .290 against left-handers). He has trouble with curves against right-handers (.202).

Starting with his fastball performance against right-handers, notice the weaknesses in his medium-high inside and high-inside locations (.268 and .142 respectively). This sector gives pitchers the best area for attack.

Downing hits .302 against medium-high outside fastballs and .325 against low-outside fastballs thrown by right-handers. The following fielding strategy charts show that every fielder needs to shift to be properly positioned for both of these pitches.

MEDIUM-HIGH OUTSIDE FASTBALLS

BATTING AVERAGE .302
Play
Left	Deep and shifted toward center field
Center	Deep in straightaway center field
Right	Deep in straightaway right field
Short	Shifted toward third base
Second	Shifted toward first base

LOW-OUTSIDE FASTBALLS

BATTING AVERAGE .325
Play
Left	Deep and shifted toward the left field line

Center	Medium-deep in straightaway center field
Right	Medium-deep and shifted toward the right line
Short	Normal position
Second	Normal position

His .421 against high-over-the-middle fastballs is excellent.

HIGH-OVER-THE-MIDDLE FASTBALLS

BATTING AVERAGE .421
Play
Left	Deep and shifted toward the left field line
Center	Medium-deep in straightaway center field
Right	Medium-deep in straightaway right field
Short	Shifted toward third base
Second	*No instances recorded*

In contrast, his .275 against low-over-the-middle fastballs is only fair.

LOW-OVER-THE-MIDDLE FASTBALLS

BATTING AVERAGE .275
Play
Left	Medium-deep and shifted toward the left field line
Center	Medium-deep in straightaway center field
Right	Deep and shifted toward center field
Short	Shifted toward third base
Second	Normal position

Downing Against Curves And Sliders

Downing hits medium-high outside curves and medium-high outside sliders extremely well but has trouble with low-outside curves and low-outside sliders. This contrast makes it apparent that right-handed pitchers should keep their breaking pitches low.

MEDIUM-HIGH OUTSIDE CURVEBALLS

BATTING AVERAGE .321

Play

Left	Deep and shifted toward the left field line
Center	Medium-deep and shifted toward left field
Right	Medium-deep and shifted toward the right line
Short	Normal position
Second	Shifted toward first base

MEDIUM-HIGH OUTSIDE SLIDERS

BATTING AVERAGE .391

Play

Left	Deep and shifted toward the left field line
Center	Deep in straightaway center field
Right	Deep in straightaway right field
Short	Up middle (shifted toward second base)
Second	*No instances recorded*

He hits low-outside sliders to the opposite field. His .178 average indicates that most of his hit balls in this location are easy outs.

LOW-OUTSIDE SLIDERS

BATTING AVERAGE .178

Play

Left	Deep and shifted toward center field
Center	Medium-deep and shifted toward right field
Right	Medium-deep and shifted toward the right line
Short	Up middle (shifted toward second base)
Second	*No instances recorded*

Downing Against Left-Handed Pitchers

Downing hits medium-high outside fastballs poorly against left-handed pitchers (.235). He hits this pitch straightaway to all fields.

MEDIUM-HIGH OUTSIDE FASTBALLS (THROWN BY LEFT-HANDED PITCHERS)

BATTING AVERAGE .235

Play

Left	Medium-deep in straightaway left field
Center	Deep in straightaway center field
Right	Deep in straightaway right field
Short	Up middle (shifted toward second base)
Second	Shifted toward first base

Both left- and right-handed pitchers tend to pitch Downing low, as indicated by the high number of instances in his low fastball locations. His low-over-the-middle average against left-handed pitchers is good — .297.

LOW-OVER-THE-MIDDLE FASTBALLS (THROWN BY LEFT-HANDED PITCHERS)

BATTING AVERAGE .297

Play

Left	Deep in straightaway left field
Center	Deep in straightaway center field
Right	Medium-deep in straightaway right field
Short	Shifted toward third base
Second	Shifted toward first base

Ahead And Behind In The Count Vs. RH

Ahead

Fastball Average .336

	Inside	Middle	Outside
High	6/0	12/416 /5	2/0
Med	15/400 /6	7/714 /5	23/217 /5
Low	7/571 /4	14/214 /3	15/400 /6

Curve Average .266

	Inside	Middle	Outside
High	0/0	0/0	0/0
Med	1/0	3/0	5/600 /3
Low	0/0	1/0	5/200 /1

Behind

Fastball Average .386

	Inside	Middle	Outside
High	3/333 /1	1/0	5/400 /2
Med	11/181 /2	4/250 /1	27/481 /13
Low	6/333 /2	8/500 /4	10/400 /4

Curve Average .250

	Inside	Middle	Outside
High	3/333 /1	3/0	0/0
Med	3/333 /1	1/0	13/307 /4
Low	0/0	2/500 /1	11/181 /2

Overall Evaluation

Against Right-Handed Pitchers

Overall Fastball	⚾⚾ ⚾⚾⚾
Overall Curve	⚾⚾
Overall Slider	⚾⚾ ⚾⚾

Against Left-Handed Pitchers

Overall Fastball	⚾⚾ ⚾⚾
Overall Curve	⚾⚾ ⚾⚾ ⚾⚾ ⚾⚾
Overall Slider	⚾⚾ ⚾⚾

Comments: Weak against low curves vs. RH. **Strengths:** High-middle, medium-middle, low-outside and low-inside fastballs, medium-outside curves and sliders vs. RH; high-middle, high-outside, medium-inside and medium-middle fastballs vs. LH. **Weaknesses:** High-inside, high-outside, and medium-inside fastballs, low curves, inside curves and low sliders vs. RH; medium-outside and low-inside fastballs vs. LH.

Glenn Hoffman Against Right-Handed Pitchers
Overall BARS Batting Average .228

Fastball Average .250

	Inside	Middle	Outside
High	8/ 250 /2	10/ 200 /2	0/ 0 /0
Med	16/ 187 /3	18/ 333 /6	25/ 200 /5
Low	3/ 333 /1	16/ 312 /5	12/ 250 /3

Curve Average .108

	Inside	Middle	Outside
High	0/ 0 /0	1/ 0 /0	0/ 0 /0
Med	5/ 400 /2	7/ 285 /2	10/ 0 /0
Low	0/ 0 /0	4/ 0 /0	10/ 0 /0

Slider Average .285

	Inside	Middle	Outside
High	1/ 0 /0	1/ 1000 /1	0/ 0 /0
Med	1/ 0 /0	3/ 1000 /3	11/ 272 /3
Low	1/ 0 /0	7/ 285 /2	10/ 100 /1

Glenn Hoffman Against Left-Handed Pitchers
Overall BARS Batting Average .171

Fastball Average .196

	Inside	Middle	Outside
High	2/ 500 /1	5/ 200 /1	2/ 1000 /2
Med	5/ 0 /0	3/ 333 /1	13/ 230 /3
Low	4/ 0 /0	12/ 166 /2	5/ 0 /0

Curve Average .071

	Inside	Middle	Outside
High	0/ 0 /0	0/ 0 /0	0/ 0 /0
Med	2/ 0 /0	1/ 0 /0	3/ 333 /1
Low	1/ 0 /0	5/ 0 /0	2/ 0 /0

Slider Average .181

	Inside	Middle	Outside
High	0/ 0 /0	1/ 0 /0	0/ 0 /0
Med	3/ 0 /0	1/ 0 /0	1/ 0 /0
Low	2/ 500 /1	0/ 0 /0	3/ 333 /1

Right-handed hitter Glenn Hoffman has two strong fastball locations against right-handed pitchers. He hits .312 against low-over-the-middle fastballs and .333 against medium-over-the-middle fastballs.

He hits low-over-the-middle fastballs medium-deep to left and center and deep to right.

LOW-OVER-THE-MIDDLE FASTBALLS

BATTING AVERAGE .312

Play

Left	Medium-deep in straightaway left field
Center	Medium-deep and shifted toward left field
Right	Deep in straightaway right field
Short	Normal position
Second	Normal position

He hits medium-over-the-middle fastballs deep to all fields. The field diagram on the opposite page shows how fielders need to shift for medium-over-the-middle fastballs compared to low-over-the-middle fastballs.

MEDIUM-OVER-THE-MIDDLE FASTBALLS

BATTING AVERAGE .333

Play

Left	Deep in straightaway left field
Center	Deep in straightaway center field
Right	Deep and shifted toward center field
Short	Shifted toward third base
Second	Normal position

Hoffman is weak against all outside and high fastballs. His .200 and .187 in the medium-high outside and inside locations bring down his overall effectiveness. He is very weak against outside curves.

He is also weak against low-outside sliders (.100) but he hits medium-high outside sliders fairly well.

MEDIUM-HIGH OUTSIDE SLIDERS

BATTING AVERAGE .272

Play

Left	Short in straightaway left field
Center	Medium-deep in straightaway center field
Right	*No instances recorded*
Short	Normal position
Second	Shifted toward first base

Hoffman has even more trouble against left-handed pitchers than he does against right-handed pitchers. He has problems with all low fastballs. He hits .230 against medium-high outside fastballs, however.

MEDIUM-HIGH OUTSIDE FASTBALLS
(THROWN BY LEFT-HANDED PITCHERS)

BATTING AVERAGE .230

Play

Left	Medium-deep in straightaway left field
Center	Medium-deep in straightaway center field
Right	Deep in straightaway right field
Short	Shifted toward third base
Second	*No instances recorded*

Dark Fielders — Low-Over-The-Middle Fastballs Vs. RH
Light Fielders — Medium-Over-The-Middle Fastballs Vs. RH

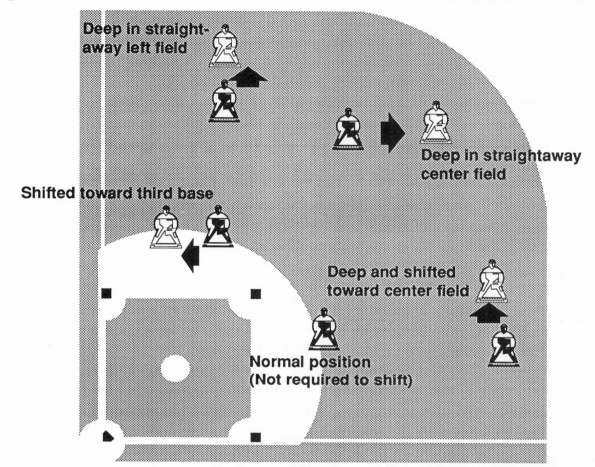

Deep in straight-away left field

Deep in straightaway center field

Shifted toward third base

Deep and shifted toward center field

Normal position
(Not required to shift)

Ahead And Behind In The Count Vs. RH

Ahead

Fastball Average .290

	Inside	Middle	Outside
High	5/ **200** /1	5/ **200** /1	0/ **0** /0
Med	11/ **272** /3	9/ **444** /4	14/ **214** /3
Low	2/ **500** /1	8/ **375** /3	1/ **0** /0

Curve Average .166

	Inside	Middle	Outside
High	0/ **0** /0	0/ **0** /0	0/ **0** /0
Med	2/ **500** /1	1/ **0** /0	1/ **0** /0
Low	0/ **0** /0	1/ **0** /0	1/ **0** /0

Behind

Fastball Average .206

	Inside	Middle	Outside
High	1/ **0** /0	1/ **0** /0	0/ **0** /0
Med	3/ **0** /0	8/ **250** /2	4/ **250** /1
Low	0/ **0** /0	5/ **400** /2	7/ **142** /1

Curve Average .117

	Inside	Middle	Outside
High	0/ **0** /0	0/ **0** /0	0/ **0** /0
Med	0/ **0** /0	4/ **500** /2	7/ **0** /0
Low	0/ **0** /0	2/ **0** /0	4/ **0** /0

Overall Evaluation
Against Right-Handed Pitchers

Overall Fastball ⚾⚾

Overall Curve ⚾⚾

Overall Slider ⚾⚾ ⚾⚾⚾

Against Left-Handed Pitchers

Overall Fastball ⚾⚾

Overall Curve ⚾⚾

Overall Slider   Not enough information

Comments: Weak against high fastballs, outside fastballs and outside curves vs. RH.

Strengths: Medium-middle and low-middle fastballs vs. RH.

Weaknesses: High fastballs, medium-high inside fastballs, outside fastballs, outside curves, low-outside sliders vs. RH; medium-outside fastballs, low fastballs vs. LH.

Jack Howell Against Right-Handed Pitchers
Overall BARS Batting Average .254

Fastball Average .261

	Outside	Middle	Inside
High	23/86 /2	13/230 /3	10/100 /1
Med	42/309 /13	4/500 /2	27/296 /8
Low	16/187 /3	24/458 /11	13/153 /2

Curve Average .232

	Outside	Middle	Inside
High	0/0 /0	4/250 /1	2/500 /1
Med	13/384 /5	4/250 /1	3/333 /1
Low	7/142 /1	1/0 /0	9/0 /0

Slider Average .243

	Outside	Middle	Inside
High	2/0 /0	1/0 /0	1/1000 /1
Med	4/0 /0	0/0 /0	7/142 /1
Low	4/250 /1	5/800 /4	13/153 /2

Jack Howell Against Left-Handed Pitchers
Overall BARS Batting Average .195

Fastball Average .235

	Outside	Middle	Inside
High	3/333 /1	2/0 /0	4/250 /1
Med	16/187 /3	7/285 /2	11/272 /3
Low	3/0 /0	2/500 /1	3/333 /1

Curve Average .187

	Outside	Middle	Inside
High	1/0 /0	1/0 /0	0/0 /0
Med	3/0 /0	1/1000 /1	5/400 /2
Low	4/0 /0	1/0 /0	0/0 /0

Slider Average .000

	Outside	Middle	Inside
High	0/0 /0	1/0 /0	1/0 /0
Med	3/0 /0	0/0 /0	0/0 /0
Low	2/0 /0	2/0 /0	1/0 /0

Left-handed hitting Jack Howell has low overall BARS averages against both right- and left-handed pitchers (.230 vs. right-handers, .187 vs. left-handers). He has some strong locations in his charts, but his many weak locations bring down his overall averages.

Against right-handers, Howell hits low-over-the-middle fastballs extremely well (.458). He hits this pitch deep down the left line (his opposite field) and into the deep right-center gap. By positioning themselves as suggested by the BARS System for pitches to this location, fielders could get to most of his hit balls and prevent base hits.

LOW-OVER-THE-MIDDLE FASTBALLS

BATTING AVERAGE .458
Play
Left   Deep and shifted toward the left field line
Center Deep in straightaway center field
Right   Deep and shifted toward center field
Short   Up middle (shifted toward second base)
Second Normal position

He hits medium-high inside fastballs fairly well (.296), scattering the pitch to all fields.

MEDIUM-HIGH INSIDE FASTBALLS

BATTING AVERAGE .296
Play
Left   Medium-deep and shifted toward the left field line
Center Deep and shifted toward left field
Right   Deep and shifted toward the right field line
Short   Normal position
Second Normal position

His .309 against medium-high outside fastballs is good. He goes with this pitch, hitting it down the left line. But he hits to the right side of the infield when he hits ground balls.

MEDIUM-HIGH OUTSIDE FASTBALLS

BATTING AVERAGE .309
Play
Left   Deep and shifted toward the left field line
Center Deep in straightaway center field
Right   Medium-deep in straightaway right field
Short   Up middle (shifted toward second base)
Second Shifted toward first base

He has trouble with all high fastballs. In addition, he has weak averages in his low-outside and low-inside fastball locations.

He hits high-outside fastballs deep and straight-away to all fields. His .086 average in this location indicates that most of his hit balls are probably easy pop flies to the outfield and easy grounders to the infield.

HIGH-OUTSIDE FASTBALLS

BATTING AVERAGE .086
Play

Left	Deep in straightaway left field
Center	Deep in straightaway center field
Right	Deep in straightaway right field
Short	Normal position
Second	Shifted toward first base

His .187 against low-outside fastballs is also weak. He hits this pitch deep to left and center, but again, these hit balls are probably easy outs.

He has trouble with low curves. However, he hits medium-high outside curves extremely well (.384).

MEDIUM-HIGH OUTSIDE CURVEBALLS

BATTING AVERAGE .384
Play

Left	Medium-deep and shifted toward the left field line
Center	Medium-deep in straightaway center field
Right	Deep and shifted toward center field
Short	*No instances recorded*
Second	Normal position

He has a lot of trouble with inside sliders. His 2-for-13 against low-inside sliders indicates a weakness.

LOW-INSIDE SLIDERS

BATTING AVERAGE .153

Play

Left	*No instances recorded*
Center	*No instances recorded*
Right	Medium-deep and shifted toward the right line
Short	Shifted toward third base
Second	Shifted toward first base

Howell Against Left-Handed Pitchers

The BARS System has recorded less information for Howell against left-handed pitchers. His records indicate that he has trouble with fastballs against left-handers.

MEDIUM-HIGH OUTSIDE FASTBALLS (THROWN BY LEFT-HANDED PITCHERS)

BATTING AVERAGE .187
Play

Left	Deep and shifted toward center field
Center	Deep in straightaway center field
Right	*No instances recorded*
Short	*No instances recorded*
Second	Shifted toward first base

His .272 against medium-high inside fastballs is better, but is still barely adequate.

MEDIUM-HIGH INSIDE FASTBALLS

BATTING AVERAGE .272
Play

Left	Deep and shifted toward center field
Center	Deep in straightaway center field
Right	Deep and shifted toward center field
Short	*No instances recorded*
Second	Normal position

Ahead And Behind In The Count Vs. RH

Ahead

Fastball Average .378

	Outside	Middle	Inside
High	6/ 333 /2	6/ 0 /0	3/ 333 /1
Med	17/ 352 /6	1/ 1000 /1	13/ 384 /5
Low	5/ 400 /2	13/ 538 /7	2/ 500 /1

Curve Average .600

	Outside	Middle	Inside
High	0/ 0 /0	1/ 1000 /1	0/ 0 /0
Med	2/ 500 /1	0/ 0 /0	1/ 0 /0
Low	1/ 1000 /1	0/ 0 /0	0/ 0 /0

Behind

Fastball Average .312

	Outside	Middle	Inside
High	2/ 0 /0	3/ 333 /1	4/ 0 /0
Med	9/ 333 /3	1/ 1000 /1	4/ 250 /1
Low	2/ 500 /1	3/ 666 /2	4/ 250 /1

Curve Average .357

	Outside	Middle	Inside
High	0/ 0 /0	0/ 0 /0	2/ 500 /1
Med	8/ 375 /3	2/ 500 /1	1/ 0 /0
Low	0/ 0 /0	0/ 0 /0	1/ 0 /0

Overall Evaluation

Against Right-Handed Pitchers

Overall Fastball ⚾⚾

Overall Curve ⚾⚾

Overall Slider ⚾⚾

Against Left-Handed Pitchers

Overall Fastball ⚾⚾

Overall Curve ⚾⚾

Overall Slider   Not enough information

Comments: Weak vs. high fastballs vs. RH, medium-outside fastballs vs. LH.

Strengths: Low-middle and medium-outside fastballs, medium-outside curves, low-middle sliders vs. RH.

Weaknesses: High fastballs, low-outside and low-inside fastballs vs. RH, low curves and inside sliders vs. RH; medium-outside and medium-inside fastballs, outside curves and sliders in general vs. LH.

Wally Joyner (Left Handed)   *California Angels*

Wally Joyner Against Right-Handed Pitchers
Overall BARS Batting Average .346

Fastball Average .364

	Outside	Middle	Inside
High	18/277 /5	20/450 /9	14/142 /2
Med	76/355 /27	7/428 /3	21/428 /9
Low	16/437 /7	26/538 /14	19/157 /3

Curve Average .238

	Outside	Middle	Inside
High	3/333 /1	4/250 /1	2/500 /1
Med	10/400 /4	4/250 /1	1/0 /0
Low	7/142 /1	4/0 /0	7/142 /1

Slider Average .375

	Outside	Middle	Inside
High	1/0 /0	3/666 /2	4/500 /2
Med	3/333 /1	0/0 /0	3/333 /1
Low	4/250 /1	2/0 /0	4/500 /2

Wally Joyner Against Left-Handed Pitchers
Overall BARS Batting Average .260

Fastball Average .307

	Outside	Middle	Inside
High	4/250 /1	13/384 /5	13/307 /4
Med	35/314 /11	8/375 /3	27/333 /9
Low	2/0 /0	8/125 /1	7/285 /2

Curve Average .095

	Outside	Middle	Inside
High	2/500 /1	2/0 /0	2/0 /0
Med	5/0 /0	1/1000 /1	4/0 /0
Low	3/0 /0	1/0 /0	1/0 /0

Slider Average .193

	Outside	Middle	Inside
High	0/0 /0	1/0 /0	0/0 /0
Med	10/100 /1	2/1000 /2	4/0 /0
Low	8/250 /2	3/333 /1	3/0 /0

Left-handed hitter Wally Joyner has an excellent overall fastball average against right-handed pitchers (.364) and a good average against left-handed pitchers (.307). Joyner's fastball chart against right-handers shows that he hits all waist-high fastballs, all over-the-middle fastballs, and low-outside fastballs very strongly.

Notice in Joyner's Ahead and Behind charts on the opposite page that he murders medium-high outside fastballs against right-handers when ahead in the count. In contrast, his .083 average when behind is exceptionally low.

MEDIUM-HIGH OUTSIDE FASTBALLS (WHEN AHEAD IN THE COUNT)

BATTING AVERAGE .475
Play

Left	Medium-deep and shifted toward the left field line
Center	Deep in straightaway center field
Right	Deep in straightaway right field
Short	Up middle (shifted toward second base)
Second	Shifted toward first base

MEDIUM-HIGH OUTSIDE FASTBALLS (WHEN BEHIND IN THE COUNT)

BATTING AVERAGE .083
Play

Left	Deep and shifted toward the left field line
Center	Deep in straightaway center field
Right	Deep in straightaway right field
Short	Up middle (shifted toward second base)
Second	Normal position

His .538 against low-over-the-middle fastballs is exceptional, as is his .450 against high-over-the-middle fastballs. Each outfielder needs to adjust specifically for these pitches. If they all did, they could prevent most of Joyner's hits from pitches to these locations.

LOW-OVER-THE-MIDDLE FASTBALLS

BATTING AVERAGE .538
Play

Left	Deep and shifted toward the left field line
Center	Medium-deep in straightaway center field
Right	Deep in straightaway right field
Short	Up middle (shifted toward second base)
Second	Shifted toward first base

HIGH-OVER-THE-MIDDLE FASTBALLS

BATTING AVERAGE .450
Play

Left	Deep in straightaway left field
Center	Deep and shifted toward left field
Right	Medium-deep in straightaway right field
Short	*No instances recorded*
Second	Shifted toward first base

He hits low-outside fastballs deep to the outfield.

LOW-OUTSIDE FASTBALLS

BATTING AVERAGE .437
Play

Left	Deep and shifted toward the left field line
Center	Deep and shifted toward right field
Right	Medium-deep and shifted toward the right line
Short	Up middle (shifted toward second base)
Second	Normal position

Joyner's .428 against medium-high inside fastballs is excellent. Again, if fielders positioned themselves properly for this pitch, they could prevent most of his base hits resulting from pitches to this location.

MEDIUM-HIGH INSIDE FASTBALLS

BATTING AVERAGE .428
Play

Left	Medium-deep in straightaway left field
Center	Deep and shifted toward left field
Right	Deep in straightaway right field
Short	Up middle (shifted toward second base)
Second	Shifted toward first base

Both right- and left-handed pitchers throw Joyner very few breaking pitches in comparison with fastballs. Considering how well Joyner hits fastballs, pitchers could hardly do worse by mixing in some curves and sliders.

Joyner Against Left-Handed Pitchers

Joyner also hits waist-high fastballs well against left-handed pitchers. His .314 against medium-high outside fastballs is good.

MEDIUM-HIGH OUTSIDE FASTBALLS (THROWN BY LEFT-HANDED PITCHERS)

BATTING AVERAGE .314
Play

Left	Medium-deep in straightaway left field
Center	Deep in straightaway center field
Right	Deep and shifted toward center field
Short	Up middle (shifted toward second base)
Second	Shifted toward first base

He hits .333 against medium-high inside fastballs and .384 against high-over-the-middle fastballs. Both of these averages are excellent.

MEDIUM-HIGH INSIDE FASTBALLS (THROWN BY LEFT-HANDED PITCHERS)

BATTING AVERAGE .333
Play

Left	Short and shifted toward the left field line
Center	Deep in straightaway center field
Right	Medium-deep in straightaway right field
Short	Normal position
Second	Shifted toward first base

HIGH-OVER-THE-MIDDLE FASTBALLS (THROWN BY LEFT-HANDED PITCHERS)

BATTING AVERAGE .384
Play

Left	*No instances recorded*
Center	Deep in straightaway center field
Right	Deep and shifted toward center field
Short	*No instances recorded*
Second	Normal position

Ahead And Behind In The Count Vs. RH

Ahead

Fastball Average .456

	Outside	Middle	Inside
High	8/375 /3	10/600 /6	4/250 /1
Med	40/475 /19	4/250 /1	10/500 /5
Low	6/666 /4	9/666 /6	12/166 /2

Curve Average .444

	Outside	Middle	Inside
High	0/0 /0	1/1000 /1	0/0 /0
Med	3/666 /2	1/0 /0	1/0 /0
Low	0/0 /0	1/0 /0	2/500 /1

Behind

Fastball Average .297

	Outside	Middle	Inside
High	4/250 /1	1/0 /0	2/0 /0
Med	12/83 /1	1/1000 /1	5/200 /1
Low	4/750 /3	6/666 /4	2/0 /0

Curve Average .250

	Outside	Middle	Inside
High	3/333 /1	0/0 /0	2/500 /1
Med	2/500 /1	2/0 /0	0/0 /0
Low	3/333 /1	2/0 /0	2/0 /0

Overall Evaluation

Against Right-Handed Pitchers

Overall Fastball	⚾⚾⚾⚾
Overall Curve	⚾
Overall Slider	⚾⚾⚾⚾

Against Left-Handed Pitchers

Overall Fastball	⚾⚾⚾
Overall Curve	⚾
Overall Slider	⚾

Comments: An excellent fastball hitter vs. RH.
Strengths: Waist-high and over-the-middle fastballs, low-outside fastballs, medium-outside curves vs. RH; waist-high fastballs and high-middle fastballs vs. LH.
Weaknesses: Four fastball corners vs. RH except low-outside, low curves vs. RH; low-middle fastballs, curves in general vs. LH.

Lance Parrish (Right Handed) — *California Angels*

Lance Parrish Against Right-Handed Pitchers
Overall BARS Batting Average .246

Fastball Average .248

	Inside	Middle	Outside
High	15/ 266 /4	33/ 242 /8	25/ 240 /6
Med	42/ 238 /10	27/ 333 /9	107/ 233 /25
Low	20/ 200 /4	59/ 322 /19	30/ 133 /4

Curve Average .150

	Inside	Middle	Outside
High	1/ 0 /0	5/ 400 /2	3/ 0 /0
Med	13/ 76 /1	9/ 444 /4	28/ 142 /4
Low	5/ 0 /0	13/ 230 /3	36/ 83 /3

Slider Average .333

	Inside	Middle	Outside
High	1/ 0 /0	4/ 750 /3	9/ 111 /1
Med	5/ 0 /0	6/ 666 /4	33/ 424 /14
Low	2/ 0 /0	9/ 666 /6	42/ 214 /9

Lance Parrish Against Left-Handed Pitchers
Overall BARS Batting Average .262

Fastball Average .272

	Inside	Middle	Outside
High	4/ 250 /1	15/ 333 /5	14/ 142 /2
Med	12/ 500 /6	14/ 500 /7	54/ 185 /10
Low	7/ 285 /2	36/ 305 /11	20/ 200 /4

Curve Average .205

	Inside	Middle	Outside
High	1/ 0 /0	0/ 0 /0	3/ 333 /1
Med	4/ 0 /0	5/ 600 /3	12/ 333 /4
Low	3/ 0 /0	5/ 0 /0	6/ 0 /0

Slider Average .272

	Inside	Middle	Outside
High	1/ 0 /0	2/ 0 /0	0/ 0 /0
Med	6/ 333 /2	1/ 1000 /1	1/ 1000 /1
Low	7/ 142 /1	4/ 250 /1	0/ 0 /0

Right-handed hitting Lance Parrish has a higher overall BARS fastball average against left-handed pitchers (.272 vs. left-handers, .248 vs. right-handers). He also hits curves better against left-handers but has an excellent .333 overall slider average against right-handers.

Starting with his performance against right-handers, notice his overall weakness against fastballs. His only strong fastball locations are low-over-the-middle (.322) and medium-over-the-middle (333).

He hits low-over-the-middle fastballs deep to left and center and medium-deep to right.

LOW-OVER-THE-MIDDLE FASTBALLS

BATTING AVERAGE .322
Play
Left   Deep in straightaway left field
Center   Deep and shifted toward left field
Right   Medium-deep in straightaway right field
Short   Up middle (shifted toward second base)
Second *No instances recorded*

Parrish hits only .233 against medium-high outside fastballs thrown by right-handers. This brings down his overall average since this is by far his most highly pitched location.

His fielding strategy shows that he drives this pitch into the deep left center and deep right center gaps. If

fielders adjusted, they could be positioned to catch these drives.

MEDIUM-HIGH OUTSIDE FASTBALLS

BATTING AVERAGE .233
Play
Left   Deep in straightaway left field
Center   Deep and shifted toward left field
Right   Deep and shifted toward center field
Short   Up middle (shifted toward second base)
Second Shifted toward first base

Parrish's .238 against medium-high inside fastballs is also low.

MEDIUM-HIGH INSIDE FASTBALLS

BATTING AVERAGE .238
Play
Left   Deep and shifted toward the left field line
Center   Deep and shifted toward left field
Right   Medium-deep in straightaway right field
Short   Normal position
Second *No instances recorded*

Pitchers do not want to throw Parrish, or any hitter, a medium-over-the-middle fastball. But it is interesting to see where Parrish hits this pitch.

MEDIUM-OVER-THE-MIDDLE FASTBALLS

BATTING AVERAGE .333
Play

Left   Deep and shifted toward the left field line
Center   Deep and shifted toward left field
Right   Deep and shifted toward the right field line
Short   Normal position
Second   *No instances recorded*

Parrish Against Curves And Sliders

Parrish has trouble in almost all curve locations against right-handed pitchers. His low, inside, and outside locations are weak.

He does hit sliders excellently overall, however. His .424 against medium-high outside sliders is very strong. He drives this pitch into the deep left center and right center alleys.

MEDIUM-HIGH OUTSIDE SLIDERS

BATTING AVERAGE .424
Play

Left   Deep in straightaway left field
Center   Deep and shifted toward left field
Right   Deep and shifted toward center field
Short   Up middle (shifted toward second base)
Second   Normal position

Parrish Against Left-Handed Pitchers

Parrish has some very strong and some very weak fastball locations against left-handed pitchers. His outside locations are weak (.142, .185, and .200, high to

low), but he hits well in his over-the-middle fastball locations (.333, .500, and .305, high to low).

LOW-OVER-THE-MIDDLE FASTBALLS
(THROWN BY LEFT-HANDED PITCHERS)

BATTING AVERAGE .305
Play

Left   Deep and shifted toward the left field line
Center   Deep in straightaway center field
Right   Deep in straightaway right field
Short   Shifted toward third base
Second   Normal position

His .500 against medium-high inside fastballs is based on a relatively low number of recorded instances (12) but is excellent nonetheless.

MEDIUM-HIGH INSIDE FASTBALLS
(THROWN BY LEFT-HANDED PITCHERS)

BATTING AVERAGE .500
Play

Left   Deep and shifted toward the left field line
Center   Medium-deep in straightaway center field
Right   Medium-deep and shifted toward center field
Short   *No instances recorded*
Second   Normal position

Parrish hits medium-high outside curves very well (.333) against left-handers. He has trouble with low curves and low sliders against lefties.

Ahead And Behind In The Count Vs. RH

Ahead

Fastball Average .333

	Inside	Middle	Outside
High	4/250 /1	20/300 /6	10/500 /5
Med	16/375 /6	15/400 /6	38/289 /11
Low	9/111 /1	26/423 /11	9/222 /2

Curve Average .304

	Inside	Middle	Outside
High	1/0 /0	1/1000 /1	2/0 /0
Med	0/0 /0	2/500 /1	8/375 /3
Low	1/0 /0	5/400 /2	3/0 /0

Behind

Fastball Average .257

	Inside	Middle	Outside
High	2/500 /1	4/250 /1	6/0 /0
Med	7/285 /2	8/250 /2	22/272 /6
Low	2/0 /0	11/363 /4	4/250 /1

Curve Average .240

	Inside	Middle	Outside
High	0/0 /0	3/0 /0	1/0 /0
Med	2/500 /1	5/400 /2	7/142 /1
Low	0/0 /0	2/500 /1	5/200 /1

Overall Evaluation

Against Right-Handed Pitchers

Overall Fastball ◯◯
Overall Curve ◯◯
Overall Slider ◯◯◯◯◯

Against Left-Handed Pitchers

Overall Fastball ◯◯
Overall Curve ◯◯
Overall Slider ◯◯

Comments: Weak against high, inside and outside fastballs vs. RH.
Strengths: Low-middle and medium-middle fastballs, medium-middle curves, over-the-middle and medium-outside sliders vs. RH; over-the-middle and medium-inside fastballs, medium-outside curves vs. LH.
Weaknesses: Fastballs except as above, inside, low, and outside curves, low-outside sliders vs. RH; outside fastballs and low curves vs. LH.

Johnny Ray (Switch Hitter) — *California Angels*

Johnny Ray Against Right-Handed Pitchers
Overall BARS Batting Average .317

	Fastball Average .334			Curve Average .298			Slider Average .191		
	Outside	Middle	Inside	Outside	Middle	Inside	Outside	Middle	Inside
High	26/192 /5	50/320 /16	32/375 /12	2/0 /0	2/1000 /2	1/0 /0	0/0 /0	0/0 /0	1/0 /0
Med	81/333 /27	23/304 /7	67/373 /25	8/125 /1	2/500 /1	13/307 /4	2/0 /0	0/0 /0	14/142 /2
Low	31/258 /8	66/348 /23	46/391 /18	9/0 /0	20/400 /8	10/400 /4	3/333 /1	10/200 /2	17/235 /4

Johnny Ray Against Left-Handed Pitchers
Overall BARS Batting Average .251

	Fastball Average .276			Curve Average .263			Slider Average .000		
	Inside	Middle	Outside	Inside	Middle	Outside	Inside	Middle	Outside
High	7/142 /1	9/222 /2	9/222 /2	0/0 /0	1/0 /0	1/1000 /1	1/0 /0	1/0 /0	0/0 /0
Med	14/500 /7	3/666 /2	48/333 /16	2/0 /0	0/0 /0	4/250 /1	1/0 /0	1/0 /0	2/0 /0
Low	12/83 /1	16/187 /3	16/187 /3	3/666 /2	7/0 /0	1/1000 /1	2/0 /0	4/0 /0	2/0 /0

Switch-hitting Johnny Ray hits fastballs excellently against right-handed pitchers (.334) but is only fair against left-handed pitchers (.276).

Looking first at his performance against right-handers, note how well he hits all inside, over-the-middle, and waist-high fastballs. He has only two weak fastball locations against right-handers (.192 high-outside and .258 low-outside).

He hits medium-high outside fastballs deep down the left line (his opposite field).

MEDIUM-HIGH OUTSIDE FASTBALLS

BATTING AVERAGE .333
Play

Left	Deep and shifted toward the left field line
Center	Medium-deep in straightaway center field
Right	Deep in straightaway right field
Short	Up middle (shifted toward second base)
Second	Normal position

He hits medium-high inside fastballs for an excellent .373 average. Notice that he also hits this pitch deep down the left line.

MEDIUM-HIGH INSIDE FASTBALLS

BATTING AVERAGE .360
Play

Left	Deep and shifted toward the left field line

Center	Short in straightaway center field
Right	Medium-deep in straightaway right field
Short	Up middle (shifted toward second base)
Second	Shifted toward first base

He hits very strongly against low-over-the-middle and low-inside fastballs. Again note that he hits both these pitches down the left line.

LOW-OVER-THE-MIDDLE FASTBALLS

BATTING AVERAGE .348
Play

Left	Deep and shifted toward the left field line
Center	Medium-deep in straightaway center field
Right	Deep in straightaway right field
Short	Normal position
Second	Normal position

LOW-INSIDE FASTBALLS

BATTING AVERAGE .391
Play

Left	Medium-deep and shifted toward the left field line
Center	Deep and shifted toward right field
Right	Deep in straightaway right field
Short	Normal position
Second	Shifted toward first base

Ray's .375 against high-inside fastballs is also top rate.

HIGH-INSIDE FASTBALLS

BATTING AVERAGE .375
Play
Left	Medium-deep and shifted toward the left line
Center	Deep in straightaway center field
Right	Deep in straightaway right field
Short	Normal position
Second	Normal position

Ray Against Curves And Sliders

Ray has a strong curve sector consisting of his low-inside, medium-high inside/medium-middle/low-over-the-middle curve locations. Right-handers want to stay away from this by throwing outside. He hits .400 against low-over-the-middle curves.

LOW-OVER-THE-MIDDLE CURVEBALLS

BATTING AVERAGE .400
Play
Left	Medium-deep and shifted toward the left field line
Center	Deep in straightaway center field
Right	Deep in straightaway right field
Short	Shifted toward third base
Second	Normal position

Ray has a reversed L-shaped sector of weakness in his slider chart consisting of the medium-high inside/low-inside/low-over-the-middle slider locations.

Ray Against Left-Handed Pitchers

Ray hits waist-high fastballs extremely well against left-handed pitchers, but he has trouble with low and high fastballs. These bands of strength and weakness serve as a clear guide for pitchers.

He hits medium-high outside fastballs at an excellent .333 clip.

MEDIUM-HIGH OUTSIDE FASTBALLS
(THROWN BY LEFT-HANDED PITCHERS)

BATTING AVERAGE .333
Play
Left	Medium-deep in straightaway left field
Center	Deep and shifted toward left field
Right	Medium-deep and shifted toward center field
Short	Up middle (shifted toward second base)
Second	Normal position

His .500 against medium-high inside fastballs is extremely good. If fielders aligned themselves as suggested by the BARS fielding strategy for this pitch, they could prevent most of his base hits resulting from pitches to this location. Notice that both the center and right fielders need to play medium-deep and the left fielder needs to play deep down the line.

MEDIUM-HIGH INSIDE FASTBALLS
(THROWN BY LEFT-HANDED PITCHERS)

BATTING AVERAGE .500
Play
Left	Deep and shifted toward the left field line
Center	Medium-deep in straightaway center field
Right	Medium-deep and shifted toward center field
Short	Shifted toward third base
Second	Normal position

Ahead And Behind In The Count Vs. RH

Ahead

Fastball Average .407

	Outside	Middle	Inside
High	11/454 /5	26/423 /11	13/307 /4
Med	37/432 /16	16/312 /5	38/421 /16
Low	12/333 /4	43/441 /19	25/400 /10

Curve Average .384

	Outside	Middle	Inside
High	0/0 /0	0/0 /0	0/0 /0
Med	2/500 /1	0/0 /0	3/666 /2
Low	0/0 /0	7/285 /2	1/0 /0

Behind

Fastball Average .322

	Outside	Middle	Inside
High	5/0 /0	6/166 /1	9/555 /5
Med	13/307 /4	2/500 /1	5/400 /2
Low	8/375 /3	7/142 /1	4/500 /2

Curve Average .250

	Outside	Middle	Inside
High	1/0 /0	2/1000 /2	0/0 /0
Med	3/0 /0	0/0 /0	5/400 /2
Low	6/0 /0	4/250 /1	3/333 /1

Overall Evaluation
Against Right-Handed Pitchers

Overall Fastball	⚾⚾⚾⚾
Overall Curve	⚾⚾⚾
Overall Slider	⚾

Against Left-Handed Pitchers

Overall Fastball	⚾⚾
Overall Curve	⚾⚾
Overall Slider	⚾

Comments: Excellent against fastballs vs. RH. **Strengths:** Fastballs vs. RH except high-outside and low-outside, low-middle, low-inside, and medium-inside curves vs. RH; all waist-high fastballs vs. LH. **Weaknesses:** High-outside and low-outside fastballs vs. RH, all outside curves and all inside sliders, low-middle sliders vs. RH; high and low fastballs, low-middle curves, sliders vs. LH.

Bill Schroeder (Right Handed)　　*California Angels*

Bill Schroeder Against Right-Handed Pitchers
Overall BARS Batting Average .256

Fastball Average .293

	Inside	Middle	Outside
High	4/ 0/0	1/ 0/0	3/ 0/0
Med	17/ 411/7	5/ 400/2	29/ 344/10
Low	2/ 0/0	8/ 250/2	6/ 166/1

Curve Average .166

	Inside	Middle	Outside
High	0/ 0/0	0/ 0/0	1/ 0/0
Med	0/ 0/0	3/ 666/2	7/ 142/1
Low	1/ 0/0	6/ 333/2	12/ 0/0

Slider Average .250

	Inside	Middle	Outside
High	0/ 0/0	0/ 0/0	1/ 0/0
Med	0/ 0/0	2/ 500/1	9/ 333/3
Low	0/ 0/0	2/ 0/0	14/ 214/3

Bill Schroeder Against Left-Handed Pitchers
Overall BARS Batting Average .302

Fastball Average .339

	Inside	Middle	Outside
High	2/ 500/1	2/ 0/0	3/ 333/1
Med	8/ 125/1	0/ 0/0	20/ 450/9
Low	2/ 0/0	9/ 555/5	10/ 200/2

Curve Average .250

	Inside	Middle	Outside
High	0/ 0/0	0/ 0/0	1/ 0/0
Med	1/ 0/0	0/ 0/0	5/ 600/3
Low	1/ 0/0	5/ 200/1	3/ 0/0

Slider Average .214

	Inside	Middle	Outside
High	1/ 1000/1	0/ 0/0	0/ 0/0
Med	3/ 333/1	0/ 0/0	2/ 0/0
Low	3/ 0/0	1/ 0/0	4/ 250/1

Right-handed hitter Bill Schroeder hits very well against fastballs thrown by right-handed pitchers (.293) and excellently against fastballs thrown by left-handed pitchers (.339). But he has trouble with curves and sliders against both.

Starting with his performance against right-handers, notice his strength against all waist-high fastballs (.411, .400, and .344, inside to outside). This is the key to his strength since he has trouble with high and low fastballs.

He hits medium-high outside fastballs deep to all fields.

MEDIUM-HIGH OUTSIDE FASTBALLS

BATTING AVERAGE .344
Play

Left	Deep in straightaway left field
Center	Deep in straightaway center field
Right	Deep and shifted toward center field
Short	Normal position
Second	Shifted toward first base

He hits medium-high inside fastballs much differently than he hits medium-high outside fastballs. Both the center and right fielder need to shift to be positioned correctly.

MEDIUM-HIGH INSIDE FASTBALLS

BATTING AVERAGE .411
Play

Left	Deep in straightaway left field
Center	Medium-deep and shifted toward left field
Right	Deep and shifted toward the right field line
Short	Normal position
Second	*No instances recorded*

Schroeder Against Curves And Sliders

Schroeder has trouble overall with curves thrown by right-handed pitchers. He is especially weak against medium-high outside (.142) and low-outside curves (.000 on 0 for 12).

He has trouble getting his bat on low-outside curves. There are few recorded instances of hit balls; he strikes out a lot on this pitch.

LOW-OUTSIDE CURVEBALLS

BATTING AVERAGE .000 (0 for 12)
Play

Left	*No instances recorded*
Center	*No instances recorded*
Right	*No instances recorded*
Short	Normal position
Second	*No instances recorded*

He has trouble with low-outside sliders (.214) but hits medium-high outside sliders excellently (.333). If fielders aligned themselves properly for medium-high outside sliders they would prevent most of his base hits from this location.

MEDIUM-HIGH OUTSIDE SLIDERS

BATTING AVERAGE .333
Play
Left	Deep in straightaway left field
Center	Medium-deep in straightaway center field
Right	Deep and shifted toward center field
Short	Up middle (shifted toward second base)
Second	*No instances recorded*

Schroeder Against Left-Handed Pitchers

Schroeder has some weak fastball locations, but overall he hits fastballs excellently against left-handed pitchers. He hits a solid .450 against medium-high outside fastballs.

MEDIUM-HIGH OUTSIDE FASTBALLS
(THROWN BY LEFT-HANDED PITCHERS)

BATTING AVERAGE .450
Play
Left	Deep and shifted toward the left field line
Center	Medium-deep in straightaway center field
Right	Deep in straightaway right field
Short	Normal position
Second	*No instances recorded*

His .555 against low-over-the-middle fastballs is extremely high. He pulls this pitch to the outfield. But note that the shortstop needs to play shifted toward second.

LOW-OVER-THE-MIDDLE FASTBALLS

BATTING AVERAGE .555
Play
Left	Deep and shifted toward the left field line
Center	Deep and shifted toward left field
Right	Medium-deep and shifted toward center field
Short	Up middle (shifted toward second base)
Second	Normal position

He hits .200 against low-outside fastballs thrown by left-handers. Most of the hit balls from this location are probably easy flies or easy grounders.

LOW-OUTSIDE FASTBALLS
(THROWN BY LEFT-HANDED PITCHERS)

BATTING AVERAGE .200
Play
Left	Deep and shifted toward the left field line
Center	Medium-deep in straightaway center field
Right	Medium-deep in straightaway right field
Short	*No instances recorded*
Second	Shifted toward first base

Schroeder hits medium-high outside curves well (.600) but he has trouble in his other curve locations against left-handers.

Ahead And Behind In The Count Vs. RH

Ahead

	Fastball Average .484			Curve Average .000		
	Inside	Middle	Outside	Inside	Middle	Outside
High	1/0 /0	0/0 /0	1/0 /0	0/0 /0	0/0 /0	1/0 /0
Med	6/666 /4	2/1000 /2	17/470 /8	0/0 /0	0/0 /0	0/0 /0
Low	0/0 /0	6/333 /2	0/0 /0	0/0 /0	1/0 /0	1/0 /0

Behind

	Fastball Average .416			Curve Average .250		
	Inside	Middle	Outside	Inside	Middle	Outside
High	0/0 /0	0/0 /0	0/0 /0	0/0 /0	0/0 /0	0/0 /0
Med	5/600 /3	1/0 /0	4/250 /1	0/0 /0	1/0 /0	3/0 /0
Low	0/0 /0	1/0 /0	1/1000 /1	0/0 /0	3/666 /2	1/0 /0

Overall Evaluation
Against Right-Handed Pitchers

Overall Fastball ⚾⚾ ⚾⚾

Overall Curve ⚾⚾

Overall Slider ⚾⚾ ⚾⚾

Against Left-Handed Pitchers

Overall Fastball ⚾⚾ ⚾⚾ ⚾⚾ ⚾⚾

Overall Curve ⚾⚾ ⚾⚾

Overall Slider ⚾⚾

Comments: Strong against medium-outside fastballs vs. both RH and LH.
Strengths: Waist-high fastballs, medium-outside sliders vs. RH; medium-outside and low-middle fastballs vs. LH.
Weaknesses: Low fastballs, outside curves, and low-outside sliders vs. RH; medium-inside and low-outside fastballs vs. LH.

Dick Schofield (Right Handed) *California Angels*

Dick Schofield Against Right-Handed Pitchers
Overall BARS Batting Average .194

	Fastball Average .240			Curve Average .155			Slider Average .150		
	Inside	Middle	Outside	Inside	Middle	Outside	Inside	Middle	Outside
High	17/176/3	19/157/3	7/285/2	1/0/0	5/400/2	3/0/0	2/0/0	2/500/1	2/0/0
Med	46/173/8	9/222/2	66/287/19	5/200/1	1/0/0	15/200/3	4/500/2	6/0/0	25/200/5
Low	27/370/10	36/361/13	39/102/4	2/0/0	7/0/0	19/157/3	6/333/2	7/142/1	26/38/1

Dick Schofield Against Left-Handed Pitchers
Overall BARS Batting Average .246

	Fastball Average .257			Curve Average .190			Slider Average .230		
	Inside	Middle	Outside	Inside	Middle	Outside	Inside	Middle	Outside
High	4/0/0	8/250/2	8/375/3	0/0/0	5/400/2	1/0/0	1/0/0	1/0/0	0/0/0
Med	12/166/2	6/333/2	49/224/11	2/0/0	1/0/0	2/0/0	5/400/2	1/1000/1	3/333/1
Low	5/200/1	20/300/6	16/375/6	1/0/0	7/285/2	2/0/0	6/166/1	5/0/0	4/250/1

Right-handed hitter Dick Schofield has weak overall BARS averages against both right- and left-handed pitchers. His fastball average of .240 against right-handers is very weak. His .257 against fastballs thrown by left-handers is better, but is still poor.

Against right-handers, Schofield has trouble with high-inside and high-over-the-middle fastballs, medium-high inside fastballs, and low-outside fastballs. By concentrating on these locations pitchers can gain an advantage.

Schofield hits .287 against medium-high outside fastballs. He hits this pitch short to left center and straightaway to center and right fields. If the fielders positioned themselves as suggested by the BARS System fielding strategy, they could prevent most of his base hits resulting from pitches to this location.

MEDIUM-HIGH OUTSIDE FASTBALLS

BATTING AVERAGE .287
Play

Left	Short and shifted toward center field
Center	Deep in straightaway center field
Right	Medium-deep in straightaway right field
Short	Up middle (shifted toward second base)
Second	Normal position

Schofield hits low-outside fastballs very poorly (.102) but he hits low-over-the-middle (.361) and low-inside fastballs (.370) excellently. These are his two best fastball locations against right-handers.

LOW-OVER-THE-MIDDLE FASTBALLS

BATTING AVERAGE .361
Play

Left	Medium-deep in straightaway left field
Center	Deep in straightaway center field
Right	Deep and shifted toward the right field line
Short	Shifted toward third base
Second	Normal position

LOW-INSIDE FASTBALLS

BATTING AVERAGE .370
Play

Left	Deep and shifted toward the left field line
Center	Medium-deep in straightaway center field
Right	Deep in straightaway right field
Short	Shifted toward third base
Second	*No instances recorded*

Schofield Against Curves And Sliders

Schofield has trouble with all outside curves and outside sliders. He hits .157 against low-outside curves and .038 against low-outside sliders.

LOW-OUTSIDE CURVEBALLS

BATTING AVERAGE .157
Play

Left	Medium-deep in straightaway left field
Center	Deep in straightaway center field
Right	Deep in straightaway right field
Short	Normal position
Second	*No instances recorded*

LOW-OUTSIDE SLIDERS

BATTING AVERAGE .038
Play

Left	*No instances recorded*
Center	Deep and shifted toward right field
Right	Deep in straightaway right field
Short	Normal position
Second	Normal position

He hits .200 against medium-high outside sliders. He scatters this pitch to all fields, but his low average indicates that most of his hit balls are probably easy outs.

MEDIUM-HIGH OUTSIDE SLIDERS

BATTING AVERAGE .200
Play

Left	Deep and shifted toward the left field line
Center	Medium-deep in straightaway center field
Right	Deep and shifted toward the right field line
Short	Up middle (shifted toward second base)
Second	Shifted toward first base

Schofield Against Left-Handed Pitchers

Schofield hits fastballs a little better against left-handed pitchers. He hits .224 against medium-high outside fastball. His low average in this highly pitched location brings down his overall average against left-handers.

MEDIUM-HIGH OUTSIDE FASTBALLS
(THROWN BY LEFT-HANDED PITCHERS)

BATTING AVERAGE .224
Play

Left	Deep in straightaway left field
Center	Deep in straightaway center field
Right	Deep and shifted toward center field
Short	Up middle (shifted toward second base)
Second	Shifted toward first base

His .375 against low-outside fastballs thrown by left-handers is excellent. Notice that he hits this pitch medium-deep to all fields. By adjusting as suggested by this BARS strategy, fielders could prevent most of the base hits resulting from pitches to this location.

LOW-OUTSIDE FASTBALLS
(THROWN BY LEFT-HANDED PITCHERS)

BATTING AVERAGE .375
Play

Left	Medium-deep in straightaway left field
Center	Medium-deep and shifted toward left field
Right	Medium-deep in straightaway right field
Short	Up middle (shifted toward second base)
Second	Normal position

Schofield has trouble with inside fastballs thrown by left-handers. His .166 against medium-high inside fastballs and .200 against low-inside fastballs give targets to pitchers.

Ahead And Behind In The Count Vs. RH

Ahead

	Fastball Average .252			Curve Average .000		
	Inside	Middle	Outside	Inside	Middle	Outside
High	8/250/2	8/0/0	1/0/0	1/0/0	0/0/0	1/0/0
Med	25/240/6	3/333/1	21/285/6	1/0/0	0/0/0	3/0/0
Low	10/400/4	19/421/8	20/100/2	0/0/0	0/0/0	1/0/0

Behind

	Fastball Average .242			Curve Average .294		
	Inside	Middle	Outside	Inside	Middle	Outside
High	2/0/0	2/0/0	2/500/1	0/0/0	1/1000/1	2/0/0
Med	7/142/1	1/0/0	10/500/5	1/0/0	1/0/0	6/500/3
Low	3/333/1	2/0/0	4/0/0	0/0/0	2/0/0	4/250/1

Overall Evaluation
Against Right-Handed Pitchers

Overall Fastball	⚾⚾
Overall Curve	⚾⚾
Overall Slider	⚾⚾

Against Left-Handed Pitchers

Overall Fastball	⚾⚾
Overall Curve	⚾⚾
Overall Slider	⚾⚾

Comments: Has a strong fastball sector vs. RH consisting of low-inside/low-middle.
Strengths: Low-middle and low-inside fastballs vs. RH; low-middle, low-outside and high-outside fastballs vs. LH.
Weaknesses: High-inside, high-middle, medium-inside, medium-middle and low-outside fastballs, curves in general, outside sliders vs. RH; inside fastballs, medium-outside fastballs vs. LH.

Claudell Washington (LH)   *California Angels*

Claudell Washington Against Right-Handed Pitchers
Overall BARS Batting Average .294

Fastball Average .328

	Outside	Middle	Inside
High	32/281 /9	37/378 /14	29/344 /10
Med	139/302 /42	40/450 /18	94/351 /33
Low	50/260 /13	103/330 /34	122/319 /39

Curve Average .212

	Outside	Middle	Inside
High	4/0 /0	9/111 /1	3/333 /1
Med	22/272 /6	17/235 /4	20/300 /6
Low	30/100 /3	43/232 /10	45/222 /10

Slider Average .243

	Outside	Middle	Inside
High	0/0 /0	5/600 /3	8/375 /3
Med	7/142 /1	3/0 /0	23/347 /8
Low	14/285 /4	16/375 /6	43/93 /4

Claudell Washington Against Left-Handed Pitchers
Overall BARS Batting Average .273

Fastball Average .292

	Outside	Middle	Inside
High	6/0 /0	8/375 /3	9/222 /2
Med	28/250 /7	10/300 /3	30/466 /14
Low	10/200 /2	17/411 /7	22/136 /3

Curve Average .187

	Outside	Middle	Inside
High	0/0 /0	2/0 /0	4/250 /1
Med	9/333 /3	5/400 /2	8/125 /1
Low	17/58 /1	10/300 /3	9/111 /1

Slider Average .370

	Outside	Middle	Inside
High	0/0 /0	0/0 /0	0/0 /0
Med	2/0 /0	3/1000 /3	2/0 /0
Low	9/111 /1	9/666 /6	2/0 /0

Against right-handed pitchers, left-handed hitting Claudell Washington hits excellently against fastballs but very poorly against curves. His weakness against curves brings his overall averages down against both right- and left-handed pitchers.

Washington hits medium-high outside fastballs deep against right-handers, but if outfielders played him to hit all pitches deep, they would be badly out of position for medium-high *inside* fastballs.

MEDIUM-HIGH OUTSIDE FASTBALLS

BATTING AVERAGE .302
Play
Left	Deep in straightaway left field
Center	Deep in straightaway center field
Right	Deep in straightaway right field
Short	Up middle (shifted toward second base)
Second	Shifted toward first base

MEDIUM-HIGH INSIDE FASTBALLS

BATTING AVERAGE .351
Play
Left	Medium-deep and shifted toward the left field line
Center	Medium-deep in straightaway center field
Right	Deep and shifted toward the right field line
Short	Up middle (shifted toward second base)
Second	Shifted toward first base

Washington Against Curves And Sliders

Washington has trouble with low curves against right-handed pitchers (.100, .232 and .222, outside to inside). Most pitchers throw curves low to him, and they're right to do so. He hits medium-inside curves at a .300 clip. If left-fielders would play him short and toward the line for this pitch they could catch most of his line drives that fall in for base hits.

MEDIUM-HIGH INSIDE CURVEBALLS

BATTING AVERAGE .300
Play
Left	Short and shifted toward the left field line
Center	Deep in straightaway center field
Right	Deep in straightaway right field
Short	Normal position
Second	Shifted toward first base

Washington hits medium-high inside sliders for a strong .347 average.

MEDIUM-HIGH INSIDE SLIDERS

BATTING AVERAGE .347
Play
Left	Medium-deep in straightaway left field
Center	Short and shifted toward left field

Right	Deep in straightaway right field
Short	Up middle (shifted toward second base)
Second	Normal position

Washington Ahead And Behind In The Count

Washington's fastball average against right-handers is significantly higher when he is ahead in the count (.401 when ahead, .239 when behind). He is thrown a lot of low-inside fastballs by right-handers. His average is almost 400 points higher in this location when he is ahead than when he is behind.

**LOW-INSIDE FASTBALLS
(WHEN AHEAD IN THE COUNT)**

BATTING AVERAGE .450
Play

Left	Deep and shifted toward the left field line
Center	Medium-deep in straightaway center field
Right	Medium-deep in straightaway right field
Short	Up middle (shifted toward second base)
Second	Normal position

**LOW-INSIDE FASTBALLS
(WHEN BEHIND IN THE COUNT)**

BATTING AVERAGE .058
Play

Left	Deep and shifted toward the left field line
Center	Deep and shifted toward left field
Right	Deep in straightaway right field
Short	Normal position
Second	Normal position

When behind in the count, it seems that Washington hits low-inside fastballs mostly for easy fly-ball outs, while hitting the ball with great authority when ahead in the count.

This means that it is very important for fielders to follow the above strategy when Washington is ahead. When behind, he probably hits a lot of lazy flies that fielders can get to even if they are out of position.

Washington Against Left-Handed Pitchers

Washington's .292 overall fastball average against left-handers is pretty good for a left-handed hitter. Against lefties he hits medium-high inside fastballs exceptionally well (.466). Left-handers should avoid throwing him this pitch. He hits medium-high outside fastballs poorly (.250), as he does low-outside (.200) and low-inside fastballs (.136).

He has a lot of trouble with low-outside curves (.058), but he hits medium-high outside curves (.333) and low-over-the-middle curves (.300) excellently.

**MEDIUM-HIGH OUTSIDE FASTBALLS
(THROWN BY LEFT-HANDED PITCHERS)**

BATTING AVERAGE .333
Play

Left	Medium-deep and shifted toward the left field line
Center	Medium-deep in straightaway center field
Right	Deep and shifted toward the right field line
Short	Up middle (shifted toward second base)
Second	Normal position

Ahead And Behind In The Count Vs. RH

Ahead

Fastball Average .401

	Outside	Middle	Inside
High	6 / 666 / 4	15 / 533 / 8	15 / 466 / 7
Med	70 / 371 / 26	22 / 363 / 8	52 / 384 / 20
Low	21 / 380 / 8	47 / 319 / 15	71 / 450 / 32

Curve Average .333

	Outside	Middle	Inside
High	1 / 0 / 0	4 / 250 / 1	2 / 500 / 1
Med	6 / 666 / 4	5 / 400 / 2	3 / 333 / 1
Low	5 / 0 / 0	14 / 285 / 4	8 / 375 / 3

Behind

Fastball Average .239

	Outside	Middle	Inside
High	5 / 200 / 1	5 / 200 / 1	3 / 333 / 1
Med	23 / 347 / 8	4 / 750 / 3	7 / 142 / 1
Low	10 / 300 / 3	18 / 166 / 3	17 / 58 / 1

Curve Average .222

	Outside	Middle	Inside
High	0 / 0 / 0	1 / 0 / 0	1 / 0 / 0
Med	5 / 400 / 2	7 / 142 / 1	6 / 333 / 2
Low	9 / 111 / 1	15 / 133 / 2	10 / 400 / 4

Overall Evaluation

Against Right-Handed Pitchers

Overall Fastball	⚾ ⚾ ⚾ ⚾
Overall Curve	⚾
Overall Slider	⚾

Against Left-Handed Pitchers

Overall Fastball	⚾ ⚾
Overall Curve	⚾
Overall Slider	⚾ ⚾ ⚾ ⚾

Comments: Washington hits fastballs well vs. RH.
Strengths: Fastballs vs. RH, medium-inside curves and sliders, low-middle sliders vs. RH; medium-inside and all over-the-middle fastballs, low-middle curves and low-middle sliders vs. LH.
Weaknesses: Low-outside fastballs, low curves, high-middle curves, low-inside sliders vs. RH; outside and low-inside fastballs, low-outside and low-inside curves, low-outside sliders vs. LH.

Devon White (Switch Hitter) — *California Angels*

Devon White Against Right-Handed Pitchers
Overall BARS Batting Average .279

Fastball Average .293

	Outside	Middle	Inside
High	13 / 230 / 3	6 / 666 / 4	10 / 300 / 3
Med	51 / 274 / 14	6 / 500 / 3	23 / 260 / 6
Low	15 / 133 / 2	25 / 320 / 8	11 / 363 / 4

Curve Average .206

	Outside	Middle	Inside
High	1 / 0 / 0	0 / 0 / 0	2 / 0 / 0
Med	8 / 250 / 2	2 / 500 / 1	4 / 0 / 0
Low	5 / 400 / 2	1 / 0 / 0	6 / 166 / 1

Slider Average .250

	Outside	Middle	Inside
High	0 / 0 / 0	0 / 0 / 0	2 / 0 / 0
Med	2 / 1000 / 2	1 / 0 / 0	2 / 500 / 1
Low	2 / 500 / 1	2 / 0 / 0	5 / 0 / 0

Devon White Against Left-Handed Pitchers
Overall BARS Batting Average .226

Fastball Average .258

	Inside	Middle	Outside
High	3 / 333 / 1	1 / 1000 / 1	4 / 250 / 1
Med	8 / 500 / 4	3 / 333 / 1	22 / 227 / 5
Low	5 / 200 / 1	11 / 90 / 1	5 / 200 / 1

Curve Average .125

	Inside	Middle	Outside
High	0 / 0 / 0	0 / 0 / 0	0 / 0 / 0
Med	0 / 0 / 0	1 / 1000 / 1	2 / 0 / 0
Low	2 / 0 / 0	3 / 0 / 0	0 / 0 / 0

Slider Average .142

	Inside	Middle	Outside
High	3 / 333 / 1	0 / 0 / 0	0 / 0 / 0
Med	3 / 333 / 1	0 / 0 / 0	0 / 0 / 0
Low	4 / 0 / 0	1 / 0 / 0	3 / 0 / 0

Switch-hitting Devon White has low BARS averages against both right- and left-handed hitters. Nonetheless, he hits .293 overall against fastballs thrown by right-handers.

He hits medium-high outside fastballs very well when ahead in the count (.380 when ahead, .250 when behind). When ahead, he hits this pitch deep to all fields and pulls the ball more than when behind.

MEDIUM-HIGH OUTSIDE FASTBALLS (WHEN AHEAD IN THE COUNT)

BATTING AVERAGE .380

Play

Left	Deep in straightaway left field
Center	Deep and shifted toward right field
Right	Deep in straightaway right field
Short	Up middle (shifted toward second base)
Second	Normal position

MEDIUM-HIGH OUTSIDE FASTBALLS (WHEN BEHIND IN THE COUNT)

BATTING AVERAGE .250

Play

Left	Medium-deep and shifted toward the left field line
Center	Medium-deep and shifted toward left field
Right	Deep in straightaway right field
Short	Normal position
Second	*No instances recorded*

His .320 against low-over-the-middle fastballs is very good. He goes to his opposite field (left field) with this pitch.

LOW-OVER-THE-MIDDLE FASTBALLS

BATTING AVERAGE .320

Play

Left	Deep and shifted toward the left field line
Center	Deep in straightaway center field
Right	Medium-deep in straightaway right field
Short	Normal position
Second	Normal position

He also hits low-inside fastballs very well (.363). Again, he goes down the left line with this pitch. If fielders adjusted properly, they could prevent most of his base hits when this pitch is thrown.

LOW-INSIDE FASTBALLS

BATTING AVERAGE .363

Play

Left	Short and shifted toward the left field line
Center	Deep and shifted toward right field
Right	Deep in straightaway right field
Short	Shifted toward third base
Second	Normal position

He hits high-inside fastballs medium-deep to the opposite field for a .300 average.

HIGH-INSIDE FASTBALLS

BATTING AVERAGE .300
Play

Left	Medium-deep and shifted toward the left field line
Center	Medium-deep and shifted toward left field
Right	Medium-deep and shifted toward center field
Short	*No instances recorded*
Second	Normal position

His .230 against high-outside fastballs indicates a weakness.

HIGH-OUTSIDE FASTBALLS

BATTING AVERAGE .230
Play

Left	Deep and shifted toward the left field line
Center	Deep in straightaway center field
Right	Deep and shifted toward center field
Short	Shifted toward third base
Second	*No instances recorded*

He hits medium-high inside fastballs more toward center field when he hits to the outfield and to the right side of the infield when he hits grounders. His average in this location is .260.

MEDIUM-HIGH INSIDE FASTBALLS

BATTING AVERAGE .260
Play

Left	Deep and shifted toward center field
Center	Medium-deep in straightaway center field
Right	Deep and shifted toward center field
Short	*No instances recorded*
Second	Shifted toward first base

White has few recorded curves and sliders against right-handed pitchers. Considering that he hits fastballs well overall, right-handers should consider throwing him more breaking pitches.

White Against Left-Handed Pitchers

Fewer instances have been recorded for White against left-handed pitchers, but it is evident that he has trouble with all outside and low fastballs.

His .227 against medium-high outside fastballs is weak.

MEDIUM-HIGH OUTSIDE FASTBALLS
(THROWN BY LEFT-HANDED PITCHERS)

BATTING AVERAGE .227
Play

Left	Deep and shifted toward the left field line
Center	Deep in straightaway center field
Right	Deep in straightaway right field
Short	Normal position
Second	Normal position

His .500 against medium-high inside fastballs is excellent.

MEDIUM-HIGH INSIDE FASTBALLS
(THROWN BY LEFT-HANDED PITCHERS)

BATTING AVERAGE .500
Play

Left	Short and shifted toward center field
Center	Medium-deep and shifted toward right field
Right	Deep and shifted toward the right field line
Short	Shifted toward third base
Second	*No instances recorded*

Ahead And Behind In The Count Vs. RH

Ahead

Fastball Average .320

	Outside	Middle	Inside
High	6/ 500 /3	0/ 0 /0	4/ 0 /0
Med	21/ 380 /8	4/ 750 /3	10/ 200 /2
Low	8/ 125 /1	16/ 250 /4	6/ 500 /3

Curve Average 1.000

	Outside	Middle	Inside
High	0/ 0 /0	0/ 0 /0	0/ 0 /0
Med	1/ 1000 /1	0/ 0 /0	0/ 0 /0
Low	0/ 0 /0	0/ 0 /0	0/ 0 /0

Behind

Fastball Average .379

	Outside	Middle	Inside
High	0/ 0 /0	3/ 1000 /3	2/ 1000 /2
Med	12/ 250 /3	0/ 0 /0	5/ 400 /2
Low	2/ 0 /0	1/ 0 /0	4/ 250 /1

Curve Average .100

	Outside	Middle	Inside
High	0/ 0 /0	0/ 0 /0	1/ 0 /0
Med	4/ 0 /0	0/ 0 /0	3/ 0 /0
Low	1/ 1000 /1	1/ 0 /0	0/ 0 /0

Overall Evaluation

Against Right-Handed Pitchers

Overall Fastball	⚾⚾ ⚾⚾
Overall Curve	⚾⚾
Overall Slider	⚾⚾ ⚾⚾

Against Left-Handed Pitchers

Overall Fastball	⚾⚾
Overall Curve	Not enough information
Overall Slider	⚾⚾

Comments: Strong against over-the-middle fastballs and low-inside fastballs vs. RH.
Strengths: Fastballs as above vs. RH; medium-inside fastballs vs. LH.
Weaknesses: Outside fastballs, medium-inside fastballs, inside curves vs. RH; low fastballs and outside fastballs vs. LH.

Boston, Daryl
Calderon, Ivan
Fisk, Carlton
Fletcher, Scott
Gallagher, Dave
Guillen, Ozzie
Johnson, Lance
Karcovice, Ron
Kittle, Ron
Lyons, Steve
Pasqua, Dan
Walker, Greg

Chicago White Sox
BARS System
Hitting Analysis

Daryl Boston (Left Handed) — *Chicago White Sox*

Daryl Boston Against Right-Handed Pitchers
Overall BARS Batting Average .274

Fastball Average .274

	Outside	Middle	Inside
High	26 / 153 / 4	19 / 263 / 5	12 / 250 / 3
Med	93 / 311 / 29	14 / 357 / 5	37 / 189 / 7
Low	25 / 320 / 8	34 / 411 / 14	17 / 58 / 1

Curve Average .333

	Outside	Middle	Inside
High	5 / 400 / 2	2 / 500 / 1	4 / 250 / 1
Med	4 / 750 / 3	4 / 500 / 2	5 / 200 / 1
Low	5 / 200 / 1	10 / 300 / 3	3 / 0 / 0

Slider Average .205

	Outside	Middle	Inside
High	4 / 0 / 0	1 / 1000 / 1	2 / 0 / 0
Med	5 / 200 / 1	1 / 1000 / 1	8 / 250 / 2
Low	1 / 0 / 0	5 / 400 / 2	12 / 83 / 1

Daryl Boston Against Left-Handed Pitchers
Overall BARS Batting Average .258

Fastball Average .333

	Outside	Middle	Inside
High	1 / 0 / 0	1 / 0 / 0	5 / 400 / 2
Med	19 / 421 / 8	1 / 0 / 0	8 / 500 / 4
Low	1 / 0 / 0	2 / 0 / 0	7 / 142 / 1

Curve Average .100

	Outside	Middle	Inside
High	0 / 0 / 0	1 / 0 / 0	0 / 0 / 0
Med	7 / 0 / 0	2 / 0 / 0	3 / 333 / 1
Low	3 / 0 / 0	4 / 250 / 1	0 / 0 / 0

Slider Average .250

	Outside	Middle	Inside
High	1 / 1000 / 1	0 / 0 / 0	0 / 0 / 0
Med	7 / 428 / 3	0 / 0 / 0	0 / 0 / 0
Low	7 / 142 / 1	4 / 0 / 0	1 / 0 / 0

Daryl Boston, left-handed hitter, has more trouble with fastballs when facing right-handers (274 overall fastball vs. right-handers, .333 overall fastball vs. left-handers). This is somewhat unusual for a left-handed hitter. He does, however, hit curves better overall against right-handed pitchers.

Looking at his fastball chart against right-handed pitchers, notice that he has some very strong and some very weak locations. His averages against inside fastballs and high fastballs are poor. But his .411 against low-over-the-middle fastballs is excellent. He hits this pitch deep to left and medium-deep to center and right.

LOW-OVER-THE-MIDDLE FASTBALLS

BATTING AVERAGE .411

Play

Left	Deep in straightaway left field
Center	Medium-deep in straightaway center field
Right	Medium-deep in straightaway right field
Short	Up middle (shifted toward second base)
Second	Normal position

Boston hits medium-high outside fastballs for a fine .311 average, sending the ball deep and straightaway to the outfield. Note, however, that the infielders need to play shifted to the right side.

MEDIUM-HIGH OUTSIDE FASTBALLS

BATTING AVERAGE .311

Play

Left	Deep in straightaway left field
Center	Deep in straightaway center field
Right	Deep in straightaway right field
Short	Up middle (shifted toward second base)
Second	Shifted toward first base

Boston's .320 against low-outside fastballs is very good. He goes to his opposite field (left field) with this pitch. There are no recorded instances of hit balls to right.

LOW-OUTSIDE FASTBALLS

BATTING AVERAGE .320

Play

Left	Medium-deep and shifted toward the left line
Center	Deep and shifted toward left field
Right	*No instances recorded*
Short	Shifted toward third base
Second	Normal position

Boston's weak inside averages offer targets for pitchers. He hits medium-high inside fastballs for a low .189 average. Most of the hit balls shown in his fielding strategy for this pitch are probably easy fly balls or grounders.

MEDIUM-HIGH INSIDE FASTBALLS

BATTING AVERAGE .189
Play

Left	Short and shifted toward center field
Center	Deep and shifted toward right field
Right	Deep in straightaway right field
Short	Up middle (shifted toward second base)
Second	Shifted toward first base

Boston hits curves excellently overall against right-handed pitchers (.333). He hits low-over-the-middle curves for a .300 average.

LOW-OVER-THE-MIDDLE CURVEBALLS

BATTING AVERAGE .300
Play

Left	Deep and shifted toward center field
Center	Medium-deep in straightaway center field
Right	Deep in straightaway right field
Short	Up middle (shifted toward second base)
Second	Normal position

He has significant problems with sliders thrown by right-handers. His low-outside and medium-high outside slider averages are weak (.083 and .250).

Boston Against Left-Handed Pitchers

The BARS System has less information for Boston against left-handed pitchers, but there is enough to determine trends.

He hits fastballs well overall against left-handers (.333). Note especially his .421 against medium-high outside fastballs and his .500 against medium-high inside fastballs. Every outfielder needs to shift to be in proper position for both pitches. This illustrates how important it is for fielders to adjust for every pitch to a batter. If they don't, they could be badly out of position.

MEDIUM-HIGH OUTSIDE FASTBALLS (THROWN BY LEFT-HANDED PITCHERS)

BATTING AVERAGE .421
Play

Left	Deep in straightaway left field
Center	Deep in straightaway center field
Right	Deep and shifted toward center field
Short	Normal position
Second	Normal position

MEDIUM-HIGH INSIDE FASTBALLS (THROWN BY LEFT-HANDED PITCHERS)

BATTING AVERAGE .500
Play

Left	Short and shifted toward the left field line
Center	Medium-deep in straightaway center field
Right	Medium-deep and shifted toward center field
Short	Normal position
Second	Shifted toward first base

Boston has trouble with outside curves and with low-outside sliders against left-handers. He does hit medium-high outside sliders very well (.428).

Ahead And Behind In The Count Vs. RH

Ahead

Fastball Average .309   Curve Average .461

	Outside	Middle	Inside		Outside	Middle	Inside
High	12/166 /2	9/333 /3	7/285 /2		2/500 /1	2/500 /1	1/0 /0
Med	36/388 /14	8/500 /4	15/200 /3		2/1000 /2	2/500 /1	3/0 /0
Low	9/333 /3	20/400 /8	10/0 /0		0/0 /0	1/1000 /1	0/0 /0

Behind

Fastball Average .333   Curve Average .312

	Outside	Middle	Inside		Outside	Middle	Inside
High	3/0 /0	3/333 /1	3/333 /1		3/333 /1	0/0 /0	1/0 /0
Med	20/350 /7	3/333 /1	11/181 /2		2/500 /1	1/1000 /1	0/0 /0
Low	5/600 /3	5/600 /3	1/0 /0		3/333 /1	5/200 /1	1/0 /0

Overall Evaluation
Against Right-Handed Pitchers

Overall Fastball ⚾⚾

Overall Curve ⚾⚾ ⚾⚾ ⚾⚾ ⚾⚾

Overall Slider ⚾⚾

Against Left-Handed Pitchers

Overall Fastball ⚾⚾ ⚾⚾ ⚾⚾

Overall Curve ⚾⚾

Overall Slider ⚾⚾ ⚾⚾

Comments: Has a strong fastball sector vs. RH low-outside/medium-outside/medium-middle/low-middle.
Strengths: Fastballs as above, low-middle curves vs. RH; medium-outside and medium-inside fastballs, medium-outside sliders vs. LH.
Weaknesses: All high and inside fastballs, inside sliders vs. RH; low-inside fastballs, outside curves, low-outside sliders vs. LH.

Ivan Calderon (Right Handed) — *Chicago White Sox*

Ivan Calderon Against Right-Handed Pitchers
Overall BARS Batting Average .291

Fastball Average .289

	Inside	Middle	Outside
High	7/142/1	8/125/1	18/111/2
Med	30/266/8	4/250/1	87/367/32
Low	5/200/1	22/409/9	23/173/4

Curve Average .250

	Inside	Middle	Outside
High	1/0/0	2/1000/2	3/333/1
Med	6/333/2	4/250/1	24/291/7
Low	1/0/0	6/333/2	13/0/0

Slider Average .354

	Inside	Middle	Outside
High	2/500/1	1/1000/1	1/1000/1
Med	2/500/1	3/666/2	15/400/6
Low	1/0/0	4/250/1	19/210/4

Ivan Calderon Against Left-Handed Pitchers
Overall BARS Batting Average .229

Fastball Average .234

	Inside	Middle	Outside
High	4/0/0	8/125/1	7/0/0
Med	17/352/6	2/500/1	32/281/9
Low	6/333/2	7/142/1	11/181/2

Curve Average .260

	Inside	Middle	Outside
High	0/0/0	0/0/0	1/0/0
Med	3/666/2	1/1000/1	8/125/1
Low	3/0/0	2/1000/2	5/0/0

Slider Average .117

	Inside	Middle	Outside
High	1/0/0	0/0/0	0/0/0
Med	3/0/0	0/0/0	3/333/1
Low	3/0/0	4/250/1	3/0/0

Right-handed hitting Ivan Calderon hits fastballs much better against right-handed than against left-handed pitchers (.289 overall fastball against right-handers, .234 overall fastball against left-handers). His main fastball strength against right-handers is his medium-high outside location, in which he hits .367. He hits this pitch deep to all fields.

MEDIUM-HIGH OUTSIDE FASTBALLS

BATTING AVERAGE .367

Play

Left	Deep in straightaway left field
Center	Deep in straightaway center field
Right	Deep and shifted toward center field
Short	Normal position
Second	Shifted toward first base

He has trouble with all high fastballs and inside fastballs thrown by right-handers. But he hits .409 against low-over-the-middle fastballs. This location, with his medium-high outside location, bolsters his overall fastball average.

LOW-OVER-THE-MIDDLE FASTBALLS

BATTING AVERAGE .409

Play

Left	Deep in straightaway left field

Center	Deep and shifted toward right field
Right	Deep in straightaway right field
Short	Normal position
Second	Shifted toward first base

He hits .266 against medium-high inside fastballs.

MEDIUM-HIGH INSIDE FASTBALLS

BATTING AVERAGE .266

Play

Left	Deep and shifted toward the left field line
Center	Medium-deep in straightaway center field
Right	Medium-deep in straightaway right field
Short	Normal position
Second	Normal position

He hits only .173 against low-outside fastballs thrown by right-handers.

LOW-OUTSIDE FASTBALLS

BATTING AVERAGE .173

Play

Left	Medium-deep and shifted toward the left field line
Center	Medium-deep in straightaway center field
Right	Deep and shifted toward center field
Short	Shifted toward third base
Second	Normal position

Calderon Against Curves And Sliders

Calderon has a lot of trouble with low-outside curves (.000 on 0 for 13) and low-outside sliders (.210) against right-handed pitchers. But he hits strongly against medium-high outside curves and sliders (.291 and .400, respectively).

MEDIUM-HIGH OUTSIDE CURVEBALLS

BATTING AVERAGE .291
Play

Left	Medium-deep in straightaway left field
Center	Deep in straightaway center field
Right	Short in straightaway right field
Short	Shifted toward third base
Second	Normal position

MEDIUM-HIGH OUTSIDE SLIDERS

BATTING AVERAGE .400
Play

Left	Deep in straightaway left field
Center	Medium-deep in straightaway center field
Right	Deep and shifted toward the right field line
Short	Up middle (shifted toward second base)
Second	Normal position

Notice Calderon's troubled with all low-outside pitches against right-handers. This pattern continues against left-handers.

Calderon Against Left-Handed Pitchers

Against left-handed pitchers, Calderon hits medium-high outside fastballs fairly well (.281). He hits this pitch deep to all fields.

MEDIUM-HIGH OUTSIDE FASTBALLS (THROWN BY LEFT-HANDED PITCHERS)

BATTING AVERAGE .281
Play

Left	Deep and shifted toward center field
Center	Deep in straightaway center field
Right	Deep in straightaway right field
Short	Up middle (shifted toward second base)
Second	Normal position

He hits an excellent .352 against medium-high inside fastballs. He pulls this pitch deep down the left line and deep into the left-center alley. Note also that the shortstop needs to play shifted toward third and that there are no recorded instances of hit balls to the second baseman.

MEDIUM-HIGH INSIDE FASTBALLS (THROWN BY LEFT-HANDED PITCHERS)

BATTING AVERAGE .352
Play

Left	Deep and shifted toward the left field line
Center	Deep and shifted toward left field
Right	Deep in straightaway right field
Short	Shifted toward third base
Second	*No instances recorded*

Calderon is weak against all high fastballs thrown by left-handers. In addition, he has trouble with low-outside fastballs (.181).

He also seems to have trouble with outside curves thrown by lefties. His .125 against medium-high outside curves and his .000 on 0 for 5 against low-outside curves show weaknesses pitchers can attack.

Ahead And Behind In The Count Vs. RH

Ahead

Fastball Average .345

	Inside	Middle	Outside
High	2/0 /0	2/500 /1	2/500 /1
Med	17/235 /4	2/500 /1	35/400 /14
Low	3/333 /1	10/400 /4	8/250 /2

Curve Average .333

	Inside	Middle	Outside
High	0/0 /0	1/1000 /1	1/0 /0
Med	1/0 /0	1/0 /0	8/375 /3
Low	0/0 /0	2/500 /1	1/0 /0

Behind

Fastball Average .370

	Inside	Middle	Outside
High	0/0 /0	0/0 /0	4/250 /1
Med	4/500 /2	1/0 /0	14/428 /6
Low	1/0 /0	2/500 /1	1/0 /0

Curve Average .263

	Inside	Middle	Outside
High	0/0 /0	0/0 /0	2/500 /1
Med	3/333 /1	0/0 /0	10/300 /3
Low	0/0 /0	2/0 /0	2/0 /0

Overall Evaluation

Against Right-Handed Pitchers

Overall Fastball ⚾⚾ ⚾⚾
Overall Curve ⚾⚾ ⚾⚾
Overall Slider ⚾⚾ ⚾⚾ ⚾⚾ ⚾⚾

Against Left-Handed Pitchers

Overall Fastball ⚾⚾
Overall Curve ⚾⚾ ⚾⚾
Overall Slider ⚾⚾

Comments: Weak vs. high and inside fastballs vs. RH.
Strengths: Medium-outside and low-middle fastballs, medium-outside curves and sliders vs. RH; medium-inside fastballs vs. LH.
Weaknesses: High and inside fastballs, low-outside fastballs, low-outside curves and low-outside sliders vs. RH; high fastballs, low-outside fastballs, outside curves vs. LH.

Carlton Fisk Against Right-Handed Pitchers
Overall BARS Batting Average .280

Fastball Average .315

	Inside	Middle	Outside
High	25/200/5	23/86/2	24/166/4
Med	51/215/11	24/458/11	134/395/53
Low	14/214/3	51/392/20	44/318/14

Curve Average .216

	Inside	Middle	Outside
High	1/0/0	7/428/3	3/0/0
Med	10/100/1	8/375/3	42/285/12
Low	3/0/0	16/312/5	44/113/5

Slider Average .216

	Inside	Middle	Outside
High	0/0/0	2/500/1	1/0/0
Med	6/166/1	4/500/2	23/217/5
Low	1/0/0	13/461/6	24/41/1

Carlton Fisk Against Left-Handed Pitchers
Overall BARS Batting Average .265

Fastball Average .259

	Inside	Middle	Outside
High	8/0/0	13/153/2	14/357/5
Med	12/250/3	12/416/5	85/329/28
Low	6/166/1	28/250/7	30/100/3

Curve Average .306

	Inside	Middle	Outside
High	1/0/0	1/0/0	3/666/2
Med	3/666/2	2/0/0	14/357/5
Low	7/0/0	13/307/4	5/400/2

Slider Average .243

	Inside	Middle	Outside
High	0/0/0	3/666/2	1/0/0
Med	4/250/1	5/800/4	4/250/1
Low	15/66/1	5/0/0	4/250/1

Right-handed veteran Carlton Fisk has an exceptional ability to hit medium-high outside fastballs thrown by right-handed pitchers. His .395 average in this location is one of the highest recorded by the BARS System, especially considering the relatively large number of recorded instances (134). Pitchers seemingly don't care if it is his strength; they just keep throwing fastballs to this location.

MEDIUM-HIGH OUTSIDE FASTBALLS

BATTING AVERAGE .395

Play

Left	Deep and shifted toward the left field line
Center	Deep and shifted toward left field
Right	Deep and shifted toward center field
Short	Normal position
Second	Shifted toward first base

He also hits low-outside fastballs well (.318). Notice that fielders need to play him differently for fastballs to this location compared to medium-high outside.

LOW-OUTSIDE FASTBALLS

BATTING AVERAGE .318

Play

Left	Deep in straightaway left field
Center	Deep in straightaway center field
Right	Deep and shifted toward center field
Short	Normal position
Second	Normal position

Fisk has trouble with inside fastballs. Against right-handers he pulls medium-high inside fastballs.

MEDIUM-HIGH INSIDE FASTBALLS

BATTING AVERAGE .215

Play

Left	Deep and shifted toward the left field line
Center	Medium-deep and shifted toward left field
Right	Short and shifted toward center field
Short	Normal position
Second	Normal position

He also has trouble with high fastballs against right-handers. In the past most pitchers have probably avoided throwing him high pitches because of his power. Now pitchers might want to exploit his low averages in the high locations.

HIGH-INSIDE FASTBALLS

BATTING AVERAGE .200

Play

Left	Deep and shifted toward the left field line
Center	Medium-deep and shifted toward left field
Right	Short and shifted toward center field
Short	Up middle (shifted toward second base)
Second	Shifted toward first base

Fisk Against Curves And Sliders

Fisk has quite a bit of trouble with low-outside curves and all outside sliders. He hits medium-high outside curves well, however (.285).

MEDIUM-HIGH OUTSIDE CURVEBALLS

BATTING AVERAGE .285

Play	
Left	Deep and shifted toward the left field line
Center	Deep and shifted toward left field
Right	Deep and shifted toward the right field line
Short	Normal position
Second	Shifted toward first base

He hits low-outside sliders deep to all fields. But his .041 average certainly indicates that his hit balls from pitches to this location are easy fly balls.

LOW-OUTSIDE SLIDERS

BATTING AVERAGE .041 (1 for 24)

Play	
Left	Deep and shifted toward the left field line
Center	Deep and shifted toward left field
Right	Deep in straightaway right field
Short	Normal position
Second	Shifted toward first base

Fisk Against Left-Handed Pitchers

Fisk's fastball average is lower against left-handed pitchers. But his .329 against medium-high outside fastballs is excellent.

MEDIUM-HIGH OUTSIDE FASTBALLS (THROWN BY LEFT-HANDED PITCHERS)

BATTING AVERAGE .329

Play	
Left	Deep in straightaway left field
Center	Deep and shifted toward left field
Right	Medium-deep and shifted toward center field
Short	Up middle (shifted toward second base)
Second	Shifted toward first base

He hits high-outside fastballs against left-handers for an excellent .357 average.

HIGH-OUTSIDE FASTBALLS (THROWN BY LEFT-HANDED PITCHERS)

BATTING AVERAGE .357

Play	
Left	Deep and shifted toward center field
Center	Deep in straightaway field
Right	Deep and shifted toward center field
Short	Shifted toward third base
Second	Normal position

He hits medium-high outside curves very well against left-handers (.357). He pulls this pitch sharply to the outfield.

MEDIUM-HIGH OUTSIDE CURVEBALLS (THROWN BY LEFT-HANDED PITCHERS)

BATTING AVERAGE .357

Play	
Left	Deep and shifted toward the left field line
Center	Deep and shifted toward left field
Right	Deep and shifted toward center field
Short	Normal position
Second	*No instances recorded*

Ahead And Behind In The Count Vs. RH

Ahead

	Fastball Average .357			Curve Average .321		
	Inside	Middle	Outside	Inside	Middle	Outside
High	5/0 /0	5/0 /0	4/0 /0	1/0 /0	2/0 /0	2/0 /0
Med	27/222 /6	14/428 /6	65/446 /29	2/0 /0	1/1000 /1	11/454 /5
Low	3/333 /1	27/370 /10	18/444 /8	1/0 /0	4/250 /1	4/500 /2

Behind

	Fastball Average .310			Curve Average .279		
	Inside	Middle	Outside	Inside	Middle	Outside
High	11/181 /2	7/285 /2	6/166 /1	0/0 /0	3/666 /2	0/0 /0
Med	11/363 /4	3/333 /1	26/384 /10	5/200 /1	2/500 /1	15/200 /3
Low	5/200 /1	7/428 /3	11/272 /3	0/0 /0	3/1000 /3	15/133 /2

Overall Evaluation

Against Right-Handed Pitchers

Overall Fastball	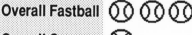
Overall Curve	
Overall Slider	

Against Left-Handed Pitchers

Overall Fastball	
Overall Curve	
Overall Slider	

Comments: Weak vs. high and inside fastballs vs. RH. Strengths: Medium-outside, medium-middle, low-middle and low-outside fastballs, over-the-middle curves and over-the-middle sliders vs. RH; high-outside, medium-outside & medium-middle fastballs, medium-outside & low-middle curves vs. LH. Weaknesses: High and inside fastballs, low-outside curves and outside sliders vs. RH; inside fastballs and low-outside fastballs, low-inside sliders vs. LH.

Scott Fletcher (Right Handed)   *Chicago White Sox*

Scott Fletcher Against Right-Handed Pitchers
Overall BARS Batting Average .257

Fastball Average .289			Curve Average .227			Slider Average .185		
Inside	Middle	Outside	Inside	Middle	Outside	Inside	Middle	Outside
High								
41/292 /12	33/393 /13	23/304 /7	5/200 /1	7/285 /2	1/1000 /1	3/333 /1	2/500 /1	2/500 /1
Med								
86/232 /20	39/512 /20	176/295 /52	10/300 /3	6/166 /1	21/285 /6	4/500 /2	2/0 /0	15/133 /2
Low								
37/297 /11	73/219 /16	61/229 /14	3/333 /1	9/111 /1	26/153 /4	5/200 /1	5/0 /0	16/125 /2

Scott Fletcher Against Left-Handed Pitchers
Overall BARS Batting Average .253

Fastball Average .257			Curve Average .250			Slider Average .250		
Inside	Middle	Outside	Inside	Middle	Outside	Inside	Middle	Outside
High								
11/90 /1	18/166 /3	9/222 /2	2/1000 /2	2/1000 /2	3/333 /1	4/250 /1	1/0 /0	0/0 /0
Med								
31/354 /11	13/461 /6	89/157 /14	4/0 /0	3/333 /1	14/0 /0	6/333 /2	3/0 /0	9/444 /4
Low								
17/235 /4	38/447 /17	23/260 /6	8/250 /2	7/428 /3	5/200 /1	5/400 /2	6/333 /2	10/0 /0

Right-handed Scott Fletcher hits fastballs pretty well overall against right-handed pitchers (.289). He has some weak fastball locations (.232 medium-high inside, .219 low-over-the-middle, and .229 low-outside) but he hits well in his other locations.

Fletcher hits .295 against medium-high outside fastballs. He hits this pitch deep and straightaway to left and center and medium-deep down the right line. Note that the infielders need to play toward the right side.

MEDIUM-HIGH OUTSIDE FASTBALLS

BATTING AVERAGE .295
Play
Left   Deep in straightaway left field
Center   Deep in straightaway center field
Right   Medium-deep and shifted toward the right line
Short   Up middle (shifted toward second base)
Second   Shifted toward first base

He hits medium-high inside fastballs medium-deep and straightaway to all fields.

MEDIUM-HIGH INSIDE FASTBALLS

BATTING AVERAGE .232
Play
Left   Medium-deep in straightaway left field
Center   Medium-deep in straightaway center field
Right   Medium-deep in straightaway right field

Short   Normal position
Second   Shifted toward first base

He tends to pull high-inside fastballs.

HIGH-INSIDE FASTBALLS

BATTING AVERAGE .292
Play
Left   Deep and shifted toward the left field line
Center   Deep and shifted toward left field
Right   Medium-deep and shifted toward center field
Short   Normal position
Second   Normal position

He hits high-over-the-middle fastballs deep down both lines.

HIGH-OVER-THE-MIDDLE FASTBALLS

BATTING AVERAGE .393
Play
Left   Deep and shifted toward the left field line
Center   Medium-deep in straightaway center field
Right   Deep and shifted toward the right field line
Short   Normal position
Second   Shifted toward first base

His .512 average in his medium-over-the-middle location is exceptional. Note that the fielding strategy for this location is similar to the strategy for his medium-high inside fastball location. His higher average indicates that he hits the ball much more sharply in the medium-over-the-middle location.

MEDIUM-OVER-THE-MIDDLE FASTBALLS

BATTING AVERAGE .512
Play

Left	Medium-deep in straightaway left field
Center	Medium-deep in straightaway center field
Right	Medium-deep in straightaway right field
Short	Up middle (shifted toward second base)
Second	Shifted toward first base

Fletcher has trouble with low curves against right-handed pitchers. His .111 against low-over-the-middle curves and .153 against low-outside curves give a good target for pitchers. He hits medium-high outside curves fairly well, however (.285). By playing him medium-deep for this pitch, fielders could prevent most of his line-drive base hits.

MEDIUM-HIGH OUTSIDE CURVEBALLS

BATTING AVERAGE .285
Play

Left	Medium-deep in straightaway left field
Center	Medium-deep in straightaway center field
Right	Medium-deep in straightaway right field
Short	Normal position
Second	Normal position

Fletcher has problems with low-outside and medium-high outside sliders.

Fletcher Against Left-Handed Pitchers

Fletcher hits high fastballs well against right-handed pitchers, but he has problems with high fastballs against left-handed pitchers (.090, .166 and .222, inside to outside).

He has a low average (.157) in the highly pitched medium-high outside fastball location. He probably hits this pitch mostly for easy pop-ups and grounders.

MEDIUM-HIGH OUTSIDE FASTBALLS (THROWN BY LEFT-HANDED PITCHERS)

BATTING AVERAGE .157
Play

Left	Deep in straightaway left field
Center	Medium-deep in straightaway center field
Right	Deep in straightaway right field
Short	Normal position
Second	Normal position

He rips low-over-the-middle fastballs thrown by left-handers for a fine .447 average. By playing medium-deep, as recommended by the BARS fielding strategy, fielders could prevent most of his line-drive base hits from this location.

LOW-OVER-THE-MIDDLE FASTBALLS (THROWN BY LEFT-HANDED PITCHERS)

BATTING AVERAGE .447
Play

Left	Medium-deep in straightaway left field
Center	Medium-deep in straightaway center field
Right	Medium-deep and shifted toward the right line
Short	Normal position
Second	Normal position

He has problems with medium-high outside curves and low-outside sliders against left-handers. He does not yet have a recorded base hit in these locations.

Ahead And Behind In The Count Vs. RH

Ahead

Fastball Average .305

	Inside	Middle	Outside
High	22/272 /6	18/388 /7	12/250 /3
Med	40/200 /8	21/571 /12	94/340 /32
Low	17/235 /4	37/243 /9	30/266 /8

Curve Average .000

	Inside	Middle	Outside
High	0/0 /0	0/0 /0	0/0 /0
Med	0/0 /0	0/0 /0	1/0 /0
Low	0/0 /0	3/0 /0	2/0 /0

Behind

Fastball Average .342

	Inside	Middle	Outside
High	5/600 /3	10/400 /4	4/750 /3
Med	18/277 /5	3/333 /1	38/315 /12
Low	11/363 /4	15/266 /4	7/285 /2

Curve Average .333

	Inside	Middle	Outside
High	3/0 /0	7/285 /2	1/1000 /1
Med	5/400 /2	3/0 /0	11/363 /4
Low	2/500 /1	4/250 /1	9/444 /4

Overall Evaluation

Against Right-Handed Pitchers

Overall Fastball	⚾⚾
Overall Curve	⚾
Overall Slider	⚾

Against Left-Handed Pitchers

Overall Fastball	⚾
Overall Curve	⚾⚾
Overall Slider	⚾⚾

Comments: Fletcher hits high fastballs well vs. RH. Strengths: High fastballs and medium-middle fastballs, medium-inside curves vs. RH; medium-inside, medium-middle and low-middle fastballs, low-middle curves and medium-outside sliders vs. LH. Weaknesses: Medium-inside, low-middle and low-outside fastballs, low-middle and low-outside curves, low-outside and medium-outside sliders vs. RH; high and outside fastballs, medium-outside curves vs. LH.

Dave Gallagher Against Right-Handed Pitchers
Overall BARS Batting Average .248

	Fastball Average .275			Curve Average .307			Slider Average .055		
	Inside	Middle	Outside	Inside	Middle	Outside	Inside	Middle	Outside
High	8/ 375 /3	4/ 500 /2	7/ 142 /1	1/ 0 /0	0/ 0 /0	0/ 0 /0	1/ 0 /0	1/ 0 /0	1/ 0 /0
Med	13/ 230 /3	6/ 0 /0	44/ 295 /13	0/ 0 /0	0/ 0 /0	4/ 500 /2	2/ 0 /0	0/ 0 /0	2/ 0 /0
Low	5/ 400 /2	7/ 428 /3	4/ 0 /0	0/ 0 /0	1/ 0 /0	7/ 285 /2	3/ 0 /0	1/ 0 /0	7/ 142 /1

Dave Gallagher Against Left-Handed Pitchers
Overall BARS Batting Average .152

	Fastball Average .161			Curve Average .100			Slider Average .200		
	Inside	Middle	Outside	Inside	Middle	Outside	Inside	Middle	Outside
High	1/ 1000 /1	1/ 0 /0	1/ 0 /0	0/ 0 /0	1/ 0 /0	1/ 0 /0	0/ 0 /0	0/ 0 /0	0/ 0 /0
Med	3/ 0 /0	1/ 0 /0	16/ 187 /3	0/ 0 /0	0/ 0 /0	3/ 0 /0	2/ 500 /1	0/ 0 /0	2/ 0 /0
Low	3/ 0 /0	1/ 1000 /1	4/ 0 /0	1/ 0 /0	1/ 1000 /1	3/ 0 /0	1/ 0 /0	0/ 0 /0	0/ 0 /0

Right-handed hitting Dave Gallagher hits fastballs fairly well against right-handed pitchers (.275 overall) but poorly against left-handed pitchers (.161 overall). It's unusual for a right-handed hitter to hit so much better against right-handed pitchers.

The following chart and the field diagram on the opposite page show how fielders need to play for medium-high outside fastballs to Gallagher.

MEDIUM-HIGH OUTSIDE FASTBALLS

BATTING AVERAGE .295
Play
Left   Deep and shifted toward center field
Center   Medium-deep in straightaway center field
Right   Deep in straightaway right field
Short   Up middle (shifted toward second base)
Second   Shifted toward first base

He hits only .230 against medium-high inside fastballs thrown by right-handers.

MEDIUM-HIGH INSIDE FASTBALLS

BATTING AVERAGE .230
Play
Left   Deep in straightaway left field
Center   Deep in straightaway center field
Right   Medium-deep in straightaway right field
Short   Up middle (shifted toward second base)
Second   Normal position

Gallagher hits a solid .375 against high-inside fastballs. He hits this pitch deep into the left-center alley and deep down the right line.

HIGH-INSIDE FASTBALLS

BATTING AVERAGE .375
Play
Left   Medium-deep in straightaway left field
Center   Deep and shifted toward left field
Right   Deep and shifted toward the right field line
Short   Normal position
Second   Normal position

He hits well against low-outside and medium-high outside curves thrown by right-handers (.285 and .500), but he has trouble with low-outside sliders (.142).

Against left-handed pitchers, he has a lot of trouble with medium-high outside fastballs.

MEDIUM-HIGH OUTSIDE FASTBALLS
(THROWN BY LEFT-HANDED PITCHERS)

BATTING AVERAGE .187
Play
Left   *No instances recorded*
Center   Deep in straightaway center field
Right   Deep and shifted toward the right field line
Short   Normal position
Second   Normal position

Medium-High Outside Fastballs
(Thrown By Right-Handed Pitchers)

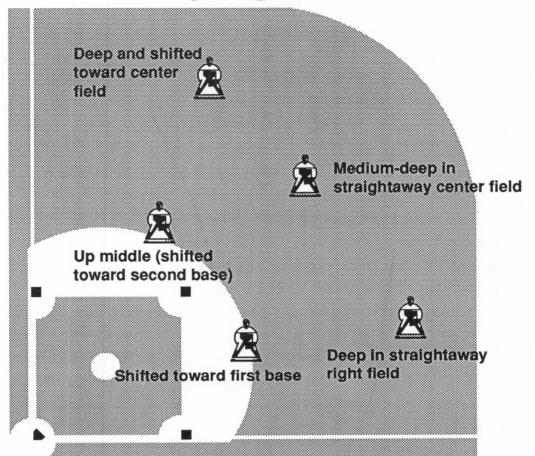

Deep and shifted toward center field

Medium-deep in straightaway center field

Up middle (shifted toward second base)

Shifted toward first base

Deep in straightaway right field

Ahead And Behind In The Count Vs. RH

Ahead

Fastball Average .219

	Inside	Middle	Outside
High	2/ 500 /1	3/ 333 /1	0/ 0 /0
Med	11/ 181 /2	3/ 0 /0	16/ 125 /2
Low	3/ 666 /2	3/ 333 /1	0/ 0 /0

Curve Average .000

	Inside	Middle	Outside
High	0/ 0 /0	0/ 0 /0	0/ 0 /0
Med	0/ 0 /0	0/ 0 /0	0/ 0 /0
Low	0/ 0 /0	0/ 0 /0	0/ 0 /0

Behind

Fastball Average .391

	Inside	Middle	Outside
High	3/ 333 /1	1/ 1000 /1	3/ 333 /1
Med	1/ 1000 /1	0/ 0 /0	14/ 285 /4
Low	0/ 0 /0	1/ 1000 /1	0/ 0 /0

Curve Average .600

	Inside	Middle	Outside
High	0/ 0 /0	0/ 0 /0	0/ 0 /0
Med	0/ 0 /0	0/ 0 /0	2/ 500 /1
Low	0/ 0 /0	1/ 0 /0	2/ 1000 /2

Overall Evaluation
Against Right-Handed Pitchers

Overall Fastball

Overall Curve

Overall Slider

Against Left-Handed Pitchers

Overall Fastball

Overall Curve   Not enough information

Overall Slider   Not enough information

Comments: Strong against medium-high outside fastballs vs. RH, weak against medium-high outside fastballs vs. LH.

Strengths: High-inside, low-middle and medium-outside fastballs, low-outside and medium-outside curves vs. RH.

Weaknesses: Medium-inside and high-outside fastballs, low-outside sliders vs. RH; medium-outside fastballs vs. LH.

Ozzie Guillen Against Right-Handed Pitchers
Overall BARS Batting Average .283

Fastball Average .286

	Outside	Middle	Inside
High	60/283 /17	45/422 /19	30/233 /7
Med	175/274 /48	16/250 /4	61/377 /23
Low	39/153 /6	54/277 /15	36/250 /9

Curve Average .247

	Outside	Middle	Inside
High	7/0 /0	7/285 /2	4/500 /2
Med	24/333 /8	3/333 /1	11/363 /4
Low	8/125 /1	13/153 /2	20/200 /4

Slider Average .313

	Outside	Middle	Inside
High	1/0 /0	4/500 /2	6/333 /2
Med	9/333 /3	2/1000 /2	15/266 /4
Low	2/0 /0	2/0 /0	10/300 /3

Ozzie Guillen Against Left-Handed Pitchers
Overall BARS Batting Average .241

Fastball Average .275

	Outside	Middle	Inside
High	12/333 /4	5/400 /2	9/333 /3
Med	58/241 /14	3/333 /1	31/258 /8
Low	7/142 /1	9/222 /2	15/400 /6

Curve Average .203

	Outside	Middle	Inside
High	6/166 /1	4/250 /1	3/666 /2
Med	17/117 /2	1/0 /0	7/142 /1
Low	18/166 /3	7/285 /2	1/1000 /1

Slider Average .148

	Outside	Middle	Inside
High	0/0 /0	1/1000 /1	0/0 /0
Med	15/66 /1	0/0 /0	2/500 /1
Low	8/125 /1	1/0 /0	0/0 /0

Left-handed hitter Ozzie Guillen hits better overall against right-handed pitchers. His fastball average of .286 against right-handers is adequate. His .377 against medium-high inside fastballs is excellent. Notice in his Ahead and Behind charts on the opposite page that he hits this pitch much better when behind in the count (.545 when behind, .281 when ahead). He hits this pitch medium-deep toward center field when behind, deeper and with more of a pull to center and right fields when ahead. This indicates that fielders in general are probably playing Guillen to pull the ball deep. If they adjusted according to the BARS System for this pitch, they could prevent most of his base hits.

MEDIUM-HIGH INSIDE FASTBALLS
(WHEN BEHIND IN THE COUNT)

BATTING AVERAGE .545
Play
Left   Medium-deep and shifted toward center field
Center   Medium-deep in straightaway center field
Right   Medium-deep and shifted toward center field
Short   Up middle (shifted toward second base)
Second   Normal position

MEDIUM-HIGH INSIDE FASTBALLS
(WHEN AHEAD IN THE COUNT)

BATTING AVERAGE .281
Play
Left   Medium-deep in straightaway left field
Center   Deep and shifted toward right field
Right   Deep and shifted toward the right field line
Short   Normal position
Second   Shifted toward first base

Guillen's .422 against high-over-the-middle fastballs is exceptional.

HIGH-OVER-THE-MIDDLE FASTBALLS

BATTING AVERAGE .422
Play
Left   Medium-deep and shifted toward center field
Center   Deep in straightaway center field
Right   Deep in straightaway right field
Short   Normal position
Second   *No instances recorded*

His .274 against medium-high outside fastballs is only fair. He goes down the left line with this pitch.

MEDIUM-HIGH OUTSIDE FASTBALLS

BATTING AVERAGE .274
Play

Left	Medium-deep and shifted toward the left field line
Center	Deep in straightaway center field
Right	Deep in straightaway right field
Short	Up middle (shifted toward second base)
Second	Normal position

Guillen Against Curves And Sliders

Guillen has trouble with low curves against right-handed pitchers (.125, .153, and .200, outside to inside). But he hits medium-high outside curves excellently.

MEDIUM-HIGH OUTSIDE CURVEBALLS

BATTING AVERAGE .333
Play

Left	Medium-deep in straightaway left field
Center	Medium-deep in straightaway center field
Right	Deep and shifted toward center field
Short	Shifted toward third base
Second	Shifted toward first base

He hits .266 against medium-high inside sliders. He pulls this pitch.

MEDIUM-HIGH INSIDE SLIDERS

BATTING AVERAGE .266
Play

Left	Deep and shifted toward center field
Center	Deep and shifted toward right field
Right	Deep and shifted toward the right field line
Short	Normal position
Second	Shifted toward first base

Guillen Against Left-Handed Pitchers

Guillen has considerable trouble overall against left-handed pitchers. His overall .275 fastball average is below average. His .241 against medium-high outside fastballs exemplifies his difficulties.

MEDIUM-HIGH OUTSIDE FASTBALLS (THROWN BY LEFT-HANDED PITCHERS)

BATTING AVERAGE .241
Play

Left	Medium-deep and shifted toward the left field line
Center	Deep in straightaway center field
Right	Medium-deep in straightaway right field
Short	Up middle (shifted toward second base)
Second	Shifted toward first base

He hits low-inside fastballs down the left line and into the deep left-center gap against left-handers. But the infielders need to play this pitch for a pull.

LOW-INSIDE FASTBALLS (THROWN BY LEFT-HANDED PITCHERS)

BATTING AVERAGE .400
Play

Left	Medium-deep and shifted toward the left field line
Center	Deep and shifted toward left field
Right	Medium-deep in straightaway right field
Short	Up middle (shifted toward second base)
Second	Shifted toward first base

He has a lot of trouble with outside curves and sliders against left-handers. In general, if left-handed pitchers throw him outside, they'll have an advantage.

Ahead And Behind In The Count Vs. RH

Ahead

Fastball Average .306

	Outside	Middle	Inside
High	35/ 285 /10	22/ 409 /9	17/ 294 /5
Med	94/ 308 /29	8/ 250 /2	32/ 281 /9
Low	13/ 230 /3	32/ 343 /11	24/ 291 /7

Curve Average .263

	Outside	Middle	Inside
High	1/ 0 /0	2/ 500 /1	1/ 1000 /1
Med	6/ 166 /1	0/ 0 /0	3/ 666 /2
Low	2/ 0 /0	1/ 0 /0	3/ 0 /0

Behind

Fastball Average .306

	Outside	Middle	Inside
High	8/ 250 /2	7/ 571 /4	9/ 222 /2
Med	33/ 272 /9	2/ 0 /0	11/ 545 /6
Low	8/ 250 /2	4/ 250 /1	6/ 166 /1

Curve Average .216

	Outside	Middle	Inside
High	3/ 0 /0	2/ 0 /0	2/ 0 /0
Med	10/ 400 /4	2/ 500 /1	3/ 333 /1
Low	2/ 500 /1	6/ 0 /0	7/ 142 /1

Overall Evaluation

Against Right-Handed Pitchers

Overall Fastball	◯◯ ◯◯
Overall Curve	◯◯
Overall Slider	◯◯ ◯◯◯ ◯◯

Against Left-Handed Pitchers

Overall Fastball	◯◯ ◯◯
Overall Curve	◯◯
Overall Slider	◯◯

Comments: Strong vs. medium-inside fastballs vs. RH.
Strengths: Medium-inside and high-middle fastballs, medium-outside and medium-inside curves, low-inside sliders vs. RH; low-inside and high-outside fastballs vs. LH.
Weaknesses: Low-inside, low-outside, medium-middle and high-inside fastballs, low curves vs. RH; outside pitches in general vs. LH (except high-outside fastballs).

Lance Johnson (Left Handed)   *Chicago White Sox*

Lance Johnson Against Right-Handed Pitchers
Overall BARS Batting Average .294

	Fastball Average .338			Curve Average .125			Slider Average .125		
	Outside	Middle	Inside	Outside	Middle	Inside	Outside	Middle	Inside
High	11/ 363 /4	5/ 800 /4	9/ 444 /4	0/ 0 /0	0/ 0 /0	1/ 0 /0	0/ 0 /0	0/ 0 /0	0/ 0 /0
Med	21/ 190 /4	3/ 0 /0	7/ 571 /4	2/ 500 /1	0/ 0 /0	1/ 0 /0	2/ 500 /1	0/ 0 /0	2/ 0 /0
Low	2/ 500 /1	1/ 0 /0	3/ 0 /0	0/ 0 /0	3/ 0 /0	1/ 0 /0	0/ 0 /0	1/ 0 /0	3/ 0 /0

Lance Johnson Against Left-Handed Pitchers
Overall BARS Batting Average .208

	Fastball Average .187			Curve Average .200			Slider Average .333		
	Outside	Middle	Inside	Outside	Middle	Inside	Outside	Middle	Inside
High	3/ 0 /0	0/ 0 /0	2/ 500 /1	1/ 1000 /1	0/ 0 /0	1/ 0 /0	0/ 0 /0	0/ 0 /0	1/ 0 /0
Med	5/ 400 /2	2/ 0 /0	2/ 0 /0	0/ 0 /0	0/ 0 /0	0/ 0 /0	1/ 0 /0	0/ 0 /0	0/ 0 /0
Low	2/ 0 /0	0/ 0 /0	0/ 0 /0	1/ 0 /0	1/ 0 /0	1/ 0 /0	1/ 1000 /1	0/ 0 /0	0/ 0 /0

Left-handed hitter Lance Johnson has some very strong fastball locations against right-handed pitchers. The BARS System has not yet recorded much information for him against left-handed pitchers, so his charts against lefties are not discussed here.

Against right-handers, Johnson hits an excellent .363 in his high-outside fastball location. He hits this pitch medium-deep down the left line (his opposite field). But notice that the infielders must be shifted to the right side. The chart below and the field diagram on the opposite page show how fielders need to play for this pitch.

HIGH-OUTSIDE FASTBALLS

BATTING AVERAGE .363
Play
Left   Medium-deep and shifted toward the left field line
Center   Medium-deep and shifted toward left field
Right   Medium-deep in straightaway right field
Short   Up middle (shifted toward second base)
Second   Shifted toward first base

He has a lot of trouble with medium-high outside fastballs. If not for his weakness in this highly pitched location, his overall fastball average would be very high.

MEDIUM-HIGH OUTSIDE FASTBALLS

BATTING AVERAGE .190

Play
Left   Deep and shifted toward center field
Center   Deep in straightaway center field
Right   Medium-deep and shifted toward center field
Short   Up middle (shifted toward second base)
Second   Shifted toward first base

In general, Johnson hits high fastballs excellently against right-handed pitchers. He hits an outstanding .444 against high-inside fastballs.

HIGH-INSIDE FASTBALLS

BATTING AVERAGE .444
Play
Left   *No instances recorded*
Center   *No instances recorded*
Right   Deep and shifted toward the right field line
Short   Shifted toward third base
Second   Shifted toward first base

His .571 against medium-high inside fastballs is also excellent.

MEDIUM-HIGH INSIDE FASTBALLS

BATTING AVERAGE .571
Play
Left   *No instances recorded*
Center   Medium-deep in straightaway center field
Right   Deep and shifted toward the right field line
Short   Normal position
Second   Normal position

High-Outside Fastballs
(Thrown By Right-Handed Pitchers)

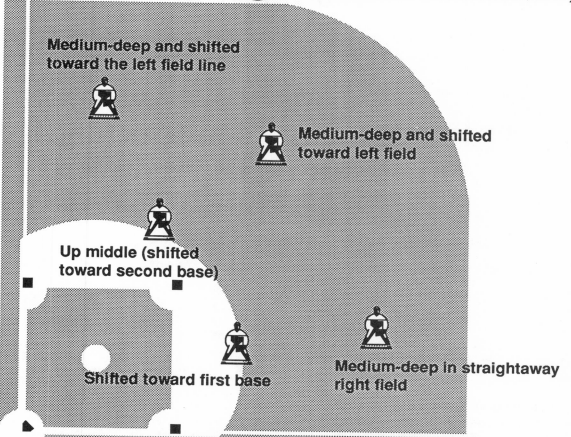

Medium-deep and shifted toward the left field line

Medium-deep and shifted toward left field

Up middle (shifted toward second base)

Shifted toward first base

Medium-deep in straightaway right field

Ahead And Behind In The Count Vs. RH

Ahead

Fastball Average .444

	Outside	Middle	Inside
High	428 $\frac{7}{3}$	800 $\frac{5}{4}$	428 $\frac{7}{3}$
Med	200 $\frac{5}{1}$	0 $\frac{1}{0}$	0 $\frac{0}{0}$
Low	1000 $\frac{1}{1}$	0 $\frac{0}{0}$	0 $\frac{1}{0}$

Curve Average .500

	Outside	Middle	Inside
	0 $\frac{0}{0}$	0 $\frac{0}{0}$	0 $\frac{0}{0}$
	1000 $\frac{1}{1}$	0 $\frac{0}{0}$	0 $\frac{1}{0}$
	0 $\frac{0}{0}$	0 $\frac{0}{0}$	0 $\frac{0}{0}$

Behind

Fastball Average .153

	Outside	Middle	Inside
High	0 $\frac{1}{0}$	0 $\frac{0}{0}$	0 $\frac{0}{0}$
Med	200 $\frac{5}{1}$	0 $\frac{1}{0}$	333 $\frac{3}{1}$
Low	0 $\frac{1}{0}$	0 $\frac{1}{0}$	0 $\frac{1}{0}$

Curve Average .000

	Outside	Middle	Inside
High	0 $\frac{0}{0}$	0 $\frac{0}{0}$	0 $\frac{0}{0}$
Med	0 $\frac{0}{0}$	0 $\frac{0}{0}$	0 $\frac{0}{0}$
Low	0 $\frac{0}{0}$	0 $\frac{0}{0}$	0 $\frac{0}{0}$

Overall Evaluation
Against Right-Handed Pitchers

Overall Fastball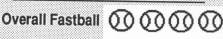

Overall Curve — Not enough information

Overall Slider — Not enough information

Against Left-Handed Pitchers

Overall Fastball

Overall Curve — Not enough information

Overall Slider — Not enough information

Comments: Strong against high fastballs vs. RH.
Strengths: High fastballs, medium-inside fastballs vs. RH.
Weaknesses: Medium-outside fastballs vs. RH.

Ron Karkovice (Right Handed) — *Chicago White Sox*

Ron Karkovice Against Right-Handed Pitchers
Overall BARS Batting Average .276

Fastball Average .365

	Inside	Middle	Outside
High	2/ 500 /1	3/ 0 /0	6/ 333 /2
Med	7/ 428 /3	2/ 0 /0	21/ 523 /11
Low	0/ 0 /0	5/ 400 /2	6/ 0 /0

Curve Average .142

	Inside	Middle	Outside
High	0/ 0 /0	0/ 0 /0	0/ 0 /0
Med	2/ 0 /0	1/ 0 /0	8/ 125 /1
Low	0/ 0 /0	1/ 0 /0	2/ 500 /1

Slider Average .000

	Inside	Middle	Outside
High	0/ 0 /0	0/ 0 /0	0/ 0 /0
Med	0/ 0 /0	1/ 0 /0	2/ 0 /0
Low	1/ 0 /0	3/ 0 /0	3/ 0 /0

Ron Karkovice Against Left-Handed Pitchers
Overall BARS Batting Average .163

Fastball Average .088

	Inside	Middle	Outside
High	2/ 0 /0	1/ 0 /0	3/ 0 /0
Med	5/ 0 /0	1/ 0 /0	11/ 181 /2
Low	1/ 0 /0	2/ 0 /0	8/ 125 /1

Curve Average .333

	Inside	Middle	Outside
High	0/ 0 /0	1/ 1000 /1	0/ 0 /0
Med	2/ 500 /1	0/ 0 /0	3/ 333 /1
Low	0/ 0 /0	0/ 0 /0	3/ 0 /0

Slider Average .333

	Inside	Middle	Outside
High	1/ 0 /0	0/ 0 /0	0/ 0 /0
Med	1/ 0 /0	0/ 0 /0	3/ 666 /2
Low	0/ 0 /0	1/ 0 /0	0/ 0 /0

Right-handed hitting Ron Karkovice has some extremely strong fastball locations against right-handed pitchers. His .523 against medium-high outside fastballs is exceptional. The chart below and the field diagram on the opposite page show how fielders need to play him for this pitch.

MEDIUM-HIGH OUTSIDE FASTBALLS

BATTING AVERAGE .523
Play

Left	Deep and shifted toward the left field line
Center	Medium-deep in straightaway center field
Right	Deep in straightaway right field
Short	Shifted toward third base
Second	Normal position

His .428 against medium-high inside fastballs thrown by right-handers is also excellent.

MEDIUM-HIGH INSIDE FASTBALLS

BATTING AVERAGE .428
Play

Left	Deep and shifted toward the left field line
Center	Medium-deep in straightaway center field
Right	Short and shifted toward center field
Short	Shifted toward third base
Second	Normal position

He has trouble with low-outside fastballs against right-handers (.000 on 0 for 6).

Against left-handed pitchers he has great difficulty in all fastball locations. It is unusual for a right-handed hitter to hit so much worse against left-handed pitchers.

He hits only .181 against medium-high outside fastballs thrown by left-handers. The following chart shows how fielders need to play for this pitch. His low average in this location indicates that most of his hit balls probably are easy outs.

MEDIUM-HIGH OUTSIDE FASTBALLS
(THROWN BY LEFT-HANDED PITCHERS)

BATTING AVERAGE .181
Play

Left	Short and shifted toward the left field line
Center	Medium-deep in straightaway center field
Right	Deep and shifted toward center field
Short	Normal position
Second	Normal position

He hits .125 on 1 for 8 against low-outside fastballs. Beside the medium-outside and low-outside locations, he does not have a recorded base hit in any of his fastball locations against lefties.

Medium-High Outside Fastballs
(Thrown By Right-Handed Pitchers)

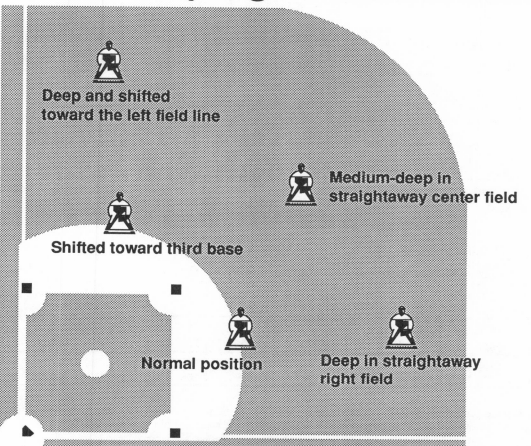

Deep and shifted toward the left field line

Medium-deep in straightaway center field

Shifted toward third base

Normal position

Deep in straightaway right field

Ahead And Behind In The Count Vs. RH

Ahead

Fastball Average .500

	Inside	Middle	Outside
High	0/0 /0	1/0 /0	2/1000 /2
Med	3/666 /2	2/0 /0	9/555 /5
Low	0/0 /0	4/500 /2	1/0 /0

Curve Average .333

	Inside	Middle	Outside
High	0/0 /0	0/0 /0	0/0 /0
Med	1/0 /0	1/0 /0	3/333 /1
Low	0/0 /0	0/0 /0	1/1000 /1

Behind

Fastball Average .222

	Inside	Middle	Outside
High	1/0 /0	0/0 /0	1/0 /0
Med	2/500 /1	0/0 /0	4/250 /1
Low	0/0 /0	1/0 /0	0/0 /0

Curve Average .000

	Inside	Middle	Outside
High	0/0 /0	0/0 /0	0/0 /0
Med	1/0 /0	0/0 /0	3/0 /0
Low	0/0 /0	0/0 /0	0/0 /0

Overall Evaluation

Against Right-Handed Pitchers

Overall Fastball

Overall Curve

Overall Slider   Not enough information

Against Left-Handed Pitchers

Overall Fastball

Overall Curve   Not enough information

Overall Slider   Not enough information

Comments: Has some very strong fastball locations against RH.
Strengths: Medium-inside, high-outside and medium-outside fastballs vs. RH.
Weaknesses: Medium-outside curves vs. RH; all fastball locations vs. LH.

Ron Kittle Against Right-Handed Pitchers
Overall BARS Batting Average .245

Fastball Average .255

	Inside	Middle	Outside
High	12/166/2	17/294/5	15/0/0
Med	38/236/9	20/300/6	55/290/16
Low	17/176/3	29/379/11	20/250/5

Curve Average .230

	Inside	Middle	Outside
High	4/0/0	8/375/3	1/0/0
Med	8/125/1	9/444/4	24/250/6
Low	1/0/0	14/357/5	31/129/4

Slider Average .230

	Inside	Middle	Outside
High	4/250/1	2/500/1	3/333/1
Med	2/0/0	2/500/1	16/375/6
Low	1/0/0	3/0/0	19/105/2

Ron Kittle Against Left-Handed Pitchers
Overall BARS Batting Average .268

Fastball Average .253

	Inside	Middle	Outside
High	6/166/1	10/400/4	8/125/1
Med	14/71/1	9/111/1	52/326/17
Low	12/250/3	25/400/10	14/0/0

Curve Average .229

	Inside	Middle	Outside
High	0/0/0	2/1000/2	0/0/0
Med	5/200/1	5/200/1	9/222/2
Low	9/111/1	6/333/2	12/166/2

Slider Average .378

	Inside	Middle	Outside
High	0/0/0	0/0/0	1/1000/1
Med	9/222/2	4/500/2	3/333/1
Low	10/300/3	7/571/4	3/333/1

Right-handed hitter Ron Kittle has similar fastball and curve averages against right- and left-handed pitchers (fastballs .255 and .253 overall against right- and left-handers respectively, curves .230 and .229 overall respectively).

Against right-handers, Kittle has trouble with inside fastballs but he hits all over-the-middle fastballs and medium-high outside fastballs well. He hits .290 against medium-high outside.

MEDIUM-HIGH OUTSIDE FASTBALLS

BATTING AVERAGE .290

Play

Left	Deep in straightaway left field
Center	Deep in straightaway center field
Right	Deep in straightaway right field
Short	Normal position
Second	Normal position

He hits only .236 against medium-high inside fastballs.

MEDIUM-HIGH INSIDE FASTBALLS

BATTING AVERAGE .236

Play

Left	Medium-deep and shifted toward the left field line
Center	Medium-deep in straightaway center field
Right	Medium-deep and shifted toward the right line
Short	Normal position
Second	Normal position

He hits a solid .379 against low-over-the-middle fastballs. Note that he hits this pitch medium-deep to straightaway left and center fields. He undoubtedly hits this pitch much harder than he hits medium-high inside fastballs, as indicated by his higher average.

LOW-OVER-THE-MIDDLE FASTBALLS

BATTING AVERAGE .379

Play

Left	Medium-deep in straightaway left field
Center	Medium-deep in straightaway center field
Right	Deep in straightaway right field
Short	Normal position
Second	*No instances recorded*

Kittle Against Curves And Sliders

Kittle has trouble with outside curves against right-handed pitchers. But he hits all over-the-middle curves excellently (.375, .444, and .357, high to low). He pulls low-over-the-middle curves. No recorded instances of hit balls to other than the left and center fielders have been recorded for this location.

LOW-OVER-THE-MIDDLE CURVEBALLS

BATTING AVERAGE .375
Play

Left	Medium-deep and shifted toward the left field line
Center	Deep in straightaway center field
Right	*No instances recorded*
Short	*No instances recorded*
Second	*No instances recorded*

He has trouble with low-outside sliders (.105 on 2 for 19) but hits an outstanding .375 against medium-high outside sliders.

MEDIUM-HIGH OUTSIDE SLIDERS

BATTING AVERAGE .375
Play

Left	Deep in straightaway left field
Center	Deep and shifted toward left field
Right	Medium-deep and shifted toward the right line
Short	Normal position
Second	*No instances recorded*

Kittle Against Left-Handed Pitchers

Kittle hits an excellent .326 against medium-high outside fastballs thrown by left-handed pitchers.

MEDIUM-HIGH OUTSIDE FASTBALLS
(THROWN BY LEFT-HANDED PITCHERS)

BATTING AVERAGE .326

Play

Left	Deep in straightaway left field
Center	Deep in straightaway center field
Right	Medium-deep in straightaway right field
Short	Normal position
Second	Normal position

His .400 against low-over-the-middle fastballs thrown by left-handers is also excellent. He hits this pitch down both lines. By positioning themselves as recommended by the BARS fielding strategy, fielders could prevent most of Kittle's hits from this location.

LOW-OVER-THE-MIDDLE FASTBALLS
(THROWN BY LEFT-HANDED PITCHERS)

BATTING AVERAGE .400
Play

Left	Deep and shifted toward the left field line
Center	Deep and shifted toward right field
Right	Medium-deep and shifted toward the right line
Short	Up middle (shifted toward second base)
Second	*No instances recorded*

He has trouble with inside fastballs against lefties (.166, .071, and .250, high to low). He also has trouble with low-outside fastballs (.000 on 0 for 14).

Kittle has weaknesses against all inside and outside curves thrown by left-handers. He has some strong locations against sliders, however. His .300 against low-inside sliders is excellent, as is the .571 against low-over-the-middle sliders. He pulls low-over-the-middle sliders.

Ahead And Behind In The Count Vs. RH

Ahead

Fastball Average .380

	Inside	Middle	Outside
High	2/1 500	9/4 444	2/0 0
Med	14/5 357	9/5 555	24/8 333
Low	7/3 428	15/5 333	10/4 400

Curve Average .300

	Inside	Middle	Outside
High	0/0 0	4/2 500	0/0 0
Med	4/1 250	3/1 333	9/3 333
Low	0/0 0	3/1 333	7/1 142

Behind

Fastball Average .277

	Inside	Middle	Outside
High	3/1 333	1/0 0	1/0 0
Med	4/1 250	5/0 0	12/6 500
Low	1/0 0	5/2 400	4/0 0

Curve Average .363

	Inside	Middle	Outside
High	3/0 0	2/0 0	0/0 0
Med	0/0 0	3/1 333	7/3 428
Low	0/0 0	3/2 666	4/2 500

Overall Evaluation

Against Right-Handed Pitchers

Overall Fastball	⚾⚾
Overall Curve	⚾⚾
Overall Slider	⚾⚾

Against Left-Handed Pitchers

Overall Fastball	⚾⚾
Overall Curve	⚾⚾
Overall Slider	⚾⚾⚾⚾⚾

Comments: Strong vs. all middle fastballs & all middle curves vs. RH.

Strengths: All middle fastballs and middle curves, medium-outside sliders vs. RH; high-middle, low-middle and medium-outside fastballs, low-inside and low-middle sliders vs. LH.

Weaknesses: Inside and outside fastballs and curves, low-outside sliders vs. RH; inside fastballs, low-outside fastballs, inside and outside curves vs. LH.

Steve Lyons Against Right-Handed Pitchers
Overall BARS Batting Average .281

Fastball Average .296

	Outside	Middle	Inside
High	16/187 /3	24/291 /7	20/400 /8
Med	120/308 /37	20/250 /5	35/314 /11
Low	24/208 /5	34/205 /7	24/458 /11

Curve Average .196

	Outside	Middle	Inside
High	5/200 /1	2/0 /0	3/333 /1
Med	18/222 /4	4/500 /2	4/500 /2
Low	8/125 /1	9/111 /1	13/76 /1

Slider Average .310

	Outside	Middle	Inside
High	1/0 /0	0/0 /0	3/0 /0
Med	2/500 /1	1/0 /0	7/428 /3
Low	1/0 /0	4/1000 /4	10/100 /1

Steve Lyons Against Left-Handed Pitchers
Overall BARS Batting Average .280

Fastball Average .342

	Outside	Middle	Inside
High	3/333 /1	3/1000 /3	11/545 /6
Med	22/500 /11	5/200 /1	14/142 /2
Low	3/0 /0	8/0 /0	4/250 /1

Curve Average .200

	Outside	Middle	Inside
High	1/0 /0	2/0 /0	1/0 /0
Med	4/250 /1	0/0 /0	4/0 /0
Low	5/200 /1	1/1000 /1	2/500 /1

Slider Average .100

	Outside	Middle	Inside
High	2/0 /0	0/0 /0	0/0 /0
Med	3/333 /1	2/0 /0	0/0 /0
Low	3/0 /0	0/0 /0	0/0 /0

The BARS System has more information for left-handed hitting Steve Lyons against right-handed pitchers than against left-handed pitchers.

He hits medium-high outside fastballs very well against right-handers. Notice in his Ahead and Behind charts on the opposite page that he hits this pitch much better when ahead in the count (.367 when ahead, .111 on 2 for 18 when behind).

MEDIUM-HIGH OUTSIDE FASTBALLS (WHEN AHEAD IN THE COUNT)

BATTING AVERAGE .367

Play

Left	Deep and shifted toward the left field line
Center	Medium-deep in straightaway center field
Right	Medium-deep in straightaway right field
Short	Up middle (shifted toward second base)
Second	Normal position

MEDIUM-HIGH OUTSIDE FASTBALLS (WHEN BEHIND IN THE COUNT)

BATTING AVERAGE .111

Play

Left	Deep in straightaway left field
Center	Medium-deep in straightaway center field
Right	Medium-deep in straightaway right field
Short	Up middle (shifted toward second base)
Second	Normal position

His .314 against medium-high inside fastballs is very good.

MEDIUM-HIGH INSIDE FASTBALLS

BATTING AVERAGE .314

Play

Left	Deep in straightaway left field
Center	Deep in straightaway center field
Right	Deep and shifted toward the right field line
Short	Up middle (shifted toward second base)
Second	Shifted toward first base

Notice Lyons' strength against all inside fastballs thrown by right-handers. His .458 against low-inside fastballs is excellent. If fielders adjusted properly they could prevent most of his base hits resulting from pitches to this location.

LOW-INSIDE FASTBALLS

BATTING AVERAGE .458

Play

Left	Medium-deep and shifted toward center field
Center	Medium-deep in straightaway center field
Right	Deep and shifted toward center field
Short	Up middle (shifted toward second base)

Second   Shifted toward first base

    Lyons hits high-over-the-middle and low-over-the-middle fastballs differently.

HIGH-OVER-THE-MIDDLE FASTBALLS

BATTING AVERAGE .291
Play

Left	Deep and shifted toward the left field line
Center	Medium-deep and shifted toward right field
Right	Deep and shifted toward the right field line
Short	Normal position
Second	Shifted toward first base

LOW-OVER-THE-MIDDLE FASTBALLS

BATTING AVERAGE .205
Play

Left	Deep and shifted toward center field
Center	Deep in straightaway center field
Right	Deep and shifted toward the right field line
Short	Up middle (shifted toward second base)
Second	Shifted toward first base

Lyons Against Curves And Sliders

    Lyons has a weakness against outside curves and low curves thrown by right-handed pitchers. His .222 average against medium-outside curves is poor.

MEDIUM-HIGH OUTSIDE CURVEBALLS

BATTING AVERAGE .222

Play

Left	Medium-deep and shifted toward center field
Center	Deep in straightaway center field
Right	Medium-deep in straightaway right field
Short	Normal position
Second	Shifted toward first base

    Notice his weakness against both low-inside curves and low-inside sliders. These are targets for pitchers.

Lyons Against Left-Handed Pitchers

    Lyons' overall fastball average of .342 against left-handed pitchers is built on his exceptional .545 average against high-inside fastballs and .500 against medium-high outside fastballs.

MEDIUM-HIGH OUTSIDE FASTBALLS (THROWN BY LEFT-HANDED PITCHERS)

BATTING AVERAGE .500
Play

Left	Medium-deep in straightaway left field
Center	Deep in straightaway center field
Right	Deep and shifted toward center field
Short	Up middle (shifted toward second base)
Second	Normal position

    He pulls high-inside fastballs (.545) deep down the left line. There is not a lot of information for Lyons against low fastballs, but his BARS records indicate possible weaknesses in these locations.

Ahead And Behind In The Count Vs. RH

Ahead

Fastball Average .333

	Outside	Middle	Inside
High	5/ 400 /2	9/ 222 /2	10/ 400 /4
Med	68/ 367 /25	8/ 375 /3	16/ 312 /5
Low	12/ 166 /2	22/ 136 /3	9/ 777 /7

Curve Average .300

	Outside	Middle	Inside
High	1/ 1000 /1	1/ 0 /0	0/ 0 /0
Med	4/ 0 /0	0/ 0 /0	1/ 1000 /1
Low	1/ 0 /0	2/ 500 /1	0/ 0 /0

Behind

Fastball Average .307

	Outside	Middle	Inside
High	3/ 0 /0	4/ 250 /1	7/ 571 /4
Med	18/ 111 /2	3/ 0 /0	4/ 750 /3
Low	5/ 400 /2	5/ 600 /3	3/ 333 /1

Curve Average .333

	Outside	Middle	Inside
High	2/ 0 /0	1/ 0 /0	1/ 1000 /1
Med	10/ 300 /3	3/ 666 /2	3/ 333 /1
Low	3/ 333 /1	2/ 0 /0	2/ 500 /1

Overall Evaluation

Against Right-Handed Pitchers

Overall Fastball	⚾⚾ ⚾⚾
Overall Curve	⚾⚾
Overall Slider	⚾⚾ ⚾⚾⚾ ⚾⚾

Against Left-Handed Pitchers

Overall Fastball	⚾⚾ ⚾⚾ ⚾⚾ ⚾⚾
Overall Curve	⚾⚾
Overall Slider	Not enough information

Comments: Strong against fastballs, weak against curves against both RH and LH.

Strengths: Inside fastballs, medium-outside fastballs, medium-inside sliders vs. RH; medium-outside and high-inside fastballs vs. LH.

Weaknesses: Low-outside, low-middle, medium-middle and high-outside fastballs, outside and low curves, low-inside sliders vs. RH; medium-inside and all low fastballs, curves and sliders in general vs. LH.

Dan Pasqua (Left Handed) — *Chicago White Sox*

Dan Pasqua Against Right-Handed Pitchers
Overall BARS Batting Average .252

Fastball Average .243

	Outside	Middle	Inside
High	31/ 258 /8	15/ 133 /2	8/ 250 /2
Med	108/ 268 /29	19/ 473 /9	32/ 156 /5
Low	22/ 136 /3	36/ 250 /9	20/ 200 /4

Curve Average .295

	Outside	Middle	Inside
High	0/ 0 /0	4/ 750 /3	2/ 0 /0
Med	12/ 500 /6	5/ 0 /0	3/ 333 /1
Low	17/ 0 /0	9/ 666 /6	9/ 222 /2

Slider Average .243

	Outside	Middle	Inside
High	0/ 0 /0	2/ 0 /0	1/ 0 /0
Med	5/ 400 /2	2/ 500 /1	7/ 142 /1
Low	4/ 250 /1	8/ 500 /4	12/ 83 /1

Dan Pasqua Against Left-Handed Pitchers
Overall BARS Batting Average .194

Fastball Average .250

	Outside	Middle	Inside
High	3/ 0 /0	0/ 0 /0	2/ 0 /0
Med	14/ 71 /1	3/ 333 /1	9/ 222 /2
Low	6/ 333 /2	6/ 666 /4	5/ 400 /2

Curve Average .111

	Outside	Middle	Inside
High	0/ 0 /0	0/ 0 /0	0/ 0 /0
Med	2/ 0 /0	2/ 1000 /2	3/ 0 /0
Low	5/ 0 /0	5/ 0 /0	1/ 0 /0

Slider Average .090

	Outside	Middle	Inside
High	0/ 0 /0	0/ 0 /0	0/ 0 /0
Med	3/ 0 /0	0/ 0 /0	2/ 500 /1
Low	5/ 0 /0	1/ 0 /0	0/ 0 /0

Left-handed hitter Dan Pasqua has trouble with fastballs thrown by right-handed pitchers (.243 overall against fastballs). He hits medium-over-the-middle fastballs well (.473), but his other fastball locations are weak. His .268 against medium-high outside fastballs is barely adequate.

He hits medium-high outside fastballs against right-handers better when he is behind in the count than when ahead. He pulls this pitch a little more when ahead (.274) than when behind (.444).

MEDIUM-HIGH OUTSIDE FASTBALLS (WHEN BEHIND IN THE COUNT)

BATTING AVERAGE .444
Play

Left	Deep in straightaway left field
Center	Deep and shifted toward right field
Right	Medium-deep in straightaway right field
Short	Normal position
Second	Normal position

MEDIUM-HIGH OUTSIDE FASTBALLS (WHEN AHEAD IN THE COUNT)

BATTING AVERAGE .274
Play

Left	Deep and shifted toward the left field line
Center	Deep in straightaway center field
Right	Deep in straightaway right field
Short	Up middle (shifted toward second base)
Second	Normal position

He has a lot of trouble with inside fastballs. He hits medium-high inside fastballs for a .156 average, scattering the ball down both lines.

MEDIUM-HIGH INSIDE FASTBALLS

BATTING AVERAGE .156
Play

Left	Deep and shifted toward the left field line
Center	Deep in straightaway center field
Right	Deep and shifted toward the right field line
Short	Up middle (shifted toward second base)
Second	Normal position

He also scatters low-inside fastballs.

LOW-INSIDE FASTBALLS

BATTING AVERAGE .200
Play

Left	Medium-deep and shifted toward the left field line
Center	Deep in straightaway center field
Right	Deep and shifted toward the right field line
Short	Up middle (shifted toward second base)
Second	Normal position

248

He goes to the opposite field with low-over-the-middle fastballs. The infielders need to play for a pull.

LOW-OVER-THE-MIDDLE FASTBALLS

BATTING AVERAGE .250
Play
Left	Deep and shifted toward the left field line
Center	Deep in straightaway center field
Right	Deep and shifted toward center field
Short	Up middle (shifted toward second base)
Second	Shifted toward first base

Pasqua hits high-outside fastballs deep to all fields and to the right side of the infield.

HIGH-OUTSIDE FASTBALLS

BATTING AVERAGE .258
Play
Left	Medium-deep in straightaway left field
Center	Deep in straightaway center field
Right	Deep in straightaway right field
Short	Up middle (shifted toward second base)
Second	Shifted toward first base

One would not want to throw Pasqua, or any hitter, a medium-over-the-middle fastball, but his strong .473 average in this location makes it interesting to look at how he hits this pitch. He hits it deep and straightaway to the outfield.

MEDIUM-OVER-THE-MIDDLE FASTBALLS

BATTING AVERAGE .473
Play
Left	Deep in straightaway left field
Center	Deep in straightaway center field
Right	Deep in straightaway right field

Short	Shifted toward third base
Second	Shifted toward first base

Pasqua Against Curves And Sliders

Pasqua hits medium-high outside curves exceptionally well (.500) but hits low-outside curves very poorly (.000 on 0 for 17). He hits medium-high outside curves deep to all fields.

MEDIUM-HIGH OUTSIDE CURVEBALLS

BATTING AVERAGE .500
Play
Left	Deep in straightaway left field
Center	Deep and shifted toward right field
Right	Deep in straightaway right field
Short	*No instances recorded*
Second	Shifted toward first base

Pasqua Against Left-Handed Pitchers

Pasqua has trouble with fastballs against left-handed pitchers. He hits medium-high outside pitches for a .071 average.

MEDIUM-HIGH OUTSIDE FASTBALLS (THROWN BY LEFT-HANDED PITCHERS)

BATTING AVERAGE .071
Play
Left	Deep in straightaway left field
Center	Deep in straightaway center field
Right	Deep and shifted toward the right field line
Short	Normal position
Second	Shifted toward first base

Ahead And Behind In The Count Vs. RH

Ahead

	Fastball Average .308			Curve Average .357		
	Outside	Middle	Inside	Outside	Middle	Inside
High	9/444 /4	5/200 /1	1/0 /0	0/0 /0	3/666 /2	1/0 /0
Med	51/274 /14	13/461 /6	11/363 /4	3/333 /1	1/0 /0	0/0 /0
Low	4/250 /1	18/277 /5	8/250 /2	2/0 /0	3/666 /2	1/0 /0

Behind

	Fastball Average .339			Curve Average .357		
	Outside	Middle	Inside	Outside	Middle	Inside
High	7/285 /2	3/0 /0	5/400 /2	0/0 /0	1/1000 /1	1/0 /0
Med	18/444 /8	1/1000 /1	5/0 /0	4/250 /1	2/0 /0	0/0 /0
Low	3/333 /1	7/285 /2	4/500 /2	1/0 /0	3/666 /2	2/500 /1

Overall Evaluation

Against Right-Handed Pitchers

Overall Fastball ⚾⚾

Overall Curve ⚾⚾ ⚾⚾⚾

Overall Slider ⚾⚾

Against Left-Handed Pitchers

Overall Fastball ⚾⚾

Overall Curve ⚾⚾

Overall Slider Not enough information

Comments: Weak against fastballs vs. RH and LH. Strengths: Medium-middle fastballs, medium-outside and low-middle curves, low-middle sliders vs. RH. Weaknesses: High, inside, outside and low fastballs, low-outside curves, inside sliders vs. RH; medium-outside fastballs, all curves and sliders in general vs. LH.

Greg Walker (Left Handed)   *Chicago White Sox*

Greg Walker Against Right-Handed Pitchers
Overall BARS Batting Average .293

Fastball Average .326

	Outside	Middle	Inside
High	34 / 176 /6	34 / 294 /10	28 / 214 /6
Med	166 / 277 /46	34 / 441 /15	69 / 347 /24
Low	43 / 372 /16	71 / 450 /32	44 / 363 /16

Curve Average .227

	Outside	Middle	Inside
High	3 / 0 /0	1 / 1000 /1	3 / 333 /1
Med	25 / 320 /8	7 / 714 /5	8 / 0 /0
Low	16 / 312 /5	20 / 100 /2	18 / 55 /1

Slider Average .200

	Outside	Middle	Inside
High	1 / 0 /0	1 / 1000 /1	2 / 0 /0
Med	8 / 250 /2	7 / 428 /3	9 / 111 /1
Low	2 / 0 /0	7 / 142 /1	13 / 153 /2

Greg Walker Against Left-Handed Pitchers
Overall BARS Batting Average .223

Fastball Average .248

	Outside	Middle	Inside
High	7 / 0 /0	11 / 272 /3	13 / 307 /4
Med	59 / 237 /14	4 / 500 /2	38 / 263 /10
Low	12 / 83 /1	36 / 333 /12	17 / 176 /3

Curve Average .203

	Outside	Middle	Inside
High	2 / 500 /1	1 / 1000 /1	1 / 0 /0
Med	14 / 357 /5	5 / 0 /0	4 / 250 /1
Low	18 / 55 /1	14 / 214 /3	0 / 0 /0

Slider Average .128

	Outside	Middle	Inside
High	1 / 0 /0	1 / 0 /0	1 / 0 /0
Med	11 / 363 /4	0 / 0 /0	4 / 0 /0
Low	12 / 83 /1	8 / 0 /0	1 / 0 /0

Greg Walker, left-handed hitter, has an excellent .326 overall BARS fastball average against right-handed pitchers. But his .248 overall fastball average against left-handers is not as strong.

Walker has only two weak fastball locations against right-handers (high-outside at .176 and high-inside at .214). All other fastball locations are solid. He hits low fastballs extremely well. His .450 average against low-over-the-middle fastballs is superb. He hits this pitch well both when ahead and when behind, but better when ahead. When ahead, he scatters this pitch to all fields.

LOW-OVER-THE-MIDDLE FASTBALLS (WHEN AHEAD IN THE COUNT)

BATTING AVERAGE .548
Play
Left — Medium-deep and shifted toward the left field line
Center — Deep and shifted toward left field
Right — Medium-deep and shifted toward the right line
Short — Up middle (shifted toward second base)
Second — Shifted toward first base

LOW-OVER-THE-MIDDLE FASTBALLS (WHEN BEHIND IN THE COUNT)

BATTING AVERAGE .375
Play
Left — Deep and shifted toward the left field line

Center — Deep in straightaway center field
Right — Deep and shifted toward center field
Short — Shifted toward third base
Second — Shifted toward first base

He also hits medium-high inside fastballs better when ahead. He hits medium-high outside fastballs, however, better when behind. When behind he goes with medium-high outside pitches, hitting them to his opposite field (left field). When ahead, he scatters this pitch to all fields.

MEDIUM-HIGH OUTSIDE FASTBALLS (WHEN BEHIND IN THE COUNT)

BATTING AVERAGE .406
Play
Left — Deep and shifted toward the left field line
Center — Deep and shifted toward left field
Right — Deep and shifted toward center field
Short — Up middle (shifted toward second base)
Second — Normal position

MEDIUM-HIGH OUTSIDE FASTBALLS (WHEN AHEAD IN THE COUNT)

BATTING AVERAGE .328
Play
Left — Deep and shifted toward the left field line

Center	Deep in straightaway center field
Right	Deep and shifted toward the right field line
Short	Normal position
Second	Shifted toward first base

Walker Against Curves And Sliders

Walker hits low-outside and medium-high outside curves excellently. He's weak against low-over-the-middle and low-inside curves. He hits medium-high outside curves deep and straightaway to all fields.

MEDIUM-HIGH OUTSIDE CURVEBALLS

BATTING AVERAGE .320

Play
Left	Deep in straightaway left field
Center	Deep in straightaway center field
Right	Deep in straightaway right field
Short	Normal position
Second	Shifted toward first base

He hits low-outside curves medium-deep to center and right.

LOW-OUTSIDE CURVEBALLS

BATTING AVERAGE .312

Play
Left	Deep in straightaway left field
Center	Medium-deep in straightaway center field
Right	Medium-deep and shifted toward center field
Short	Up middle (shifted toward second base)
Second	Normal position

Walker has a lot of trouble with low sliders. His

.153 average against low-inside sliders is a weakness pitchers can focus on.

Walker Against Left-Handed Pitchers

Walker has trouble with low-outside fastballs (1 for 12) and high-outside fastballs (0 for 7) thrown by left-handed pitchers. His .237 against medium-high outside fastballs is also weak.

MEDIUM-HIGH OUTSIDE FASTBALLS (THROWN BY LEFT-HANDED PITCHERS)

BATTING AVERAGE .237

Play
Left	Deep in straightaway left field
Center	Deep in straightaway center field
Right	Medium-deep in straightaway right field
Short	Up middle (shifted toward second base)
Second	Normal position

He hits .333 against low-over-the-middle fastballs against left-handers.

LOW-OVER-THE-MIDDLE FASTBALLS (THROWN BY LEFT-HANDED PITCHERS)

BATTING AVERAGE .333

Play
Left	Deep and shifted toward center field
Center	Medium-deep in straightaway center field
Right	Deep in straightaway right field
Short	Shifted toward third base
Second	Normal position

Ahead And Behind In The Count Vs. RH

Ahead

	Fastball Average .422			Curve Average .296		
	Outside	Middle	Inside	Outside	Middle	Inside
High	4/750 /3	14/428 /6	5/400 /2	2/0 /0	0/0 /0	2/500 /1
Med	73/328 /24	22/409 /9	30/466 /14	5/600 /3	3/333 /1	1/0 /0
Low	14/571 /8	31/548 /17	20/350 /7	3/666 /2	8/125 /1	3/0 /0

Behind

	Fastball Average .387			Curve Average .321		
	Outside	Middle	Inside	Outside	Middle	Inside
High	12/166 /2	12/333 /4	7/428 /3	0/0 /0	0/0 /0	1/0 /0
Med	32/406 /13	2/500 /1	19/368 /7	8/375 /3	4/1000 /4	5/0 /0
Low	10/400 /4	16/375 /6	6/833 /5	5/400 /2	3/0 /0	2/0 /0

Kansas City Royals

Boone, Bob
Brett, George
Buckner, Bill
Eisenreich, Jim
Jackson, Bo
Perry, Gerald
Seitzer, Kevin
Stillwell, Kurt
Tabler, Pat
Tartabull, Danny
White, Frank
Wilson, Willie

Kansas City Royals
BARS System
Hitting Analysis

Bob Boone Against Right-Handed Pitchers
Overall BARS Batting Average .233

	Fastball Average .239			Curve Average .194			Slider Average .260		
	Inside	Middle	Outside	Inside	Middle	Outside	Inside	Middle	Outside
High	21/142 /3	28/428 /12	10/500 /5	3/666 /2	8/500 /4	3/333 /1	3/666 /2	4/250 /1	2/0 /0
Med	52/269 /14	20/150 /3	62/209 /13	10/200 /2	3/0 /0	26/76 /2	6/500 /3	0/0 /0	14/214 /3
Low	11/272 /3	31/161 /5	20/150 /3	1/0 /0	9/222 /2	9/111 /1	2/0 /0	7/285 /2	12/166 /2

Bob Boone Against Left-Handed Pitchers
Overall BARS Batting Average .245

	Fastball Average .245			Curve Average .133			Slider Average .333		
	Inside	Middle	Outside	Inside	Middle	Outside	Inside	Middle	Outside
High	9/222 /2	10/200 /2	13/230 /3	1/0 /0	0/0 /0	0/0 /0	2/500 /1	2/500 /1	0/0 /0
Med	19/315 /6	16/437 /7	34/205 /7	0/0 /0	3/333 /1	1/0 /0	2/0 /0	1/1000 /1	1/1000 /1
Low	3/0 /0	27/259 /7	20/150 /3	1/0 /0	4/250 /1	5/0 /0	0/0 /0	5/400 /2	5/0 /0

Right-handed Bob Boone has similar overall BARS averages against right- and left-handed pitchers. And he hits fastballs for about the same average overall (.239 against right-handers, .245 against left-handers).

He has a strong sector in his fastball chart against right-handed pitchers. He hits .428 against high-over-the-middle fastballs and .500 against high-outside fastballs. These are the two strong locations in his fastball grid against right-handers.

He hits high-over-the-middle fastballs deep down the left line and medium-deep to center and right.

HIGH-OVER-THE-MIDDLE FASTBALLS

BATTING AVERAGE .428
Play

Left	Deep and shifted toward the left field line
Center	Medium-deep in straightaway center field
Right	Medium-deep in straightaway right field
Short	Normal position
Second	*No instances recorded*

He hits high-outside fastballs medium-deep into the left-center alley and deep into the right-center alley. Every outfielder needs to play differently for a high-over-the-middle compared to a high-outside fastball.

HIGH-OUTSIDE FASTBALLS

BATTING AVERAGE .500
Play

Left	Medium-deep and shifted toward center field
Center	Deep and shifted toward right field
Right	Deep in straightaway right field
Short	*No instances recorded*
Second	Shifted toward first base

Boone hits .269 against medium-high inside fastballs. His Ahead and Behind charts on the opposite page show that he hits this pitch better when behind in the count (.300 when behind, .200 when ahead).

MEDIUM-HIGH INSIDE FASTBALLS
(WHEN BEHIND IN THE COUNT)

BATTING AVERAGE .300
Play

Left	Medium-deep and shifted toward the left field line
Center	Medium-deep in straightaway center field
Right	*No instances recorded*
Short	Shifted toward third base
Second	Normal position

MEDIUM-HIGH INSIDE FASTBALLS
(WHEN AHEAD IN THE COUNT)

BATTING AVERAGE .200
  Play
Left   Medium-deep and shifted toward the left field line
Center   Medium-deep and shifted toward left field
Right   Short in straightaway right field
Short   Shifted toward third base
Second   Normal position

He hits only .209 in his medium-high outside fast-ball location.

MEDIUM-HIGH OUTSIDE FASTBALLS

BATTING AVERAGE .209
  Play
Left   Deep and shifted toward the left field line
Center   Medium-deep in straightaway center field
Right   Medium-deep in straightaway right field
Short   Up middle (shifted toward second base)
Second   Normal position

Except for the three high locations, Boone has trouble against all curves against right-handed pitchers.

He hits a little better overall against sliders. His .214 and .166 in the medium-high and low-outside slider locations are weak, but he hits .285 against low-over-the-middle sliders and .500 against medium-high inside sliders.

Boone Against Left-Handed Pitchers

Boone has trouble with all outside, high, and low fastballs thrown by left-handed pitchers. His strong sector consists of the medium-high inside (.315) and medium-over-the-middle (.437) locations. If left-handers keep fastballs away from these locations, they should have an edge on him. He hits medium-high inside fastballs deep down the left line.

MEDIUM-HIGH INSIDE FASTBALLS (THROWN BY LEFT-HANDED PITCHERS)

BATTING AVERAGE .315
  Play
Left   Deep and shifted toward the left field line
Center   Deep in straightaway center field
Right   *No instances recorded*
Short   Shifted toward third base
Second   Normal position

He hits medium-over-the-middle fastballs straight-away to all fields, but note that the outfielders need to play medium-deep or short. If they did, they could prevent most of his base hits from this location.

MEDIUM-OVER-THE-MIDDLE FASTBALLS (THROWN BY LEFT-HANDED PITCHERS)

BATTING AVERAGE .437
  Play
Left   Medium-deep in straightaway left field
Center   Medium-deep in straightaway center field
Right   Short in straightaway right field
Short   Normal position
Second   *No instances recorded*

Ahead And Behind In The Count Vs. RH

Ahead

Fastball Average .264

	Inside	Middle	Outside
High	7/ 0/0	13/ 384/5	3/ 1000/3
Med	20/ 200/4	13/ 153/2	24/ 250/6
Low	5/ 400/2	16/ 187/3	5/ 600/3

Curve Average .125

	Inside	Middle	Outside
High	0/ 0/0	2/ 1000/2	0/ 0/0
Med	4/ 0/0	0/ 0/0	5/ 0/0
Low	0/ 0/0	3/ 0/0	2/ 0/0

Behind

Fastball Average .269

	Inside	Middle	Outside
High	5/ 0/0	7/ 571/4	2/ 500/1
Med	10/ 300/3	4/ 250/1	9/ 222/2
Low	3/ 333/1	8/ 250/2	4/ 0/0

Curve Average .190

	Inside	Middle	Outside
High	1/ 0/0	3/ 0/0	1/ 0/0
Med	2/ 500/1	1/ 0/0	8/ 125/1
Low	0/ 0/0	3/ 333/1	2/ 500/1

Overall Evaluation

Against Right-Handed Pitchers

Overall Fastball ⚾⚾
Overall Curve ⚾⚾
Overall Slider ⚾⚾ ⚾

Against Left-Handed Pitchers

Overall Fastball ⚾⚾
Overall Curve ⚾⚾
Overall Slider ⚾⚾ ⚾⚾ ⚾⚾ ⚾⚾

Comments: Has a strong fastball sector high-middle/high-outside vs. RH.
Strengths: Fastballs as above, high-middle curves vs. RH; medium-inside & medium-middle fastballs vs. LH.
Weaknesses: Fastballs except high-middle and high-outside, waist-high and low curves, outside sliders vs. RH; fastballs except medium-inside and medium-middle vs. LH.

George Brett (Left Handed)   *Kansas City Royals*

George Brett Against Right-Handed Pitchers
Overall BARS Batting Average .348

Fastball Average .356			Curve Average .302			Slider Average .354		
Outside	Middle	Inside	Outside	Middle	Inside	Outside	Middle	Inside
High 47/255/12	96/312/30	20/350/7	8/250/2	9/666/6	2/0/0	0/0/0	7/428/3	4/500/2
Med 180/377/68	92/489/45	81/283/23	37/351/13	19/421/8	22/363/8	8/250/2	10/700/7	24/250/6
Low 53/320/17	120/358/43	23/391/9	10/0/0	29/137/4	16/312/5	7/285/2	17/235/4	19/421/8

George Brett Against Left-Handed Pitchers
Overall BARS Batting Average .305

Fastball Average .318			Curve Average .286			Slider Average .276		
Outside	Middle	Inside	Outside	Middle	Inside	Outside	Middle	Inside
High 10/400/4	37/540/20	23/391/9	6/500/3	16/312/5	5/400/2	5/400/2	7/428/3	1/0/0
Med 99/272/27	31/354/11	52/307/16	34/323/11	15/400/6	20/250/5	17/235/4	4/750/3	2/0/0
Low 18/111/2	34/264/9	16/250/4	14/142/2	20/250/5	6/0/0	11/0/0	12/416/5	6/166/1

Left-handed hitting George Brett, first baseman for the Royals and one of the league's finest hitters over the last decade, hits better against right-handed than left-handed pitchers (.323 overall against right-handers, .286 overall against left-handers). But it should be noted that his .318 against fastballs and .286 against curves thrown by left-handers are very good for a left-handed hitter.

Brett's .356 overall fastball average against right-handed pitchers is excellent. His .377 in the frequently pitched medium-high outside location is top rate. He hits this pitch deep to all fields.

MEDIUM-HIGH OUTSIDE FASTBALLS

BATTING AVERAGE .377
Play
Left   Deep and shifted toward the left field line
Center   Deep in straightaway center field
Right   Deep and shifted toward center field
Short   Up middle (shifted toward second base)
Second   Normal position

Brett has the characteristic of hitting many fly balls and line drives to the opposite field (left field) while pulling ground balls to the right side of the infield. This is true of both inside and outside fastballs. This shows how badly some fielders could be out of position when they don't follow the BARS fielding strategy.

LOW-OUTSIDE FASTBALLS

BATTING AVERAGE .320
Play
Left   Deep and shifted toward the left field line
Center   Deep and shifted toward left field
Right   Deep and shifted toward center field
Short   Up middle (shifted toward second base)
Second   Shifted toward first base

LOW-INSIDE FASTBALLS

BATTING AVERAGE .391
Play
Left   Medium-deep shifted toward the left field line
Center   Deep and shifted toward left field
Right   Medium-deep and shifted toward center field
Short   Up middle (shifted toward second base)
Second   Shifted toward first base

Brett's extremely high medium-over-the-middle fastball average (.489 on 45 for 92) is a stern warning to pitchers not to throw over the heart of the plate. He pulls these pitches deep to the outfield and infield.

The high number of recorded instances in Brett's medium-over-the-middle location (92) shows that he is a patient hitter. He knows that if he waits long enough, he will get a good pitch to hit. This is a good example for other hitters to follow.

He hits a solid .351 against medium-high outside curves thrown by right-handers. He scatters these pitches deep to all fields.

MEDIUM-HIGH OUTSIDE CURVEBALLS

BATTING AVERAGE .351
Play

Left	Deep and shifted toward the left field line
Center	Deep and straightaway in center field
Right	Deep and shifted toward the right field line
Short	Up middle (shifted toward second base)
Second	Shifted toward first base

Brett hits well overall against sliders. His .421 against low-inside sliders is excellent. His .250 against medium-high inside and .235 against low-over-the-middle are below par for him, however.

The Ahead and Behind charts below show that Brett hits both fastballs and curves better when ahead in the count than when behind in the count against right-handed pitchers. His BARS fielding strategy shows that he hits inside fastballs with greater authority when ahead.

Although a pitcher would usually not want to throw Brett a medium-over-the-middle fastball, he doesn't have a high average in that location when he's behind (.142).

Brett Against Left-Handed Pitchers

Against left-handed pitchers, Brett tends to hit fastballs similarly to the way he hits them against right-handed pitchers — fairly straightaway or slightly toward the opposite field when he hits fly balls, and to the right side of the infield when he hits grounders.

MEDIUM-HIGH OUTSIDE FASTBALLS (THROWN BY LEFT-HANDED PITCHERS)

BATTING AVERAGE .272
Play

Left	Deep in straightaway left field
Center	Deep in straightaway center field
Right	Deep in straightaway right field
Short	Up middle (shifted toward second base)
Second	Shifted toward first base

MEDIUM-HIGH INSIDE FASTBALLS (THROWN BY LEFT-HANDED PITCHERS)

BATTING AVERAGE .307
Play

Left	Medium-deep in straightaway left field
Center	Deep and shifted toward left field
Right	Deep and straightaway in right field
Short	Normal position
Second	Shifted toward first base

He has trouble with low-outside curves and low-over-the-middle curves against left-handers (.142 and .250, respectively) but he hits medium-high outside curves excellently (.323).

MEDIUM-HIGH OUTSIDE CURVEBALLS (THROWN BY LEFT-HANDED PITCHERS)

BATTING AVERAGE .323
Play

Left	Deep in straightaway left field
Center	Deep in straightaway center field
Right	Deep in straightaway right field
Short	Up middle (shifted toward second base)
Second	Shifted toward first base

Ahead And Behind In The Count Vs. RH

Ahead

Fastball Average .397

	Outside	Middle	Inside
High	16/250/4	45/333/15	9/333/3
Med	100/440/44	60/600/36	56/321/18
Low	23/391/9	70/314/22	11/363/4

Curve Average .404

	Outside	Middle	Inside
High	1/1000/1	3/666/2	1/0/0
Med	12/416/5	5/200/1	8/500/4
Low	2/0/0	9/222/2	6/666/4

Behind

Fastball Average .343

	Outside	Middle	Inside
High	9/666/6	14/214/3	6/166/1
Med	25/360/9	7/142/1	11/90/1
Low	4/500/2	20/450/9	3/666/2

Curve Average .282

	Outside	Middle	Inside
High	3/0/0	4/1000/4	0/0/0
Med	10/200/2	4/250/1	5/400/2
Low	1/0/0	10/100/1	2/500/1

Overall Evaluation
Against Right-Handed Pitchers

Overall Fastball ⚾⚾⚾⚾⚾

Overall Curve ⚾⚾⚾⚾⚾

Overall Slider ⚾⚾⚾⚾⚾

Against Left-Handed Pitchers

Overall Fastball ⚾⚾⚾

Overall Curve ⚾⚾⚾

Overall Slider ⚾⚾⚾

Comments: Very strong against fastballs vs. RH. Strengths: Fastballs vs. RH except high-outside, waist-high and low-outside curves, low-inside and medium-middle sliders vs. RH; medium-middle and all high fastballs, medium-outside, high-middle and medium-middle curves, low-middle sliders vs. LH. Weaknesses: High-outside fastballs, low-outside and low-middle curves, low-middle sliders vs. RH; low fastballs, low curves and low-outside sliders vs. LH.

Bill Buckner (Left Handed)   *Kansas City Royals*

Bill Buckner Against Right-Handed Pitchers
Overall BARS Batting Average .289

Fastball Average .296

	Outside	Middle	Inside
High	51 / 274 / 14	50 / 260 / 13	17 / 352 / 6
Med	231 / 320 / 74	42 / 428 / 18	57 / 263 / 15
Low	58 / 275 / 16	117 / 273 / 32	52 / 230 / 12

Curve Average .270

	Outside	Middle	Inside
High	10 / 400 / 4	14 / 428 / 6	6 / 166 / 1
Med	38 / 210 / 8	11 / 454 / 5	16 / 312 / 5
Low	17 / 235 / 4	29 / 172 / 5	18 / 277 / 5

Slider Average .259

	Outside	Middle	Inside
High	2 / 0 / 0	1 / 0 / 0	2 / 0 / 0
Med	2 / 500 / 1	1 / 0 / 0	8 / 500 / 4
Low	8 / 125 / 1	12 / 250 / 3	18 / 277 / 5

Bill Buckner Against Left-Handed Pitchers
Overall BARS Batting Average .279

Fastball Average .258

	Outside	Middle	Inside
High	8 / 375 / 3	27 / 185 / 5	16 / 250 / 4
Med	91 / 296 / 27	21 / 285 / 6	39 / 282 / 11
Low	13 / 230 / 3	41 / 219 / 9	26 / 192 / 5

Curve Average .316

	Outside	Middle	Inside
High	4 / 500 / 2	7 / 428 / 3	3 / 333 / 1
Med	19 / 210 / 4	1 / 0 / 0	10 / 300 / 3
Low	18 / 111 / 2	12 / 583 / 7	5 / 600 / 3

Slider Average .254

	Outside	Middle	Inside
High	1 / 0 / 0	2 / 0 / 0	0 / 0 / 0
Med	22 / 318 / 7	4 / 250 / 1	6 / 0 / 0
Low	13 / 153 / 2	8 / 500 / 4	3 / 333 / 1

Bill Buckner, left-handed batter, hits better overall against right-handed pitchers (.277 overall against right-handers, .258 overall against left-handers).

Buckner's .296 overall fastball average against right-handed pitchers is pretty good. His .320 average in the medium-high outside location is solid, especially considering the high number of recorded instances in that location (231).

He hits medium-high outside fastballs deep to all fields. Notice that he hits these fastballs down both lines.

MEDIUM-HIGH OUTSIDE FASTBALLS

BATTING AVERAGE .320
Play
Left	Deep and shifted toward the left field line
Center	Deep in straightaway center field
Right	Deep and shifted toward the right field line
Short	Up middle (shifted toward second base)
Second	Normal position

The next chart shows that Buckner hits low-over-the-middle fastballs medium-deep to left and center fields. This emphasizes the point that if the outfielders play Buckner deep for all pitches to him, some will be out of position when low pitches are thrown.

LOW-OVER-THE-MIDDLE FASTBALLS

BATTING AVERAGE .273
Play
Left	Medium-deep and shifted toward center field
Center	Medium-deep in straightaway center field
Right	Deep and shifted toward center field
Short	Up middle (shifted toward second base)
Second	Normal position

Note in the above chart that all outfielders need to shift when a low-over-the-middle fastball is thrown. The infielders do not need to shift.

Buckner Against Curves And Sliders

In his curve chart against right-handed pitchers, Buckner has a weak L-shaped sector in the medium-high outside (.210), low-outside (.235) and low-over-the-middle (.172) curve locations. Buckner pulls low-over-the-middle curves, hits low-outside curves to the opposite field, and hits medium-high outside curves straightaway to the outfield.

MEDIUM-HIGH OUTSIDE CURVEBALLS

BATTING AVERAGE .210

Play

Left   Deep in straightaway left field
Center   Medium-deep in straightaway center field
Right   Medium-deep in straightaway right field
Short   Up middle (shifted toward second base)
Second   Normal position

LOW-OUTSIDE CURVEBALLS

BATTING AVERAGE .235

Play

Left   Deep and shifted toward the left field line
Center   Medium-deep and shifted toward left field
Right   Medium-deep in straightaway right field
Short   *No instances recorded*
Second   Normal position

LOW-OVER-THE-MIDDLE CURVEBALLS

BATTING AVERAGE .172

Play

Left   Deep and shifted toward center field
Center   Deep in straightaway center field
Right   Deep and shifted toward the right field line
Short   Up middle (shifted toward second base)
Second   Shifted toward first base

Buckner hits sliders only adequately (.259 overall). His .277 against low-inside sliders is fairly good and his .500 against medium-high inside sliders is excellent, but he has trouble in other slider locations.

Buckner Against Left-Handed Pitchers

Against left-handed pitchers, Buckner's fastball average is lower than it is against right-handed pitchers, but his curve average is higher (this is somewhat unusual for a left-handed hitter). Buckner is probably looking for curves and pitchers don't realize it. This is a good case in which left-handers could learn from the BARS charts. Managers might consider bringing Buckner in to pinch hit against a left-handed pitcher.

Notice Buckner's weaknesses against low fastballs thrown by left-handed pitchers (.192, .219 and .230, inside to outside).

He hits medium-high fastballs better. The following charts show that the center and right fielders must position themselves differently for medium-high inside and medium-high outside fastballs.

MEDIUM-HIGH OUTSIDE FASTBALLS (THROWN BY LEFT-HANDED PITCHERS)

BATTING AVERAGE .296

Play

Left   Deep in straightaway left field
Center   Deep in straightaway center field
Right   Deep and shifted toward center field
Short   Up middle (shifted toward second base)
Second   Normal position

MEDIUM-HIGH INSIDE FASTBALLS (THROWN BY LEFT-HANDED PITCHERS)

BATTING AVERAGE .282

Play

Left   *No instances recorded*
Center   Medium-deep in straightaway center field
Right   Medium-deep and shifted toward the right
Short   Normal position
Second   Shifted toward first base

Ahead And Behind In The Count Vs. RH

Ahead

Fastball Average .324

	Outside	Middle	Inside
High	12/333 /4	19/315 /6	4/500 /2
Med	126/341 /43	25/440 /11	33/303 /10
Low	24/208 /5	59/305 /18	22/272 /6

Curve Average .325

	Outside	Middle	Inside
High	3/666 /2	4/750 /3	1/0 /0
Med	6/0 /0	1/0 /0	7/285 /2
Low	4/250 /1	10/400 /4	4/250 /1

Behind

Fastball Average .289

	Outside	Middle	Inside
High	17/352 /6	17/235 /4	6/333 /2
Med	53/339 /18	6/333 /2	8/250 /2
Low	14/285 /4	29/206 /6	9/222 /2

Curve Average .357

	Outside	Middle	Inside
High	5/200 /1	5/200 /1	0/0 /0
Med	6/333 /2	4/500 /2	4/500 /2
Low	5/400 /2	5/200 /1	8/500 /4

Overall Evaluation

Against Right-Handed Pitchers

Overall Fastball ⚾⚾
Overall Curve ⚾⚾
Overall Slider ⚾⚾

Against Left-Handed Pitchers

Overall Fastball ⚾
Overall Curve ⚾⚾⚾⚾
Overall Slider ⚾⚾

Comments: Hits fastballs better overall against RH, curves better against LH.

Strengths: High-inside, medium-middle and medium-outside fastballs vs. RH, high-middle, high-outside, medium-middle and medium-inside curves vs. RH.

Weaknesses: All fastballs except as above vs. RH, low curves and medium-outside curves, low sliders vs. RH; high-middle and all low fastballs, low-outside & medium-outside curves, low-outside sliders vs. LH.

Jim Eisenreich (Left Handed)　　　*Kansas City Royals*

Jim Eisenreich Against Right-Handed Pitchers
Overall BARS Batting Average .226

Fastball Average .237			Curve Average .293			Slider Average .260		
Outside	Middle	Inside	Outside	Middle	Inside	Outside	Middle	Inside
High 14/142 /2	15/133 /2	11/90 /1	2/0 /0	5/200 /1	3/0 /0	1/1000 /1	1/0 /0	1/0 /0
Med 65/200 /13	14/357 /5	35/342 /12	17/294 /5	1/1000 /1	12/416 /5	2/0 /0	0/0 /0	3/333 /1
Low 11/90 /1	24/333 /8	13/307 /4	6/500 /3	6/333 /2	6/0 /0	4/250 /1	3/666 /2	8/125 /1

Left-handed hitter Jim Eisenreich has a low overall fastball average against right-handed pitchers (.237), but he hits curves and sliders well (.293 and .260). The BARS System has little information for Eisenreich against left-handed pitchers, so only his charts against right-handers are included here.

Against right-handers, Eisenreich has a strong fastball sector consisting of his low-inside (.307)/medium-high inside (.342)/medium-over-the-middle (.357)/low-over-the-middle (.333) locations. Right-handers should avoid this sector because he is weak against all outside and all high fastballs.

His .342 against medium-high inside fastballs is excellent. He hits this pitch straightaway to the outfield while pulling it to the right side of the infield. Please see the field diagram opposite.

MEDIUM-HIGH INSIDE FASTBALLS

BATTING AVERAGE .342
Play
Left　　　Medium-deep in straightaway left field
Center　Deep in straightaway center field
Right　　Deep in straightaway right field
Short　　Up middle (shifted toward second base)
Second　Shifted toward first base

His .333 against low-over-the-middle fastballs is also excellent. Notice that he hits this pitch down the left line and into left-center. But the infielders need to play for a pull.

LOW-OVER-THE-MIDDLE FASTBALLS

BATTING AVERAGE .333
Play
Left　　　Medium-deep and shifted toward the left line
Center　Deep and shifted toward left field
Right　　Medium-deep in straightaway right field
Short　　Up middle (shifted toward second base)
Second　Shifted toward first base

Eisenreich's .200 against medium-high outside fastballs is a weakness. His low average in this location indicates that he hits this pitch mostly for easy pop flies and ground outs.

MEDIUM-HIGH OUTSIDE FASTBALLS

BATTING AVERAGE .200
Play
Left　　　Deep in straightaway left field
Center　Deep in straightaway center field
Right　　Deep and shifted toward the right field line
Short　　Up middle (shifted toward second base)
Second　Shifted toward first base

Eisenreich Against Curves And Sliders

Eisenreich hits a strong .294 against medium-high outside curves thrown by right-handers.

MEDIUM-HIGH OUTSIDE CURVEBALLS

BATTING AVERAGE .294
Play
Left　　　Deep in straightaway left field
Center　Medium-deep in straightaway center field
Right　　Deep in straightaway right field
Short　　Up middle (shifted toward second base)
Second　Normal position

His .416 against medium-high inside curves is very strong.

MEDIUM-HIGH INSIDE CURVEBALLS

BATTING AVERAGE .416
Play
Left　　　Short in straightaway left field
Center　Medium-deep and shifted toward right field
Right　　Deep in straightaway right field
Short　　Normal position
Second　Shifted toward first base

He hits sliders pretty well overall against right-handers but has trouble with low-inside sliders (.125).

Medium-High Inside Fastballs
(Thrown By Right-Handed Pitchers)

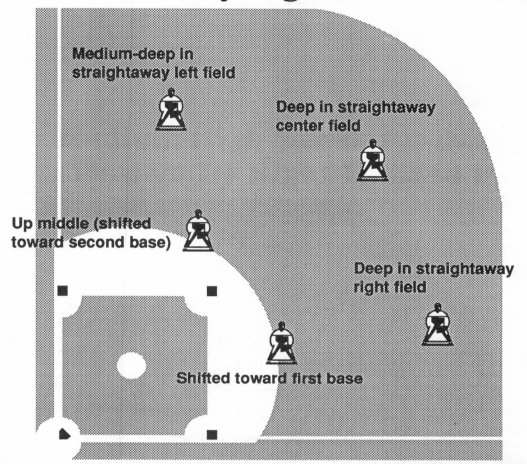

Medium-deep in straightaway left field

Deep in straightaway center field

Up middle (shifted toward second base)

Deep in straightaway right field

Shifted toward first base

Ahead And Behind In The Count Vs. RH

Ahead

	Fastball Average .326			Curve Average .285		
	Outside	Middle	Inside	Outside	Middle	Inside
High	3/ 666 /2	6/ 166 /1	3/ 0 /0	1/ 0 /0	2/ 0 /0	0/ 0 /0
Med	14/ 285 /4	4/ 250 /1	11/ 363 /4	1/ 0 /0	0/ 0 /0	3/ 666 /2
Low	1/ 0 /0	8/ 375 /3	2/ 1000 /2	0/ 0 /0	0/ 0 /0	0/ 0 /0

Behind

	Fastball Average .195			Curve Average .368		
	Outside	Middle	Inside	Outside	Middle	Inside
High	5/ 0 /0	1/ 0 /0	2/ 500 /1	0/ 0 /0	1/ 0 /0	1/ 0 /0
Med	15/ 200 /3	2/ 0 /0	7/ 285 /2	5/ 600 /3	0/ 0 /0	4/ 250 /1
Low	3/ 0 /0	7/ 285 /2	4/ 250 /1	4/ 500 /2	1/ 1000 /1	3/ 0 /0

Overall Evaluation
Against Right-Handed Pitchers

Overall Fastball ⚾

Overall Curve ⚾ ⚾ ⚾

Overall Slider ⚾ ⚾

Against Left-Handed Pitchers

Overall Fastball ⚾

Overall Curve — Not enough information

Overall Slider ⚾ ⚾ ⚾ ⚾

Comments: Strong fastball sector low-inside/medium-inside/medium-middle/low-middle vs. RH.
Strengths: Fastballs as above, medium-outside, low-outside and medium-inside curves vs. RH.
Weaknesses: All high fastballs and outside fastballs, high-middle and low-inside curves, low-inside sliders vs. LH.

Bo Jackson (Right Handed)   *Kansas City Royals*

Bo Jackson Against Right-Handed Pitchers
Overall BARS Batting Average .257

Fastball Average .292

	Inside	Middle	Outside
High	26/115/3	16/312/5	13/0/0
Med	42/309/13	12/416/5	52/346/18
Low	15/200/3	30/466/14	20/250/5

Curve Average .154

	Inside	Middle	Outside
High	2/0/0	4/500/2	0/0/0
Med	5/0/0	8/375/3	13/76/1
Low	2/500/1	7/142/1	30/100/3

Slider Average .245

	Inside	Middle	Outside
High	1/1000/1	4/500/2	3/333/1
Med	4/250/1	3/333/1	11/363/4
Low	1/0/0	4/0/0	30/166/5

Bo Jackson Against Left-Handed Pitchers
Overall BARS Batting Average .260

Fastball Average .273

	Inside	Middle	Outside
High	6/166/1	10/100/1	7/285/2
Med	11/181/2	3/333/1	38/421/16
Low	5/200/1	3/333/1	12/83/1

Curve Average .173

	Inside	Middle	Outside
High	0/0/0	2/500/1	1/0/0
Med	1/0/0	2/0/0	3/333/1
Low	4/0/0	2/1000/2	8/0/0

Slider Average .277

	Inside	Middle	Outside
High	4/0/0	1/1000/1	0/0/0
Med	3/333/1	0/0/0	0/0/0
Low	6/166/1	3/666/2	1/0/0

Right-handed Bo Jackson hits fastballs better against right-handed than against left-handed pitchers (.292 vs. right-handers, .273 vs. left-handers). But overall he hits a little better against left-handers (.260 vs. left-handers, .246 against right-handers).

Jackson's fastball chart against right-handed pitchers shows that he hits medium-high outside fastballs and high-over-middle fastballs very well (.346 and .312 respectively). He hits low-over-the-middle (.466) and medium-over-the-middle fastballs (.416) excellently.

His fastball weaknesses are on the corners. His 0-for-13 against high-outside fastballs, .115 against high-inside, .200 against low-inside and .250 against low-outside are all weak.

The BARS fielding strategy required for Jackson shows how necessary it is to adjust for him on a pitch-by-pitch basis. The fielders need to change for almost every fastball location.

MEDIUM-HIGH OUTSIDE FASTBALLS

BATTING AVERAGE .346
Play

Left	Deep in straightaway left field
Center	Medium-deep in straightaway center field
Right	Deep in straightaway right field
Short	Normal position
Second	Shifted toward first base

LOW-OVER-THE-MIDDLE FASTBALLS

BATTING AVERAGE .466
Play

Left	Medium-deep in straightaway left field
Center	Deep and shifted toward left field
Right	Medium-deep in straightaway right field
Short	Up middle (shifted toward second base)
Second	Shifted toward first base

MEDIUM-HIGH INSIDE FASTBALLS

BATTING AVERAGE .309
Play

Left	Medium-deep and shifted toward the left field line
Center	Deep in straightaway center field
Right	Short and shifted toward center field
Short	Up middle (shifted toward second base)
Second	Shifted toward first base

HIGH-OVER-THE-MIDDLE FASTBALLS

BATTING AVERAGE .312
Play

Left	Deep and shifted toward the left field line
Center	Deep in straightaway center field
Right	Deep in straightaway right field
Short	Normal position
Second	*No instances recorded*

The BARS fielding strategy for those four pitches shows that if the outfielders and the shortstop took a position and held it for all pitches thrown to Jackson, they would be out of position for some of the pitches. Only the second baseman is not required to shift.

Jackson Against Curves

Jackson's BARS charts point out his overall weakness against curves thrown by right-handed pitchers. His .076 against medium-high outside and .100 against low-outside present an area of great weakness for pitchers to concentrate on.

He hits medium-high outside curves deep to all fields, but his low average in this location indicates that he does not hit them with great authority.

MEDIUM-HIGH OUTSIDE CURVEBALLS

BATTING AVERAGE .076
Play

Left   Deep in straightaway left field
Center   Deep in straightaway center field
Right   Deep and shifted toward center field
Short   Normal position
Second   *No instances recorded*

Jackson Against Left-Handed Pitchers

Against left-handers, Jackson's .273 overall fastball average consists of one location of great strength (.421 against medium-high outside) and many locations of weakness, most notably the .083 against low-outside, the .100 against high-over-the-middle, and the .181 against medium-high inside. This fastball chart clearly shows that if a pitcher throws Jackson an outside fastball, he should keep it low. He would do much better throwing inside fastballs.

Jackson hits medium-high outside fastballs deep to all fields.

MEDIUM-HIGH OUTSIDE FASTBALLS (THROWN BY LEFT-HANDED PITCHERS)

BATTING AVERAGE .421
Play

Left   Deep in straightaway left field
Center   Deep and shifted toward left field
Right   Deep and shifted toward the right field line
Short   Normal position
Second   Normal position

He hits medium-high inside fastballs to medium-deep left and center.

MEDIUM-HIGH INSIDE FASTBALLS (THROWN BY LEFT-HANDED PITCHERS)

BATTING AVERAGE .181
Play

Left   Medium-deep in straightaway left field
Center   Medium-deep and shifted toward right field
Right   *No instances recorded*
Short   Normal position
Second   Shifted toward first base

Jackson has great trouble with curves thrown by left-handed pitchers, especially low-outside and low-inside curves. In general, keeping pitches low-outside gives pitchers an edge over Jackson.

Ahead And Behind In The Count Vs. RH

Ahead

Fastball Average .400

	Inside	Middle	Outside
High	9/111 /1	4/1000 /4	0/0 /0
Med	19/368 /7	3/333 /1	19/315 /6
Low	3/333 /1	8/750 /6	5/400 /2

Curve Average .187

	Inside	Middle	Outside
High	0/0 /0	0/0 /0	0/0 /0
Med	2/0 /0	3/666 /2	4/0 /0
Low	0/0 /0	1/0 /0	6/166 /1

Behind

Fastball Average .400

	Inside	Middle	Outside
High	4/500 /2	2/0 /0	1/0 /0
Med	10/300 /3	0/0 /0	12/500 /6
Low	4/250 /1	10/500 /5	2/500 /1

Curve Average .583

	Inside	Middle	Outside
High	0/0 /0	1/1000 /1	0/0 /0
Med	0/0 /0	1/1000 /1	3/333 /1
Low	1/1000 /1	2/500 /1	4/500 /2

Overall Evaluation

Against Right-Handed Pitchers

Overall Fastball ⚾⚾
Overall Curve ⚾
Overall Slider ⚾

Against Left-Handed Pitchers

Overall Fastball ⚾
Overall Curve ⚾
Overall Slider ⚾⚾⚾

Comments: Strong vs. waist-high and over-the-middle fastballs vs. RH, medium-outside fastballs vs. LH.
Strengths: All waist-high fastballs and all over-the-middle fastballs vs. RH, medium-middle curves, medium-outside sliders vs. RH; medium-outside fastballs vs. LH.
Weaknesses: Four fastball corners, outside curves and low sliders vs. RH; inside fastballs, high-middle and low-outside fastballs vs. LH, low-outside curves vs. LH.

Gerald Perry Against Right-Handed Pitchers
Overall BARS Batting Average .274

Fastball Average .277

	Outside	Middle	Inside
High	37/ 243 /9	70/ 342 /24	36/ 333 /12
Med	126/ 293 /37	20/ 400 /8	70/ 300 /21
Low	35/ 200 /7	65/ 276 /18	42/ 71 /3

Curve Average .250

	Outside	Middle	Inside
High	7/ 285 /2	15/ 466 /7	11/ 90 /1
Med	11/ 90 /1	12/ 416 /5	31/ 225 /7
Low	6/ 500 /3	12/ 166 /2	15/ 133 /2

Slider Average .307

	Outside	Middle	Inside
High	1/ 0 /0	7/ 428 /3	5/ 400 /2
Med	5/ 400 /2	3/ 0 /0	13/ 230 /3
Low	4/ 250 /1	3/ 666 /2	11/ 272 /3

Gerald Perry Against Left-Handed Pitchers
Overall BARS Batting Average .242

Fastball Average .250

	Outside	Middle	Inside
High	18/ 277 /5	11/ 272 /3	23/ 173 /4
Med	23/ 217 /5	0/ 0 /0	25/ 320 /8
Low	11/ 0 /0	9/ 111 /1	16/ 500 /8

Curve Average .196

	Outside	Middle	Inside
High	6/ 166 /1	11/ 272 /3	7/ 285 /2
Med	13/ 307 /4	1/ 1000 /1	2/ 0 /0
Low	14/ 0 /0	3/ 333 /1	4/ 0 /0

Slider Average .333

	Outside	Middle	Inside
High	0/ 0 /0	1/ 0 /0	1/ 0 /0
Med	5/ 600 /3	1/ 0 /0	4/ 500 /2
Low	2/ 0 /0	4/ 250 /1	0/ 0 /0

Left-handed hitter Gerald Perry has some strong fastball, curve and slider locations in his charts, but he has several distinct sectors of weakness. Against right-handed pitchers, Perry has a strong fastball sector consisting of his medium-over-the-middle/high-middle/high-inside/medium-high inside locations. Right-handers should steer away from this sector.

Perry hits medium-high outside fastballs for a fairly good .293 average. The chart below and the field diagram on the opposite page show how fielders should play for this pitch..

MEDIUM-HIGH OUTSIDE FASTBALLS

BATTING AVERAGE .293
Play

Left	Deep and shifted toward the left field line
Center	Deep and shifted toward right field
Right	Deep in straightaway right field
Short	Up middle (shifted toward second base)
Second	Shifted toward first base

He hits .342 vs. high-over-the-middle fastballs.

HIGH-OVER-THE-MIDDLE FASTBALLS

BATTING AVERAGE .342
Play

Left	Deep and shifted toward the left field line
Center	Deep and shifted toward right field

Right	Deep in straightaway right field
Short	Normal position
Second	Normal position

Perry is weak against low fastballs thrown by right-handers (.200, .276, and .071, outside to inside). If right-handers keep their fastballs to him low, they will have an edge.

Perry has weaknesses in many of his curve and slider locations against right-handers. He is especially vulnerable in his inside curve locations. He hits only .090 in his high-inside curve location, but he hits high-over-the-middle curves for a .466 average.

Perry is weak against outside fastballs thrown by left-handed pitchers (.277, .217, and .000 on 0 for 11, high to low). He is also weak against high-over-the-middle and high-inside fastballs. His strongest fastball sector is medium-high inside/low-inside. He hits .500 against low-inside fastballs.

LOW-INSIDE FASTBALLS
(THROWN BY LEFT-HANDED PITCHERS)

BATTING AVERAGE .500
Play

Left	Medium-deep and shifted toward the left line
Center	Deep and shifted toward right field
Right	Deep in straightaway right field
Short	Shifted toward third base
Second	Shifted toward first base

Medium-High Outside Fastballs (Thrown By Right-Handed Pitchers)

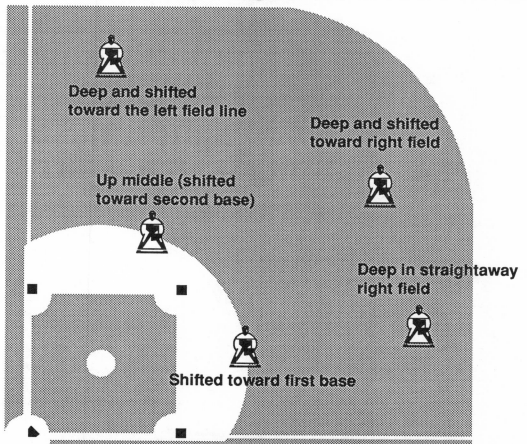

Deep and shifted toward the left field line

Deep and shifted toward right field

Up middle (shifted toward second base)

Deep in straightaway right field

Shifted toward first base

Ahead And Behind In The Count Vs. RH

Ahead

Fastball Average .309

	Outside	Middle	Inside
High	16/ 187 /3	45/ 355 /16	23/ 217 /5
Med	72/ 305 /22	9/ 666 /6	42/ 380 /16
Low	10/ 300 /3	42/ 333 /14	22/ 90 /2

Curve Average .200

	Outside	Middle	Inside
High	2/ 0 /0	5/ 600 /3	5/ 0 /0
Med	3/ 333 /1	6/ 166 /1	9/ 111 /1
Low	2/ 500 /1	6/ 166 /1	2/ 0 /0

Behind

Fastball Average .311

	Outside	Middle	Inside
High	3/ 333 /1	11/ 363 /4	4/ 1000 /4
Med	23/ 304 /7	3/ 333 /1	14/ 357 /5
Low	7/ 0 /0	7/ 285 /2	5/ 0 /0

Curve Average .312

	Outside	Middle	Inside
High	4/ 500 /2	2/ 500 /1	2/ 0 /0
Med	1/ 0 /0	5/ 600 /3	11/ 181 /2
Low	2/ 500 /1	0/ 0 /0	5/ 200 /1

Overall Evaluation

Against Right-Handed Pitchers

Overall Fastball ⚾⚾ ⚾⚾

Overall Curve ⚾⚾ ⚾⚾

Overall Slider ⚾⚾ ⚾⚾ ⚾⚾ ⚾⚾

Against Left-Handed Pitchers

Overall Fastball ⚾⚾

Overall Curve ⚾⚾

Overall Slider ⚾⚾ ⚾⚾ ⚾⚾ ⚾⚾

Comments: RH pitchers should keep fastballs away from the sector consisting of medium-middle, high-middle, high-inside and medium-high inside.
Strengths: Fastballs as above, high-middle and medium-middle curves vs. RH; medium-inside fastballs, medium-outside curves vs. LH.
Weaknesses: Low fastballs, high-outside fastballs, inside, medium-outside and low-middle curves vs. RH; outside and high fastballs, low-outside curves vs. LH.

Kevin Seitzer (Right Handed)   *Kansas City Royals*

Kevin Seitzer Against Right-Handed Pitchers
Overall BARS Batting Average .336

	Fastball Average .349			Curve Average .333			Slider Average .271		
	Inside	Middle	Outside	Inside	Middle	Outside	Inside	Middle	Outside
High	29/ 275 /8	29/ 344 /10	15/ 133 /2	4/ 250 /1	5/ 400 /2	5/ 0 /0	3/ 0 /0	5/ 400 /2	3/ 333 /1
Med	48/ 604 /29	17/ 411 /7	106/ 339 /36	4/ 500 /2	6/ 500 /3	20/ 450 /9	2/ 0 /0	5/ 400 /2	11/ 181 /2
Low	27/ 296 /8	53/ 358 /19	31/ 161 /5	1/ 1000 /1	12/ 416 /5	18/ 111 /2	4/ 500 /2	10/ 500 /5	27/ 185 /5

Kevin Seitzer Against Left-Handed Pitchers
Overall BARS Batting Average .369

	Fastball Average .378			Curve Average .461			Slider Average .235		
	Inside	Middle	Outside	Inside	Middle	Outside	Inside	Middle	Outside
High	8/ 125 /1	7/ 428 /3	3/ 333 /1	1/ 0 /0	1/ 1000 /1	0/ 0 /0	0/ 0 /0	1/ 0 /0	0/ 0 /0
Med	9/ 444 /4	5/ 600 /3	50/ 440 /22	1/ 1000 /1	1/ 0 /0	5/ 400 /2	5/ 0 /0	1/ 1000 /1	4/ 500 /2
Low	5/ 0 /0	19/ 421 /8	13/ 230 /3	0/ 0 /0	4/ 500 /2	0/ 0 /0	2/ 0 /0	2/ 500 /1	2/ 0 /0

Right-handed Kevin Seitzer hits extremely well overall against fastballs and curves, against both right- and left-handed pitchers. He has trouble with sliders against left-handers, but hits them well (.271) against right-handers.

Against right-handers, Seitzer's overall .349 fastball average is excellent. He has trouble with low-outside (.161), high-outside (.133) and high-inside (.275) fastballs, but all other locations are solid. His .604 against medium-high inside fastballs is phenomenal, especially considering the relatively high number of recorded instances in this location (48).

MEDIUM-HIGH INSIDE FASTBALLS

BATTING AVERAGE .604
Play
Left   Deep and shifted toward the left field line
Center   Medium-deep in straightaway center field
Right   Medium-deep and shifted toward center field
Short   Up middle (shifted toward second base)
Second   Normal position

Seitzer tends to hit both low-outside and medium-high outside fastballs fairly straightaway to the outfield and to the opposite side (the right side) of the infield.

Seitzer pulls high-over-the-middle fastballs, but he hits low-over-the-middle fastballs to the opposite field.

HIGH-OVER-THE-MIDDLE FASTBALLS

BATTING AVERAGE .344
Play
Left   Deep and shifted toward the left field line
Center   Medium-deep and straightaway in center field
Right   Deep in straightaway right field
Short   Shifted toward third base
Second   *No instances recorded*

LOW-OVER-THE-MIDDLE FASTBALLS

BATTING AVERAGE .358
Play
Left   *No instances recorded*
Center   Deep in straightaway center field
Right   Medium-deep in straightaway right field
Short   Up middle (shifted toward second base)
Second   Shifted toward first base

Seitzer Against Curves And Sliders

Seitzer hits curves against right-handed pitchers very well (.333 overall). His weak .111 average in the low-outside location and his 0-for-5 in the high-outside location bring down his overall average, but these weaknesses are bolstered by his strong .450 in the medium-high outside location and .416 in the low-over-the-middle location.

MEDIUM-HIGH OUTSIDE CURVEBALLS

BATTING AVERAGE .450
Play

Left	Medium-deep in straightaway left field
Center	Deep and shifted toward left field
Right	Medium-deep in straightaway right field
Short	Normal position
Second	Shifted toward first base

An interesting trend is found in the fielding strategy for Seitzer's low-over-the-middle curve location. He tends to hit this pitch up the middle. If center fielders and shortstops adjusted, they could probably take away a lot of Seitzer's singles.

LOW-OVER-THE-MIDDLE CURVEBALLS

BATTING AVERAGE .416
Play

Left	Medium-deep and shifted toward center field
Center	Medium-deep in straightaway center field
Right	*No instances recorded*
Short	Up middle (shifted toward second base)
Second	*No instances recorded*

Seitzer's overall .271 against sliders is adequate. He tends to hit low-outside sliders up the middle, as he does low-over-the-middle curves. If the center fielder, the right fielder and the shortstop adjusted, they could take away Seitzer's alley on this pitch and lower his slider average even more.

LOW-OUTSIDE SLIDERS

BATTING AVERAGE .185
Play

Left	*No instances recorded*
Center	Medium-deep in straightaway center field
Right	Medium-deep and shifted toward center field
Short	Up middle (shifted toward second base)
Second	Normal position

Seitzer Against Left-Handed Pitchers

Seitzer hits even better against left-handed pitchers. His overall .378 fastball average is built on a solid .440 in the medium-high outside location.

MEDIUM-HIGH OUTSIDE FASTBALLS (THROWN BY LEFT-HANDED PITCHERS)

BATTING AVERAGE .440
Play

Left	Deep and shifted toward center field
Center	Deep in straightaway center field
Right	Deep in straightaway right field
Short	Up middle (shifted toward second base)
Second	Normal position

Ahead And Behind In The Count Vs. RH

Ahead

Fastball Average .355

	Inside	Middle	Outside
High	13/307 /4	14/285 /4	4/0 /0
Med	21/714 /15	11/363 /4	51/294 /15
Low	10/300 /3	27/407 /11	15/200 /3

Curve Average .384

	Inside	Middle	Outside
High	0/0 /0	0/0 /0	0/0 /0
Med	3/666 /2	0/0 /0	5/400 /2
Low	0/0 /0	1/0 /0	4/250 /1

Behind

Fastball Average .416

	Inside	Middle	Outside
High	5/200 /1	3/1000 /3	3/333 /1
Med	5/600 /3	3/666 /2	23/391 /9
Low	6/333 /2	7/428 /3	5/200 /1

Curve Average .500

	Inside	Middle	Outside
High	3/333 /1	1/1000 /1	2/0 /0
Med	0/0 /0	2/500 /1	8/625 /5
Low	0/0 /0	7/714 /5	5/200 /1

Overall Evaluation
Against Right-Handed Pitchers

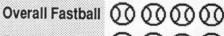

Overall Fastball	⚾⚾⚾⚾
Overall Curve	⚾⚾⚾⚾
Overall Slider	⚾⚾

Against Left-Handed Pitchers

Overall Fastball	⚾⚾⚾⚾
Overall Curve	⚾⚾⚾⚾
Overall Slider	⚾

Comments: Excellent fastball and curve hitter vs. both RH and LH and when ahead and behind.
Strengths: All waist-high and over-the-middle fastballs vs. RH and LH; medium-outside curves, low-middle curves and low-middle sliders vs. RH.
Weaknesses: Low-outside and high-outside fastballs vs. RH, low-outside curves vs. RH, low-outside and medium-outside sliders vs. RH; low-outside and high-inside fastballs vs. LH.

Kurt Stillwell (Switch Hitter)   *Kansas City Royals*

Kurt Stillwell Against Right-Handed Pitchers
Overall BARS Batting Average .286

	Fastball Average .306			Curve Average .258			Slider Average .105		
	Outside	Middle	Inside	Outside	Middle	Inside	Outside	Middle	Inside
High	18/388 /7	31/258 /8	12/250 /3	3/0 /0	3/666 /2	0/0 /0	0/0 /0	2/0 /0	0/0 /0
Med	53/358 /19	23/217 /5	19/421 /8	5/600 /3	3/333 /1	3/666 /2	1/0 /0	0/0 /0	5/200 /1
Low	11/181 /2	29/310 /9	16/250 /4	4/0 /0	4/0 /0	6/0 /0	1/0 /0	4/0 /0	6/166 /1

Kurt Stillwell Against Left-Handed Pitchers
Overall BARS Batting Average .228

	Fastball Average .241			Curve Average .100			Slider Average .250		
	Inside	Middle	Outside	Inside	Middle	Outside	Inside	Middle	Outside
High	6/166 /1	6/166 /1	9/444 /4	0/0 /0	0/0 /0	0/0 /0	0/0 /0	0/0 /0	0/0 /0
Med	11/90 /1	4/1000 /4	30/200 /6	2/0 /0	3/0 /0	2/500 /1	1/0 /0	0/0 /0	0/0 /0
Low	4/250 /1	6/166 /1	11/181 /2	1/0 /0	2/0 /0	0/0 /0	1/0 /0	1/1000 /1	1/0 /0

Switch-hitting Kurt Stillwell has a higher overall average when batting left-handed against right-handed pitchers (.253 against right-handers, .213 against left-handers). His .306 overall fastball average against right-handers is very respectable. It is 65 points higher than his overall .241 fastball average when batting right-handed against left-handed pitchers.

Stillwell's .306 overall fastball average is built on some very steady locations. His .421 against medium-high inside fastballs, .388 against high-outside fastballs, .358 against medium-high outside and .310 against low-over-the-middle fastballs are solid. His .181 against low-outside fastballs, his .250 against low-inside and high-inside, his .258 against high-over-the-middle and, strangely, his .217 against medium-over-the-middle are his significant weaknesses.

The differences between how he hits medium-high outside and low-outside fastballs are interesting.

MEDIUM-HIGH OUTSIDE FASTBALLS

BATTING AVERAGE .358
Play
Left   Medium-deep and shifted toward the left field line
Center   Deep and shifted toward left field
Right   Deep and shifted toward the right field line
Short   Up middle (shifted toward second base)
Second   Normal position

LOW-OUTSIDE FASTBALLS

BATTING AVERAGE .181
Play
Left   Medium-deep and shifted toward the left field line
Center   Deep and shifted toward left field
Right   Medium-deep and shifted toward center field
Short   Normal position
Second   Shifted toward first base

Stillwell pulls high-outside fastballs down the line when he hits to right field.

HIGH-OUTSIDE FASTBALLS

BATTING AVERAGE .388
Play
Left   Deep in straightaway left field
Center   Deep in straightaway center field
Right   Deep and shifted toward the right field line
Short   Up middle (shifted toward second base)
Second   Normal position

He hits all three inside fastball locations down the line to left. Notice in the following charts that if all the fielders played Stillwell to pull, or if they all played him to go to the opposite field, some of the fielders would be badly out of position on some of the pitches.

HIGH-INSIDE FASTBALLS

BATTING AVERAGE .250
Play

Left	Short and shifted toward the left field line
Center	Short in straightaway center field
Right	Deep in straightaway right field
Short	Normal position
Second	Shifted toward first base

MEDIUM-HIGH INSIDE FASTBALLS

BATTING AVERAGE .421
Play

Left	Medium-deep and shifted toward the left field line
Center	Medium-deep and shifted toward right field
Right	Deep and shifted toward the right field line
Short	Up middle (shifted toward second base)
Second	Shifted toward first base

LOW-INSIDE FASTBALLS

BATTING AVERAGE .250
Play

Left	Medium-deep and shifted toward the left field line
Center	Deep and shifted toward right field
Right	Deep and shifted toward the right field line
Short	Up middle (shifted toward second base)
Second	Shifted toward first base

Notice how few curves Stillwell is thrown in comparison to fastballs. Pitchers should throw him more curves, especially with his apparent weakness against low curves. It may be that he knows he has trouble with breaking pitches and holds off until he has to swing at them.

Stillwell Against Left-Handed Pitchers

Since left-handed pitchers also throw Stillwell very few curves (or since he swings at very few curves and sliders thrown by left-handers), his overall average against left-handers is primarily built on his fastball performance.

Batting right-handed against left-handed pitchers, Stillwell hits .200 in the medium-high outside location and .090 in the medium-high inside location.

He hits medium-high outside fastballs straightaway to center and right fields and to the right side (his opposite side) of the infield. He pulls medium-high inside fastballs down the line to left.

MEDIUM-HIGH OUTSIDE FASTBALLS
(THROWN BY LEFT-HANDED PITCHERS)

BATTING AVERAGE .200
Play

Left	Deep and shifted toward center field
Center	Medium-deep in straightaway center field
Right	Medium-deep in straightaway right field
Short	Up middle (shifted toward second base)
Second	Shifted toward first base

MEDIUM-HIGH INSIDE FASTBALLS

BATTING AVERAGE .090
Play

Left	Medium-deep and shifted toward the left field line
Center	Short in straightaway center field
Right	Deep in straightaway right field
Short	Shifted toward third base
Second	*No instances recorded*

Ahead And Behind In The Count Vs. RH

Ahead

Fastball Average .320

	Outside	Middle	Inside
High	5/600 /3	17/294 /5	7/428 /3
Med	24/333 /8	15/133 /2	10/600 /6
Low	4/250 /1	15/266 /4	6/166 /1

Curve Average .500

	Outside	Middle	Inside
High	0/0 /0	1/1000 /1	0/0 /0
Med	1/1000 /1	0/0 /0	1/0 /0
Low	0/0 /0	1/0 /0	0/0 /0

Behind

Fastball Average .358

	Outside	Middle	Inside
High	0/0 /0	7/285 /2	1/0 /0
Med	15/333 /5	3/333 /1	2/500 /1
Low	2/0 /0	7/571 /4	2/500 /1

Curve Average .363

	Outside	Middle	Inside
High	2/0 /0	0/0 /0	0/0 /0
Med	2/1000 /2	3/333 /1	1/1000 /1
Low	2/0 /0	1/0 /0	0/0 /0

Overall Evaluation

Against Right-Handed Pitchers

Overall Fastball ⚾⚾ ⚾⚾ ⚾⚾

Overall Curve ⚾⚾ ⚾⚾

Overall Slider ⚾⚾

Against Left-Handed Pitchers

Overall Fastball ⚾⚾

Overall Curve Not enough information

Overall Slider Not enough information

Comments: Has some very strong fastball locations vs. RH, has difficulty with curves and sliders.
Strengths: Medium-outside, high-outside, low-middle and medium-inside fastballs, waist-high curves vs. RH; high-outside fastballs vs. LH.
Weaknesses: High-middle, high-inside, medium-middle, low-outside and low-inside fastballs vs. RH, low curves and sliders vs. RH; fastballs vs. LH except high-outside and medium-middle.

Pat Tabler (Right Handed)   *Kansas City Royals*

Pat Tabler Against Right-Handed Pitchers
Overall BARS Batting Average .323

Fastball Average .333

	Inside	Middle	Outside
High	16/ 187 /3	29/ 310 /9	13/ 461 /6
Med	49/ 408 /20	30/ 400 /12	82/ 243 /20
Low	15/ 400 /6	44/ 454 /20	13/ 76 /1

Curve Average .325

	Inside	Middle	Outside
High	0/ 0 /0	8/ 500 /4	4/ 500 /2
Med	5/ 800 /4	6/ 500 /3	17/ 294 /5
Low	2/ 0 /0	19/ 210 /4	19/ 210 /4

Slider Average .255

	Inside	Middle	Outside
High	2/ 500 /1	2/ 500 /1	1/ 0 /0
Med	9/ 333 /3	3/ 333 /1	11/ 363 /4
Low	0/ 0 /0	5/ 0 /0	14/ 142 /2

Pat Tabler Against Left-Handed Pitchers
Overall BARS Batting Average .270

Fastball Average .270

	Inside	Middle	Outside
High	7/ 142 /1	15/ 333 /5	8/ 125 /1
Med	15/ 266 /4	8/ 250 /2	51/ 352 /18
Low	12/ 250 /3	18/ 166 /3	14/ 214 /3

Curve Average .277

	Inside	Middle	Outside
High	2/ 500 /1	2/ 500 /1	3/ 666 /2
Med	5/ 400 /2	2/ 0 /0	4/ 0 /0
Low	3/ 0 /0	8/ 250 /2	7/ 285 /2

Slider Average .200

	Inside	Middle	Outside
High	0/ 0 /0	1/ 0 /0	0/ 0 /0
Med	4/ 250 /1	1/ 0 /0	2/ 1000 /2
Low	6/ 0 /0	8/ 125 /1	3/ 333 /1

Right-handed hitter Pat Tabler has an excellent overall fastball average against right-handed pitchers (.333) and is very effective against curves thrown by right-handers (.325). He is not as effective, however, against fastballs thrown by left-handers (.270). This is somewhat unusual for a right-handed hitter.

One of the most significant strengths of Tabler's overall fastball chart against right-handed pitchers is his .408 average against medium-high inside fastballs and his weak .243 average against medium-high outside fastballs. Most good hitters have a much higher medium-high outside fastball average than Tabler.

Tabler has a weakness in his medium-high outside/low-outside fastball sector. He has difficulty even hitting low-outside fastballs. He hits medium-high outside fastballs deep to all fields. His low average in this location indicates that he hits mostly easy fly outs.

MEDIUM-HIGH OUTSIDE FASTBALLS

BATTING AVERAGE .243
Play

Left	Deep in straightaway left field
Center	Deep and shifted toward left field
Right	Deep in straightaway right field
Short	Normal position
Second	Shifted toward first base

He hits medium-high inside fastballs medium-deep

to all fields. If the outfielders would play him medium-deep when he is thrown this type of pitch, they might be able to catch some of the line drives that now fall in for base hits.

MEDIUM-HIGH INSIDE FASTBALLS

BATTING AVERAGE .408
Play

Left	Medium-deep and shifted toward the left field line
Center	Medium-deep and shifted toward right field
Right	Medium-deep in straightaway right field
Short	Normal position
Second	Shifted toward first base

Tabler slaps low-over-the-middle fastballs to the right side of the infield. The proper positioning of fielders for this pitch could cut off some of his ground-ball singles through the infield.

LOW-OVER-THE-MIDDLE FASTBALLS

BATTING AVERAGE .454
Play

Left	Deep in straightaway left field
Center	Deep in straightaway center field
Right	Deep and shifted toward center field
Short	Up middle (shifted toward second base)
Second	Shifted toward first base

Tabler Against Curves

Tabler hits strongly against curves thrown by right-handed pitchers. He has weaknesses in the low-over-the-middle and low-outside curve locations (.210 in both locations), but is solid in the other locations.

By keeping curves low to Tabler, pitchers can gain a significant advantage. This weak sector in his curve chart is in contrast to the strength shown in his medium-high and high curve locations.

LOW-OVER-THE-MIDDLE CURVEBALLS

BATTING AVERAGE .210
Play
Left	Medium-deep and shifted toward the left field line
Center	Medium-deep and shifted toward right field
Right	*No instances recorded*
Short	Shifted toward third base
Second	Normal position

LOW-OUTSIDE CURVEBALLS

BATTING AVERAGE .210
Play
Left	*No instances recorded*
Center	Medium-deep and shifted toward left field
Right	Deep and shifted toward the right field line
Short	Normal position
Second	Normal position

Tabler Against Left-Handed Pitchers

Against left-handers, Tabler hits .270 overall against fastballs. He hits a strong .352 against medium-high outside fastballs, but a weak .214 against low-outside and an extremely weak .166 against low-over-the-middle. He has trouble with all inside fastballs.

Tabler pulls medium-high inside fastballs thrown by left-handers. He hits medium-high outside fastballs fairly straightaway to left and center, and down the line to right.

MEDIUM-HIGH INSIDE FASTBALLS
(THROWN BY LEFT-HANDED PITCHERS)

BATTING AVERAGE .266
Play
Left	Deep and shifted toward the left field line
Center	Deep and shifted toward left field
Right	Medium-deep and shifted toward center field
Short	Normal position
Second	Normal position

MEDIUM-HIGH OUTSIDE FASTBALLS
(THROWN BY LEFT-HANDED PITCHERS)

BATTING AVERAGE .352
Play
Left	Deep in straightaway left field
Center	Medium-deep in straightaway center field
Right	Deep and shifted toward the right field line
Short	Up middle (shifted toward second base)
Second	Normal position

Ahead And Behind In The Count Vs. RH

Ahead

Fastball Average .435

	Inside	Middle	Outside
High	6/166 /1	10/300 /3	8/500 /4
Med	22/454 /10	15/533 /8	35/400 /14
Low	6/333 /2	20/550 /11	2/500 /1

Curve Average .222

	Inside	Middle	Outside
High	0/0 /0	1/0 /0	2/500 /1
Med	1/1000 /1	1/0 /0	4/250 /1
Low	0/0 /0	7/142 /1	2/0 /0

Behind

Fastball Average .208

	Inside	Middle	Outside
High	0/0 /0	4/500 /2	2/0 /0
Med	7/142 /1	4/250 /1	19/105 /2
Low	2/500 /1	9/333 /3	1/0 /0

Curve Average .500

	Inside	Middle	Outside
High	0/0 /0	2/500 /1	2/500 /1
Med	3/666 /2	5/600 /3	6/500 /3
Low	0/0 /0	4/250 /1	4/500 /2

Overall Evaluation

Against Right-Handed Pitchers

Overall Fastball	⚾⚾⚾⚾
Overall Curve	⚾⚾⚾⚾
Overall Slider	⚾⚾

Against Left-Handed Pitchers

Overall Fastball	⚾
Overall Curve	⚾⚾⚾
Overall Slider	⚾

Comments: Strong vs. fastballs and curves vs. RH.
Strengths: Medium-inside, low-inside, high-outside and all over-the-middle fastballs vs. RH, medium-outside curves and sliders vs. RH; medium-outside fastballs vs. LH.
Weaknesses: Low-outside, medium-outside and high-inside fastballs vs. RH, low curves and low sliders vs. RH; all low and all inside fastballs vs. LH, low-middle and low-inside sliders vs. LH.

Danny Tartabull (Right Handed) *Kansas City Royals*

Danny Tartabull Against Right-Handed Pitchers
Overall BARS Batting Average .323

Fastball Average .364

	Inside	Middle	Outside
High	19/ 157 /3	36/ 472 /17	15/ 266 /4
Med	39/ 256 /10	21/ 571 /12	119/ 403 /48
Low	28/ 250 /7	57/ 385 /22	36/ 333 /12

Curve Average .261

	Inside	Middle	Outside
High	1/ 0 /0	10/ 500 /5	5/ 400 /2
Med	7/ 285 /2	7/ 285 /2	13/ 230 /3
Low	2/ 500 /1	15/ 200 /3	24/ 166 /4

Slider Average .204

	Inside	Middle	Outside
High	2/ 0 /0	4/ 750 /3	2/ 0 /0
Med	5/ 400 /2	6/ 333 /2	28/ 285 /8
Low	2/ 500 /1	7/ 0 /0	32/ 62 /2

Danny Tartabull Against Left-Handed Pitchers
Overall BARS Batting Average .287

Fastball Average .338

	Inside	Middle	Outside
High	4/ 500 /2	10/ 500 /5	8/ 375 /3
Med	11/ 363 /4	6/ 333 /2	42/ 380 /16
Low	4/ 0 /0	23/ 217 /5	13/ 307 /4

Curve Average .217

	Inside	Middle	Outside
High	1/ 0 /0	1/ 0 /0	3/ 333 /1
Med	1/ 0 /0	0/ 0 /0	9/ 333 /3
Low	2/ 0 /0	2/ 500 /1	4/ 0 /0

Slider Average .086

	Inside	Middle	Outside
High	2/ 0 /0	2/ 0 /0	1/ 0 /0
Med	5/ 200 /1	2/ 0 /0	3/ 333 /1
Low	6/ 0 /0	1/ 0 /0	1/ 0 /0

Danny Tartabull is an excellent fastball hitter, but he has trouble with curves and sliders against right- and left-handed pitchers.

Tartabull's .364 overall fastball average against right-handers is top rate. His solid .403 against medium-high outside (built on a high number of recorded instances — 119) stands as a warning to pitchers who think they can get him out with an outside fastball. He also hits high-over-the-middle and low-over-the-middle fastballs excellently (.472 and .385 respectively). His .571 against medium-over-the-middle should convince pitchers to think only of the corners when throwing Tartabull a fastball.

The fielding strategy below shows that Tartabull pulls medium-over-the-middle fastballs deep to all fields. When the BARS System batting grids include the number of home runs hit in each of the locations (coming soon), it will be interesting to see how many homers Tartabull hits in this location.

MEDIUM-OVER-THE-MIDDLE FASTBALLS

BATTING AVERAGE .571
Play

Left	Deep and shifted toward the left field line
Center	Deep and shifted toward left field
Right	Deep and shifted toward center field
Short	Shifted toward third base
Second	*No instances recorded*

He hits medium-high outside fastballs much the same as he hits medium-over-the-middle (and for a high average — .403), but he hits medium-high inside fastballs differently (for a lower average — .256).

MEDIUM-HIGH OUTSIDE FASTBALLS

BATTING AVERAGE .403
Play

Left	Deep and shifted toward the left field line
Center	Deep in straightaway center field
Right	Deep and shifted toward center field
Short	Up middle (shifted toward second base)
Second	Normal position

MEDIUM-HIGH INSIDE FASTBALLS

BATTING AVERAGE .256
Play

Left	Deep and shifted toward the left field line
Center	Medium-deep in straightaway center field
Right	Short and shifted toward the right field line
Short	Normal position
Second	Normal position

Tartabull Against Curves And Sliders

When facing right-handed pitchers, Tartabull has trouble against both curves and sliders, especially in the low-outside locations (.166 against low-outside curves, .062 against low-outside sliders). He also has trouble in the low-over-the-middle location against curves and sliders. Pitchers should focus on this area.

Fielders should be aware of how Tartabull hits medium-high outside sliders as opposed to low-outside sliders.

LOW-OUTSIDE SLIDERS

BATTING AVERAGE .062
Play

Left	*No instances recorded*
Center	Medium-deep and shifted toward left field
Right	*No instances recorded*
Short	Normal position
Second	*No instances recorded*

MEDIUM-HIGH OUTSIDE SLIDERS

BATTING AVERAGE .285
Play

Left	Deep and shifted toward the left field line
Center	Deep and shifted toward left field
Right	Deep and shifted toward center field
Short	Up middle (shifted toward second base)
Second	Shifted toward first base

Tartabull Against Left-Handed Pitchers

Against left-handers, Tartabull hits fastballs very well (.338 overall), but has even more trouble with curves and sliders than he does against right-handers. Tartabull is unusual in that he, a right-handed hitter, hits better overall against right-handed pitchers.

Tartabull's fastball chart against lefties shows that he hits all outside fastballs well. His .380 against medium-high outside fastballs is high, as are his .375 against high-outside and .307 against low-outside.

It is interesting to see how differently Tartabull hits low-over-the-middle and low-outside fastballs thrown by left-handers. Even this slight difference in the strike zone makes a significant difference in how the fielders need to be positioned.

LOW-OVER-THE-MIDDLE FASTBALLS
(THROWN BY LEFT-HANDED PITCHERS)

BATTING AVERAGE .217
Play

Left	Deep and shifted toward center field
Center	Deep in straightaway center field
Right	Deep and shifted toward center field
Short	Normal position
Second	Normal position

LOW-OUTSIDE FASTBALLS
(THROWN BY LEFT-HANDED PITCHERS)

BATTING AVERAGE .307
Play

Left	Deep in straightaway left field
Center	Deep and shifted toward right field
Right	Deep in straightaway right field
Short	Up middle (shifted toward second base)
Second	Shifted toward first base

Every fielder is required to shift for a low-outside fastball as compared to a low-over-the-middle fastball. Again, this underscores the importance of accurate, pitch-by-pitch fielding strategy.

Ahead And Behind In The Count Vs. RH

Ahead

Fastball Average .472

	Inside	Middle	Outside
High	4/0 /0	17/588 /10	6/166 /1
Med	14/357 /5	15/733 /11	57/473 /27
Low	10/300 /3	26/500 /13	14/500 /7

Curve Average .461

	Inside	Middle	Outside
High	0/0 /0	3/333 /1	2/500 /1
Med	0/0 /0	2/500 /1	2/0 /0
Low	0/0 /0	3/666 /2	1/1000 /1

Behind

Fastball Average .373

	Inside	Middle	Outside
High	8/250 /2	5/600 /3	3/666 /2
Med	12/416 /5	2/0 /0	20/400 /8
Low	8/125 /1	10/500 /5	7/285 /2

Curve Average .384

	Inside	Middle	Outside
High	0/0 /0	5/400 /2	3/333 /1
Med	2/500 /1	3/0 /0	4/250 /1
Low	1/1000 /1	2/500 /1	6/500 /3

Overall Evaluation
Against Right-Handed Pitchers

Overall Fastball	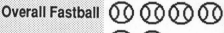
Overall Curve	⚾⚾
Overall Slider	⚾

Against Left-Handed Pitchers

Overall Fastball	⚾⚾ ⚾⚾ ⚾⚾
Overall Curve	⚾
Overall Slider	⚾⚾

Comments: Tartabull is an excellent fastball hitter.
Strengths: Medium-outside, all over-the-middle fastballs and low-outside fastballs, high middle curves vs. RH, waist-high and outside fastballs vs. LH.
Weaknesses: Inside fastballs, high-outside fastballs, low-middle and low-outside curves, medium-outside curves, low-outside and low-middle sliders vs. RH; low-middle fastballs vs. LH.

Frank White (Right Handed)　　　*Kansas City Royals*

Frank White Against Right-Handed Pitchers
Overall BARS Batting Average .248

Fastball Average .266

	Inside	Middle	Outside
High	37/ 189 /7	79/ 265 /21	41/ 268 /11
Med	106/ 283 /30	94/ 361 /34	212/ 268 /57
Low	40/ 175 /7	109/ 284 /31	78/ 179 /14

Curve Average .240

	Inside	Middle	Outside
High	7/ 285 /2	34/ 470 /16	14/ 214 /3
Med	24/ 250 /6	30/ 466 /14	76/ 144 /11
Low	4/ 250 /1	39/ 179 /7	34/ 88 /3

Slider Average .190

	Inside	Middle	Outside
High	8/ 250 /2	27/ 222 /6	5/ 0 /0
Med	10/ 400 /4	17/ 176 /3	52/ 134 /7
Low	5/ 200 /1	35/ 257 /9	62/ 161 /10

Frank White Against Left-Handed Pitchers
Overall BARS Batting Average .297

Fastball Average .311

	Inside	Middle	Outside
High	4/ 0 /0	26/ 500 /13	18/ 222 /4
Med	26/ 423 /11	33/ 333 /11	107/ 242 /26
Low	10/ 300 /3	56/ 357 /20	35/ 285 /10

Curve Average .296

	Inside	Middle	Outside
High	0/ 0 /0	10/ 300 /3	5/ 200 /1
Med	9/ 333 /3	10/ 300 /3	30/ 266 /8
Low	2/ 0 /0	16/ 312 /5	9/ 444 /4

Slider Average .224

	Inside	Middle	Outside
High	3/ 0 /0	2/ 500 /1	1/ 0 /0
Med	10/ 0 /0	3/ 0 /0	13/ 230 /3
Low	7/ 285 /2	10/ 400 /4	9/ 333 /3

Right-handed Frank White hits fastballs and curves very well against left-handed pitchers, but has difficulty against right-handed pitchers. His overall average of .291 against left-handers is much higher than his overall .231 against right-handers.

Against right-handers, White has trouble with many fastball locations. His .179 against low-outside fastballs, the .175 against low-inside and the .189 against high-inside give pitchers targets on the corners.

The differences in fielding strategies between White's weak low-outside and relatively strong low-over-the-middle fastball locations are instructive.

LOW-OUTSIDE FASTBALLS

BATTING AVERAGE .179
Play

Left	Medium-deep in straightaway left field
Center	Medium-deep in straightaway center field
Right	Medium-deep and shifted toward right line
Short	Normal position
Second	Shifted toward first base

LOW-OVER-THE-MIDDLE FASTBALLS

BATTING AVERAGE .284
Play

Left	Deep and shifted toward the left field line
Center	Deep in straightaway center field
Right	Medium-deep and shifted toward center field
Short	Up middle (shifted toward second base)
Second	Shifted toward first base

White hits medium-over-the-middle fastballs deep to all fields. He hits a lot of these (34 out of 94 instances). This shows that he's probably a patient hitter and waits for his pitch.

MEDIUM-OVER-THE-MIDDLE FASTBALLS

BATTING AVERAGE .361
Play

Left	Deep in straightaway left field
Center	Deep in straightaway center field
Right	Deep and shifted toward center field
Short	Up middle (shifted toward second base)
Second	Normal position

White Against Curves And Sliders

Against right-handed pitchers, White has trouble with curves (.240 overall) and sliders (.190 overall).

In his curve chart against right-handers, White has a weak sector consisting of the low-outside (.088), low-over-the-middle (.179), medium-high outside (.144) and high-outside (.214) locations. This presents a dramatic weakness for pitchers to attack.

This weak area is in contrast to the stronger area consisting of the high-over-the-middle (.470), medium-over-the-middle (.466), medium-high inside (.250), and high-inside (.285) locations.

White pulls low-outside curves down the line and into the left-center gap. Many players do not pull low-outside curves as much as White does. Notice also in the following chart that he hits these pitches to the right side of the infield when he hits grounders.

LOW-OUTSIDE CURVEBALLS

BATTING AVERAGE .470
Play

Left	Deep and shifted toward the left field line
Center	Short in straightaway center field
Right	Deep and shifted toward center field
Short	Normal position
Second	Shifted toward first base

White's slider chart has many weak locations. He hits low-outside sliders toward center field.

LOW-OUTSIDE SLIDERS

BATTING AVERAGE .161
Play

Left	Deep and shifted toward center field
Center	Medium-deep in straightaway center field
Right	Medium-deep and shifted toward center field
Short	Normal position
Second	Normal position

White Ahead And Behind In The Count

White is known to be a good clutch hitter. His Ahead and Behind in the count charts shown below clearly indicate that he has higher overall averages against both fastballs and curves when behind.

White Against Left-Handed Pitchers

White hits fastballs and curves much better against left-handers than he does against right-handers. His .311 overall fastball average against lefties is very good, as is his .296 overall curve average.

He hits medium-over-the-middle fastballs (.333), low-over-the-middle fastballs (.357), medium-high inside fastballs (.423) and high-over-the-middle fastballs (.500) extremely well.

However, he has weaknesses against medium-high outside (.242) and high-outside fastballs (.222).

White tends to pull medium-high and high-outside fastballs thrown by left-handers, but he tends to hit low-outside fastballs fairly straightaway.

LOW-OUTSIDE FASTBALLS

BATTING AVERAGE .285
Play

Left	Deep and shifted toward center field
Center	Deep in straightaway center field
Right	Medium-deep in straightaway right field
Short	Up middle (shifted toward second base)
Second	Normal position

White's .296 overall average against curves thrown by left-handed pitchers is very good. Notice that not many low-outside curves have been thrown to him by left-handers. It will be interesting to see if he can continue his high average (.444) against these pitches as the number of recorded instances goes up.

Ahead And Behind In The Count Vs. RH

Ahead

Fastball Average .291

	Inside	Middle	Outside
High	12/333/4	39/282/11	14/357/5
Med	46/260/12	48/354/17	104/307/32
Low	16/125/2	55/309/17	23/173/4

Curve Average .243

	Inside	Middle	Outside
High	2/0/0	15/533/8	4/0/0
Med	8/250/2	11/454/5	22/45/1
Low	1/1000/1	14/214/3	5/0/0

Behind

Fastball Average .312

	Inside	Middle	Outside
High	6/166/1	16/312/5	13/307/4
Med	20/350/7	16/437/7	34/264/9
Low	6/166/1	19/368/7	14/285/4

Curve Average .269

	Inside	Middle	Outside
High	4/250/1	10/400/4	3/666/2
Med	5/0/0	8/375/3	20/300/6
Low	0/0/0	9/111/1	4/0/0

Overall Evaluation

Against Right-Handed Pitchers

Overall Fastball	⚾
Overall Curve	⚾
Overall Slider	⚾

Against Left-Handed Pitchers

Overall Fastball	⚾ ⚾ ⚾
Overall Curve	⚾ ⚾ ⚾
Overall Slider	⚾

Comments: Weak vs. outside and high fastballs vs. RH. Strengths: Medium-middle fastballs and curves, high-middle curves, medium-inside sliders vs. RH; over-the-middle fastballs, medium-inside fastballs, medium-inside and over-the-middle curves, low sliders vs. LH. Weaknesses: Fastballs and curves except as above vs. RH, sliders in general vs. RH; outside fastballs vs. LH, medium-inside and medium-outside sliders vs. LH.

Willie Wilson (Switch Hitter) — *Kansas City Royals*

Willie Wilson Against Right-Handed Pitchers
Overall BARS Batting Average .296

Fastball Average .303

	Outside	Middle	Inside
High	38 / 394 / 15	94 / 340 / 32	46 / 239 / 11
Med	193 / 326 / 63	124 / 354 / 44	213 / 314 / 67
Low	44 / 45 / 2	180 / 316 / 57	130 / 238 / 31

Curve Average .299

	Outside	Middle	Inside
High	9 / 444 / 4	9 / 222 / 2	2 / 500 / 1
Med	41 / 268 / 11	19 / 368 / 7	42 / 380 / 16
Low	13 / 307 / 4	42 / 238 / 10	30 / 233 / 7

Slider Average .225

	Outside	Middle	Inside
High	0 / 0 / 0	2 / 0 / 0	5 / 0 / 0
Med	5 / 400 / 2	6 / 500 / 3	41 / 243 / 10
Low	3 / 333 / 1	18 / 444 / 8	44 / 90 / 4

Willie Wilson Against Left-Handed Pitchers
Overall BARS Batting Average .295

Fastball Average .307

	Inside	Middle	Outside
High	14 / 285 / 4	31 / 451 / 14	18 / 55 / 1
Med	44 / 340 / 15	36 / 250 / 9	102 / 352 / 36
Low	29 / 137 / 4	79 / 392 / 31	27 / 111 / 3

Curve Average .291

	Inside	Middle	Outside
High	2 / 0 / 0	4 / 0 / 0	4 / 750 / 3
Med	7 / 714 / 5	8 / 375 / 3	22 / 227 / 5
Low	2 / 0 / 0	38 / 289 / 11	9 / 111 / 1

Slider Average .227

	Inside	Middle	Outside
High	8 / 125 / 1	3 / 333 / 1	2 / 0 / 0
Med	14 / 142 / 2	4 / 250 / 1	3 / 0 / 0
Low	17 / 352 / 6	13 / 230 / 3	2 / 500 / 1

Switch-hitting Willie Wilson hits a little better when batting right-handed against left-handed pitchers (.290 overall against left-handers, .274 overall against right-handers). He hits fastballs, curves and sliders about equally well against both; the difference in his overall averages is caused primarily by how well he hits change-ups and other types of pitches that are not included here.

Against right-handed pitchers, Wilson's .303 fastball average is good. He hits solidly in the three medium-high locations (.326, .354 and .314, outside to inside). He also hits well in the low-over-the-middle (.316), high-over-the-middle (.340), and high-outside locations (.394).

He has weaknesses in the high- and low-inside locations (.239 and .238), and an extreme weakness in the low-outside location (.045 on 2 for 44).

Wilson hits medium-high inside and medium-high outside fastballs very differently.

MEDIUM-HIGH INSIDE FASTBALLS

BATTING AVERAGE .314
Play

Left — Medium-deep and shifted toward center field
Center — Medium-deep in straightaway center field
Right — Deep and shifted toward the right field line
Short — Up middle (shifted toward second base)
Second — Shifted toward first base

MEDIUM-HIGH OUTSIDE FASTBALLS

BATTING AVERAGE .326
Play

Left — Medium-deep and shifted toward the left field line
Center — Deep in straightaway center field
Right — Deep in straightaway right field
Short — Up middle (shifted toward second base)
Second — Shifted toward first base

Wilson tends to hit low-over-the-middle fastballs up the middle.

LOW-OVER-THE-MIDDLE FASTBALLS

BATTING AVERAGE .316
Play

Left — Medium-deep and shifted toward center field
Center — Medium-deep in straightaway center field
Right — Deep and shifted toward center field
Short — Up middle (shifted toward second base)
Second — Shifted toward first base

Wilson Against Curves And Sliders

Wilson hits medium-high inside curves thrown by right-handers for a fine .380 average. He tends to pull these pitches to the infield (the right side), while tending to hit fly balls to the opposite field.

MEDIUM-HIGH INSIDE CURVEBALLS

BATTING AVERAGE .380
Play
Left	Medium-deep in straightaway left field
Center	Medium-deep and shifted toward left field
Right	Medium-deep and shifted toward center field
Short	Up middle (shifted toward second base)
Second	Shifted toward first base

Wilson tends to hit low-inside curves (one of his weakest curve locations) deep and scattered to all fields. The fact that his average is low in this location indicates that his deep fly balls are easy outs.

LOW-INSIDE CURVEBALLS

BATTING AVERAGE .233
Play
Left	Deep and shifted toward the left field line
Center	Deep and shifted toward left field
Right	Deep and shifted toward the right field line
Short	Up middle (shifted toward second base)
Second	Shifted toward first base

Wilson hits sliders poorly overall. He hits low-over-the-middle sliders excellently (.444) but has great difficulty in the highly pitched medium-high inside and low-inside slider locations (.243 and .090 respectively).

Wilson Against Left-Handed Pitchers

Against left-handed pitchers, Wilson hits medium-high outside fastballs very well, driving the ball strongly to all fields. His weakness against high-outside fastballs, however, lowers his overall average.

MEDIUM-HIGH OUTSIDE FASTBALLS (THROWN BY LEFT-HANDED PITCHERS)

BATTING AVERAGE .352
Play
Left	Deep in straightaway left field
Center	Deep and shifted toward left field
Right	Deep in straightaway right field
Short	Up middle (shifted toward second base)
Second	Shifted toward first base

HIGH-OUTSIDE FASTBALLS (THROWN BY LEFT-HANDED PITCHERS)

BATTING AVERAGE .055
Play
Left	*No instances recorded*
Center	Deep and shifted toward right field
Right	*No instances recorded*
Short	Up middle (shifted toward second base)
Second	Normal position

Wilson scatters low curves thrown by left-handers.

LOW-OVER-THE-MIDDLE CURVEBALLS (THROWN BY LEFT-HANDED PITCHERS)

BATTING AVERAGE .289
Play
Left	Deep and shifted toward the left field line
Center	Medium-deep and shifted toward right field
Right	Short and shifted toward the right field line
Short	Shifted toward third base
Second	Normal position

Ahead And Behind In The Count Vs. RH

Ahead

	Fastball Average .352			Curve Average .345		
	Outside	Middle	Inside	Outside	Middle	Inside
High	10/500/5	34/470/16	15/400/6	1/0/0	2/0/0	1/0/0
Med	88/352/31	60/400/24	96/364/35	7/714/5	8/250/2	16/437/7
Low	16/125/2	74/337/25	61/262/16	2/0/0	10/200/2	8/375/3

Behind

	Fastball Average .306			Curve Average .352		
	Outside	Middle	Inside	Outside	Middle	Inside
High	10/600/6	25/280/7	16/187/3	5/600/3	4/250/1	0/0/0
Med	42/357/15	22/318/7	49/285/14	12/250/3	3/666/2	14/357/5
Low	3/0/0	33/242/8	22/363/8	7/428/3	12/250/3	11/363/4

Overall Evaluation

Against Right-Handed Pitchers

Overall Fastball	⚾⚾ ⚾⚾⚾ ⚾⚾
Overall Curve	⚾⚾ ⚾⚾⚾ ⚾⚾
Overall Slider	⚾⚾

Against Left-Handed Pitchers

Overall Fastball	⚾⚾ ⚾⚾⚾ ⚾⚾
Overall Curve	⚾⚾ ⚾⚾⚾ ⚾⚾
Overall Slider	⚾⚾

Comments: Good fastball hitter vs. both RH and LH. Strengths: Waist-high , high-outside , high- and low-middle fastballs vs. RH, medium-inside, medium-middle, low-outside and high-outside curves vs. RH, low-middle sliders vs. RH; medium-outside, low-middle, high-middle & medium-inside fastballs vs. LH. Weaknesses: Fastball corners except high-outside vs. RH, low-inside curves and inside sliders vs. RH; four fastballs corners, medium-inside sliders vs. LH.

Minnesota Twins

Backman, Wally
Bush, Randy
Castillo, Carmen
Dwyer, Jim
Gaetti, Gary
Gagne, Greg
Gladden, Dan
Harper, Brian
Hrbek, Kent
Laudner, Tim
Larkin, Gene
Newman, Al
Puckett, Kirby

Minnesota Twins
BARS System
Hitting Analysis

Wally Backman (Switch Hitter) — *Minnesota Twins*

Wally Backman Against Right-Handed Pitchers
Overall BARS Batting Average .294

Fastball Average .324

	Outside	Middle	Inside
High	34/ 235 /8	68/ 485 /33	53/ 283 /15
Med	96/ 281 /27	38/ 342 /13	107/ 327 /35
Low	17/ 235 /4	65/ 369 /24	61/ 262 /16

Curve Average .283

	Outside	Middle	Inside
High	2/ 0 /0	9/ 666 /6	6/ 333 /2
Med	11/ 181 /2	4/ 0 /0	16/ 437 /7
Low	12/ 0 /0	22/ 272 /6	24/ 291 /7

Slider Average .222

	Outside	Middle	Inside
High	0/ 0 /0	0/ 0 /0	5/ 200 /1
Med	3/ 333 /1	1/ 0 /0	17/ 411 /7
Low	1/ 0 /0	5/ 0 /0	22/ 136 /3

Wally Backman Against Left-Handed Pitchers
Overall BARS Batting Average .177

Fastball Average .202

	Inside	Middle	Outside
High	2/ 0 /0	5/ 400 /2	5/ 0 /0
Med	7/ 428 /3	4/ 0 /0	22/ 181 /4
Low	5/ 200 /1	14/ 285 /4	5/ 0 /0

Curve Average .181

	Inside	Middle	Outside
High	1/ 0 /0	1/ 0 /0	1/ 1000 /1
Med	0/ 0 /0	2/ 0 /0	1/ 0 /0
Low	0/ 0 /0	2/ 500 /1	3/ 0 /0

Slider Average .100

	Inside	Middle	Outside
High	1/ 0 /0	0/ 0 /0	0/ 0 /0
Med	1/ 1000 /1	0/ 0 /0	0/ 0 /0
Low	1/ 0 /0	6/ 0 /0	1/ 0 /0

Switch-hitting Wally Backman has a much higher overall fastball average against right-handed pitchers (.324 overall against right-handers, .202 overall against left-handers).

Notice how well Backman hits over-the-middle fastballs against right-handers (.485, .342 and .369, high to low). This strong sector, along with his medium-high inside fastball location (.327), bolsters his overall average.

He hits high-over-the-middle fastballs medium-deep down the left line and straightaway to the other fields when he hits fly balls and to the right side of the infield when he hits grounders.

HIGH-OVER-THE-MIDDLE FASTBALLS

BATTING AVERAGE .485

Play

Left	Medium-deep and shifted toward the left field line
Center	Medium-deep in straightaway center field
Right	Deep in straightaway right field
Short	Up middle (shifted toward second base)
Second	Shifted toward first base

Backman's strong .369 average in his low-over-the-middle location is built on drives deep to the outfield.

LOW-OVER-THE-MIDDLE FASTBALLS

BATTING AVERAGE .369

Play

Left	Deep and shifted toward the left field line
Center	Deep and shifted toward left field
Right	Deep in straightaway right field
Short	Up middle (shifted toward second base)
Second	Normal position

He hits a strong .327 against medium-high inside fastballs against right-handers. His high number of instances in this location (107) shows that pitchers are throwing him fastballs inside. But he has a higher average in each of his inside fastball locations than in the corresponding outside fastball locations. Because of this, pitchers should consider throwing him a greater number of outside fastballs than they have been.

MEDIUM-HIGH INSIDE FASTBALLS

BATTING AVERAGE .327

Play

Left	Deep and shifted toward the left field line
Center	Medium-deep in straightaway center field
Right	Deep in straightaway right field
Short	Up middle (shifted toward second base)
Second	Normal position

Overall against fastballs, Backman is weakest in

his outside locations when facing right-handers. He has a solid enough .281 average against medium-high outside fastballs thrown by right-handers.

MEDIUM-HIGH OUTSIDE FASTBALLS

BATTING AVERAGE .281

Play

Left	Deep and shifted toward the left field line
Center	Medium-deep in straightaway center field
Right	Medium-deep in straightaway right field
Short	Up middle (shifted toward second base)
Second	Shifted toward first base

Backman Against Curves And Sliders

Backman hits inside curves very strongly against right-handed pitchers. His .437 against medium-high inside curves is excellent.

MEDIUM-HIGH INSIDE CURVEBALLS

BATTING AVERAGE .437

Play

Left	Medium-deep and shifted toward the left field line
Center	Deep in straightaway center field
Right	Medium-deep and shifted toward the right line
Short	Normal position
Second	Shifted toward first base

He hits low-inside curves for a good .291 average. He goes deep down the left line (his opposite field) with this pitch.

LOW-INSIDE CURVEBALLS

BATTING AVERAGE .291

Play

Left	Deep and shifted toward the left field line
Center	Medium-deep and shifted toward left field
Right	Medium-deep in straightaway right field
Short	Up middle (shifted toward second base)
Second	Normal position

He is weak against all outside curves against right-handers. His 2-for-11 against medium-high outside and 0-for-12 against low-outside curves give a distinct sector for pitchers to focus on.

He hits well against medium-high inside sliders (.411) but very poorly against low-inside sliders (.136).

MEDIUM-HIGH INSIDE SLIDERS

BATTING AVERAGE .411

Play

Left	Medium-deep and shifted toward the left line
Center	Medium-deep and shifted toward left field
Right	Medium-deep in straightaway right field
Short	Normal position
Second	Normal position

Fewer instances have been recorded for Backman against left-handed pitchers. His 4-for-22 against medium-outside fastballs indicates a weakness, but his .285 against low-over-the-middle fastballs and .428 on 3 for 7 against medium-high inside fastballs are strong.

Ahead And Behind In The Count Vs. RH

Ahead

Fastball Average .362

	Outside	Middle	Inside
High	10/ 500 /5	37/ 540 /20	21/ 333 /7
Med	50/ 300 /15	25/ 400 /10	57/ 315 /18
Low	3/ 333 /1	38/ 368 /14	32/ 281 /9

Curve Average .142

	Outside	Middle	Inside
High	0/ 0 /0	1/ 1000 /1	0/ 0 /0
Med	1/ 0 /0	0/ 0 /0	3/ 0 /0
Low	0/ 0 /0	1/ 0 /0	1/ 0 /0

Behind

Fastball Average .358

	Outside	Middle	Inside
High	6/ 166 /1	9/ 666 /6	11/ 272 /3
Med	17/ 352 /6	5/ 200 /1	15/ 400 /6
Low	7/ 428 /3	8/ 375 /3	14/ 285 /4

Curve Average .355

	Outside	Middle	Inside
High	1/ 0 /0	5/ 600 /3	6/ 333 /2
Med	4/ 250 /1	1/ 0 /0	7/ 428 /3
Low	5/ 0 /0	6/ 500 /3	10/ 400 /4

Overall Evaluation

Against Right-Handed Pitchers

Overall Fastball	⚾ ⚾ ⚾ ⚾
Overall Curve	⚾ ⚾ ⚾ ⚾
Overall Slider	⚾

Against Left-Handed Pitchers

Overall Fastball	⚾
Overall Curve	Not enough information
Overall Slider	Not enough information

Comments: Hits fastballs well vs. RH — very strong against over-the-middle fastballs.

Strengths: Medium-inside fastballs and all over-the-middle fastballs, medium-inside and low-inside curves, medium-inside sliders vs. RH.

Weaknesses: High-outside, low-outside and low-inside fastballs, outside curves and low sliders vs. RH; outside fastballs vs. LH.

Randy Bush (Left Handed) — *Minnesota Twins*

Randy Bush Against Right-Handed Pitchers
Overall BARS Batting Average .272

Fastball Average .302

	Outside	Middle	Inside
High	23/ 217 /5	14/ 214 /3	14/ 71 /1
Med	91/ 318 /29	11/ 363 /4	46/ 326 /15
Low	21/ 238 /5	33/ 484 /16	18/ 222 /4

Curve Average .102

	Outside	Middle	Inside
High	4/ 0 /0	2/ 500 /1	2/ 0 /0
Med	9/ 0 /0	2/ 0 /0	6/ 166 /1
Low	4/ 0 /0	3/ 666 /2	7/ 0 /0

Slider Average .208

	Outside	Middle	Inside
High	1/ 0 /0	1/ 0 /0	0/ 0 /0
Med	6/ 333 /2	0/ 0 /0	3/ 333 /1
Low	3/ 333 /1	5/ 200 /1	5/ 0 /0

The BARS System has few recorded instances against left-handed pitchers for Randy Bush, so only his charts against right-handers are shown here.

The left-handed hitting Bush has a strong .302 overall fastball average against right-handed pitchers. He hits excellently against waist-high fastballs (.318, .363 and .326, outside to inside) but has trouble with high fastballs (.217, .214 and .071, outside to inside).

He hits medium-high outside fastballs deep to the outfield.

MEDIUM-HIGH OUTSIDE FASTBALLS

BATTING AVERAGE .318
Play

Left	Deep and shifted toward center field
Center	Deep in straightaway center field
Right	Deep in straightaway right field
Short	Up middle (shifted toward second base)
Second	Normal position

He hits medium-high inside fastballs down both lines. The diagram on the opposite page shows how fielders need to play to be properly positioned for a medium-high inside fastball thrown to Bush.

MEDIUM-HIGH INSIDE FASTBALLS

BATTING AVERAGE .326
Play

Left	Medium-deep and shifted toward the left line
Center	Medium-deep in straightaway center field
Right	Deep and shifted toward the right field line
Short	Up middle (shifted toward second base)
Second	Shifted toward first base

Bush hits a resounding .484 against low-over-the-middle fastballs.

LOW-OVER-THE-MIDDLE FASTBALLS

BATTING AVERAGE .484
Play

Left	Deep in straightaway left field
Center	Medium-deep in straightaway center field
Right	Deep and shifted toward the right field line
Short	*No instances recorded*
Second	Normal position

He hits high-outside fastballs deep to all fields.

HIGH-OUTSIDE FASTBALLS

BATTING AVERAGE .217
Play

Left	Deep and shifted toward center field
Center	Deep in straightaway center field
Right	Deep in straightaway right field
Short	Up middle (shifted toward second base)
Second	Normal position

He has trouble with outside and inside curves. His 0-for-9 against medium-high outside curves and 0-for-7 against low-inside curves indicate significant weaknesses. Right-handers should try throwing him more curves, especially since he hits fastballs well overall.

Right-handers also throw him few sliders. His 0-for-5 against low-inside sliders indicates a weakness.

Medium-High Inside Fastballs
(Thrown By Right-Handed Pitchers)

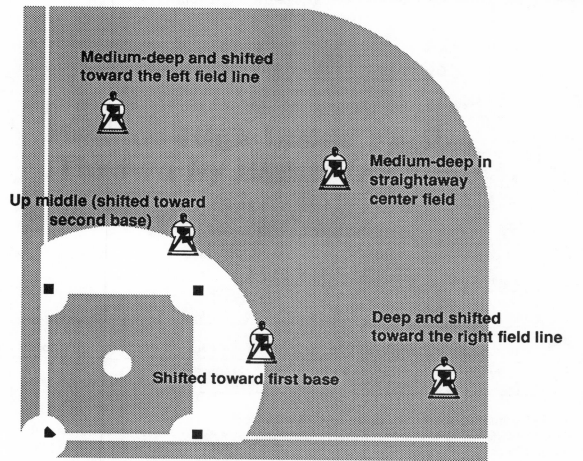

Medium-deep and shifted toward the left field line

Medium-deep in straightaway center field

Up middle (shifted toward second base)

Deep and shifted toward the right field line

Shifted toward first base

Ahead And Behind In The Count Vs. RH

Ahead

Fastball Average .302

	Outside	Middle	Inside
High	10/200 /2	9/222 /2	2/0 /0
Med	40/350 /14	6/500 /3	25/200 /5
Low	8/250 /2	14/500 /7	5/200 /1

Curve Average .000

	Outside	Middle	Inside
High	0/0 /0	0/0 /0	0/0 /0
Med	1/0 /0	1/0 /0	1/0 /0
Low	1/0 /0	0/0 /0	0/0 /0

Behind

Fastball Average .212

	Outside	Middle	Inside
High	2/500 /1	3/333 /1	6/0 /0
Med	20/300 /6	3/333 /1	5/200 /1
Low	5/0 /0	2/0 /0	1/0 /0

Curve Average .083

	Outside	Middle	Inside
High	3/0 /0	1/0 /0	1/0 /0
Med	3/0 /0	0/0 /0	3/333 /1
Low	0/0 /0	0/0 /0	1/0 /0

Overall Evaluation
Against Right-Handed Pitchers

Overall Fastball	
Overall Curve	
Overall Slider	

Against Left-Handed Pitchers

Overall Fastball	Not enough information
Overall Curve	Not enough information
Overall Slider	Not enough information

Comments: Weak against high fastballs vs. RH.
Strengths: Waist-high fastballs vs. RH, low-middle fastballs vs. RH.
Weaknesses: High fastballs vs. RH, low-outside and low-inside fastballs vs. RH, outside curves, low-inside and medium-inside curves, low-inside sliders vs. RH.

Carmen Castillo (Right Handed) — *Minnesota Twins*

Carmen Castillo Against Right-Handed Pitchers
Overall BARS Batting Average .175

Fastball Average .172

	Inside	Middle	Outside
High	4/ 250 /1	3/ 0 /0	4/ 0 /0
Med	8/ 125 /1	1/ 1000 /1	22/ 45 /1
Low	0/ 0 /0	7/ 285 /2	9/ 444 /4

Curve Average .294

	Inside	Middle	Outside
High	1/ 0 /0	1/ 0 /0	0/ 0 /0
Med	1/ 0 /0	0/ 0 /0	6/ 333 /2
Low	1/ 0 /0	0/ 0 /0	7/ 428 /3

Slider Average .100

	Inside	Middle	Outside
High	0/ 0 /0	0/ 0 /0	0/ 0 /0
Med	3/ 0 /0	0/ 0 /0	8/ 250 /2
Low	0/ 0 /0	1/ 0 /0	8/ 0 /0

Carmen Castillo Against Left-Handed Pitchers
Overall BARS Batting Average .259

Fastball Average .284

	Inside	Middle	Outside
High	2/ 500 /1	8/ 250 /2	9/ 333 /3
Med	7/ 285 /2	5/ 800 /4	30/ 300 /9
Low	7/ 142 /1	23/ 217 /5	11/ 181 /2

Curve Average .200

	Inside	Middle	Outside
High	0/ 0 /0	1/ 1000 /1	1/ 1000 /1
Med	2/ 0 /0	0/ 0 /0	5/ 400 /2
Low	4/ 0 /0	4/ 0 /0	3/ 0 /0

Slider Average .142

	Inside	Middle	Outside
High	1/ 0 /0	1/ 0 /0	0/ 0 /0
Med	2/ 500 /1	0/ 0 /0	6/ 166 /1
Low	2/ 0 /0	1/ 0 /0	1/ 0 /0

Right-handed hitter Carmen Castillo has trouble with fastballs against right-handed pitchers (.172 overall) but he hits fastballs pretty well against left-handed pitchers (.284 overall).

Notice Castillo's .045 average in his medium-high outside fastball location against right-handers. This is one of the weakest medium-high outside fastball averages recorded by the BARS System. Most hitters are fairly strong in this location. Castillo hits this pitch deep to left and center fields, but his low average probably means he hits the ball for easy outs.

MEDIUM-HIGH OUTSIDE FASTBALLS

BATTING AVERAGE .045
Play

Left	Deep and shifted toward the left field line
Center	Deep in straightaway center field
Right	Medium-deep in straightaway right field
Short	Normal position
Second	Shifted toward first base

In contrast, he hits .444 against low-outside fastballs. This is unusual in light of his weak medium-high outside location, but shows that every hitter is unique.

LOW-OUTSIDE FASTBALLS

BATTING AVERAGE .444
Play

Left	*No instances recorded*
Center	Deep in straightaway center field
Right	Deep in straightaway right field
Short	Normal position
Second	*No instances recorded*

Castillo's weak against inside fastballs thrown by right-handers. He has strong averages against low-outside and medium-high outside curves (.428 and .333). He hits medium-high outside sliders pretty well (.250) but has trouble with low-outside sliders (.000 on 0 for 8).

Against left-handed pitchers Castillo hits an even .300 against medium-high outside fastballs.

MEDIUM-HIGH OUTSIDE FASTBALLS
(THROWN BY LEFT-HANDED PITCHERS)

BATTING AVERAGE .300
Play

Left	Deep and shifted toward the left field line
Center	Medium-deep in straightaway center field
Right	Deep in straightaway right field
Short	Normal position
Second	Normal position

He has trouble with low fastballs against left-handers, but hits high fastballs well overall.

His curve and slider charts show a lot of weak sectors for left-handers to attack.

Medium-High Outside Fastballs
(Thrown By Left-Handed Pitchers)

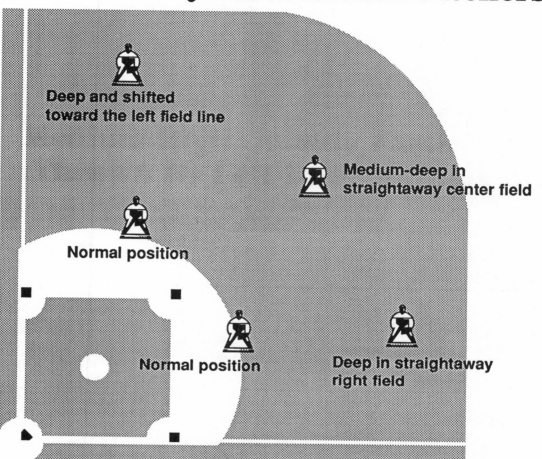

Deep and shifted toward the left field line

Medium-deep in straightaway center field

Normal position

Normal position

Deep in straightaway right field

Ahead And Behind In The Count Vs. RH

Ahead

Fastball Average .250

	Inside	Middle	Outside
High	2/500 /1	2/0 /0	1/0 /0
Med	1/0 /0	1/1000 /1	10/100 /1
Low	0/0 /0	3/0 /0	4/750 /3

Curve Average .250

	Inside	Middle	Outside
High	0/0 /0	0/0 /0	0/0 /0
Med	1/0 /0	0/0 /0	2/0 /0
Low	0/0 /0	0/0 /0	1/1000 /1

Behind

Fastball Average .076

	Inside	Middle	Outside
High	1/0 /0	0/0 /0	0/0 /0
Med	1/1000 /1	0/0 /0	9/0 /0
Low	0/0 /0	0/0 /0	2/0 /0

Curve Average .285

	Inside	Middle	Outside
High	1/0 /0	0/0 /0	0/0 /0
Med	0/0 /0	0/0 /0	2/500 /1
Low	0/0 /0	0/0 /0	4/250 /1

Overall Evaluation

Against Right-Handed Pitchers

Overall Fastball ⚾⚾

Overall Curve ⚾⚾ ⚾⚾⚾

Overall Slider ⚾⚾

Against Left-Handed Pitchers

Overall Fastball ⚾⚾ ⚾⚾

Overall Curve ⚾⚾

Overall Slider ⚾⚾

Comments: Very weak against medium-outside fastballs vs. RH.

Strengths: Low-outside fastballs, low-outside and medium-outside curves vs. RH; waist-high and high-outside fastballs vs. LH.

Weaknesses: Inside fastballs, high fastballs, medium-outside fastballs, low-outside sliders vs. RH; low fastballs, low curves and medium-outside sliders vs. LH.

Jim Dwyer (Left Handed)

Minnesota Twins

Jim Dwyer Against Right-Handed Pitchers
Overall BARS Batting Average .261

Fastball Average .261

	Outside	Middle	Inside
High	19 / 210 / 4	10 / 600 / 6	8 / 125 / 1
Med	111 / 243 / 27	30 / 366 / 11	30 / 200 / 6
Low	14 / 214 / 3	37 / 243 / 9	16 / 312 / 5

Curve Average .293

	Outside	Middle	Inside
High	2 / 500 / 1	3 / 333 / 1	4 / 250 / 1
Med	11 / 272 / 3	6 / 166 / 1	6 / 500 / 3
Low	4 / 0 / 0	11 / 272 / 3	11 / 363 / 4

Slider Average .181

	Outside	Middle	Inside
High	1 / 0 / 0	2 / 0 / 0	1 / 0 / 0
Med	2 / 0 / 0	1 / 1000 / 1	6 / 166 / 1
Low	3 / 0 / 0	4 / 250 / 1	2 / 500 / 1

Jim Dwyer Against Left-Handed Pitchers
Overall BARS Batting Average .272

Fastball Average .187

	Outside	Middle	Inside
High	1 / 0 / 0	0 / 0 / 0	1 / 1000 / 1
Med	8 / 125 / 1	0 / 0 / 0	2 / 0 / 0
Low	0 / 0 / 0	3 / 333 / 1	1 / 0 / 0

Curve Average .600

	Outside	Middle	Inside
High	0 / 0 / 0	1 / 1000 / 1	0 / 0 / 0
Med	0 / 0 / 0	2 / 1000 / 2	0 / 0 / 0
Low	0 / 0 / 0	1 / 0 / 0	1 / 0 / 0

Slider Average .000

	Outside	Middle	Inside
High	0 / 0 / 0	0 / 0 / 0	0 / 0 / 0
Med	0 / 0 / 0	0 / 0 / 0	0 / 0 / 0
Low	0 / 0 / 0	0 / 0 / 0	0 / 0 / 0

Left-handed hitter Jim Dwyer has many more recorded instances against right-handed pitchers so we won't go into his performance against left-handers in these pages.

Dwyer has trouble with outside fastballs against right-handers (.210, .243, and .214, high to low). He hits medium-high outside fastballs deep to all fields, but his low average in this location indicates that he doesn't hit the ball hard. Most of his hit balls are probably easy fly balls or easy grounders.

MEDIUM-HIGH OUTSIDE FASTBALLS

BATTING AVERAGE .243

Play

Left	Deep and shifted toward the left field line
Center	Deep in straightaway center field
Right	Deep in straightaway right field
Short	Up middle (shifted toward second base)
Second	Normal position

Right-handers throw him so many medium-high outside fastballs (111 — three times his next-highest location) that he could really just expect them and tee off, hitting more sharply and raising his average.

He hits .200 against medium-high inside fastballs.

MEDIUM-HIGH INSIDE FASTBALLS

BATTING AVERAGE .200

Play

Left	Medium-deep and shifted toward the left field line
Center	Deep in straightaway center field
Right	Short in straightaway right field
Short	Normal position
Second	Shifted toward first base

His strong fastball locations are high-over-the-middle (.600), medium-over-the-middle (.366), and low-inside (.312).

He hits a relatively high number of medium-over-the-middle fastballs (30). He hits this pitch deep to the outfield, and his high average indicates that he probably hits the ball hard. The field diagram on the opposite page indicates how fielders should play him for this pitch.

MEDIUM-OVER-THE-MIDDLE FASTBALLS

BATTING AVERAGE .366

Play

Left	Deep in straightaway left field
Center	Deep in straightaway center field
Right	Deep and shifted toward the right field line
Short	Normal position
Second	Shifted toward first base

He hits medium-high outside curves and low-over-the middle curves pretty well (.272 in each location). His .363 against low-inside curves is excellent.

Medium-Over-The-Middle Fastballs (Thrown By Right-Handed Pitchers)

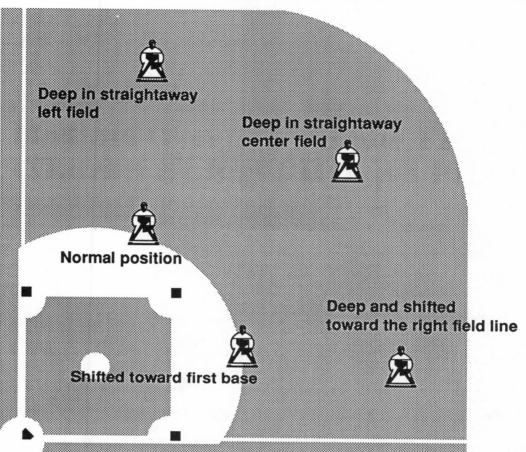

Deep in straightaway left field

Deep in straightaway center field

Normal position

Deep and shifted toward the right field line

Shifted toward first base

Ahead And Behind In The Count Vs. RH

Ahead

Fastball Average .343

	Outside	Middle	Inside
High	7/ 571 /4	7/ 714 /5	0/ 0 /0
Med	50/ 280 /14	20/ 400 /8	15/ 333 /5
Low	4/ 500 /2	19/ 157 /3	9/ 444 /4

Curve Average .571

	Outside	Middle	Inside
High	1/ 0 /0	2/ 500 /1	0/ 0 /0
Med	2/ 500 /1	1/ 1000 /1	2/ 500 /1
Low	0/ 0 /0	3/ 666 /2	3/ 666 /2

Behind

Fastball Average .372

	Outside	Middle	Inside
High	3/ 0 /0	1/ 1000 /1	2/ 500 /1
Med	19/ 368 /7	4/ 750 /3	5/ 200 /1
Low	2/ 0 /0	3/ 666 /2	4/ 250 /1

Curve Average .222

	Outside	Middle	Inside
High	0/ 0 /0	1/ 0 /0	1/ 0 /0
Med	4/ 500 /2	2/ 0 /0	2/ 0 /0
Low	1/ 0 /0	4/ 250 /1	3/ 333 /1

Overall Evaluation

Against Right-Handed Pitchers

Overall Fastball

Overall Curve ⚾ ⚾ ⚾ ⚾

Overall Slider ⚾

Against Left-Handed Pitchers

Overall Fastball ⚾

Overall Curve — Not enough information

Overall Slider — Not enough information

Comments: Weak against outside fastballs vs. RH.
Strengths: High-middle, medium-middle and low-inside fastballs, low-inside curves vs. RH.
Weaknesses: Outside fastballs, low-middle, high-inside and medium-inside fastballs, medium-inside sliders vs. RH; medium-outside fastballs vs. LH.

Gary Gaetti Against Right-Handed Pitchers
Overall BARS Batting Average .272

Fastball Average .284

	Inside	Middle	Outside
High	10/ 100 /1	19/ 473 /9	16/ 125 /2
Med	38/ 263 /10	22/ 500 /11	114/ 289 /33
Low	13/ 307 /4	42/ 309 /13	39/ 153 /6

Curve Average .268

	Inside	Middle	Outside
High	4/ 0 /0	4/ 0 /0	4/ 250 /1
Med	5/ 0 /0	5/ 0 /0	34/ 323 /11
Low	5/ 200 /1	12/ 666 /8	20/ 200 /4

Slider Average .219

	Inside	Middle	Outside
High	2/ 0 /0	2/ 500 /1	1/ 1000 /1
Med	5/ 200 /1	9/ 111 /1	19/ 421 /8
Low	2/ 500 /1	13/ 230 /3	20/ 0 /0

Gary Gaetti Against Left-Handed Pitchers
Overall BARS Batting Average .243

Fastball Average .251

	Inside	Middle	Outside
High	3/ 0 /0	7/ 714 /5	9/ 111 /1
Med	20/ 250 /5	5/ 600 /3	54/ 259 /14
Low	8/ 125 /1	13/ 153 /2	16/ 187 /3

Curve Average .285

	Inside	Middle	Outside
High	0/ 0 /0	0/ 0 /0	2/ 0 /0
Med	0/ 0 /0	2/ 500 /1	9/ 444 /4
Low	4/ 250 /1	6/ 166 /1	12/ 250 /3

Slider Average .130

	Inside	Middle	Outside
High	0/ 0 /0	0/ 0 /0	0/ 0 /0
Med	6/ 166 /1	1/ 1000 /1	3/ 0 /0
Low	4/ 0 /0	2/ 0 /0	7/ 142 /1

Right-handed hitter Gary Gaetti has an overall fastball average of .284 against right-handed pitchers, .251 against left-handed pitchers. It's somewhat unusual for a right-handed hitter to hit so much better against right-handed pitchers. He does hit curves better against lefties, however.

Notice in Gaetti's fastball chart against right-handed pitchers how strong he is against all three over-the-middle locations (.473, .500 and .309, high to low). He hits low-over-the-middle fastballs medium-deep to all fields, pulling the ball down the left line.

LOW-OVER-THE-MIDDLE FASTBALLS

BATTING AVERAGE .309
Play
Left   Medium-deep and shifted toward the left line
Center   Medium-deep in straightaway center field
Right   Medium-deep and shifted toward center field
Short   Up middle (shifted toward second base)
Second   Normal position

He scatters high-over-the-middle fastballs. If fielders positioned themselves according to the BARS fielding strategy, they could prevent most of his base hits from this location.

HIGH-OVER-THE-MIDDLE FASTBALLS

BATTING AVERAGE .473
Play
Left   Deep and shifted toward the left field line
Center   Deep and shifted toward left field
Right   Medium-deep and shifted toward the right line
Short   Shifted toward third base
Second   *No instances recorded*

He hits medium-high outside fastballs thrown by right-handers deep to all fields.

MEDIUM-HIGH OUTSIDE FASTBALLS

BATTING AVERAGE .289
Play
Left   Deep in straightaway left field
Center   Deep in straightaway center field
Right   Deep and shifted toward center field
Short   Up middle (shifted toward second base)
Second   Normal position

He hits medium-high inside fastballs down both lines against right-handers.

MEDIUM-HIGH INSIDE FASTBALLS

BATTING AVERAGE .263
Play

Left	Deep and shifted toward the left field line
Center	Medium-deep in straightaway center field
Right	Short and shifted toward the right field line
Short	Shifted toward third base
Second	Shifted toward first base

Gaetti Against Curves And Sliders

Against right-handed pitchers Gaetti has trouble with low-outside curves (.200) and low-outside sliders (.000 on 0 for 20). But he hits medium-high outside curves and sliders well (.323 and .421 respectively).

He pulls medium-high outside curves and sliders.

MEDIUM-HIGH OUTSIDE CURVES

BATTING AVERAGE .323
Play

Left	Medium-deep and shifted toward the left field line
Center	Deep and shifted toward left field
Right	Deep and shifted toward center field
Short	Normal position
Second	Shifted toward first base

MEDIUM-HIGH OUTSIDE SLIDERS

BATTING AVERAGE .421
Play

Left	Deep and shifted toward the left field line
Center	Deep and shifted toward left field
Right	Deep and shifted toward center field
Short	Shifted toward third base
Second	Normal position

Gaetti Against Left-Handed Pitchers

Gaetti hits .251 overall against fastballs thrown by left-handed pitchers. He hits only .259 against medium-high outside fastballs, sending this pitch deep to all fields.

MEDIUM-HIGH OUTSIDE FASTBALLS (THROWN BY LEFT-HANDED PITCHERS)

BATTING AVERAGE .259
Play

Left	Deep in straightaway left field
Center	Deep in straightaway center field
Right	Deep in straightaway right field
Short	Shifted toward third base
Second	Normal position

Gaetti tends to pull medium-high inside fastballs thrown by left-handers

MEDIUM-HIGH INSIDE FASTBALLS (THROWN BY LEFT-HANDED PITCHERS)

BATTING AVERAGE .250
Play

Left	Medium-deep in straightaway left field
Center	Deep and shifted toward left field
Right	*No instances recorded*
Short	Shifted toward third base
Second	Normal position

Gaetti's fastball chart shows his difficulties with all low and all inside fastballs against left-handers. These difficulties carry over to curves and sliders. His .250 against low-outside curves is fair. His .142 against low-outside sliders indicates a weakness.

Ahead And Behind In The Count Vs. RH

Ahead

Fastball Average .396

	Inside	Middle	Outside
High	3/0	7/4 — 571	5/1 — 200
Med	11/5 — 454	14/8 — 571	48/19 — 395
Low	8/3 — 375	20/9 — 450	15/3 — 200

Curve Average .388

	Inside	Middle	Outside
High	1/0	1/0	1/1 — 1000
Med	2/0	2/0	14/5 — 357
Low	1/0	11/7 — 636	3/1 — 333

Behind

Fastball Average .272

	Inside	Middle	Outside
High	1/0	4/2 — 500	4/0
Med	12/3 — 250	2/0	18/6 — 333
Low	1/0	8/2 — 250	5/2 — 400

Curve Average .166

	Inside	Middle	Outside
High	1/0	2/0	2/0
Med	2/0	1/0	5/1 — 200
Low	1/1 — 1000	0/0	4/1 — 250

Overall Evaluation

Against Right-Handed Pitchers

Overall Fastball	⚾⚾ ⚾⚾
Overall Curve	⚾⚾ ⚾⚾
Overall Slider	⚾⚾

Against Left-Handed Pitchers

Overall Fastball	⚾⚾
Overall Curve	⚾⚾ ⚾⚾ ⚾⚾
Overall Slider	⚾⚾

Comments: Weak against low-outside pitches. **Strengths:** Over-the-middle fastballs, low-inside fastballs, medium-outside and low-middle curves, medium-outside sliders vs. RH; high-middle & medium-middle fastballs, medium-outside curves vs. LH. **Weaknesses:** Medium-inside and low-outside fastballs, low-outside curves, low-outside and low-middle sliders vs. RH; inside fastballs, low fastballs, low curves and low sliders vs. LH.

Greg Gagne Against Right-Handed Pitchers
Overall BARS Batting Average .258

Fastball Average .257

	Inside	Middle	Outside
High	7/ 0/0	10/ 200/2	14/ 0/0
Med	34/ 205/7	10/ 300/3	60/ 283/17
Low	14/ 285/4	26/ 423/11	15/ 333/5

Curve Average .181

	Inside	Middle	Outside
High	1/ 0/0	3/ 333/1	0/ 0/0
Med	2/ 500/1	3/ 333/1	14/ 71/1
Low	0/ 0/0	4/ 750/3	17/ 58/1

Slider Average .358

	Inside	Middle	Outside
High	0/ 0/0	1/ 0/0	0/ 0/0
Med	2/ 500/1	0/ 0/0	12/ 250/3
Low	2/ 500/1	2/ 500/1	20/ 400/8

Greg Gagne Against Left-Handed Pitchers
Overall BARS Batting Average .250

Fastball Average .252

	Inside	Middle	Outside
High	11/ 181/2	8/ 375/3	6/ 166/1
Med	17/ 176/3	4/ 0/0	39/ 333/13
Low	5/ 200/1	14/ 214/3	7/ 285/2

Curve Average .250

	Inside	Middle	Outside
High	0/ 0/0	0/ 0/0	1/ 0/0
Med	3/ 0/0	1/ 0/0	6/ 500/3
Low	4/ 0/0	4/ 250/1	5/ 400/2

Slider Average .235

	Inside	Middle	Outside
High	0/ 0/0	0/ 0/0	1/ 0/0
Med	2/ 500/1	0/ 0/0	6/ 166/1
Low	4/ 250/1	1/ 0/0	3/ 333/1

Greg Gagne, right-handed hitter, has comparable overall fastball averages against right- and left-handed pitchers (.257 overall fastball vs. right-handers, .252 overall fastball vs. left-handers).

Against right-handers, Gagne hits medium-high outside fastballs (.283) deep down the left line, medium-deep and straightaway to center and into the right-center gap.

MEDIUM-HIGH OUTSIDE FASTBALLS

BATTING AVERAGE .283
Play
Left   Deep and shifted toward the left field line
Center   Medium-deep in straightaway center field
Right   Deep and shifted toward center field
Short   Normal position
Second   Normal position

Notice how well Gagne hits low fastballs against right-handed pitchers. He pulls low-over-the-middle fastballs (.423) when hitting to the outfield, but the shortstop needs to shift toward second base.

LOW-OVER-THE-MIDDLE FASTBALLS

BATTING AVERAGE .423
Play
Left   Medium-deep and shifted toward the left line

Center   Deep and shifted toward left field
Right   Deep and shifted toward center field
Short   Up middle (shifted toward second base)
Second   Normal position

Gagne hits low-outside fastballs (.333) medium-deep down the left line, medium-deep into the left-center gap, and medium-deep down the right line. The second baseman needs to shift toward first.

LOW-OUTSIDE FASTBALLS

BATTING AVERAGE .333
Play
Left   Medium-deep and shifted toward the left line
Center   Medium-deep and shifted toward left field
Right   Medium-deep and shifted toward the right line
Short   Normal position
Second   Shifted toward first base

Gagne is weak against high fastballs thrown by right-handers (.000 on 0 for 7, .200, and .000 on 0 for 14). By keeping fastballs high or medium-high inside, right-handers could do well against him.

Gagne Against Curves And Sliders

Gagne has tremendous difficulty with outside

curves. His 1-for-14 against medium-high outside and 1-for-17 against low-outside curves offer an excellent target for right-handed pitchers.

Low-outside sliders are a different story. Gagne hits this pitch excellently (.400). His BARS fielding strategy indicates that he pulls the ball medium-deep to all fields. If fielders followed this strategy, they could get to most of his line-drive base hits.

LOW-OUTSIDE SLIDERS

BATTING AVERAGE .400
Play

Left	Medium-deep and shifted toward the left field line
Center	Medium-deep and shifted toward left field
Right	Medium-deep and shifted toward center field
Short	*No instances recorded*
Second	*No instances recorded*

Gagne Against Left-Handed Pitchers

Gagne hits medium-high outside fastballs strongly against left-handed pitchers (.333). He hits this pitch straightaway to the outfield.

MEDIUM-HIGH OUTSIDE FASTBALLS
(THROWN BY LEFT-HANDED PITCHERS)

BATTING AVERAGE .333
Play

Left	Medium-deep in straightaway left field
Center	Medium-deep in straightaway center field

Right	Deep in straightaway right field
Short	Normal position
Second	Normal position

He has a weak .214 average against low-over-the-middle fastballs. He hits this pitch toward center field.

LOW-OVER-THE-MIDDLE FASTBALLS
(THROWN BY LEFT-HANDED PITCHERS)

BATTING AVERAGE .214
Play

Left	Deep and shifted toward center field
Center	Deep in straightaway center field
Right	Deep and shifted toward center field
Short	Normal position
Second	*No instances recorded*

Gagne has trouble with inside fastballs and low fastballs against left-handers (with the exception of low-outside, .285). He hits .176 against medium-high inside fastballs.

MEDIUM-HIGH INSIDE FASTBALLS
(THROWN BY LEFT-HANDED PITCHERS)

BATTING AVERAGE .176
Play

Left	Deep in straightaway left field
Center	Medium-deep in straightaway center field
Right	Deep and shifted toward center field
Short	Up middle (shifted toward second base)
Second	Shifted toward first base

Ahead And Behind In The Count Vs. RH

Ahead

Fastball Average .282

	Inside	Middle	Outside
High	3/0 /0	5/400 /2	2/0 /0
Med	18/222 /4	6/333 /2	23/304 /7
Low	6/166 /1	12/416 /5	3/333 /1

Curve Average .300

	Inside	Middle	Outside
High	0/0 /0	1/1000 /1	0/0 /0
Med	0/0 /0	1/0 /0	5/200 /1
Low	0/0 /0	1/1000 /1	2/0 /0

Behind

Fastball Average .263

	Inside	Middle	Outside
High	3/0 /0	1/0 /0	5/0 /0
Med	6/333 /2	0/0 /0	13/230 /3
Low	1/1000 /1	7/428 /3	2/500 /1

Curve Average .181

	Inside	Middle	Outside
High	1/0 /0	1/0 /0	0/0 /0
Med	1/1000 /1	1/1000 /1	3/0 /0
Low	0/0 /0	0/0 /0	4/0 /0

Overall Evaluation
Against Right-Handed Pitchers

Overall Fastball	⚾⚾
Overall Curve	⚾⚾
Overall Slider	⚾⚾ ⚾⚾ ⚾

Against Left-Handed Pitchers

Overall Fastball	⚾⚾
Overall Curve	⚾⚾ ⚾⚾
Overall Slider	⚾⚾

Comments: Hits low fastballs well, high fastballs poorly vs. RH. Weak against outside curves vs. RH. **Strengths:** Low fastballs, medium-middle fastballs, over-the-middle curves, low sliders vs. RH; medium-outside and high-middle fastballs, medium-outside curves vs. LH. **Weaknesses:** High fastballs, medium-inside fastballs, outside curves vs. RH; inside fastballs and low-middle fastballs, inside curves vs. LH.

Dan Gladden (Right Handed) — *Minnesota Twins*

Dan Gladden Against Right-Handed Pitchers
Overall BARS Batting Average .297

Fastball Average .356

	Inside	Middle	Outside
High	21/428 /9	32/343 /11	7/142 /1
Med	41/365 /15	16/312 /5	83/373 /31
Low	15/266 /4	34/441 /15	26/269 /7

Curve Average .277

	Inside	Middle	Outside
High	1/1000 /1	6/333 /2	0/0 /0
Med	7/428 /3	2/0 /0	24/333 /8
Low	3/333 /1	5/200 /1	24/166 /4

Slider Average .250

	Inside	Middle	Outside
High	0/0 /0	2/1000 /2	0/0 /0
Med	3/333 /1	1/0 /0	22/272 /6
Low	0/0 /0	8/250 /2	16/125 /2

Dan Gladden Against Left-Handed Pitchers
Overall BARS Batting Average .273

Fastball Average .293

	Inside	Middle	Outside
High	8/375 /3	12/583 /7	10/200 /2
Med	15/133 /2	6/333 /2	33/333 /11
Low	8/125 /1	9/222 /2	15/266 /4

Curve Average .222

	Inside	Middle	Outside
High	1/0 /0	2/1000 /2	2/0 /0
Med	1/1000 /1	0/0 /0	6/333 /2
Low	3/0 /0	7/142 /1	5/0 /0

Slider Average .428

	Inside	Middle	Outside
High	0/0 /0	1/1000 /1	0/0 /0
Med	2/1000 /2	0/0 /0	0/0 /0
Low	7/142 /1	2/500 /1	2/500 /1

For a right-handed hitter, Dan Gladden's .356 overall fastball average against right-handed pitchers is exceptional. His .293 overall fastball average against left-handers is lower, but still isn't bad.

Gladden has some very strong fastball locations against right-handers. He hits .373 against medium-high outside fastballs. If the left fielder played him more in the left-center gap and the center and right fielders played him medium-deep, as indicated by the BARS fielding strategy shown below, they would be able to prevent most of his base hits.

MEDIUM-HIGH OUTSIDE FASTBALLS

BATTING AVERAGE .373
Play

Left	Deep and shifted toward center field
Center	Medium-deep in straightaway center field
Right	Medium-deep in straightaway right field
Short	Up middle (shifted toward second base)
Second	Normal position

He hits a strong .365 against medium-high inside fastballs.

MEDIUM-HIGH INSIDE FASTBALLS

BATTING AVERAGE .365
Play

Left	Deep in straightaway left field
Center	Medium-deep in straightaway center field
Right	Deep and shifted toward center field
Short	Normal position
Second	Shifted toward first base

He hits low-over-the-middle fastballs for a high .441 average.

LOW-OVER-THE-MIDDLE FASTBALLS

BATTING AVERAGE .441
Play

Left	Deep and shifted toward the left field line
Center	Deep and shifted toward left field
Right	Deep and shifted toward center field
Short	Normal position
Second	Shifted toward first base

Gladden tends to hit high-inside fastballs more to right field, while pulling high-over-the-middle fastballs down the left line. He has excellent averages in both locations.

HIGH-INSIDE FASTBALLS

BATTING AVERAGE .428
Play

Left	Medium-deep in straightaway left field

Center	Medium-deep and shifted toward right field
Right	Medium-deep and shifted toward the right line
Short	Up middle (shifted toward second base)
Second	Normal position

HIGH-OVER-THE-MIDDLE FASTBALLS

BATTING AVERAGE .343
Play

Left	Deep and shifted toward the left field line
Center	Medium-deep in straightaway center field
Right	Deep in straightaway right field
Short	Shifted toward third base
Second	Normal position

Gladden Against Curves And Sliders

Gladden has trouble with low-outside curves (.166) and low-outside sliders (.125), but he hits medium-high outside curves (.333) and medium-high outside sliders (.272) well.

He pulls medium-high outside curves.

MEDIUM-HIGH OUTSIDE CURVEBALLS

BATTING AVERAGE .333
Play

Left	Deep and shifted toward the left field line
Center	Medium-deep in straightaway center field
Right	Medium-deep and shifted toward center field
Short	Normal position
Second	*No instances recorded*

Gladden Against Left-Handed Pitchers

Gladden's .293 overall fastball average against left-handed pitchers is built on three strong locations: medium-high outside (.333), high-over-the-middle (.583) and high-inside (.375).

He hits medium-high outside fastballs straightaway to all fields. He hits high-over-the-middle fastballs deep down the line to left and medium-deep to center and right.

HIGH-OVER-THE-MIDDLE FASTBALLS
(THROWN BY LEFT-HANDED PITCHERS)

BATTING AVERAGE .583
Play

Left	Deep and shifted toward the left field line
Center	Medium-deep in straightaway center field
Right	Medium-deep in straightaway right field
Short	Up middle (shifted toward second base)
Second	*No instances recorded*

His .133 against medium-high inside fastballs hurts his overall average. His BARS fielding strategy indicates that he hits this pitch weakly.

MEDIUM-HIGH INSIDE FASTBALLS
(THROWN BY LEFT-HANDED PITCHERS)

BATTING AVERAGE .133
Play

Left	Medium-deep in straightaway left field
Center	*No instances recorded*
Right	Short and shifted toward the right field line
Short	Up middle (shifted toward second base)
Second	*No instances recorded*

Ahead And Behind In The Count Vs. RH

Ahead

Fastball Average .381

	Inside	Middle	Outside
High	750 4/3	461 13/6	0 4/0
Med	400 20/8	600 5/3	358 39/14
Low	0 5/0	384 13/5	428 7/3

Curve Average .375

	Inside	Middle	Outside
High	0 0/0	500 2/1	0 0/0
Med	1000 1/1	0 1/0	166 6/1
Low	0 0/0	333 3/1	666 3/2

Behind

Fastball Average .452

	Inside	Middle	Outside
High	500 4/2	250 4/1	0 1/0
Med	400 10/4	666 3/2	466 15/7
Low	0 0/0	555 9/5	428 7/3

Curve Average .294

	Inside	Middle	Outside
High	0 0/0	0 1/0	0 0/0
Med	500 2/1	0 0/0	400 10/4
Low	0 0/0	0 0/0	0 4/0

Overall Evaluation
Against Right-Handed Pitchers

Overall Fastball	⚾⚾⚾⚾
Overall Curve	⚾⚾⚾
Overall Slider	⚾⚾

Against Left-Handed Pitchers

Overall Fastball	⚾⚾
Overall Curve	⚾
Overall Slider	⚾⚾⚾⚾

Comments: Right-handed pitchers should keep fastballs down and in or low and away.
Strengths: Waist-high fastballs, over-the-middle fastballs, high-inside fastballs, medium-outside curves vs. RH; medium-outside, high-middle and high-inside fastballs vs. LH.
Weaknesses: Low-inside and low-outside fastballs, low-outside curves, low sliders vs. RH; low fastballs, medium-inside fastballs, low curves vs. LH.

Brian Harper (Right Handed) — *Minnesota Twins*

Brian Harper Against Right-Handed Pitchers
Overall BARS Batting Average .354

Fastball Average .366

	Inside	Middle	Outside
High	3 / 333/1	5 / 400/2	0 / 0/0
Med	3 / 0/0	3 / 0/0	9 / 666/6
Low	2 / 0/0	3 / 333/1	2 / 500/1

Curve Average .500

	Inside	Middle	Outside
High	2 / 0/0	1 / 0/0	1 / 1000/1
Med	1 / 0/0	0 / 0/0	5 / 600/3
Low	1 / 1000/1	3 / 666/2	6 / 500/3

Slider Average .266

	Inside	Middle	Outside
High	0 / 0/0	1 / 1000/1	0 / 0/0
Med	0 / 0/0	1 / 0/0	4 / 250/1
Low	1 / 0/0	1 / 0/0	7 / 285/2

Brian Harper Against Left-Handed Pitchers
Overall BARS Batting Average .273

Fastball Average .258

	Inside	Middle	Outside
High	4 / 0/0	6 / 0/0	5 / 400/2
Med	3 / 0/0	1 / 0/0	24 / 416/10
Low	2 / 0/0	8 / 250/2	5 / 200/1

Curve Average .266

	Inside	Middle	Outside
High	0 / 0/0	1 / 1000/1	0 / 0/0
Med	3 / 0/0	1 / 1000/1	3 / 333/1
Low	1 / 0/0	3 / 333/1	3 / 0/0

Slider Average .363

	Inside	Middle	Outside
High	0 / 0/0	1 / 1000/1	0 / 0/0
Med	0 / 0/0	0 / 0/0	1 / 0/0
Low	3 / 0/0	3 / 333/1	3 / 666/2

Right-handed hitter Brian Harper seems to hit medium-high outside fastballs very well against right-handed pitchers (.666 on 6 for 9). He hits this pitch medium-deep to left and center fields and short to right field. Fielders could take away most of his base hits by adjusting according to the following BARS strategy.

MEDIUM-HIGH OUTSIDE FASTBALLS

BATTING AVERAGE .666

Play

Left	Medium-deep in straightaway left field
Center	Medium-deep in straightaway center field
Right	Short and shifted toward the right field line
Short	Normal position
Second	Shifted toward first base

He also has strong averages in his medium-high outside and low-outside curve locations against right-handers (.600 and .500). And he's pretty strong in these two locations against sliders thrown by right-handers (.250 and .285).

When facing left-handed pitchers, Harper hits very strongly against medium-high outside fastballs (.416). By positioning themselves as indicated in the BARS fielding strategy for this pitch (shown in the following chart and on the field diagram on the opposite page) fielders could prevent most of his base hits from this location.

MEDIUM-HIGH OUTSIDE FASTBALLS
(THROWN BY LEFT-HANDED PITCHERS)

BATTING AVERAGE .416

Play

Left	Deep in straightaway left field
Center	Deep and shifted toward left field
Right	Short and shifted toward the right field line
Short	Up middle (shifted toward second base)
Second	Normal position

Against left-handers Harper has a weak block consisting of all his inside and over-the-middle fastball locations. Left-handers could have quite an edge by avoiding his strong high-outside and medium-high outside fastball locations.

He hits low-over-the-middle fastballs for a barely adequate .250.

LOW-OVER-THE-MIDDLE FASTBALLS
(THROWN BY LEFT-HANDED PITCHERS)

BATTING AVERAGE .250

Play

Left	Deep in straightaway left field
Center	Medium-deep in straightaway center field
Right	Medium-deep and shifted toward center field
Short	Up middle (shifted toward second base)
Second	Normal position

Medium-High Outside Fastballs
(Thrown By Left-Handed Pitchers)

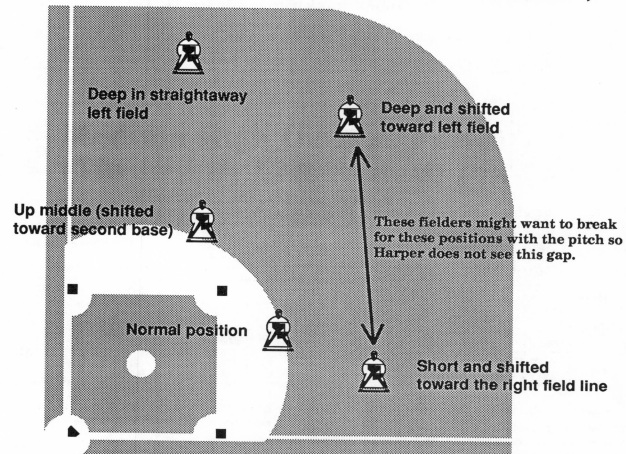

Deep in straightaway
left field

Deep and shifted
toward left field

Up middle (shifted
toward second base)

These fielders might want to break
for these positions with the pitch so
Harper does not see this gap.

Normal position

Short and shifted
toward the right field line

Ahead And Behind In The Count Vs. RH

Ahead

Fastball Average .312

	Inside	Middle	Outside
High	1 / 0 /0	3 / 666 /2	0 / 0 /0
Med	2 / 0 /0	1 / 0 /0	6 / 500 /3
Low	1 / 0 /0	1 / 0 /0	1 / 0 /0

Curve Average .666

	Inside	Middle	Outside
High	0 / 0 /0	0 / 0 /0	0 / 0 /0
Med	0 / 0 /0	0 / 0 /0	1 / 1000 /1
Low	1 / 1000 /1	1 / 0 /0	0 / 0 /0

Behind

Fastball Average .600

	Inside	Middle	Outside
High	0 / 0 /0	0 / 0 /0	0 / 0 /0
Med	0 / 0 /0	0 / 0 /0	1 / 1000 /1
Low	1 / 0 /0	2 / 500 /1	1 / 1000 /1

Curve Average .500

	Inside	Middle	Outside
High	2 / 0 /0	1 / 0 /0	0 / 0 /0
Med	0 / 0 /0	0 / 0 /0	2 / 500 /1
Low	0 / 0 /0	0 / 0 /0	3 / 1000 /3

Overall Evaluation
Against Right-Handed Pitchers

Overall Fastball	⚾⚾⚾⚾⚾
Overall Curve	⚾⚾⚾⚾
Overall Slider	⚾⚾

Against Left-Handed Pitchers

Overall Fastball	⚾
Overall Curve	⚾⚾
Overall Slider	⚾⚾⚾⚾

Comments: Strong against medium-high outside
fastballs vs. LH.
Strengths: Medium-outside fastballs, medium-outside
and low-outside curves, low-outside sliders vs. RH;
medium-outside fastballs vs. LH.
Weaknesses: Inside fastballs, over-the-middle
fastballs vs. LH.

Kent Hrbek (Left Handed)   *Minnesota Twins*

Kent Hrbek Against Right-Handed Pitchers
Overall BARS Batting Average .284

Fastball Average .323

	Outside	Middle	Inside
High	35 / 285 /10	33 / 393 /13	8 / 250 /2
Med	122 / 344 /42	25 / 520 /13	44 / 318 /14
Low	29 / 310 /9	39 / 179 /7	24 / 250 /6

Curve Average .245

	Outside	Middle	Inside
High	5 / 200 /1	7 / 571 /4	1 / 0 /0
Med	11 / 181 /2	6 / 833 /5	5 / 200 /1
Low	5 / 0 /0	7 / 142 /1	10 / 0 /0

Slider Average .218

	Outside	Middle	Inside
High	0 / 0 /0	1 / 0 /0	1 / 0 /0
Med	8 / 500 /4	0 / 0 /0	4 / 250 /1
Low	5 / 0 /0	5 / 0 /0	8 / 250 /2

Kent Hrbek Against Left-Handed Pitchers
Overall BARS Batting Average .240

Fastball Average .297

	Outside	Middle	Inside
High	9 / 111 /1	14 / 285 /4	7 / 142 /1
Med	34 / 352 /12	7 / 714 /5	26 / 307 /8
Low	15 / 133 /2	17 / 294 /5	19 / 315 /6

Curve Average .137

	Outside	Middle	Inside
High	2 / 0 /0	3 / 333 /1	3 / 0 /0
Med	11 / 181 /2	2 / 500 /1	11 / 272 /3
Low	18 / 0 /0	5 / 200 /1	3 / 0 /0

Slider Average .148

	Outside	Middle	Inside
High	1 / 0 /0	2 / 0 /0	0 / 0 /0
Med	8 / 375 /3	2 / 500 /1	0 / 0 /0
Low	10 / 0 /0	2 / 0 /0	2 / 0 /0

Kent Hrbek, left-handed hitter, has steady fastball averages of .323 against right-handed pitchers and .297 against left-handed pitchers. His .297 against lefties is very good for a left-handed hitter. He hits well in all three outside fastball locations against right-handers and against medium-high outside fastballs thrown by left-handers.

Against right-handers Hrbek hits medium-high outside fastballs deep and straightaway to all fields.

MEDIUM-HIGH OUTSIDE FASTBALLS

BATTING AVERAGE .344
Play

Left	Deep in straightaway left field
Center	Deep in straightaway center field
Right	Deep in straightaway right field
Short	Up middle (shifted toward second base)
Second	Normal position

His low-outside fastball average against right-handers is very good (.310). This again shows not all hitters have trouble with this pitch.

LOW-OUTSIDE FASTBALLS

BATTING AVERAGE .310
Play

Left	Deep and shifted toward the left field line
Center	Deep and shifted toward left field
Right	Deep and shifted toward the right field line

Short	Up middle (shifted toward second base)
Second	Shifted toward first base

Hrbek hits high-over-the-middle fastballs extremely well. He pulls this pitch to the right side of the infield, but the right fielder needs to shift toward center.

HIGH-OVER-THE-MIDDLE FASTBALLS

BATTING AVERAGE .393
Play

Left	Deep in straightaway left field
Center	Medium-deep in straightaway center field
Right	Deep and shifted toward center field
Short	Up middle (shifted toward second base)
Second	Shifted toward first base

Hrbek hits medium-high inside fastballs deep to all fields.

MEDIUM-HIGH INSIDE FASTBALLS

BATTING AVERAGE .318
Play

Left	Deep in straightaway left field
Center	Deep and shifted toward right field
Right	Deep in straightaway right field
Short	Up middle (shifted toward second base)
Second	Shifted toward first base

Hrbek's weakest fastball sector is low-over-the-middle/low-inside (.179 and .250 respectively). By keeping fastballs low and in to Hrbek, right-handed pitchers have the best chance to get him out.

The same is true with curves. In fact, he has trouble with all low curves and low sliders, and he has low averages against all outside and inside curves. It is remarkable that right-handed pitchers throw Hrbek so many more fastballs than curves, especially considering how well he hits most fastball locations.

Hrbek Against Left-Handed Pitchers

Hrbek hits medium-high outside fastballs extremely well against left-handed pitchers (.352). He hits this pitch straightaway to left field, into the right-center gap, straightaway to right field, and to the right side of the infield.

MEDIUM-HIGH OUTSIDE FASTBALLS
(THROWN BY LEFT-HANDED PITCHERS)

BATTING AVERAGE .352

Play

Left	Deep in straightaway left field
Center	Deep and shifted toward right field
Right	Deep in straightaway right field
Short	Up middle (shifted toward second base)
Second	Shifted toward first base

In contrast, he hits very poorly against low-outside fastballs thrown by left-handers (.133).

LOW-OUTSIDE FASTBALLS
(THROWN BY LEFT-HANDED PITCHERS)

BATTING AVERAGE .133

Play

Left	Medium-deep and shifted toward the left field line
Center	Deep and shifted toward right field
Right	Medium-deep in straightaway right field
Short	Normal position
Second	Shifted toward first base

He hits medium-high inside fastballs for a solid .307 average.

MEDIUM-HIGH INSIDE FASTBALLS
(THROWN BY LEFT-HANDED PITCHERS)

BATTING AVERAGE .307

Play

Left	Short in straightaway left field
Center	Deep and shifted toward right field
Right	Deep in straightaway right field
Short	Up middle (shifted toward second base)
Second	Normal position

Hrbek has trouble with low curves and low sliders against left-handers. He also has trouble with medium-high outside curves (.181), although he hits medium-high outside sliders strongly (.375).

MEDIUM-HIGH OUTSIDE SLIDERS
(THROWN BY LEFT-HANDED PITCHERS)

BATTING AVERAGE .375

Play

Left	Deep and shifted toward center field
Center	Deep and shifted toward right field
Right	Deep in straightaway right field
Short	*No instances recorded*
Second	*No instances recorded*

Ahead And Behind In The Count Vs. RH

Ahead

Fastball Average .359

	Outside	Middle	Inside
High	12/ 333 /4	15/ 600 /9	4/ 250 /1
Med	62/ 354 /22	16/ 562 /9	22/ 409 /9
Low	15/ 266 /4	24/ 166 /4	11/ 272 /3

Curve Average .000

	Outside	Middle	Inside
High	0/ 0 /0	2/ 0 /0	0/ 0 /0
Med	2/ 0 /0	0/ 0 /0	1/ 0 /0
Low	1/ 0 /0	4/ 0 /0	2/ 0 /0

Behind

Fastball Average .308

	Outside	Middle	Inside
High	11/ 181 /2	10/ 200 /2	3/ 333 /1
Med	23/ 478 /11	1/ 0 /0	6/ 333 /2
Low	5/ 600 /3	4/ 0 /0	5/ 0 /0

Curve Average .444

	Outside	Middle	Inside
High	2/ 500 /1	2/ 1000 /2	1/ 0 /0
Med	6/ 166 /1	3/ 1000 /3	2/ 0 /0
Low	0/ 0 /0	2/ 500 /1	0/ 0 /0

Overall Evaluation
Against Right-Handed Pitchers

Overall Fastball

Overall Curve

Overall Slider

Against Left-Handed Pitchers

Overall Fastball

Overall Curve

Overall Slider

Comments: Has trouble with low curves and sliders.
Strengths: Waist-high fastballs, high-middle fastballs, low-outside fastballs, high-middle and medium-middle curves, medium-outside sliders vs. RH; waist-high fastballs, medium-outside sliders vs. LH.
Weaknesses: Low-middle, high-inside and low-inside fastballs, low curves, outside curves, low sliders vs. RH; low-outside and high-outside fastballs, low curves, outside curves, low sliders vs. LH.

Tim Laudner (Right Handed) — *Minnesota Twins*

Tim Laudner Against Right-Handed Pitchers
Overall BARS Batting Average .163

Fastball Average .184

	Inside	Middle	Outside
High	5/ 200 /1	8/ 0 /0	8/ 125 /1
Med	21/ 95 /2	4/ 250 /1	38/ 289 /11
Low	6/ 333 /2	24/ 250 /6	16/ 0 /0

Curve Average .142

	Inside	Middle	Outside
High	0/ 0 /0	0/ 0 /0	0/ 0 /0
Med	1/ 0 /0	1/ 1000 /1	3/ 0 /0
Low	1/ 0 /0	7/ 285 /2	8/ 0 /0

Slider Average .076

	Inside	Middle	Outside
High	2/ 0 /0	1/ 0 /0	2/ 0 /0
Med	1/ 0 /0	0/ 0 /0	6/ 333 /2
Low	3/ 0 /0	1/ 0 /0	10/ 0 /0

Tim Laudner Against Left-Handed Pitchers
Overall BARS Batting Average .307

Fastball Average .346

	Inside	Middle	Outside
High	2/ 500 /1	5/ 200 /1	13/ 384 /5
Med	5/ 600 /3	5/ 600 /3	43/ 279 /12
Low	6/ 333 /2	12/ 416 /5	7/ 285 /2

Curve Average .230

	Inside	Middle	Outside
High	0/ 0 /0	0/ 0 /0	0/ 0 /0
Med	2/ 500 /1	4/ 500 /2	3/ 0 /0
Low	2/ 0 /0	7/ 428 /3	8/ 0 /0

Slider Average .166

	Inside	Middle	Outside
High	2/ 500 /1	0/ 0 /0	0/ 0 /0
Med	3/ 0 /0	1/ 0 /0	2/ 500 /1
Low	5/ 0 /0	2/ 500 /1	3/ 0 /0

Right-handed hitter Tim Laudner hits much better against left-handed pitchers. His fastball average of .346 against left-handers is excellent; his .184 fastball average against right-handers is weak.

Laudner hits .289 against medium-high outside fastballs thrown by right-handers. The small diagram on the opposite page illustrates the fielding strategy.

MEDIUM-HIGH OUTSIDE FASTBALLS

BATTING AVERAGE .289
Play
Left	Medium-deep and shifted toward the left line
Center	Deep and shifted toward right field
Right	Deep in straightaway right field
Short	Normal position
Second	Shifted toward first base

Laudner hits a weak .095 against medium-high inside fastballs. His .250 in the low-over-the-middle fastball location isn't too bad.

LOW-OVER-THE-MIDDLE FASTBALLS

BATTING AVERAGE .250
Play
Left	Deep and shifted toward the left field line
Center	Medium-deep and shifted toward left field
Right	Deep in straightaway right field
Short	Normal position
Second	*No instances recorded*

Laudner has difficulty against low-outside pitches in general. Against right-handers the BARS System has him at 0-for-16 against low-outside fastballs, 0-for-8 against low-outside curves and 0-for-10 against low-outside sliders.

Against left-handed pitchers he hits medium-high outside fastballs for a .279 average. Please see the diagram on the opposite page.

MEDIUM-HIGH OUTSIDE FASTBALLS
(THROWN BY LEFT-HANDED PITCHERS)

BATTING AVERAGE .279
Play
Left	Medium-deep in straightaway left field
Center	Deep and shifted toward left field
Right	Deep in straightaway right field
Short	Up middle (shifted toward second base)
Second	Shifted toward first base

Laudner hits a strong .416 against low-over-the-middle fastballs thrown by left-handers.

LOW-OVER-THE-MIDDLE FASTBALLS
(THROWN BY LEFT-HANDED PITCHERS)

BATTING AVERAGE .416
Play
Left	Deep in straightaway left field
Center	Deep and shifted toward left field
Right	Medium-deep in straightaway right field
Short	Up middle (shifted toward second base)
Second	Normal position

Medium-High Outside Fastballs
(Thrown By Left-Handed Pitchers)

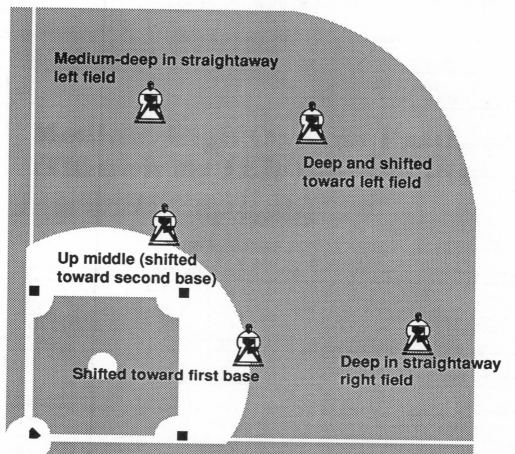

Medium-deep in straightaway left field

Deep and shifted toward left field

Up middle (shifted toward second base)

Shifted toward first base

Deep in straightaway right field

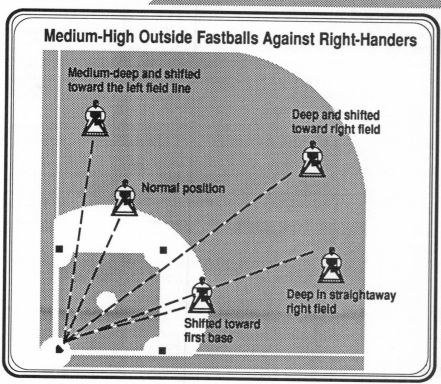

Medium-High Outside Fastballs Against Right-Handers

Medium-deep and shifted toward the left field line

Deep and shifted toward right field

Normal position

Shifted toward first base

Deep in straightaway right field

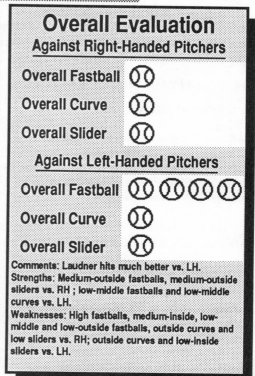

Overall Evaluation
Against Right-Handed Pitchers

Overall Fastball ⚾

Overall Curve ⚾

Overall Slider ⚾

Against Left-Handed Pitchers

Overall Fastball ⚾⚾⚾⚾

Overall Curve ⚾

Overall Slider ⚾

Comments: Laudner hits much better vs. LH.
Strengths: Medium-outside fastballs, medium-outside sliders vs. RH ; low-middle fastballs and low-middle curves vs. LH.
Weaknesses: High fastballs, medium-inside, low-middle and low-outside fastballs, outside curves and low sliders vs. RH; outside curves and low-inside sliders vs. LH.

Gene Larkin Against Right-Handed Pitchers
Overall BARS Batting Average .200

Fastball Average .224

	Outside	Middle	Inside
High	5 / 200 / 1	7 / 142 / 1	2 / 500 / 1
Med	36 / 194 / 7	2 / 500 / 1	17 / 235 / 4
Low	7 / 428 / 3	13 / 230 / 3	9 / 111 / 1

Curve Average .000

	Outside	Middle	Inside
High	0 / 0 / 0	1 / 0 / 0	0 / 0 / 0
Med	2 / 0 / 0	0 / 0 / 0	1 / 0 / 0
Low	1 / 0 / 0	0 / 0 / 0	1 / 0 / 0

Slider Average .000

	Outside	Middle	Inside
High	0 / 0 / 0	0 / 0 / 0	1 / 0 / 0
Med	0 / 0 / 0	0 / 0 / 0	1 / 0 / 0
Low	0 / 0 / 0	0 / 0 / 0	2 / 0 / 0

Gene Larkin Against Left-Handed Pitchers
Overall BARS Batting Average .352

Fastball Average .345

	Inside	Middle	Outside
High	2 / 500 / 1	6 / 166 / 1	3 / 0 / 0
Med	8 / 250 / 2	1 / 1000 / 1	21 / 428 / 9
Low	6 / 500 / 3	6 / 333 / 2	2 / 0 / 0

Curve Average .666

	Inside	Middle	Outside
High	0 / 0 / 0	0 / 0 / 0	0 / 0 / 0
Med	0 / 0 / 0	0 / 0 / 0	2 / 500 / 1
Low	1 / 1000 / 1	0 / 0 / 0	0 / 0 / 0

Slider Average .375

	Inside	Middle	Outside
High	0 / 0 / 0	1 / 0 / 0	0 / 0 / 0
Med	3 / 666 / 2	1 / 1000 / 1	1 / 0 / 0
Low	2 / 0 / 0	0 / 0 / 0	0 / 0 / 0

Switch-hitting Gene Larkin has trouble with fastballs against right-handed pitchers (.224 overall) but hits fastballs excellently against left-handed pitchers (.345 overall).

Larkin's BARS records show him hitting .194 against medium-high outside fastballs thrown by right-handers. The field diagram on the opposite page shows how fielders need to be positioned for this pitch.

MEDIUM-HIGH OUTSIDE FASTBALLS

BATTING AVERAGE .194
Play
Left	Medium-deep in straightaway left field
Center	Deep in straightaway center field
Right	Deep and shifted toward center field
Short	Shifted toward third base
Second	Normal position

He hits low-over-the-middle fastballs straightaway to left and center and into the right-center gap.

LOW-OVER-THE-MIDDLE FASTBALLS

BATTING AVERAGE .230
Play
Left	Deep in straightaway left field
Center	Deep in straightaway center field
Right	Deep and shifted toward center field
Short	Up middle (shifted toward second base)
Second	Normal position

Larkin's record indicates that he has a weakness against medium-high inside fastballs (.235) and low-inside fastballs (.111) thrown by right-handers.

Right-handed pitchers throw Larkin so few curves and sliders in comparison to fastballs that it is difficult to obtain information on these pitches. It will be interesting to see how Larkin's average shapes up as the BARS System gets more information on him in coming years.

Larkin Against Left-Handed Pitchers

Batting right-handed against left-handed pitchers, Larkin has an excellent .428 average in his medium-high outside location. He pulls this pitch to the outfield, but the shortstop needs to play shifted toward second base.

MEDIUM-HIGH OUTSIDE FASTBALLS
(THROWN BY LEFT-HANDED PITCHERS)

BATTING AVERAGE .428
Play
Left	Deep and shifted toward the left field line
Center	Deep and shifted toward left field
Right	Deep in straightaway right field
Short	Up middle (shifted toward second base)
Second	*No instances recorded*

Medium-High Outside Fastballs
(Thrown By Right-Handed Pitchers)

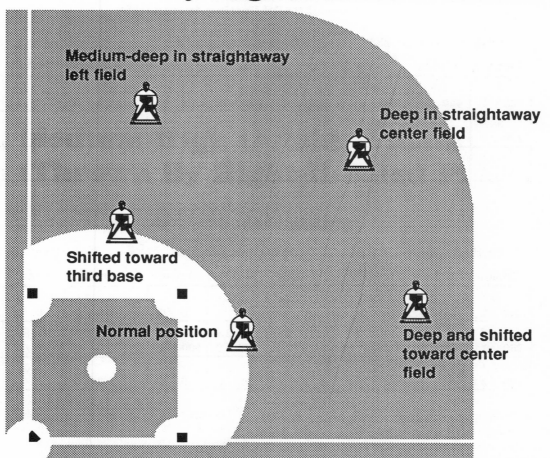

Medium-deep in straightaway left field

Deep in straightaway center field

Shifted toward third base

Normal position

Deep and shifted toward center field

Ahead And Behind In The Count Vs. RH

Ahead

Fastball Average .229

	Outside	Middle	Inside
High	3 / 333 /1	2 / 0 /0	2 / 500 /1
Med	12 / 83 /1	1 / 0 /0	10 / 300 /3
Low	3 / 666 /2	7 / 285 /2	8 / 125 /1

Curve Average .000

	Outside	Middle	Inside
High	0 / 0 /0	0 / 0 /0	0 / 0 /0
Med	0 / 0 /0	0 / 0 /0	0 / 0 /0
Low	0 / 0 /0	0 / 0 /0	0 / 0 /0

Behind

Fastball Average .142

	Outside	Middle	Inside
High	0 / 0 /0	0 / 0 /0	0 / 0 /0
Med	3 / 0 /0	0 / 0 /0	2 / 500 /1
Low	0 / 0 /0	1 / 0 /0	1 / 0 /0

Curve Average .000

	Outside	Middle	Inside
High	0 / 0 /0	1 / 0 /0	0 / 0 /0
Med	0 / 0 /0	0 / 0 /0	1 / 0 /0
Low	0 / 0 /0	0 / 0 /0	0 / 0 /0

Overall Evaluation

Against Right-Handed Pitchers

Overall Fastball

Overall Curve — Not enough information

Overall Slider — Not enough information

Against Left-Handed Pitchers

Overall Fastball

Overall Curve — Not enough information

Overall Slider — Not enough information

Comments: Larkin hits .428 against medium-outside fastballs vs. LH.

Strengths: Low-outside fastballs vs. RH; medium-high outside, low-inside and low-middle fastballs vs. LH.

Weaknesses: Medium-outside, low-middle, high-middle, medium-inside and low-inside fastballs vs. RH; medium-inside fastballs vs. LH.

Al Newman Against Right-Handed Pitchers
Overall BARS Batting Average .229

	Fastball Average .233			Curve Average .187			Slider Average .200		
	Outside	Middle	Inside	Outside	Middle	Inside	Outside	Middle	Inside
High	11/272 /3	15/400 /6	9/111 /1	0/0 /0	1/1000 /1	0/0 /0	0/0 /0	0/0 /0	2/0 /0
Med	39/230 /9	2/0 /0	13/153 /2	4/0 /0	1/1000 /1	3/333 /1	4/250 /1	0/0 /0	1/0 /0
Low	9/111 /1	16/312 /5	6/166 /1	4/0 /0	2/0 /0	1/0 /0	0/0 /0	0/0 /0	3/333 /1

Al Newman Against Left-Handed Pitchers
Overall BARS Batting Average .293

	Fastball Average .296			Curve Average .428			Slider Average .000		
	Inside	Middle	Outside	Inside	Middle	Outside	Inside	Middle	Outside
High	7/142 /1	8/500 /4	5/400 /2	1/0 /0	1/1000 /1	0/0 /0	1/0 /0	0/0 /0	0/0 /0
Med	4/250 /1	1/1000 /1	22/318 /7	1/0 /0	2/1000 /2	1/1000 /1	2/0 /0	0/0 /0	3/0 /0
Low	5/400 /2	7/142 /1	5/0 /0	2/0 /0	3/666 /2	3/0 /0	1/0 /0	0/0 /0	1/0 /0

Switch-hitting Al Newman has a higher overall fastball average against left-handed pitchers than against right-handed pitchers (.296 vs. left-handers, .233 vs. right-handers).

Batting left-handed, Newman hits .230 against medium-high outside fastballs thrown by right-handed pitchers.

MEDIUM-HIGH OUTSIDE FASTBALLS

BATTING AVERAGE .230
Play

Left	Deep and shifted toward the left field line
Center	Medium-deep in straightaway center field
Right	Deep in straightaway right field
Short	Up middle (shifted toward second base)
Second	Normal position

He hits high-over-the-middle fastballs against right-handers for an excellent .400 average. He hits this pitch deep to straightaway left and center and medium-deep to straightaway right. Both the shortstop and the second baseman need to be positioned for Newman to pull the ball to the right side of the infield.

HIGH-OVER-THE-MIDDLE FASTBALLS

BATTING AVERAGE .400
Play

Left	Deep in straightaway left field

Center	Deep in straightaway center field
Right	Medium-deep in straightaway right field
Short	Up middle (shifted toward second base)
Second	Shifted toward first base

He hits .312 against low-over-the-middle fastballs. He hits this pitch deep to straightaway left and deep into the left-center gap.

LOW-OVER-THE-MIDDLE FASTBALLS

BATTING AVERAGE .312
Play

Left	Deep in straightaway left field
Center	Deep in straightaway center field
Right	Deep and shifted toward center field
Short	Up middle (shifted toward second base)
Second	Normal position

Newman's .153 against medium-high inside fastballs indicates a weakness. He hits this pitch deep into the left-center gap and deep down the right line.

MEDIUM-HIGH INSIDE FASTBALLS

BATTING AVERAGE .153
Play

Left	Medium-deep in straightaway left field
Center	Deep and shifted toward left field

Right	Deep and shifted toward the right field line
Short	Normal position
Second	Normal position

His .111 against high-inside fastballs is also weak. He hits this pitch mostly to right field down the line when he gets it out of the infield.

HIGH-INSIDE FASTBALLS

BATTING AVERAGE .111
Play

Left	*No instances recorded*
Center	*No instances recorded*
Right	Medium-deep and shifted toward the right line
Short	Shifted toward third base
Second	Shifted toward first base

Newman Against Left-Handed Pitchers

Batting right-handed against left-handed pitchers, Newman hits fastballs .296 overall. His .318 against medium-high outside fastballs is strong.

MEDIUM-HIGH OUTSIDE FASTBALLS
(THROWN BY LEFT-HANDED PITCHERS)

BATTING AVERAGE .318
Play

Left	Deep in straightaway left field
Center	Deep in straightaway center field
Right	Medium-deep and shifted toward the right line
Short	Up middle (shifted toward second base)
Second	Shifted toward first base

He is 4 for 8 against high-over-the-middle fastballs when facing left-handers.

HIGH-OVER-THE-MIDDLE FASTBALLS
(THROWN BY LEFT-HANDED PITCHERS)

BATTING AVERAGE .500
Play

Left	Deep and shifted toward center field
Center	Deep in straightaway center field
Right	Deep and shifted toward center field
Short	Normal position
Second	*No instances recorded*

Newman is 1-for-7 against low-over-the-middle fastballs and 0-for-5 against low-outside fastballs thrown by left-handers. This is not a large number of instances to go on, but these two locations seem weak.

Ahead And Behind In The Count Vs. RH

Ahead

Fastball Average .218

	Outside	Middle	Inside
High	4/250 /1	8/375 /3	6/166 /1
Med	18/222 /4	1/0 /0	8/125 /1
Low	2/0 /0	5/200 /1	3/333 /1

Curve Average .500

	Outside	Middle	Inside
High	0/0 /0	0/0 /0	0/0 /0
Med	0/0 /0	1/1000 /1	1/0 /0
Low	0/0 /0	0/0 /0	0/0 /0

Behind

Fastball Average .259

	Outside	Middle	Inside
High	2/0 /0	4/250 /1	1/0 /0
Med	9/333 /3	0/0 /0	5/200 /1
Low	2/500 /1	4/250 /1	0/0 /0

Curve Average .500

	Outside	Middle	Inside
High	0/0 /0	1/1000 /1	0/0 /0
Med	0/0 /0	0/0 /0	1/1000 /1
Low	1/0 /0	1/0 /0	0/0 /0

Overall Evaluation
Against Right-Handed Pitchers

Overall Fastball	
Overall Curve	
Overall Slider	Not enough information

Against Left-Handed Pitchers

Overall Fastball	
Overall Curve	
Overall Slider	Not enough information

Comments: Newman has problems with right-handed pitchers.
Strengths: High-middle and low-middle fastballs vs. RH; high-middle and medium-outside fastballs vs. LH.
Weaknesses: Outside and inside fastballs, outside curves vs. RH; high-inside and low-middle fastballs vs. LH.

Kirby Puckett Against Right-Handed Pitchers
Overall BARS Batting Average .299

Fastball Average .312

	Inside	Middle	Outside
High	16/ 187 /3	25/ 280 /7	16/ 312 /5
Med	45/ 355 /16	26/ 423 /11	125/ 328 /41
Low	18/ 166 /3	34/ 323 /11	31/ 258 /8

Curve Average .283

	Inside	Middle	Outside
High	5/ 400 /2	5/ 600 /3	6/ 333 /2
Med	7/ 428 /3	9/ 555 /5	38/ 342 /13
Low	0/ 0 /0	14/ 71 /1	29/ 103 /3

Slider Average .269

	Inside	Middle	Outside
High	1/ 0 /0	2/ 500 /1	4/ 0 /0
Med	1/ 0 /0	5/ 200 /1	23/ 391 /9
Low	2/ 0 /0	18/ 222 /4	33/ 272 /9

Kirby Puckett Against Left-Handed Pitchers
Overall BARS Batting Average .303

Fastball Average .305

	Inside	Middle	Outside
High	8/ 750 /6	9/ 222 /2	11/ 272 /3
Med	20/ 150 /3	5/ 800 /4	51/ 313 /16
Low	10/ 300 /3	14/ 285 /4	16/ 187 /3

Curve Average .333

	Inside	Middle	Outside
High	1/ 0 /0	0/ 0 /0	3/ 333 /1
Med	5/ 400 /2	1/ 0 /0	10/ 400 /4
Low	3/ 333 /1	8/ 375 /3	11/ 272 /3

Slider Average .266

	Inside	Middle	Outside
High	2/ 500 /1	4/ 500 /2	0/ 0 /0
Med	6/ 333 /2	1/ 1000 /1	6/ 166 /1
Low	14/ 142 /2	8/ 375 /3	4/ 0 /0

Right-handed Kirby Puckett's averages may differ a little in this section from his averages in the introductory chapter of this book. The BARS System continually updates its records; the statistics on these two pages are the latest available for Puckett at the time of publication.

Notice that Puckett hits .328 against medium-high outside fastballs thrown by right-handers. His Ahead and Behind charts on the opposite page show that he hits this pitch better when ahead than when behind in the count.

MEDIUM-HIGH OUTSIDE FASTBALLS (WHEN AHEAD IN THE COUNT)

BATTING AVERAGE .340
Play

Left	Deep in straightaway left field
Center	Deep in straightaway center field
Right	Deep and shifted toward the right field line
Short	Up middle (shifted toward second base)
Second	Shifted toward first base

MEDIUM-HIGH OUTSIDE FASTBALLS (WHEN BEHIND IN THE COUNT)

BATTING AVERAGE .300
Play

Left	*No instances recorded*
Center	Deep and shifted toward right field
Right	Medium-deep in straightaway right field
Short	Normal position
Second	Normal position

Puckett hits a blazing .355 against medium-high inside fastballs.

MEDIUM-HIGH INSIDE FASTBALLS

BATTING AVERAGE .355
Play

Left	Deep in straightaway left field
Center	Medium-deep in straightaway center field
Right	Medium-deep and shifted toward center field
Short	Up middle (shifted toward second base)
Second	Normal position

Puckett's .258 average against low-outside fastballs thrown by right-handers is low. Most of his hit balls in this location are probably easy pop-ups and ground outs.

LOW-OUTSIDE FASTBALLS

BATTING AVERAGE .258
Play

Left	Short in straightaway left field
Center	Deep and shifted toward left field
Right	Deep in straightaway right field
Short	Up middle (shifted toward second base)
Second	Normal position

Puckett has trouble with low curves in general against right-handers (.071 low-over-middle and .103 low-outside). But he hits medium-high outside curves for a strong .342 average.

MEDIUM-HIGH OUTSIDE CURVEBALLS

BATTING AVERAGE .342
Play

Left	Medium-deep and shifted toward center field
Center	Deep and shifted toward left field
Right	Deep and shifted toward center field
Short	Shifted toward third base
Second	Normal position

He hits low-outside sliders well enough (.272) but he murders medium-high outside sliders (.391).

MEDIUM-HIGH OUTSIDE SLIDERS

BATTING AVERAGE .391
Play

Left	Medium-deep and shifted toward the left line
Center	Deep in straightaway center field
Right	Deep in straightaway right field
Short	Normal position
Second	Normal position

Puckett Against Left-Handed Pitchers

Puckett hits medium-high outside fastballs at a .313 clip against left-handed pitchers.

MEDIUM-HIGH OUTSIDE FASTBALLS
(THROWN BY LEFT-HANDED PITCHERS)

BATTING AVERAGE .313
Play

Left	Medium-deep in straightaway left field

Center	Deep and shifted toward left field
Right	Deep in straightaway right field
Short	Up middle (shifted toward second base)
Second	Normal position

He hits low-over-the-middle fastballs against left-handers deep to all fields.

LOW-OVER-THE-MIDDLE FASTBALLS
(THROWN BY LEFT-HANDED PITCHERS)

BATTING AVERAGE .285
Play

Left	Deep in straightaway left field
Center	Deep in straightaway center field
Right	Deep and shifted toward the right field line
Short	Up middle (shifted toward second base)
Second	Normal position

Puckett hits low-outside curves only moderately well against left-handers (.272). But he has a strong .400 average against medium-high outside curves and .375 against low-over-the-middle curves.

LOW-OVER-THE-MIDDLE CURVEBALLS
(THROWN BY LEFT-HANDED PITCHERS)

BATTING AVERAGE .375
Play

Left	Deep and shifted toward the left field line
Center	Deep and shifted toward right field
Right	Deep in straightaway right field
Short	Normal position
Second	Up middle (shifted toward second base)

Puckett has trouble with low-inside sliders against lefties (.142). But he hits .375 against low-over-the-middle sliders.

Ahead And Behind In The Count Vs. RH

Ahead

	Fastball Average .377			Curve Average .333		
	Inside	Middle	Outside	Inside	Middle	Outside
High	10/200 /2	15/400 /6	4/750 /3	1/0 /0	3/666 /2	3/333 /1
Med	26/461 /12	16/312 /5	50/340 /17	2/500 /1	4/500 /2	12/500 /6
Low	8/375 /3	21/285 /6	9/666 /6	0/0 /0	7/0 /0	4/0 /0

Behind

	Fastball Average .293			Curve Average .517		
	Inside	Middle	Outside	Inside	Middle	Outside
High	3/333 /1	4/250 /1	4/250 /1	1/1000 /1	1/1000 /1	1/1000 /1
Med	6/0 /0	6/666 /4	20/300 /6	2/500 /1	3/1000 /3	10/600 /6
Low	5/0 /0	7/571 /4	3/0 /0	0/0 /0	3/0 /0	8/250 /2

Overall Evaluation
Against Right-Handed Pitchers

Overall Fastball	⚾⚾⚾
Overall Curve	⚾⚾⚾
Overall Slider	⚾⚾

Against Left-Handed Pitchers

Overall Fastball	⚾⚾⚾
Overall Curve	⚾⚾⚾⚾
Overall Slider	⚾⚾

Comments: Very strong waist-high hitter vs. RH.
Strengths: Waist-high fastballs, low-middle fastballs, waist-high curves, high curves, medium-outside sliders vs. RH; medium-outside and low-inside fastballs, medium-outside curves vs. LH.
Weaknesses: High-inside, low-inside and low-outside fastballs, low curves, low-middle sliders vs. RH; medium-inside and low-outside fastballs, low-inside sliders vs. LH.

Canseco, Jose
Gallego, Mike
Hassey, Ron
Henderson, Dave
Henderson, Rickey
Javier, Stan
Lansford, Carney
McGwire, Mark
Steinbach, Terry
Weiss, Walt

Oakland Athletics
BARS System
Hitting Analysis

Jose Canseco (Right Handed)　　　*Oakland Athletics*

Jose Canseco Against Right-Handed Pitchers
Overall BARS Batting Average .269

Fastball Average .275

	Inside	Middle	Outside
High	12/ 83 /1	18/ 333 /6	18/ 333 /6
Med	31/ 258 /8	10/ 400 /4	51/ 313 /16
Low	11/ 181 /2	19/ 263 /5	19/ 210 /4

Curve Average .278

	Inside	Middle	Outside
High	3/ 666 /2	7/ 428 /3	2/ 500 /1
Med	4/ 250 /1	2/ 500 /1	13/ 230 /3
Low	1/ 1000 /1	9/ 333 /3	20/ 100 /2

Slider Average .235

	Inside	Middle	Outside
High	3/ 333 /1	2/ 500 /1	2/ 500 /1
Med	1/ 1000 /1	1/ 1000 /1	16/ 250 /4
Low	1/ 0 /0	5/ 200 /1	20/ 100 /2

Jose Canseco Against Left-Handed Pitchers
Overall BARS Batting Average .298

Fastball Average .327

	Inside	Middle	Outside
High	4/ 500 /2	9/ 222 /2	7/ 285 /2
Med	18/ 222 /4	2/ 1000 /2	39/ 307 /12
Low	6/ 500 /3	14/ 428 /6	8/ 250 /2

Curve Average .357

	Inside	Middle	Outside
High	0/ 0 /0	0/ 0 /0	2/ 1000 /2
Med	3/ 0 /0	0/ 0 /0	4/ 750 /3
Low	3/ 0 /0	1/ 0 /0	1/ 0 /0

Slider Average .100

	Inside	Middle	Outside
High	0/ 0 /0	0/ 0 /0	0/ 0 /0
Med	7/ 0 /0	0/ 0 /0	6/ 166 /1
Low	2/ 0 /0	0/ 0 /0	5/ 200 /1

Jose Canseco, right-handed outfielder, hits better against left-handed than against right-handed pitchers. His overall slider average is higher against right-handers, but his fastball and curve averages are significantly higher against left-handers.

Against right-handers, Canseco hits medium-high outside fastballs very well (.313 overall). A glance at his Ahead and Behind charts on the opposite page shows that he hits this pitch better when he is ahead in the count. He also hits it different distances and directions when ahead and behind.

**MEDIUM-HIGH OUTSIDE FASTBALLS
(WHEN BEHIND IN THE COUNT)**

BATTING AVERAGE .307
Play
Left　　　*No instances recorded*
Center　Deep and shifted toward right field
Right　　Deep in straightaway right field
Short　　Normal position
Second　Normal position

**MEDIUM-HIGH OUTSIDE FASTBALLS
(WHEN AHEAD IN THE COUNT)**

BATTING AVERAGE .421
Play
Left　　　Deep and shifted toward center field
Center　Deep in straightaway center field

Right　　Deep and shifted toward the right field line
Short　　Normal position
Second　Shifted toward first base

Notice Canseco's low average in his low-outside fastball location (.210). His averages are low in each of his low fastball locations.

His .333 average against high-over-the-middle fastballs is excellent. He hits this pitch down both lines. The following BARS fielding strategy for a high-over-the-middle fastball shows that if every fielder played Canseco to pull the ball when the pitch is to this location, the right fielder, shortstop and second baseman would be out of position.

HIGH-OVER-THE-MIDDLE FASTBALLS

BATTING AVERAGE .333
Play
Left　　　Deep and shifted toward the left field line
Center　Deep and shifted toward left field
Right　　Medium-deep and shifted toward the right line
Short　　Up middle (shifted toward second base)
Second　Normal position

Canseco pulls medium-high inside fastballs deep down the left line, but he has trouble with high-inside fastballs, punching them into right field.

MEDIUM-HIGH INSIDE FASTBALLS

BATTING AVERAGE .258
Play

Left	Deep and shifted toward the left field line
Center	Deep in straightaway center field
Right	Deep in straightaway right field
Short	Up middle (shifted toward second base)
Second	Normal position

HIGH-INSIDE FASTBALLS

BATTING AVERAGE .083
Play

Left	*No instances recorded*
Center	Medium-deep and shifted toward right field
Right	Deep and shifted toward the right field line
Short	*No instances recorded*
Second	Shifted toward first base

Canseco Against Curves And Sliders

Canseco takes advantage of high curves (.666, .428, and .500), but he hits poorly in his two most highly pitched curve locations (.100 low-outside and .230 medium-high outside).

MEDIUM-HIGH OUTSIDE CURVEBALLS

BATTING AVERAGE .230
Play

Left	Deep and shifted toward the left field line
Center	Deep in straightaway center field
Right	Medium-deep in straightaway right field
Short	Shifted toward third base
Second	*No instances recorded*

Canseco hits weakly against low-outside sliders (.100) and medium-high outside sliders (.266).

Canseco Against Left-Handed Pitchers

Overall, Canseco hits fastballs excellently against left-handers. But he has several weak fastball locations. The .222 in his medium-high inside and high-over-the-middle locations indicates weaknesses. But he hits medium-high outside and low-over-the-middle fastballs well (.307 and .428 respectively).

As against right-handers, Canseco hits medium-high outside fastballs thrown by left-handers much better when he is ahead in the count. He hits this pitch with more authority and pulls the ball more when ahead.

MEDIUM-HIGH OUTSIDE FASTBALLS (THROWN BY LEFT-HANDED PITCHERS WHEN CANSECO IS BEHIND IN THE COUNT)

BATTING AVERAGE .142
Play

Left	*No instances recorded*
Center	Short in straightaway center field
Right	Medium-deep and shifted toward the right line
Short	Up middle (shifted toward second base)
Second	Normal position

MEDIUM-HIGH OUTSIDE FASTBALLS (THROWN BY LEFT-HANDED PITCHERS WHEN CANSECO IS AHEAD IN THE COUNT)

BATTING AVERAGE .411
Play

Left	Deep and shifted toward the left field line
Center	Deep in straightaway center field
Right	Medium-deep in straightaway right field
Short	Shifted toward third base
Second	Normal position

Ahead And Behind In The Count Vs. RH

Ahead

Fastball Average .402

	Inside	Middle	Outside
High	2/ 0/0	6/ 166/1	7/ 714/5
Med	10/ 400/4	5/ 400/2	19/ 421/8
Low	4/ 500/2	11/ 363/4	3/ 333/1

Curve Average .400

	Inside	Middle	Outside
High	1/ 0/0	1/ 1000/1	1/ 0/0
Med	0/ 0/0	1/ 1000/1	3/ 333/1
Low	0/ 0/0	0/ 0/0	3/ 333/1

Behind

Fastball Average .325

	Inside	Middle	Outside
High	2/ 500/1	6/ 666/4	5/ 0/0
Med	7/ 285/2	2/ 500/1	13/ 307/4
Low	0/ 0/0	2/ 0/0	3/ 333/1

Curve Average .200

	Inside	Middle	Outside
High	0/ 0/0	4/ 250/1	0/ 0/0
Med	2/ 500/1	0/ 0/0	4/ 0/0
Low	0/ 0/0	2/ 500/1	3/ 0/0

Overall Evaluation

Against Right-Handed Pitchers

Overall Fastball	⚾⚾
Overall Curve	⚾ ⚾⚾
Overall Slider	⚾

Against Left-Handed Pitchers

Overall Fastball	⚾⚾⚾⚾
Overall Curve	⚾⚾⚾⚾
Overall Slider	⚾

Comments: Canseco hits fastballs extremely well against LH (hitting better when ahead in the count). **Strengths:** Medium-outside, medium-middle and high-over-the-middle fastballs vs. RH; medium-outside and low-over-the-middle fastballs vs. LH. **Weaknesses:** Low fastballs and inside fastballs, medium-outside and low-outside curves and sliders vs. RH; high-over-the-middle and medium-inside fastballs, sliders in general vs. LH.

Mike Gallego (Right Handed)   *Oakland Athletics*

Mike Gallego Against Right-Handed Pitchers
Overall BARS Batting Average .234

Fastball Average .233

	Inside	Middle	Outside
High	5/400 /2	2/500 /1	5/0 /0
Med	19/263 /5	4/750 /3	22/181 /4
Low	3/333 /1	9/111 /1	8/125 /1

Curve Average .250

	Inside	Middle	Outside
High	1/0 /0	0/0 /0	1/1000 /1
Med	1/1000 /1	0/0 /0	4/250 /1
Low	0/0 /0	3/0 /0	2/0 /0

Slider Average .200

	Inside	Middle	Outside
High	0/0 /0	0/0 /0	0/0 /0
Med	1/0 /0	0/0 /0	1/0 /0
Low	0/0 /0	2/500 /1	1/0 /0

Mike Gallego Against Left-Handed Pitchers
Overall BARS Batting Average .216

Fastball Average .225

	Inside	Middle	Outside
High	0/0 /0	1/0 /0	4/0 /0
Med	4/250 /1	0/0 /0	15/266 /4
Low	1/1000 /1	3/333 /1	3/0 /0

Curve Average .000

	Inside	Middle	Outside
High	0/0 /0	1/0 /0	0/0 /0
Med	1/0 /0	0/0 /0	0/0 /0
Low	0/0 /0	1/0 /0	1/0 /0

Slider Average .500

	Inside	Middle	Outside
High	0/0 /0	0/0 /0	0/0 /0
Med	0/0 /0	0/0 /0	1/0 /0
Low	1/1000 /1	0/0 /0	0/0 /0

Right-handed hitter Mike Gallego has low BARS averages against fastballs thrown both by right- and left-handed pitchers (.233 and .225, respectively).

He hits only .181 against medium-high inside fastballs thrown by right-handers. He hits this pitch deep to all fields, but his low average in this location indicates that most of his hit balls are probably easy outs.

MEDIUM-HIGH OUTSIDE FASTBALLS

BATTING AVERAGE .181
Play

Left	Deep and shifted toward the left field line
Center	Deep in straightaway center field
Right	Deep and shifted toward center field
Short	Normal position
Second	Normal position

He hits .263 against medium-high outside fastballs against right-handers. He hits this pitch short down the right line. Notice in the field diagram on the opposite page that the right fielder needs to play completely differently for medium-high inside and medium-high outside fastballs. In fact, the right fielder needs to shift about 90 feet to be correctly positioned for each of these pitches.

MEDIUM-HIGH INSIDE FASTBALLS

BATTING AVERAGE .263
Play

Left	Medium-deep and shifted toward the left line
Center	Medium-deep in straightaway center field
Right	Short and shifted toward the right field line
Short	Normal position
Second	Normal position

He has problems with low-over-the-middle fastballs against right-handers (.111).

LOW-OVER-THE-MIDDLE FASTBALLS

BATTING AVERAGE .111
Play

Left	*No instances recorded*
Center	Deep in straightaway center field
Right	Deep in straightaway right field
Short	Up middle (shifted toward second base)
Second	Shifted toward first base

Gallego hits .266 against medium-high outside fastballs thrown by left-handed pitchers.

MEDIUM-HIGH OUTSIDE FASTBALLS
(THROWN BY LEFT-HANDED PITCHERS)

BATTING AVERAGE .266
Play

Left	Medium-deep and shifted toward center field
Center	Deep in straightaway center field
Right	Deep in straightaway right field
Short	Shifted toward third base
Second	Shifted toward first base

Dark Fielders — Medium-High Outside Fastballs Vs. RH
Light Fielders — Medium-High Inside Fastballs Vs. RH

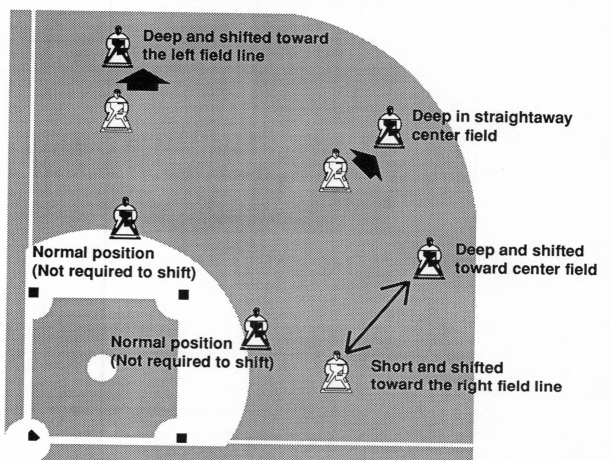

Deep and shifted toward the left field line

Deep in straightaway center field

Normal position (Not required to shift)

Deep and shifted toward center field

Normal position (Not required to shift)

Short and shifted toward the right field line

Ahead And Behind In The Count Vs. RH

Ahead

Fastball Average .205

	Inside	Middle	Outside
High	2/ 0/0	1/ 1000/1	2/ 0/0
Med	8/ 250/2	2/ 500/1	9/ 333/3
Low	1/ 0/0	6/ 0/0	3/ 0/0

Curve Average .500

	Inside	Middle	Outside
High	0/ 0/0	0/ 0/0	0/ 0/0
Med	1/ 1000/1	0/ 0/0	1/ 0/0
Low	0/ 0/0	0/ 0/0	0/ 0/0

Behind

Fastball Average .357

	Inside	Middle	Outside
High	2/ 1000/2	1/ 0/0	1/ 0/0
Med	3/ 0/0	1/ 1000/1	4/ 250/1
Low	1/ 1000/1	1/ 0/0	0/ 0/0

Curve Average .500

	Inside	Middle	Outside
High	1/ 0/0	0/ 0/0	1/ 1000/1
Med	0/ 0/0	0/ 0/0	1/ 1000/1
Low	0/ 0/0	1/ 0/0	0/ 0/0

Overall Evaluation
Against Right-Handed Pitchers

Overall Fastball ⚾⚾

Overall Curve ⚾⚾ ⚾⚾

Overall Slider — Not enough information

Against Left-Handed Pitchers

Overall Fastball ⚾⚾

Overall Curve — Not enough information

Overall Slider — Not enough information

Comments: Weak vs. outside fastballs vs. RH and LH.
Strengths: High-inside fastballs, medium-middle fastballs vs. RH.
Weaknesses: Outside fastballs, low-middle fastballs vs. RH; outside fastballs vs. LH.

Ron Hassey (Left Handed)   *Oakland Athletics*

Ron Hassey Against Right-Handed Pitchers
Overall BARS Batting Average .341

Fastball Average .348

	Outside	Middle	Inside
High	16/ 375 /6	21/ 523 /11	13/ 230 /3
Med	88/ 375 /33	25/ 480 /12	39/ 256 /10
Low	24/ 333 /8	57/ 263 /15	24/ 375 /9

Curve Average .333

	Outside	Middle	Inside
High	1/ 0 /0	2/ 0 /0	0/ 0 /0
Med	9/ 222 /2	5/ 600 /3	4/ 500 /2
Low	4/ 0 /0	18/ 277 /5	8/ 625 /5

Slider Average .289

	Outside	Middle	Inside
High	1/ 1000 /1	0/ 0 /0	2/ 500 /1
Med	7/ 0 /0	5/ 200 /1	10/ 500 /5
Low	1/ 0 /0	6/ 166 /1	6/ 333 /2

Ron Hassey Against Left-Handed Pitchers
Overall BARS Batting Average .161

Fastball Average .189

	Outside	Middle	Inside
High	1/ 0 /0	6/ 166 /1	4/ 250 /1
Med	16/ 312 /5	3/ 0 /0	11/ 90 /1
Low	4/ 0 /0	10/ 200 /2	3/ 333 /1

Curve Average .120

	Outside	Middle	Inside
High	1/ 1000 /1	1/ 0 /0	1/ 0 /0
Med	6/ 333 /2	3/ 0 /0	0/ 0 /0
Low	6/ 0 /0	2/ 0 /0	5/ 0 /0

Slider Average .100

	Outside	Middle	Inside
High	0/ 0 /0	1/ 0 /0	0/ 0 /0
Med	4/ 0 /0	0/ 0 /0	1/ 1000 /1
Low	3/ 0 /0	1/ 0 /0	0/ 0 /0

Left-handed hitter Ron Hassey hits extremely well overall against fastballs thrown by right-handed pitchers (.348). He also hits curves and sliders well against right-handers (.333 and .289 respectively).

Against left-handers, however, it's another story. He hits poorly against fastballs (.189), curves (.120) and sliders (.100).

Hassey hits extremely well against outside fastballs thrown by right-handers (.375, .375 and .333, high to low). He hits medium-high outside fastballs straightaway to the outfield.

MEDIUM-HIGH OUTSIDE FASTBALLS

BATTING AVERAGE .375
Play
Left	Deep in straightaway left field
Center	Deep in straightaway center field
Right	Deep in straightaway right field
Short	Normal position
Second	Shifted toward first base

He hits high-outside and low-outside fastballs much differently than he hits medium-high outside fastballs. The center and right fielders would need to shift for pitches to each of these three locations to be correctly positioned for these two pitches.

HIGH-OUTSIDE FASTBALLS

BATTING AVERAGE .375
Play
Left	Deep and shifted toward the left field line
Center	Medium-deep and shifted toward left field
Right	Deep and shifted toward center field
Short	Shifted toward third base
Second	Shifted toward first base

LOW-OUTSIDE FASTBALLS

BATTING AVERAGE .333
Play
Left	Deep and shifted toward the left field line
Center	Medium-deep in straightaway center field
Right	Deep and shifted toward the right field line
Short	Shifted toward third base
Second	Shifted toward first base

Hassey has a strong .375 average against low-inside fastballs.

LOW-INSIDE FASTBALLS

BATTING AVERAGE .375
Play
Left	Deep in straightaway left field
Center	Deep and shifted toward left field
Right	*No instances recorded*

Short	Shifted toward third base
Second	Shifted toward first base

He hits high-over-the-middle fastballs at a .523 clip.

HIGH-OVER-THE-MIDDLE FASTBALLS

BATTING AVERAGE .523
Play

Left	Medium-deep and shifted toward the left field line
Center	Deep in straightaway center field
Right	Deep and shifted toward center field
Short	Up middle (shifted toward second base)
Second	*No instances recorded*

Hassey Against Curves And Sliders

Hassey has several strong curve locations against right-handers. He hits .625 against low-inside curves, pulling the ball deep down the right line. But the .222 in his medium-high outside curve location indicates a possible weakness.

He also has trouble with medium-high outside sliders (0 for 7). In contrast, he hits medium-high inside sliders very well (.500). He pulls this pitch deep to right center and down the right line.

MEDIUM-HIGH INSIDE SLIDERS

BATTING AVERAGE .500
Play

Left	Medium-deep and shifted toward center field
Center	Deep and shifted toward right field
Right	Deep and shifted toward the right field line
Short	Shifted toward third base
Second	Shifted toward first base

Hassey Against Left-Handed Pitchers

Against left-handed pitchers, Hassey hits medium-high outside fastballs fairly well (.312). In contrast, he hits medium-high inside fastballs very poorly (.090). The BARS fielding strategies show how differently fielders need to play for these two locations.

MEDIUM-HIGH OUTSIDE FASTBALLS (THROWN BY LEFT-HANDED PITCHERS)

BATTING AVERAGE .312
Play

Left	Deep in straightaway left field
Center	Medium-deep in straightaway center field
Right	Medium-deep in straightaway right field
Short	Up middle (shifted toward second base)
Second	Normal position

MEDIUM-HIGH INSIDE FASTBALLS (THROWN BY LEFT-HANDED PITCHERS)

BATTING AVERAGE .090
Play

Left	Medium-deep and shifted toward the left field line
Center	Deep in straightaway center field
Right	*No instances recorded*
Short	Shifted toward third base
Second	Normal position

Hassey seems to have trouble with low-outside curves thrown by left-handers (0 for 6). In fact, he does not have a recorded base hit in the three low-curve locations against left-handers.

Ahead And Behind In The Count Vs. RH

Ahead

Fastball Average .387

	Outside	Middle	Inside
High	4/250 /1	12/583 /7	6/333 /2
Med	46/456 /21	14/500 /7	27/296 /8
Low	9/222 /2	30/333 /10	12/333 /4

Curve Average .315

	Outside	Middle	Inside
High	1/0 /0	1/0 /0	0/0 /0
Med	2/0 /0	2/500 /1	4/500 /2
Low	1/0 /0	5/0 /0	3/1000 /3

Behind

Fastball Average .365

	Outside	Middle	Inside
High	3/666 /2	4/500 /2	4/250 /1
Med	13/384 /5	4/250 /1	5/400 /2
Low	2/500 /1	12/250 /3	5/400 /2

Curve Average .285

	Outside	Middle	Inside
High	0/0 /0	1/0 /0	0/0 /0
Med	4/0 /0	1/1000 /1	0/0 /0
Low	0/0 /0	6/333 /2	2/500 /1

Overall Evaluation

Against Right-Handed Pitchers

Overall Fastball	⚾⚾ ⚾⚾ ⚾⚾ ⚾⚾
Overall Curve	⚾⚾ ⚾⚾ ⚾⚾ ⚾⚾
Overall Slider	⚾⚾ ⚾⚾ ⚾⚾

Against Left-Handed Pitchers

Overall Fastball	⚾⚾
Overall Curve	⚾⚾
Overall Slider	Not enough information

Comments: A top-rate fastball hitter against RH, Hassey has only three weak fastball locations. Strengths: Fastballs in general vs. RH, low-inside curves and medium-high inside sliders vs. RH; medium-high outside fastballs vs. LH. Weaknesses: Low-middle, medium-inside and high-inside fastballs vs. RH, outside curves and outside sliders vs. RH; medium-inside fastballs, over-the-middle fastballs and low curves vs. LH.

Dave Henderson (Right Handed) *Oakland Athletics*

Dave Henderson Against Right-Handed Pitchers
Overall BARS Batting Average .245

Fastball Average .238

	Inside	Middle	Outside
High	14/142 /2	26/269 /7	21/190 /4
Med	30/233 /7	11/636 /7	67/238 /16
Low	13/230 /3	27/333 /9	26/38 /1

Curve Average .238

	Inside	Middle	Outside
High	1/1000 /1	5/400 /2	2/0 /0
Med	4/250 /1	5/600 /3	39/230 /9
Low	6/0 /0	12/166 /2	31/225 /7

Slider Average .296

	Inside	Middle	Outside
High	2/500 /1	2/0 /0	1/0 /0
Med	4/250 /1	5/600 /3	13/384 /5
Low	1/0 /0	7/428 /3	19/157 /3

Dave Henderson Against Left-Handed Pitchers
Overall BARS Batting Average .281

Fastball Average .292

	Inside	Middle	Outside
High	2/0 /0	11/181 /2	9/222 /2
Med	12/416 /5	9/777 /7	37/216 /8
Low	2/500 /1	12/250 /3	12/250 /3

Curve Average .290

	Inside	Middle	Outside
High	0/0 /0	2/500 /1	1/0 /0
Med	5/400 /2	4/750 /3	7/285 /2
Low	2/0 /0	6/166 /1	4/0 /0

Slider Average .187

	Inside	Middle	Outside
High	0/0 /0	1/1000 /1	1/0 /0
Med	5/400 /2	0/0 /0	1/0 /0
Low	4/0 /0	4/0 /0	0/0 /0

Right-handed Dave Henderson hits a little better against left-handed than against right-handed pitchers. His BARS fastball average is 54 points higher against left-handers (.292 vs. left-handers, .238 vs. right-handers) and his curve chart is 52 points higher (.290 vs. left-handers, .238 vs. right-handers).

Henderson's only truly strong fastball location against right-handed pitchers is medium-over-the-middle (.636). Since pitchers seldom throw to that location, Henderson has an overall weakness against fastballs thrown by right-handers. Note especially his weaknesses on the four fastball corners (.142, .190, .038 and .230, clockwise from high-inside).

He hits medium-high outside fastballs for a higher average when he is ahead in the count than when he is behind (.142 when behind, .333 when ahead). He pulls the ball much more when ahead.

MEDIUM-HIGH OUTSIDE FASTBALLS
(WHEN AHEAD IN THE COUNT)

BATTING AVERAGE .333
Play
Left	Deep and shifted toward the left field line
Center	Deep in straightaway center field
Right	Deep and shifted toward center field
Short	Normal position
Second	Normal position

MEDIUM-HIGH OUTSIDE FASTBALLS
(WHEN BEHIND IN THE COUNT)

BATTING AVERAGE .142
Play
Left	Deep and shifted toward center field
Center	Deep in straightaway center field
Right	Deep and shifted toward the right field line
Short	Up middle (shifted toward second base)
Second	Shifted toward first base

Henderson also hits low-over-the-middle fastballs for a higher average and pulls the ball more when ahead than when behind. This is the case with many of Henderson's fastball and curve locations.

LOW-OVER-THE-MIDDLE FASTBALLS
(WHEN AHEAD IN THE COUNT)

BATTING AVERAGE .428
Play
Left	Deep and shifted toward the left field line
Center	Deep and shifted toward left field
Right	No instances recorded
Short	Normal position
Second	Normal position

LOW-OVER-THE-MIDDLE FASTBALLS (WHEN BEHIND IN THE COUNT)

BATTING AVERAGE .285

Play

Left	Medium-deep in straightaway left field
Center	Deep and shifted toward right field
Right	Medium-deep in straightaway right field
Short	Up middle (shifted toward second base)
Second	Normal position

MEDIUM-HIGH INSIDE FASTBALLS (WHEN AHEAD IN THE COUNT)

BATTING AVERAGE .454

Play

Left	Deep and shifted toward the left field line
Center	Deep and shifted toward right field
Right	Medium-deep in straightaway right field
Short	Normal position
Second	*No instances recorded*

MEDIUM-HIGH INSIDE FASTBALLS (WHEN BEHIND IN THE COUNT)

BATTING AVERAGE .125

Play

Left	*No instances recorded*
Center	Deep and shifted toward left field
Right	Medium-deep in straightaway right field
Short	Normal position
Second	Normal position

Henderson Against Curves And Sliders

Henderson has problems with all low and outside curve locations against right-handed pitchers. If pitchers kept their curves low they would have little trouble with him.

He hits medium-high outside sliders very well against right-handers (.384), although he has problems with low-outside sliders (.157).

MEDIUM-HIGH OUTSIDE SLIDERS

BATTING AVERAGE .384

Play

Left	Medium-deep and shifted toward the left field line
Center	Deep and shifted toward left field
Right	Medium-deep and shifted toward center field
Short	Up middle (shifted toward second base)
Second	*No instances recorded*

Henderson Against Left-Handed Pitchers

Henderson hits medium-high inside and medium-over-the-middle fastballs very well against left-handers (.416 and .777 respectively). He has trouble with all outside and all high fastballs.

He hits medium-high outside fastballs straightaway to all fields but hits medium-high inside fastballs deep down both lines.

MEDIUM-HIGH INSIDE FASTBALLS (THROWN BY LEFT-HANDED PITCHERS)

BATTING AVERAGE .416

Play

Left	Deep and shifted toward the left field line
Center	Deep in straightaway center field
Right	Deep and shifted toward the right field line
Short	Normal position
Second	Shifted toward first base

Ahead And Behind In The Count Vs. RH

Ahead

Fastball Average .358

	Inside	Middle	Outside
High	6/ 333 /2	12/ 333 /4	8/ 250 /2
Med	11/ 454 /5	6/ 666 /4	24/ 333 /8
Low	5/ 200 /1	14/ 428 /6	6/ 166 /1

Curve Average .388

	Inside	Middle	Outside
High	1/ 1000 /1	1/ 1000 /1	0/ 0 /0
Med	1/ 1000 /1	1/ 0 /0	11/ 181 /2
Low	0/ 0 /0	0/ 0 /0	3/ 666 /2

Behind

Fastball Average .190

	Inside	Middle	Outside
High	1/ 0 /0	3/ 0 /0	1/ 0 /0
Med	8/ 125 /1	2/ 1000 /2	14/ 142 /2
Low	3/ 333 /1	7/ 285 /2	3/ 0 /0

Curve Average .416

	Inside	Middle	Outside
High	0/ 0 /0	0/ 0 /0	1/ 0 /0
Med	1/ 0 /0	1/ 1000 /1	12/ 500 /6
Low	0/ 0 /0	4/ 250 /1	5/ 400 /2

Overall Evaluation

Against Right-Handed Pitchers

Overall Fastball	⚾⚾
Overall Curve	⚾⚾
Overall Slider	⚾⚾ ⚾⚾⚾

Against Left-Handed Pitchers

Overall Fastball	⚾⚾ ⚾⚾
Overall Curve	⚾⚾ ⚾⚾⚾ ⚾⚾
Overall Slider	⚾⚾

Comments: Henderson has large areas pitchers can focus on to gain an advantage (outside fastballs vs. RH and LH, low curves vs. RH, etc.).

Strengths: Medium over-the-middle and low-over-the-middle fastballs vs. RH, medium-high outside sliders vs. RH; medium-inside and medium-over-the-middle fastballs vs. LH, all medium-high curves vs. LH.

Weaknesses: All fastball locations except as above, low & outside curves vs. RH, low-outside sliders vs. RH.

Rickey Henderson (Right Handed) *Oakland Athletics*

Rickey Henderson Against Right-Handed Pitchers
Overall BARS Batting Average .299

Fastball Average .329

	Inside	Middle	Outside
High	32/ 281 /9	37/ 351 /13	18/ 166 /3
Med	71/ 338 /24	72/ 444 /32	157/ 343 /54
Low	22/ 318 /7	94/ 361 /34	58/ 155 /9

Curve Average .201

	Inside	Middle	Outside
High	3/ 333 /1	5/ 600 /3	4/ 250 /1
Med	10/ 100 /1	9/ 333 /3	27/ 148 /4
Low	3/ 333 /1	15/ 266 /4	28/ 107 /3

Slider Average .244

	Inside	Middle	Outside
High	0/ 0 /0	9/ 333 /3	1/ 0 /0
Med	3/ 0 /0	9/ 222 /2	27/ 333 /9
Low	8/ 250 /2	18/ 277 /5	52/ 192 /10

Rickey Henderson Against Left-Handed Pitchers
Overall BARS Batting Average .320

Fastball Average .338

	Inside	Middle	Outside
High	5/ 400 /2	17/ 411 /7	11/ 363 /4
Med	35/ 285 /10	19/ 263 /5	79/ 291 /23
Low	12/ 500 /6	41/ 439 /18	26/ 307 /8

Curve Average .237

	Inside	Middle	Outside
High	1/ 0 /0	1/ 0 /0	2/ 500 /1
Med	9/ 444 /4	1/ 0 /0	12/ 250 /3
Low	11/ 90 /1	7/ 428 /3	15/ 133 /2

Slider Average .333

	Inside	Middle	Outside
High	1/ 1000 /1	2/ 1000 /2	1/ 0 /0
Med	2/ 0 /0	5/ 200 /1	5/ 600 /3
Low	6/ 166 /1	5/ 200 /1	3/ 333 /1

Right-handed Rickey Henderson is an excellent fastball hitter who has considerable trouble with curves. He hits fastballs so well, however, that his overall BARS average against right-handed pitchers is .299 and against left-handed pitchers is .320.

Henderson's .329 overall fastball average against right-handed pitchers is excellent. He does have two weak locations (.155 in the low-outside location and .166 in the high-outside location) but hits solidly in all other locations. His .343 in the medium-high outside location is very strong.

MEDIUM-HIGH OUTSIDE FASTBALLS

BATTING AVERAGE .343
Play

Left	Deep in straightaway left field
Center	Deep in straightaway center field
Right	Deep in straightaway right field
Short	Normal position
Second	Shifted toward first base

He hits low-over-the-middle fastballs for an excellent .361 average.

LOW-OVER-THE-MIDDLE FASTBALLS

BATTING AVERAGE .361
Play

Left	Deep and shifted toward center field
Center	Deep in straightaway center field
Right	Medium-deep in straightaway right field
Short	Shifted toward third base
Second	Normal position

Notice in the chart above that left fielders need to play Henderson deep and shifted toward center field for low-over-the-middle fastballs. Most of the time they probably play him deep and shifted toward the line — and are not able to get to a lot of his hit balls. That's why his average is .361 in this location. The chart below shows that left fielders need to play medium-deep and shifted toward the line for low-outside fastballs. Left fielders are probably playing correctly for this pitch and can get to most of his hit balls — as a result his average is a low .155 in this location.

This emphasizes the necessity for fielders to adjust on a pitch-by-pitch basis.

LOW-OUTSIDE FASTBALLS

BATTING AVERAGE .155
Play

Left	Medium-deep and shifted toward the left field line
Center	Deep in straightaway center field
Right	Medium-deep in straightaway right field
Short	Normal position
Second	Normal position

Henderson has extreme difficulty with curves

thrown by right-handed pitchers. But look how few curves are thrown in comparison to fastballs. Why don't right-handed pitchers throw him more curves, considering that he hits .329 overall against fastballs? Good question.

He pulls low-over-the-middle curves.

LOW-OVER-THE-MIDDLE CURVEBALLS

BATTING AVERAGE .266
Play

Left	Deep and shifted toward the left field line
Center	Deep and shifted toward left field
Right	Deep and shifted toward center field
Short	Normal position
Second	*No instances recorded*

He hits medium-high outside sliders well (.333) but hits low-outside sliders very poorly (.192).

MEDIUM-HIGH OUTSIDE SLIDERS

BATTING AVERAGE .333
Play

Left	Deep and shifted toward the left field line
Center	Deep in straightaway center field
Right	Medium-deep and shifted toward the right line
Short	Shifted toward third base
Second	Normal position

Henderson Against Left-Handed Pitchers

Henderson also hits fastballs extremely well against left-handed pitchers. He blisters low-over-the-middle and high-over-the-middle fastballs (.439 and .411).

LOW-OVER-THE-MIDDLE FASTBALLS (THROWN BY LEFT-HANDED PITCHERS)

BATTING AVERAGE .439
Play

Left	Deep and shifted toward the left field line
Center	Medium-deep in straightaway center field
Right	Deep and shifted toward center field
Short	Up middle (shifted toward second base)
Second	Normal position

He hits medium-high outside fastballs for a .291 average.

MEDIUM-HIGH OUTSIDE FASTBALLS (THROWN BY LEFT-HANDED PITCHERS)

BATTING AVERAGE .291
Play

Left	Medium-deep in straightaway left field
Center	Deep in straightaway center field
Right	Deep in straightaway right field
Short	Normal position
Second	Normal position

Henderson has trouble with low-outside curves (.133), low-inside curves (.090), and medium-high outside curves (.250) against left-handers. He hits medium-high inside curves very well (.444).

He has trouble with low-inside and low-over-the-middle sliders against lefties (.166 and .200, respectively). He hits medium-high outside sliders very well, however (.600 on 3 for 5).

Ahead And Behind In The Count Vs. RH

Ahead

Fastball Average .352

	Inside	Middle	Outside
High	11 / 181 / 2	19 / 368 / 7	7 / 285 / 2
Med	35 / 371 / 13	41 / 414 / 17	69 / 362 / 25
Low	6 / 500 / 3	64 / 390 / 25	20 / 100 / 2

Curve Average .222

	Inside	Middle	Outside
High	0 / 0 / 0	0 / 0 / 0	0 / 0 / 0
Med	1 / 0 / 0	2 / 500 / 1	2 / 0 / 0
Low	0 / 0 / 0	1 / 0 / 0	3 / 333 / 1

Behind

Fastball Average .370

	Inside	Middle	Outside
High	9 / 444 / 4	1 / 1000 / 1	1 / 0 / 0
Med	13 / 384 / 5	9 / 555 / 5	25 / 360 / 9
Low	7 / 285 / 2	7 / 285 / 2	9 / 222 / 2

Curve Average .222

	Inside	Middle	Outside
High	2 / 500 / 1	2 / 500 / 1	2 / 500 / 1
Med	4 / 0 / 0	5 / 400 / 2	17 / 235 / 4
Low	0 / 0 / 0	8 / 250 / 2	14 / 71 / 1

Overall Evaluation

Against Right-Handed Pitchers

Overall Fastball	⚾⚾⚾⚾
Overall Curve	⚾
Overall Slider	⚾

Against Left-Handed Pitchers

Overall Fastball	⚾⚾⚾⚾
Overall Curve	⚾
Overall Slider	⚾⚾⚾⚾

Comments: Excellent fastball hitter.
Strengths: All waist-high and all over-the-middle fastballs vs. RH, low-inside fastballs vs. RH, medium-outside sliders vs. RH; all high fastballs and all low fastballs vs. LH.
Weaknesses: Low-outside and high-outside fastballs, outside curves, low-outside sliders vs. RH; medium-outside, low-outside and low-inside curves vs. LH.

Stan Javier (Switch Hitter) — *Oakland Athletics*

Stan Javier Against Right-Handed Pitchers
Overall BARS Batting Average .248

Fastball Average .301

	Outside	Middle	Inside
High	7/142 /1	3/333 /1	7/285 /2
Med	32/312 /10	1/1000 /1	15/266 /4
Low	7/285 /2	9/444 /4	12/250 /3

Curve Average .111

	Outside	Middle	Inside
High	1/0 /0	2/0 /0	1/0 /0
Med	4/0 /0	0/0 /0	2/0 /0
Low	1/1000 /1	5/200 /1	2/0 /0

Slider Average .272

	Outside	Middle	Inside
High	0/0 /0	2/500 /1	1/0 /0
Med	2/0 /0	0/0 /0	2/500 /1
Low	0/0 /0	1/0 /0	3/333 /1

Stan Javier Against Left-Handed Pitchers
Overall BARS Batting Average .156

Fastball Average .147

	Inside	Middle	Outside
High	1/0 /0	4/0 /0	0/0 /0
Med	1/1000 /1	1/0 /0	15/66 /1
Low	0/0 /0	6/166 /1	6/333 /2

Curve Average .142

	Inside	Middle	Outside
High	0/0 /0	0/0 /0	1/1000 /1
Med	0/0 /0	1/0 /0	1/0 /0
Low	0/0 /0	2/0 /0	2/0 /0

Slider Average .250

	Inside	Middle	Outside
High	1/0 /0	0/0 /0	0/0 /0
Med	0/0 /0	0/0 /0	1/1000 /1
Low	2/0 /0	0/0 /0	0/0 /0

Switch-hitting Stan Javier has a good .301 overall fastball average against right-handed pitchers. This is built on his strong .312 medium-high outside fastball location. But he hits only .147 overall against left-handed pitchers, mostly as a result of his weak .066 medium-high outside average.

He hits medium-high outside fastballs uniquely against right-handers.

MEDIUM-HIGH OUTSIDE FASTBALLS

BATTING AVERAGE .312
Play

Left	Medium-deep and shifted toward center field
Center	Deep and shifted toward left field
Right	Medium-deep and shifted toward the right line
Short	Normal position
Second	Shifted toward first base

In contrast, he hits only .266 against medium-high inside fastballs thrown by right-handers. The field diagram on the opposite page illustrates how differently fielders need to play him for medium-high inside and medium-high outside fastballs.

MEDIUM-HIGH INSIDE FASTBALLS

BATTING AVERAGE .266
Play

Left	Medium-deep in straightaway left field
Center	Medium-deep in straightaway center field
Right	Deep in straightaway right field
Short	Up middle (shifted toward second base)
Second	Normal position

He is also weak against low-inside fastballs against right-handers. The medium-high inside/low-inside sector is a good target for right-handers.

LOW-INSIDE FASTBALLS

BATTING AVERAGE .250
Play

Left	Deep in straightaway left field
Center	Medium-deep and shifted toward left field
Right	*No instances recorded*
Short	Shifted toward third base
Second	Shifted toward first base

Against left-handed pitchers, Javier hits a poor .066 on 1 for 15 in his medium-high outside fastball location. His low average indicates that most of his hit balls in this location are probably easy outs.

MEDIUM-HIGH OUTSIDE FASTBALLS
(THROWN BY LEFT-HANDED PITCHERS)

BATTING AVERAGE .066
Play

Left	Deep and shifted toward center field
Center	Medium-deep in straightaway center field
Right	Deep and shifted toward the right field line
Short	Shifted toward third base
Second	Normal position

Dark Fielders — Medium-High Outside Fastballs
Light Fielders — Medium-High Inside Fastballs

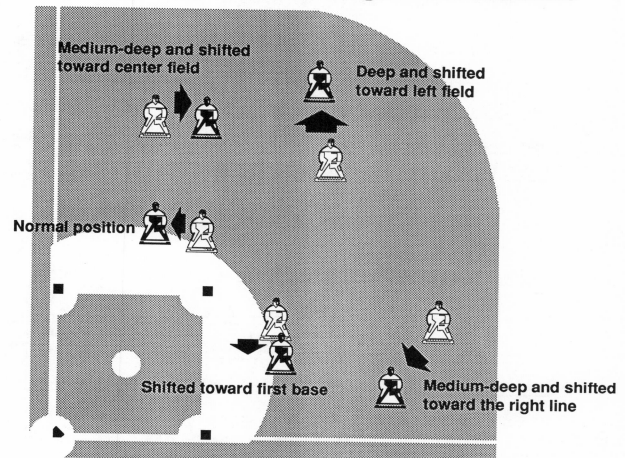

Medium-deep and shifted toward center field

Deep and shifted toward left field

Normal position

Shifted toward first base

Medium-deep and shifted toward the right line

Ahead And Behind In The Count Vs. RH

Ahead

Fastball Average .416

	Outside	Middle	Inside
High	1/ 1000 /1	1/ 1000 /1	2/ 500 /1
Med	12/ 500 /6	0/ 0 /0	6/ 500 /3
Low	1/ 0 /0	5/ 400 /2	8/ 125 /1

Curve Average .000

	Outside	Middle	Inside
High	0/ 0 /0	1/ 0 /0	0/ 0 /0
Med	1/ 0 /0	0/ 0 /0	1/ 0 /0
Low	0/ 0 /0	1/ 0 /0	0/ 0 /0

Behind

Fastball Average .227

	Outside	Middle	Inside
High	3/ 0 /0	1/ 0 /0	1/ 0 /0
Med	5/ 400 /2	0/ 0 /0	4/ 250 /1
Low	4/ 250 /1	3/ 333 /1	1/ 0 /0

Curve Average .250

	Outside	Middle	Inside
High	1/ 0 /0	0/ 0 /0	0/ 0 /0
Med	1/ 0 /0	0/ 0 /0	0/ 0 /0
Low	0/ 0 /0	2/ 500 /1	0/ 0 /0

Overall Evaluation

Against Right-Handed Pitchers

Overall Fastball ⚾⚾ ⚾⚾⚾ ⚾⚾

Overall Curve ⚾⚾

Overall Slider ⚾⚾ ⚾⚾

Against Left-Handed Pitchers

Overall Fastball ⚾⚾

Overall Curve — Not enough information

Overall Slider — Not enough information

Comments: Hits fastballs well vs. RH.
Strengths: Medium-outside fastballs, low-middle fastballs vs. RH; low-outside fastballs vs. LH.
Weaknesses: Medium-inside, low-inside and high-outside fastballs, curves in general vs. RH; medium-outside and low-middle fastballs vs. LH.

Carney Lansford (Right Handed)　　*Oakland Athletics*

Carney Lansford Against Right-Handed Pitchers
Overall BARS Batting Average .305

Fastball Average .305

	Inside	Middle	Outside
High	25 / 160 / 4	24 / 500 / 12	9 / 111 / 1
Med	52 / 365 / 19	21 / 333 / 7	85 / 258 / 22
Low	24 / 208 / 5	49 / 448 / 22	28 / 178 / 5

Curve Average .329

	Inside	Middle	Outside
High	3 / 333 / 1	5 / 600 / 3	2 / 0 / 0
Med	7 / 428 / 3	11 / 181 / 2	21 / 333 / 7
Low	3 / 666 / 2	22 / 363 / 8	14 / 214 / 3

Slider Average .254

	Inside	Middle	Outside
High	1 / 0 / 0	5 / 400 / 2	1 / 0 / 0
Med	3 / 333 / 1	2 / 1000 / 2	15 / 200 / 3
Low	2 / 500 / 1	8 / 125 / 1	14 / 214 / 3

Carney Lansford Against Left-Handed Pitchers
Overall BARS Batting Average .261

Fastball Average .236

	Inside	Middle	Outside
High	8 / 125 / 1	7 / 428 / 3	9 / 111 / 1
Med	21 / 238 / 5	5 / 200 / 1	34 / 264 / 9
Low	22 / 318 / 7	24 / 250 / 6	18 / 111 / 2

Curve Average .303

	Inside	Middle	Outside
High	1 / 1000 / 1	2 / 500 / 1	1 / 0 / 0
Med	3 / 333 / 1	1 / 0 / 0	5 / 400 / 2
Low	2 / 500 / 1	9 / 222 / 2	9 / 222 / 2

Slider Average .363

	Inside	Middle	Outside
High	1 / 0 / 0	0 / 0 / 0	0 / 0 / 0
Med	4 / 250 / 1	0 / 0 / 0	4 / 500 / 2
Low	6 / 166 / 1	6 / 666 / 4	1 / 0 / 0

Carney Lansford hits .305 against fastballs thrown by right-handed pitchers but only .236 against fastballs thrown by left-handed pitchers. He is one of several right-handed hitters on the team who hit better against right-handed pitchers. This could make Oakland a team that hits better against right-handers than would normally be expected.

He hits low-over-the-middle fastballs straightaway to left and center and into right center.

LOW-OVER-THE-MIDDLE FASTBALLS

BATTING AVERAGE .448
Play
Left　　Deep in straightaway left field
Center　Medium-deep in straightaway center field
Right　Deep and shifted toward center field
Short　Shifted toward third base
Second　Normal position

His .500 against high-over-the-middle fastballs is exceptional.

HIGH-OVER-THE-MIDDLE FASTBALLS

BATTING AVERAGE .500
Play
Left　　Deep and shifted toward the left field line
Center　Deep in straightaway center field
Right　Medium-deep in straightaway right field
Short　Shifted toward third base

Second　Shifted toward first base

He hits .365 against medium-high inside fastballs thrown by right-handers.

MEDIUM-HIGH INSIDE FASTBALLS

BATTING AVERAGE .365
Play
Left　　Deep and shifted toward the left field line
Center　Medium-deep in straightaway center field
Right　Deep and shifted toward center field
Short　Shifted toward third base
Second　Normal position

He hits medium-high outside fastballs deep down the left line and straightaway to the other positions.

MEDIUM-HIGH OUTSIDE FASTBALLS

BATTING AVERAGE .258
Play
Left　　Deep and shifted toward the left field line
Center　Medium-deep in straightaway center field
Right　Deep in straightaway right field
Short　Normal position
Second　Normal position

Lansford's fastball weaknesses are on the four corners. He pulls high-inside fastballs to all fields, hits high-outside fastballs to the opposite field, goes with low-outside fastballs to straightaway center and right, and hits low-inside fastballs straightaway to deep left and left center. His low averages in the four corner corners indicate that most of his hits balls in these locations are easy fly balls or grounders.

Lansford Against Curves And Sliders

Lansford hits curves thrown by right-handers excellently overall. His .333 against medium-high outside and .363 against low-over-the-middle curves are very strong. But he has trouble against low-outside (.214) and medium-over-the-middle curves (.181).

MEDIUM-HIGH OUTSIDE CURVEBALLS

BATTING AVERAGE .333

Play	
Left	Deep and shifted toward the left field line
Center	Medium-deep and shifted toward left field
Right	Medium-deep in straightaway right field
Short	Normal position
Second	Normal position

LOW-OVER-THE-MIDDLE CURVEBALLS

BATTING AVERAGE .363

Play	
Left	Medium-deep in straightaway left field
Center	Deep and shifted toward left field
Right	Deep and shifted toward center field
Short	Normal position
Second	Normal position

Lansford has problems with outside sliders and low-over-the-middle sliders thrown by right-handers. His .214 average against low-outside sliders is poor; his .200 in the medium-high outside and .125 in the low-over-the-middle slider locations are very weak.

Lansford Against Left-Handed Pitchers

Lansford has much more difficulty with fastballs against left-handers than against right-handers.

His .318 in the low-inside fastball location is good, as is the .428 (on fewer instances) in the high-over-the-middle location. His other fastball locations are adequate at best.

Lansford pulls low-inside fastballs and hits medium-high inside fastballs straightaway.

LOW-INSIDE FASTBALLS (THROWN BY LEFT-HANDED PITCHERS)

BATTING AVERAGE .318

Play	
Left	Deep and shifted toward the left field line
Center	Deep in straightaway center field
Right	Deep and shifted toward center field
Short	Normal position
Second	Normal position

MEDIUM-HIGH OUTSIDE FASTBALLS (THROWN BY LEFT-HANDED PITCHERS)

BATTING AVERAGE .264

Play	
Left	Deep in straightaway left field
Center	Deep in straightaway center field
Right	Deep in straightaway right field
Short	Normal position
Second	Normal position

He has trouble with low-outside, high-outside, and high-inside fastballs thrown by left-handers. In addition, he has trouble with low-outside and low-over-the-middle curves thrown by lefties (.222 in each).

Ahead And Behind In The Count Vs. RH

Ahead

Fastball Average .207

	Inside	Middle	Outside
High	2/ 0 /0	1/ 0 /0	4/ 0 /0
Med	10/ 200 /2	4/ 250 /1	19/ 157 /3
Low	16/ 312 /5	16/ 312 /5	5/ 0 /0

Curve Average .200

	Inside	Middle	Outside
High	1/ 1000 /1	1/ 1000 /1	0/ 0 /0
Med	1/ 0 /0	1/ 0 /0	2/ 0 /0
Low	0/ 0 /0	4/ 0 /0	5/ 200 /1

Behind

Fastball Average .222

	Inside	Middle	Outside
High	1/ 0 /0	4/ 500 /2	0/ 0 /0
Med	5/ 400 /2	1/ 0 /0	5/ 200 /1
Low	2/ 0 /0	3/ 0 /0	6/ 166 /1

Curve Average .333

	Inside	Middle	Outside
High	0/ 0 /0	0/ 0 /0	1/ 0 /0
Med	1/ 0 /0	0/ 0 /0	2/ 500 /1
Low	1/ 1000 /1	3/ 333 /1	1/ 0 /0

Overall Evaluation

Against Right-Handed Pitchers

Overall Fastball	⚾⚾ ⚾⚾ ⚾⚾
Overall Curve	⚾⚾ ⚾⚾ ⚾⚾ ⚾⚾
Overall Slider	⚾⚾ ⚾⚾

Against Left-Handed Pitchers

Overall Fastball	⚾⚾
Overall Curve	⚾⚾ ⚾⚾ ⚾⚾ ⚾⚾
Overall Slider	⚾⚾ ⚾⚾ ⚾⚾ ⚾⚾

Comments: Lansford hits fastballs much better vs. right-handed pitchers.
Strengths: Over-the-middle and medium-high inside fastballs vs. RH, low-over-the-middle and medium-high outside curves vs. RH, low-inside and high-over-the-middle fastballs vs. LH.
Weaknesses: The four fastball corners vs. RH, low-outside curves vs. RH, medium-high outside sliders vs. RH, all fastball locations vs. LH except as above.

Mark McGwire (Right Handed)   *Oakland Athletics*

Fastball Average .285

	Inside	Middle	Outside
High	11/90 /1	11/181 /2	12/0 /0
Med	14/428 /6	11/363 /4	53/339 /18
Low	13/461 /6	20/300 /6	16/187 /3

Curve Average .263

	Inside	Middle	Outside
High	3/333 /1	2/1000 /2	3/333 /1
Med	3/333 /1	1/0 /0	12/166 /2
Low	3/0 /0	3/333 /1	8/250 /2

Slider Average .250

	Inside	Middle	Outside
High	0/0 /0	0/0 /0	2/500 /1
Med	0/0 /0	2/0 /0	3/333 /1
Low	0/0 /0	2/1000 /2	7/0 /0

Mark McQwire Against Left-Handed Pitchers
Overall BARS Batting Average .291

Fastball Average .294

	Inside	Middle	Outside
High	3/333 /1	5/400 /2	1/0 /0
Med	9/333 /3	4/500 /2	27/296 /8
Low	6/500 /3	5/200 /1	8/0 /0

Curve Average .333

	Inside	Middle	Outside
High	0/0 /0	0/0 /0	3/333 /1
Med	0/0 /0	1/0 /0	1/0 /0
Low	0/0 /0	6/500 /3	1/0 /0

Slider Average .230

	Inside	Middle	Outside
High	0/0 /0	0/0 /0	1/0 /0
Med	2/500 /1	0/0 /0	3/333 /1
Low	3/333 /1	1/0 /0	3/0 /0

Right-handed hitter Mark McGwire hits all waist-high fastballs strongly against both right- and left-handed pitchers. He has trouble, however, with high fastballs thrown by right-handers.

McGwire's .339 average in the medium-high outside fastball location is excellent. He hits this pitch deep to all fields.

MEDIUM-HIGH OUTSIDE FASTBALLS

BATTING AVERAGE .339
Play

Left	Deep in straightaway left field
Center	Deep and shifted toward left field
Right	Deep in straightaway right field
Short	Up middle (shifted toward second base)
Second	Normal position

His .428 medium-high inside fastball average is also excellent. He hits this pitch deep down both lines.

MEDIUM-HIGH INSIDE FASTBALLS

BATTING AVERAGE .428
Play

Left	Deep and shifted toward the left field line
Center	Deep and shifted toward left field
Right	Deep and shifted toward the right field line
Short	Normal position
Second	Normal position

The differences in the required fielding strategy for McGwire's low-inside and low-over-the-middle fastballs locations are striking. McGwire pulls low-inside fastballs down the left line, while going more to right field with low-over-the-middle fastballs.

LOW-INSIDE FASTBALLS

BATTING AVERAGE .461
Play

Left	Deep and shifted toward the left field line
Center	Deep in straightaway center field
Right	Medium-deep in straightaway right field
Short	Shifted toward third base
Second	Normal position

LOW-OVER-THE-MIDDLE FASTBALLS

BATTING AVERAGE .300
Play

Left	Deep in straightaway left field
Center	Deep in straightaway center field
Right	Deep and shifted toward the right field line
Short	Normal position
Second	Shifted toward first base

The .187 average in McGwire's low-outside fastball location seems to indicate that he hits this pitch mostly for easy pop-ups and ground outs.

LOW-OUTSIDE FASTBALLS

BATTING AVERAGE .187
Play

Left	Medium-deep in straightaway left field
Center	Deep in straightaway center field
Right	Medium-deep and shifted toward the right line
Short	Up middle (shifted toward second base)
Second	Normal position

McGwire's weaknesses in the high fastball locations give pitchers targets for attack. Rather than throw so many low and medium-high fastballs, they should try high fastballs. He hits few of these pitches out of the infield.

McGwire Against Curves And Sliders

He seems to have difficulty with outside curves. The .166 in his medium-high outside location and the .250 in his low-outside location indicate this.

He hits medium-high outside curves to deep left and center fields.

MEDIUM-HIGH OUTSIDE CURVEBALLS

BATTING AVERAGE .166
Play

Left	Deep and shifted toward center field
Center	Deep in straightaway center field
Right	Medium-deep in straightaway right field
Short	Normal position
Second	*No instances recorded*

He has significant trouble with low-outside sliders (.000 on 0 for 7).

McGwire Against Left-Handed Pitchers

McGwire hits well against waist-high fastballs thrown by left-handed pitchers. He hits .296 against medium-high outside fastballs.

MEDIUM-HIGH OUTSIDE FASTBALLS (THROWN BY LEFT-HANDED PITCHERS)

BATTING AVERAGE .296
Play

Left	Medium-deep and shifted toward center field
Center	Deep in straightaway center field
Right	Deep in straightaway right field
Short	Up middle (shifted toward second base)
Second	Normal position

He hits medium-high inside fastballs thrown by left-handers deep down the left line, short into straightaway center field, and medium-deep to straightaway right field. If centerfielders prefer not to play him short, they could play medium-deep anticipating the likelihood of a ball hit short. This way they would be able to cover deep drives and still be prepared to cover shorter hits.

MEDIUM-HIGH INSIDE FASTBALLS (THROWN BY LEFT-HANDED PITCHERS)

BATTING AVERAGE .333
Play

Left	Deep and shifted toward the left field line
Center	Short in straightaway center field
Right	Medium-deep in straightaway right field
Short	*No instances recorded*
Second	*No instances recorded*

Ahead And Behind In The Count Vs. RH

Ahead

Fastball Average .320

	Inside	Middle	Outside
High	200 5/1	0 4/0	0 3/0
Med	444 9/4	1000 2/2	322 31/10
Low	250 4/1	416 12/5	200 5/1

Curve Average .307

	Inside	Middle	Outside
High	0 0/0	0 0/0	500 2/1
Med	500 2/1	0 1/0	0 4/0
Low	0 1/0	0 0/0	666 3/2

Behind

Fastball Average .347

	Inside	Middle	Outside
High	0 0/0	400 5/2	0 3/0
Med	500 2/1	250 4/1	250 4/1
Low	1000 1/1	500 2/1	500 2/1

Curve Average .500

	Inside	Middle	Outside
High	0 0/0	1000 2/2	0 1/0
Med	0 0/0	0 0/0	333 3/1
Low	0 0/0	0 0/0	0 0/0

Overall Evaluation

Against Right-Handed Pitchers

Overall Fastball	⚾⚾
Overall Curve	⚾⚾
Overall Slider	⚾⚾

Against Left-Handed Pitchers

Overall Fastball	⚾⚾
Overall Curve	⚾⚾⚾⚾
Overall Slider	⚾

Comments: Avoid throwing McGwire waist-high fastballs.

Strengths: All waist-high fastballs vs. RH and LH pitchers, low-inside fastballs vs. RH and LH.

Weaknesses: All high fastballs vs. RH, low-outside fastballs, medium-high outside curves, and low-outside sliders vs. RH; low-outside fastballs vs. LH.

Terry Steinbach (Right Handed) — *Oakland Athletics*

Terry Steinbach Against Right-Handed Pitchers
Overall BARS Batting Average .271

Fastball Average .318

	Inside	Middle	Outside
High	4/ 0/0	7/ 142/1	4/ 250/1
Med	13/ 307/4	1/ 1000/1	42/ 404/17
Low	4/ 250/1	5/ 200/1	8/ 250/2

Curve Average .235

	Inside	Middle	Outside
High	1/ 0/0	1/ 1000/1	0/ 0/0
Med	1/ 1000/1	2/ 500/1	4/ 250/1
Low	0/ 0/0	1/ 0/0	7/ 0/0

Slider Average .214

	Inside	Middle	Outside
High	1/ 1000/1	0/ 0/0	0/ 0/0
Med	1/ 0/0	0/ 0/0	4/ 500/2
Low	0/ 0/0	2/ 0/0	6/ 0/0

Terry Steinbach Against Left-Handed Pitchers
Overall BARS Batting Average .354

Fastball Average .377

	Inside	Middle	Outside
High	4/ 500/2	1/ 0/0	3/ 666/2
Med	3/ 666/2	6/ 333/2	26/ 346/9
Low	1/ 0/0	3/ 666/2	6/ 166/1

Curve Average .333

	Inside	Middle	Outside
High	0/ 0/0	0/ 0/0	0/ 0/0
Med	0/ 0/0	0/ 0/0	2/ 0/0
Low	0/ 0/0	1/ 1000/1	0/ 0/0

Slider Average .142

	Inside	Middle	Outside
High	1/ 0/0	0/ 0/0	0/ 0/0
Med	0/ 0/0	1/ 1000/1	2/ 0/0
Low	1/ 0/0	0/ 0/0	2/ 0/0

Right-handed Terry Steinbach hits fastballs well against right-handed pitchers (.318 overall) and excellently against left-handed pitchers (.377).

Against right-handed pitchers, Steinbach hits .404 against medium-high outside fastballs. He hits this pitch deep to left and center fields and medium-deep to right field.

MEDIUM-HIGH OUTSIDE FASTBALLS

BATTING AVERAGE .404
Play

Left	Deep and shifted toward center field
Center	Deep in straightaway center field
Right	Medium-deep in straightaway right field
Short	Up middle (shifted toward second base)
Second	Normal position

He hits medium-high inside fastballs for a .307 average. Notice how differently fielders need to align themselves for this pitch compared to a medium-high outside fastball.

MEDIUM-HIGH INSIDE FASTBALLS

BATTING AVERAGE .307
Play

Left	*No instances recorded*
Center	Medium-deep and shifted toward right field
Right	Short in straightaway right field
Short	Up middle (shifted toward second base)
Second	Shifted toward first base

Steinbach has trouble with all high fastballs and all low fastballs against right-handers. He also has trouble with low-outside curves (.000 on 0 for 7) and low-outside sliders (.000 on 0 for 6).

Steinbach Against Left-Handed Pitchers

Steinbach's fastball chart against left-handed pitchers is scattered with high averages. He hits .346 against medium-high outside fastballs, hitting the ball to deep left center and deep right center.

MEDIUM-HIGH OUTSIDE FASTBALLS
(THROWN BY LEFT-HANDED PITCHERS)

BATTING AVERAGE .346
Play

Left	Medium-deep in straightaway left field
Center	Deep and shifted toward left field
Right	Deep and shifted toward center field
Short	Normal position
Second	Normal position

In contrast with his performance against right-handed pitchers, Steinbach hits medium-high outside fastballs against left-handers very well when ahead in the count (.333 on 3 for 9).

Medium-High Outside Fastballs
(Thrown By Right-Handed Pitchers)

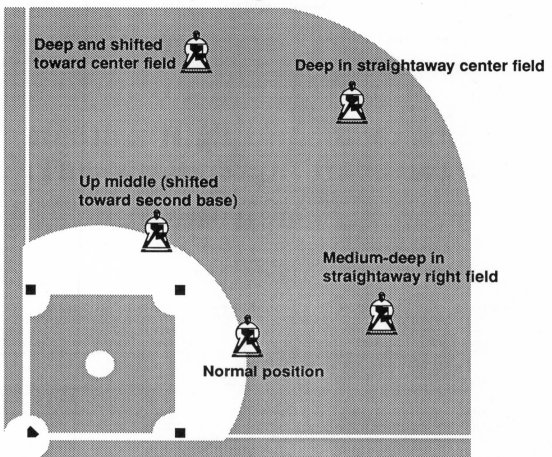

Deep and shifted toward center field

Deep in straightaway center field

Up middle (shifted toward second base)

Medium-deep in straightaway right field

Normal position

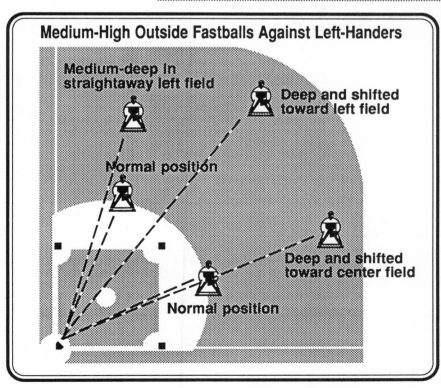

Medium-High Outside Fastballs Against Left-Handers

Medium-deep in straightaway left field

Deep and shifted toward left field

Normal position

Deep and shifted toward center field

Normal position

Overall Evaluation
Against Right-Handed Pitchers

Overall Fastball	⚾⚾ ⚾⚾ ⚾⚾
Overall Curve	⚾⚾
Overall Slider	⚾⚾

Against Left-Handed Pitchers

Overall Fastball	⚾⚾ ⚾⚾ ⚾⚾ ⚾⚾
Overall Curve	Not enough information
Overall Slider	Not enough information

Comments: Steinbach hits medium-high outside fastballs excellently against both RH and LH pitchers.
Strengths: Medium-high outside fastballs, possibly several other fastball locations vs. LH.
Weaknesses: Low and high fastballs vs. RH, outside curves and low sliders vs. RH; low-outside fastballs vs. LH.

Walt Weiss Against Right-Handed Pitchers
Overall BARS Batting Average .252

Fastball Average .291

	Outside	Middle	Inside
High	5/ 200 /1	7/ 428 /3	7/ 285 /2
Med	17/ 235 /4	3/ 333 /1	13/ 538 /7
Low	5/ 0 /0	8/ 250 /2	7/ 142 /1

Curve Average .000

	Outside	Middle	Inside
High	0/ 0 /0	0/ 0 /0	0/ 0 /0
Med	1/ 0 /0	0/ 0 /0	0/ 0 /0
Low	1/ 0 /0	0/ 0 /0	2/ 0 /0

Slider Average .000

	Outside	Middle	Inside
High	0/ 0 /0	0/ 0 /0	0/ 0 /0
Med	0/ 0 /0	0/ 0 /0	2/ 0 /0
Low	0/ 0 /0	0/ 0 /0	0/ 0 /0

Walt Weiss Against Left-Handed Pitchers
Overall BARS Batting Average .333

Fastball Average .320

	Inside	Middle	Outside
High	1/ 1000 /1	0/ 0 /0	3/ 0 /0
Med	1/ 0 /0	4/ 250 /1	8/ 500 /4
Low	2/ 0 /0	6/ 333 /2	0/ 0 /0

Curve Average 1.000

	Inside	Middle	Outside
High	0/ 0 /0	0/ 0 /0	0/ 0 /0
Med	0/ 0 /0	0/ 0 /0	0/ 0 /0
Low	1/ 1000 /1	0/ 0 /0	0/ 0 /0

Slider Average .000

	Inside	Middle	Outside
High	0/ 0 /0	0/ 0 /0	0/ 0 /0
Med	0/ 0 /0	0/ 0 /0	1/ 0 /0
Low	0/ 0 /0	0/ 0 /0	0/ 0 /0

Switch-hitting Walt Weiss hits fastballs well against both right- and left-handed pitchers (.291 overall against right-handers, .320 overall against left-handers).

He hits medium-high outside fastballs at .235 overall against right-handers. He hits this pitch deep to all fields.

MEDIUM-HIGH OUTSIDE FASTBALLS

BATTING AVERAGE .235
Play

Left	Deep and shifted toward center field
Center	Deep in straightaway center field
Right	Deep in straightaway right field
Short	Normal position
Second	Normal position

He hits medium-high inside fastballs for a sparkling .538 average. The chart below and the field diagram on the opposite page show how fielders need to play for this pitch.

MEDIUM-HIGH INSIDE FASTBALLS

BATTING AVERAGE .538
Play

Left	Deep and shifted toward the left field line
Center	Medium-deep in straightaway center field
Right	Deep and shifted toward the right field line
Short	Normal position
Second	Normal position

Weiss Against Left-Handed Pitchers

Few recorded instances in this category were available for Weiss as of this printing. Batting right-handed against left-handed pitchers, he seems to hit medium-high outside fastballs well (.500). See the field diagram at bottom of opposite page.

MEDIUM-HIGH OUTSIDE FASTBALLS (THROWN BY LEFT-HANDED PITCHERS)

BATTING AVERAGE .500
Play

Left	Medium-deep in straightaway left field
Center	Medium-deep in straightaway center field
Right	*No instances recorded*
Short	Up middle (shifted toward second base)
Second	Shifted toward first base

He also hits low-over-the-middle fastballs well.

LOW-OVER-THE-MIDDLE FASTBALLS (THROWN BY LEFT-HANDED PITCHERS)

BATTING AVERAGE .333
Play

Left	Deep in straightaway left field
Center	Short and shifted toward left field
Right	Medium-deep and shifted toward center field
Short	Normal position
Second	Normal position

Medium-High Inside Fastballs
(Thrown By Right-Handed Pitchers)

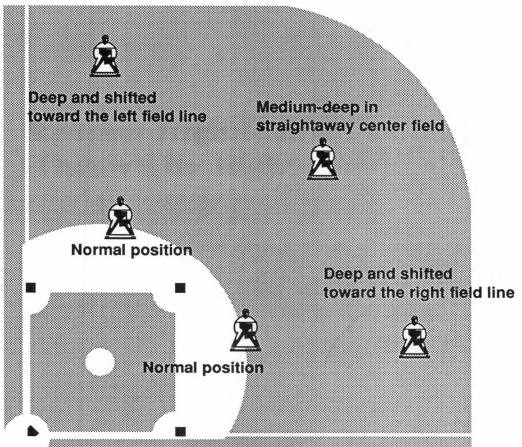

Deep and shifted toward the left field line

Medium-deep in straightaway center field

Normal position

Deep and shifted toward the right field line

Normal position

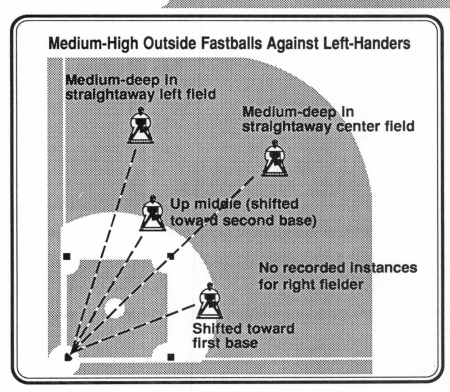

Medium-High Outside Fastballs Against Left-Handers

Medium-deep in straightaway left field

Medium-deep in straightaway center field

Up middle (shifted toward second base)

No recorded instances for right fielder

Shifted toward first base

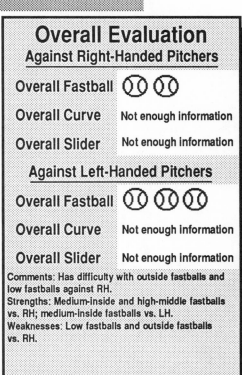

Overall Evaluation
Against Right-Handed Pitchers

Overall Fastball	⚾⚾
Overall Curve	Not enough information
Overall Slider	Not enough information

Against Left-Handed Pitchers

Overall Fastball	⚾⚾⚾
Overall Curve	Not enough information
Overall Slider	Not enough information

Comments: Has difficulty with outside fastballs and low fastballs against RH.
Strengths: Medium-inside and high-middle fastballs vs. RH; medium-inside fastballs vs. LH.
Weaknesses: Low fastballs and outside fastballs vs. RH.

Bradley, Scott
Brantley, Mickey
Coles, Darnell
Cotto, Henry
Davis, Alvin
Kingery, Mike
Leonard, Jeff
O'Brien, Pete
Presley, Jim
Quinones, Rey
Reynolds, Harold
Valle, Dave

Seattle Mariners
BARS System
Hitting Analysis

Scott Bradley (Left Handed) — *Seattle Mariners*

Scott Bradley Against Right-Handed Pitchers
Overall BARS Batting Average .288

Fastball Average .301

	Outside	Middle	Inside
High	26/ 307 /8	15/ 466 /7	9/ 111 /1
Med	67/ 298 /20	13/ 307 /4	11/ 363 /4
Low	12/ 250 /3	14/ 285 /4	9/ 222 /2

Curve Average .259

	Outside	Middle	Inside
High	1/ 0 /0	4/ 250 /1	1/ 1000 /1
Med	9/ 222 /2	1/ 0 /0	2/ 500 /1
Low	2/ 0 /0	4/ 250 /1	3/ 333 /1

Slider Average .200

	Outside	Middle	Inside
High	0/ 0 /0	5/ 200 /1	2/ 0 /0
Med	1/ 0 /0	0/ 0 /0	2/ 0 /0
Low	0/ 0 /0	3/ 333 /1	2/ 500 /1

Scott Bradley Against Left-Handed Pitchers
Overall BARS Batting Average .268

Fastball Average .291

	Outside	Middle	Inside
High	1/ 0 /0	1/ 0 /0	2/ 0 /0
Med	8/ 500 /4	2/ 0 /0	3/ 333 /1
Low	2/ 500 /1	5/ 200 /1	0/ 0 /0

Curve Average .363

	Outside	Middle	Inside
High	0/ 0 /0	1/ 1000 /1	0/ 0 /0
Med	0/ 0 /0	0/ 0 /0	3/ 1000 /3
Low	2/ 0 /0	2/ 0 /0	3/ 0 /0

Slider Average .000

	Outside	Middle	Inside
High	0/ 0 /0	0/ 0 /0	0/ 0 /0
Med	1/ 0 /0	0/ 0 /0	0/ 0 /0
Low	3/ 0 /0	1/ 0 /0	1/ 0 /0

Left-handed hitting Scott Bradley has a fine .301 overall fastball average against right-handed pitchers. The BARS System has many more instances for Bradley against right-handers so his charts against left-handers are not discussed here.

Against right-handers, Bradley hits medium-high outside fastballs pretty well (.298 overall). His Ahead and Behind charts on the opposite page show that he hits this pitch better when ahead in the count. He hits the ball deep when he is ahead.

MEDIUM-HIGH OUTSIDE FASTBALLS (WHEN AHEAD IN THE COUNT)

BATTING AVERAGE .272
Play

Left	Deep and shifted toward the left field line
Center	Deep in straightaway center field
Right	Deep in straightaway right field
Short	Normal position
Second	Normal position

MEDIUM-HIGH OUTSIDE FASTBALLS (WHEN BEHIND IN THE COUNT)

BATTING AVERAGE .187
Play

Left	Deep and shifted toward the left field line
Center	Medium-deep in straightaway center field

Right	Medium-deep in straightaway right field
Short	Normal position
Second	Normal position

Notice that right-handers throw Bradley many more outside than inside fastballs. It is vital that fielders be properly positioned when he is thrown outside fastballs because he hits these pitches well overall.

He hits high-outside fastballs deep and straightaway to the outfield. But the infielders need to play him to pull this pitch.

HIGH-OUTSIDE FASTBALLS

BATTING AVERAGE .307
Play

Left	Deep in straightaway left field
Center	Deep in straightaway center field
Right	Deep in straightaway right field
Short	Up middle (shifted toward second base)
Second	Shifted toward first base

He hits high-over-the-middle fastballs very well (.466).

HIGH-OVER-THE-MIDDLE FASTBALLS

BATTING AVERAGE .466
Play

Left	Deep in straightaway left field

Center	Deep in straightaway center field
Right	Deep in straightaway right field
Short	Normal position
Second	Shifted toward first base

His .285 against low-over-the-middle fastballs is adequate. He tends to hit this pitch to left center and right center. Note that the shortstop and second baseman need to be positioned shifted toward third and first, respectively.

LOW-OVER-THE-MIDDLE FASTBALLS

BATTING AVERAGE .285
Play

Left	Deep in straightaway left field
Center	Deep and shifted toward left field
Right	Deep and shifted toward center field
Short	Shifted toward third base
Second	Shifted toward first base

Bradley hits medium-over-the-middle fastballs at a .307 clip. He pulls this pitch to the right side of the infield, but more to his opposite field when hitting to the outfield.

MEDIUM-OVER-THE-MIDDLE FASTBALLS

BATTING AVERAGE .307
Play

Left	Deep and shifted toward the left field line
Center	Deep and shifted toward left field
Right	Deep and shifted toward center field
Short	Up middle (shifted toward second base)
Second	Shifted toward first base

He hits low-outside fastballs straightaway to the outfield. The infielders, however, need to adjust individually for this pitch.

LOW-OUTSIDE FASTBALLS

BATTING AVERAGE .250
Play

Left	Deep in straightaway left field
Center	Deep in straightaway center field
Right	Deep in straightaway right field
Short	Shifted toward third base
Second	Shifted toward first base

Bradley hits .363 against medium-inside fastballs against right-handers. He tends to hit this pitch to right field and to the right side of the infield.

Bradley Against Curves

Bradley hits .222 against medium-high outside curves thrown by right-handed pitchers. His fielding strategy shows no instances in which he hit this pitch out of the infield.

MEDIUM-HIGH OUTSIDE CURVEBALLS

BATTING AVERAGE .222
Play

Left	*No instances recorded*
Center	*No instances recorded*
Right	*No instances recorded*
Short	*No instances recorded*
Second	Normal position

Ahead And Behind In The Count Vs. RH

Ahead

	Fastball Average .354			Curve Average .400		
	Outside	Middle	Inside	Outside	Middle	Inside
High	13/461 /6	7/571 /4	5/200 /1	0/0 /0	2/500 /1	1/1000 /1
Med	33/272 /9	9/444 /4	6/500 /3	2/500 /1	1/0 /0	2/500 /1
Low	5/200 /1	8/375 /3	7/285 /2	1/0 /0	1/0 /0	0/0 /0

Behind

	Fastball Average .185			Curve Average .400		
	Outside	Middle	Inside	Outside	Middle	Inside
High	3/0 /0	1/1000 /1	1/0 /0	0/0 /0	1/0 /0	0/0 /0
Med	16/187 /3	2/0 /0	2/0 /0	1/1000 /1	0/0 /0	0/0 /0
Low	1/1000 /1	0/0 /0	1/0 /0	0/0 /0	2/500 /1	1/0 /0

Overall Evaluation
Against Right-Handed Pitchers

Overall Fastball

Overall Curve

Overall Slider

Against Left-Handed Pitchers

Overall Fastball

Overall Curve   Not enough information

Overall Slider   Not enough information

Comments: Hits waist-high fastballs well vs. RH.
Strengths: All fastballs vs. RH except high-inside, low-inside and low-outside; medium-outside fastballs vs. LH.
Weaknesses: Fastballs as noted above vs. RH, medium-outside curves vs. RH.

Mickey Brantley (Right Handed)　　*Seattle Mariners*

Mickey Brantley Against Right-Handed Pitchers
Overall BARS Batting Average .270

Fastball Average .322

	Inside	Middle	Outside
High	7 / 428 / 3	5 / 400 / 2	8 / 250 / 2
Med	9 / 444 / 4	4 / 250 / 1	46 / 304 / 14
Low	3 / 0 / 0	8 / 500 / 4	6 / 166 / 1

Curve Average .142

	Inside	Middle	Outside
High	1 / 0 / 0	1 / 0 / 0	0 / 0 / 0
Med	0 / 0 / 0	0 / 0 / 0	14 / 214 / 3
Low	0 / 0 / 0	4 / 250 / 1	8 / 0 / 0

Slider Average .200

	Inside	Middle	Outside
High	0 / 0 / 0	0 / 0 / 0	0 / 0 / 0
Med	0 / 0 / 0	1 / 0 / 0	8 / 250 / 2
Low	0 / 0 / 0	2 / 0 / 0	4 / 250 / 1

Mickey Brantley Against Left-Handed Pitchers
Overall BARS Batting Average .275

Fastball Average .255

	Inside	Middle	Outside
High	2 / 0 / 0	2 / 0 / 0	6 / 333 / 2
Med	2 / 500 / 1	2 / 1000 / 2	19 / 210 / 4
Low	2 / 0 / 0	3 / 0 / 0	5 / 400 / 2

Curve Average .285

	Inside	Middle	Outside
High	0 / 0 / 0	0 / 0 / 0	0 / 0 / 0
Med	0 / 0 / 0	0 / 0 / 0	3 / 333 / 1
Low	0 / 0 / 0	1 / 1000 / 1	3 / 0 / 0

Slider Average .375

	Inside	Middle	Outside
High	1 / 0 / 0	1 / 1000 / 1	0 / 0 / 0
Med	2 / 500 / 1	1 / 0 / 0	1 / 1000 / 1
Low	0 / 0 / 0	1 / 0 / 0	1 / 0 / 0

Right-handed hitting Mickey Brantley has a strong .322 overall fastball average against right-handed pitchers. His .255 overall fastball average against left-handed pitchers is not as strong.

Notice in his Ahead and Behind charts on the opposite page that he hits medium-high outside fastballs better when behind in the count than when ahead (.533 when behind, .294 when ahead). When behind, he scatters the ball to all fields. When ahead, he pulls it to left. This indicates that fielders are playing him to pull and are properly positioned when he does. By shifting as suggested by the BARS System on a pitch-by-pitch basis, fielders could prevent most of his base hits.

MEDIUM-HIGH OUTSIDE FASTBALLS
(WHEN BEHIND IN THE COUNT)

BATTING AVERAGE .533
Play

Left	Deep and shifted toward the left field line
Center	Deep and shifted toward right field
Right	Medium-deep and shifted toward the right line
Short	Up middle (shifted toward second base)
Second	Shifted toward first base

MEDIUM-HIGH OUTSIDE FASTBALLS
(WHEN AHEAD IN THE COUNT)

BATTING AVERAGE .294
Play

Left	Deep and shifted toward the left field line
Center	Deep and shifted toward left field
Right	Deep in straightaway right field
Short	Normal position
Second	Shifted toward first base

He has fewer instances in his other locations, but his fielding strategy for medium-high inside fastballs indicates that he pulls this pitch. There are no recorded instances of hit balls to center or right fields.

MEDIUM-HIGH INSIDE FASTBALLS

BATTING AVERAGE .444
Play

Left	Medium-deep and shifted toward the left line
Center	*No instances recorded*
Right	*No instances recorded*
Short	Shifted toward third base
Second	Shifted toward first base

He scatters low-over-the-middle fastballs against right-handers (.500).

LOW-OVER-THE-MIDDLE FASTBALLS

BATTING AVERAGE .500
Play

Left	Medium-deep and shifted toward the left line
Center	Deep and shifted toward left field
Right	Deep and shifted toward the right field line
Short	Up middle (shifted toward second base)
Second	*No instances recorded*

Brantley Against Curves And Sliders

Brantley hits a weak .214 against medium-high outside curves thrown by right-handed pitchers. He hits this pitch mostly to deep straightaway left field.

MEDIUM-HIGH OUTSIDE CURVEBALLS

BATTING AVERAGE .214
Play
Left Deep in straightaway left field
Center Deep in straightaway center field
Right *No instances recorded*
Short Up middle (shifted toward second base)
Second *No instances recorded*

Brantley's 0-for-8 against low-outside curves indicates a weakness. He hits this pitch medium-deep to left center and straightaway right.

LOW-OUTSIDE CURVEBALLS

BATTING AVERAGE .000 (0 for 8)
Play
Left *No instances recorded*
Center Medium-deep and shifted toward left field
Right Medium-deep in straightaway right field
Short Up middle (shifted toward second base)
Second *No instances recorded*

His .250 average against medium-high outside sliders is adequate.

Brantley Against Left-Handed Pitchers

Brantley hits only .255 overall against fastballs thrown by left-handed pitchers. He hits medium-high outside fastballs better when ahead in the count than when behind.

MEDIUM-HIGH OUTSIDE FASTBALLS (WHEN AHEAD IN THE COUNT)

BATTING AVERAGE .300
Play
Left Deep in straightaway left field
Center *No instances recorded*
Right Deep and shifted toward the right field line
Short Up middle (shifted toward second base)
Second *No instances recorded*

MEDIUM-HIGH OUTSIDE FASTBALLS (WHEN BEHIND IN THE COUNT)

BATTING AVERAGE .200
Play
Left Deep in straightaway left field
Center *No instances recorded*
Right Medium-deep in straightaway right field
Short *No instances recorded*
Second Normal position

Ahead And Behind In The Count Vs. RH

Ahead

Fastball Average .307

	Inside	Middle	Outside
High	4/250 /1	2/500 /1	3/666 /2
Med	3/333 /1	3/0 /0	17/294 /5
Low	2/0 /0	5/400 /2	0/0 /0

Curve Average .000

	Inside	Middle	Outside
High	1/0 /0	0/0 /0	0/0 /0
Med	0/0 /0	0/0 /0	2/0 /0
Low	0/0 /0	2/0 /0	1/0 /0

Behind

Fastball Average .444

	Inside	Middle	Outside
High	2/500 /1	1/1000 /1	3/0 /0
Med	4/500 /2	0/0 /0	15/533 /8
Low	0/0 /0	0/0 /0	2/0 /0

Curve Average .428

	Inside	Middle	Outside
High	0/0 /0	0/0 /0	0/0 /0
Med	0/0 /0	0/0 /0	5/400 /2
Low	0/0 /0	1/1000 /1	1/0 /0

Overall Evaluation

Against Right-Handed Pitchers

Overall Fastball   ⚾ ⚾⚾ ⚾⚾
Overall Curve   ⚾
Overall Slider   ⚾⚾

Against Left-Handed Pitchers

Overall Fastball   ⚾⚾
Overall Curve   Not enough information
Overall Slider   Not enough information

Comments: Hits fastballs very well overall vs. RH.
Strengths: High-inside, medium-inside, low-middle and medium-outside fastballs vs. RH.
Weaknesses: Low-outside fastballs, outside curves vs. RH; medium-outside fastballs vs. LH.

Darnell Coles (Right Handed)

Darnell Coles Against Right-Handed Pitchers
Overall BARS Batting Average .266

Fastball Average .302

	Inside	Middle	Outside
High	8/ 125/1	13/ 307/4	12/ 333/4
Med	38/ 421/16	15/ 200/3	74/ 297/22
Low	21/ 380/8	21/ 190/4	13/ 230/3

Curve Average .162

	Inside	Middle	Outside
High	0/ 0/0	2/ 0/0	3/ 333/1
Med	4/ 250/1	3/ 666/2	10/ 200/2
Low	4/ 0/0	3/ 0/0	8/ 0/0

Slider Average .181

	Inside	Middle	Outside
High	1/ 0/0	3/ 0/0	0/ 0/0
Med	3/ 333/1	1/ 0/0	11/ 363/4
Low	2/ 500/1	5/ 200/1	18/ 55/1

Darnell Coles Against Left-Handed Pitchers
Overall BARS Batting Average .266

Fastball Average .301

	Inside	Middle	Outside
High	4/ 0/0	11/ 363/4	11/ 272/3
Med	4/ 250/1	4/ 250/1	27/ 333/9
Low	6/ 166/1	11/ 454/5	15/ 266/4

Curve Average .214

	Inside	Middle	Outside
High	0/ 0/0	0/ 0/0	2/ 0/0
Med	0/ 0/0	1/ 1000/1	11/ 181/2
Low	3/ 0/0	9/ 333/3	2/ 0/0

Slider Average .206

	Inside	Middle	Outside
High	2/ 0/0	2/ 500/1	0/ 0/0
Med	9/ 111/1	1/ 1000/1	2/ 0/0
Low	5/ 200/1	4/ 500/2	4/ 0/0

Right-handed hitting Darnell Coles hits fastballs for about the same average overall against right-handed and left-handed pitchers (.302 vs. right-handers, .301 vs. left-handers).

Against right-handers, notice that Coles hits an excellent .421 against medium-high inside fastballs. This, along with his strong low-inside fastball location, forms a strong sector. Notice how differently he hits pitches to these locations even though they are adjacent in the strike zone.

MEDIUM-HIGH INSIDE FASTBALLS

BATTING AVERAGE .421

Play

Left	Deep in straightaway left field
Center	Deep and shifted toward left field
Right	Deep and shifted toward the right field line
Short	Shifted toward third base
Second	Shifted toward first base

LOW-INSIDE FASTBALLS

BATTING AVERAGE .380

Play

Left	Deep and shifted toward the left field line
Center	Deep and shifted toward left field
Right	Deep and shifted toward center field
Short	Normal position
Second	*No instances recorded*

He tends to pull medium-high outside fastballs (.297) down the left line and into left center.

MEDIUM-HIGH OUTSIDE FASTBALLS

BATTING AVERAGE .297

Play

Left	Deep and shifted toward the left field line
Center	Deep and shifted toward left field
Right	Deep in straightaway right field
Short	Normal position
Second	Shifted toward first base

He hits low-over-the-middle fastballs for a weak .190 average.

LOW-OVER-THE-MIDDLE FASTBALLS

BATTING AVERAGE .190

Play

Left	Medium-deep and shifted toward center field
Center	Deep in straightaway center field
Right	Deep and shifted toward center field
Short	Normal position
Second	*No instances recorded*

He hits high-outside fastballs deep to left and center fields.

HIGH-OUTSIDE FASTBALLS

BATTING AVERAGE .333

Play

Left	Deep and shifted toward center field
Center	Deep in straightaway center field
Right	*No instances recorded*
Short	Shifted toward third base
Second	*No instances recorded*

Coles Against Curves And Sliders

Coles has trouble with low curves and with low-outside sliders. His .200 average against medium-high outside curves is also low, but his .363 against medium-high outside sliders is excellent.

MEDIUM-HIGH OUTSIDE SLIDERS

BATTING AVERAGE .363

Play

Left	Medium-deep in straightaway left field
Center	Deep in straightaway center field
Right	Deep and shifted toward the right field line
Short	Normal position
Second	Shifted toward first base

His 1-for-18 against low-outside sliders indicates a weakness. He hits this pitch medium-deep to right field and to the right side of the infield. Most of his hits balls in this location are probably easy outs.

LOW-OUTSIDE SLIDERS

BATTING AVERAGE .055

Play

Left	*No instances recorded*
Center	*No instances recorded*
Right	Medium-deep in straightaway right field
Short	Up middle (shifted toward second base)
Second	Shifted toward first base

Coles Against Left-Handed Pitchers

Coles hits a fine .333 against medium-high outside fastballs thrown by left-handed pitchers. He hits this pitch better when ahead than when behind in the count. He hits this pitch with more authority when ahead.

MEDIUM-HIGH OUTSIDE FASTBALLS (THROWN BY LEFT-HANDED PITCHERS WHEN COLES IS AHEAD IN THE COUNT)

BATTING AVERAGE .466

Play

Left	Deep in straightaway left field
Center	Deep and shifted toward right field
Right	Deep and shifted toward the right field line
Short	Normal position
Second	*No instances recorded*

MEDIUM-HIGH OUTSIDE FASTBALLS (THROWN BY LEFT-HANDED PITCHERS WHEN COLES IS BEHIND IN THE COUNT)

BATTING AVERAGE .285

Play

Left	Short and shifted toward the left field line
Center	Deep and shifted toward left field
Right	Deep and shifted toward the right field line
Short	Shifted toward third base
Second	*No instances recorded*

His .454 average against low-over-the-middle fastballs and .363 against high-over-the-middle fastballs are excellent. He pulls high-over-the-middle fastballs deep to the outfield. He pulls low-over-the-middle fastballs deep down the left line and medium-deep into the left-center gap.

Ahead And Behind In The Count Vs. RH

Ahead

Fastball Average .361

	Inside	Middle	Outside
High	333 3/1	400 5/2	666 3/2
Med	411 17/7	250 8/2	361 36/13
Low	428 7/3	285 14/4	0 1/0

Curve Average .333

	Inside	Middle	Outside
High	0 0/0	0 0/0	1000 1/1
Med	0 2/0	1000 1/1	0 0/0
Low	0 2/0	0 0/0	0 0/0

Behind

Fastball Average .282

	Inside	Middle	Outside
High	0 4/0	500 2/1	333 3/1
Med	333 9/3	0 2/0	300 20/6
Low	333 3/1	0 1/0	500 2/1

Curve Average .166

	Inside	Middle	Outside
High	0 0/0	0 1/0	0 2/0
Med	500 2/1	0 1/0	333 3/1
Low	0 1/0	0 0/0	0 2/0

Overall Evaluation

Against Right-Handed Pitchers

Overall Fastball	⚾⚾⚾
Overall Curve	⚾
Overall Slider	⚾

Against Left-Handed Pitchers

Overall Fastball	⚾⚾⚾
Overall Curve	⚾
Overall Slider	⚾

Comments: Strong down and in vs. RH.
Strengths: Medium-inside, low-inside, high-middle and high-outside fastballs, medium-outside sliders vs. RH; medium-outside, low-middle and high-middle fastballs vs. LH.
Weaknesses: Low-outside and low-middle fastballs, low-outside and medium-outside curves, low-outside sliders vs. RH; Inside fastballs, outside curves, inside sliders vs. LH.

Henry Cotto Against Right-Handed Pitchers
Overall BARS Batting Average .300

Fastball Average .382

	Inside	Middle	Outside
High	5 / 200 / 1	9 / 222 / 2	9 / 111 / 1
Med	11 / 727 / 8	3 / 333 / 1	60 / 383 / 23
Low	5 / 400 / 2	14 / 571 / 8	7 / 142 / 1

Curve Average .033

	Inside	Middle	Outside
High	0 / 0 / 0	2 / 500 / 1	3 / 0 / 0
Med	2 / 0 / 0	0 / 0 / 0	8 / 0 / 0
Low	2 / 0 / 0	2 / 0 / 0	11 / 0 / 0

Slider Average .176

	Inside	Middle	Outside
High	0 / 0 / 0	1 / 1000 / 1	0 / 0 / 0
Med	0 / 0 / 0	0 / 0 / 0	9 / 111 / 1
Low	0 / 0 / 0	1 / 0 / 0	6 / 166 / 1

Henry Cotto Against Left-Handed Pitchers
Overall BARS Batting Average .297

Fastball Average .302

	Inside	Middle	Outside
High	6 / 166 / 1	9 / 555 / 5	6 / 333 / 2
Med	9 / 444 / 4	8 / 375 / 3	41 / 243 / 10
Low	4 / 0 / 0	19 / 421 / 8	7 / 0 / 0

Curve Average .250

	Inside	Middle	Outside
High	0 / 0 / 0	0 / 0 / 0	0 / 0 / 0
Med	1 / 0 / 0	0 / 0 / 0	4 / 750 / 3
Low	4 / 0 / 0	2 / 0 / 0	1 / 0 / 0

Slider Average .300

	Inside	Middle	Outside
High	0 / 0 / 0	0 / 0 / 0	1 / 1000 / 1
Med	1 / 1000 / 1	1 / 1000 / 1	0 / 0 / 0
Low	3 / 0 / 0	3 / 0 / 0	1 / 0 / 0

Right-handed hitting Henry Cotto has an excellent overall fastball average against right-handed pitchers (.382). He has some very weak fastball locations, but he also has some very strong locations.

His .383 against medium-high outside fastballs thrown by right-handers is top rate. His Ahead and Behind charts on the following page show that he hits this pitch at a .583 rate when behind in the count.

MEDIUM-HIGH OUTSIDE FASTBALLS (WHEN BEHIND IN THE COUNT)

BATTING AVERAGE .583
Play
Left Deep and shifted toward center field
Center Medium-deep in straightaway center field
Right Deep and shifted toward center field
Short Normal position
Second *No instances recorded*

MEDIUM-HIGH OUTSIDE FASTBALLS (WHEN AHEAD IN THE COUNT)

BATTING AVERAGE .344
Play
Left Deep and shifted toward the left field line
Center Deep and shifted toward right field
Right Short and shifted toward the right field line
Short Normal position
Second Shifted toward first base

His .571 overall against low-over-the-middle fastballs is exceptional.

LOW-OVER-THE-MIDDLE FASTBALLS

BATTING AVERAGE .571
Play
Left Deep and shifted toward the left field line
Center Deep in straightaway center field
Right *No instances recorded*
Short Shifted toward third base
Second Shifted toward first base

There are fewer instances in Cotto's medium-high inside fastball location, but his .727 average sounds more like an airplane than a batting average.

MEDIUM-HIGH INSIDE FASTBALLS

BATTING AVERAGE .727
Play
Left Medium-deep and shifted toward center field
Center Medium-deep in straightaway center field
Right Short in straightaway right field
Short Up middle (shifted toward second base)
Second Shifted toward first base

Cotto Against Curves and Sliders

Cotto has a severe weakness against breaking pitches thrown by right-handed pitchers. His 0-for-8 against medium-high outside curves and 0-for-11 against low-outside curves show this weakness. He has trouble hitting low-outside curves out of the infield.

LOW-OUTSIDE CURVEBALLS

BATTING AVERAGE .000 (0 for 11)
Play
Left   *No instances recorded*
Center   *No instances recorded*
Right   *No instances recorded*
Short   Normal position
Second   *No instances recorded*

Cotto Against Left-Handed Pitchers

Cotto hits only .243 against medium-high outside fastballs thrown by left-handed pitchers. He hits this pitch better when behind in the count (.285 when behind, .263 when ahead).

MEDIUM-HIGH OUTSIDE FASTBALLS (THROWN BY LEFT-HANDED PITCHERS WHEN COTTO IS BEHIND IN THE COUNT)

BATTING AVERAGE .285
Play
Left   Medium-deep in straightaway left field
Center   Deep and shifted toward right field
Right   Short in straightaway right field
Short   Shifted toward third base
Second   *No instances recorded*

MEDIUM-HIGH OUTSIDE FASTBALLS (THROWN BY LEFT-HANDED PITCHERS WHEN COTTO IS AHEAD IN THE COUNT)

BATTING AVERAGE .263
Play
Left   Deep and shifted toward center field
Center   Medium-deep in straightaway center field
Right   Medium-deep in straightaway right field
Short   Normal position
Second   *No instances recorded*

Cotto's .421 against low-over-the-middle fastballs is excellent. If fielders played him medium-deep for this pitch, as indicated by the following BARS fielding strategy, they would be able to take away most of his base hits resulting from this location.

LOW-OVER-THE-MIDDLE FASTBALLS (THROWN BY LEFT-HANDED PITCHERS)

BATTING AVERAGE .421
Play
Left   Medium-deep in straightaway left field
Center   Medium-deep in straightaway center field
Right   Medium-deep and shifted toward the right line
Short   Normal position
Second   Shifted toward first base

Cotto's .444 average against medium-high inside fastballs thrown by lefties is also excellent.

MEDIUM-HIGH INSIDE FASTBALLS (THROWN BY LEFT-HANDED PITCHERS)

BATTING AVERAGE .444
Play
Left   Deep and shifted toward the left field line
Center   Deep and shifted toward left field
Right   *No instances recorded*
Short   Normal position
Second   Normal position

Ahead And Behind In The Count Vs. RH

Ahead

	Fastball Average .410			Curve Average .000		
	Inside	Middle	Outside	Inside	Middle	Outside
High	1/0 / 0	4/500 / 2	4/250 / 1	0/0 / 0	0/0 / 0	1/0 / 0
Med	6/833 / 5	3/333 / 1	29/344 / 10	0/0 / 0	0/0 / 0	0/0 / 0
Low	1/0 / 0	7/571 / 4	1/0 / 0	0/0 / 0	0/0 / 0	1/0 / 0

Behind

	Fastball Average .500			Curve Average .000		
	Inside	Middle	Outside	Inside	Middle	Outside
High	1/0 / 0	4/0 / 0	0/0 / 0	0/0 / 0	1/0 / 0	2/0 / 0
Med	2/500 / 1	0/0 / 0	12/583 / 7	0/0 / 0	0/0 / 0	5/0 / 0
Low	3/666 / 2	3/1000 / 3	1/0 / 0	0/0 / 0	1/0 / 0	0/0 / 0

Overall Evaluation

Against Right-Handed Pitchers

Overall Fastball ⚾ ⚾ ⚾ ⚾
Overall Curve   ⚾
Overall Slider   ⚾

Against Left-Handed Pitchers

Overall Fastball ⚾ ⚾ ⚾
Overall Curve   ⚾ ⚾
Overall Slider   Not enough information

Comments: Weak against low-outside pitches. Problems with curves vs. RH.
Strengths: Medium-outside, low-middle and medium-inside fastballs vs. RH; over-the-middle fastballs, medium-inside fastballs, medium-outside curves vs. LH.
Weaknesses: High fastballs, low-outside fastballs, all curves and sliders vs. RH; medium-outside and low-outside fastballs vs. LH.

Alvin Davis (Left Handed) — *Seattle Mariners*

Alvin Davis Against Right-Handed Pitchers
Overall BARS Batting Average .362

Fastball Average .377

	Outside	Middle	Inside
High	16 / 375 / 6	22 / 363 / 8	14 / 642 / 9
Med	98 / 377 / 37	31 / 387 / 12	42 / 238 / 10
Low	12 / 333 / 4	54 / 462 / 25	29 / 310 / 9

Curve Average .166

	Outside	Middle	Inside
High	1 / 0 / 0	3 / 333 / 1	1 / 0 / 0
Med	10 / 0 / 0	7 / 571 / 4	5 / 200 / 1
Low	5 / 0 / 0	4 / 0 / 0	6 / 166 / 1

Slider Average .500

	Outside	Middle	Inside
High	1 / 0 / 0	3 / 1000 / 3	2 / 1000 / 2
Med	2 / 500 / 1	2 / 1000 / 2	7 / 142 / 1
Low	2 / 1000 / 2	2 / 500 / 1	5 / 200 / 1

Alvin Davis Against Left-Handed Pitchers
Overall BARS Batting Average .238

Fastball Average .259

	Outside	Middle	Inside
High	8 / 0 / 0	14 / 285 / 4	16 / 312 / 5
Med	35 / 257 / 9	7 / 428 / 3	24 / 250 / 6
Low	9 / 222 / 2	12 / 250 / 3	6 / 333 / 2

Curve Average .200

	Outside	Middle	Inside
High	1 / 1000 / 1	3 / 0 / 0	2 / 0 / 0
Med	4 / 0 / 0	2 / 0 / 0	7 / 571 / 4
Low	8 / 0 / 0	3 / 666 / 2	5 / 0 / 0

Slider Average .193

	Outside	Middle	Inside
High	0 / 0 / 0	0 / 0 / 0	0 / 0 / 0
Med	7 / 571 / 4	0 / 0 / 0	2 / 0 / 0
Low	17 / 117 / 2	5 / 0 / 0	0 / 0 / 0

Bolstered by eight strong fastball locations, left-handed hitter Alvin Davis has an excellent overall fastball average of .377 against right-handed pitchers. His .259 overall fastball average against left-handed pitchers is weak.

Starting against right-handers, his .377 average against medium-high outside fastballs is excellent. He hits this pitch for a higher average when ahead in the count. When ahead he hits it deep and straightaway to all fields.

MEDIUM-HIGH OUTSIDE FASTBALLS (WHEN AHEAD IN THE COUNT)

BATTING AVERAGE .386

Play

Left	Deep in straightaway left field
Center	Deep in straightaway center field
Right	Deep in straightaway right field
Short	Up middle (shifted toward second base)
Second	Shifted toward first base

MEDIUM-HIGH OUTSIDE FASTBALLS (WHEN BEHIND IN THE COUNT)

BATTING AVERAGE .318

Play

Left	Deep and shifted toward center field
Center	Medium-deep and shifted toward right field
Right	Medium-deep in straightaway right field

Short	Up middle (shifted toward second base)
Second	Shifted toward first base

He hits low-over-the-middle fastballs (.462) deep and straightaway to all fields.

LOW-OVER-THE-MIDDLE FASTBALLS

BATTING AVERAGE .462

Play

Left	Deep in straightaway left field
Center	Deep in straightaway center field
Right	Deep in straightaway right field
Short	Normal position
Second	Shifted toward first base

He hits an excellent .642 against high-inside fastballs, going deep to his opposite field (left field).

HIGH-INSIDE FASTBALLS

BATTING AVERAGE .642

Play

Left	Deep and shifted toward the left field line
Center	Deep and shifted toward left field
Right	Deep and shifted toward center field
Short	Normal position
Second	Shifted toward first base

His .363 against high-over-the-middle fastballs is also top rate.

HIGH-OVER-THE-MIDDLE FASTBALLS

BATTING AVERAGE .363
Play
Left	Medium-deep in straightaway left field
Center	Deep in straightaway center field
Right	Deep in straightaway right field
Short	Up middle (shifted toward second base)
Second	Normal position

He hits only .238 against medium-high inside fastballs against right-handers.

MEDIUM-HIGH INSIDE FASTBALLS

BATTING AVERAGE .238
Play
Left	Deep in straightaway left field
Center	Deep and shifted toward left field
Right	Deep in straightaway right field
Short	Normal position
Second	Shifted toward first base

It's hard to understand why right-handed pitchers throw Davis so few curves and sliders considering his outstanding fastball strength. He is weak against all outside and low curves.

Davis Against Left-Handed Pitchers

Davis' fastball average against left-handed pitchers is much lower than against right-handed pitchers. He has trouble against outside fastballs. His .257 medium-high outside and his .250 medium-high inside fastball averages against left-handers are both poor.

MEDIUM-HIGH OUTSIDE FASTBALLS
(THROWN BY LEFT-HANDED PITCHERS)

BATTING AVERAGE .257
Play
Left	Deep and shifted toward the left field line
Center	Medium-deep in straightaway center field
Right	Deep and shifted toward center field
Short	Up middle (shifted toward second base)
Second	Normal position

MEDIUM-HIGH INSIDE FASTBALLS
(THROWN BY LEFT-HANDED PITCHERS)

BATTING AVERAGE .250
Play
Left	Deep in straightaway left field
Center	Deep and shifted toward left field
Right	Deep in straightaway right field
Short	Shifted toward third base
Second	Normal position

His .285 high-over-the-middle fastball average is pretty good.

HIGH-OVER-THE-MIDDLE FASTBALLS
(THROWN BY LEFT-HANDED PITCHERS)

BATTING AVERAGE .285
Play
Left	Deep and shifted toward the left field line
Center	Medium-deep in straightaway center field
Right	Deep and shifted toward center field
Short	*No instances recorded*
Second	*No instances recorded*

He has a weakness against outside curves thrown by left-handed pitchers. His low-outside slider average is also weak (.117), although he hits medium-high outside sliders excellently (.571).

Ahead And Behind In The Count Vs. RH

Ahead

Fastball Average .421
	Outside	Middle	Inside
High	7/ 428 /3	11/ 363 /4	7/ 714 /5
Med	44/ 386 /17	24/ 416 /10	21/ 238 /5
Low	6/ 500 /3	31/ 483 /15	15/ 533 /8

Curve Average .333
	Outside	Middle	Inside
High	0/ 0 /0	1/ 1000 /1	1/ 0 /0
Med	2/ 0 /0	3/ 666 /2	1/ 0 /0
Low	0/ 0 /0	1/ 0 /0	0/ 0 /0

Behind

Fastball Average .400
	Outside	Middle	Inside
High	3/ 666 /2	5/ 600 /3	2/ 500 /1
Med	22/ 318 /7	2/ 0 /0	6/ 500 /3
Low	3/ 333 /1	8/ 625 /5	4/ 0 /0

Curve Average .142
	Outside	Middle	Inside
High	1/ 0 /0	2/ 0 /0	0/ 0 /0
Med	2/ 0 /0	1/ 1000 /1	0/ 0 /0
Low	0/ 0 /0	1/ 0 /0	0/ 0 /0

Overall Evaluation

Against Right-Handed Pitchers

Overall Fastball	⚾ ⚾ ⚾ ⚾
Overall Curve	⚾
Overall Slider	⚾ ⚾ ⚾ ⚾

Against Left-Handed Pitchers

Overall Fastball	⚾
Overall Curve	⚾
Overall Slider	⚾

Comments: Excellent against fastballs vs. RH.
Strengths: All fastballs vs. RH except medium-inside, medium-middle curves vs. RH; high-inside and medium-middle fastballs, medium-inside curves and medium-outside sliders vs. LH.
Weaknesses: Medium-inside fastballs, all curves except medium-middle and high-middle, medium-inside and low-inside sliders vs. RH; low-outside fastballs, curves and sliders vs. LH.

Mike Kingery Against Right-Handed Pitchers
Overall BARS Batting Average .309

	Fastball Average .340			Curve Average .173			Slider Average .000		
	Outside	Middle	Inside	Outside	Middle	Inside	Outside	Middle	Inside
High	12/250 /3	16/375 /6	9/333 /3	3/0 /0	1/1000 /1	0/0 /0	0/0 /0	0/0 /0	1/0 /0
Med	59/322 /19	8/375 /3	20/500 /10	7/0 /0	3/666 /2	3/0 /0	1/0 /0	0/0 /0	0/0 /0
Low	11/272 /3	23/347 /8	21/285 /6	1/0 /0	3/333 /1	2/0 /0	2/0 /0	1/0 /0	3/0 /0

Left-handed hitter Mike Kingery has an excellent .340 overall fastball average against right-handed pitchers. His curve and slider averages are much lower. He hits so infrequently against left-handers it's hard to get information on him. For this reason his records against lefties are not included here.

He hits a solid .322 against medium-high outside fastballs thrown by right-handers. His Ahead and Behind charts on the opposite page show that he hits this pitch better when ahead in the count. Notice that the leftfielder, rightfielder, and shortstop need to shift to be correctly positioned for this pitch when Kingery is ahead and behind in the count.

MEDIUM-HIGH OUTSIDE FASTBALLS (WHEN AHEAD IN THE COUNT)

BATTING AVERAGE .323
Play
Left	Deep and shifted toward center field
Center	Deep in straightaway center field
Right	Deep and shifted toward center field
Short	Normal position
Second	Normal position

MEDIUM-HIGH OUTSIDE FASTBALLS (WHEN BEHIND IN THE COUNT)

BATTING AVERAGE .272
Play
Left	Medium-deep and shifted toward the left line
Center	Deep in straightaway center field
Right	Deep in straightaway right field
Short	Up middle (shifted toward second base)
Second	Normal position

He hits a blazing .500 against medium-high inside fastballs thrown by right-handers.

MEDIUM-HIGH INSIDE FASTBALLS

BATTING AVERAGE .500

Play
Left	Medium-deep and shifted toward the left field line
Center	Deep and shifted toward right field
Right	Medium-deep in straightaway right field
Short	Shifted toward third base
Second	Normal position

Kingery is excellent against all over-the-middle fastballs (.375, .375, and .347, high to low). He hits low-over-the-middle fastballs deep into the left-center gap and to the right side of the infield.

LOW-OVER-THE-MIDDLE FASTBALLS

BATTING AVERAGE .347
Play
Left	Deep and shifted toward center field
Center	Medium-deep in straightaway center field
Right	Deep in straightaway right field
Short	Up middle (shifted toward second base)
Second	Shifted toward first base

He hits high-over-the-middle fastballs medium-deep down the left line and deep into the right-center gap.

HIGH-OVER-THE-MIDDLE FASTBALLS

BATTING AVERAGE .375
Play
Left	Medium-deep and shifted toward the left field line
Center	Deep and shifted toward right field
Right	Deep in straightaway right field
Short	*No instances recorded*
Second	Normal position

Kingery has trouble with medium-high outside curves thrown by right-handed pitchers. Notice how few breaking balls he is thrown in comparison with fastballs. Since he hits fastballs excellently overall, right-handers should try mixing in more breaking pitches to him.

Medium-High Outside Fastballs Vs. RH

Dark Fielders — Ahead In The Count
Light Fielders — Behind In The Count

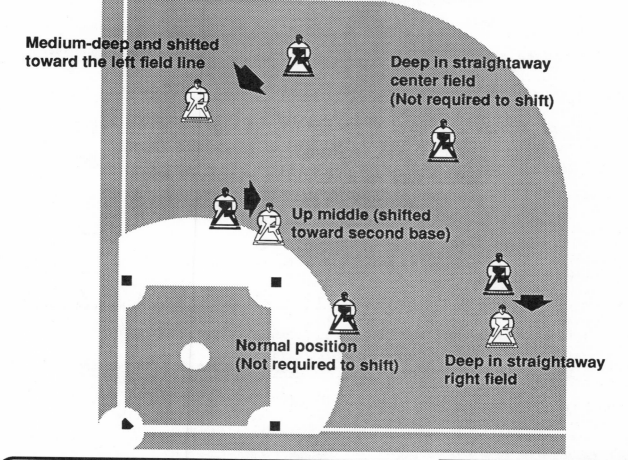

Medium-deep and shifted toward the left field line

Deep in straightaway center field (Not required to shift)

Up middle (shifted toward second base)

Normal position (Not required to shift)

Deep in straightaway right field

Ahead And Behind In The Count Vs. RH

Ahead

Fastball Average .361

	Outside	Middle	Inside
High	4/250 /1	4/250 /1	2/0 /0
Med	34/323 /11	3/666 /2	12/416 /5
Low	3/333 /1	10/400 /4	11/454 /5

Curve Average .500

	Outside	Middle	Inside
High	0/0 /0	0/0 /0	0/0 /0
Med	0/0 /0	1/1000 /1	0/0 /0
Low	0/0 /0	0/0 /0	1/0 /0

Behind

Fastball Average .405

	Outside	Middle	Inside
High	2/500 /1	4/750 /3	2/500 /1
Med	11/272 /3	1/0 /0	3/666 /2
Low	5/400 /2	5/400 /2	4/250 /1

Curve Average .125

	Outside	Middle	Inside
High	2/0 /0	1/1000 /1	0/0 /0
Med	3/0 /0	0/0 /0	2/0 /0
Low	0/0 /0	0/0 /0	0/0 /0

Overall Evaluation
Against Right-Handed Pitchers

Overall Fastball	
Overall Curve	
Overall Slider	Not enough information

Against Left-Handed Pitchers

Overall Fastball	Not enough information
Overall Curve	Not enough information
Overall Slider	Not enough information

Comments: Very strong against waist-high and over-the-middle fastballs vs. RH.

Strengths: Waist-high and over-the-middle fastballs vs. RH.

Weaknesses: High-outside fastballs, outside curves vs. RH.

Jeff Leonard (Right Handed) — *Seattle Mariners*

Jeff Leonard Against Right-Handed Pitchers
Overall BARS Batting Average .252

Fastball Average .285

	Inside	Middle	Outside
High	26/ 269 /7	16/ 125 /2	15/ 133 /2
Med	44/ 272 /12	19/ 315 /6	72/ 319 /23
Low	27/ 370 /10	60/ 350 /21	36/ 194 /7

Curve Average .259

	Inside	Middle	Outside
High	1/ 0 /0	4/ 500 /2	4/ 250 /1
Med	5/ 600 /3	6/ 333 /2	33/ 333 /11
Low	1/ 0 /0	15/ 200 /3	35/ 142 /5

Slider Average .161

	Inside	Middle	Outside
High	1/ 0 /0	4/ 500 /2	2/ 0 /0
Med	2/ 500 /1	1/ 0 /0	20/ 150 /3
Low	2/ 0 /0	11/ 181 /2	25/ 120 /3

Jeff Leonard Against Left-Handed Pitchers
Overall BARS Batting Average .303

Fastball Average .298

	Inside	Middle	Outside
High	9/ 444 /4	5/ 400 /2	3/ 0 /0
Med	11/ 90 /1	5/ 600 /3	29/ 344 /10
Low	9/ 111 /1	16/ 375 /6	10/ 200 /2

Curve Average .454

	Inside	Middle	Outside
High	0/ 0 /0	1/ 0 /0	0/ 0 /0
Med	2/ 1000 /2	3/ 0 /0	5/ 400 /2
Low	2/ 1000 /2	7/ 428 /3	2/ 500 /1

Slider Average .260

	Inside	Middle	Outside
High	1/ 0 /0	0/ 0 /0	0/ 0 /0
Med	5/ 200 /1	0/ 0 /0	1/ 0 /0
Low	8/ 500 /4	6/ 0 /0	2/ 500 /1

Jeff Leonard, right-handed hitter, has a .285 overall fastball average against right-handers and a .298 overall fastball average against left-handers. He has trouble with high fastballs thrown by right-handers, but has some very strong locations in his charts.

Leonard hits medium-high outside fastballs at a .319 clip against right-handers. He tends to pull this pitch deep down the left line.

MEDIUM-HIGH OUTSIDE FASTBALLS

BATTING AVERAGE .319
Play

Left	Deep and shifted toward the left field line
Center	Medium-deep in straightaway center field
Right	Deep and shifted toward center field
Short	Up middle (shifted toward second base)
Second	Shifted toward first base

The high number of recorded instances in Leonard's low fastball locations indicates that pitchers often try to throw him low. This is fine if they hit the low-outside location (.194). But pitchers will be in trouble if they wander to the low-over-the-middle (.350) or low-inside (.370) locations.

Leonard hits low-over-the-middle fastballs deep down both lines.

LOW-OVER-THE-MIDDLE FASTBALLS

BATTING AVERAGE .350

Play

Left	Deep and shifted toward the left field line
Center	Deep in straightaway center field
Right	Deep and shifted toward the right field line
Short	Normal position
Second	Normal position

He tends to pull low-inside fastballs.

LOW-INSIDE FASTBALLS

BATTING AVERAGE .370
Play

Left	Deep and shifted toward the left field line
Center	Medium-deep and shifted toward left field
Right	Medium-deep in straightaway right field
Short	Normal position
Short	*No instances recorded*

In contrast, he hits low-outside fastballs to right field and to the right side of the infield. His low average in this location indicates that most of these hit balls are easy outs.

LOW-OUTSIDE FASTBALLS

BATTING AVERAGE .194
Play

Left	*No instances recorded*
Center	Deep and shifted toward right field
Right	Deep in straightaway right field
Short	Up middle (shifted toward second base)
Second	Shifted toward first base

Leonard hits medium-high inside fastballs fairly well (.272).

MEDIUM-HIGH INSIDE FASTBALLS

BATTING AVERAGE .272
Play
Left   Deep and shifted toward the left field line
Center Deep in straightaway center field
Right   Medium-deep in straightaway right field
Short   Up middle (shifted toward second base)
Second Shifted toward first base

Leonard Against Curves And Sliders

Leonard hits medium-high outside curves excellently against right-handers (.333). But he hits low-outside and low-over-the-middle curves poorly (.142 low-outside, .200 low-over-the-middle). Note in his Ahead And Behind charts how much better he hits medium-high outside and low-outside curves when behind in the count. He obviously is expecting these pitches when behind and is teeing off on them.

The following BARS strategies show that each of the outfielders needs to shift to be correctly positioned for medium-high outside curves when Leonard is ahead and behind.

MEDIUM-HIGH OUTSIDE CURVEBALLS (WHEN BEHIND IN THE COUNT)

BATTING AVERAGE .384
Play
Left   Deep in straightaway left field
Center Deep and shifted toward left field
Right   Deep in straightaway right field

Short   Normal position
Second *No instances recorded*

MEDIUM-HIGH OUTSIDE CURVEBALLS (WHEN AHEAD IN THE COUNT)

BATTING AVERAGE .222
Play
Left   Medium-deep and shifted toward the left field line
Center Deep in straightaway center field
Right   Deep and shifted toward center field
Short   Normal position
Second Normal position

He has trouble in the reversed L-shaped slider sector down and outside. Pitchers seem to be aware of this because there are a relatively high number of recorded instances in these three locations.

Leonard Against Left-Handed Pitchers

Leonard has trouble with medium-high inside and low-inside fastballs against left-handed pitchers, but he hits very well against low-over-the-middle, high-inside and medium-high outside fastballs.

MEDIUM-HIGH OUTSIDE FASTBALLS (THROWN BY LEFT-HANDED PITCHERS)

BATTING AVERAGE .320
Play
Left   Medium-deep in straightaway left field
Center Deep and shifted toward left field
Right   Deep in straightaway right field
Short   Up middle (shifted toward second base)
Second Shifted toward first base

Ahead And Behind In The Count Vs. RH

Ahead

Fastball Average .384

	Inside	Middle	Outside
High	10/300 /3	6/333 /2	6/333 /2
Med	22/363 /8	9/333 /3	29/448 /13
Low	11/636 /7	35/314 /11	10/400 /4

Curve Average .275

	Inside	Middle	Outside
High	1/0 /0	1/1000 /1	2/0 /0
Med	4/500 /2	2/500 /1	9/222 /2
Low	1/0 /0	3/333 /1	6/166 /1

Behind

Fastball Average .400

	Inside	Middle	Outside
High	5/200 /1	3/0 /0	0/0 /0
Med	9/222 /2	1/0 /0	11/545 /6
Low	5/200 /1	8/750 /6	3/666 /2

Curve Average .393

	Inside	Middle	Outside
High	0/0 /0	2/500 /1	0/0 /0
Med	1/1000 /1	1/1000 /1	13/384 /5
Low	0/0 /0	6/166 /1	10/400 /4

Overall Evaluation
Against Right-Handed Pitchers

Overall Fastball ⚾⚾ ⚾⚾
Overall Curve   ⚾⚾ ⚾⚾
Overall Slider   ⚾⚾

Against Left-Handed Pitchers

Overall Fastball ⚾⚾ ⚾⚾
Overall Curve   ⚾⚾ ⚾⚾ ⚾⚾
Overall Slider   ⚾⚾ ⚾⚾

Comments: Strong vs. curves vs. RH when behind.
Strengths: Medium-outside, medium-middle, low-middle and low-inside fastballs, medium-outside curves vs. RH; medium-outside, high-inside and low-middle fastballs, low-middle curves, low-inside sliders vs. LH.
Weaknesses: High fastballs, low-outside fastballs, low curves, all low and all outside sliders vs. RH; medium-inside, low-inside and low-outside fastballs vs. LH.

Pete O'Brien (Left Handed) — *Seattle Mariners*

Pete O'Brien Against Right-Handed Pitchers
Overall BARS Batting Average .279

Fastball Average .294				Curve Average .193				Slider Average .236		
	Outside	Middle	Inside	Outside	Middle	Inside		Outside	Middle	Inside
High	39/205 /8	60/283 /17	19/210 /4	1/0 /0	6/500 /3	2/500 /1		3/333 /1	2/0 /0	3/0 /0
Med	215/283 /61	63/412 /26	83/349 /29	19/157 /3	11/181 /2	13/307 /4		4/0 /0	4/500 /2	9/333 /3
Low	39/205 /8	84/273 /23	44/318 /14	17/117 /2	14/214 /3	10/0 /0		4/250 /1	3/666 /2	6/0 /0

Pete O'Brien Against Left-Handed Pitchers
Overall BARS Batting Average .235

Fastball Average .215				Curve Average .267				Slider Average .195		
	Outside	Middle	Inside	Outside	Middle	Inside		Outside	Middle	Inside
High	7/142 /1	20/350 /7	19/52 /1	3/333 /1	9/333 /3	4/250 /1		3/0 /0	2/500 /1	1/0 /0
Med	64/187 /12	19/315 /6	32/375 /12	24/208 /5	14/285 /4	8/375 /3		9/222 /2	3/666 /2	5/200 /1
Low	9/0 /0	25/80 /2	9/333 /3	15/133 /2	5/800 /4	4/0 /0		10/100 /1	9/111 /1	4/250 /1

Left-handed hitting Pete O'Brien hits fastballs significantly better against right-handed than against left-handed pitchers (.294 vs. right-handers, .215 vs. left-handers) but he hits curves better against left-handers (.267 vs. left-handers, .193 vs. right-handers).

O'Brien's .283 against medium-high outside fastballs is fairly good, but his .412 against medium-over-the-middle and .349 against medium-high inside are excellent. He's strong against waist-high fastballs.

He hits medium-high outside fastballs straight-away to the outfield and to the right side of the infield.

MEDIUM-HIGH OUTSIDE FASTBALLS

BATTING AVERAGE .283
Play

Left	Deep in straightaway left field
Center	Deep in straightaway center field
Right	Deep in straightaway right field
Short	Up middle (shifted toward second base)
Second	Shifted toward first base

As a side note, he hits medium-high outside fastballs for a higher average when ahead in the count than when behind. He hits this pitch deeper when ahead in the count.

He hits medium-high inside fastballs toward center field when he hits to the outfield, and toward the right side of the infield when he hits grounders.

MEDIUM-HIGH INSIDE FASTBALLS

BATTING AVERAGE .349
Play

Left	Deep and shifted toward center field
Center	Medium-deep in straightaway center field
Right	Deep and shifted toward center field
Short	Up middle (shifted toward second base)
Second	Shifted toward first base

His .318 average against low-inside fastballs is strong. He tends to pull this pitch to the outfield. But note that the shortstop needs to be shifted toward third base.

LOW-INSIDE FASTBALLS

BATTING AVERAGE .318
Play

Left	Medium-deep and shifted toward center field
Center	Deep and shifted toward right field
Right	Deep and shifted toward the right field line
Short	Shifted toward third base
Second	Shifted toward first base

O'Brien hits low-over-the-middle pitches much differently when ahead and when behind in the count. When ahead, he tends to hit it toward center field. When behind, he pulls the ball deep down the right line.

LOW-OVER-THE-MIDDLE FASTBALLS
(WHEN AHEAD IN THE COUNT)

BATTING AVERAGE .290
Play

Left	Deep and shifted toward center field
Center	Deep in straightaway center field
Right	Deep and shifted toward center field
Short	Up middle (shifted toward second base)
Second	Shifted toward first base

LOW-OVER-THE-MIDDLE FASTBALLS
(WHEN BEHIND IN THE COUNT)

BATTING AVERAGE .100
Play

Left	Deep in straightaway left field
Center	Deep in straightaway center field
Right	Deep and shifted toward the right field line
Short	Up middle (shifted toward second base)
Second	Shifted toward first base

O'Brien has lots of problems with curves against right-handers. He is strong location against medium-high inside curves. He pulls this pitch to right field.

MEDIUM-HIGH INSIDE CURVEBALLS

BATTING AVERAGE .307
Play

Left	*No instances recorded*
Center	Deep in straightaway center field
Right	Medium-deep in straightaway right field
Short	Up middle (shifted toward second base)
Second	Shifted toward first base

O'Brien Against Left-Handed Pitchers

O'Brien has extreme problems with outside fastballs against left-handers (.142, .187 and 0-for-9, high to low). In addition, he has trouble with low-over-the-middle (.080 on 2 for 25) and high-inside fastballs (.052 on 1 for 19) against left-handers.

He hits medium-high inside fastballs very well.

MEDIUM-HIGH INSIDE FASTBALLS
(THROWN BY LEFT-HANDED PITCHERS)

BATTING AVERAGE .375
Play

Left	Medium-deep in straightaway left field
Center	Deep in straightaway center field
Right	Deep and shifted toward the right line
Short	Shifted toward third base
Second	Normal position

With the exception of the center fielder, every fielder needs to shift for a medium-high outside fastball as compared with a medium-high inside fastball.

MEDIUM-HIGH OUTSIDE FASTBALLS
(THROWN BY LEFT-HANDED PITCHERS)

BATTING AVERAGE .187
Play

Left	Deep and shifted toward center field
Center	Deep in straightaway center field
Right	Medium-deep in straightaway right field
Short	Up middle (shifted toward second base)
Second	Shifted toward first base

Ahead And Behind In The Count Vs. RH

Ahead

Fastball Average .336

	Outside	Middle	Inside
High	20/200 /4	29/344 /10	9/222 /2
Med	120/300 /36	37/459 /17	46/391 /18
Low	14/500 /7	55/290 /16	24/375 /9

Curve Average .062

	Outside	Middle	Inside
High	1/0 /0	1/0 /0	0/0 /0
Med	6/0 /0	2/0 /0	2/0 /0
Low	1/0 /0	3/333 /1	0/0 /0

Behind

Fastball Average .224

	Outside	Middle	Inside
High	4/250 /1	12/166 /2	3/0 /0
Med	36/222 /8	8/250 /2	13/384 /5
Low	2/0 /0	10/100 /1	10/300 /3

Curve Average .250

	Outside	Middle	Inside
High	0/0 /0	0/0 /0	1/1000/1
Med	5/400 /2	4/250 /1	4/250 /1
Low	6/166 /1	5/200 /1	3/0 /0

Overall Evaluation
Against Right-Handed Pitchers

Overall Fastball	⚾⚾
Overall Curve	⚾
Overall Slider	⚾

Against Left-Handed Pitchers

Overall Fastball	⚾
Overall Curve	⚾⚾
Overall Slider	⚾

Comments: Hits fastballs better against RH; curves better against LH.

Strengths: Waist-high fastballs and low-inside fastballs, medium-inside curves and sliders vs. RH; medium-inside fastballs and curves against LH.

Weaknesses: High-outside, high-inside and low-outside fastballs, all outside and all low curves vs. RH; outside fastballs, low-middle and high-inside fastballs, medium-outside & low-outside curves & sliders vs LH.

Jim Presley (Right Handed) — *Seattle Mariners*

Jim Presley Against Right-Handed Pitchers
Overall BARS Batting Average .221

Fastball Average .256

	Inside	Middle	Outside
High	15/ 66 /1	19/ 368 /7	21/ 190 /4
Med	30/ 300 /9	12/ 250 /3	96/ 239 /23
Low	18/ 277 /5	33/ 393 /13	21/ 142 /3

Curve Average .132

	Inside	Middle	Outside
High	1/ 0 /0	1/ 0 /0	2/ 500 /1
Med	4/ 250 /1	5/ 400 /2	24/ 83 /2
Low	1/ 0 /0	14/ 71 /1	31/ 129 /4

Slider Average .191

	Inside	Middle	Outside
High	1/ 0 /0	2/ 0 /0	1/ 0 /0
Med	3/ 0 /0	4/ 0 /0	20/ 200 /4
Low	1/ 0 /0	9/ 444 /4	27/ 185 /5

Jim Presley Against Left-Handed Pitchers
Overall BARS Batting Average .324

Fastball Average .358

	Inside	Middle	Outside
High	3/ 333 /1	5/ 400 /2	8/ 125 /1
Med	10/ 300 /3	4/ 750 /3	37/ 351 /13
Low	6/ 333 /2	17/ 470 /8	16/ 312 /5

Curve Average .222

	Inside	Middle	Outside
High	0/ 0 /0	0/ 0 /0	3/ 333 /1
Med	3/ 0 /0	2/ 0 /0	8/ 500 /4
Low	7/ 142 /1	2/ 0 /0	2/ 0 /0

Slider Average .277

	Inside	Middle	Outside
High	1/ 0 /0	1/ 1000 /1	0/ 0 /0
Med	2/ 0 /0	0/ 0 /0	3/ 333 /1
Low	6/ 333 /2	3/ 333 /1	2/ 0 /0

Right-handed hitting Jim Presley has a significantly higher overall fastball average against left-handed pitchers (.358 overall vs. left-handers, .256 overall vs. right-handers).

He has a weak .239 average against medium-high outside fastballs thrown by right-handed pitchers. His Ahead and Behind charts on the opposite page show that he hits this pitch much better when ahead in the count (.322 when ahead, .250 when behind). Notice in the following fielding strategies that each fielder is required to shift for this pitch when Presley is ahead and behind in the count.

MEDIUM-HIGH OUTSIDE FASTBALLS (WHEN AHEAD IN THE COUNT)

BATTING AVERAGE .322
Play
Left	Medium-deep in straightaway left field
Center	Deep in straightaway center field
Right	Deep and shifted toward the right field line
Short	Up middle (shifted toward second base)
Second	Shifted toward first base

MEDIUM-HIGH OUTSIDE FASTBALLS (WHEN BEHIND IN THE COUNT)

BATTING AVERAGE .250
Play
Left	Short in straightaway left field
Center	Medium-deep in straightaway center field

Right	Deep in straightaway right field
Short	Normal position
Second	Normal position

Presley hits low-over-the-middle fastballs extremely well against right-handers (.393).

LOW-OVER-THE-MIDDLE FASTBALLS

BATTING AVERAGE .393
Play
Left	Deep in straightaway left field
Center	Deep and shifted toward left field
Right	Deep and shifted toward center field
Short	Up middle (shifted toward second base)
Second	Normal position

He has trouble with low-outside fastballs (.142), high-outside fastballs (.190), and high-inside fastballs (.066). He hits medium-high inside fastballs very well, however, (.300).

MEDIUM-HIGH INSIDE FASTBALLS

BATTING AVERAGE .300
Play
Left	Deep in straightaway left field
Center	Medium-deep in straightaway center field
Right	Deep in straightaway right field
Short	Normal position
Second	Normal position

His .368 against high-over-the-middle fastballs is excellent. He hits this pitch deep and straightaway to left field, deep into center field toward right, and deep down the right line.

Presley Against Curves And Sliders

Presley has tremendous difficulties with curves and sliders thrown by right-handed pitchers. His .129 low-outside curve average and .083 medium-high inside curve average offer a weak sector to right-handers.

LOW-OUTSIDE CURVEBALLS

BATTING AVERAGE .129

Play

Left	Deep in straightaway left field
Center	*No instances recorded*
Right	Medium-deep and shifted toward the right line
Short	Normal position
Second	Normal position

His .185 low-outside slider and .200 medium-high outside slider averages give an attractive target to pitchers.

Presley Against Left-Handed Pitchers

Notice Presley's strong .351 average in his medium-high outside fastball location against left-handed pitchers. He hits this pitch straightaway to left and right fields, and to deep right-center field.

MEDIUM-HIGH OUTSIDE FASTBALLS
(THROWN BY LEFT-HANDED PITCHERS)

BATTING AVERAGE .351

Play

Left	Medium-deep in straightaway left field
Center	Deep and shifted toward right field
Right	Deep in straightaway right field
Short	Normal position
Second	Shifted toward first base

He hits .312 against low-outside fastballs thrown by left-handers. He hits this pitch deep down the left line and into the left-center gap.

LOW-OUTSIDE FASTBALLS
(THROWN BY LEFT-HANDED PITCHERS)

BATTING AVERAGE .312

Play

Left	Deep and shifted toward the left field line
Center	Deep and shifted toward left field
Right	Deep in straightaway right field
Short	Normal position
Second	*No instances recorded*

Presley hits low-over-the-middle fastballs exceptionally well against left-handers (.470). He also pulls this pitch deep down the left line. (Recall that he also hits this pitch excellently against right-handers.)

LOW-OVER-THE-MIDDLE FASTBALLS
(THROWN BY LEFT-HANDED PITCHERS)

BATTING AVERAGE .470

Play

Left	Deep and shifted toward the left field line
Center	Medium-deep in straightaway center field
Right	Deep in straightaway right field
Short	Normal position
Second	*No instances recorded*

Ahead And Behind In The Count Vs. RH

Ahead

Fastball Average .315

	Inside	Middle	Outside
High	5/0 — 0/0	7/428 — 3	7/285 — 2
Med	13/384 — 5	6/333 — 2	31/322 — 10
Low	5/400 — 2	16/375 — 6	5/0 — 0

Curve Average .352

	Inside	Middle	Outside
High	1/0 — 0/0	0/0 — 0/0	1/1000 — 1
Med	1/0 — 0/0	1/1000 — 1	5/200 — 1
Low	0/0 — 0/0	3/0 — 0	5/600 — 3

Behind

Fastball Average .311

	Inside	Middle	Outside
High	4/250 — 1	6/500 — 3	6/166 — 1
Med	5/400 — 2	3/0 — 0	24/250 — 6
Low	3/0 — 0	8/625 — 5	2/500 — 1

Curve Average .133

	Inside	Middle	Outside
High	0/0 — 0/0	0/0 — 0/0	0/0 — 0/0
Med	1/1000 — 1	1/0 — 0	4/0 — 0
Low	0/0 — 0/0	4/0 — 0	5/200 — 1

Overall Evaluation
Against Right-Handed Pitchers

Overall Fastball ⚾⚾
Overall Curve ⚾⚾
Overall Slider ⚾⚾

Against Left-Handed Pitchers

Overall Fastball ⚾⚾ ⚾⚾ ⚾⚾ ⚾⚾
Overall Curve ⚾⚾
Overall Slider ⚾⚾ ⚾⚾ ⚾⚾

Comments: Hits fastballs excellently overall vs. LH. **Strengths:** Low-middle, medium-inside and high-middle fastballs, low-middle sliders vs. RH; medium-outside, low-middle and all inside fastballs, medium-outside curves vs. LH. **Weaknesses:** Outside fastballs, high-inside fastballs, low-outside, low-middle and medium-outside curves, outside sliders vs. RH, high-outside fastballs and low-inside curves vs. LH.

Rey Quinones (Right Handed)   *Seattle Mariners*

Rey Quinones Against Right-Handed Pitchers
Overall BARS Batting Average .258

Fastball Average .251

	Inside	Middle	Outside
High	12/ 0/0	13/ 153/2	10/ 300/3
Med	18/ 222/4	5/ 200/1	68/ 308/21
Low	8/ 375/3	14/ 285/4	19/ 210/4

Curve Average .195

	Inside	Middle	Outside
High	2/ 0/0	1/ 0/0	2/ 0/0
Med	2/ 0/0	2/ 0/0	14/ 285/4
Low	2/ 0/0	4/ 0/0	12/ 333/4

Slider Average .392

	Inside	Middle	Outside
High	0/ 0/0	1/ 0/0	1/ 0/0
Med	2/ 500/1	0/ 0/0	9/ 555/5
Low	0/ 0/0	2/ 1000/2	13/ 230/3

Rey Quinones Against Left-Handed Pitchers
Overall BARS Batting Average .298

Fastball Average .283

	Inside	Middle	Outside
High	2/ 0/0	5/ 0/0	3/ 333/1
Med	5/ 600/3	2/ 500/1	33/ 242/8
Low	7/ 142/1	17/ 470/8	7/ 142/1

Curve Average .466

	Inside	Middle	Outside
High	0/ 0/0	0/ 0/0	0/ 0/0
Med	0/ 0/0	2/ 1000/2	6/ 333/2
Low	4/ 500/2	2/ 500/1	1/ 0/0

Slider Average .125

	Inside	Middle	Outside
High	0/ 0/0	1/ 0/0	0/ 0/0
Med	1/ 0/0	0/ 0/0	2/ 0/0
Low	3/ 333/1	0/ 0/0	1/ 0/0

Right-handed hitting Rey Quinones has a higher overall fastball average against left-handed than against right-handed pitchers (.283 vs. left-handers, .251 vs. right-handers).

Starting with his performance against right-handers, notice that Quinones hits medium-high outside fastballs for a good .308 average. His Ahead and Behind charts on the opposite page show that he hits this pitch better when behind in the count. He pulls this pitch more to the outfield when he is behind than when ahead. This is unusual — hitters usually pull the ball more when ahead.

MEDIUM-HIGH OUTSIDE FASTBALLS (WHEN BEHIND IN THE COUNT)

BATTING AVERAGE .333
Play
Left   Deep and shifted toward the left field line
Center   Deep in straightaway center field
Right   Deep and shifted toward center field
Short   Shifted toward third base
Second   Shifted toward first base

MEDIUM-HIGH OUTSIDE FASTBALLS (WHEN AHEAD IN THE COUNT)

BATTING AVERAGE .250
Play
Left   Deep in straightaway left field

Center   Deep in straightaway center field
Right   Deep in straightaway right field
Short   Normal position
Second   Normal position

He hits low-over-the-middle fastballs against right-handers deep and straightaway to all fields.

LOW-OVER-THE-MIDDLE FASTBALLS

BATTING AVERAGE .285
Play
Left   Deep in straightaway left field
Center   Deep in straightaway center field
Right   Deep in straightaway right field
Short   Up middle (shifted toward second base)
Second   Normal position

Quinones has trouble with medium-high inside fastballs against right-handers, hitting only .222.

MEDIUM-HIGH INSIDE FASTBALLS

BATTING AVERAGE .222
Play
Left   Medium-deep in straightaway left field
Center   Deep and shifted toward left field
Right   Medium-deep and shifted toward center field
Short   Normal position
Second   Normal position

He goes down the right line and to the right side of the infield with low-outside fastballs, but his low average in this location (.210) indicates that he does not hit this pitch sharply.

LOW-OUTSIDE FASTBALLS

BATTING AVERAGE .210
Play
Left	Medium-deep in straightaway left field
Center	Medium-deep in straightaway center field
Right	Deep and shifted toward the right field line
Short	Up middle (shifted toward second base)
Second	Shifted toward first base

Quinones Against Curves And Sliders

Quinones hits low-outside curves excellently against right-handed pitchers (.333). If fielders positioned themselves according to the BARS fielding strategy for this pitch they would undoubtedly be able to prevent most of his base hits.

LOW-OUTSIDE CURVEBALLS

BATTING AVERAGE .333
Play
Left	Medium-deep and shifted toward the left field line
Center	Short in straightaway center field
Right	Medium-deep in straightaway right field
Short	Up middle (shifted toward second base)
Second	Normal position

He also hit medium-high outside curves well (.285). Notice how differently fielders need to be positioned for this pitch compared with low-outside curves. The center and right fielders need to shift to be properly positioned for these two pitches.

MEDIUM-HIGH OUTSIDE CURVEBALLS

BATTING AVERAGE .285
Play
Left	Medium-deep and shifted toward the left field line
Center	Deep and shifted toward left field
Right	Short and shifted toward the right field line
Short	Up middle (shifted toward second base)
Second	Normal position

Quinones Against Left-Handed Pitchers

Quinones has a weak .242 average in his medium-high outside fastball location when facing left-handed pitchers.

MEDIUM-HIGH OUTSIDE FASTBALLS (THROWN BY LEFT-HANDED PITCHERS)

BATTING AVERAGE .242
Play
Left	Medium-deep in straightaway left field
Center	Deep in straightaway center field
Right	Deep and shifted toward the right field line
Short	Up middle (shifted toward second base)
Second	Normal position

His strong .470 average against low-over-the-middle fastballs shows he can hit low fastballs against lefties. He hits this pitch deep and straightaway to left field, deep to center shifted toward left, and deep to right shifted toward center.

Ahead And Behind In The Count Vs. RH

Ahead

	Fastball Average .226			Curve Average .400		
	Inside	Middle	Outside	Inside	Middle	Outside
High	4/ 0 /0	5/ 200 /1	4/ 250 /1	0/ 0 /0	0/ 0 /0	0/ 0 /0
Med	9/ 333 /3	2/ 0 /0	32/ 250 /8	1/ 0 /0	0/ 0 /0	6/ 333 /2
Low	1/ 0 /0	8/ 125 /1	10/ 300 /3	0/ 0 /0	0/ 0 /0	3/ 666 /2

Behind

	Fastball Average .419			Curve Average .272		
	Inside	Middle	Outside	Inside	Middle	Outside
High	1/ 0 /0	0/ 0 /0	3/ 333 /1	0/ 0 /0	0/ 0 /0	2/ 0 /0
Med	2/ 0 /0	1/ 1000 /1	12/ 333 /4	0/ 0 /0	1/ 0 /0	3/ 333 /1
Low	4/ 750 /3	3/ 1000 /3	5/ 200 /1	0/ 0 /0	1/ 0 /0	4/ 500 /2

Overall Evaluation
Against Right-Handed Pitchers

Overall Fastball	⚾⚾
Overall Curve	⚾⚾
Overall Slider	⚾⚾⚾⚾⚾

Against Left-Handed Pitchers

Overall Fastball	⚾⚾
Overall Curve	⚾⚾⚾⚾⚾
Overall Slider	Not enough information

Comments: Hits medium-outside fastballs and low-outside curves well vs. RH.
Strengths: Medium-outside, high-outside and low-inside fastballs, medium-outside and low-outside curves, medium-outside sliders vs. RH; low-middle fastballs, medium-outside curves vs. LH.
Weaknesses: High-inside, high-middle, low-outside and medium-inside fastballs, low-outside sliders vs. RH; medium-outside fastballs vs. LH.

Harold Reynolds (Switch Hitter)   *Seattle Mariners*

Harold Reynolds Against Right-Handed Pitchers
Overall BARS Batting Average .305

Fastball Average .306

	Outside	Middle	Inside
High	22/ 272 /6	17/ 470 /8	14/ 214 /3
Med	110/ 327 /36	15/ 266 /4	35/ 285 /10
Low	13/ 461 /6	22/ 181 /4	16/ 250 /4

Curve Average .241

	Outside	Middle	Inside
High	4/ 250 /1	0/ 0 /0	0/ 0 /0
Med	10/ 200 /2	1/ 1000 /1	2/ 0 /0
Low	5/ 200 /1	4/ 250 /1	3/ 333 /1

Slider Average .375

	Outside	Middle	Inside
High	0/ 0 /0	1/ 1000 /1	0/ 0 /0
Med	1/ 1000 /1	0/ 0 /0	6/ 500 /3
Low	0/ 0 /0	1/ 0 /0	7/ 142 /1

Harold Reynolds Against Left-Handed Pitchers
Overall BARS Batting Average .282

Fastball Average .291

	Inside	Middle	Outside
High	6/ 333 /2	13/ 384 /5	9/ 222 /2
Med	11/ 181 /2	3/ 666 /2	32/ 281 /9
Low	5/ 200 /1	9/ 444 /4	8/ 125 /1

Curve Average .181

	Inside	Middle	Outside
High	0/ 0 /0	0/ 0 /0	1/ 0 /0
Med	3/ 0 /0	0/ 0 /0	2/ 500 /1
Low	1/ 0 /0	2/ 500 /1	2/ 0 /0

Slider Average .300

	Inside	Middle	Outside
High	3/ 333 /1	0/ 0 /0	0/ 0 /0
Med	4/ 500 /2	1/ 0 /0	2/ 0 /0
Low	0/ 0 /0	0/ 0 /0	0/ 0 /0

Switch-hitting Harold Reynolds hits fastballs a little better against right-handed pitchers (.306 vs. right-handers, .291 vs. left-handers).

Looking first at Reynolds' charts against right-handers, notice his fine .327 average against medium-high outside fastballs. He hits this pitch medium-deep and straightaway to the outfield. If outfielders adjusted according to the following BARS fielding strategy, they would prevent most of Reynolds' base hits from pitches to this location.

MEDIUM-HIGH OUTSIDE FASTBALLS

BATTING AVERAGE .327
Play
Left — Medium-deep in straightaway left field
Center — Medium-deep in straightaway center field
Right — Medium-deep in straightaway right field
Short — Up middle (shifted toward second base)
Second — Shifted toward first base

He also hits medium-high inside fastballs medium-deep and straightaway to all fields. Fielders should take note of this.

MEDIUM-HIGH INSIDE FASTBALLS

BATTING AVERAGE .285
Play
Left — Medium-deep in straightaway left field
Center — Medium-deep in straightaway center field
Right — Medium-deep in straightaway right field
Short — Up middle (shifted toward second base)
Second — Normal position

Reynolds' highest fastball average is in his high-over-the-middle location (.470). He hits this pitch medium-deep to center and right and deep down the left line. The infield should play for a pull.

HIGH-OVER-THE-MIDDLE FASTBALLS

BATTING AVERAGE .470
Play
Left — Deep and shifted toward the left field line
Center — Medium-deep in straightaway center field
Right — Medium-deep in straightaway right field
Short — Up middle (shifted toward second base)
Second — Shifted toward first base

Reynolds hits low-outside fastballs medium-deep down the left line and into left center. Fielders need to pay special attention to this. Pitchers may throw him low-outside, thinking they can gain an advantage, but if fielders are not properly positioned, all advantage will be lost. His high average in this location (.461) indicates that fielders are not playing him properly for this pitch.

LOW-OUTSIDE FASTBALLS

BATTING AVERAGE .461
Play

Left	Medium-deep and shifted toward the left field line
Center	Medium-deep and shifted toward left field
Right	*No instances recorded*
Short	Normal position
Second	Normal position

Reynolds hits high-outside fastballs down both lines.

HIGH-OUTSIDE FASTBALLS

BATTING AVERAGE .272
Play

Left	Medium-deep and shifted toward the left line
Center	Deep in straightaway center field
Right	Deep and shifted toward the right field line
Short	Up middle (shifted toward second base)
Second	Normal position

Notice how few curves and sliders are thrown to Reynolds in comparison with fastballs. Considering that Reynolds hits fastballs well overall, pitchers should blend in more breaking pitches.

Reynolds Against Left-Handed Pitchers

Batting right-handed, Reynolds has a .281 average against medium-high outside fastballs thrown by left-handed pitchers. He pulls this pitch deep down the left line and into left center.

MEDIUM-HIGH OUTSIDE FASTBALLS
(THROWN BY LEFT-HANDED PITCHERS)

BATTING AVERAGE .281
Play

Left	Deep and shifted toward the left field line
Center	Deep and shifted toward left field
Right	Deep in straightaway right field
Short	Up middle (shifted toward second base)
Second	Shifted toward first base

He hits a strong .384 against high-over-the-middle fastballs thrown by lefties. Again, notice that he hits this pitch medium-deep to the outfield. By adjusting, fielders could take away most of his base hits.

HIGH-OVER-THE-MIDDLE FASTBALLS
(THROWN BY LEFT-HANDED PITCHERS)

BATTING AVERAGE .384
Play

Left	Medium-deep in straightaway left field
Center	Medium-deep in straightaway center field
Right	Medium-deep and shifted toward the right line
Short	Shifted toward third base
Second	Shifted toward first base

Ahead And Behind In The Count Vs. RH

Ahead

Fastball Average .325

	Outside	Middle	Inside
High	10/300 /3	10/500 /5	5/200 /1
Med	44/340 /15	9/444 /4	19/315 /6
Low	8/250 /2	6/166 /1	9/222 /2

Curve Average .333

	Outside	Middle	Inside
High	0/0 /0	0/0 /0	0/0 /0
Med	2/500 /1	0/0 /0	0/0 /0
Low	0/0 /0	0/0 /0	1/0 /0

Behind

Fastball Average .302

	Outside	Middle	Inside
High	6/166 /1	4/500 /2	4/500 /2
Med	17/294 /5	1/0 /0	4/0 /0
Low	1/1000 /1	3/333 /1	3/333 /1

Curve Average .200

	Outside	Middle	Inside
High	2/0 /0	0/0 /0	0/0 /0
Med	4/250 /1	0/0 /0	1/0 /0
Low	1/0 /0	2/500 /1	0/0 /0

Overall Evaluation
Against Right-Handed Pitchers

Overall Fastball	⚾ ⚾ ⚾
Overall Curve	⚾
Overall Slider	⚾ ⚾ ⚾ ⚾

Against Left-Handed Pitchers

Overall Fastball	⚾ ⚾
Overall Curve	Not enough information
Overall Slider	Not enough information

Comments: Fielders need to play medium-deep for many pitches to Reynolds.
Strengths: Medium-outside, low-outside and high-middle fastballs, medium-inside sliders vs. RH; all over-the-middle fastballs vs. LH.
Weaknesses: Low-middle, medium-middle, low-inside and high-inside fastballs, outside curves, low-inside sliders vs. RH; medium-inside, low-inside, high-outside and low-outside fastballs vs. LH.

Dave Valle (Right Handed)   *Seattle Mariners*

Dave Valle Against Right-Handed Pitchers
Overall BARS Batting Average .185

Fastball Average .194

	Inside	Middle	Outside
High	6 / 166 / 1	5 / 200 / 1	7 / 142 / 1
Med	7 / 285 / 2	2 / 0 / 0	28 / 250 / 7
Low	2 / 0 / 0	7 / 0 / 0	3 / 333 / 1

Curve Average .133

	Inside	Middle	Outside
High	0 / 0 / 0	0 / 0 / 0	0 / 0 / 0
Med	0 / 0 / 0	0 / 0 / 0	6 / 166 / 1
Low	0 / 0 / 0	3 / 0 / 0	6 / 166 / 1

Slider Average .153

	Inside	Middle	Outside
High	0 / 0 / 0	1 / 0 / 0	0 / 0 / 0
Med	0 / 0 / 0	1 / 0 / 0	6 / 333 / 2
Low	1 / 0 / 0	0 / 0 / 0	4 / 0 / 0

Dave Valle Against Left-Handed Pitchers
Overall BARS Batting Average .337

Fastball Average .351

	Inside	Middle	Outside
High	4 / 250 / 1	5 / 200 / 1	5 / 800 / 4
Med	4 / 250 / 1	3 / 666 / 2	20 / 400 / 8
Low	4 / 0 / 0	3 / 333 / 1	6 / 166 / 1

Curve Average .250

	Inside	Middle	Outside
High	0 / 0 / 0	0 / 0 / 0	0 / 0 / 0
Med	2 / 500 / 1	0 / 0 / 0	3 / 0 / 0
Low	1 / 0 / 0	2 / 500 / 1	0 / 0 / 0

Slider Average .333

	Inside	Middle	Outside
High	2 / 500 / 1	1 / 1000 / 1	0 / 0 / 0
Med	3 / 333 / 1	0 / 0 / 0	0 / 0 / 0
Low	2 / 0 / 0	2 / 0 / 0	2 / 500 / 1

Right-handed hitter Dave Valle has a weak .194 overall fastball average against right-handed pitchers, but he hits a solid .351 overall against fastballs thrown by left-handed pitchers.

Starting with right-handers, Valle hits .250 against medium-high outside fastballs. Notice in his Ahead and Behind charts on the opposite page how much trouble he has with medium-high outside fastballs when ahead in the count (.000 on 0 for 11). This is very unusual. When ahead he hits this pitch straightaway to the outfield, but he must hit the ball very weakly because of his .000 average. When behind he tends to go to the opposite field with this pitch.

MEDIUM-HIGH OUTSIDE FASTBALLS (WHEN AHEAD IN THE COUNT)

BATTING AVERAGE .000 (0 for 11)

Play
Left	Deep in straightaway left field
Center	Short in straightaway center field
Right	Deep in straightaway right field
Short	Normal position
Second	*No instances recorded*

MEDIUM-HIGH OUTSIDE FASTBALLS (WHEN BEHIND IN THE COUNT)

BATTING AVERAGE .600 (3 for 5)

Play
Left	*No instances recorded*
Center	*No instances recorded*
Right	Deep and shifted toward center field
Short	Up middle (shifted toward second base)
Second	Shifted toward first base

Valle hits medium-high inside fastballs for a .285 average. He has trouble with all high fastballs and with low-over-the-middle fastballs. He also seems to have trouble with outside curves. His .166 averages against low-outside and medium-high outside curves indicate weaknesses.

Valle hits an excellent .400 against medium-high outside fastballs thrown by left-handed pitchers. His high average in this location indicates that he hits this pitch hard, making it difficult for fielders to get to the ball. If fielders positioned themselves as suggested by the BARS fielding strategy for this pitch, they could prevent most of his base hits from this location.

MEDIUM-HIGH OUTSIDE FASTBALLS (THROWN BY LEFT-HANDED PITCHERS)

BATTING AVERAGE .400

Play
Left	Deep in straightaway left field
Center	Medium-deep in straightaway center field
Right	Deep in straightaway right field
Short	Up middle (shifted toward second base)
Second	Shifted toward first base

Medium-High Outside Fastballs (Thrown By Left-Handed Pitchers)

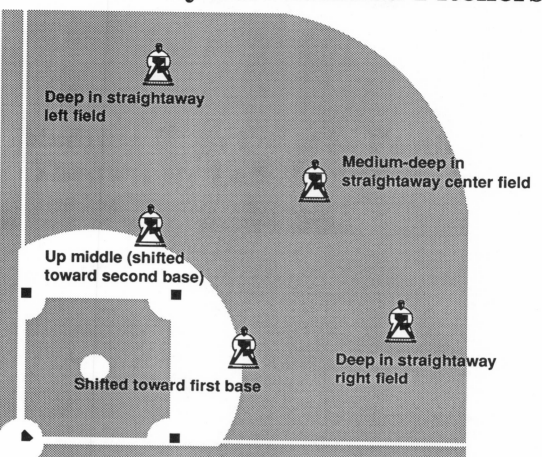

Deep in straightaway left field

Medium-deep in straightaway center field

Up middle (shifted toward second base)

Shifted toward first base

Deep in straightaway right field

Ahead And Behind In The Count Vs. RH

Ahead

Fastball Average .034

	Inside	Middle	Outside
High	3/ 0 /0	3/ 0 /0	2/ 0 /0
Med	2/ 0 /0	1/ 0 /0	11/ 0 /0
Low	0/ 0 /0	4/ 0 /0	3/ 333 /1

Curve Average .000

	Inside	Middle	Outside
High	0/ 0 /0	0/ 0 /0	0/ 0 /0
Med	0/ 0 /0	0/ 0 /0	0/ 0 /0
Low	0/ 0 /0	1/ 0 /0	0/ 0 /0

Behind

Fastball Average .461

	Inside	Middle	Outside
High	1/ 1000 /1	1/ 1000 /1	1/ 0 /0
Med	3/ 333 /1	0/ 0 /0	5/ 600 /3
Low	0/ 0 /0	2/ 0 /0	0/ 0 /0

Curve Average .400

	Inside	Middle	Outside
High	0/ 0 /0	0/ 0 /0	0/ 0 /0
Med	0/ 0 /0	0/ 0 /0	2/ 500 /1
Low	0/ 0 /0	0/ 0 /0	3/ 333 /1

Overall Evaluation

Against Right-Handed Pitchers

Overall Fastball ⚾⚾

Overall Curve ⚾⚾

Overall Slider ⚾⚾

Against Left-Handed Pitchers

Overall Fastball ⚾⚾ ⚾⚾ ⚾⚾ ⚾⚾

Overall Curve Not enough information

Overall Slider ⚾⚾ ⚾⚾ ⚾⚾ ⚾⚾

Comments: Has trouble in general vs. RH.
Strengths: Medium-outside sliders vs. RH; medium-outside fastballs vs. LH.
Weaknesses: High fastballs, low-middle fastballs, medium-outside fastballs, outside curves vs. RH; inside fastballs, low-outside fastballs vs. LH.

Baines, Harold
Buechele, Steve
Espy, Cecil
Franco, Julio
Incaviglia, Pete
Leach, Rick
Manrique, Fred
Palmeiro, Rafael
Petralli, Geno
Pettis, Gary
Sierra, Ruben

Texas Rangers
BARS System
Hitting Analysis

Harold Baines (Left Handed) — *Texas Rangers*

Harold Baines Against Right-Handed Pitchers
Overall BARS Batting Average .314

Fastball Average .342

	Outside	Middle	Inside
High	41/ 317 /13	48/ 395 /19	14/ 214 /3
Med	205/ 375 /77	40/ 500 /20	78/ 294 /23
Low	39/ 256 /10	84/ 309 /26	32/ 250 /8

Curve Average .208

	Outside	Middle	Inside
High	10/ 300 /3	10/ 300 /3	2/ 500 /1
Med	38/ 289 /11	9/ 222 /2	19/ 263 /5
Low	19/ 0 /0	18/ 277 /5	24/ 41 /1

Slider Average .309

	Outside	Middle	Inside
High	2/ 0 /0	4/ 250 /1	5/ 0 /0
Med	12/ 416 /5	4/ 0 /0	14/ 571 /8
Low	7/ 0 /0	12/ 416 /5	24/ 291 /7

Harold Baines Against Left-Handed Pitchers
Overall BARS Batting Average .302

Fastball Average .326

	Outside	Middle	Inside
High	7/ 142 /1	25/ 280 /7	16/ 500 /8
Med	76/ 381 /29	13/ 230 /3	28/ 357 /10
Low	16/ 125 /2	27/ 333 /9	25/ 280 /7

Curve Average .284

	Outside	Middle	Inside
High	6/ 500 /3	10/ 500 /5	4/ 250 /1
Med	33/ 303 /10	8/ 250 /2	12/ 333 /4
Low	28/ 178 /5	11/ 181 /2	4/ 250 /1

Slider Average .235

	Outside	Middle	Inside
High	5/ 0 /0	1/ 1000 /1	1/ 0 /0
Med	13/ 153 /2	2/ 500 /1	2/ 500 /1
Low	16/ 125 /2	10/ 400 /4	1/ 1000 /1

Left-handed hitting Harold Baines has excellent overall fastball averages against right-handed pitchers (.342) and left-handed pitchers (.326). His overall average against left-handed pitchers (.292) is very high for a left-handed batter. Starting with right-handers, he hits .375 against medium-high outside fastballs.

MEDIUM-HIGH OUTSIDE FASTBALLS

BATTING AVERAGE .375
Play

Left	Deep in straightaway left field
Center	Deep in straightaway center field
Right	Deep and shifted toward the right field line
Short	Up middle (shifted toward second base)
Second	Shifted toward first base

He hits .294 against medium-high inside fastballs thrown by right-handers.

MEDIUM-HIGH INSIDE FASTBALLS

BATTING AVERAGE .294
Play

Left	Deep in straightaway left field
Center	Deep and shifted toward left field
Right	Medium-deep and shifted toward center field
Short	Up middle (shifted toward second base)
Second	Normal position

He hits low-over-the-middle fastballs deep to all fields.

LOW-OVER-THE-MIDDLE FASTBALLS

BATTING AVERAGE .309
Play

Left	Deep in straightaway left field
Center	Deep in straightaway center field
Right	Deep and shifted toward center field
Short	Normal position
Second	Normal position

He hits high-outside fastballs deep down the opposite line (the left line for Baines).

HIGH-OUTSIDE FASTBALLS

BATTING AVERAGE .317
Play

Left	Deep and shifted toward the left field line
Center	Deep and shifted toward left field
Right	Deep in straightaway right field
Short	Normal position
Second	Shifted toward first base

He has trouble with low-outside fastballs, scattering them to all fields (.256).

LOW-OUTSIDE FASTBALLS

BATTING AVERAGE .256
Play

Left	Medium-deep and shifted toward the left field line
Center	Deep and shifted toward left field

Right	Medium-deep and shifted toward the right line
Short	Normal position
Second	Normal position

Baines Against Curves And Sliders

Baines hits some of his curve locations very well, but he has trouble with low-inside (.041) and low-outside (.000 on 0 for 19) curves. He hits medium-high outside curves fairly well (.289).

MEDIUM-HIGH OUTSIDE CURVEBALLS

BATTING AVERAGE .289

Play

Left	Deep and shifted toward the left field line
Center	Medium-deep in straightaway center field
Right	Deep and shifted toward center field
Short	Normal position
Second	Shifted toward first base

Baines has excellent averages in some of his slider locations. He hits low-inside sliders for a solid .291.

LOW-INSIDE SLIDERS

BATTING AVERAGE .291

Play

Left	Medium-deep in straightaway left field
Center	Deep in straightaway center field
Right	Deep and shifted toward the right field line
Short	Up middle (shifted toward second base)
Second	Shifted toward first base

Notice how well he hits medium-high inside sliders (.571). He pulls this pitch deep down the right line.

Baines Against Left-Handed Pitchers

Baines hits fastballs and curves very well overall against left-handed pitchers. He hits medium-high outside fastballs at a .381 clip. He hits a strong .357 against medium-high inside fastballs. Note in the following fielding strategies that the outfielders and the shortstop need to shift to be correctly positioned for both inside and outside medium-high fastballs.

MEDIUM-HIGH OUTSIDE FASTBALLS
(THROWN BY LEFT-HANDED PITCHERS)

BATTING AVERAGE .381

Play

Left	Deep in straightaway left field
Center	Deep and shifted toward left field
Right	Deep in straightaway right field
Short	Normal position
Second	Shifted toward first base

MEDIUM-HIGH INSIDE FASTBALLS
(THROWN BY LEFT-HANDED PITCHERS)

BATTING AVERAGE .357

Play

Left	Medium-deep and shifted toward the left field line
Center	Deep in straightaway center field
Right	Deep and shifted toward center field
Short	Up middle (shifted toward second base)
Second	Shifted toward first base

Baines has trouble with low curves and low-outside sliders against left-handers. He hits medium-high outside and medium-high inside curves excellently, however (.303 and .333, respectively).

Ahead And Behind In The Count Vs. RH

Ahead

Fastball Average .409

	Outside	Middle	Inside
High	16/312 /5	15/533 /8	4/500 /2
Med	106/424 /45	16/625 /10	41/390 /16
Low	16/312 /5	46/369 /17	16/312 /5

Curve Average .274

	Outside	Middle	Inside
High	2/500 /1	4/500 /2	1/1000 /1
Med	15/333 /5	2/0 /0	11/272 /3
Low	2/0 /0	6/166 /1	8/125 /1

Behind

Fastball Average .427

	Outside	Middle	Inside
High	10/500 /5	14/357 /5	4/250 /1
Med	29/551 /16	11/636 /7	16/250 /4
Low	8/500 /4	13/230 /3	5/400 /2

Curve Average .277

	Outside	Middle	Inside
High	4/500 /2	2/500 /1	1/0 /0
Med	9/222 /2	3/0 /0	4/500 /2
Low	6/0 /0	6/500 /3	1/0 /0

Overall Evaluation

Against Right-Handed Pitchers

Overall Fastball	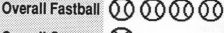
Overall Curve	
Overall Slider	

Against Left-Handed Pitchers

Overall Fastball	
Overall Curve	
Overall Slider	

Comments: An excellent fastball hitter vs. RH and LH. Strengths: Waist-high fastballs, over-the-middle fastballs, high-outside fastballs, high curves, medium-inside, medium-outside and low-middle sliders vs. RH; medium-outside, low-middle and inside fastballs, medium-outside curves, low-middle sliders vs. LH. Weaknesses: Low-outside and low-inside fastballs, low-outside and low-inside curves vs. RH; low-outside fastballs, low curves and outside sliders vs. LH.

Steve Buechele Against Right-Handed Pitchers
Overall BARS Batting Average .231

Fastball Average .245

	Inside	Middle	Outside
High	18/222 /4	21/428 /9	14/214 /3
Med	46/152 /7	15/533 /8	115/234 /27
Low	7/142 /1	34/382 /13	48/125 /6

Curve Average .176

	Inside	Middle	Outside
High	4/250 /1	3/333 /1	1/0 /0
Med	5/400 /2	5/600 /3	23/173 /4
Low	1/0 /0	7/0 /0	19/52 /1

Slider Average .220

	Inside	Middle	Outside
High	0/0 /0	0/0 /0	3/333 /1
Med	8/250 /2	1/1000 /1	16/250 /4
Low	0/0 /0	5/400 /2	17/58 /1

Steve Buechele Against Left-Handed Pitchers
Overall BARS Batting Average .311

Fastball Average .354

	Inside	Middle	Outside
High	4/500 /2	9/444 /4	13/307 /4
Med	12/333 /4	10/700 /7	71/352 /25
Low	5/200 /1	10/200 /2	10/200 /2

Curve Average .212

	Inside	Middle	Outside
High	0/0 /0	0/0 /0	3/333 /1
Med	3/0 /0	2/500 /1	9/333 /3
Low	2/0 /0	7/142 /1	7/142 /1

Slider Average .157

	Inside	Middle	Outside
High	0/0 /0	0/0 /0	0/0 /0
Med	1/0 /0	1/0 /0	5/200 /1
Low	5/400 /2	6/0 /0	1/0 /0

Steve Buechele, right-handed hitter, has a high overall fastball average against left-handed pitchers (.354). His overall fastball average against right-handed pitchers is 109 points lower (.245).

Buechele has trouble with outside and inside fastballs thrown by right-handed pitchers. His fastball strength is in the over-the-middle locations.

Buechele hits low-over-the-middle fastballs for a strong .382 average. He goes deep down the left line with this pitch.

LOW-OVER-THE-MIDDLE FASTBALLS

BATTING AVERAGE .382
Play

Left	Deep and shifted toward the left field line
Center	Deep in straightaway center field
Right	Medium-deep in straightaway right field
Short	Normal position
Second	*No instances recorded*

He hits high-over-the-middle fastballs for an even more impressive .428. He hits this pitch to the right side of the infield, straightaway to medium-deep left and center fields, and to deep right-center field.

HIGH-OVER-THE-MIDDLE FASTBALLS

BATTING AVERAGE .428
Play

Left	Medium-deep in straightaway left field
Center	Medium-deep in straightaway center field

Right	Deep and shifted toward center field
Short	Up middle (shifted toward second base)
Second	Shifted toward first base

He hits medium-high outside fastballs straightaway to all fields.

MEDIUM-HIGH OUTSIDE FASTBALLS

BATTING AVERAGE .234
Play

Left	Deep in straightaway left field
Center	Deep in straightaway center field
Right	Deep in straightaway right field
Short	Normal position
Second	Normal position

Buechele hits low-outside fastballs to right field (his opposite field). His low average in this location (.125) indicates that he hits this pitch mostly for easy pop-ups and grounders.

LOW-OUTSIDE FASTBALLS

BATTING AVERAGE .125
Play

Left	Medium-deep and shifted toward center field
Center	Deep and shifted toward right field
Right	Deep in straightaway right field
Short	Up middle (shifted toward second base)
Second	Normal position

He has a low average in his medium-high inside fastball location (.152). He hits this pitch down the left line and straightaway to the other fields.

MEDIUM-HIGH INSIDE FASTBALLS

BATTING AVERAGE .152
Play

Left	Deep and shifted toward the left field line
Center	Medium-deep in straightaway center field
Right	Deep in straightaway right field
Short	Normal position
Second	Normal position

Buechele has tremendous difficulty with curves and sliders against right-handed pitchers. In particular look at his low-outside curve and low-outside slider locations. Ahead or behind, pitchers could gain an edge by throwing him these pitches.

Buechele Against Left-Handed Pitchers

Note his high averages in the waist-high locations against left-handers (.333, .700, and .352, inside to outside). He hits medium-high outside fastballs deep to left center and center.

MEDIUM-HIGH OUTSIDE FASTBALLS
(THROWN BY LEFT-HANDED PITCHERS)

BATTING AVERAGE .352
Play

Left	Deep and shifted toward center field
Center	Deep in straightaway center field
Right	Medium-deep in straightaway right field

Short	Normal position
Second	Normal position

The left fielder and the shortstop would have to change position for a high-outside fastball as compared to a medium-high outside fastball.

HIGH-OUTSIDE FASTBALLS
(THROWN BY LEFT-HANDED PITCHERS)

BATTING AVERAGE .333
Play

Left	Deep in straightaway left field
Center	Deep in straightaway center field
Right	Medium-deep in straightaway right field
Short	Shifted toward third base
Second	*No instances recorded*

Pitchers would not want to throw Buechele a medium-over-the-middle fastball (.700), but it's interesting to see how he hits this pitch.

MEDIUM-OVER-THE-MIDDLE FASTBALLS
(THROWN BY LEFT-HANDED PITCHERS)

BATTING AVERAGE .700
Play

Left	Medium-deep in straightaway left field
Center	Deep in straightaway center field
Right	*No instances recorded*
Short	Shifted toward third base
Second	*No instances recorded*

Buechele has trouble with low curves and low-middle sliders against left-handers. He seems to hit medium-high outside curves well (.333 on 3 for 9).

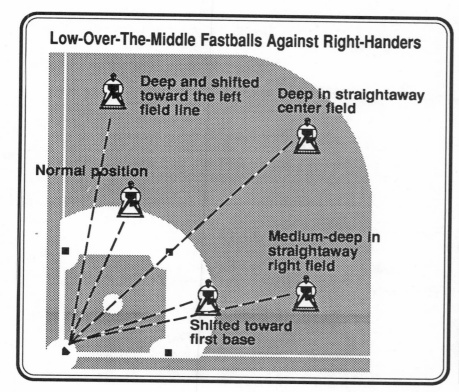

Low-Over-The-Middle Fastballs Against Right-Handers

Deep and shifted toward the left field line

Deep in straightaway center field

Normal position

Medium-deep in straightaway right field

Shifted toward first base

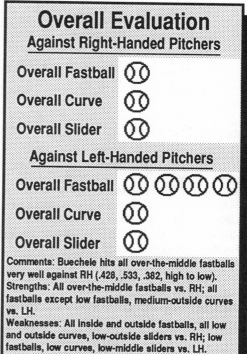

Overall Evaluation
Against Right-Handed Pitchers

Overall Fastball
Overall Curve
Overall Slider

Against Left-Handed Pitchers

Overall Fastball
Overall Curve
Overall Slider

Comments: Buechele hits all over-the-middle fastballs very well against RH (.428, .533, .382, high to low).
Strengths: All over-the-middle fastballs vs. RH; all fastballs except low fastballs, medium-outside curves vs. LH.
Weaknesses: All inside and outside fastballs, all low and outside curves, low-outside sliders vs. RH; low fastballs, low curves, low-middle sliders vs. LH.

Cecil Espy Against Right-Handed Pitchers
Overall BARS Batting Average .197

Fastball Average .192

	Outside	Middle	Inside
High	11/ 181 /2	2/ 500 /1	4/ 0 /0
Med	52/ 288 /15	10/ 100 /1	17/ 58 /1
Low	7/ 142 /1	14/ 214 /3	8/ 0 /0

Curve Average .210

	Outside	Middle	Inside
High	1/ 0 /0	0/ 0 /0	0/ 0 /0
Med	9/ 222 /2	0/ 0 /0	1/ 1000 /1
Low	4/ 0 /0	2/ 0 /0	2/ 500 /1

Slider Average .000

	Outside	Middle	Inside
High	1/ 0 /0	0/ 0 /0	0/ 0 /0
Med	1/ 0 /0	0/ 0 /0	2/ 0 /0
Low	0/ 0 /0	0/ 0 /0	3/ 0 /0

Cecil Espy Against Left-Handed Pitchers
Overall BARS Batting Average .125

Fastball Average .111

	Inside	Middle	Outside
High	0/ 0 /0	0/ 0 /0	1/ 0 /0
Med	2/ 0 /0	0/ 0 /0	8/ 125 /1
Low	1/ 0 /0	5/ 200 /1	1/ 0 /0

Curve Average .000

	Inside	Middle	Outside
High	0/ 0 /0	0/ 0 /0	0/ 0 /0
Med	0/ 0 /0	0/ 0 /0	1/ 0 /0
Low	0/ 0 /0	0/ 0 /0	0/ 0 /0

Slider Average .200

	Inside	Middle	Outside
High	1/ 1000 /1	0/ 0 /0	0/ 0 /0
Med	0/ 0 /0	0/ 0 /0	1/ 0 /0
Low	3/ 0 /0	0/ 0 /0	0/ 0 /0

Switch-hitting Cecil Espy has trouble with fastballs against both right- and left-handed pitchers (.192 overall vs. right-handers, .111 overall vs. left-handers).

He has weaknesses in all his inside and low fastball locations against right-handers. His strongest fastball location against right-handers is medium-high outside. This is his most highly pitched locations and buoys up his entire average.

The chart below and the field diagram on the opposite page show how fielders need to play for this pitch.

MEDIUM-HIGH OUTSIDE FASTBALLS

BATTING AVERAGE .288
Play

Left	Medium-deep in straightaway left field
Center	Deep and shifted toward left field
Right	Medium-deep in straightaway right field
Short	Up middle (shifted toward second base)
Second	Shifted toward first base

He hits only .058 on 1 for 17 against medium-high inside fastballs.

MEDIUM-HIGH INSIDE FASTBALLS

BATTING AVERAGE .058
Play

Left	Medium-deep and shifted toward the left field line
Center	*No instances recorded*
Right	Deep and shifted toward the right field line
Short	Normal position
Second	Normal position

He hits .214 against low-over-the-middle fastballs.

LOW-OVER-THE-MIDDLE FASTBALLS

BATTING AVERAGE .214
Play

Left	Deep and shifted toward the left field line
Center	Deep in straightaway center field
Right	Medium-deep in straightaway right field
Short	Normal position
Second	Shifted toward first base

His batting average against fastballs thrown by left-handers is very weak (.111). He hits .125 against medium-high outside fastballs thrown by lefties.

MEDIUM-HIGH OUTSIDE FASTBALLS
(THROWN BY LEFT-HANDED PITCHERS)

BATTING AVERAGE .125
Play

Left	*No instances recorded*
Center	Deep and shifted toward right field
Right	*No instances recorded*
Short	Normal position
Second	Shifted toward first base

Medium-High Outside Fastballs
(Thrown By Right-Handed Pitchers)

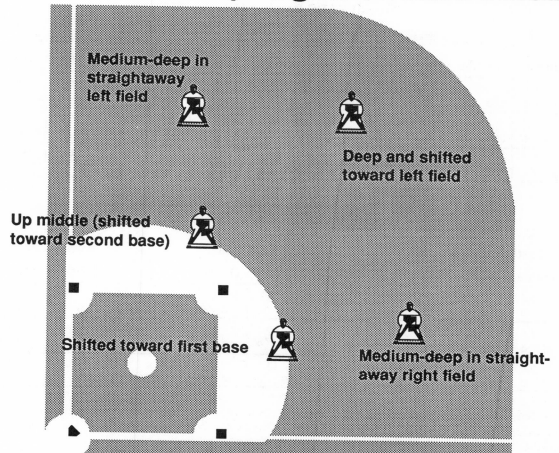

Medium-deep in straightaway left field

Deep and shifted toward left field

Up middle (shifted toward second base)

Shifted toward first base

Medium-deep in straight-away right field

Ahead And Behind In The Count Vs. RH

Ahead

Fastball Average .226

	Outside	Middle	Inside
High	7/285/2	0/0/0	0/0/0
Med	24/291/7	2/0/0	6/0/0
Low	3/333/1	8/250/2	3/0/0

Curve Average .600

	Outside	Middle	Inside
High	0/0/0	0/0/0	0/0/0
Med	4/500/2	0/0/0	1/1000/1
Low	0/0/0	0/0/0	0/0/0

Behind

Fastball Average .200

	Outside	Middle	Inside
High	3/0/0	2/500/1	2/0/0
Med	8/375/3	0/0/0	3/0/0
Low	1/0/0	1/0/0	0/0/0

Curve Average .200

	Outside	Middle	Inside
High	0/0/0	0/0/0	0/0/0
Med	1/0/0	0/0/0	0/0/0
Low	2/0/0	1/0/0	1/1000/1

Overall Evaluation
Against Right-Handed Pitchers

Overall Fastball ⚾⚾

Overall Curve ⚾⚾

Overall Slider — Not enough information

Against Left-Handed Pitchers

Overall Fastball ⚾⚾

Overall Curve — Not enough information

Overall Slider — Not enough information

Comments: Weak against inside fastballs and low fastballs vs. RH.
Strengths: Medium-outside fastballs vs. RH.
Weaknesses: Inside fastballs, low fastballs, high-outside fastballs, medium-middle fastballs, outside curves vs. RH; medium-outside fastballs vs. LH.

Julio Franco (Right Handed)   *Texas Rangers*

Julio Franco Against Right-Handed Pitchers
Overall BARS Batting Average .328

Fastball Average .345

	Inside	Middle	Outside
High	14/ 285 /4	37/ 351 /13	23/ 173 /4
Med	46/ 282 /13	36/ 388 /14	138/ 369 /51
Low	18/ 444 /8	59/ 474 /28	28/ 107 /3

Curve Average .300

	Inside	Middle	Outside
High	2/ 1000 /2	4/ 1000 /4	2/ 0 /0
Med	9/ 333 /3	4/ 500 /2	21/ 190 /4
Low	3/ 666 /2	13/ 307 /4	22/ 136 /3

Slider Average .263

	Inside	Middle	Outside
High	2/ 1000 /2	6/ 0 /0	1/ 1000 /1
Med	4/ 250 /1	0/ 0 /0	24/ 333 /8
Low	1/ 0 /0	6/ 333 /2	28/ 178 /5

Julio Franco Against Left-Handed Pitchers
Overall BARS Batting Average .281

Fastball Average .283

	Inside	Middle	Outside
High	1/ 0 /0	13/ 230 /3	17/ 117 /2
Med	14/ 285 /4	11/ 181 /2	63/ 301 /19
Low	6/ 166 /1	26/ 423 /11	8/ 375 /3

Curve Average .282

	Inside	Middle	Outside
High	0/ 0 /0	1/ 0 /0	0/ 0 /0
Med	2/ 500 /1	2/ 1000 /2	12/ 250 /3
Low	4/ 500 /2	11/ 272 /3	7/ 0 /0

Slider Average .260

	Inside	Middle	Outside
High	0/ 0 /0	2/ 0 /0	0/ 0 /0
Med	6/ 500 /3	0/ 0 /0	7/ 142 /1
Low	4/ 250 /1	4/ 250 /1	0/ 0 /0

Right-handed hitting Julio Franco has an exceptionally strong .345 overall fastball average against right-handed pitchers. This is much stronger than his .283 overall fastball average against left-handed pitchers. Notice that he also hits curves and sliders better against right-handers. This is somewhat unusual for a right-handed hitter.

Against right-handers he hits .369 against medium-high outside fastballs. He hits this pitch better when ahead in the count (see his Ahead and Behind charts on the opposite page).

MEDIUM-HIGH OUTSIDE FASTBALLS (WHEN AHEAD IN THE COUNT)

BATTING AVERAGE .466
Play
Left   Deep in straightaway left field
Center   Medium-deep in straightaway center field
Right   Deep in straightaway right field
Short   Up middle (shifted toward second base)
Second   Normal position

MEDIUM-HIGH OUTSIDE FASTBALLS (WHEN BEHIND IN THE COUNT)

BATTING AVERAGE .322
Play
Left   Deep and shifted toward the left field line
Center   Deep in straightaway center field
Right   Deep in straightaway right field

Short   Up middle (shifted toward second base)
Second   Normal position

Franco is strong against all fastballs thrown over-the-middle (.351, .388, and .474, high to low). He hits medium-over-the-middle fastballs straight-away to all fields. He hits high-over-the-middle fastballs somewhat to his opposite field (deep into the left-center alley and medium-deep down the right line).

HIGH-OVER-THE-MIDDLE FASTBALLS

BATTING AVERAGE .351
Play
Left   Deep and shifted toward center field
Center   Medium-deep in straightaway center field
Right   Medium-deep and shifted toward the right line
Short   Up middle (shifted toward second base)
Second   Normal position

He pulls low-over-the-middle fastballs. Note, however, that the shortstop needs to play shifted toward second base.

LOW-OVER-THE-MIDDLE FASTBALLS

BATTING AVERAGE .474
Play
Left   Deep and shifted toward the left field line
Center   Medium-deep in straightaway center field
Right   Medium-deep and shifted toward center field

Short	Up middle (shifted toward second base)
Second	Normal position

He goes to his opposite field with medium-high inside fastballs. But the shortstop needs to be shifted toward third base. This shows the importance of aligning each fielder on a pitch-by-pitch basis according to the BARS System.

MEDIUM-HIGH INSIDE FASTBALLS

BATTING AVERAGE .282
Play

Left	Deep and shifted toward center field
Center	Medium-deep in straightaway center field
Right	Deep and shifted toward the right field line
Short	Shifted toward third base
Second	Normal position

Franco has trouble with outside curves and with low-outside sliders against right-handers. He hits low-over-the-middle curves and medium-high outside sliders excellently, however (.307 and .333).

MEDIUM-HIGH OUTSIDE SLIDERS

BATTING AVERAGE .333
Play

Left	Medium-deep in straightaway left field
Center	Deep and shifted toward right field
Right	Medium-deep in straightaway right field
Short	Normal position
Second	*No instances recorded*

Franco Against Left-Handed Pitchers

Franco hits for lower fastball averages against left-handed pitchers. His .301 against medium-high outside fastballs is solid enough, but not spectacular like his .369 average in this location against right-handers.

MEDIUM-HIGH OUTSIDE FASTBALLS (THROWN BY LEFT-HANDED PITCHERS)

BATTING AVERAGE .301
Play

Left	Deep in straightaway left field
Center	Deep in straightaway center field
Right	Deep and shifted toward the right field line
Short	Normal position
Second	Normal position

His .423 against low-over-the-middle fastballs is top rate.

LOW-OVER-THE-MIDDLE FASTBALLS (THROWN BY LEFT-HANDED PITCHERS)

BATTING AVERAGE .423
Play

Left	Medium-deep in straightaway left field
Center	Deep and shifted toward right field
Right	Medium-deep in straightaway right field
Short	Shifted toward third base
Second	*No instances recorded*

Franco has trouble with high-outside and high-over-the-middle fastballs against left-handers (.117 and .230). He also has trouble with low-outside curves (.000 on 0 for 7) and medium-high outside sliders (.142). He hits medium-high outside and low-over-the-middle curves adequately (.250 and .272).

Ahead And Behind In The Count Vs. RH

Ahead

Fastball Average .388

	Inside	Middle	Outside
High	2/0 0/0	19/315 6	8/250 2
Med	30/300 9	21/428 9	60/466 28
Low	9/333 3	29/482 14	10/200 2

Curve Average .294

	Inside	Middle	Outside
High	0/0 0/0	2/1000 2	1/0 0/0
Med	2/500 1	0/0 0/0	8/250 2
Low	0/0 0/0	1/0 0/0	3/0 0/0

Behind

Fastball Average .333

	Inside	Middle	Outside
High	4/250 1	10/400 4	6/166 1
Med	4/250 1	5/400 2	31/322 10
Low	1/0 0/0	8/625 5	3/0 0/0

Curve Average .400

	Inside	Middle	Outside
High	1/1000 1	2/1000 2	1/0 0/0
Med	4/250 1	3/666 2	2/0 0/0
Low	2/1000 2	6/333 2	9/222 2

Overall Evaluation

Against Right-Handed Pitchers

Overall Fastball	⚾⚾⚾⚾
Overall Curve	⚾⚾⚾⚾
Overall Slider	⚾⚾

Against Left-Handed Pitchers

Overall Fastball	⚾⚾
Overall Curve	⚾⚾⚾
Overall Slider	⚾⚾

Comments: Weak vs. low-outside fastballs vs. RH. Strengths: Fastballs except low-outside and high-outside, low-middle curves and medium-outside sliders vs. RH; low-middle, low-outside and medium-outside fastballs against LH. Weaknesses: High outside and low-outside fastballs, outside curves and low-outside sliders vs. RH; high fastballs, medium-middle fastballs, outside curves and medium-outside sliders vs. LH.

Pete Incaviglia (Right Handed) — *Texas Rangers*

Pete Incaviglia Against Right-Handed Pitchers
Overall BARS Batting Average .225

Fastball Average .222

	Inside	Middle	Outside
High	20/ 100/2	19/ 105/2	20/ 100/2
Med	40/ 225/9	7/ 428/3	112/ 250/28
Low	14/ 214/3	24/ 375/9	31/ 193/6

Curve Average .206

	Inside	Middle	Outside
High	2/ 0/0	2/ 0/0	4/ 250/1
Med	4/ 500/2	3/ 666/2	47/ 234/11
Low	3/ 0/0	7/ 428/3	25/ 40/1

Slider Average .266

	Inside	Middle	Outside
High	2/ 0/0	4/ 500/2	2/ 500/1
Med	3/ 333/1	2/ 500/1	14/ 357/5
Low	1/ 1000/1	5/ 200/1	27/ 148/4

Pete Incaviglia Against Left-Handed Pitchers
Overall BARS Batting Average .347

Fastball Average .370

	Inside	Middle	Outside
High	7/ 0/0	4/ 500/2	12/ 0/0
Med	12/ 166/2	2/ 1000/2	61/ 475/29
Low	7/ 142/1	13/ 615/8	9/ 333/3

Curve Average .281

	Inside	Middle	Outside
High	1/ 0/0	3/ 666/2	1/ 0/0
Med	2/ 0/0	2/ 0/0	10/ 400/4
Low	3/ 666/2	6/ 166/1	4/ 0/0

Slider Average .354

	Inside	Middle	Outside
High	0/ 0/0	1/ 1000/1	0/ 0/0
Med	5/ 600/3	0/ 0/0	9/ 555/5
Low	9/ 111/1	7/ 142/1	0/ 0/0

Incaviglia doesn't hit fastballs well against right-handers. His average is almost 150 points higher against fastballs thrown by left-handed pitchers. Note his low averages against right-handers in the three high fastball locations (.100, .105 and .100, inside to outside). He also has trouble with medium-high inside (.225), low-inside (.214) and low-outside (.193).

He hits .250 against medium-high outside fastballs thrown by right-handers. He hits this pitch straight-away to the outfield.

MEDIUM-HIGH OUTSIDE FASTBALLS

BATTING AVERAGE .250
Play

Left	Deep in straightaway left field
Center	Deep in straightaway center field
Right	Deep in straightaway right field
Short	Up middle (shifted toward second base)
Second	Normal position

He hits low-over-the-middle fastballs at a .375 clip.

LOW-OVER-THE-MIDDLE FASTBALLS

BATTING AVERAGE .375
Play

Left	Medium-deep in straightaway left field
Center	Deep and shifted toward right field
Right	Deep in straightaway right field
Short	Shifted toward third base
Second	Normal position

He pulls medium-high inside fastballs to the outfield but tends to go to the right side of the infield.

MEDIUM-HIGH INSIDE FASTBALLS

BATTING AVERAGE .225
Play

Left	Deep and shifted toward the left field line
Center	Deep in straightaway center field
Right	Medium-deep and shifted toward center field
Short	Up middle (shifted toward second base)
Second	Normal position

Incaviglia Against Curves And Sliders

Incaviglia hits low-outside curves very poorly (.040 on 1 for 25). It seems that he mostly strikes out on low-outside curves because the only recorded hit balls in this location are to shortstop toward third base.

Incaviglia hits medium-high outside curves for a .234 average.

MEDIUM-HIGH OUTSIDE CURVEBALLS

BATTING AVERAGE .234
Play

Left	Deep in straightaway left field

Center	Deep in straightaway center field
Right	Deep and shifted toward center field
Short	Normal position
Second	Normal position

He has trouble with low-outside sliders (.148) but hits medium-high outside sliders very well (.357).

MEDIUM-HIGH OUTSIDE SLIDERS

BATTING AVERAGE .357
Play
Left	Deep in straightaway left field
Center	Medium-deep and shifted toward left field
Right	Medium-deep in straightaway right field
Short	Up middle (shifted toward second base)
Second	Shifted toward first base

Incaviglia Against Left-Handed Pitchers

Incaviglia has a much higher average against left-handed than against right-handed pitchers. His fastball, curve and slider averages all are higher against left-handers.

Notice the strong .475 average in his medium-high outside fastball location against left-handers. This is strong enough to boost his overall fastball average against left-handers to a lofty .370.

He hits this pitch short to straightaway left and deep into the right-center gap.

MEDIUM-HIGH OUTSIDE FASTBALLS
(THROWN BY LEFT-HANDED PITCHERS)

BATTING AVERAGE .475
Play
Left	Short in straightaway left field
Center	Medium-deep in straightaway center field
Right	Deep and shifted toward center field
Short	Up middle (shifted toward second base)
Second	Normal position

Since this fielding strategy is based on a relatively high number of instances (61 in the medium-high outside fastball location), it is safe to say that fielders could position themselves with great accuracy for this pitch and prevent a lot of Incaviglia's hits.

Note that Incaviglia has trouble in the adjacent high-outside fastball location (0 for 12). All in all, pitchers try to throw outside to him (as indicated by the high number of instances in his outside locations), but they need to keep the ball up since he does so well in the other outside locations.

Incaviglia hits low-over-the-middle fastballs extremely well against lefties.

LOW-OVER-THE-MIDDLE FASTBALLS
(THROWN BY LEFT-HANDED PITCHERS)

BATTING AVERAGE .615
Play
Left	Deep and shifted toward center field
Center	Deep in straightaway center field
Right	Deep and shifted toward center field
Short	Shifted toward third base
Second	*No instances recorded*

Note that Incaviglia also hits medium-high outside curves and sliders for high averages (.400 for curves, .555 for sliders).

Ahead And Behind In The Count Vs. RH
Ahead

Fastball Average .233
	Inside	Middle	Outside
High	6/166 /1	5/200 /1	4/500 /2
Med	18/166 /3	3/333 /1	40/250 /10
Low	5/200 /1	12/250 /3	10/200 /2

Curve Average .227
	Inside	Middle	Outside
High	0/0 /0	0/0 /0	4/250 /1
Med	0/0 /0	0/0 /0	12/250 /3
Low	0/0 /0	3/0 /0	3/333 /1

Behind

Fastball Average .333
	Inside	Middle	Outside
High	2/0 /0	1/1000 /1	0/0 /0
Med	4/0 /0	3/333 /1	14/357 /5
Low	2/1000 /2	4/500 /2	3/0 /0

Curve Average .352
	Inside	Middle	Outside
High	1/0 /0	1/0 /0	0/0 /0
Med	2/1000 /2	1/1000 /1	11/272 /3
Low	0/0 /0	0/0 /0	1/0 /0

Overall Evaluation
Against Right-Handed Pitchers

Overall Fastball	⚾⚾
Overall Curve	⚾⚾
Overall Slider	⚾⚾ ⚾⚾

Against Left-Handed Pitchers

Overall Fastball	⚾⚾ ⚾⚾ ⚾⚾ ⚾⚾
Overall Curve	⚾⚾ ⚾⚾ ⚾⚾
Overall Slider	⚾⚾ ⚾⚾ ⚾⚾ ⚾⚾

Comments: Has many fastball weaknesses against RH; very strong against fastballs vs. LH.

Strengths: Low-middle fastballs and medium-outside sliders vs. RH; medium-outside, low-middle and low-outside fastballs, medium-outside curves and medium-outside sliders vs. LH.

Weaknesses: All inside, outside and high fastballs, outside curves, low-outside sliders vs. RH; inside fastballs and high-outside fastballs, low-sliders vs. LH.

Rick Leach (Left Handed)   *Texas Rangers*

Rick Leach Against Right-Handed Pitchers
Overall BARS Batting Average .305

Fastball Average .305

	Outside	Middle	Inside
High	20/ 350 /7	11/ 545 /6	9/ 333 /3
Med	50/ 260 /13	8/ 500 /4	20/ 250 /5
Low	7/ 142 /1	15/ 200 /3	4/ 500 /2

Curve Average .307

	Outside	Middle	Inside
High	1/ 0 /0	5/ 400 /2	0/ 0 /0
Med	3/ 333 /1	3/ 666 /2	3/ 333 /1
Low	6/ 0 /0	4/ 500 /2	1/ 0 /0

Slider Average .300

	Outside	Middle	Inside
High	0/ 0 /0	0/ 0 /0	1/ 0 /0
Med	0/ 0 /0	0/ 0 /0	2/ 0 /0
Low	4/ 500 /2	0/ 0 /0	3/ 333 /1

Left-handed hitter Rick Leach has a solid .305 overall fastball average against right-handed pitchers. This is primarily built on his strength against high fastballs (.350, .545, and .333, outside to inside). His charts against left-handed pitchers are not shown because so little information is available for Leach against left-handers.

He hits high-outside fastballs deep down the left line and to the shortstop in the hole.

HIGH-OUTSIDE FASTBALLS

BATTING AVERAGE .350
Play

Left	Deep and shifted toward the left field line
Center	Medium-deep in straightaway center field
Right	Medium-deep in straightaway right field
Short	Shifted toward third base
Second	Normal position

His .545 against high-over-the-middle fastballs is excellent. He goes to his opposite field with this pitch when hitting to the outfield (deep down the left line and medium-deep into the right-center gap). But the infielders need to play to the right side. The chart below and the field diagram on the opposite page show how fielders should play for this pitch.

HIGH-OVER-THE-MIDDLE FASTBALLS

BATTING AVERAGE .545
Play

Left	Deep and shifted toward the left field line
Center	Deep in straightaway center field
Right	Medium-deep and shifted toward center field
Short	Up middle (shifted toward second base)
Second	Shifted toward first base

He hits high-inside fastballs short to left and deep to the other fields.

HIGH-INSIDE FASTBALLS

BATTING AVERAGE .333
Play

Left	Short in straightaway left field
Center	Deep in straightaway center field
Right	Deep and shifted toward the right field line
Short	Normal position
Second	*No instances recorded*

He hits .260 in his highly pitched medium-high outside fastball location. He goes deep down the left line and into the deep right-center alley. But again the infielders need to play shifted toward the right side.

MEDIUM-HIGH OUTSIDE FASTBALLS

BATTING AVERAGE .260
Play

Left	Deep and shifted toward the left field line
Center	Medium-deep in straightaway center field
Right	Deep and shifted toward center field
Short	Up middle (shifted toward second base)
Second	Shifted toward first base

His .250 against medium-high inside fastballs shows a weakness.

MEDIUM-HIGH INSIDE FASTBALLS

BATTING AVERAGE .250
Play

Left	Deep and shifted toward the left field line
Center	Medium-deep in straightaway center field
Right	Deep and shifted toward the right field line
Short	Up middle (shifted toward second base)
Second	Shifted toward first base

Leach does well against curves, although there are fewer instances recorded. He seems to have trouble with low-outside curves (0 for 6). This is also his weakest fastball location (.142).

High-Over-The-Middle Fastballs
(Thrown By Right-Handed Pitchers)

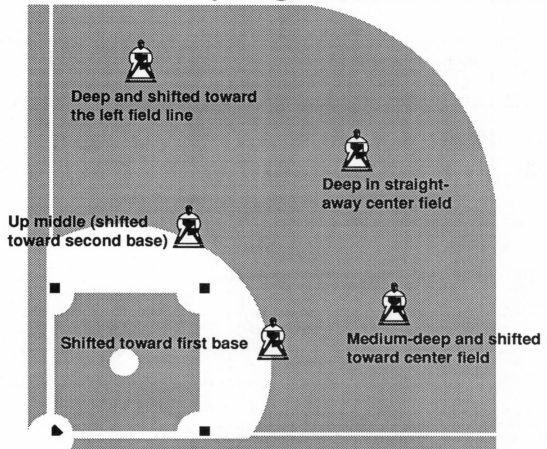

Deep and shifted toward the left field line

Deep in straight-away center field

Up middle (shifted toward second base)

Shifted toward first base

Medium-deep and shifted toward center field

Ahead And Behind In The Count Vs. RH

Ahead

Fastball Average .362

	Outside	Middle	Inside
High	7/428 /3	5/200 /1	2/1000 /2
Med	25/400 /10	5/400 /2	10/200 /2
Low	2/0 /0	11/272 /3	2/1000 /2

Curve Average .600

	Outside	Middle	Inside
High	1/0 /0	3/666 /2	0/0 /0
Med	1/1000 /1	0/0 /0	2/500 /1
Low	1/0 /0	2/1000 /2	0/0 /0

Behind

Fastball Average .294

	Outside	Middle	Inside
High	6/500 /3	2/1000 /2	5/200 /1
Med	11/272 /3	0/0 /0	4/250 /1
Low	1/0 /0	3/0 /0	2/0 /0

Curve Average .200

	Outside	Middle	Inside
High	0/0 /0	1/0 /0	0/0 /0
Med	0/0 /0	1/1000 /1	0/0 /0
Low	1/0 /0	2/0 /0	0/0 /0

Overall Evaluation
Against Right-Handed Pitchers

Overall Fastball ⚾⚾ ⚾⚾ ⚾⚾

Overall Curve ⚾⚾ ⚾⚾ ⚾⚾ ⚾⚾

Overall Slider   Not enough information

Against Left-Handed Pitchers

Overall Fastball   Not enough information

Overall Curve   Not enough information

Overall Slider   Not enough information

Comments: Strong against high fastballs vs. RH.
Strengths: High fastballs, medium-middle fastballs, over-the-middle curves vs. RH.
Weaknesses: Low-outside, low-middle and medium-inside fastballs, low-outside curves vs. RH.

367

Fred Manrique Against Right-Handed Pitchers
Overall BARS Batting Average .236

Fastball Average .261

	Inside	Middle	Outside
High	7 / 0 / 0	13 / 538 / 7	6 / 500 / 3
Med	18 / 333 / 6	4 / 250 / 1	67 / 194 / 13
Low	8 / 125 / 1	13 / 461 / 6	17 / 176 / 3

Curve Average .142

	Inside	Middle	Outside
High	2 / 0 / 0	0 / 0 / 0	0 / 0 / 0
Med	2 / 500 / 1	0 / 0 / 0	8 / 250 / 2
Low	1 / 0 / 0	3 / 333 / 1	12 / 0 / 0

Slider Average .192

	Inside	Middle	Outside
High	0 / 0 / 0	4 / 500 / 2	0 / 0 / 0
Med	0 / 0 / 0	2 / 0 / 0	7 / 142 / 1
Low	2 / 0 / 0	4 / 250 / 1	7 / 142 / 1

Fred Manrique Against Left-Handed Pitchers
Overall BARS Batting Average .279

Fastball Average .319

	Inside	Middle	Outside
High	6 / 500 / 3	6 / 500 / 3	8 / 250 / 2
Med	6 / 333 / 2	4 / 500 / 2	39 / 333 / 13
Low	5 / 200 / 1	13 / 307 / 4	7 / 0 / 0

Curve Average .083

	Inside	Middle	Outside
High	0 / 0 / 0	0 / 0 / 0	2 / 0 / 0
Med	2 / 500 / 1	0 / 0 / 0	3 / 0 / 0
Low	1 / 0 / 0	2 / 0 / 0	2 / 0 / 0

Slider Average .166

	Inside	Middle	Outside
High	0 / 0 / 0	0 / 0 / 0	0 / 0 / 0
Med	0 / 0 / 0	0 / 0 / 0	4 / 500 / 2
Low	6 / 0 / 0	2 / 0 / 0	0 / 0 / 0

Right-handed hitter Fred Manrique has a higher BARS fastball average against left-handed than against right-handed pitchers (.319 overall fastball vs. left-handers, .261 overall fastball vs. right-handers). This reflects in his overall averages of .279 vs. left-handers, .236 vs. right-handers.

Manrique's .194 average in his medium-high outside fastball location against right-handed pitchers is weak.

MEDIUM-HIGH OUTSIDE FASTBALLS

BATTING AVERAGE .194
Play
Left	Deep and shifted toward the left field line
Center	Medium-deep in straightaway center field
Right	Deep and shifted toward right field
Short	Normal position
Second	Shifted toward first base

He hits this pitch about the same when ahead as when behind in the count. It's interesting to see how his Ahead and Behind fielding strategies combine to make up his overall fielding strategy for this location as shown above. Remember that his even-count pitches are not included in his Ahead and Behind averages.

MEDIUM-HIGH OUTSIDE FASTBALLS (WHEN BEHIND IN THE COUNT)

BATTING AVERAGE .214
Play
Left	Deep and shifted toward the left field line
Center	Deep and shifted toward left field
Right	*No instances recorded*
Short	Up middle (shifted toward second base)
Second	Normal position

MEDIUM-HIGH OUTSIDE FASTBALLS (WHEN AHEAD IN THE COUNT)

BATTING AVERAGE .216
Play
Left	Deep and shifted toward the left field line
Center	Medium-deep in straightaway center field
Right	Medium-deep in straightaway right field
Short	Normal position
Second	Shifted toward first base

He hits low-over-the-middle fastballs at an excellent .461 clip.

LOW-OVER-THE-MIDDLE FASTBALLS

BATTING AVERAGE .461
Play
Left	Deep in straightaway left field
Center	Medium-deep in straightaway center field
Right	Medium-deep in straightaway right field
Short	*No instances recorded*
Second	Normal position

He hits an exceptional .538 against high-over-the-middle fastballs.

HIGH-OVER-THE-MIDDLE FASTBALLS

BATTING AVERAGE .538
Play

Left   Medium-deep and shifted toward the left field line
Center   Medium-deep in straightaway center field
Right   Medium-deep and shifted toward center field
Short   Shifted toward third base
Second   *No instances recorded*

He hits .333 against medium-high inside fastballs.

MEDIUM-HIGH INSIDE FASTBALLS

BATTING AVERAGE .333
Play

Left   Deep in straightaway left field
Center   Medium-deep in straightaway center field
Right   Medium-deep and shifted toward center field
Short   Normal position
Second   Shifted toward first base

Manrique Against Curves And Sliders

Manrique's 0-for-12 against low-outside curves indicates a weakness, but he hits medium-high outside curves fairly well (.250). The fielding strategy against medium-high outside curves is unique. There are no recorded instances of hit balls other than deep to the left fielder down the line and to the shortstop shifted

toward third base.

MEDIUM-HIGH OUTSIDE CURVEBALLS

BATTING AVERAGE .250
Play

Left   Deep and shifted toward the left field line
Center   *No instances recorded*
Right   *No instances recorded*
Short   Shifted toward third base
Second   *No instances recorded*

Manrique Against Left-Handed Pitchers

Against left-handers, Manrique hits a solid .333 against medium-high outside fastballs. He hits this pitch deep to all fields.

MEDIUM-HIGH OUTSIDE FASTBALLS (THROWN BY LEFT-HANDED PITCHERS)

BATTING AVERAGE .333
Play

Left   Deep and shifted toward the left field line
Center   Deep in straightaway center field
Right   Deep in straightaway right field
Short   Up middle (shifted toward second base)
Second   Normal position

Manrique is weak against low-outside fastballs (0 for 7). He hits low-over-the-middle fastballs for a solid .307 average. He hits this pitch deep down the left line and deep into the right-center gap.

Ahead And Behind In The Count Vs. RH

Ahead

Fastball Average .346

	Inside	Middle	Outside
High	0/0 0	7/4 571	3/3 1000
Med	5/4 800	3/1 333	37/8 216
Low	3/0 0	10/4 400	7/2 285

Curve Average .250

	Inside	Middle	Outside
High	0/0 0	0/0 0	0/0 0
Med	1/0 0	0/0 0	2/1 500
Low	0/0 0	0/0 0	1/0 0

Behind

Fastball Average .217

	Inside	Middle	Outside
High	3/0 0	2/1 500	0/0 0
Med	2/0 0	0/0 0	14/3 214
Low	1/1 1000	0/0 0	1/0 0

Curve Average .300

	Inside	Middle	Outside
High	1/0 0	0/0 0	0/0 0
Med	1/1 1000	0/0 0	3/1 333
Low	0/0 0	2/1 500	3/0 0

Overall Evaluation

Against Right-Handed Pitchers

Overall Fastball ⚾⚾
Overall Curve ⚾⚾
Overall Slider ⚾⚾

Against Left-Handed Pitchers

Overall Fastball ⚾⚾ ⚾⚾ ⚾⚾
Overall Curve Not enough information
Overall Slider Not enough information

Comments: Has problems with low-outside and medium-outside fastballs vs. RH.
Strengths: Low-middle, high-middle and medium-inside fastballs vs. RH; medium-outside and all over-the-middle fastballs vs. LH.
Weaknesses: Medium-outside and low-outside fastballs, low-inside and high-inside fastballs, low-outside curves and outside sliders vs. RH; low-outside fastballs vs. LH.

Rafael Palmeiro (Left Handed) — *Texas Rangers*

Rafael Palmeiro Against Right-Handed Pitchers
Overall BARS Batting Average .323

Fastball Average .358

	Outside	Middle	Inside
High	29/241 /7	24/291 /7	27/370 /10
Med	65/430 /28	5/200 /1	60/383 /23
Low	40/250 /10	50/420 /21	51/372 /19

Curve Average .266

	Outside	Middle	Inside
High	1/0 /0	6/166 /1	10/400 /4
Med	12/166 /2	2/0 /0	1/1000 /1
Low	11/363 /4	17/411 /7	15/66 /1

Slider Average .148

	Outside	Middle	Inside
High	0/0 /0	2/500 /1	2/0 /0
Med	4/250 /1	0/0 /0	9/111 /1
Low	3/333 /1	5/0 /0	22/136 /3

Rafael Palmeiro Against Left-Handed Pitchers
Overall BARS Batting Average .305

Fastball Average .341

	Outside	Middle	Inside
High	7/428 /3	4/250 /1	12/166 /2
Med	15/533 /8	0/0 /0	19/368 /7
Low	1/1000 /1	11/181 /2	13/307 /4

Curve Average .200

	Outside	Middle	Inside
High	0/0 /0	1/0 /0	3/0 /0
Med	4/500 /2	1/0 /0	0/0 /0
Low	15/133 /2	4/500 /2	2/0 /0

Slider Average .333

	Outside	Middle	Inside
High	2/500 /1	0/0 /0	0/0 /0
Med	2/500 /1	1/0 /0	0/0 /0
Low	1/0 /0	3/333 /1	0/0 /0

Left-handed hitter Rafael Palmeiro hits fastballs exceptionally well against both right- and left-handed pitchers (.358 against right-handers, .341 against left-handers). His .341 is excellent for a left-handed hitter.

Starting with his performance against right-handers, note his strength against inside fastballs (.370, .383 and .372, high to low). Pitchers who try to throw him fastballs inside are making a mistake.

He pulls low-inside fastballs down the right line and to the right side of the infield. But note that the center fielder needs to play shifted toward left.

LOW-INSIDE FASTBALLS

BATTING AVERAGE .372
Play

Left	Deep in straightaway left field
Center	Deep and shifted toward left field
Right	Medium-deep and shifted toward the right line
Short	Up middle (shifted toward second base)
Second	Shifted toward first base

He hits .383 against medium-high inside fastballs.

MEDIUM-HIGH INSIDE FASTBALLS

BATTING AVERAGE .383
Play

Left	Medium-deep and shifted toward the left line
Center	Deep in straightaway center field
Right	Deep and shifted toward the right line
Short	Up middle (shifted toward second base)
Second	Shifted toward first base

He also hits low-over-the-middle fastballs extremely well (.420). He hits this pitch down the left line and into the right-center gap.

LOW-OVER-THE-MIDDLE FASTBALLS
BATTING AVERAGE .420
Play

Left	Medium-deep and shifted toward the left line
Center	Deep in straightaway center field
Right	Deep and shifted toward center field
Short	Up middle (shifted toward second base)
Second	Shifted toward first base

He hits medium-high outside fastballs for an outstanding .430 average. He hits this pitch medium-deep to all fields. By positioning themselves properly, fielders could prevent most of his base hits resulting from this location.

MEDIUM-HIGH OUTSIDE FASTBALLS

BATTING AVERAGE .430
Play

Left	Medium-deep and shifted toward the left field line

Center	Medium-deep in straightaway center field
Right	Medium-deep in straightaway right field
Short	Shifted toward third base
Second	Shifted toward first base

Palmeiro has three weak fastball locations against right-handers: low-outside (.250), high-outside (.241) and medium-over-the-middle (.200).

Palmeiro Against Curves And Sliders

Palmeiro has trouble with low-inside curves against right-handers (.066), but he hits low-outside and low-over-the-middle curves excellently (.363 and .411 respectively).

LOW-OVER-THE-MIDDLE CURVEBALLS

BATTING AVERAGE .411
Play

Left	Deep and shifted toward center field
Center	Medium-deep in straightaway center field
Right	Deep and shifted toward center field
Short	Up middle (shifted toward second base)
Second	Shifted toward first base

He has trouble with inside sliders against right-handers. This gives a target for attack.

Palmeiro Against Left-Handed Pitchers

There are fewer BARS instances recorded for Palmeiro against left-handed pitchers, but it is evident that he hits medium-high inside fastballs (.368) and medium-high outside fastballs (.533) excellently.

MEDIUM-HIGH INSIDE FASTBALLS
(THROWN BY LEFT-HANDED PITCHERS)

BATTING AVERAGE .368
Play

Left	Deep and shifted toward the left field line
Center	Deep and shifted toward left field
Right	Medium-deep and shifted toward center field
Short	Up middle (shifted toward second base)
Second	Normal position

MEDIUM-HIGH OUTSIDE FASTBALLS
(THROWN BY LEFT-HANDED PITCHERS)

BATTING AVERAGE .533
Play

Left	Medium-deep and shifted toward the left line
Center	Deep in straightaway center field
Right	Deep and shifted toward center field
Short	Shifted toward third base
Second	Shifted toward first base

Palmeiro has trouble with low-outside curves against lefties (.133).

LOW-OUTSIDE CURVEBALLS
(THROWN BY LEFT-HANDED PITCHERS)

BATTING AVERAGE .133
Play

Left	Deep in straightaway left field
Center	Deep and shifted toward right field
Right	Deep and shifted toward the right field line
Short	Up middle (shifted toward second base)
Second	Shifted toward first base

Ahead And Behind In The Count Vs. RH

Ahead

Fastball Average .397

	Outside	Middle	Inside
High	12/333 / 4	11/272 / 3	10/400 / 4
Med	32/406 / 13	2/0 / 0	36/444 / 16
Low	18/333 / 6	29/482 / 14	21/380 / 8

Curve Average .166

	Outside	Middle	Inside
High	0/0 / 0	0/0 / 0	1/0 / 0
Med	2/0 / 0	0/0 / 0	0/0 / 0
Low	2/500 / 1	4/250 / 1	3/0 / 0

Behind

Fastball Average .413

	Outside	Middle	Inside
High	3/333 / 1	5/200 / 1	4/500 / 2
Med	12/666 / 8	1/0 / 0	5/400 / 2
Low	8/250 / 2	8/250 / 2	12/500 / 6

Curve Average .448

	Outside	Middle	Inside
High	1/0 / 0	3/333 / 1	4/500 / 2
Med	5/400 / 2	0/0 / 0	1/1000 / 1
Low	4/500 / 2	7/571 / 4	4/250 / 1

Overall Evaluation
Against Right-Handed Pitchers

Overall Fastball ⚾⚾⚾⚾
Overall Curve ⚾⚾
Overall Slider ⚾

Against Left-Handed Pitchers

Overall Fastball ⚾⚾⚾⚾
Overall Curve ⚾
Overall Slider   Not enough information

Comments: Very strong vs. inside fastballs vs. RH.
Strengths: Inside fastballs, low-middle and medium-outside fastballs, low-outside and low-middle curves vs. RH; medium-inside and medium-outside fastballs vs. LH.
Weaknesses: Low-outside and high-outside fastballs, low-inside and medium-outside curves, inside sliders vs. RH; high-inside and low-middle fastballs, low-outside curves vs. LH.

Geno Petralli Against Right-Handed Pitchers
Overall BARS Batting Average .313

Fastball Average .329

	Outside	Middle	Inside
High	13/230/3	15/266/4	11/272/3
Med	93/322/30	13/384/5	33/393/13
Low	13/153/2	29/517/15	23/217/5

Curve Average .275

	Outside	Middle	Inside
High	0/0/0	2/500/1	1/1000/1
Med	8/375/3	2/500/1	3/0/0
Low	4/250/1	4/250/1	5/0/0

Slider Average .142

	Outside	Middle	Inside
High	0/0/0	0/0/0	1/0/0
Med	0/0/0	1/1000/1	4/250/1
Low	1/0/0	3/333/1	11/0/0

Geno Petralli Against Left-Handed Pitchers
Overall BARS Batting Average .250

Fastball Average .187

	Outside	Middle	Inside
High	1/0/0	1/0/0	0/0/0
Med	4/250/1	0/0/0	7/285/2
Low	1/0/0	1/0/0	1/0/0

Curve Average .400

	Outside	Middle	Inside
High	0/0/0	0/0/0	0/0/0
Med	1/1000/1	0/0/0	1/0/0
Low	0/0/0	2/0/0	1/1000/1

Slider Average .000

	Outside	Middle	Inside
High	0/0/0	0/0/0	0/0/0
Med	0/0/0	0/0/0	1/0/0
Low	0/0/0	0/0/0	0/0/0

Geno Petralli, left-handed hitter, has many more recorded instances against right-handed pitchers. His overall fastball average of .329 against right-handers is excellent. It is made up of some very high and some very low averages within his fastball chart.

Petralli hits a solid enough .322 against medium-high outside fastballs thrown by right-handers.

MEDIUM-HIGH OUTSIDE FASTBALLS

BATTING AVERAGE .322
Play

Left	Deep in straightaway left field
Center	Deep in straightaway center field
Right	Deep and shifted toward center field
Short	Up middle (shifted toward second base)
Second	Normal position

He hits low-over-the-middle fastballs for an exceptional .517.

LOW-OVER-THE-MIDDLE FASTBALLS

BATTING AVERAGE .517
Play

Left	Medium-deep and shifted toward the left field line
Center	Medium-deep in straightaway center field
Right	Deep in straightaway right field
Short	*No instances recorded*
Second	Normal position

He hits .393 against medium-high inside fastballs.

MEDIUM-HIGH INSIDE FASTBALLS

BATTING AVERAGE .393
Play

Left	Medium-deep and shifted toward the left field line
Center	Medium-deep in straightaway center field
Right	Deep in straightaway right field
Short	Normal position
Second	Normal position

Petralli hits the ball differently in each of his high fastball locations. The more accurately pitchers can throw to these specific locations, the more accurately fielders could position themselves by following the BARS fielding strategy.

He hits high-inside fastballs down both lines.

HIGH-INSIDE FASTBALLS

BATTING AVERAGE .272
Play

Left	Medium-deep and shifted toward the left field line
Center	Deep and shifted toward left field
Right	Deep and shifted toward the right field line
Short	Up middle (shifted toward second base)
Second	Normal position

He pulls high-over-the-middle fastballs down the

right line and to left center. But note that the shortstop needs to play shifted toward third base for this pitch.

HIGH-OVER-THE-MIDDLE FASTBALLS

BATTING AVERAGE .266
Play

Left	Deep and shifted toward center field
Center	Deep in straightaway center field
Right	Medium-deep and shifted toward the right line
Short	Shifted toward third base
Second	Normal position

Petralli goes medium deep to left field (his opposite field) and to center field with high-outside fastballs. But notice that he hits this pitch to the right side of the infield.

HIGH-OUTSIDE FASTBALLS

BATTING AVERAGE .230
Play

Left	Medium-deep and shifted toward the left field line
Center	Medium-deep in straightaway center field
Right	*No instances recorded*
Short	Up middle (shifted toward second base)
Second	Shifted toward first base

Petralli Against Curves

Petralli hits .375 against medium-high outside curves thrown by right-handers.

MEDIUM-HIGH OUTSIDE CURVEBALLS

BATTING AVERAGE .375
Play

Left	Medium-deep in straightaway left field
Center	Deep and shifted toward left field
Right	Short in straightaway right field
Short	Normal position
Second	Normal position

He has a lot of trouble with low-inside sliders against right-handers (.000 on 0 for 11).

Petralli Against Left-Handed Pitchers

Against left-handed pitchers, Petralli hits medium-high inside fastballs fairly well (.285). He pulls this ball strongly to right. Notice that he has no recorded instances of hit balls to left or center.

MEDIUM-HIGH INSIDE FASTBALLS (THROWN BY LEFT-HANDED PITCHERS)

BATTING AVERAGE .285
Play

Left	*No instances recorded*
Center	*No instances recorded*
Right	Deep and shifted toward the right field line
Short	Up middle (shifted toward second base)
Second	Normal position

Ahead And Behind In The Count Vs. RH

Ahead

Fastball Average .367

	Outside	Middle	Inside
High	6 / 0 / 0	12 / 250 / 3	5 / 200 / 1
Med	44 / 386 / 17	10 / 500 / 5	17 / 411 / 7
Low	3 / 0 / 0	15 / 600 / 9	16 / 312 / 5

Curve Average .500

	Outside	Middle	Inside
High	0 / 0 / 0	1 / 1000 / 1	0 / 0 / 0
Med	1 / 1000 / 1	0 / 0 / 0	0 / 0 / 0
Low	0 / 0 / 0	0 / 0 / 0	2 / 0 / 0

Behind

Fastball Average .380

	Outside	Middle	Inside
High	3 / 666 / 2	1 / 0 / 0	1 / 0 / 0
Med	22 / 409 / 9	0 / 0 / 0	2 / 500 / 1
Low	1 / 0 / 0	8 / 500 / 4	4 / 0 / 0

Curve Average .444

	Outside	Middle	Inside
High	0 / 0 / 0	0 / 0 / 0	0 / 0 / 0
Med	3 / 666 / 2	1 / 0 / 0	1 / 0 / 0
Low	2 / 500 / 1	2 / 500 / 1	0 / 0 / 0

Overall Evaluation

Against Right-Handed Pitchers

Overall Fastball	⚾⚾ ⚾⚾⚾ ⚾⚾
Overall Curve	⚾⚾ ⚾⚾⚾
Overall Slider	⚾⚾

Against Left-Handed Pitchers

Overall Fastball	⚾⚾
Overall Curve	Not enough Information
Overall Slider	Not enough Information

Comments: Petralli is strong against all waist-high fastballs thrown by RH.
Strengths: All waist-high fastballs, low-middle fastballs, medium-outside curves vs. RH.
Weaknesses: All high fastballs, low-inside and low-outside fastballs, low-inside sliders vs. RH.

Gary Pettis (Switch Hitter) — *Texas Rangers*

Gary Pettis Against Right-Handed Pitchers
Overall BARS Batting Average .245

Fastball Average .239

	Outside	Middle	Inside
High	17/ 176 /3	22/ 136 /3	8/ 250 /2
Med	104/ 230 /24	24/ 416 /10	41/ 365 /15
Low	37/ 54 /2	61/ 295 /18	41/ 195 /8

Curve Average .229

	Outside	Middle	Inside
High	2/ 0 /0	2/ 500 /1	0/ 0 /0
Med	15/ 266 /4	1/ 0 /0	8/ 375 /3
Low	4/ 250 /1	10/ 100 /1	6/ 166 /1

Slider Average .357

	Outside	Middle	Inside
High	1/ 0 /0	0/ 0 /0	2/ 1000 /2
Med	2/ 0 /0	2/ 0 /0	5/ 600 /3
Low	5/ 0 /0	8/ 500 /4	3/ 333 /1

Gary Pettis Against Left-Handed Pitchers
Overall BARS Batting Average .252

Fastball Average .272

	Inside	Middle	Outside
High	3/ 0 /0	20/ 300 /6	11/ 181 /2
Med	16/ 375 /6	10/ 500 /5	32/ 218 /7
Low	9/ 111 /1	37/ 351 /13	16/ 125 /2

Curve Average .250

	Inside	Middle	Outside
High	0/ 0 /0	2/ 500 /1	3/ 0 /0
Med	3/ 666 /2	0/ 0 /0	2/ 500 /1
Low	3/ 0 /0	3/ 333 /1	4/ 0 /0

Slider Average .100

	Inside	Middle	Outside
High	2/ 0 /0	1/ 0 /0	0/ 0 /0
Med	5/ 0 /0	1/ 0 /0	1/ 0 /0
Low	6/ 166 /1	4/ 250 /1	0/ 0 /0

Switch-hitter Gary Pettis has trouble with fastballs and curves against right-handed pitchers (.239 overall fastballs, .229 overall curves). He hits these pitches better against left-handed pitchers (.272 overall fastballs, .250 overall curves). He hits sliders better against right-handers (.357 overall vs. right-handers, .100 overall vs. left-handers).

Starting with his fastball chart against right-handers, note his trouble in the outside locations (.176, .230, and .054, high to low). he also has trouble with high fastballs (.176, .136, and .250, outside to inside).

Pettis hits medium-high outside fastballs deep down the left line against right-handers.

MEDIUM-HIGH OUTSIDE FASTBALLS

BATTING AVERAGE .230

Play

Left	Deep and shifted toward the left field line
Center	Medium-deep in straightaway center field
Right	Medium-deep in straightaway right field
Short	Up middle (shifted toward second base)
Second	Normal position

In contrast, he hits .365 against medium-high inside fastballs thrown by right-handers. By positioning themselves according to the BARS fielding strategy for this pitch fielders could prevent most of his base hits from this location.

MEDIUM-HIGH INSIDE FASTBALLS

BATTING AVERAGE .365

Play

Left	Medium-deep in straightaway left field
Center	Medium-deep in straightaway center field
Right	Deep and shifted toward the right field line
Short	Up middle (shifted toward second base)
Second	Shifted toward first base

He hits .295 against low-over-the-middle fastballs thrown by right-handers. Notice that he goes to left field with this pitch when he hits to the outfield (his opposite field, batting left-handed against right-handers), but that the shortstop needs to play shifted toward second base.

LOW-OVER-THE-MIDDLE FASTBALLS

BATTING AVERAGE .295

Play

Left	Medium-deep and shifted toward the left field line
Center	Deep and shifted toward left field

Right	Deep and shifted toward center field
Short	Up middle (shifted toward second base)
Second	Normal position

Pettis is weak against low-inside fastballs (.195). Right-handers throw him a relatively high number of low-inside fastballs (41), but since he hits well in adjacent locations, it would be better to throw him outside or high fastballs.

Pettis hits medium-high inside curves well against right-handed pitchers (.375), but he has trouble with low curves — especially low-over-the-middle curves (.100). He has trouble with outside sliders, but hits low-over-the-middle sliders very strongly (.500).

LOW-OVER-THE-MIDDLE SLIDERS

BATTING AVERAGE .500
Play

Left	Deep in straightaway left field
Center	Deep in straightaway center field
Right	*No instances recorded*
Short	Shifted toward third base
Second	Shifted toward first base

Pettis Against Left-Handed Pitchers

Against left-handed pitchers, Pettis hits all over-the-middle fastballs extremely well (.300, .500, and .351, high to low). Left-handers throw him a lot of low-over-the-middle fastballs. They should either keep the ball away from this location or make sure the fielders are positioned as follows:

LOW-OVER-THE-MIDDLE FASTBALLS (THROWN BY LEFT-HANDED PITCHERS)

BATTING AVERAGE .351
Play

Left	Medium-deep in straightaway left field
Center	Deep in straightaway center field
Right	Deep and shifted toward center field
Short	Shifted toward third base
Second	Shifted toward first base

He has trouble with medium-high outside fastballs against lefties (.218) but he hits medium-high inside fastballs for an excellent .375 average.

MEDIUM-HIGH INSIDE FASTBALLS (THROWN BY LEFT-HANDED PITCHERS)

BATTING AVERAGE .375
Play

Left	Medium-deep and shifted toward the left field line
Center	Medium-deep and shifted toward left field
Right	*No instances recorded*
Short	Normal position
Second	Normal position

The best fastball area for pitchers to attack against Pettis is his low-outside/medium-high outside sector.

Ahead And Behind In The Count Vs. RH

Ahead

Fastball Average .374

	Outside	Middle	Inside
High	3 / 0 /0	9 / 333 /3	5 / 400 /2
Med	43 / 372 /16	12 / 583 /7	21 / 380 /8
Low	7 / 285 /2	25 / 400 /10	14 / 285 /4

Curve Average .333

	Outside	Middle	Inside
High	0 / 0 /0	0 / 0 /0	0 / 0 /0
Med	2 / 0 /0	0 / 0 /0	0 / 0 /0
Low	0 / 0 /0	0 / 0 /0	1 / 1000 /1

Behind

Fastball Average .250

	Outside	Middle	Inside
High	0 / 0 /0	2 / 0 /0	0 / 0 /0
Med	14 / 357 /5	1 / 0 /0	5 / 600 /3
Low	4 / 0 /0	11 / 181 /2	3 / 0 /0

Curve Average .500

	Outside	Middle	Inside
High	1 / 0 /0	1 / 1000 /1	0 / 0 /0
Med	4 / 500 /2	0 / 0 /0	3 / 666 /2
Low	1 / 1000 /1	3 / 333 /1	1 / 0 /0

Overall Evaluation

Against Right-Handed Pitchers

Overall Fastball ⚾⚾

Overall Curve ⚾⚾

Overall Slider ⚾⚾⚾⚾⚾

Against Left-Handed Pitchers

Overall Fastball ⚾⚾

Overall Curve ⚾⚾⚾

Overall Slider ⚾⚾

Comments: Weak against outside fastballs vs. RH and LH. Strong against medium-inside pitches.
Strengths: Medium-inside, medium-middle and low-middle fastballs, medium-inside curves, medium-inside and low-middle sliders vs. RH; over-the-middle and medium-inside fastballs vs. LH.
Weaknesses: Outside fastballs, low-inside fastballs, low curves and outside sliders vs. RH; outside fastballs, low-inside fastballs vs. LH.

Ruben Sierra (Switch Hitter)   *Texas Rangers*

Ruben Sierra Against Right-Handed Pitchers
Overall BARS Batting Average .258

Fastball Average .284

	Outside	Middle	Inside
High	43/139 /6	23/173 /4	20/100 /2
Med	152/315 /48	20/600 /12	28/321 /9
Low	20/200 /4	33/212 /7	27/444 /12

Curve Average .151

	Outside	Middle	Inside
High	9/333 /3	3/0 /0	0/0 /0
Med	11/363 /4	4/250 /1	4/250 /1
Low	5/0 /0	12/83 /1	18/0 /0

Slider Average .160

	Outside	Middle	Inside
High	1/1000 /1	1/1000 /1	1/0 /0
Med	3/0 /0	2/0 /0	6/166 /1
Low	1/0 /0	3/333 /1	7/0 /0

Ruben Sierra Against Left-Handed Pitchers
Overall BARS Batting Average .280

Fastball Average .275

	Inside	Middle	Outside
High	6/166 /1	5/400 /2	21/285 /6
Med	14/428 /6	6/0 /0	50/220 /11
Low	8/750 /6	7/285 /2	10/100 /1

Curve Average .375

	Inside	Middle	Outside
High	0/0 /0	0/0 /0	0/0 /0
Med	2/0 /0	0/0 /0	14/571 /8
Low	1/0 /0	2/500 /1	5/0 /0

Slider Average .208

	Inside	Middle	Outside
High	0/0 /0	2/500 /1	0/0 /0
Med	5/400 /2	1/0 /0	4/0 /0
Low	6/166 /1	5/200 /1	1/0 /0

Switch-hitting Ruben Sierra has very distinct strengths and weaknesses against right-handed pitchers. He has trouble with high fastballs (.139, .173 and .100, outside to inside) but hits all waist-high fastballs well (.315, .600 and .321, outside to inside).

Notice in the Ahead and Behind charts on the opposite page that he hits medium-high outside fastballs for a higher average when ahead in the count than when behind (.397 ahead, .266 behind.) Notice also that every fielder except the shortstop needs to shift for this pitch when Sierra is ahead and behind.

**MEDIUM-HIGH OUTSIDE FASTBALLS
(WHEN AHEAD IN THE COUNT)**

BATTING AVERAGE .397
Play
Left   Deep and shifted toward the left field line
Center   Deep in straightaway center field
Right   Deep in straightaway right field
Short   Up middle (shifted toward second base)
Second   Shifted toward first base

**MEDIUM-HIGH OUTSIDE FASTBALLS
(WHEN BEHIND IN THE COUNT)**

BATTING AVERAGE .266

Play
Left   Deep in straightaway left field
Center   Deep and shifted toward right field
Right   Medium-deep in straightaway right field
Short   Up middle (shifted toward second base)
Second   Normal position

Sierra's high-outside fastball location has the second-highest number of recorded instances in his fastball chart (43). Pitchers are wise to throw to this location: the .139 average here is low.

He hits medium-high inside fastballs down the left line and into the left-center alley. He spreads the ball out to the infield, forcing the shortstop toward third base and the second baseman toward first.

MEDIUM-HIGH INSIDE FASTBALLS

BATTING AVERAGE .321
Play
Left   Deep and shifted toward the left field line
Center   Deep and shifted toward left field
Right   Deep in straightaway right field
Short   Shifted toward third base
Second   Shifted toward first base

He is extremely effective against low-inside fastballs (.444).

LOW-INSIDE FASTBALLS

BATTING AVERAGE .444
Play

Left	Deep and shifted toward the left field line
Center	Deep and shifted toward left field
Right	Medium-deep in straightaway right field
Short	Up middle (shifted toward second base)
Second	Normal position

Sierra Against Curves And Sliders

Sierra is very weak against low-curves. (0-for-5, 1-for-12, and 0-for-18, outside to inside). This gives pitchers a wide target against him.

He hits medium-high outside curves well (.363).

MEDIUM-HIGH OUTSIDE CURVEBALLS

BATTING AVERAGE .363
Play

Left	Deep in straightaway left field
Center	*No instances recorded*
Right	Deep and shifted toward the right field line
Short	Shifted toward third base
Second	Normal position

Sierra Against Left-Handed Pitchers

Sierra is weak against medium-high outside fastballs (.220) and low-outside fastballs (.100) thrown by left-handed pitchers. But he hits .428 against medium-high inside fastballs. Batting right-handed, he pulls this pitch deep down the left line and hits it straight-away to the other fields.

MEDIUM-HIGH INSIDE FASTBALLS
(THROWN BY LEFT-HANDED PITCHERS)

BATTING AVERAGE .428
Play

Left	Deep and shifted toward the left field line
Center	Medium-deep in straightaway center field
Right	Medium-deep in straightaway right field
Short	Normal position
Second	Normal position

He scatters medium-outside fastballs thrown by left-handers to all fields, but his low average in this location indicates that he doesn't hit this pitch with great authority.

MEDIUM-HIGH OUTSIDE FASTBALLS
(THROWN BY LEFT-HANDED PITCHERS)

BATTING AVERAGE .220
Play

Left	Deep and shifted toward the left field line
Center	Deep in straightaway center field
Right	Medium-deep and shifted toward center field

Ahead And Behind In The Count Vs. RH

Ahead

Fastball Average .363

	Outside	Middle	Inside
High	12/ 333 /4	11/ 272 /3	5/ 200 /1
Med	78/ 397 /31	12/ 583 /7	16/ 312 /5
Low	8/ 250 /2	12/ 166 /2	11/ 454 /5

Curve Average .294

	Outside	Middle	Inside
High	2/ 1000 /2	2/ 0 /0	0/ 0 /0
Med	1/ 1000 /1	2/ 500 /1	2/ 500 /1
Low	0/ 0 /0	4/ 0 /0	4/ 0 /0

Behind

Fastball Average .333

	Outside	Middle	Inside
High	9/ 222 /2	2/ 500 /1	6/ 166 /1
Med	15/ 266 /4	3/ 1000 /3	6/ 666 /4
Low	2/ 0 /0	10/ 200 /2	4/ 500 /2

Curve Average .190

	Outside	Middle	Inside
High	3/ 333 /1	1/ 0 /0	0/ 0 /0
Med	6/ 500 /3	1/ 0 /0	2/ 0 /0
Low	1/ 0 /0	3/ 0 /0	4/ 0 /0

Overall Evaluation
Against Right-Handed Pitchers

Overall Fastball	⚾⚾ ⚾⚾
Overall Curve	⚾⚾
Overall Slider	⚾⚾

Against Left-Handed Pitchers

Overall Fastball	⚾⚾ ⚾⚾
Overall Curve	⚾⚾ ⚾⚾ ⚾⚾
Overall Slider	⚾⚾

Comments: Sierra has very distinct areas of weakness (high fastballs vs. RH, low curves vs. RH, etc.). **Strengths:** Waist-high fastballs and low-inside fastballs, medium-outside curves vs. RH; medium-inside fastballs and medium-outside curves vs. LH. **Weaknesses:** High fastballs, low-outside and low-middle fastballs, low curves and inside sliders vs. RH; medium-outside and low-outside fastballs vs. LH.

Updating The BARS Records

The BARS System gathers information continually throughout the year. During the season, many games are scouted live on TV, but many are taped for later scouting. Most games for a particular season are recorded into the BARS computer by October or November. Some scouts, however, work through the winter catching up on games they did not have time to scout during the season.

This continual updating of information adds to the statistics of every player in the majors. Information for a certain year (such as the 1988 season or the 1989 season) is final when all available games for that year have been scouted, but the cumulative BARS statistics for hitters and pitchers are ongoing — they are never absolutely final.

It is interesting to look at how hitters' cumulative averages change as information is added from year to year. Several chapters in *The Tenth Man* (the previous BARS book) compare numerous players' single-season BARS records from one year to the next. In this chapter, we'll compare several cumulative BARS batting records, showing how players' records change as additional information is gathered.

Darryl Strawberry, New York Mets

The following two fastball grids for Darryl Strawberry show how his records have progressed as information has been gathered over the last few years.

Previous
Fastball Average .320

	Outside	Middle	Inside
High	24/208 / 5	43/418 / 18	19/157 / 3
Med	64/312 / 20	26/423 / 11	35/342 / 12
Low	31/193 / 6	44/386 / 17	17/294 / 5

Recent
Fastball Average .313

	Outside	Middle	Inside
High	49/285 / 14	66/393 / 26	39/230 / 9
Med	104/317 / 33	29/448 / 13	61/327 / 20
Low	50/200 / 10	59/372 / 22	41/219 / 9

Note that there are many more recorded instances in Strawberry's recent chart, which contains his complete BARS fastball record through the end of the 1989 season. His recorded instances have increased from 64 to 104 in his medium-high outside location, from 35 to 61 in his medium-high inside location, from 24 to 49 in his high-outside location, etc.

His average has changed slightly in each location. This is inevitable as additional at-bats and base hits are recorded. In some locations his average has increased, in some his average has decreased. His overall fastball average, however, stayed about the same (.320 and .313).

Though his averages in the nine locations changed, they remained fairly relative to each other. For instance, he is weak against low-outside fastballs in each chart, (.193 and .200). And he is strong against medium-high inside fastballs (.342 and .327).

One significant change is the increase in his high-outside location (.208 and .285). In his earlier chart he was 5 for 24 in this location. In his latest chart he is 14 for 49. This means that in the 25 additional instances recorded he got 9 hits. Several years ago it was a good bet to throw him a high-outside fastball. It seems that now he's learned to hit it.

In contrast, his low-inside location dropped from .294 to .219. In 24 additional at-bats, he's gotten only four hits. It seems his gain against high-outside pitches was made at the expense of low-inside pitches.

The BARS fielding strategy may also change slightly for hitters over the years. The following fielding charts compare earlier and recent strategies for Strawberry's medium-high outside fastball location.

MEDIUM-HIGH OUTSIDE FASTBALLS

Batting Average .312
Play

Left	Deep and shifted toward the left field line
Center	Medium-deep in straightaway center field
Right	Deep in straightaway right field
Short	Normal position
Second	Normal position

MEDIUM-HIGH OUTSIDE FASTBALLS

Batting Average .317
Play

Left	Deep and shifted toward the left field line
Center	Deep in straightaway center field
Right	Deep in straightaway right field
Short	Normal position
Second	Shifted toward first base

The fielding strategies for the centerfielder and the second baseman have changed. The strategies for the other fielders have stayed the same.

The BARS System has a lot of information for players like George Brett, who has been active for a number of years.

Brett's recent fastball and curve charts are compared below with his charts of several years ago.

Previous

Fastball Average .370

	Outside	Middle	Inside
High	24/166 /4	62/274 /17	14/428 /6
Med	110/400 /44	82/500 /41	57/315 /18
Low	33/333 /11	86/360 /31	18/444 /8

Curve Average .308

	Outside	Middle	Inside
High	4/250 /1	4/500 /2	2/0 /0
Med	27/444 /12	17/352 /6	20/400 /8
Low	7/0 /0	26/153 /4	13/307 /4

Recent

Fastball Average .358

	Outside	Middle	Inside
High	46/239 /11	91/318 /29	20/350 /7
Med	175/382 /67	91/494 /45	80/275 /22
Low	53/320 /17	116/362 /42	23/391 /9

Curve Average .304

	Outside	Middle	Inside
High	8/250 /2	9/666 /6	2/0 /0
Med	37/351 /13	19/421 /8	21/380 /8
Low	10/0 /0	29/137 /4	16/312 /5

Note that, for the most part, Brett's strengths and weaknesses remain the same in the charts. His medium-high outside fastball average fell slightly (.400 to .382), his high-outside fastball average rose (.166 to .239), and his medium-high inside average fell (.315 to .275). Overall, his fastball average stayed about the same (.370 and .358).

His curve charts are very similar: he remains hitless against low-outside curves, is still weak against low-over-the-middle curves, and is still strong against low-inside curves. His overall curve averages were .308 and .304.

The more information that the BARS System has for a player, the more stable the cumulative fielding strategy is from year to year. The following charts show the fielding strategies for Brett's medium-high outside locations in the two charts.

MEDIUM-HIGH OUTSIDE FASTBALLS

Batting Average .400

Play

Left	Deep and shifted toward the left field line
Center	Deep in straightaway center field
Right	Deep and shifted toward center field
Short	Up middle (shifted toward second base)
Second	Shifted toward first base

MEDIUM-HIGH OUTSIDE FASTBALLS

Batting Average .382

Play

Left	Deep and shifted toward the left field line
Center	Deep in straightaway center field
Right	Deep and shifted toward center field
Short	Up middle (shifted toward second base)
Second	Shifted toward first base

BARS Records For Every Player

The BARS System has complete records for every player in the majors. This information is constantly updated so that the most complete records can be generated.

The BARS System itself is progressing. Soon we will have an additional statistic in each location of the batting grids. This will indicate the number of home runs hit off pitches to that particular location. This will increase the practical value of the BARS batting records. If a hitter has a low average in a certain location but has a high number of home runs, pitchers will be able to adjust accordingly. The BARS fielding strategy is right over 90 percent of the time, but if a hit ball doesn't stay in the park, even the most accurate strategy will be useless.

The Increasing Precision In Modern Sports

Everything evolves and changes. It's the nature of men and women to try to improve their performances — whatever they're involved in. A person who has a hobby like golf or bowling is continually trying to improve. The same is true with professional sports. It's not so much the money involved; people just want to do better each time they try something.

Athletes have become bigger, stronger and faster over the years. Some of this is due to training techniques, some to general trends in the population. In every sport that has fixed measurements of achievement, such as the number of seconds it takes to run a mile or swim 100 meters, the general performance of athletes has improved over the years. Twelve-year-olds today swim faster than Johnny Weissmuller did at his peak. Even high-school pole vaulters go over sixteen feet, although for years the fifteen-foot mark was considered unreachable.

The same is true of all track and field events. It is only in sports such as football and baseball, in which there are no direct measurements of performance, that any argument still exists that old-time athletes may have been superior to the stars of today. The natural talents of a Babe Ruth, Ty Cobb, or Joe DiMaggio would make them stars in any era, but if the performance of track and field athletes is any indication, the average ballplayer of today is superior to the average ballplayer of thirty or forty years ago.

A lot of this is due to training and conditioning techniques. The scientific knowledge focussed on sports performance today allows an athlete to develop himself to a higher level, and to maintain his peak for a greater number of years.

The overall strategy of sports evolves also. The strategies involved in sports such as golf, skiing, basketball, football and others are much more sophisticated today than they were even ten years ago. How many set shots do you see in basketball today? Even quick jump shots are often blocked. The pace is faster, the scouting more complex and accurate, and the strategy of team coordination much more effective.

Increasing Precision In Football

During the last decade people have begun to realize that football is a precision game that loses a lot when played in less than ideal conditions. Fans used to think that football was at its best when two teams slogged it out on a field that was so muddy runners couldn't cut, quarterbacks couldn't grip the ball properly to pass, and receivers couldn't hold on to the ball if it did get to them. Fans used to say that such conditions gave the better team a chance to excel.

But gradually people realized that playing in bad weather doesn't really give the better team an edge: it throws both teams into a survival-type offense and defense and takes away much of the refinement of the game. During the last decade this has been generally accepted by everyone, especially with the increased use of sophisticated defensive and offensive strategies and the computerized scouting of opponents.

For this reason the Super Bowl will never again be played in a situation that is likely to produce extreme weather conditions. A lot of regular season and playoff games in the East and Midwest are played in open air stadiums where winter temperatures often fall into the single digits, but Super Bowl games are being scheduled in cities that have warmer climates or domed stadiums. Fans enjoy the complicated alignments and sophisticated passing game that characterizes football today.

Baseball has never been good in cold or wet weather. For over a hundred years it's been recognized that baseball is not baseball when it rains. But unlike football, which has highly coordinated offensive and defensive strategies, baseball has a fielding strategy that is still a fairly loose affair. Fielders position themselves when a hitter comes to the plate, then hold those positions through all the pitches to him, even though there's no way a hitter is likely to hit a low-outside fastball the same way he's going to hit a low-inside fastball or a low-inside curve.

Anyone who has read *The Tenth Man* and the introductory chapters of this book knows how important it is for fielders to position themselves correctly for every pitch. When they use the BARS System fielding strategy to do this, they'll become as coordinated as the offensive and defensive units in professional football.

Two Main Objections

The two main objections to implementing the BARS System seem to be (1) pitchers can't throw the ball exactly where they want, so why bother, and (2) what managers really want is information based on how a hitter has performed against specific pitchers.

The first objection is easy to answer. It may be true that some pitchers will never be able to throw specifically to the medium-high outside location instead of to the low-outside or high-outside locations. But the fact is that the fielders have to be positioned *somewhere* on every pitch. They should be positioned so that their effectiveness can have the greatest potential. The pitcher may in fact not throw the ball to the medium-high outside location, but positioning the fielders accordingly will optimize the chance that they will be in the best positions to field balls hit in their directions.

The second objection is just as easy to answer. Sure, everyone would love to have batting and fielding strategy information that is 90 percent accurate for hitters against specific pitchers. Every manager would love to have it. I'd love to have it. But the fact is that it takes a lot of information to be able to get into the 90-plus percentage range of accuracy like the BARS System does. And there's no way to get enough information for how hitters do against specific pitchers. Hitters don't face the same pitcher that often. Maybe they face a certain pitcher 20 or 30 at-bats in a season, but usually not even that often. BARS batting grids for how one hitter has done against a specific pitcher would be mostly zeros, especially in the curve and slider charts. Even in the fastball charts there wouldn't be much information, and that could be dangerous. A little information can sometimes be worse than no information at all.

That's why the BARS System uses two main categories for the Super Summary charts: a hitter's performance against left-handed pitchers and against right-handed pitchers. As we get more information in the next few years, we may try to chart hitters and pitchers one-on-one. But for now, we'll stick to the two categories. We get over 90 percent accuracy using them, so we must be doing something right.

Home Runs

As I've mentioned before, because the BARS fielding strategy is accurate more than 90 percent of the time, it's often better to throw to a location in which a hitter has a high average, if there are a large number of instances recorded in that location. This is because of the greater probability that the fielding strategy will be correct when the BARS System has recorded a large number of instances in a certain location. A batter may be hitting .400 in a location, but if you know how to position the fielders for pitches to that location, you'll get him out when he hits the ball.

One thing I am going to do very soon is show the number of home runs that a player has hit off pitches to specific locations. The number of home runs will be shown at the bottom left of every location in every BARS batting grid. Not only will this be valuable in a general sense, to show the areas of the strike zone in which a hitter tends to hit home runs, but it will also show specific locations to pitch away from in tight situations. The BARS fielding strategy shows where to position fielders, but there's no way to field a homer.

I'll work on this during the next year. It will be an added plus to the BARS System, and well worth the effort.

The Heart Of Baseball

The vital central spark of baseball involves the interaction between the pitcher and the hitter, and the overall coordinated effort of fielders positioning themselves correctly on a pitch-by-pitch basis. These factors determine how often pitches are hit and whether fielders are in position to field the hits, the number of runs scored, and ultimately whether games are won or lost.

Over the course of a season, these factors — along with the capabilities of the players on a team and certain intangibles such as motivation and momentum — determine whether a team is a winner or an also-ran.

The interaction between the pitcher and the hitter includes three basic aspects:

(1) where the ball goes over the plate;
(2) what type of pitch is thrown;
(3) whether the batter is ahead, behind or even in the count.

The location of pitches, the types of pitches, and even the count on the batter will affect how he hits the ball. The BARS System has found that, as a rule, hitters tend to pull fastballs more when they are ahead in the count than when they are behind. But when ahead and behind, the same batter will hit varying types and locations of pitches differently.

It is strange to say that almost all baseball fans, announcers and writers are entirely unaware of how important and fundamental these aspects are in determining the proper positioning of fielders. It seems that even baseball managers, coaches and players are unaware — because the fielders rarely shift once they assume positions for a hitter.

Part of the reason for this may be that it's difficult for fans at the ballpark to accurately see where the pitch comes in over the plate. A lot of seats are far away, and even fans sitting right behind the plate are often blocked by the catcher, the umpire or the netting of the screen.

It's also hard for fans to know what type of pitch is thrown every time. The difference between fastballs and curves can be obvious when watching closely, but sometimes the action is so fast that it's nearly impossible to tell what type of pitch was thrown, not to mention whether it was to the low-inside section of the strike zone or to the medium-high inside section. Even radio and TV announcers from their vantage points have difficulty telling what the types and locations of pitches are. They're wrong a surprising amount of the time.

Aside from standing right behind the catcher or the pitcher, the best way to see where the ball comes in over the plate is the center field camera on TV. A lot of the zest of baseball is missed on TV, but there's nothing better for getting a close look at this vital element of the game.

Instant replays allow fans watching TV (or at the fortunate stadiums that have instant replays on the scoreboard) to study in slow motion where the ball came in over the plate, what type of pitch was thrown, and where the fielders were positioned at the time of the pitch. Only by studying these factors can a fan really see all the elements that relate to the BARS System.

It's instructive to follow along with the BARS batting charts and fielding strategy charts while watching an actual game, whether at the ball park or on TV. Time after time it will be seen that fielders were out of position for balls hit in their direction, considering the type and location of pitch and the count on the batter. Time and time again infielders dive and barely miss ground balls that could easily have been fielded if they had been shifted to the left or right according to the BARS System. Outfielders charge hard and barely miss catching line drives that could easily have been caught if they had been positioned according to the BARS fielding strategy.

Following along with the BARS batting charts and fielding strategy shows how often fielders are out of position, and how dramatic the difference will be when every fielder is part of an integrated strategy that adapts for different types and locations of pitches on different counts. The time is approaching when players, coaches and managers will have to put in a great deal of time studying statistics like those presented in this book.

BARS Batting Grids And Fielding Strategy On Television

Television is the best way for the BARS System to be followed in actual-game situations. TV announcers could superimpose the BARS batting grids over the strike zone right on screen as a player comes to the plate. That way fans could see at a glance where the batter's strengths and weaknesses are.

Then, after a ball is hit, announcers could replay the pitch and the hit, showing where the ball came in over the plate, the type of pitch thrown, and where the fielders were positioned at the time of the pitch. The announcers could then determine if the fielders were positioned correctly, according to the BARS fielding strategy for the particular type and location of pitch and the count on the batter. This would allow fans to become involved in the intricacies of the game as never before.

Even The Best Fielders Are Handicapped When Out Of Position

Fielders take their positions when a batter comes to the plate, playing him to pull the ball, to hit it straightaway, or to hit it toward the opposite field. But when the strategy between the pitcher and catcher is to throw a series of fastballs, curves and other types of pitches to various parts of the strike zone, the batter is being thrown pitches that he will tend to hit different distances and directions.

By taking their positions and holding them through all the varying pitches to a batter, fielders are fooling themselves. Without a coordinated effort by a team, using fielding strategy on a pitch-by-pitch basis, the defending against hitters is essentially random. Using traditional major league fielding strategy, fielders are positioned correctly only about 75 percent of the time.

This percentage is even lower for sharply-hit balls, because it's usually only when a ball is hit hard (or hit to a very unusual spot) that the positioning of fielders is put to a test. Easy grounders to the infielders or lazy pop flies to the outfielders are fairly routine, no matter where the fielders are positioned. But rockets through the hole between short and third or line shots into the gaps between outfielders are the acid tests of fielding strategy. At these times a fielder is either in the right position or not. If not, the ball is past him. Today's artificial surfaces increase the speed of hit balls, making fielding strategy even more important than it has been in the past.

The large amount of information collected by the BARS System and coordinated by the powerful BARS mainframe IBM 4331 computer allows each fielder to be positioned most effectively on every pitch. The BARS fielding strategy is accurate more than 90 percent of the time. This means that fielders will be in their right positions nine out of ten times for balls hit in their areas.

Since fielders are in the right position about 75 percent of the time following traditional major league fielding strategy and over 90 percent of the time when following BARS fielding strategy, by using the BARS strategy each team could prevent an average of two to three base hits that are now being allowed every game. Many of these hits go for extra bases, set up run-producing rallies and drive in game-winning RBIs. Over the course of a season, preventing an average of two to three hits per game would make a tremendous difference in a team's final standing.

How To Prevent One-Third Of All Base Hits

In The Tenth Man, the previously-published BARS book, over 100 base hits and extra-base hits that occurred in actual major league games are analyzed to show how fielders could have prevented the hits by following the BARS fielding strategy. Examples are taken from games involving the Yankees, Mets, Dodgers, Angels, Cubs, White Sox, Red Sox, Royals, Reds, Braves and other major league teams.

Understanding the importance of the BARS statistics for performance on the team level will make the BARS records for individual players more interesting and valuable. Understanding the fielding strategy and the BARS hitting charts for every player will make baseball more interesting for the fans. At this stage of major league strategy, it will allow fans to know more about the strengths and weaknesses of players than the players and managers themselves.

How The BARS System Scouts Games

The single most crucial factor of the BARS System is that the initial data gathered by the BARS scouts be entirely accurate. A saying about computers is "garbage in, garbage out," meaning that if the data put into the computer isn't accurate, the resulting statistics won't be reliable. That's why we put so much emphasis on making sure that our scouts get accurate information. The proof is the 90 percent accuracy we get regularly in the Super Summary fielding strategy. If the scouts weren't doing things right, we couldn't have this high percentage of accuracy in a statistic that coordinates so many variables: type of pitch, location of pitch, ball-and-strike count on which the pitch is delivered, and distance and direction of hit balls.

When we started scouting, we were working with the Kansas City Royals. A BARS scout sat with the Royals' pitcher who would be starting the following day. The pitcher's job was to call the type and location of pitches, while the BARS scout recorded the direction and distance of hits, how the runners advanced, and all the other information we record. This was not an extra duty for the pitcher, since most major league teams ask the pitcher who will be starting the next day to chart pitches.

We soon found that the pitchers were doing such a poor job that their information was useless for our purposes. We had to stop using them. They didn't care about accuracy. They didn't take it seriously. Even today most pitchers probably don't take this responsibility seriously. If pitchers today do the same kind of job they did then, their information couldn't be used as the basis of any scouting system.

The BARS Scouts

We train our scouts rigorously. Not all the people we've trained have been able to maintain our high standards. Any major league team that tries to gather information for a system similar to the BARS System is going to run into the difficulty of finding reliable individuals who will take the necessary time and effort. Experienced baseball people (former players or coaches) are not necessarily the best scouts because often they have their own way of looking at things. Certainly our BARS scouts love the game, but an eye for accuracy and attention to detail is as important as having extensive baseball knowledge or experience.

Lately there's been some mention in the press about a combined effort in which scouted information for all teams would be gathered into one complete system. From experience we can say that finding the proper people to carry out the details of this job will not be easy.

The BARS Scouting Report

To facilitate the work of our scouts and to make their job easier, we have designed a special Scouting Report for recording all the information the BARS System requires. This form has been designed for ease, completeness, and accuracy of reporting. It gives the scout a clearly designated and repeatable system to record each game on a pitch-by-pitch basis with complete accuracy.

The Scouting Report is the most important document in the BARS System. Several major league managers and scouts have commented that accuracy in the Scouting Report is one of their primary concerns, and because of that, great effort has been taken to insure that the details of every pitch, swing or miss, and all the ensuing activities of fielding and base running are recorded with exactness.

At first we sat in the stands behind the catcher and umpire so we could see where the pitch came in over the plate. But with the increasing number of televised games in the last few years, and the with the availability of satellite dishes that let our scouts pick up games from all over the country, most of our scouting now is done from TV. The center field camera lets us see very clearly the type and location of pitch, and VCRs let us play back questionable situations so we can be completely accurate. The center field camera used on TV lets us see the type and location of pitch more accurately even than announcers sitting in the press box. The announcers are wrong a surprising amount of the time.

Explanation of the Scouting Report

The form shown on the opposite page is the first page of the Scouting Report. The information on the left side of the form is self-explanatory. The date of the game, the designated stadium number, the field condition at playing time, the weather, the wind direction and speed, the temperature at game time, and the time of day are factors that conceivably could affect a player's performance. A manager may want this information to analyze how well or poorly a particular player performs in certain situations. Double-headers, opposing team, attendance and the final score are also recorded.

The right side of the first page of the Scouting Report gives space for the batting order of each team to be recorded. The correct batting order is important because the BARS system has the capacity for determining how each hitter does in accordance with his position in the batting order.

Each player's information is stored in the BARS computer according to his uniform number. In addition

Page One of The BARS Scouting Report

Scouting Report
Game Information

Date (MMDDYY) _____

Stadium Number _____

Field Condition
Astroturf   1 _____
Fast   2 _____
Average   3 _____
Slow   4 _____

Weather
Indoor   1 _____
Sunny   2 _____
Overcast   3 _____
Light Precipitation   4 _____
Night   5 _____

Wind Direction
No Wind   0 _____
In   1 _____
Out   2 _____
Across, 3rd to 1st   3 _____
Across, 1st to 3rd   4 _____

Wind Speed (MPH) _____

Temperature (Degrees F) _____

Time of Day (Not Daylight Savings Time) _____

Double Header
No   0 _____
Yes   1 _____

Double Header Game # _____

Opposing Team # _____

Attendance _____

Final Score
Home _____
_____ _____

Batter Lineup
Number   *Name*

1. _____
2. _____
3. _____
4. _____
5. _____
6. _____
7. _____
8. _____
9. _____

1. _____
2. _____
3. _____
4. _____
5. _____
6. _____
7. _____
8. _____
9. _____

to the uniform number, each player has a unique number that remains the same even when the player is traded. By using specific numbers to designate each player, it is easy to record what each hitter does on every pitch and to break down the information according to the count on the batter, pitch location, and who and where the base runners are.

Recording Information on a Pitch-by-Pitch Basis

The second and ensuing pages of the Scouting Report allow the recording of specific information on a pitch-by-pitch basis. The chart below is an exact representation of the second and ensuing pages of the BARS Scouting Report.

A new page is started each time the next hitter in the lineup comes to bat. At the top of the page, the date of the game, the pitcher number, the catcher number, the inning number, and the batter number are recorded. The inning number would have T1 recorded for the top of the first inning, B1 for the bottom of the first inning, etc. The page number of the Scouting Report is recorded to assure the continuity of the entire game report.

The next item is the pitch number. There is a column for each pitch thrown, from the first pitch to the fifteenth.

In the columns below each pitch, results are recorded according to designated codes. The first item of concern (line 47) is whether the batter is a designated hitter, pinch hitter or regular hitter in the lineup. If the batter was a regular hitter in the batting order, a "0" would be put in the first column of line 47. For a designated hitter, a "1" would be put in the space, and for a pinch hitter, a "2".

Baseball Input

Date _____   Inning No. _____

Pitcher No. _____   Page No. _____

Catcher No. _____   Batter No. _____

Pitch Number	1	2	3	4	5	6	7	8	9	10	11	12	13	14	15
47 Designated/Pinch Hitter															
48 Number of Outs															
49 Base Situation															
50-51 Count Ball															
Strike															
52 Type of Pitch															
53 Location															
54 Call Hit 1															
Foul 2															
Strike Swing 3															
Strike No Swing 4															
Ball 5															
Pitchout 6															
Walk 7															
Balk 8															
Bunt 9															
Bunt Attempt 0															
Hit By Pitch A															
Interference B															
Wild-Pitch C															
Pitch Off To First Base D															
55-56 Angle															
57-59 Initial Distance															
60-62 Final Distance															
63 Fielder of Ball (Position #)															
64 Type of Hit															
65 Base Gained (Base Hit)															
66 Sacrifice Bunt/Sacrifice Fly															
67-74 Runner Scored First															
Second															
Third															
Fourth															
75 Error (Position #)															
76 Ball Thrown to Base Number															
77 Accuracy of Throw/Good Play															
78-79 Stolen Base (Player #)															
80 Covering Second															

The next two rows, 'Number of Outs' (line 48) and 'Base Situation' (line 49) may change with each pitch. For instance, when the first pitch is delivered, there could be no outs and a runner on first base. On that pitch, the runner could be thrown out while attempting to steal second. In such a situation, at the delivery of the second pitch there would be one out and no one on base.

The number of outs, 0, 1 or 2, is recorded in the space in the first column. This doesn't need to be changed until another out is made. For the base situation, the following codes are used to record the exact runners-on-base situation for each pitch:

Base Situation

No one on base	0
1st	1
2nd	2
3rd	3
1st and 2nd	4
2nd and 3rd	5
1st and 3rd	6
1st, 2nd and 3rd	7

The next two lines (50-51) are used to record the count. Before the delivery of the first pitch, there is always a count of 0 balls and 0 strikes. If the first pitch was a ball, a "1" would be put in column two along the line designated for ball, and a "0" would be put in column two along the line designated for strikes. The opposite would be the case if the first pitch was a strike. This proceeds along pitch by pitch.

The type of pitch is recorded in the columns along the next row (line 52). The code for each pitch is:

Type of Pitch

Fast	1
Curve	2
Slider	3
Knuckle	4
Screwball	5
Sinker/split-fingered fastball	6
Change-up/curve	7
Change-up/fast	8

The location of each pitch over the plate is recorded on line 53. The strike zone and the area around the strike zone is divided into a nine-location grid, so that the location of each pitch can be recorded exactly.

Location

High Inside	1
High Over Middle	2
High Outside	3
Medium-High Inside	4
Medium-High Over Middle	5
Medium-High Outside	6
Low Inside	7
Low Over Middle	8
Low Outside	9

Every pitch will have a result. The specific result, listed as 'Call' (line 54), is recorded for each pitch in one of the following categories:

Hit	Balk
Foul	Bunt
Strike Swing	Bunt Attempt
Strike No Swing	Hit By Pitch
Ball	Interference
Pitchout	Wild Pitch
Walk	Pitch Off To First Base

For greater speed and accuracy, the 'Call' categories are recorded differently than the preceding categories. Instead of using a numerical code system, all the possibilities are listed and the scout checks the proper column adjacent to the proper 'Call' category. Thus, a check next to 'Foul' in the column under pitch number one means that the batter fouled off the first pitch. A check next to 'Ball' under pitch number two means that the batter took the second pitch for a ball. The count then would be 1 ball and 1 strike going into the third pitch.

All the terms listed under the 'Call' category are baseball terms that are easily understood, but to achieve consistency the following explanations are given:

Hit – A ball hit into fair territory, whether the batter gets on base or not. This should not be confused with a base hit (single, double, triple or home run), because a base hit is only one type of a hit ball.

Foul – A ball hit into foul territory.

Strike Swing – A swing and miss on a pitch thrown in the strike zone.

Strike No Swing – A pitch that is called a strike when the batter does not swing. This information is included to determine if there is a pattern to the pitches that a batter takes for called strikes.

Ball – A pitch that is called a ball when the batter does not swing.

Pitchout – A pitch purposefully thrown out of the strike zone in anticipation of a base runner attempting to steal.

Walk – This column is marked on ball 4 instead of putting a check adjacent to 'Ball,' as would have been done on the three previous balls.

Balk – Marked when a pitcher commits a balk.

Bunt – This is checked only when the pitch is bunted into fair territory.

Bunt Attempt - Marked when the batter attempts to bunt but misses.

Hit By Pitch - Marked when batter is hit by pitch and advances to first base.

Interference – This is marked when there is an interference play.

Wild Pitch – A poorly thrown pitch that the catcher cannot handle and which allows a base runner to advance. For a passed ball, the scout would designate that the catcher (position #1) made an error.

Pitch Off To First Base – This is checked when the pitcher throws to first base to hold a base runner closer to the first base bag.

Pitch-by-Pitch Example

The chart below is a facsimile of a page from an actual Scouting Report.

Baseball Input

Date _____   Inning No. _____T1_____

Pitcher No. _____   Page No. _____

Catcher No. _____   Batter No. _____

Pitch Number	1	2	3	4	5	6	7	8	9	10	11	12	13	14	15
47 Designated/Pinch Hitter	0														
48 Number of Outs	1														
49 Base Situation	2														
50-51 Count　　　　Ball	0	0	1	1											
Strike	0	1	1	2											
52 Type of Pitch	1	2	2	1											
53 Location	6	9	7	2											
54 Call　　　　　Hit 1				✔											
Foul 2	✔														
Strike Swing 3			✔												
Strike No Swing 4															
Ball 5		✔													
Pitchout 6															
Walk 7															
Balk 8															
Bunt 9															
Bunt Attempt 0															
Hit By Pitch A															
Interference B															
Wild Pitch C															
Pitch Off to First Base D															
55-56 Angle				72											
57-59 Initial Distance				300											
60-62 Final Distance				300											
63 Fielder of Ball (Position #)				7											
64 Type of Hit				3											
65 Base Gained (Base Hit)															
66 Sacrifice Bunt/Sacrifice Fly															
67-74 Runner Scored　　First															
Second															
Third															
Fourth															
75 Error (Position #)															
76 Ball Thrown to Base Number															
77 Accuracy of Throw/Good Play															
78-79 Stolen Base (Player #)															
80 Covering Second															

Following along with the chart on the opposite page, notice that the batter came to bat in the top of the first inning (1T in the upper right hand corner of the page). He was a regular hitter in the batting order (0 recorded on line 47). There was one out when he came to the plate (line 48). There was a runner on second base (line 49), and the count naturally was 0 balls and 0 strikes at the time of the first pitch.

The first pitch was a fastball (indicated by the 1 in the first column of row 52, 'Type of Pitch'). The fastball was medium high on the outside part of the plate (indicated by the 6 in the first column of row 53, 'Location').

The batter fouled off the first pitch (indicated by the check mark beside 'Foul' underneath the 0-0 count pitch). This made the count 0 balls and 1 strike for the second pitch (line 50-51).

The second pitch, a curveball low and outside, was a ball, bringing the count even at 1 ball and 1 strike. The third pitch was also a curve, low over the inside part of the plate, at which the batter swung and missed, bringing the count to 1 ball and 2 strikes. The fourth pitch was a fastball high over the middle of the plate, which the batter hit.

Recording Hit Information on The Scouting Report

When a ball is hit into fair territory, a variety of information is recorded regarding the location and result of the hit. Recording the angle of the hit (line 55-56) and the distance the ball travels (line 60-62) are important, because this information is used in two of the reports generated by the BARS system — the Hit Location Report and the Super Summary Report. The angle is recorded to the nearest degree possible.

The angles are assigned as: 0 degrees to the first base line, 45 degrees to second base (straightaway center field), and 90 degrees to the third base line. Referring to the Scouting Report shown on the opposite page, a hit recorded at 72 degrees (indicated in column 4 of row 55-56, 'Angle') would be roughly in the direction between the third baseman and the shortstop.

The 'Initial Distance' (line 57-59) refers to the point where the ball first touches the ground or a player. The 'Final Distance' (line 60-62) designates the point where the ball comes to a stop. In the Scouting Report on the opposite page, the batter hit a fly ball to left field which was caught (indicated by 300 feet in rows 57-59, 'Initial Distance,' and rows 60-62, 'Final Distance'). The left fielder caught the ball (indicated by the 7 in row 53, 'Fielder of Ball').

The point of reception was both the 'Initial Distance' and the 'Final Distance' since the left fielder caught the ball on the fly. If the ball had been lined over the shortstop's head for a base hit, the point where the ball first touched the ground would be the 'Initial Distance' and the point where the left fielder first touched the ball would be the 'Final Distance.'

Each time a ball is hit in fair territory, the position number of the player who fielded the ball is recorded (line 63). The identification system used in baseball is: 1 for pitcher, 2 for catcher, 3 for first baseman, 4 for second baseman, 5 for third baseman, 6 for shortstop, 7 for left fielder, 8 for center fielder and 9 for right fielder.

Three categories are used for recording the type of hit (line 64): 1 for ground ball, 2 for line drive and 3 for fly ball.

'Base Gained' (line 65) indicates whether a hitter had a single (1), double (2), triple (3) or home run (4). If a hitter gets on base due to an error, this space is left blank, and an error is recorded below (line 75).

'Sacrifice Bunt' (line 66) is registered only when the batter successfully advances a runner by bunting the ball into fair territory. The code that is inserted into this category is based on which fielder charges the bunt attempt. The code numbers are: (1) First baseman charges; (2) Second baseman charges; (3) Third baseman charges; (4) First and Third basemen charge; (5) Second and Third basemen charge. A sacrifice fly is designated by a '6.'

The base runner's uniform number is recorded in the proper column along the 'Runner Scored' lines (67-74) when the runner scores. The base which the runner occupied when the pitch was thrown is designated by First, Second, Third and Fourth. For example, if there were base runners on second and third and a base hit scored both, the number of the runner who scored from third would be recorded in the column of the last pitch after 'Third.' The number of the runner who scored from second would be listed after 'Second.' If the bases were loaded and the batter hit a home run, all the columns would be recorded, with the hitter's uniform number recorded after 'Fourth.'

When a fielder commits an error, his player position number is recorded on line 75. For example, if the shortstop commits an error, a 6 is recorded in line 75.

'Ball Thrown to Base Number' (line 76) and 'Accuracy of Throw' (line 77) record the accuracy of throws from the catcher to second or third base on steals and throws from infielders and outfielders to first, second, third or home plate. First base is designated '1', second '2' and third '3'. In line 77, a '1' designates a throw that is on target and a '2' designates a throw that is off target. An exceptionally good play is designated by a '3'.

When a player steals a base, his uniform number is recorded in line 78-79. When second base is stolen, a '1' is recorded on line 80 if the second baseman covers second, and a '2' is recorded if the shortstop covers.

Continued

Comprehensive Information Available

By recording such information on a pitch-by-pitch basis, extremely exact and complete records can be kept. The BARS System information and computer analysis allows unique and comprehensive statistics to be generated.

The comprehensive information about each pitch and the ensuing results allow tremendous flexibility in the recording of statistics. Individual managers and players may require unique information in attempts to spot specific trends. The BARS system allows widely diverse information about hitters and pitchers to be studied.

Recording The BARS System Information Into The Computer

As seen in the preceding chapter which described the Scouting Report, a large amount of information is gathered for every game scouted by the BARS System. In fact, a large amount of information is gathered for every pitch of a scouted game.

It is crucial for this information to be entered accurately into the central BARS System computer, because it is the basis for all charts and analyses generated by the BARS System. To insure complete accuracy, guidelines have been established for the checking and re-checking of information, and for the systematic entering of information into the computer.

Initial Checking of the Scouting Reports

When Scouting Reports are sent to the BARS System Computer Center, the games are first divided into two categories: American League games and National League games. Each team has a unique identifying number, and an ongoing file of Scouting Reports is kept for each team.

Attached to the Scouting Report is a batting lineup for each of the two teams that played. Every player in the lineup is checked to make sure that he is recorded correctly according to the BARS System Master Player File. The Master Player File lists all players in each league alpabetically, designating each player with a specific number that remains the same even when the player is traded to another team. Also checked is the actual number the player wears; whether he hits right-handed, left-handed or is a switch hitter; and whether he is a left-handed or right-handed pitcher.

After checking all players in the batting lineup against the Master Player File for the league, the Scouting Report is checked to make sure that the innings are in correct sequence and that there is a top and bottom for each inning. If the pages of the Scouting Report have not been numbered by the BARS System scout, they are numbered by the person checking the report.

This initial inspection, which takes approximately 20 minutes for each game, takes place before the Scouting Report is given to the computer operator who inputs the data into the computer. The thoroughness of this checking process is the first step in assuring accuracy for every BARS System detail.

Entry of the Information: A 60-Minute Procedure for Each Game

The Scouting Report, along with any changes or additions to The Master Player File, is then given to the BARS System data entry personnel. The information for each game scouted is entered on diskette, with six games per diskette.

Depending on the length of the game, it takes approximately 30 minutes to enter the pitch-by-pitch information. After one data entry operator has entered the information for a game, a second operator repeats the process, entering all information without reference to the work of the first operator. This second process takes another 30 minutes.

The two reports are then compared by computer. In the comparison, the smallest discrepancy or omission will be noted. If there is a variance of even a single numeral or letter, the computer will note it. The operators check and correct any errors before making a final record of the game. This attention to detail assures the accuracy required by the BARS System.

The first part of the record for each game is called The Header, which consists of the following: the date of the game, the stadium number (which is the same as the number for the home team), the field condition, the weather, the wind direction, the wind speed (miles per hour), the temperature, the time the game started, whether or not the game was a double-header, the opposing team's number, the attendance and the final score.

After The Header has been completed for a game, information is entered on a pitch-by-pitch basis starting with the top of the first inning. Entered for each pitch is a 'T' or a 'B' for top or bottom of an inning, the inning number, page number of the Scouting Report, the batter's actual number, the pitcher's actual number, whether the batter is a designated or pinch hitter, number of outs, runners-on-base situation, ball-and-strike count, type of pitch, location of pitch and whether the pitch was called a ball or a strike.

When a ball is hit, the following information is entered: the angle of the hit, the initial distance the ball travelled before striking the ground, the total distance the ball travelled before it was fielded, the position number of the fielder of the ball, the outcome of the hit (single, double, triple or home run), whether the hit was a sacrifice fly or sacrifice bunt, runners scored (using the runner's actual number), whether the hit resulted in an error (designating the position number of the fielder committing the error), the base to which the ball was thrown and the accuracy of the throw.

If a base is stolen on a pitch, the runner's number is recorded, along with the position (shortstop or second baseman) of the player covering second base.

The Master File for Quick and Easy Access To Information

When the six games on each diskette are entered into the Master File, each game becomes a part of the permanent record of the BARS System. A separate Master File is kept for each baseball season. Records for players or teams can be drawn out of the computer for individual years or for the summation of all years.

Controlling The Destiny Of a Game

Adopting the BARS System in regular play would allow a team to control the destiny of a game much more than before.

Baseball is unique in that the defense (the team on the field) initiates the action when the pitcher throws the ball. In football, basketball, hockey and other sports, teams take a defensive alignment without really knowing what their opponents are planning offensively.

In football, for example, the defensive team can adjust its strategy according to the setup of the offensive team at the line of scrimmage, but the defensive team never really knows if the play is going to be a pass or a run, or to what part of the field the pass or run will go.

In baseball the pitcher initiates the play, and by using the BARS System, the team on the field can coordinate fielders with the type and location of pitch. The BARS fielding strategy is right over 90 percent of the time. This high percentage of accuracy brings a new dimension to the game and opens speculation about how the style of play will change once teams begin using the BARS System regularly.

Larger Players May Become The Norm

When a fielder is in just the right position for each pitch, he won't have to move as far to field the ball. The effectiveness of fielders with greater mobility will be increased also — their range will enable them to cover an even greater area using the BARS System — but, overall, mediocre fielders will benefit most.

Fielders don't have to be as fast when they're perfectly positioned, so teams may go to larger fielders when they start using the BARS fielding strategy. Shortstops and second basemen are usually among the smaller players on a team because they need to be quick and agile. At present we're seeing players like Ozzie Smith or Alfredo Griffen who are like gymnasts on the field. The necessity for this may change as the BARS System is implemented. Both infielders and outfielders could become larger and even slower when a team uses a fielding strategy that positions players in the best possible position 90 percent of the time.

If the BARS System had been used in the past, it's possible that some of the power hitters that were considered too bulky and slow to play proper defense may have made it in the major leagues. If the BARS System had allowed them to use a fielding strategy that would have positioned them closer to where the ball would be hit, they wouldn't have been such a defensive liability.

The Ways To Beat The System

The best way to beat the BARS System is to hit the ball out of the park. You can't field a home run. This may also encourage teams to go with larger, stronger players — the power hitters who can hit the ball out of the park.

On the opposite side, implementing the BARS System may encourage hitters to emphasize increased bat control and placing the ball. Not every player can hit home runs, and when the high-average hitters suddenly find that there's always a fielder where they hit the ball, they're going to try to adjust.

Getting Every Edge Possible

Teams could make the most out of the BARS System fielding strategy in several ways. One would be to have fielders break toward their correct positions as the pitch is delivered. This would confuse the batter and make it more difficult for him to know beforehand where to place the ball. Shifting and stunting is common for defensive alignments in football. It confuses the offense and makes play changes more difficult.

Teams can also have their players use the BARS System to increase the percentages of making a play. For example, even though the BARS fielding strategy suggests that an outfielder play a hitter short for a particular type and location of pitch, the outfielder may not want to play short, thinking that the batter could possibly hit a deep drive. In this situation the outfielder could increase his chance of being in the right position by playing medium-deep to guard against deep drives while anticipating the likelihood that the ball may be hit short. In this way he could guard against both possibilities.

All in all, the BARS System will bring about many changes in the game once it is implemented by even a single team. Baseball will become much more coordinated and exacting, with the result that both offensive and defensive strategies will have to become more flexible than they are now.

The BARS System will make the game even more exciting and interesting for the fans. The most important overall consideration for excellence will be a team's level of coordination between players. This will be a major advancement in the evolution of baseball, and teams that do not adjust to the new strategies will fall to the bottom of the standings.

Index Of Players